THE YOUNG CALVIN

Alexandre Ganoczy

Translated by
David Foxgrover
and
Wade Provo

The Westminster Press
Philadelphia

Page 30 (*top*): Portrait of Calvin in the Dutch-Walloon church in
Hanau, Germany.
(*bottom*): Portrait of Calvin in the Tronchin collection in Geneva.

Book design by Christine Schueler

First American Edition

Published by The Westminster Press®
Philadelphia, Pennsylvania

PRINTED IN THE UNITED STATES OF AMERICA
2   4   6   8   9   7   5   3   1

Library of Congress Cataloging-in-Publication Data

Ganoczy, Alexandre.
The young Calvin.

Translation of: Le jeune Calvin.
Bibliography: p.
1. Calvin, Jean, 1509–1564. 2. Calvin, Jean,
1509–1564. Institutio Christianae religionis.
I. Title.
BX9418.G313 1987   284'.2'0924   87-10516
ISBN 0-664-21840-7

CONTENTS

Preface to the English Translation   7

Acknowledgments   14

Foreword by Joseph Lortz   15

Abbreviations   27

Introduction   31

Part One   A Historical Inquiry Into Calvin's Religious Development Between 1523 and 1539

1. Paris and Reformism in France Around 1523   49
2. Calvin at the Collège de Montaigu, 1523–1527   57
3. Calvin in Orléans and Bourges, 1528–1531   63
4. The Second Period in Paris and Orléans, 1531–1533   71
5. The Events of Autumn 1533 and the Stay in Saintonge   76
6. The Year of Wandering, 1534   83
7. Calvin in Basle, 1535–1536   91
8. Travels Between Basle, Ferrara, and Paris, 1536   102
9. Calvin in Geneva, 1536–1538   106
10. Crisis in Geneva and Exile to Strasbourg, 1538   120
11. Conclusion to Part One   127

Part Two   The Sources of the First Edition of the *Institutes*   133

12. Luther   137
13. Melanchthon   146
14. Zwingli   151
15. Bucer   158
16. Scholastic Theology   168
17. Calvin and Humanist Thought   178

Part Three   The Content of the First Edition of the *Institutes*   **183**

18. The Dialectical Structure of Calvin's Thought   185
19. The Major Constructive Principles of Calvin's Thought   188
20. Critique and Ideal of Piety   194
21. Critique and Ideal of Doctrine   209
22. Critique and Ideal of the Ecclesiastical Structures   215
23. The Outline of Calvin's Plan for Reformation   225
24. Conclusion to Part Three   231

Part Four   The Problems of Conversion, Schism, and Vocation

25. The Problem of the Conversion   241
26. The Problem of Schism   266
27. Calvin's Consciousness of a Divine Call   287
28. Summary and Conclusions   307

Notes   **313**

Bibliography   **399**

PREFACE

This English translation of my book is the result of the initiative of The Westminster Press, to whom I wish to express my gratitude. The translation gives me an opportunity to deal with several issues raised by the discussion of this book in scholarly circles. The Franz Steiner Verlag has provided me with reviews of my book and several monographs that have reacted to it, negatively or positively, and my response is based on this material. (See the list of reviews and monographs immediately following.)

The majority of the reviews are in general agreement with my basic position. Jacobs called my book a new portrait of the young Calvin, similar to that presented by Reformed scholars. In 1974 at the European Congress for Calvin Research in Amsterdam, Nauta said that my study cast "a quite different light on 'the riddle of Calvin's conversion' " and that I am probably correct in the way I frame the questions. He also said that I have "clarified many questions pertaining to Calvin's development" (p. 75). Strasser agreed with my chosen method of preferring documents contemporary with Calvin to later statements by or about the reformer. In his opinion, my research "made it possible to abandon the assumption that at an early date (probably before 1528) Calvin had experienced a 'conversion' to Evangelical Christianity and to the role of reformer" (p. 122).

The scholars devoted their most intensive efforts to the question of the event which Calvin many years later in his Psalms Commentary of 1557 characterized as *"subita conversio"* ("sudden conversion"). In his excellent biography of Calvin, T. H. L. Parker took into account only this retrospective comment of the reformer. Nevertheless he reached the same conclusion I did: that the "conversion" of the young humanist from Noyon could neither be dated precisely nor described as sudden. The adjective *"subita"* probably refers to the totally unexpected nature of a process that took place over a specific period (pp. 162f.). Strasser agrees with this conclusion. It was not conversion as a momentary experience (Jacobs) nor one that could be pinned down historically (Scholl), but an inward development (Nauta, Nijenhus), a process (Thurneysen) in the young reformer's life that he himself traced to God's powerful work.

This formal aspect of a change of direction (Thurneysen) that extended over a long period of time corresponds to the material aspect of the truly unforeseen, unanticipated new *awareness* that he was called by God to be a reformer of the Church, after the model of Luther and Bucer (Nauta). Thus "conversion" and "calling" fall together as one event (Conzemius, Dufour). And both find their orientation in the theological content so clearly expressed in the first edition of the *Institutes,* written in 1535 (Dufour). Such a theoretical foundation of Calvin's concept of reform agrees quite specifically with his consciousness of his prophetic role (Iserloh, Lecler, Miller, Scholl, Strasser, Thurneysen).

The young Calvin's motivation also seems to have been shaped by this prophetic aspect. It was not concern for his own personal salvation, as was the case with Luther, but concern for the fate of the Church as it suffered under manifold "deformations" that drove him to his increasingly radical affinity with the "Evangelical party" (Iserloh, Nijenhus).

In answer to the question of the period of time in which this change may have taken place, two scholars gave an answer that clearly differs from mine. While I first discern with full clarity the development of Calvin's "vocation as reformer" in the first edition of the *Institutes* (1536), Parker concludes from Calvin's statement in his Psalms Commentary (1557) that "if Calvin has remembered the sequence of events correctly, his conversion must be placed during his legal studies. . . . The latter end of 1529 or early in 1530 seems to be indicated" (p. 165). In my opinion this hypothesis would stand on a firmer basis if it were not derived from an isolated analysis of this late work by Calvin. Moreover, the few documents surviving from the years between 1529 and 1536 give few indications that support Parker's hypothesis. Parker remains remarkably cautious and appears reluctant to abandon the little sympathy he has "with those whose aim is primarily to fix a date" (p. 162). Ultimately, however, he settles on a relatively precise time span.

Saxer, who criticizes several of my theses quite sharply, is more decided in his views. He begins with Calvin's first published work, his commentary on Seneca's *De Clementia,* from the year 1532. It contains numerous quotations from the Church Fathers, especially Augustine, with the help of which the young humanist shows how unsubstantial "superstition" is. In these quotations and the commentary attached to them, Saxer finds a concealed rejection of "Catholic piety," which has been totally corrupted by superstition. Thus he concludes that Calvin "came to the Reformation through the authority of the Fathers" (p. 216). Augustine's influence he regarded as particularly strong (pp. 211, 276). In this way he dates the young Calvin's conversion to 1532.

I must confess my amazement at Saxer's boldness in projecting back into Calvin's humanist period his critique of piety, which he first set forth clearly in the first edition of the *Institutes.* Scholl, building on the work of R. Peter, expresses strong reservations against that position (pp. 109, fn. 345) and

comments, "Saxer's understanding of the term *'superstitio'* is too extreme."
In any case, it cannot simply be regarded as in accord with the *Institutes*
of 1535. Calvin himself did not reduce his criticism of the Church so
exclusively to a simple negative principle, especially not to one involving the
Church's piety in that period. As I myself have shown, he combined his
critique of "papist" superstition with other criticisms, which relate above
all to doctrine. Moreover, these criticisms were closely combined with
"positive principles" such as *"soli Deo gloria"* and *"solus Christus"* (pp.
107f., fn. 337).

The debate between the two Reformed Calvin scholars Saxer and Scholl
became rather heated over my statement that Calvin's sense of reformation,
conversion, and calling cannot simply be explained as a *break* with the
catholic Church. The historian is forced to accept a different interpretation
by the terminology of Calvin's polemic against "papistry," in which he
never uses the term "catholic" to refer to his opponents, and even more by
his constantly expressed concern for the unity of the Church of Jesus Christ.

Saxer places less emphasis on historical factors and contexts than on a
thoroughgoing analysis of the concepts "superstition," "hypocrisy," and
"piety" in various of Calvin's writings. Thus Saxer (p. 49) sees the word
"superstition" as having a quite distinctive "basic meaning" in "Calvin's
polemic against the papal Church." This results quite logically in a "basic
condemnation of Catholic piety" (p. 187, fn. 185), which, however, is not
as "total" as that of Zwingli (p. 221). Calvin always held that "still in every
form of superstition and impiety" there remained "a core of true religion,"
and for this reason Calvin "again and again sought for union with the
Catholic religion" *(sic)* (pp. 192f.). Even so, we should not hesitate to
discern in his conversion a "break with the Church" or a "separation from
the Catholic Church" (p. 187, fn. 185). I am said to have wiped out the
"distinctive reformation nature" of this conversion by portraying Calvin as
a "reformer who basically did not move beyond the structure of Catholicism" (see also Tron, p. 219).

Scholl challenges Saxer's theory of a "break" in that along with Calvin's
critique of piety he also takes into consideration his critique of the theological positions of the "Roman" or "papist" party. From this point of view
the "break with Rome" becomes apparent for the first time in the first
edition of the *Institutes,* where Calvin lays out his program (p. 99). To be
sure, this does not signify a "break with the Catholic Church" (Scholl, p.
109), nor an intention to "establish a new Church" (p. 99) into which those
converted to the Gospel would be received by a new baptism. "Calvin's
knowledge of the one church" prevented "any talk of a break with the
church and thus of a sectarian understanding of his 'conversion' " (p. 109).
In a similar vein, Balke (p. 151) explains that "to repent is to place your
trust in God, not to break with the Church." Consequently it is wrong to
interpret the young Calvin's radical acceptance of the Gospel anachronisti-

cally as joining another denomination (cf. Thurneysen, p. 487). I am happy
to agree, for I have always felt that Calvin's call to be a reformer did not
lead him out of the *una sancta.* His "conversion" has the same meaning as
the biblical *metanoia;* that is, a change of one's mind-set, which results in
a turning from sin to God.

Does saying this make his rejection of *"superstitiones papatus"* (see
Parker, p. 164) harmless and sweep him into the fold of the Catholic
"denomination"? That was not the intention of my book, as most of the
other reviewers have recognized. To quote my sharpest critic, Saxer, Calvin
knew the difference between "what had to be abandoned as superstition and
what should remain" (p. 66; cf. p. 192). But, I would like to add, he was
concerned with such differences not only in reference to baptism and the
Lord's Supper but also in reference to the Church. Therefore it is, objectively seen, erroneous to want to place him outside the "catholic Church"
as he understood it.

In my book there is another issue about which I am happy to modify my
position and bring it closer to that of my critics. It involves the following
statement: "The young Calvin did not have the Catholic understanding of
the sacrament. His prophetic protest led him to separate the divine and the
human to an excessive degree and to experience an implacable aversion to
anything that seemed to bind grace to 'carnal elements' " (p. 237).

This could give the impression that I had included Calvin in the category
of "spiritualists" (see Saxer, p. 67, fn. 259). That is not at all what I meant.
In addition to the present book, my dissertation (Paris, 1964) and its
modified German form (Freiburg, 1968) contain enough information about
Calvin's rejection of the anabaptists and spiritualists of his time to deflate
any such misunderstanding. The pronounced "churchliness" (Lortz) of the
French reformers prevented him, even in his younger years, from denigrat-
ing infant baptism and robbing the real presence in the Eucharist of its
meaning (cf. Strasser, p. 124).

On the other hand, my statement that the young Calvin did not possess
the "Catholic understanding of the sacrament" could easily be misunderstood, all the more so since I seemed to imply that it was "catholic" to tie
grace to the external elements; that is, to the signs. At best such a statement
approached a neoscholastic doctrine of sacramental causality which ritua-
listically abbreviated the principle of *ex opere operato.* Scholl, who has
carefully studied my earlier as well as my later writings, holds that in
positions I have taken on Calvin's Christology I have "only with hesitation
succeeded in freeing myself from neo-Thomistic modes of thought" (1974:
p. 135). And in as far as I have succeeded in this, I owe my success to the
critique formulated by Willis (pp. 5, 99).

This verdict is essentially correct. Earlier I indeed carried too far the
analogy between the hypostatic union of deity and humanity in Christ and
the relationship of the divine and the human in the sacrament. All too

readily I required of Calvin a "theandric synthesis" (Nijenhus, p. 99; see also Ganoczy 1964 and Scholl's critique, 1974: p. 105) in the sacramental realm, which, viewed objectively, could result in a distortion of the genuine Catholic tradition. We need only to think of the "holiness through works" (Nijenhus, p. 99) of Calvin's contemporaries or that abuse of divine grace for human purposes from which the reformer attempted to free the Church in the name of the Gospel. This attempt was not uncatholic, but catholic in the truest sense of the word.

As the result of this discussion I am happy to retract my statement about the absence of the "Catholic understanding of the sacrament" in the writings of the young Calvin. I do, however, continue to regard part of the Calvinist doctrine of the sacraments as deviating from a doctrinal tradition which must be termed catholic in a nonsectarian sense. Other Catholic Calvin scholars such as K. McDonnell and H. Schützeichel are of the same opinion. Viewed in a careful manner, the understanding of the sacraments of both the younger and the older Calvin must be acknowledged as in accord with tradition and thus as catholic. By this I mean above all his doctrine of the real presence of Christ in the Lord's Supper through the activity of the Holy Spirit (cf. my *Ecclesia Ministrans* 72). On this point, according to the most recent research, even the Council of Trent could take no exception to Calvin's teaching. We could say today that Calvin's pneumatology serves not only to affirm God's absolute freedom in his saving acts but also to support a dynamic understanding of the sacraments, which in many ways is quite close to the doctrine of the Eucharist in the Eastern Churches. It makes possible a theology of epiclesis.

In conclusion I shall mention a few points that my book makes. First, what Calvin learned from Luther—a long-acknowledged fact—without making him out to be an epigone of the German reformer (Iserloh, p. 185). Much the same can be said for the increased emphasis on Zwingli's influence on Calvin's critique of the Roman Mass (Dufour, p. 786). The formerly popular opinion that the Scottish theologian John Major acquainted Calvin with elements of nominalist theology during his years of study in Paris is now regarded as scarcely tenable. Miller (p. 93) writes, "Ganoczy also proves conclusively that Calvin could not possibly have got his ideas from John Major, at least before 1535." For indeed the young man from Noyon studied only scholastic philosophy in Paris, not theology.

But according to the research of Rotts (pp. 291–311) my surmise that Calvin was not the author of the address given by Nicolas Cop, 1 November, 1530, at the Sorbonne, is unlikely to be correct (cf. Saxer, p. 209, fn. 253). In any case, no final agreement has yet been reached on this much disputed issue. The ecumenical character of my book, though generally perceived as not directly intended but rather the result of objective research, is expressed in the final sentence, which I still affirm and which has been cited approvingly by many reviewers: "Calvin's calling as a reformer, a factor in division for the past four centuries, may in some way now become a factor in reunion."

The sources of the original Latin and French Calvin texts are cited in the notes as OC (Opera Calvini) and OS (Opera Selecta). Luther texts are cited as WA (Weimarer Ausgabe) and those of other Reformers as CR (Corpus Reformatorum).

Important parallels of terms, expressions, and sentences between two different sources (e.g., between Zwingli and Calvin) are indicated by italics.

I am grateful for the high standard of the translation by Dr. David Foxgrover and Dr. Wade Provo. I also wish to thank Miss Anette Zillenbiller and Mr. Gisbert Nolte for their faithful work in assisting me in checking the translation.

ALEXANDRE GANOCZY

Würzburg, March 4, 1987

Reviews and Monographs

W. Balke, in *Wapenweld* 17 (1967), pp. 148–151.

V. Conzemius, in *Revue d'Histoire ecclésiastique* 62 (1967), pp. 849–851.

A. Dufour, in *Bibliothèque d'Humanisme et de Renaissance* 29 (1967), pp. 785–787.

A. Ganoczy. *Calvin, théologien de l'église et du ministère* (Paris, 1964).

―――. *Ecclesia Ministrans* (Freiburg, 1968).

E. Iserloh, in *Erasmus* 20 (1968), pp. 184–187.

P. Jacobs, in *Reformierte Kirchenzeitung* 1967, No. 5; in: *Das historisch-politische Buch* 16 (1968), pp. 76f.

J. Lecler, in *Recherches de Science religieuse* 50 (1962), pp. 301–303.

S. v. d. L., in *Theologia Reformata* 10 (1967), pp. 38f.

S. J. Miller, in *Catholic Historical Review,* April 1969, pp. 92ff.

D. Nauta, in *Stand der Calvinforschung,* in: W. H. Neuser (ed.), *Calvinus theologus. Die Referate des Europäischen Kongresses für Calvinforschung* from 16 to 19 September 1974 in Amsterdam (Neukirchen-Vluyn, 1976), p. 75.

W. Nijenhus, in *Kerk en Theologie* 19, pp. 19f.

T. H. L. Parker. *John Calvin: A Biography* (London, 1975), pp. 162–165.

R. Peter. Cited in Scholl, *CC.*

J. Rotts, in *RHPhR* 44 (1964).

E. Saxer. *Aberglaube, Heuchelei und Frömmigkeit. Eine Untersuchung zu Calvins reformatorischer Eigenart* (Zurich, 1970). This book enters into extensive debate with Ganoczy's theses in *Le jeune Calvin.*

H. Scholl, in *Kirchenblatt für die reformierte Schweiz* 124 (1968), pp. 97–100.

————. *Calvinus Catholicus. Die katholische Calvinforschung im 20. Jahrhundert* (cited in Scholl, *CC*) (Freiburg-Basel-Wien 1974). (See references under Ganoczy in the index of names.)

A. **Segovia,** in *Archivo Teológico Granadino* 30 (1967), pp. 335f.

O. E. **Strasser,** in *Theologische Literaturzeitung* 93 (1968), pp. 121–124.

M. **Thurneysen,** in *Historische Zeitschrift* 206, pp. 486f.

M. C. **Tron,** in *Protestantesimo,* 1967, No. 3–4, pp. 218–220.

E. D. **Willis.** *Calvin's Catholic Christology* (Leiden, 1966).

ACKNOWLEDGMENTS

We wish to acknowledge our debt of gratitude to two of our colleagues whose help was indispensable: Dr. Donald Martin of the Rockford College Classics Department, who checked the Latin translations in the text and notes; and Marjean Silberhorn, the secretary of Fisher Chapel, Rockford College, who typed the entire manuscript at each stage of our work.

DAVID FOXGROVER
WADE PROVO

Rockford College

FOREWORD

This book was prepared and published in Germany, a country where Calvin is, of course, less often the subject of scientific inquiry than Martin Luther. Thus there is all the more reason for me to rejoice in being able to present to the scholarly world (so soon after the work of Pastor Léopold Schummer, *Le ministère pastoral dans l'Institution Chrétienne de Calvin à la lumière du troisième sacrement,* [1] which appeared in our collection and will no doubt give rise to many debates) this new contribution to the study of Calvin, which appears belatedly among the works appropriate for the Jubilee Year of 1964. Its author is a young Hungarian priest of French nationality who has come to work with us.

1. Whoever considers European history, especially the history of Christianity, cannot fail to be obsessed with the following question: How did the reform of the sixteenth century come about? How did the breakup of the community of faith and the Western Church take place? How was it possible? We know that the causes go back much farther than the sixteenth century and that they prepare the way so thoroughly that a revolutionary reform had become historically necessary and inevitable. But we also know that in spite of these historical causes, the reform was due mainly to the initiative of those whom we call the Reformers, especially Martin Luther and John Calvin.

All history is complicated; the causes that prepared and made possible a theological and ecclesiastical separation do not at all preclude any fundamental connection between what was being abandoned and what was being created. To this day, an agreement on what may be considered the basis of the reform movement cannot be reached. The word "reformer," in any case, does not mean purely and simply "anti-Catholic" or "non-Catholic." Besides, when using the term "Catholic," one must not forget that the Catholic confession of faith underwent an important development. It is precisely our period—under the influence of Vatican II and the biblical studies movement which have renewed exegesis and teaching in contemporary Catholicism— that has learned to understand clearly how Catholic ideals can be obscured in some instances. Proclaiming these ideals does not lead us back to the formulations of the late Middle Ages or to neoscholastic schematizations which were excessively objective. Much more strongly than other generations, we perceive once again the possibility of presenting Catholic ideals with the help of scriptural categories and by using all the riches of the Bible. Granted that the reform in general was an effort to hold to the Scriptures, we should admit at least the possibility of the survival of Catholicism in the Protestant secession of the sixteenth century, in spite of its vehement reaction against Rome.

2. This conception of historical development which allows us to remain open to a positive evaluation of the reform and the reformers is particularly important and useful regarding the subject of this book: Calvin's *development* as a reformer.

Luther's and Calvin's awareness of being called to be reformers is less well known than their characteristics as "mature" reformers. It is even more difficult to describe this awareness for Calvin than for Luther, for the documentation is much more limited. Certainly Calvin spares us the difficulties inherent in Luther's "reminiscences" which are so disconcerting in their ambiguity and which complicate any attempt to describe his evolution. With Calvin we no longer have to confront the troublesome paradoxes that underlie Luther's assertions.

The paucity of documentation does not absolve us of considering this pressing question: How did Calvin *become* a reformer? I consider the present monograph to have special value because it approaches the subject in a new way. Ganoczy deserves our approval when he asserts the necessity of knowing not only the "mature" Calvin but the Calvin who is "becoming," the man who was first completely "imbued with the spirit of Erasmus" (p. 288), an apostle of Stoic even-mindedness ("a former humanist champion of the virtue of clemency," p. 131), and then who turned little by little (but also, so inexplicably, quickly) toward the inexorable rigor of an intolerant leader of the Church. In spite of what we have just said, this rigor is rooted in his character and develops more and more in the name of God into "acts of religious intolerance comparable to those of the Inquisition of the Sorbonne" (p. 301). And all of this happened well before Calvin's career reached its climax.

3. Ganoczy's *objective* is to gather young Calvin's ideas from the texts with the greatest possible precision, in order to set forth the origins and evolution of his calling as a reformer.

We recognize Ganoczy's extensive knowledge of the reformer's writings; his exposition does not leave any obvious gaps. The references to parallel sources from Luther, Melanchthon, Zwingli, and especially Bucer add to the quality of the analysis. We see that they are not simply mentioned but their significance is conscientiously determined before the author gives his interpretation. Ganoczy's many considerations of Calvin's evolution always manifest extreme prudence in exegesis and judgment. He prefers to resign himself to lengthy inquiries rather than risk a statement that is insufficiently founded. The dividing line between hypothesis and carefully established fact is rigorously respected. Ganoczy notes his sources with a care that is equaled only by that with which he uses them (cf. pp. 68ff., 73ff., 79ff.). He never forces the meaning of a text, and he never succumbs to the temptation of drawing from the texts and the facts more than they actually contain (cf. p. 69), or to examine them from only one point of view. Should the documentation not allow him to take a definite position, on a date for example, he settles on what is "most likely" (p. 88). "Faced with obscurities in the documents," he says, "we prefer to leave everything in the realm of possibility."

This concern to build only on a solid basis and to give the most careful analysis possible never turns into a cold detachment toward the object of research. On the contrary, one feels that the analysis is handled by a man who is "involved" and gifted with a vigor of mind that captivates the reader in many passages of the book.

The authors studied are also the object of precise discussions, not only on well-known points but also on many others. Documents are included that up to now have been considered only rarely, such as Calvin's second preface to Olivétan's translation of the Bible, which Ganoczy calls "a document of capital importance" (p. 98).

The quality of the work is seen in that at each stage of the analysis Ganoczy orders and presents his material in such a way that the reader is able to confirm easily and quickly the progressive elaboration of its main ideas.

The analysis itself unfolds in a strictly chronological order; it appears to develop progressively and—quite naturally—to reach a point where all the elements taken into account find their place. Moreover, the analysis has the tremendous advantage of placing the texts in the setting of contemporary events of Church history (e.g., those of Paris and Bourges; cf. pp. 69ff.).

Certain parts deserve special praise. One may call masterful the remarkable objectivity (imbued with a restrained passion) with which various developments are brought together; for example, Ganoczy takes into account both the internal and the subjective elements as well as the external factors surrounding Nicolas Cop's rectoral address (pp. 81ff.; cf. pp. 44–45).

For those who want a clear illustration of Ganoczy's method, I recommend the reading of chapter 25 on Calvin's conversion. The masterful analysis of the steps of Calvin's path gradually leads to a recognition of the nature of this conversion, and at the same time the meaning of the words *convertere* and *conversio* in Calvin's writings becomes more clear. As a result, the meaning of Calvin's own "sudden conversion" (pp. 252–266) is elucidated.[2]

1. It is very gratifying to learn that with this method Calvin's growth comes to light in detail, right up to the establishment of what Ganoczy elegantly names Calvin's "incurably impatient character" as well as his "passionately intellectual temperament" (p. 288); but we are spared the terrible conflicts that later on will weigh upon Calvin's reform activities in Geneva. In the course of the narrative and the analysis of events, one moves effortlessly in a climate of perfect objectivity from the image of the humanist reformer, to the biblical reformer, and then to the evangelical reformer. In this evolution Calvin moves out of the traditional Church without realizing it (p. 90: "without knowing it"). In this process an unwavering "confidence in God" (p. 292) is allied with a very sensitive conscience and even a pronounced and persistent mistrust of himself. This was a period of rigorous self-control, and the experiences of this period allowed Calvin later to be very precise in his descriptions of the ordinary and extraordinary ecclesiastical ministries.

2. The reform took place because at the beginning of the sixteenth century the true nature of the Church appeared only in very inadequate ways. It was difficult to recognize all of its richness, and an independent mind may well have been tempted to separate from it, precisely in the name of the Gospel.

Such was the case with Calvin. Theologically and philosophically (his dependence on the nominalism [?] of John Major; see pp. 174ff.), the most important thing is that he was not familiar with scholasticism. This is why Gratian and Lombard were for him little more than objects of polemics (pp. 168ff.); all scholasticism seemed to him to be no more than pure *curiositas,* which was careful to define but not to listen (p. 210). Calvin's attitude is exactly the opposite. The obvious proof of this is the *Institutes,* the first edition of which is the culminating point of the evolution that made Calvin a reformer.

One will notice how the stage of theological and spiritual development that Calvin reached at this point is defined with meticulous precision in relationship to the preceding stage and described with many detailed comparisons (pp. 174ff.). This concern for precision meant that Calvin defined his fundamental theological concepts very gradually. The process of definition was not complete by the time of the first *Institutes.*

It is typical of the care that Ganoczy devotes to his work that he consciously refuses all simplistic schematizations (p. 195), for it is characteristic of Calvin's thought that "in spite of its clarity, unity, and systematic structure, [it] never loses its fluidity and variations" (p. 203). Calvin's language is clear and his style is mature, but his terminology is not always precise.

3. But *how* did Calvin become a reformer? His astonishingly rapid inner growth (see above) reveals one of the most important differences between

Calvin and Luther, who (in spite of the "tower experience" in the monastery) had to pay a much more painful price for the discoveries that he made during the course of his long journey. By age twenty-seven, when he wrote his first *Institutes,* Calvin had obviously received a great deal of intellectual stimulation from his studies, experiences, and relationships. He had been impressed by the reports of evangelical martyrs who died at the stake, and his flight to Basle presupposes a whole series of experiences. But Ganoczy proves that at the time when Calvin was writing his masterpiece, he still lacked "any experience as a reformer or pastor" (p. 226).

4. What pushed Calvin onward was what Ganoczy terms his "prophetic call." This concept is established in accord with L. Bouyer's views (p. 307) by the unusually rich and thorough analysis of Calvin's evolution and work, which anyone may examine. After the completion of his "philosophical," humanistic, and legal training, there developed in Calvin the noble awareness that God had called him to be a "prophet." Here is a key idea that allows us to synthesize and harmonize the details of Calvin's evolution, seen in their "prophetic tone"—to use Ganoczy's admirable words (p. 290; cf. p. 293). Basically, Calvin's theology convinced him that God may at any moment raise up a prophet within his Church in opposition to the ministerial hierarchy; the Lord did this with the prophets of the Old Testament, where often the true faith and the Church were embodied in a single prophet such as Micaiah or Jeremiah (p. 229). Thus there are also "modern 'prophets' " (p. 299), "taught by the Spirit of God" (p. 301), like Calvin. He is absolutely convinced of it. His conception of himself and the Reformation depends entirely upon this supposition, which also accords with the basis of his piety (he does not belong to himself but to God; p. 298).

Reformation alone remained the way to save the Church, since the call of the pope was uncertain and the call of God became more pressing (p. 299). But divine intervention did not cause Calvin to forget that there is only one Church, the ancient Church, and that all his zeal should be aimed at preserving its unity. He definitely granted a central place to Eph. 4:11: "God makes some prophets, and others evangelists, pastors, and teachers." But legitimate authority must be respected: *respect must be granted the priesthood, and great is the danger of disregarding regular power.* Isaiah, Jeremiah, Joel, and Habakkuk did not break with the "corrupt community."

The prophetic call by which one would purify the Church is thus distinguished as clearly and carefully as possible from that of the "false prophets," the anabaptists and catabaptists, who were severely criticized (p. 229). We shall return to this concept of the *one* Church (see p. 22 of this Foreword).

5. We have already spoken of the difficulties encountered in analyzing the personal evolution of the reformer Martin Luther and interpreting his reminiscences. However, if we recognize the basic truth of these testimonies—which we must if we are not to turn Luther into a babbler who made

a travesty of the facts—we may say that his religious and reformist evolution essentially stems from his terrifying and unique crisis of conscience in the convent when "brother Martin Luther" sought a merciful God.

There is nothing comparable in Calvin to this extraordinary subjectivity!

Calvin's "Latin character," highly refined by his legal studies, manifests itself in an entirely different form of religious expression. His progressive awareness of his prophetic calling testifies to his intense objectivity, and it is this vocation—animated by the hidden or manifest inspiration of the prophet—which characterizes the entire development of Calvin the Reformer. This is why the glory of God, the Church, and the ministry remained central values for Calvin.

6. To verify these views, it is especially helpful to examine the famous testimony of Calvin on his *"subita conversio"* in the preface to his commentary on the Psalms. The way Ganoczy carefully approaches the study of this central theme (p. 131) and the way he introduces it at the heart of his research show the thoroughly systematic character of his thought. The complexity of this *conversion*—its "ecclesiastical dimension" (p. 42)—is seen in Calvin's own reflections. The theme is judiciously clarified in all aspects and then progressively analyzed until a precise synthesis is attained. Ganoczy's use of earlier research to interpret the word "conversion" is proof of the sound and certain method we mentioned (pp. 41ff.), the care with which it is developed, and the skillful and guarded way in which its historical method is formulated.

The explanation of the *"subita conversio"* should be sought in the reformist concerns that dominated Calvin, the precocious, young lay theologian. We can hardly speak of a conversion from sin, a " 'conversion' in the pietistic sense" (pp. 291ff.), or even of a theological discovery (as with Luther). What we have is the awakening to a call to reform the concrete Church, a vocation nurtured by the call of God. The "sudden conversion" is recognized as a prophetic sign of an eternal theological truth, a sign independent of all considerations of time (cf. esp. pp. 263ff.). It deals with an idea, central to Calvin, that divine might is more powerful than any human resistance (p. 263); as in the case of the prophets, Calvin's reference to his conversion is not a piece of information but a testimony (pp. 263–264). We have seen that Calvin's emphasis is not on the sudden break with papal superstition but the awareness of the all-powerful intervention of God's grace. That is why this conversion is at the same time a reform of the Church to which one belongs; one does not leave the Church but purifies it (p. 266).

We admire the way Ganoczy puts before us this primary aspect of the reformer's evolution. His critical judgment does not leave out any authentic element of this growth and does not distort the facts to "prove" a thesis.

7. In a profound way, the reform is a protest movement against the ills and weaknesses of the papal Church. The polemics of the reform were quite

strident (one may say the same of the Catholic reaction, which was generally quite unsatisfactory). But this is not what is really important, especially for Calvin's Reformation. Certainly Luther also considered the positive aspect of his new teaching to be primary. But his teaching depended so much upon polemics in its origin as well as its content that whoever goes from Luther to Calvin is especially impressed by the *positive* character of Calvin's zeal.

The question of ecclesiastical abuses—which Ganoczy sums up in the expression "an 'evangelical decline' without precedence" (p. 308)—naturally comes up several times. This well-worn subject is treated in an original way with the help of numerous illustrations drawn from the sources. With a very careful eye, Ganoczy closely follows Calvin and directs our attention to doctrine rather than morals: lack of theological clarity, opposition between conciliarists and papists (opposition of the conciliarists to the Roman see), between national episcopates and that of Rome, and between reform humanists and theological faculties. Ganoczy notes that the plague of rash excommunications and doctrinal condemnations pronounced too easily and without discernment gave rise to an increasing sense of theological uncertainty. Everyone struggled against everyone else, infecting the entire Church so that "the ancient authority of the Church was not universally recognized and followed."

Ganoczy clearly points out the insufficient basis of "papist" theology, especially in controversy, where at best there was a superficial accumulation of biblical quotes that were not even used in a proper theological way. Thus appears the elementary fact that if the Catholics had understood that the central Christian preoccupation of the reform was to return the papal Church to a more pure form of the people of God, a true break with Rome would not have been necessary or even likely. We know that the question of "what might have been" cannot be dealt with in a perfunctory manner. But the historian can verify that many rich and valuable Catholic traditions continued to be important to the reformers. Then if he takes into account how excesses (along with misunderstandings over legitimate concerns) naturally lead to an overreaction, he may correctly conceive (exercising great prudence) that there could have been a truly revolutionary reform without any essential break with Rome.

An exhaustive study of the confrontation between the Catholic theologians of the sixteenth century and Calvin requires an entire work of its own. This is not the aim of the present study. It is obvious that such a study would not be easy. Moreover, we find in the evolution of young Calvin an important episode that directly shows the fatal inadequacy of the theology of Catholic humanists and members of the Curia: Sadolet's appeal to the Genevans.

No doubt Cardinal Sadolet was a signer of the *Consilium de emendanda ecclesia;* he held a very independent view of scholasticism and demonstrated an authentic, conciliatory spirit (e.g., in regard to Melanchthon). But his appeal to the Genevans was seen as a superficial attack which dishonored him (pp. 279ff). It is moving to see how Calvin denounced its inadequacy, while insisting on remaining within the unity of the Church of Christ at any cost.

8. There is still no agreement about the role of Luther's influence on Calvin's evolution.[3] Ganoczy succeeds in showing the surprising importance of this influence, but the difference in the intellectual and spiritual character of these two men is also highlighted. Adhering to a strictly chronological order, Ganoczy competently points out similarities (especially the influence of Luther's *Small Catechism* (pp. 137–145). Once again, one is led to believe that Calvin left the Church gradually and without premeditation (cf. p. 308; p. 18 of this Foreword). This implies that "nothing allows us to assert that this change meant for him an abandonment of Catholicism, a break with the *Una Sancta,* or even a conversion in the contemporary, confessional sense of the word" (p. 308).[4]

9. We are now brought back to a problem to which we have already alluded: the positive importance of Calvin from the Catholic point of view. To elucidate this aspect of Calvin's "grand attempt" (p. 308) is one of the major preoccupations and merits of this book. What was Calvin's purpose and the focus of his work? "A recollection and a living witness of the transcendence of God, of the absolute sovereignty of the Word, of the unique priesthood of Christ and his place as the one Mediator, of the nature of the ministry as service, of its Christ-centered collegiality, and of the role of the laity which is at the heart of the idea of the priesthood of the people of God" (p. 311). As Ganoczy's first book[5] leads us to expect, it is not "private" or personal themes but the themes of community and the Church which appear to be most significant in the evolution of the young Calvin. With du Tillet, a longtime friend of the reformer, we must obviously stress that Calvin did not receive his ecclesiastical mission from a legitimate Church authority but at the invitation of his brothers in Christ at Geneva. But as may be seen in similar cases, Calvin did not seek official sanction for long. Convinced of the importance of his cause both for religion and for the Church, he clearly saw that the mission entrusted to him was an expression of the will of God (pp. 292–293). In the face of the advanced corruption of the Church, one argument played an important role for Calvin and the entire Reformation: "Necessity makes the law" (p. 297).

To emphasize again what Ganoczy has said in all of this, the great concern for the unity of the Church was not long-lived (pp. 41ff.). Calvin recognized his duty to remain within this unity; we see the conflict arise within the reformer who is torn between his preoccupation with Church unity and his condemnations of the popes. For Calvin, there is no reason to speak of a new Church (p. 272) or to oppose a "true Church" to a "false Church," and no possibility of speaking of a "salutary schism" (pp. 273ff.,

276). For the abuses are *within the Church of God.* That is to say, for Calvin the Reformation was a "grand work of reconstruction" of the Church (p. 275). "Both the Calvin of Ratisbon and the Calvin of the first *Institutes* never intended to break with what was most essential in the Catholic doctrine of the Church" (see chapter 26, n. 156). "The most basic points of their preaching" come from this living tradition of the "Church founded by Christ, which continues to exist as such even under outward distortions and corruptions."

"Regarding those matters which concerned him, Calvin was subjectively persuaded that the entire work of his life was not aimed at breaking with the Church but at re-establishing continuity with the true Church of Christ and his apostles."[6] With Calvin there is evident "a sense of stability" (p. 298). He recognized the importance of structure, and one of his fundamental ideas is the need for order and tradition and for offices to uphold them. The Church is an objective reality where the *opus operatum* has its place: "The promise of God inevitably comes to pass, even if those who transmit it or receive it lack true faith" (p. 226).

10. The first edition of the *Institutes* also includes the Catholic idea that the episcopate is essential to the Church (p. 223), and the fundamental characteristic of the episcopate is service *(diakonia).*

But, to be sure, the Church is not made up of two categories of members; it includes not only those who are ordained and tonsured, not only the priests, but "the whole people of God, united in his [Christ's] name" (p. 218). *All* have received their lot *(kleros),* all the baptized are of equal importance and power.

To understand correctly the basis of Calvin's theology, it is very important to notice how clearly he declares himself in favor of frequent communion (p. 113), "the supreme act of worship," without which the life of the Church would not be well ordered. But however important it might be to demonstrate "piety" in formal Christian worship, it is one's attitude which is decisive (as characteristic of Luther): "Worship for Calvin . . . is essentially adoration" (p. 207). Calvin insists that this adoration by nature is founded upon personal faith, but it culminates in the "great celebration of the act of grace, the Eucharist" (p. 208), which (as in all personal prayer) "should be filled with a communal and public spirit."

But there is a limit to Calvin's Catholicism: "Young Calvin did not have the Catholic understanding of the sacrament" (cf. pp. 208–209, 237); his concept of the Church was severed from its sacramental dimension.

11. One of the most important questions that the evolution of the reform poses for us is the place of theology within the framework of proclaiming the Gospel. This point is of considerable importance for determining the essence of Calvin's vision of the reform and for ecumenical dialogue.

In a general way, both Luther and Calvin consider the role of theology to be essential. It is fortunate that neither of the two reformers hesitates to insist that faith, upon which all must finally rest, be fully accessible to the humble and ignorant and that theologians themselves must come to a childlike faith. In spite of his vigorous affirmations, Luther did not uniformly follow this line of thought. The depth and purity required of faith (*omnibus viribus, in hilaritate,* perfect love) means that most often faith is beyond the reach of the average Christian. While Luther's description of faith and piety is often complicated by his well-known paradoxes, Calvin on this point remains nearer to the tone of the Gospels, which are often obscure regarding details but generally clear to him, as they were to Luther. The "simplicity of Scripture" is Calvin's ideal (pp. 199, 214). It follows that preaching should embrace all the riches of revelation, but in such a way that it is accessible to the "poor little Church," to the "simple people," to the *uneducated,* who are "much more sensitive to the pure teaching of the Word of God than one might think." They are the ones especially "taught by God." Moreover, insistence on dogma does not stop Calvin from believing that "the virtue of religion consists principally in submitting to the divine will" (p. 198), and he expressly describes this virtue as capable of growth. This belief cannot help recalling Luther's first thesis on indulgences: "The entire life of the Christian ought to be a meditation on piety."

1. Of all the scholarly Catholic publications on the reform of the sixteenth century, this book constitutes a new and welcome example of the objective, historical understanding that we Catholics have acquired of the forces and principal reformers of the sixteenth century as well as the goals of the evangelicals. It is up to the specialist to say to what extent one may subscribe in detail to Ganoczy's analysis. Without ending up with a bland interconfessionalism, this work by a Catholic priest does not allow polemical passions or any misguided defensiveness to assert itself. The problems posed by Calvin are approached in a climate of total freedom. What has prevented us for a long time from properly understanding the reform, its leaders and theology, is our external approach. That is, we have persisted in approaching this prodigious and complex history through categories and ideas from either post-Trent or post-Vatican theology. The author's attitude is simply that of a scholar, a historian. The researcher is inspired by a passionate yet measured enthusiasm, and he encounters his famous subject with the requisite esteem for the man and his work. At the same time, Ganoczy freely criticizes Calvin's ideas, albeit with reserve and sobriety. He knows that Calvin "often lacked objectivity and the spirit of dialogue" (p. 187).[7] Moreover, he is not afraid to present the reformer of Geneva as "a true instrument of the Spirit of God" and to praise him as a "prophet of the Lord" (p. 306), just as Theodore Beza and Nicolas Colladon did. What undoubtedly justified Calvin's prophetic call is recognized with all objectivity. (The reformers themselves, in spite of their awareness of their mission,

remained conscious of what distinguished them from the prophets of the
Old and the New Testament.)

2. I do not contradict myself when I note the ecumenical spirit that
inspires this book. In this sense, it serves a cause. But this is certainly no
reason to contest its rigorously scientific character. Although it may seem
that in this study we return to an unfortunate example of historical positiv-
ism, which now seems outdated, we must understand it in its proper function: to clear the way for reflection by detailed and precise work.[8]

Ganoczy's thoroughly scientific study understands in a truly historical
sense the young Calvin's development and therefore his faithfulness to
Christianity and to the Church; that is, he asks himself to what extent this
section of history, of which Calvin is the center and focus, contains elements
that still concern us (cf. p. 15 of this Foreword).

In a time when ecumenism has become fashionable, it is necessary to
realize that at best we can say some edifying words of little weight about
the *Una Sancta,* and at worst we might encourage a dangerous attitude of
indifference, if there was not actually some common ground among all the
separated Churches.

Ganoczy proves once again the reality of a common patrimony in the
young Calvin, which stems from the universal priesthood of all baptized
believers.

But is this a "posthumous and arbitrary 'integration' "? Ganoczy asks.
After carefully and precisely weighing the facts, he answers "No." And in
this answer we find at least a reply "to one of his [Calvin's] deepest intentions" (p. 312): "Calvin's calling as a reformer, a factor in division for the
past four centuries, may in some way now become a factor in reunion" (p.
312).

3. This question of the Catholic "integration" of the reform may basically
be resolved in terms of its doctrine of Church and ministry, to which we
have already alluded. What determines everything else is the meaning given
to the well-known exclusive expressions: faith *alone,* Scripture *alone,* etc.

After the important start made by W. Stählin (*Allein. Recht und Grenze
einer polemischen Formel;* Stuttgart, 1950), both Catholics and Protestants
lacked the boldness to continue investigating this question. One sees more
clearly today, even among our Protestant brethren, the degree to which
Scripture is an expression of tradition. But the profound question of the one
mediator and the many ways in which his grace is mediated has not, to my
knowledge, been seriously explored. Research may lead us farther on this
point.

Moreover, Calvin expressed his principles "consistently with the help of
the adjective 'alone' " (p. 188) to such a degree that Ganoczy can say that
the expression "glory to God alone" underlies everything, even though it
cannot expressly be found in the first *Institutes* (pp. 188ff. et passim).

But in fact "alone" is not understood by Calvin as absolutely as the word may suggest. Even in the most troublesome point, "Scripture *alone,*" the meaning of "alone" is considerably limited by tradition ("especially that of the Fathers"),[9] which is frequently invoked without question. It is obvious, as we have seen, that the "ancient" Church of the apostles and the Fathers plays an absolutely normative role in elaborating the doctrine of the Church that Calvin draws from Scripture alone.[10]

4. This beautiful book awakens in us a concern about the division of the Church. By taking into account the mysterious nature of this division, it invites us not to despair of a positive solution and not to be blind to the deep relationship between the ancient apostolic and Roman Church, which today is being renewed, and the Church of the Reform, which Calvin so often asserted was part of this same ancient Church: one, holy, and catholic.

5. This book was developed in our Institute of European History in Mainz (the Department of Western Religious History[11]) and represents an outstanding example of our objectives. Young Catholic and Protestant researchers from all nations live together with us, and in a spirit of complete equality they discuss the problems of the reform and its consequences. They do not ignore the powerful impulse that the faith of their respective churches gives them, but they consider it and properly use it as a creative impetus, by which they seek (we seek) objective historical reality with scientific, critical methods.

The present study succeeds in being objective and impartial, but it does not exclude sympathetic or enthusiastic involvement. I consider this book to be very important. This is the work of a *historian* who is also capable of skillfully mastering *theological* problems. The analyst's touch may sometimes be firm and even inflexible. But no one can deny that he succeeds in building a solid synthesis and presenting the necessary cross sections of the work and life of young Calvin. Thus the functional nature of Calvin's thought—that is, the concepts and their practical results—becomes quite clear. In summary, one may say that this book succeeds because of its original way of posing questions and resolving them.

The author seems to me especially qualified to render great service to the study of the reformation led by Calvin and to the French setting of the "Gospel" in which it took root. His name will not be forgotten.

JOSEPH LORTZ

Mainz, Domus universitatis
Summer 1965

ABBREVIATIONS

Primary Sources

Allen
P. S. Allen. *Opus epistolarum Desiderii Erasmi Roterdami.* Oxford, 1922ff.

BL
J. Calvin. *Institution de la Religion Chrestienne* (1541). Edited by J. Pannier. 2d ed. 4 vols. Paris, Les Belles-Lettres, 1961.

BSLK
Bekenntnisschriften der evangelisch-lutherischen Kirche. 2d ed. Göttingen, 1952.

CCath
Corpus Catholicorum. 28 vols. Münster in Westfalen, 1919ff.

CR
Corpus Reformatorum. Braunschweig and Berlin, 1834ff.; Leipzig, 1906ff.

Denz
H. Denzinger and A. Schönmetzer. *Enchiridion Symbolorum, Definitionum et declarationum de rebus fidei et morum.* 32d ed. Freiburg im Breisgau, 1963.

EN
M. Bucer. *Enarrationes perpetuae in sacra quatuor evangelia, recognitae nuper et locis compluribus auctae.* Strasbourg, 1530.

Er Op
Desiderii Erasmi Opera Omnia. 10 vols. Leiden, 1705.

IC
J. Calvin. *Institution Chrestienne* (1560).

IRC
J. Calvin. *Institutio Religionis Christianae* (1536, 1539, 1543, 1559).

LC
Ph. Melanchthon. *Loci Communes.* Edited by D. Th. Kolde according to G. L. Plitt's edition. Leipzig, 1900.

Mansi
S. D. Mansi. *Sacrorum conciliorum nova et amplissima collectio.* Edited by L. Petit and J.-B. Martin. 60 vols. Paris 1899ff.

OC
Ioannis Calvini Opera quae supersunt omnia. Edited in CR by G. Baum, E. Cunitz, and E. Reuss. 55 vols. Braunschweig and Berlin, 1863–1890.

OS
Joannis Calvini Opera Selecta. Edited by P. Barth, W. Niesel, D. Scheuner. Vol. 1 (1926), vol. 2 (1952), vol. 3 (2d ed., 1957), vol. 4 (2d ed., 1959), vol. 5 (2d ed., 1962). Munich.

PL
J. P. Migne. Patrologia latina. 217 vols. Paris, 1878ff.

WA
M. Luther. *Werke.* Weimar, 1883ff.

WA Br   M. Luther. *Briefwechsel.* Weimar, 1930ff.
WA DB   M. Luther. *Die deutsche Bibel.* Weimar, 1906ff.

Journals, Reference Works, and Collections

AElsKG   Archiv für elsässische Kirchengeschichte. Rixheim (1926–1946). Strasbourg, 1946–.
AEPHE   *Annuaire de l'Ecole pratique des Hautes Etudes.* Paris.
AHR   *American Historical Review.* New York.
AN   Archives Nationales de Paris.
ARG   *Archiv für Reformationsgeschichte.* (Leipzig) Gütersloh.
BHPF   *Bulletin d'Histoire du Protestantisme français.* Paris.
BN   Bibliothèque Nationale de Paris.
BZThS   *Bonner Zeitschrift für Theologie und Seelsorge.* Düsseldorf, 1924–1931.
EvTh   *Evangelische Theologie.* Munich.
HJ   *Historisches Jahrbuch der Görres-Gesellschaft.* (Cologne) Munich.
JR   *Journal of Religion.* Chicago.
LThK   *Lexikon für Theologie und Kirche.* 2d ed. Freiburg im Breisgau, 1957ff.
NGG   *Nachrichten von der (Königlichen) Gesellschaft der Wissenschaften zu Göttingen.* Berlin, 1845–1940.
RE   *Realencyklopädie für protestantische Theologie und Kirche.* 3d ed. 24 vols. Leipzig, 1896–1913.
RGG   *Die religion in Geschichte und Gegenwart.* 3d ed. Tübingen, 1956ff.
RH   *Revue historique.* Paris.
RHPhR   *Revue d'Historie et de Philosophie religieuses.* Strasbourg.
RMM   *Revue de Métaphysique et de Morale.* Paris.
RThPh   *Revue de Théologie et de Philosophie.* Lausanne.
RThQR   *Revue de Théologie et des Questions religieuses.* Montauban.
StG   *Studia Gratiana.* Bologna.
StGThK   *Studien zur Geschichte der Theologie und der Kirche.* Leipzig, 1897–1908.
SVRG   Schriften des Vereins für Reformationsgeschichte. Gütersloh.
ThEx   *Theologische Existenz heute.* Munich.
ThLZ   *Theologische Literaturzeitung.* Leipzig.
ThQ   *Theologische Quartalschrift.* (Tübingen) Stuttgart.
ThStK   *Theologische Studien und Kritiken.* (Hamburg) Gotha.
TThZ   *Trierer Theologische Zeitschrift.*
ZHTh   *Zeitschrift für die historische Theologie.* Leipzig-Gotha, 1832–1875.
ZKG   *Zeitschrift für Kirchengeschichte.* Gotha (Stuttgart).
ZKTh   *Zeitschrift für Katholische Theologie.* (Innsbruck) Vienna.

The translation of this book from the French
was made possible by a generous gift from

Mr. Donald E. Hall

INTRODUCTION

The State of the Question

Two portraits of Calvin come to mind: the first shows us the young scholar of Paris[1] and the other the reformer of Geneva at age fifty-three.[2]

The first is a painting that presents a frontal view of a distinguished and engaging person who radiates sensitivity and intellectual curiosity. The facial characteristics are not very pronounced. Lively and piercing, the gaze seems fixed on the observer. The hands draw our attention. The right hand rests on the table. The left, with the index finger raised, makes a gesture of one who has just asked a question. It holds a pair of gloves which leads one to suppose that the young humanist is often on a journey. This is certainly the Calvin who is still searching.

The second is an old engraving that shows the profile of a man of mature age. The face is emaciated, nervous, angular; it reflects the determination and desire to persuade someone. The lips are pressed together. The glance seems to be fixed on a distant point or upon an invisible listener. Above the head is a motto: "Prompt and sincere." Nothing suggests movement. One has the impression that this man is advanced in age and scarcely moves anymore; he is seated, and his listeners come to him. This is certainly the Calvin of Geneva, the uncontested head of the premier Reformed Church.

The second painting, with others that resemble it, is better known and more widespread than the first. It is the very model of the stereotype of the reformer, the one that appears before the eyes of most of his faithful followers or his adversaries—the true Calvin.

These portraits correspond to the idea that one generally has of Calvin. When his name comes up in the course of a conversation, one thinks almost automatically of the Genevan "theocracy," of the protagonist of absolute predestination, of the ingenious organizer of the Protestant movement, of the harsh and inflexible man who sent Servetus to the stake and the libertines to prison, and finally of the initiator of a rigid and uncompromising Puritan morality.

The majority of historians also prefer to devote themselves to the study of the Genevan activities of the reformer. In order to show the considerable influence that the head of Geneva has had upon both religious and world history,[3] they write from the perspective determined by the relationship "Calvin-history." Thus they explain how the present is related to the past, how the Reformed churches of today are heirs or beneficiaries of the doctrines and structures established by the author of *The Institutes of the Christian Religion* and the *Ecclesiastical Ordinances of Geneva.*

The majority of theologians naturally observe a similar attitude. In order to present, comment upon, and explicate the teachings of Calvin, they are generally drawn to study them in their definitive form as found in the Latin text of 1559 and in the 1560 French version of the *Institutes.* J. D. Benoit, for example, is of the opinion that "it is the 1560 edition which gives us the final form of Calvin's thinking and theology. . . . It is there that one ought to go to obtain a complete view."[4] This is also the view of J. Cadier, who wrote, "It is natural to make use of his last edition, as it is natural to know a man according to his mature age rather than according to his childhood."[5]

This manner of studying Calvin is completely normal and legitimate if one stops at the relationship "Calvin-history." But if one considers that before he was able to influence later history, Calvin himself was influenced by earlier and contemporary history, one must also take into account the relationship "history-Calvin." Certainly it is the fully developed personality and the clearly established work of the reformer at a mature age which expound what one calls "Calvinism" and the "Calvinist tradition." But in order to understand the reformer himself, it is also necessary to study the conditions in which his personality took shape and in which his work evolved. As with every man and every great historical personality, the Geneva reformer is at the same time "cause" and "effect," "tree" and "fruit." Thus, in order to obtain a truly complete view of the man and his thought, it is not sufficient to know him in his adult age, but one must also describe the road traveled between his childhood and the height of his career.

It is such a study that I propose to undertake. From the existential point of view of Calvin's development and relationships, I wish to reply to this question: How did he become a reformer? More precisely: What were the genesis and the evolution of his calling as a reformer?

As we seek to reply to this question, we must first discover the essential characteristics of Calvin's times. Then we must describe how he is related to his milieu, to other men, to events and ideas that were likely to condition his intellectual and spiritual development. In this regard, we shall pay particular attention to ecclesiastical factors, for it is more important to understand the evolution of the future reformer of the Church than to trace some spiritual journey. In principle, one does not become a reformer by oneself or for oneself. An entire series of causes coming from the religious community prepare and stimulate such a vocation; an entire series of results in turn affect the life of the Church. The existential situation of a community can have considerable repercussions on a member, and an existential change in a member can exercise a profound influence on the entire community. One of our principal aims, then, will be to uncover the relationship between the personal history of Calvin and the history of the Church of his time. Finally, when we have established with some degree of certainty how and why Calvin became a reformer, we can then attempt to grasp the significance of this personal *and* ecclesiastical transformation for the history of the universal Church as well as for Calvin himself.

These are the ideas guiding our work. We will return to them again, but we will first establish the spirit in which we desire to work and summarize the studies already published on this question.

The Spirit of Our Study

The way one speaks of a reformer depends in large part on the image that one has of him. If one sees above all a man dedicated by vocation to restoring the Church of his time to its original purity and form, one easily tends toward praise or panegyric. Several historians of Calvin, among whom Theodore Beza is the earliest and Emile Doumergue is one of the most important among the moderns, have largely given way to this tendency. But if one assumes that a reformer must be a heretic and schismatic, perhaps well intentioned but blinded by impatience and polemics, one easily tends to interpret the facts according to the classical methods of an apologetic style. Almost all the Catholic theological manuals and many historical works have moved in the latter direction.[6]

Often the two ways of presenting a reformer depend, more or less directly, on the confessional position—or even the nationality—of the writer. The great separations that occurred during the reform movements of the sixteenth century not only divided Christianity into different confessions but resulted—even within the same denomination—in a wide variety of theological, spiritual, and institutional traditions. These in turn strongly conditioned the thought, concerns, judgment, and vocabulary of different historians. Thus we have many versions of the history of Calvin: Calvinist, Lutheran, liberal Protestant, Roman Catholic, and so forth. In addition, several works that were written for the most part during and after World War I go so far as to reflect specific national antagonisms: a French Protestant speaks one way of his great compatriot, while a German Protestant . . .

Of course, it is difficult a priori to detach oneself completely from this type of writing. As all mortals, historians are subject to the different spiritual, intellectual, and psychological influences that arise from their milieu and background. However, since their mission is the objective description of the past, they should not restrict themselves to a *pro domo* study. Historians must strive as much as possible for complete impartiality.

Several recent historians of Calvin, especially Protestants imbued with an ecumenical spirit, have accomplished real progress in this regard. Overcoming the temptation to make systematic pronouncements for or against Calvin, they recognize the complexity of things and refuse to simplify the life of the great reformer and thereby to schematize it.

I hope our study will be impartial and alert to the complexity of our topic. To reply to the question, How did Calvin become a reformer? we will stand apart from a confessional perspective as much as possible. Without recourse to the well-worn paths of the "Calvinist" tradition, we will seek to rediscover Calvin directly. Without recourse to Roman Catholic dictionaries and manuals, written according to the demands of the Counter-Reformation (still uncorrected!), without appealing to "selected passages" chosen to present a particular understanding of Calvin, we shall study the entire range of Calvin's own writings. I am convinced that it is not the heritage of the dead Calvin that will lead us to the living Calvin, nor will the elder Calvin lead us to the younger Calvin. The proper method consists of approaching him through the milieu from which he emerges, then accompanying him on the paths of his youth in the light of contemporary documents, and finally arriving with him at the moment when he becomes fully conscious of his calling as a reformer. In sum, we shall try to understand Calvin from both the outside and the inside. We will willingly grant Calvin the sympathy that this attempt demands. The criticisms that will emerge by virtue of an unchanging order of values we will address to him without anger or prejudice. And we will apply to him only the terms that he himself would not have refused.

This initial option of objectivity and impartiality does not mean that we will conduct our study in a spirit of complete neutrality. The drama of Calvin is a drama of faith. The history of Calvin belongs to the history of the Church. The future reformer received the faith within the form of the Church of his time, lived it with intensity, and was led to contrast its expressions with those of the early Church. This he did under the influence of several reform trends, and in the end he allied himself completely with the reform movement. Understanding this transformation would be impossible for someone studying Calvin from an absolutely neutral position, that is, by ignoring the very mysteries that were working within his soul throughout his entire life. Such an approach would reduce the study to sociological, psychological, philosophical, and political phenomena[7] and would lose sight of the essence of the problem, which is to understand that Calvin was fundamentally a religious man and a man of the Church. A historian of Calvin must recognize in each moment of his research the religious and ecclesiastical context. This is the only way he can serve the cause to which all the reformers were dedicated: the re-formation of the one and indivisible Church of Christ.

This is the spirit in which I desire that we undertake our study on the origin and evolution of Calvin's calling as a reformer. I do not hide the fact that understanding the young Calvin is not an end in itself. In retracing his "development," in establishing the role of the absolute and relative, and in constructing the relationship between continuity and opposition, we shall always keep in mind our present situation in which separated Christians work together to reduce opposition and to establish continuity. The history of Calvin, with its shadows and lights, can still teach us much today.

Survey of Previous Studies

An examination of the works published up to now on the youth of Calvin reveals that there is not one Catholic study specifically devoted to this subject. The irrevocable judgment pronounced on the hereterodoxy of several of Calvin's ideas has probably led Roman Catholic historians to lose interest almost completely in the study of the young Calvin. Without doubt it was more important to present him as a heretic than to try to explain how and why he developed his views. The exceptions are very few. The research of J. Lortz on the religious evolution of Martin Luther[8] still does not have its counterpart for Calvin.

Protestant works come to various conclusions on particular aspects of Calvin's religious transformation, but they almost unanimously qualify this transformation as conversion. To describe and date it, some authors have used as a principal source the *Life of Calvin,* published in three successive editions by Theodore Beza, the disciple and successor of Calvin as the head of the church of Geneva, and by his collaborator, Nicolas Colladon.[9] According to Beza's thesis, which has become classic, Calvin—under the sole influence of his relative, Pierre Robert—would have abandoned the papacy for the Gospel before beginning his study of law in 1528. Others have reservations about the scientific value of this document, which the editors of the *Calvini Opera* assert is a "panegyric rather than a biography in the true sense of the word."[10] They complement it or replace it with other sources, particularly with those "autobiographical" passages in the earliest pieces of Calvin's correspondence. Among the "autobiographical" texts, the majority of these authors prefer the Preface of the *Commentary on the Psalms,* where Calvin's famous *hapax* is found: *"subita conversione."*[11]

Moreover, Protestant historians seek to determine who among Calvin's family acquaintances in Noyon exerted a decisive evangelical influence: his relative Pierre Robert, called Olivétan; the German Hellenist, Melchior Wolmar; or Gérard Roussel, the preacher of the Queen of Navarre. Finally, they try to learn whether Nicolas Cop's rectoral discourse, with its Lutheran tendencies, delivered in Paris on 1 November 1533, was written by Calvin, who was Cop's friend. Now let us examine these works in detail.

In 1863, E. Staehelin, in the fourth volume of his work *Leben und ausgewählte Schriften der Väter und Begründer der reformirten Kirche,*[12] gives his opinions on Calvin's development. He does not seek new evidence, and his animated language reflects his admiration for the principal "father and founder" of the Reformed Church. Staehelin affirms first that Calvin's spiritual progress was like the growth of a plant, regular and without any violent jolts: "Very seldom does there appear a man so even-tempered as he, developing in the most constant and regular manner."[13] In Staehelin's view, this does not exclude the possibility that at some moment the mighty hand of God abruptly seized the young university student to convert him to the truth. He is very confident: "1533 is the year of Calvin's conversion to the truth of the Gospel and to the Saviour of his soul."[14] After this event, Calvin is indeed a reformer, and as such he urges Cop to publish his manifesto of evangelical teaching which he wrote with him. When this first attempt failed, Calvin agreed to a short rest at Angoulême, in order to prepare himself for additional evangelical struggles.[15]

In 1869, F. W. Kampschulte, a learned German Catholic who in 1870 became a member of the Old Catholic Confession, in the first part of his work on the religious and political activity of Calvin in Geneva,[16] tried to combat the traditional opinion which goes back as far as Beza. He wrote: "The traditional view, that Calvin during his university years was already won over to the Reformation and even came forward with great success as its public defender and advocate, is entirely erroneous."[17] The author believes that he is able to date Calvin's decisive transformation (he prefers "decisive transformation" to "conversion") in the second half of the year 1532.[18] His hypothesis is founded primarily on the earliest letters of the future reformer. He also takes account of the multiplicity of influences and the complexity of Calvin's spiritual transformation. Although Kampschulte's work stresses the "heretical" aspects of Calvin, its concern for objectivity represents a notable advance in comparison to the polemical tone or even the systematic denigration characteristic of earlier Catholic works.

Allard Pierson, in his *Studien over Johannes Kalvijn* (Amsterdam, 1881), devotes some fifty pages[19] to refuting Beza's opinion with even more resolve than Kampschulte. He refuses to attribute Cop's discourse to Calvin, and he declares that there cannot be found a single irrefutable testimony to Calvin's "conversion" before the first edition of the *Institutes,* whose preface is dated August 1535.

But several years later the traditional view found a perceptive defender in Abel Lefranc and his work *La jeunesse de Calvin.* His principal contribution was to uncover several documents in the archives of Noyon and to succeed in reconstructing the familial, social, and religious setting of Calvin's childhood. Lefranc insists particularly on the decisive impact of these various influences, especially that of Olivétan.[20] He also thinks that Calvin's friends in Paris and Orléans helped to bring him nearer to evangelical ideas.[21] Calvin's conversion, which he saw as the result of a long struggle "of logic and reflection where feeling had no role,"[22] he dated during the second half of 1532. Lefranc also affirmed that Cop's discourse was written by the young convert.[23]

The Swiss historian Henri Lecoultre, in his 1890 article entitled "La conversion de Calvin,"[24] attacked Lefranc's thesis. He believed that one could not establish either the existence of a Lutheran circle at Noyon before 1534 or an evangelical influence from Calvin's own family. Only Olivétan could have been his first mentor. In turn, Lecoultre proposed the following theory: It was during his university studies that the future reformer became "convinced about Protestant doctrine." However, he acquired a "ready resolve" to combat "the errors which he had already renounced in the depths of his heart" only at the moment of his "conversion," properly speaking. Calvin made this conversion clearly known by renouncing his ecclesiastical benefices on 4 May 1534.[25] Thus it was by a "conversion of the will,"[26] not the intellect as Lefranc affirmed, that Calvin was "converted to Protestantism."[27] Henceforth, his attitude toward the Catholic Church was clear: "He understood that he must work at combating and replacing it rather than amending it."[28] The statements of Lecoultre are explicit but often lack cohesion.[29]

A reaction against this thesis came from a German scholar, August Lang of Halle, in his study "Die Bekehrung Johannes Calvins," which appeared in 1897.[30] Lang is of the opinion that as an energetic and uncompromising man, Calvin could not be convinced of a truth without immediately drawing its practical consequences.[31] For Lang, Calvin's conversion had to have been sudden and complete. Beginning with this assumption, Lang seeks to support his hypothesis with solid proofs and attributes major importance to the so-called autobiographical passages *(Selbstzeugnisse)*, especially the Preface to the *Commentary on the Psalms*.[32] On the question of influences, Lang is a minimalist; he refuses to accept as proven the idea that the milieu of Noyon, Olivétan, or even Wolmar were able to direct the religious evolution of the young student. For Calvin, the religious question simply would not have arisen before the middle of 1532 or even 1533. The immediate instrument of "divine intervention" that brought about the conversion of the future reformer could only have been Gérard Roussel, whose sermons of 1533 shocked the circle to which he belonged.[33] Calvin was suddenly converted and made aware that God speaks in the Scriptures.[34] In a few weeks he would have devoured the Bible and several of Luther's writings; thus Calvin would have already been sufficiently initiated in Luther's thought to write Cop's discourse. Lang certainly rendered a great service to historical research in revealing what the French reformer owed to Luther. But his thesis reduces considerably the evolutionary process in order to defend the expression *"subita conversione."*

Emil Doumergue, in the first volume of his monumental work on Calvin which appeared in 1899,[35] takes up the traditional thesis of the "sudden conversion" and attributes it to Olivétan's influence. However, to express more accurately what actually happened, he resorts to the ingenious expression: a "conversion suddenly begun."[36] This permits him to describe the entire "history" of this transformation.[37] He utilizes all the documents and reconciles them with each other to derive the maximum amount of information. This process also permits him to take into account the complexity of the events and influences that were exerted on the future reformer. For instance, Doumergue underlines the respective roles that Erasmian thought, the circle of Lefèvre, Olivétan, Wolmar, Roussel, and—of course—Lutheran writings had on the development of Calvin's thought. But in his excessive enthusiasm, he releases a torrent of hypotheses that are not all supported by scholarly research. His far too laudatory tone tends to evoke in the reader more distrust than his work deserves.

Professor Karl Müller of Tübingen published a work on the same subject in 1905.[38] With careful attention to chronology and precise documentation, he analyzed in detail the earliest sources, the letters of the young Calvin. He concludes that Calvin's interest in religious matters is not dominant, but neither is it absent.[39] The German professor recognizes the influence of Olivétan and Wolmar,[40] but he stresses even more the impact of Erasmian thought and the circle of Lefèvre d'Etaples and Marguerite d'Angoulême. Müller is aware of the merely relative historical value of the famous passage from the *Commentary on the Psalms,* written twenty-five years after these events. According to Müller, there was "development" in Calvin, not a sudden conversion. There was no sudden break, but a slow and peaceful "growth" of an awareness of the ideas and interests of reformist circles.[41] According to Müller, it is obvious that the positive movement toward adherence to reform was stronger than the negative movement away from the church. The decisive break would only have consisted in Calvin's ceasing to participate in the sacraments of the official Church. Calvin would have made that decision in August 1533, after participating for the last time in the public prayers at Noyon.[42] After a meticulous examination of the two manuscript copies of Cop's discourse, the German scholar refuses to admit that Calvin was the author.[43]

Written along the same critical lines were two articles published in 1906 and 1910 by Paul Wernle, a professor at the University of Basle.[44] Wernle notes first that to understand Calvin's conversion, the best method is to examine the earliest sources (letters, documents from Noyon, first publications) and only then to refer to the *Commentary on the Psalms* and Beza. It seems probable that the "autobiographical" passage of the *Commentary* does not contain a historical account but is a theological declaration: the reformer, already fifty years old, glances at his past and affirms that God alone was the author of his conversion.[45] Wernle shows how Beza used this passage to establish the plan of his *Vita Calvini* and then how he corrected it by omitting the words *"subita conversione."* In spite of this, Wernle did not wish—even on a historical level—to renounce entirely the sudden nature of the young Calvin's change.[46] This abrupt change—thus the hypothesis is formulated—would have occurred during a sermon by Gérard Roussel, at the end of 1533 or the beginning of 1534.

The numerous works that were published in 1909 to commemorate the four hundredth anniversary of Calvin's birth did not bring any new elements into the debate. Nevertheless I must mention two names: Williston Walker and Theodore Werdermann.

The first, a professor at Yale University, wrote an excellent biography of the reformer for the Jubilee Year.[47] It contains a good review of the main positions—so divergent—on Calvin's conversion. Walker declares that he does not agree with any of the proposed interpretations.[48] His own proposal is a model of balance and prudence. He goes so far as to place the term "conversion" in parentheses to express his reservations about its sudden nature.[49] Finally, he strongly underlines the role played by "the human instruments of this transformation."[50]

Werdermann introduced his study of Calvin's ecclesiastical doctrine[51] with some considerations of Calvin's conversion. He writes: "For us the issue is primarily determining the content of Calvin's conversion, because it is probable that the character of his conversion is important not only for his piety and theology but also for his doctrine of the Church."[52] A little farther on, he declares that the decisive motif of the conversion was Calvin's discovery of the glory of God. God's glory had been clouded by attempts to deify the creature, and now Calvin must make this glory shine again by reforming the corrupt Church.[53] This approach of putting the religious evolution of Calvin in its *ecclesiastical context* could be very fruitful for both historical and theological research.

In an article by J. Pannier written in 1924,[54] we find a position similar to that of Doumergue. The author takes as his starting point Beza's *Life* and the *Commentary on the Psalms,* but he underlines as well the progressive character of Calvin's transformation and the impact on it of several mentors. He suspects that there was "a slow detachment, a progressive tearing away and then an accelerated movement. It is a long time after the events that Calvin spoke of a 'sudden conversion.' Perhaps an *involuntary exaggeration* is involved there. Besides, 'sudden' does not always mean 'in an instant,' but also 'in a rapid progression.' " Pannier adds that this expression could simply mean: "after I experienced a transformation."[55] This exegesis points out how much historians are embarrassed by Calvin's famous *hapax.*

The works of P. Imbart de la Tour (1935),[56] F. Wendel (1950),[57] and W. F. Dankbaar (1959)[58] do not claim to bring new solutions to this complex problem. But they are marked by a desire to situate the evolution of the future reformer within the thought of the late Middle Ages. Thus they emphasize the probable influence of nominalist philosophy on the student of the Collège de Montaigu. They are followed on this point by K. Reuter, who, in his recent book on Calvin's theology,[59] tries to demonstrate Calvin's close dependence on several representatives of the *theologia moderna* such as John Major, Bradwardine, and Gregory of Rimini.

Paul Sprenger's study is entitled *Das Rätsel um die Bekehrung Calvins.*[60] The title clearly announces that the author's concern is to decipher the "enigma" of Calvin's conversion, which after four centuries of research is not yet resolved. Sprenger believes that it is possible to approach the problem from two points of view: the theological and the biographical-historical. The historian's task is particularly arduous: he needs to conduct an investigation and to sketch a psychological portrait with the few documents at his disposal. According to Sprenger, the work of the theologian is easier and also more important, for without his results the historical problem could not be resolved. Accordingly, Sprenger proposes to undertake a theological study. He begins with the text of the *Commentary on the Psalms,* where he finds a "judgment of faith," a testimony to the reformer's faith in the divine origin of his conversion.[61] The work analyzes each of the main terms of the text in order to reconstruct the original meaning of Calvin's concepts. But the fact that the author uses almost exclusively late "theological sources" restricts him to a *schematization* of the facts. For example, in taking literally the language that Calvin at age fifty uses to condemn the hardening of the young Calvin under the papacy ("too obstinately addicted to papal superstitions"; "my heart, which was excessively hardened for such an age"), he tries to establish the notion that Calvin—between fifteen and eighteen years of age!—was a fanatical partisan of the papacy and a fanatical adversary of new doctrine.[62] This notion also highlights the miraculous character of the "sudden conversion" by which God would have tamed the violent and intolerant young papist and placed in his heart a sweet evangelical docility.[63]

To interpret the expression "too obstinately addicted to papal superstitions," Sprenger offers a thorough analysis of the concept "superstition." But he studies this only in the 1559 *Institutes,* and this limitation permits him to affirm at the end that for Calvin "superstition" refers above all to the worship of the saints and their images and not the ceremonies of the Mass.[64] We know that in his other writings the reformer did not hesitate to call the celebration of the eucharistic sacrifice a superstition.[65] Sprenger believes that he can simply neglect these passages because his purpose is primarily to explain how Calvin, already a "convert," was able to continue to attend Mass without hypocrisy.

In order to date the future reformer's conversion, Sprenger proposes the period between 1527 and 1528, the time when the young master of arts, age eighteen, left Paris for Orléans.[66] But this sudden transition from fanaticism to docility would only have been a *beginning,* just as the miracle of the road to Damascus was only the first shock that moved Saul to listen to the word of God. A long period of apprenticeship and faithful listening to the divine teachings had to follow.

However, in his conclusion Sprenger notices the permanent desire of the young "convert" to remain in the Catholic Church, for he could not imagine that there might be several Churches.[67]

As we end our survey, we discover two principal tendencies in the works we examined: one stresses the tradition of Beza and the *Commentary on the Psalms* (Lang, Sprenger) and the other prefers to begin with the earlier documents that are contemporary with the events (Kampschulte, Müller, Wernle, Walker). The first curtails the time of preparation, has little concern with the "human instruments," and resolutely affirms that in fact the conversion was sudden. The second group is more sensitive to the notion of Calvin's evolution, attributes an important role to various influences, and does not take literally the adjective *"subita."* Several authors are inclined to accept both tendencies (Lecoultre, Lefranc, Pannier). Finally, Doumergue makes a grand attempt to draw out all the implications of both views.

An Ecclesiastical Perspective

The diversity of explanations raises several critical questions that permit us to get closer to the central problem of our study. First, is it really the term "conversion" that the historian should use to describe how Calvin became a reformer, and if so, what meaning should one attribute to it?

Should we understand by "conversion" a spiritual "turnaround," a true *metanoia* which would have made the superficially religious and disinterested student into a fervent and evangelistic believer? Or was it an extraordinary encounter with the living God which prompted him to pass from the despair of the sinner to the *fides fiducialis?* Or is it, rather, a matter of a radical change from a fanatical adversary of the Gospel to one who is suddenly disposed to serve this same Gospel? In a word, are we actually dealing with an intimate and personal religious experience?

One might object that a positive reply to any of these questions presupposes a theological interpretation of the facts and that the historians cannot enter into an analysis of conscience anymore than they can speak of "divine interventions." But these objections would only have a relative value in the sense that these trustworthy documents do reveal and attest to such an experience. Among these documents, one finds contemporary references to the event and others that contain, as it were, "glimpses of the past." The first assuredly would have more value for the historian than the second, for, as a general rule, the closer an account is to the event, the more likely it is to be spontaneous and true.

However, even if the contemporary documents allow us to affirm a religious experience equivalent to a conversion, we will still not have found an adequate reply to the question that concerns us. We need to study the development of a *reformer* who is by vocation a man of the community. Therefore we must go beyond the strictly personal level.

A reformer's life is characterized by the tension between the defective state of the Church to which he belongs and the ideal state that he wishes to establish. The reformer always occupies a position at the "crossroads." He discovers that the road traveled by the Church was in the beginning straight and clear and that later on it became twisted and cluttered. This vision arouses within him a type of "prophetic" vocation to make straight and smooth the "way of the Lord." He wants to "re-form," which supposes that he is conscious of relations between the different forms—past, present, and future—of the one Church. He also knows that according to the faith the Church is a mystery and the different states of the Church (Calvin would say "forms of the Church") are relative to this mystery: they reveal it or hide it; they are in harmony with it or are in contradiction to it.

If Calvin became a man of the Church in becoming a reformer, it is impossible to study this transformation from a purely individual point of view. The inquiry must have an *"ecclesiastical dimension."* Therefore one must raise the following questions: To what extent is there a "personal conversion" and to what extent a "call to reform"? Is the "conversion" necessarily identified with the "vocation" or "call"? Does it at least coincide with it? Is it possible to perceive two distinct moments in the same process? Which of the two appears fundamental and decisive in the documents?

From the moment one emphasizes the ecclesiastical aspect of Calvin's transformation, one is necessarily confronted with the alternative: *sudden break or slow evolution.* We have already established that historians are divided on this point. For this reason we ourselves will proceed with a great deal of care and investigate all the available documents. Only in this way will we have any chance of bringing new elements into the debate and explaining to what extent it is or is not permissible to call Calvin's development "conversion" or "schism" or the awakening of a new "vocation." This is the only way we will be able to understand what was essential for Calvin in his abandoning certain doctrines and structures of the Church of his time and in his attraction to the reform. Only in this way will we be able to understand what constituted his "yes" to the Gospel and his "no" to the papacy, and finally the role of the *absolute* and the *relative* in his position.

The Problem of Terminology

In examining earlier works, we have observed that authors often use an anachronistic vocabulary. In principle, the historian should avoid designating men, ideas, movements, and past events by modern terms whose origin and meaning are later than the age under study. It is advisable that the historian use expressions of the period, determine as necessary their exact meaning, and explain them to the modern reader. This is particularly important when one is writing the history of the reform. Four centuries of separation have strongly "confessionalized" the language of separated Christians. In our times, the best Catholic and non-Catholic authors sometimes use expressions that show an unconscious tendency to justify their own confession of faith.

It would be impossible to obtain absolute perfection in this matter. It would also be a grave error to try at all costs to relate the facts of the reform exclusively in the terminology of the sixteenth century. But as much as possible, we must at least try to avoid using expressions *that the men of that era would certainly have rejected* because they would not express their thoughts or desires. (For example, as much as it seems justified to call Calvin a "reformer," a name he certainly would have accepted, it would be unjust to call him "the founder of the Reformed Church," a title he probably would have rejected.)

To designate the reformers and their followers, historians generally use the adjective "Protestant," as opposed to "Catholic." When one speaks of "the conversion of Calvin to Protestantism," of his "conviction on the subject of Protestant dogma,"[68] one evokes the idea of Calvin's adherence to a "complete Protestantism."[69] We also read that before a certain date he was "still Catholic" and participated "for the last time in a Catholic religious service,"[70] that "Catholic doctrine never was a living reality for him," that he elaborated "his point of view in opposition to the Catholic Church," and that he turned "completely against the Catholic concept of the Church" from which "he had broken away."[71] Another scholar writes that in one of Calvin's letters the reformer's "conviction of faith" is best expressed as "opposition to Catholicism."[72]

We will ignore passages in which we learn, for example, that on such and such a date Calvin "openly proclaims himself a Huguenot" *(sic),*[73] and consider the use of specific adjectives by our authors to describe religious communities and beliefs. In this regard we most frequently encounter: "the new doctrine" as opposed to "the ancient faith,"[74] and "Protestantism" as opposed to the "earlier Church."[75] Of the latter it is often said that Calvin wanted to "fight it and replace it,"[76] or again that he wanted to "reform the Church in spite of the Church."[77]

I contend that this terminology is anachronistic and inadequate, for not only was it not used by Calvin and his companions in the struggle but it was implicitly and explicitly rejected by them. We will have occasion to see[78] how profoundly positive and sacred to the reformer was the adjective "catholic." The epithet "Protestant" is not found anywhere in his work in the confessional sense we use today. In rare cases when Calvin uses it, he applies it to the group of *German* Lutherans who sided with the princes and of the cities that protested against the religious politics of the emperor, such as the Diet of Speyer in 1529. The context of these passages is not confes-

sional but *political and religious.* Besides, the term that is generally opposed
to *protestantes* is never *catholici* but—and this is significant—*pontificii.*[79]
The noun "Protestantism" is totally unknown to Calvin, and we know that
it is not found in French documents before 1623.[80]

Concerning the pair of adjectives "new-ancient," we shall see in the
course of our study[81] that the reformer always criticized those who brought
forth doctrinal novelties and that he applied the term "ancient Church"
exclusively to the Christian community of the early centuries, which was
in his view the ideal "form of the Church."

To designate the men, ideas, and communities that confronted each other
in the conflicts of the reform, Calvin and his followers referred to the "true
clarity of the Gospel" in opposition to the "shadows of superstition";[82] the
more radical reformers contrasted "evangelical doctrine" to "papist" dogmas or to the "papal" sacramental system.[83] In addition to these expressions, Calvin himself regularly used contrasting expressions, as in the 1536
Institutes: "superstition" and "religion,"[84] "idolatry" and "true religion,"[85]
"the wicked" and "the pious,"[86] "adversaries" or "a faction of adversaries"
and defenders of "sound doctrine,"[87] the "papal kingdom" and the "kingdom of God" or the "kingdom of Christ,"[88] the "empty title of Church" and
the "true Church," the Church in a state of "ruin" or "deformity" and the
Church restored according to the Gospel.[89] All these contrasting expressions were understood by him to have come forth from the bosom of the
one and the same true catholic Church.

Civil and religious authorities who persecuted the followers of the reform
continually stigmatized them with the following names: "Lutherans," "the
sect of Luther,"[90] the "cursed Lutheran sect,"[91] "innovators," "creators of
new things."[92]

Therefore in matters of terminology I hold to the following rules. I will
avoid using the expressions "Protestant" and "Protestantism" for those
who were opposed to the "Catholic" Church and "Catholicism." To describe the spiritual and intellectual currents within which Calvin's vocation
took form, I prefer the term "reformist," to which I shall add, according
to the circumstances, the adjectives "moderate," "radical," "Fabrisian," or
"Lutheran." Although the words derived from the term "reform" were not
universally applied to the Calvinist movement until the end of the sixteenth
century, I do not hesitate to use the word "reform" itself, for it expresses
very well the guiding idea of this movement. In addition, I shall adopt in
our vocabulary the name that was dominant among the French followers
of Luther: *"evangelical"* or "the party of the Gospel." As far as the context
and emotional factors allow, I shall even use the epithets by which the
antagonists designated each other: "Lutherans," "dissidents," "papists,"
"sophists," "doctors of the Sorbonne," and so on.

I respect the extreme fluidity of the bounds between the different parties
and reformist ideas, and therefore I shall set aside all expressions that

suggest that there was a clear-cut separation between churches and dogmas, at least as far as the period before the Council of Trent is concerned.

A terminology that avoids anachronisms as much as possible should help in doing a better job of presenting the period in all of its complexity.

Plan and Method

The considerations that I have offered already show my conception of the justification for and the aim of this study. I need only indicate in a summary way the plan and method.

The study is divided into four parts. The purpose of Part One is to follow chronologically the events of Calvin's youth that are likely to shed light on his religious transformation, while keeping in mind their general historical context. This part obviously will include the exegesis of a rather large number of documents, especially the correspondence and the first books of the future reformer.

Part Two will try to discover the sources of the first edition of the *Institutes* to see which ideas could have influenced the young theologian. I will call special attention to the numerous passages that follow closely several texts of Luther, Melanchthon, Zwingli, and Bucer. I will also try to evaluate the influence of the scholastic background—philosophical or theological—that Calvin received at the Collège de Montaigu.

Part Three will summarize the content of the first *Institutes,* with the aim of establishing the general outlines of the doctrine that Calvin elaborated under the influence of his sources and in view of his reform program. First, I shall emphasize the structure of his theological thought; then I shall present its guiding principles: "glory to God alone," "Christ alone," and "the Word of God alone." Then I shall treat the criticisms and the positive proposals of the young reformer on piety, theological doctrine, and ecclesiastical structures. Finally, I shall attempt to see how he conceived the theoretical and practical plan of carrying out the reformation itself.

In Part Four, chapter 19 will deal with the problem of conversion, chapter 20 with schism, and chapter 21 with the vocation of the reformer. I shall treat these three points in close relationship, depending on the historical documents, to discover the personal and ecclesiastical significance of the great transformation, which was first of all experienced and then propagated by the genius who was Jean Calvin.

For the sake of impartiality and objectivity, I shall refrain from criticizing Calvin. Above all, the facts and the sources should speak for themselves. Occasionally, however, I shall point out doctrinal positions that clearly deviate from the Catholic tradition as well as those ideas which, apart from their polemical tone, are in perfect agreement with tradition.

In principle, this work will limit itself to the most interesting period from the point of view of Calvin's evolution. The point of departure will be the year 1523, when the youth from Noyon arrived at the Ecole de la Marche in Paris; and we shall not go beyond 1539, the year when the reformer who had been expelled from Geneva took up his pastoral ministry in Strasbourg. The latest document to be considered is the *Reply to Sadolet* (1539), a work I consider to be a synthesis of the personal and ecclesiastical problems resolved by Calvin in the course of his religious transformation. I shall use later texts only to illuminate more fully the impact of certain facts and ideas referred to in the material from before 1539.

To define the exact meaning of a concept, I shall use the comparative method, that is, I shall consider several contemporary sources where the concept in question is used. The conceptual element that remains unchanged in the various contexts will be the essential factor.

In this way, I hope to take into account the intimate interdependence of life and ideas, events and texts. Thus, I will follow closely the special character of the sixteenth century, so full of contradictions, tensions, and rifts between sons of the same civilization and the one Christian church. To repeat again, it is the true Calvin, the man of his time, who interests us, and not one whom different confessions have seen or would like to see. It is the events, writings, and men of Calvin's own times that must teach us why and how Calvin became a reformer.

PART ONE

A Historical Inquiry Into Calvin's Religious Development Between 1523 and 1539

CHAPTER ONE
Paris and Reformism in France Around 1523

In August 1523, John Calvin, fourteen years old, arrived in Paris. On the eighth day of the same month, the Augustinian monk Jean Vallière was burned alive in front of the entrance of Saint-Honoré. Accused of connivance with "the party of the heretic Luther," and charged with having read and commented on Lutheran books, he was condemned to death by the Parlement of Paris.[1] On the day of his execution, he was led before Notre-Dame, where, without crossing the threshold, he was forced to attend Mass; then he was led outside the city to the pig market, where they cut off his tongue. He was then tied to the stake and burned alive.[2] At the same time, the Parlement ordered the public burning of all Lutheran books.

We do not know what impression this tragic event left on the youth from Noyon. It would only be conjecture to affirm that here his religious convictions experienced their first shock. In any case, the burning of Jean Vallière can be considered a characteristic manifestation of the tense atmosphere that reigned in the city where the young Calvin was to live and study. The Lutheran problem had been a reality for some time, and the name of the Saxon reformer was on everyone's lips.

A number of contemporary witnesses affirm[3] that from the beginning of the year 1519 the intellectual elite of Paris were reading, appreciating, and discussing the works of Martin Luther which were arriving by the hundreds from the printing presses of Basle. It is certain that in the beginning even a group of Sorbonne theologians greeted them with interest.[4] These men, as well as the foremost Christian humanists, were aware of the urgent need for reform in the Church—even if they were very hesitant about the method to follow. One understands why not only Johannes Eck but Luther himself would agree to submit to the University of Paris the doctrinal dispute which had divided them at the Leipzig Disputation in June 1519.[5] Documents containing the controversial questions arrived in Paris on 20 January 1520, but the judgment of the Sorbonne was announced only fifteen months later, on 15 April 1521.[6]

Why so late? Why such a long silence? Professor J. Lortz finds that the hesitation was due to the extreme doctrinal confusion that reigned in all the theological faculties of Europe.[7] Nothing could be more true. Statements by

Luther and Karlstadt at Leipzig, such as the fallibility of the pope and the councils, would not at first glance have appeared to the theologians of the Sorbonne to be heterodox; they had a very long tradition of conciliarism and antipapalism behind them.[8] At the same time, this business would strike them as very inconvenient; it was not so much a matter of an academic reading and discussion but of rendering a judgment on doctrinal statements. Therefore, since they knew they were unable to give a clear and precise reply, they preferred to wait for others to assume responsibility for the decision. Given the circumstances, they looked first to the Roman Curia (so little respected elsewhere) and then to the universities of Cologne and Louvain. In fact, Paris made no pronouncement until after the promulgation of the bull *Exsurge Domine,* dated 15 June 1520, which was followed on 3 January 1521 by the excommunication of Luther. One can assume that some doctors of the Sorbonne still had reservations about the content of *Exsurge Domine.* In reality, among the forty-one Lutheran propositions condemned in the bull, only four had been the object of debate at Leipzig, where only the Faculty was invited to render a judgment. Although the authority of this pontifical document could not be contested, its meaning was not always clear. In the text, the censure was not added to each particular proposition but only at the end of the entire list in a sweeping manner, leaving lots of room for multiple interpretations with its numerous uses of "either . . . or" and "both . . . and."[9] Erasmus himself believed the promulgation of the bull was an unfortunate act, and he continued for some time to praise and defend Luther.[10]

It is certain that during this long delay the writings of Luther, especially the text of the Disputation, continued to circulate freely among the literary circles of Paris. Even in the autumn of 1520, when Noël Bédier (or Beda), a fervent anti-Lutheran, became the syndic of the Faculty of Theology[11] and pronounced on 15 April 1521 the *Determination* condemning Luther,[12] and even when the Parlement published on 3 August a decree forbidding, under the penalty of fine and imprisonment, the reading of Lutheran books, many intellectuals persisted in behaving as if nothing had been forbidden. The heavy-handed approach of Bédier did not exert much influence on minds used to drawing subtle distinctions and nuances. The syndic attacked without discrimination[13] both moderate and radical reformists, including Erasmus, Lefèvre d'Etaples, Luther, and Melanchthon in the same condemnation. He defended with equal ferocity the temporal rights of the Roman see and several scholastic teachings as well as the essential articles of the Catholic faith.[14] Failing to find support among the intellectuals of Paris, Bédier began to depend on the police and the Parlement. This move was, after all, a traditional one, in that for some time the Paris Faculty of Theology had filled the function of the Inquisition in the realm of France.[15]

Opposing the Faculty, which had become a citadel of rigidly conservative forces thanks in large part to Bédier, we find Erasmus and Lefèvre d'Etaples in the forefront. The former enjoyed an authority without equal among the humanists of Paris.[16] His Latin version of the New Testament, which was based on the original Greek and also edited by him, and his "paraphrases" attracted the admiration of the learned. The magnificent irony of his criticism of superstitions and his tolerance, however careless, in dogmatic matters, pleased the men of letters. For Noël Bédier, Erasmus was an idol to be overthrown; but this idol knew how to defend itself. At first, Erasmus went as far as to support Luther. Later, while recognizing the danger of the German reformer's verbal violence, he declared it to be inadvisable to condemn Luther. And even when the great humanist turned resolutely against Luther, he continued to repulse with contempt Bédier's furious attacks.

Lefèvre d'Etaples,[17] on the other hand, represented a Christian humanism that tended to be more humble and at the same time more mystical and pastoral. His biblical translations and commentaries were directed not only to the elite but also to priests engaged in pastoral ministry. He was deeply committed to the Church and desired its inner reform. And—a phenomenon so characteristic of the period—it is from this perspective that he read Luther and Melanchthon! In spite of the bull *Exsurge* and the excommunication of the Saxon reformer, and in spite of the measures taken by the authorities in Paris, Lefèvre certainly did not consider Luther and Melanchthon heretical.

In 1508 the illustrious biblical scholar had been installed at St.-Germaindes-Prés by one of his former pupils, Guillaume Briçonnet,[18] at that time titular head of the abbey. There he gathered around him a coterie of young Christians interested in the Bible, the spiritual life, and reform of the Church. As soon as Bédier entered the scene, the Faculty made this little society the target of its attacks, and Lefèvre, who was suspected of Lutheran sympathies, had to leave the outskirts of Paris. Between April and June of 1521 he retired with his followers to Meaux, once again at the home of Guillaume Briçonnet, who in the meantime had become the bishop of that city. The men who surrounded him there and paid him visits included the impetuous Guillaume Farel, who later became the first reformer of Geneva; Gérard Roussel, theologian, Hellenist, and talented preacher; Michel d'Arande, an Augustinian monk; Martial Mazurier, former principal of the Collège de St. Michel in Paris; Pierre Caroli, canon of Sens and a doctor at the Sorbonne; François Vatable, the famous Hebrew scholar, who later became a reader at the Collège Royal; and Josse Clichtove, the eminent philosopher and patrologist. All were zealous priests who desired reform.[19] Their protector, the Bishop of Meaux, used several of them as preachers in his diocese. This true pastor of souls, who visited his priests and the faithful of his diocese and energetically combated moral abuses and religious ignorance, knew how to use these elite men in the work of effective evangelization that he had undertaken in 1516. But this unique undertaking was at first hindered and then checked by the repeated interventions of the Sorbonne and by the resistance of a large part of the local clergy. Nothing demonstrates better the tragic narrow-mindedness of the Faculty than the suit that it instigated in 1521 against Mazurier. It accused him of having supported in a sermon the opinion of Lefèvre that Mary Magdalene and Mary of Bethany were not the same person. By such quibbling, they blocked one of the rare pastoral undertakings of Catholic reform.[20]

However, Lefèvre and the circle of Meaux enjoyed in the person of the King's sister, Marguerite d'Angoulême, Duchess of Alençon,[21] a protector who was faithful as well as highly positioned. A cultivated woman with a mystical soul, the princess intervened on many occasions before her brother, Francis I, to block the denunciations made by the Sorbonne. She subsidized the publications of Lefèvre and his friends, secured prohibited books for them, and until 1521 remained in constant correspondence with Briçonnet. And later, when pressures from the conservative traditionalists became more and more serious, she opened her home to the persecuted reformers.

As for the King, one can say that he was hardly interested in religious matters, except of course when he was pushed by some political reason. Above all, he wanted peace and order in his kingdom, and for that he relied upon those who presented themselves as the authoritative defenders of Catholic traditions. At the same time, he showed appreciation for humanistic culture, and for this reason willingly favored men like Lefèvre. But mystical or, more properly, ecclesiastical preoccupations did not take root in his mind. This characteristic of "the most Christian King" was to have fatal consequences, because the Sorbonne, which was at first curious and then openly hostile to the German reformer, became a power more and more independent and formidable in the capital of this king, who was more political than Christian. The Sorbonne maintained a strict orthodoxy, whose predominant characteristic was what J. Lortz likes to call a "negative correctness," a faithfulness to tradition that is more negative than positive, a simple "lack of any dogmatic errors." It made no errors in doctrine, but neither did it offer a living and Christ-centered explication of revelation. Strongly tainted with a nominalist, eclectic, and juridical spirit, this theology no longer knew how to distinguish between essential and subordinate matters. At times it defended a practice such as the veneration of images with the same fervor as it would a principal truth of faith such as the real presence. And the battle that it raised against translating the Bible into the popular language forces us to point out how much more it was concerned with "defending" (in both senses of the word in French: "maintaining" and "prohibiting") the Word than in proclaiming it. In fact, the Faculty held the maintenance of the traditional text more important than the missionary proclamation of the divine word. This negative orthodoxy constantly resorted to repressive police methods. The spectacle of a Maillard or a Le Picard, doctors of the Faculty, riding alongside the wagon of Lutherans condemned to death, arguing right up to the foot of the gallows to convince them of their errors,[22] reveals clearly the true face of this aggressive theology. Its protagonists were certainly capable of acting in very good faith. This was definitely true of Bédier. What he did was true to the traditional principles of the Inquisition: it was perfectly permissible to cut off those members of the Christian body infected with gangrene. Nevertheless, this "material sin" had long-lasting, disastrous consequences. It certainly paralyzed all initiatives for internal reform, without being able to stop the continuous diffusion of Lutheran ideas in France.

In 1522, a French translation of part of Luther's *Betbüchlein,*[23] produced in Basle, penetrated the royal territory, after which other evangelical writings arrived from Anvers and Strasbourg. Beginning in the same year, several French monks, such as François Lambert and Guillaume Dumolin, began to visit the University of Wittenberg.[24] In 1523, Farel published his *Somme* and his *Sommaire,* works destined to play "in the history of the French reform a role analogous to that of the *Loci Communes* of Melanchthon in Germany."[25] One can document the fact that many Lutheran pamphlets, such as the *Litaneia Germanorum,* began to be found in the country as early as 1521. These were forerunners of a whole literature of songs and satirical antipapal leaflets.[26] Although the Bishop of Meaux was gravely shaken in 1523 in his reformist idealism, he continued to protect the members of his group, and he did not deal severely with those, such as Farel, whose permit to preach had to be revoked.[27] Moderate reform was surviving while the radical reform was gaining ground. In spite of the burning of Jean Vallière and others, the Sorbonne failed in its first attempt to eradicate Lutheran ideas. The men most faithful to the Church continued to assimilate Luther's thought.

These are the facts and events, but what were their causes? How can we explain the prodigious speed with which the writings and the ideas of the man from Wittenberg spread in France, found an elite audience, and moved some enthusiastic followers to martyrdom? On the other hand, how do we explain the brutal reaction of ecclesiastical power, which in this case was manifested more by the theologians of the Sorbonne than by the bishops?

To answer the first question, we must recognize that at the beginning of the sixteenth century, France—as many countries of the Christian West— was a ground well prepared to receive the Lutheran seed. People consciously or unconsciously were craving forceful denunciations of the evils of the times and peaceful proclamations of salvation—a salvation that was both spiritual and temporal. They desired not only collective salvation but a salvation for the individual which reconciled a man with himself and put him into direct contact with his creator. In other words, a multitude of individuals were waiting for a message that was thoroughly human and thoroughly religious.

In spite of the "pagan" aspects of the Renaissance, in spite of the optimistic naturalism of some humanists, and in spite of the continual surge of the laity and the more or less latent anticlericalism which it contained, the France of Francis I, and soon of Rabelais, was still essentially religious. (By that I do not mean a conformity regarding the dogma and laws of the Christian religion but rather an elementary and spontaneous religious feeling that penetrated the daily existence of man and put him in intimate contact with the supernatural.)

Certainly the royal power, which had become more and more absolute as a result of Louis XI's military successes and the work of his lawyers, did not hesitate to stand up against pontifical power. There were even military conflicts between the pope and the king of France. But that did not at all prevent the monarch from priding himself on his title of "most Christian King," regularly carrying out his religious duties, and relying heavily upon the politically competent members of the high clergy. Even a Francis I, who personally was concerned very little with matters of faith, did not stray from this general rule. Many writers who would soon recognize their "princes" in Rabelais, creator of the "religion of Gargantua," and in Dolet, the herald of libertine life, made great sport of pious traditions, exalted the forces of nature, and relativized doctrine. But in spite of everything, they maintained faith in God and in Christ. Gargantua was an avid reader of the Gospel.[28] The rich, dynamic, intelligent, cultured bourgeoisie of the cities could flaunt their emancipation before the men of the Church whose guardianship they no longer tolerated. But they would not open their houses to Christian humanists, and they continued to send their daughters to the convent and their sons into ecclesiastical careers. The artisans were satisfied with the new flourishing of their crafts and the requests that the great men of the world made of them, but they were to become the most zealous apostles of the evangelical movement. And the peasants? These poor people were so exposed to the ravages of incessant wars and overcome with material cares; crude, ignorant, and often very poorly Christianized, they also showed, even in their unorthodox practices and superstitions, a thirst for the absolute that often pushed them to collective mystical enthusiasm.

This entire society was drawn between the material and the spiritual and between pride in its progress and the anguish of perpetual conflicts; it was extremely sensitive to ill fortune and hope and haunted by apocalyptic thoughts and images. In brief, it was in full transition between the end of the Middle Ages and the beginning of modern times. French society was waiting for a message as substantial as its problems, as inflamed as its desires, as powerful as its ambitions, and as religious as its most profound needs. It is a fact that no one could respond better to these "messianic" expectations than the monk of Wittenberg, Martin Luther.

In these circumstances, one understands that everything that the men of letters, the bourgeoisie, the students, the artisans, and the peasants could have read about Luther or heard about him appeared to a great many of them as words of truth: "the word which was needed"—"the man who was needed."

To be sure, around 1523 few French admirers of Luther understood the central content of his message or the risks of dogmatic deviation that it included. Perhaps with the single exception of Farel, no one had yet thought of conveying his ideas in catechetical form or of immediately putting his program of reform into practice. The elite of the nation were still content to listen to the long-awaited voice of the "prophet" and to translate, read, and comment on his writings. They took pleasure in calling attention to the similarities between the criticisms and the demands formulated by Erasmus, Lefèvre, and the reform preachers of Meaux. One can hardly detect any differences. But the people were to react in a provincial manner: the Christ-centered messages of the preachers pushed them to iconoclastic acts, and their new faith brought them at times to the point of martyrdom.

In facing this situation, the representatives of the established Church showed themselves to be on the whole inadequate for the task. By all rights, they should have spoken the words of truth and salvation, as adapted to the necessities of the new times. They had the mission of bringing about the indispensable reforms by beginning to reform themselves. In fact, much had been done in this area. Much, but not enough—either in depth or in time.

During the course of the fifteenth century, the Church of France had no lack of leading reform personalities. With few exceptions, these were not bishops who normally had pastoral responsibilities but theologians without any ordinary pastoral mission, such as Jean Gerson and Pierre d'Ailly. It was they who opposed the qualitative and quantitative deviations of popular piety, excessive worship of saints, superstitions, various manifestations of enthusiasm, and the spiritual bankruptcy of the preachers. They did not cease to emphasize the need for a religion more pure, more personal, and more centered on the Bible and the liturgy. The Brethren of the Common Life were the determined proponents of the *devotio moderna.* Through the aid of their disciple Jean Standonck, the austere restorer of clerical formation in Paris, and with the rapid spread of Thomas à Kempis' *Imitation of Christ,* they exercised in France an influence that was on the whole quite salutary—even if their ecclesiastical spirit proved to be insufficient. The greatest representatives of Christian humanism owed a great deal to this school of spirituality. We should add that certain religious orders that "never had to be reformed because they were never deformed," such as the Carthusians, and others that were energetically restored to their original ideals, such as groups of Augustinians and Dominicans, were equally effective in increasing the ranks of the reformists.

Nevertheless, this admirable effort did not measure up to the needs of the time. The reforms that were proposed or brought about proved to be incomplete, inadequately organized, and not sufficiently radical. An important detail is that they were most often brought about by an elite—theologians, monks, humanists, people of high nobility—and they did not reach either the summit or the base of the ecclesiastical structure. The failure of greatest consequence was the fact that the papacy and the episcopate had been unable, as a whole, to reform themselves and to give an enlightened and adequate response to the "messianic" aspirations of the people.

After the councils of Constance and Basle, the dispute between the papists and conciliarists or Gallicans continued to consume precious energy. The popes were too distant, too worldly, too political, and too often prisoners of their curial organization; they were severely criticized in all circles and were unable to inspire the multitude of the faithful. Their promises of reform were constantly repeated but never truly kept, and therefore they aroused skepticism in the best minds. For the most part, the French bishops were such great secular lords that they were too busy to carry out the duties of their calling, that is, to serve the flock entrusted to them. They rarely preached, they no longer administered the sacraments, and they had little real contact with the faithful. In addition, there were no serious attempts to suppress the abuses of the *commendam,* the plurality of benefices, exemptions, and patronage. The parish clergy, composed mostly of "ordained sacristans" rather than men who had a true apostolic calling and formation, continued to vegetate materially, spiritually, and morally. The begging monks, called *validi mendicantes,* had more influence on the people, but their preaching tended too often to flatter the audience's crude taste without answering their real problems. The preachers of indulgences did nothing at all to free popular piety from its defects. On the contrary, they profited from them.

The times were changing, but the ecclesiastical institution was stagnant. The laity were being emancipated and wanted to hear Christian proclamation, while the clergy were becoming more secular, paying more attention to earthly than to heavenly matters. The reformists were multiplying, but general reform was delayed. The pervasive intellectual, spiritual, and moral bankruptcy of the priests created a void which—once again—could be filled only by the voice of a "prophet." The audience of Martin Luther was assured in advance.

As we have already seen, the doctors of the Sorbonne took a long time to assess the gravity of the situation. In addition, they made the error of resorting to classical methods of censure, of polemics, and of repression. These were only palliatives. To be sure, their intellectual, spiritual, and creative inadequacies, as well as their incapacity to change, made it difficult for them not to resort to worldly power. Unable to understand the present, they applied the methods of the past. The Inquisition, the heritage of the late Middle Ages, was to be used to safeguard the traditions shaken by the nascent modern age. Representatives of a scholastic theology strongly colored by nominalism wanted to prevent the renovators of biblical and patristic theology from making their voices heard. The doctrinal system of a Bédier, which was clearly inferior to that of Gerson, had to confront the ideas of the "prophetic" Luther. This orthodox but outmoded way of thinking, with no life and no audience, faced a vital and convincing message that was both contemporary and likely to be followed. In terms of spiritual strength, the outcome of the conflict was never in doubt.

This review, I believe, has highlighted the direct and indirect causes of the events that marked the spiritual atmosphere of Paris at the end of the summer of 1523, when the young Calvin arrived to begin his advanced studies.[29]

CHAPTER TWO
Calvin at the Collège de Montaigu, 1523–1527

The young Calvin had a precocious intellect and was anxious to learn. Since he had lived for several years at Noyon in contact with the aristocratic de Hangest family[1] who were devoted to moderate reform, one might suppose that Calvin immediately showed an interest in the current topics of discussion in the capital. The Collège de la Marche, which Calvin began to attend, was imbued with a humanistic spirit. Its best-known "master of grammar" was Mathurin Cordier, whom one might rightfully call one of the fathers of modern pedagogy.[2] This outstanding priest was definitely a partisan of pervasive reform, both in teaching methods and education which he wanted to base on trust and not constraint, and all aspects of piety, which he hoped would be less formal and more Christ-centered. Cordier proved himself to be an heir of biblical humanism and of the *devotio moderna*.[3] He wanted students to be initiated not only in grammar but at the same time in piety and in love of Christ, his word and his laws.[4] Although the young Calvin spent only a few months in the school of this illustrious master, Cordier had a profound influence on him.[5]

The tutor of the de Hangest children had also responsibility for directing John Calvin's studies, and by the end of 1523 had him enter the Collège de Montaigu. The future reformer was to spend four years of his youth there to prepare himself for religious service, in accord with his father's wishes. He received the tonsure at the age of twelve and enjoyed an ecclesiastical benefice which helped finance his studies. If his teacher chose Montaigu for him, it was for good reason: the institution possessed a very solid reputation as an austere and demanding ecclesiastical school.

The majority of Calvin's biographers, inspired by the testimonies of Erasmus and Rabelais,[6] describe the Collège de Montaigu in rather grim terms. They emphasize the unhealthy premises, the poor food, and the inhuman nature of its regimentation. But what interests us is the ethos of the establishment and the intellectual and spiritual formation that was disseminated there. These are the factors that were to influence the religious evolution of our student between the ages of fourteen and eighteen, a very important period for the development of every personality.

In his two studies that deal with Montaigu, Marcel Godet brings to light the role of Jean Standonck in the restoration of this institution.[7] Founded in 1314, it had for some time fallen into decline. Godet affirms that Standonck, a great Flemish ascetic, "was a model restorer of orthodoxy."[8] He was one of those men of the Church who endeavored to remedy the extreme spiritual poverty of the clergy and the people at the end of the Middle Ages. Standonck reestablished the ascetic rigor and discipline that constituted the greatness of Christianity in preceding centuries. Inspired directly by the Brethren of the Common Life and by the monastic orders that remained faithful to their early constitutions, such as the Dominicans and the Carthusians, and also influenced by François de Paule, the founder of the Minims, Standonck decided to make Montaigu a vital center of clerical development. The goal envisioned and partly attained by the austere reformer was to form irreproachable priests of an apostolic spirit, who were well prepared for the ministry of preaching, "a missionary phalanx destined to renew the Church."[9] Between 1490 and 1503 numerous students of the Collège entered religious orders that were still sound or had already undergone reform, and others became good diocesan priests.

The community was comprised of two "houses," the "poor" and the "rich." Those called "poor" or "disciples" were students who benefited from free lodging, food, and education but who in exchange had to promise temporal obedience, wear a gray robe (the uniform of the congregation of Montaigu), carry out the menial duties of the house, and restrict themselves to the most demanding ascetic and pious practices. The "rich," on the other hand, were pensioners, who were in principle not obligated to comply with all the demands imposed upon the "disciples." They lived in separate buildings, the nave of the chapel was reserved for them, and they were forbidden to mingle with the "poor." However, their regimentation was equally demanding. They had to make confession at fixed times and attend Mass and obligatory sermons. "Poor" and "rich" lived in almost complete isolation from the external world; only the theology students could leave the Collège in order to go—in pairs—to their classes. In this way, they would be preserved from the moral laxity that was so pervasive at that time in the Latin Quarter.

The dominant form of spirituality in the community was that of the *devotio moderna,* practiced according to the teachings of Gérard de Groote and Thomas à Kempis.[10] Among the required readings, the *Imitation* was primary. The principal spiritual practices of this community consisted of meditation, examination of conscience, fraternal admonitions, confession, and bodily mortification.

We must not think, however, that the essential element of the *devotio moderna* was its practices. Quite the contrary: it was born of a healthy reaction against the all too numerous pious, external exercises of the late Middle Ages. Struggling against the dispersion of spiritual energy on secondary matters or inauthentic forms of religion, it tried to relate everything to "God alone," emphasizing the inner nature of personal faith. Its most fundamental characteristic was certainly its God- and Christ-centered emphasis, which was nourished by the reading of Scripture in general and the Pauline epistles in particular.[11] Among the great spiritual masters, Augustine and Bernard exercised a dominant influence.

Sustained by these sources, followers of the *devotio* gave priority to what was later called "religion of the heart." The *Imitation* invited the faithful to encounter Jesus Christ in their hearts, to celebrate with him there mystical nuptials. However, this intimate and heartfelt dialogue between the soul and the Master was not to stop at contemplation or to aim at ecstasy but to lead to a practical imitation of the different states and virtues of the Lord. For example, as Jesus had lived in poverty, his disciples should do likewise.

In its serious personal, practical, and moralizing nature, this spirituality manifested some connections with Stoic ethics.[12] Its exaltation of the spiritual over the corporeal revealed Neoplatonist tendencies,[13] which caused it to consider the body as the prison of the soul and to neglect the fundamental dogma of the resurrection of the flesh. The devotee was invited to consider the world only as a place of passage to which one should be attached as little as possible.[14]

This characteristic weakening of the "incarnation" theme in the *devotio moderna* was coupled with its individualistic tendency. By strongly emphasizing the individual's love of God, it often warned against unnecessary association with others. In its devotion to the Eucharist, personal adoration of and union with Christ, it saw little need to emphasize the sacrament of the community and the unity of the Church. Nevertheless, its representation of the people of God as a fraternity of the disciples of Christ, both laity and priests, constituted a healthy reaction against a conception of the Church that was too hierarchical and legalistic.[15]

We cannot be sure just how much these characteristics of the *devotio moderna* still effectively influenced the religious education at Montaigu when Calvin arrived. One might suppose that its original healthy and balanced spirit was altered somewhat by the rigid mind-set that was dominant there.

Education was divided into two different sections: grammar and art classes and classes in theology. The two sections were assigned respectively to the Faculty of Arts and the Faculty of Theology at the Sorbonne. For four to five years, students of the arts learned logic, metaphysics, ethics, the "sciences," and rhetoric.[16] The treatises of Aristotle, Boethius, and other authors were used as basic texts, and each professor commented upon these writings according either to Thomas Aquinas, Duns Scotus, William of Ockham, or Buridan.[17] For five to six years the students of theology studied the Holy Scriptures and the *Sentences* of Peter Lombard.[18] During the period that interests us, a form of nominalism was the dominant tendency at the Collège in the teaching of both philosophy and theology.

When Calvin arrived at Montaigu, the methods of study and religious formation were essentially the same. The apostolic and reforming spirit of Standonck no longer reigned at Montaigu as it had during the lifetime of the holy man. His successors, Noël Bédier and Pierre Tempête, were clearly inadequate to the task. They preserved the severity of Standonck, but they did not inherit his greatness of soul. Under the direction of Bédier between 1504 and 1513, the institution was enriched, but it lost its missionary spirit and its spiritual fervor weakened.[19] The spiritual mortifications that had lost their character of voluntary sacrifice accepted in the love for God began to discourage the students. Enrollments declined. In 1503, there were still two hundred "disciples" in the community of the "poor," but in 1509 their number did not exceed 122.[20]

During the year 1513, Bédier was no longer fulfilling his role of principal. His theological tasks took more and more of his time. The students began to murmur against this lack of leadership, which resulted in Bédier's stepping down and the election of Pierre Tempête in his place. During his fourteen years of administration between 1514 and 1528, Tempête faithfully carried out the wishes of his predecessor—to whom he owed his election. Tempête was sometimes inhuman with his students, and he devoted much energy to disputing with the Chapter of Notre-Dame which had the authority to review the Collège.[21] Calvin's stay at Montaigu coincided with the last four years of the administration of this principal. What effect might this have had on Calvin's religious evolution?

The problem is not easy to solve. We do not possess a single document of Calvin from this period, either correspondence or personal notes. Nor do we possess any contemporary accounts that could inform us about Calvin's life as a student. All that we know is that Calvin was a pensioner and resided at the house of the "rich," where he was preparing for the licentiate in arts. Colladon affirmed in 1565 that the young student worked "in class under a teacher of Spanish origin, and also in the chamber of a Spanish teacher who later became a doctor of medicine."[22] In 1575, Beza spoke only of one Spaniard who taught Calvin grammar.[23] Moreover, we know that the Collège had at that time a professor of logic who was a terminist, Antonio Coronel, and he too was Spanish.[24] Is it the same person in all three cases? Or were there two: a grammarian and a philosopher? Or were there three different persons? These questions demonstrate how much we are reduced to conjecture.

Did Bédier and the famous theologian John Major—a Scotist according to some[25] and a pure nominalist according to others[26]—influence the young Calvin? This is a most delicate question. Both of them taught theology in particular, but Calvin was obligated to take courses only for students of the arts. Moreover, during this time Bédier was no longer the principal of the Collège. As far as Major is concerned, we shall have the opportunity later on to examine the value of K. Reuter's thesis, which attributes much importance to the Scotist professor for the theological formation of the future reformer.[27] In any case, we cannot affirm anything with certitude about the influences on Calvin's studies. The nearly complete obscurity that surrounds this period of Calvin's youth remains to our day.

All that we can say with any degree of probability is that an intelligent and gifted youth of fourteen from the provinces, whom the canons of Noyon deemed worthy of their patronage, arrived in Paris in accord with his father's instructions. He was a sincere, conscientious, and pious lad, even if we do not take literally the slightly hyperbolic statement of Beza: "His heart leaned entirely toward theology."[28] He probably sensed something of the tense religious atmosphere that reigned in the capital and heard of the martyrdom of Jean Vallière. However, he applied himself with confidence to the learned teaching of Mathurin Cordier, and he did not even rebel when, at the end of several months, he had to go to a less elegant place of residence: the austere Collège de Montaigu. There, in his capacity as a "rich" student, he suffered fewer deprivations than his "poor" companions. An ardent scholar, he quickly assimilated grammar, logic, ethics, and metaphysics. Conscientious in the extreme, he conformed to the rules and regularly fulfilled the exercises of piety.[29] He wished to do all he could to prepare himself for religious service, following the spirit and methods of the *devotio moderna*. Very gifted in disputation, the young Calvin excelled in exercises of formal dialectic, and one may assume that on occasion he effectively defended his ideas about contemporary religious questions. But what ideas? The fiercely antireformist and anti-Lutheran traditional ideas of his educators?[30] Had he adopted these ideas for his own? Or did he accept the ideas of some friends who read Erasmus, Lefèvre, and Luther? Who can tell? Among his friends, besides Joachim, Yves, and Claude de Hangest[31] and Nicolas Cop,[32] there was his relative, Pierre Robert, called Olivetanus. The sources reveal the name of Olivetanus only much later, but since he studied in Paris at the same time as Calvin, nothing excludes the possibility that the two young men from Noyon met in Paris sometime between 1523 and 1527. If the thick walls of Montaigu served as an obstacle to frequent meetings, nothing would have stopped them from spending long hours together during their vacations at Noyon.[33] Did they always agree in their discussions? Probably not. It is normal that each defended with fervor the ideas he received from his professors or discovered in his readings. There is no reason to suppose that Calvin at this age had a rebellious attitude and still less a doctrinal position opposed to the faith of his family and his masters.[34] He was certainly an intellectually vigorous youth who was gifted with a critical sense; but this child was, above all, an obedient son and a respectful student. It is quite possible that the reform already interested him in a theoretical way, that Lutheran martyrs commanded his admiration, that Erasmus and Lefèvre appeared to him more and more as models to imitate; but it is also certain that he remained attached to traditional beliefs and religious practices. And let us note that in this attachment there is not a single trace of fanaticism.[35]

An image comes to mind: the young Calvin marched along the straight path indicated by his educators, while taking note of troubling facts that he saw at the edge of the road and in the surrounding countryside. Much later, these observations could possibly reappear in his memory, and then, clothed with new significance, they could serve as arguments to justify a rebellion which by that time was already accomplished. But for the time being, the young man seems only to observe.

This is all that we can say with some degree of likelihood about the state of mind of Calvin the student.

During these same years, 1524 to 1527, the battle between the Sorbonne party and the reformists of all tendencies was pursued with tenacity. In 1524 the stream of Lutheran writings continued to flow into France. The sister of the King received the *De votis monasticis* of Luther[36] and read it without offense. In the following year, there arrived copies of Bucer's Latin translation of sermons by the German reformer.[37]

Then on 24 February 1525, Francis I was defeated at Pavie and was led away as a prisoner to Madrid. Without the presence of her brother, the Duchess of Alençon found it impossible to oppose effectively the attacks of the Sorbonne and Parlement, who took advantage of the situation. They went into action with the support of the Queen Mother, who was named regent, and with the encouragement of a papal pastoral letter dated 20 May 1525, which invited French authorities to extirpate "the damned sect and heresy." At the end of May the terrible peasant revolt in Alsace, which was bathed in blood by Duke Antoine of Lorraine,[38] furnished them with an easy justification. Was it not necessary to deal severely with these Lutherans who were inciting the people and endangering the peace of the kingdom? The first blow ought to be against the most dangerous enemy: the circle of Meaux. In June, they lodged a charge of heresy against Bishop Briçonnet.[39] During the trial this great pastor of souls was deeply humiliated. They broke his resistance and forced him to attack Lutherans and moderate reformists in his diocese. Although the King had ordered that no decision regarding translations of the Bible be made before his return, in August the Faculty censured the *Epîtres et Evangiles des cinquante-deux dimanches de l'année,* which had just been published by Lefèvre.[40] In October, the prosecutor general at Paris made numerous arrests in Meaux. Lefèvre, Roussel, and Caroli did not wait their turn, but fled to Strasbourg.[41] The inquiry organized by Parlement in December revealed that some Christians at Meaux were reticent about auricular confession, had reservations about the worship of saints, had difficulty believing in purgatory, and hummed tunes that were offensive to the clergy, the judges, and the religion of the state.[42] During the same year, John Major began to attack Luther's doctrines in his theology classes by comparing them to those of Wycliffe and Hus. The year 1526 saw the polemics between Erasmus and Bédier rekindled. Erasmus ridiculed his adversary's *Paraphrases* on the Gospel of Luke, and Bédier criticized Erasmus and Lefèvre in his *Annotations* which the King, after his return from captivity, was eager to suppress in order to establish peace.[43] On 5 February, a parliamentary decree prohibited for the first time not only the printing of Luther's works but also translations of Paul's epistles, the Apocalypse, and other books of the Scriptures.[44] During these two years, several persons were burned at the stake: at Metz, the Augustinian monk Jean Chastellain and the lay preacher Jean Leclerc; at Paris, Guillaume Joubert, son of the King's lawyer at La Rochelle, and Jacques Pavannes, a young cleric of Meaux, and another Augustinian monk from Livry, Jean Guibert. In the documents of the trial one can read that they were accused of refusing to venerate images of the saints, of breaking statutes, of criticizing the Mass in Latin, of translating books or preaching heretical doctrines, and of refusing to confess to a priest and to pray for the dead.[45] All died with exemplary courage and an exalted faith in the one Mediator.

Some of these events must have made an impression on our young student during his years of studies at Montaigu.

CHAPTER THREE
Calvin in Orléans and Bourges, 1528–1531

Calvin probably remained at the famous Paris Collège until the end of 1527 or even the beginning of 1528. His father had been quarreling with the canons of Noyon, his son's patrons. At this time the father decided that his son John would not study theology to become a priest, but law in order to pursue the more lucrative career of a jurist.[1] That was the father's intention. What did the son think of it?

This is precisely the point where historians who follow Beza and the Preface to the *Commentary on the Psalms* interject a statement relating to

Calvin's conversion. We come again to the text of the Preface. It emphasizes the sudden nature and divine origin of the conversion and makes no allusion to Olivétan. However, Beza's account does not speak of a "sudden conversion" but emphasizes the role played by Olivétan. In our historical inquiry, we acknowledged that the work of Beza has only relative importance. According to the opinion of many historians, its apologetic and panegyric tone invites reservations about its value as a reliable historical document. Having said this, let us see how Beza presents Olivétan.

In the first edition of the *Life of Calvin* we read: "His father was continually set upon his studying law, and he also developed such a desire through his relative and friend, master Pierre Robert, known as Olivetanus, who later translated the Hebrew Bible into French (published at Neufchâtel) and tasted something of pure religion and was beginning to be disturbed by papal superstitions. It was because of his singular reverence for his father that he agreed to go to Orléans."[2] At this point in reediting Beza's text, Colladon adds: "He agreed to study law rather than theology, for at the time theology was corrupted in the schools."[3] Finally, the last edition of Beza explains the change in studies by a sudden change of mind that took place simultaneously in both father and son: "The minds of both were changed." For the father, Beza notes the new ambition to procure a profession that would enrich his son. For the son, on the contrary, there was a more pure motive: "But the son was urged . . . by a certain relative of his, Pierre Robert Olivétan, concerning true religion, to devote himself to the reading of the sacred books and to abhor superstitions; and accordingly he began to separate himself from those sacred rites."[4]

When we compare the three texts, a first impression becomes clear: we are witnessing a variation and a reinforcement of themes. Only the role of Olivétan is presented without variation. First of all, two themes are noted: first, the will of the father and the corresponding obedience of the son; second, the fact that Calvin detached himself from "papal superstitions" in order to learn a little more about "pure religion." The second text reveals a third motive: Calvin prefers law to theology, which he believes is corrupted. Finally, in the third text the author ignores this last motive, retains the other two, and powerfully reinforces them by elaborating the second one which is of great concern to Calvin. In this student's soul, it is the "will" that is transformed; his attention was fixed upon "true religion," he immersed himself in reading holy books, and he turned away in horror from superstitions, until he gradually stopped attending Mass ("to separate from those sacred rites"). This progression of themes appears to be explained by the desire of the apologist to argue more and more convincingly. But the historian seeks to be convinced by facts and not by arguments of this kind. Therefore we will attempt to draw from all these statements a central core which seems quite realistic: the role played by Olivétan.

Who was this Olivétan? We have already had occasion to speak of him, but we must give a more complete picture. Is this possible? Doumergue notes that Olivétan is a "mysterious figure, as if covered by a veil which nothing can penetrate."[5] In fact, all that research presently can tell us about him can be summarized in a few words. He was from Noyon, and a lawyer's son. He was living in Paris at the time his relative was studying at Montaigu, and then they found themselves together again at Orléans, at least for a time, at the same university. He must have concentrated on classical languages, including Greek and Hebrew, early in his studies in order to accomplish his demanding enterprise of translating the Bible from the original texts. For this French Bible, published in 1535, Calvin wrote a Latin preface in which Olivétan is described as a "relative" of the author and an "intimate friend of long standing." He knew him well and was able to praise his great modesty.[6] But it is important to note that in this reference Calvin makes no allusion to Olivétan's introducing him to evangelical views. Shortly after leaving Orléans, Olivétan left the country to join the ranks of Lutheran reformists, but nothing allows us to affirm with certainty that Olivétan was already a Lutheran when he visited his relative in Paris and Orléans. That is only probable.[7] In any case, it is purely hypothetical to argue that Olivétan is the young man from Noyon whom Bucer describes in a letter to Farel of 1 May 1528, as having fled to Strasbourg to escape persecution in Orléans.[8] A. L. Herminjard and K. Müller defend this hypothesis,[9] but other historians, such as H. Eells, are more reserved.[10]

In my view, several indications argue against identifying this young man with Olivétan. Note especially that according to the letter the young man in question has "studied literature," but he was still "completely ignorant" of Greek and Hebrew. But by 1528, Pierre Robert, who was a few years older than Calvin, probably had completed his studies in the arts and several years of literary studies besides, during which he could not fail to have studied Greek and Hebrew, since he was preparing to translate the Bible. Moreover, the expression "completely ignorant" must have appeared embarrassing to an early commentator, for in the original manuscript these two words were crossed out and replaced by a milder expression: "in which he was not yet thoroughly educated."[11] It seems wise not to be too insistent about the hypothesis of Olivétan's flight to Strasbourg at the beginning of 1528. After all, the aim of the hypothesis is to shore up Beza's thesis that, as will be recalled, Pierre Robert played a decisive role in the conversion of Calvin before his departure for Orléans. In view of the obscurity of the documents, I prefer to leave this in the realm of possibility.[12]

More certain evidence of Olivétan's adherence to the radical reform appears only at the beginning of 1535,[13] found in his letters and the list of Zwinglian and Lutheran works that were in his library at the time when he died unexpectedly in 1538 at Ferrara.[14] Besides Beza, no other contemporary witness affirms that Olivétan was a militant evangelical before 1528, and I have already emphasized that the statements of this author are of limited value.

Let us return to Calvin himself. We do not know whether it was with joy or only in obedience to his father's order that Calvin, a *licencié en arts* fresh from Montaigu,[15] arrived early in 1528 at the Faculty of Law at Orléans. There he became a student of the famous professor, Pierre de l'Estoile. Who was this man? According to some historians, he was "the best French jurist of the times."[16] He was a man of piety and integrity. After the death of his wife, he entered a religious order. When the future reformer met him, he was vicar-general in the diocese of Orléans. A man of the Church, he proved himself to be strongly attached to orthodoxy and tradition.[17] When the council of the ecclesiastical province of Sens—to which the bishops of Meaux, Paris, and Orléans,[18] among others, belonged—was convened on 3 February 1528, at the Church of the Grand Augustinians in Paris, de l'Estoile went there to represent his bishop.[19] Presiding over the council was Cardinal Antoine du Prat, chancellor of the King and a fervent enemy of the Lutherans,[20] who enacted severe laws against heretics as well as against translators, printers, editors, and readers of the French Bible. The council also intended to consider ecclesiastical reforms to deal severely with abuses, such as nonresident priests, priestly concubines, improper use of excommunication, and confusing forms of popular piety. They also insisted upon a simple preaching of the Gospel to the people.[21] After the Inquisition-like orders of the Sorbonne and the Parlement, this council of the French episcopate, which up to this time was rather sluggish, was simultaneously "reformist" and "antireformist."[22] The council intensified the persecution, but its effectiveness was negligible in terms of Christian renewal. It was to this synod, then, that Pierre de l'Estoile in good faith contributed his support. If the young Calvin had been truly "converted" at this time, or at least on the road of "pure religion," he doubtless would have disapproved of the attitude of his professor. But what do we find? The respectful and fervent devotion of a good student to his master. And this was a lasting devotion, for in 1531 it resulted in a public defense of his professor against the attacks of the brilliant Italian jurist and humanist, Andreas Alciati.

This apology is the very first composition of Calvin intended for publication. It is in the form of a preface and frontispiece to the *Antapologia* written by a friend of Calvin, Nicolas Duchemin, the aim of which was to prove that Alciati's alleged facts in his encounter with de l'Estoile were inaccurate. We read Calvin's praise of de l'Estoile's knowledge: "For he possessed an acute mind, industry, and of course knowledge of the law. There is no question that he occupies the principal position in this field, with one or two others." But we also read Calvin's testimony to his moral qualities: his serenity, his patience, and his tranquil conscience under the blows of calumny.[23] There is not a single allusion to the antievangelical role played by the vicar-general of Orléans or to his responsibility in instigating the persecution of the Lutherans!

We note in passing that even Beza's panegyric contains only praise for de l'Estoile, "this excellent man," who is nevertheless clearly called "President of the court of the Parlement of Paris."[24] It is true that this rather awkward title disappears in the last Latin edition, but the praise remains and this time is expressed almost in the language of Calvin himself: "Pierre de l'Estoile, without question, the Prince of French lawyers."[25]

In 1528, the year of the councils of Sens and Bourges, there were also tragic events that our student would have observed more easily than the dramas that occurred while he was living within the walls of Montaigu. Various reform movements were active at Orléans. The persecution there represented a permanent threat, and the news from Paris spread from mouth to mouth in Orléans. It was learned that on 3 July, Denis de Rieux, a resident of Meaux who was accused of Lutheran propagandizing and criticizing the Mass, had been burned in the market square of the city. People spoke as much of the superhuman courage of this martyr as of the cruelty of his executioners.[26] There was another execution in Paris on 15 December of the same year, when a boatman, also originally from Meaux, was condemned for having mutilated an image of the Virgin Mary.[27] All these acts of repression could not stop the spread of Lutheran ideas; from that time on, the works of the German reformer found—right in the capital—a very competent translator, Louis de Berquin,[28] and a printer of the first order, Simon Dubois.[29] Berquin, in spite of his stature as a learned humanist and his good relations with the court, paid for his audacity on 17 April 1529, when he was burned at the stake.[30]

Then the historic moment arrived when Francis I himself ran out of patience and, at the instigation of the traditionalists, began to contend with rigor against the "Lutheran sect," especially in Picardy, the district of Calvin's birth,[31] and in Normandy, which many were already accustomed to calling "Little Germany."[32] It was the same period when the two catechisms of Luther (the *Little Catechism* under the title of *Quatre Instructions*[33]), the *Articles of Marburg,* and "confessions of faith" by Luther and by Bucer were published in France.[34] While our young jurist was advancing brilliantly in his studies,[35] he had numerous dramatic events to observe.

At Orléans, a university city where the atmosphere was no doubt more free than at Paris, Calvin counted among his friends the German Hellenist Melchior Wolmar and among his fellow students at the Faculty of Law François Daniel, François de Connan, and Nicolas Duchemin. With them Calvin could discuss not only studies but the religious situation.

Wolmar was born in 1496 in Württemberg. After completing in brilliant fashion his studies in Paris, he became a professor of Greek.[36] According to C. E. Bulaeus, Wolmar's reformist opinions, which were influenced by ideas of Luther and which he expressed quite freely, made his stay in Paris very dangerous.[37] Therefore he left the capital for Orléans about 1527 and opened a boarding house for students.[38] The majority of historians hold that Calvin met the learned man from Württemberg shortly after his arrival in Orléans.[39] But these authors are far from agreeing about the kind of influence that Wolmar exercised on him. Florimond de Raemond, an anti-Lutheran chronicler and a contemporary of the reformer, affirmed that Wolmar "was the first to give him a taste of heresy."[40] Catholic historians, for the most part, have adopted this opinion. A. Lefranc attributes to the Hellenist a predominant role in Calvin's conversion,[41] while A. Lang does not believe that such a religious influence can be proved.[42] Likewise, F. Wendel notes that the reformer, who often wrote of Wolmar and to him,[43] has not "left one line that alludes to any such influence" of this friend "in the religious realm." Wendel adds: "There is not a single document to fill this gap, so that we have to confess that nothing justifies the hypotheses that are constructed to show that the conversion of Calvin began during his stay at Orléans and was due principally to Wolmar."[44] What is proven is that the professor from Württemberg had been a friend of the future reformer and had initiated him into the rudiments of Greek and no doubt other humanist learning.[45] Beza himself does not venture beyond this statement.[46]

With Wolmar, then, we have a case similar to that of Olivétan. He will definitely become a Lutheran later on,[47] but it would be impossible to show that during the time he was in contact with Calvin he was already a Lutheran or that he had a "Lutheran" influence upon Calvin. Once again, we cannot go beyond the realm of conjecture.

Calvin's other friends at Orléans had in common with him not only an interest in the science of law but also, it seems, a passion for humanism. They knew Rabelais, if not personally[48] at least through his writings. They considered Erasmus and Lefèvre as their spiritual guides. François Daniel lived with his relatives, his brothers and sisters at Orléans, and he often invited into this family circle his friend from Noyon. François de Connan was a Parisian whose father was a director at the Chamber of the Treasury. Nicolas Duchemin, a jurist who was a little older than Calvin, lived for a time under the same roof with Calvin.[49] The earliest letters that we have from the future reformer were addressed to his friends, especially to Daniel. We shall study them later in detail. Here we note only that none of these friends followed Calvin into the radical reform. Because of lack of courage or because of loyalty, they remained on the path of the moderate reform of Christian humanism. Examining these letters, we will learn that for several more years, Calvin—at least in his correspondence—reveals no differences of opinion with and no criticisms of his fellow students. Like the others, he seems to have reconciled without much difficulty his affection for a professor such as Pierre de l'Estoile and his passion for biblical humanism.

The dreadful recriminations inflicted upon the evangelicals certainly must have impressed them but without driving them into open rebellion against the established Church.

It is probable that our young jurist stayed in Orléans until the spring of 1529, when the famous Italian, Andreas Alciati, arrived at the University of Bourges.[50] This brilliant man, whom Erasmus himself held in great esteem, "appeared as an innovator, explaining the laws of history and of social life."[51] He awakened the interest of Calvin, who after the summer vacation of 1529 went to Bourges to take Alciati's courses. At the end of 1530, Wolmar transferred his residence there at the invitation of Marguerite d'Angoulême, who by 1527 had become the Queen of Navarre and the Duchess of Berry, and consequently the protector of the University of Bourges. François Daniel also rejoined his friend[52] to take advantage of Alciati's teaching. In all probability Duchemin also joined the two of them at Meillan, a district next to Bourges, where Calvin had his lodging.

The teachings of the Italian professor captured their attention for about a year and a half in spite of the fact that they were full of sarcasm aimed at Pierre de l'Estoile, their venerable master. It is true that Duchemin defended him in his *Antapologia*—as we have already mentioned—which he probably drafted around 1529 but did not publish with Calvin's preface until 1531.[53] Our young jurists knew very well how to take things into account. As Calvin says in his preface, they criticized Alciati for the injustice of his attacks, but they nevertheless owed him a "debt of honor which was not overlooked in their preliminary remarks."[54] It was one thing for them to recognize that the knowledge of this learned man was without equal and quite another to allow him to humiliate their master from Orléans. They felt obligated to raise their voice against these unjust dealings, but their protest contained not a single trace of a partisan spirit or religious prejudice. What is more, whereas de l'Estoile was on the side of intolerant orthodoxy, Alciati belonged to a university where, thanks to the protection of Marguerite, the reformists enjoyed complete freedom. However, our friends entered the fray against Alciati in order to defend de l'Estoile![55] The importance of this observation may be seen if one is willing to retrace the religious evolution of the future reformer without taking sides.

In Paris, one of the most remarkable incidents of the year 1530 was the publication of the new *Determinatio Facultatis,* dated 30 April, in which the Sorbonne took the offensive against the readers of the recently established Collège Royal. The readers were Guillaume Budé, the famous humanist; Nicolas Cop, the son of a friend of Erasmus; the Hellenist Pierre Danès; and the Hebrew scholar François Vatable, a disciple of Lefèvre. All of them were a part of the "Fabrist group,"[56] and all were convinced of the need for a scientific exegesis of the original texts to understand the Bible better. Two propositions condemned by the Faculty were expressed in these words:

"First proposition: Holy Scripture cannot be understood properly without Greek, Hebrew, and other similar languages. Censura: this proposition is imprudent and scandalous. Second proposition: no preacher can explain the truth of an epistle or Gospel without the aforementioned languages. Censura: this proposition is false, impious, and prevents in a pernicious manner Christian people from hearing the Word of God. Moreover, the authors of these assertions are strongly suspected of *Lutheranism.* "[57] It is interesting to note that although the royal readers never fell into formal heresy, they were suspected of Lutheranism. As we have seen, such a suspicion could lead persons as eminent as Louis de Berquin to the gallows. The power of the Faculty was now formidable. During the same year, Bédier published a writing against the "secret Lutherans." Erasmus felt singled out and replied with irritation.[58]

At Bourges, Calvin probably heard people speak of these measures that might endanger some of his Parisian friends and that were contrary to the goals pursued by the Christian humanists, among whom he no doubt began to number himself. Nevertheless, it is possible that the optimism that reigned at that time in the university milieu of Bourges reassured him. The influence of the Queen of Navarre had already proven on many occasions to be effective with her brother, the King. Could not her influence be enlisted once again in favor of the royal readers?

The first letter by Calvin that we possess is dated from Meillan on 13 September 1530. It is addressed to his "incomparable friend," François Daniel, who was at that time in Orléans.[59] The tone of the letter is witty and its style lively, but it deals only with mundane matters, which is quite normal between friends. Among the greetings that it contains, there is one for Wolmar.

Colladon affirms that before leaving Bourges, Calvin preached several times at Lignières, a district of the duchy of Berry.[60] In his last edition, Beza repeats this observation in summary form. He also alludes to the scriptural readings by which the future reformer prepared himself for these sermons.[61] Doumergue has the distinction of having checked these assertions with the local tradition of Lignières and with old monographs dedicated to the history of Berry. According to the famous historian of Calvin, this statement by Colladon deserves more credit than others, since the author had lived in the region.[62] Therefore we can be sure that we are dealing with an established fact. Besides, in a period when abbots, bishops, and parish priests retained their positions without having received priestly ordination, it is not at all inconceivable that a simple cleric, such as Calvin, who held an ecclesiastical benefice, would give sermons in a country church. Moreover, according to Colladon, the seigneur of the area invited him there.[63] It is obviously impossible to comment on the content or viewpoint of these early sermons by Calvin. Doumergue himself recognizes that by preaching,

Calvin "did not pass himself off as a Protestant" and that he kept the "appearance of an ordinary pastor, a Catholic priest."[64] In the same vein, W. F. Dankbaar rejects any easy solution and assumes there would be nothing "anti-Roman" in the sermons of a young jurist of Bourges, who was more likely to reflect the spirit of the Fabrisian humanists.[65]

CHAPTER FOUR
The Second Period in Paris and Orléans, 1531–1533

In March 1531, Calvin returned to Paris with his preface to the *Antapologia* in order to have Duchemin's work published. There he received alarming news about his father's health. He quickly left the capital for Noyon. Nicolas Duchemin, whose book was in press, became very uneasy about the unexpected silence of his friend. But when Calvin arrived in his native city, he did not delay in explaining the situation.

In examining this letter, several historians have been disturbed by the contrast they find between the dispassionate mention of his father's imminent death and the affectionate words addressed to his friend ("my friend, dearer than life").[1] We find nothing astonishing in this. A proud and reserved man of Picardy always hides his grief. This extreme reserve in expression enabled him to deal in a becoming manner with his anguish. It seems very likely that Calvin was profoundly saddened to see the agony of his father, whom he loved and revered. It is precisely for that reason that he refrained from showing his feelings and was happy to demonstrate his normal tenderness toward his friend.

Gérard Cauvin died on 26 May 1531. The circumstances were painful. The excommunication, which was pronounced by the Chapter of Noyon with which Cauvin had quarreled, weighed heavily upon the old man. The very next morning, Charles, the oldest of Calvin's brothers, had to negotiate with the canons to obtain posthumous absolution and permission to bury the body in consecrated ground. Since Charles himself had just undergone the blow of excommunication—at this time this penalty was easily inflicted[2]—the negotiations must have been quite painful and humiliating for the bereaved family. Even if we do not attribute as much importance to this heartbreaking incident as does Lefranc,[3] we believe it quite possible that it left wounds in the future reformer's soul that would likely be reopened at the next demonstration of ecclesiastical severity.[4] In any case, the reformer would later on have very harsh words to say against the abuse of spiritual measures in the temporal realm.[5]

After a short stay at Orléans,[6] our jurist once again returned to Paris in order to devote himself more fully to classical humanist studies. He lodged first at the house of the Coiffart family, then at Chaillot on the outskirts of the capital, and finally at the Collège de Fortet in the middle of the Latin Quarter.[7] He went there to follow the course of study at the Collège Royal; and in view of the recent threats of the Sorbonne, this move was certainly a proof of courage or at least a demonstration of optimism. The lessons of the royal readers brought him into profound and prolonged contact with the humanism of Erasmus and Lefèvre. No doubt these new Parisian acquaintances developed in his mind all the seeds sown by men as diverse as Cordier, Olivétan, Wolmar, Alciati, and his friends at Orléans and Bourges. It is quite possible that Calvin also met at this time Gérard Roussel, who had returned from exile in Strasbourg and had been given the title of preacher at the Paris court of the Queen of Navarre.[8] He also renewed his relationship with the family of Nicolas Cop and with Etienne de la Forge, the generous evangelical merchant.[9] Colladon and Beza attribute a rather important role to de la Forge in their account of the reformer's life.[10]

From this same period[11] a most interesting letter of Calvin's has survived. It is dated 23 June and addressed to François Daniel. Our young Bible scholar gives an account of the results of an interview he had with a sister of Daniel. She was a novice in a Paris convent and was preparing to take her vows. According to his friend's wishes, Calvin and one of the Cop brothers (probably Nicolas) went to the nuns to ask the date when the novice was to make her profession. The expression used in the letter is the following: "that . . . I might determine with the nuns the day when your sister would fulfill her vows *(voti se damnaret)*." Some authors see here a negative meaning; but it seems that is incorrect, for the classical and technical sense of *voti se damnare* is "to accept an obligation according to one's own desires."[12] The remainder of the text also has no hostile allusions to monastic life. One finds nothing more than a true desire to respect the freedom of God's children.

Calvin relates in a straightforward manner that he asked the young lady whether she was about to receive the yoke of religious profession freely and in all spiritual "meekness." He also tells that he exhorted her to speak quite frankly about everything that troubled her and that finally he found her confident and joyful at the thought of pronouncing her vows. And he adds: "I did not want to turn her away from her view of things; I did not come with that intention. But I did warn her in a few words neither to depend too much on her own strength nor in any way to have an exaggerated confidence in herself; but above all to rest in the power of God, in whom we live and have our being."[13] The letter ends with a few words about the hospitality of the Coiffart family and the lessons of the Hellenist Pierre Danès. I agree with Paul Wernle[14] and K. Müller[15] that this document contains nothing Lutheran in it, but at most reveals a profoundly religious, Fabrist spirit.[16]

At this time our young scholar does not seem to be moving in a radical direction at all. Moreover, in a letter dated 27 December, his friend Daniel could propose—without risk of offense—that Calvin would intercede with a bishop originally from Picardy (perhaps the recently consecrated Claude de Hangest) in order to obtain for him an ecclesiastical judgeship or a similar honor.[17] There is no sign at all that Daniel imagined he might receive an indignant refusal from Calvin.

The spiritual portrait of the future reformer can be completed by reading his first book, a commentary on the *De Clementia* of Seneca, published in Paris in April 1532.[18]

Its preface is dedicated to the "most holy and most learned prelate Claude de Hangest, Abbot of St. Eloi of Noyon."[19] With recourse to some-what artificial formulas of modesty that according to humanist tradition should be respected at the beginning of a work, the author declares without pretense that it is his intention to develop, among other things, certain details that escaped the notice of Erasmus, who had already written two commentaries on the same subject. Furthermore, the entire composition reveals characteristics of the twenty-three-year-old author that will be confirmed as time goes on. This young man knows his Greek and Roman classics quite well, along with Augustine's *City of God,*[20] which he quotes quite appropriately. It displays genuine sympathy for the noble Stoicism of Seneca,[21] who when faced with Nero's tyranny had been able to write—in an artfully "subtle manner"—an apology for the virtue of clemency. How-ever, Calvin did not exploit this theme in order to attack the contemporary religious persecutions. This is quite surprising, since Calvin shows in this work, among other things, a genuine interest in contemporary issues.

I shall try to explain this enigma in the following manner. For Calvin at this stage of his intellectual development, each human community worthy of the name is a living organism that is well organized by virtue of its subordination to a single direction. According to the thesis of Plutarch, the head or the organ holding public power possesses an authority of divine origin: "The prince is the minister of God, for the welfare and care of the people." This is also true according to the teachings of Christianity: "It is also the confession of our religion that there is no power except from God." In these statements one can also find the influence of the "royal jurists," who created in France the theory of absolute monarchy, as well as a reflection of the social thought of Plato.[22] Then Calvin quotes the thirteenth chapter of Romans.[23] The head of the social body, the prince or the king who is vested with divine authority, is indispensable to the normal life of the human community: "A body without a head is a useless piece of earth."[24] The social body has an absolute need to be directed by sovereign authority: "The prince is to the republic what the soul is to the body. As the soul rules or moderates all the actions of its members, so those subordinate to the command of the prince observe and attend to all their duties."[25] In this context where the emphasis is placed so strongly on the need for a strong central authority, we can easily understand why our young humanist did not think of criticizing the persecution which the King of France himself had unleased, or at least approved, against the Lutherans.[26]

I do not wish to insinuate that Calvin had accepted or even considered the execution of heretics to be a necessary evil. In my opinion, one who attached such great importance to the virtue of clemency would have suffered deeply at the sight of the harsh measures against the heretics; but at the same time he would have remained completely loyal to the sovereign and the established order. We know that later on, even in his polemical and antipapal writings, Calvin always considered the persecutors, Francis I and Charles V, as legitimate princes who were invested with authority by God. There is every reason to assume that the same attitude would be found in the young Calvin.

The *De Clementia* gives us a testimony of the social and civic thought of an author who put order very high on his scale of values. What the *De Clementia* does not reveal is whether the author sympathized with the persecuted. Calvin's sense of order and sympathy no doubt made him uneasy, but he would not go so far as to make his views known in a public statement.

The rest of the commentary on the *De Clementia* bears the mark of Erasmian moralism, and in the manner of the Stoics exalts providence "which excludes chance and directs princes."[27] It contains some criticism of superstitions opposed to "religion,"[28] but it contains nothing of an evangelical character.[29] Beza himself does not try to present it as such. He only praises the moral earnestness of the young author.[30]

The sale of the book, which Calvin printed at his own expense, cost him a great deal of suffering. A letter addressed to his friend Daniel and dated from Paris, 22 April 1532, bears testimony of this.[31] At the time, Calvin was frequently short of money because his brother Charles was not very conscientious or regular in sending monthly installments. The future reformer was forced to borrow from Cop or Duchemin.[32] Some health problems increased his difficulties even more. Only the intervention of a good doctor succeeded in eliminating them.[33]

In one of the letters in which Calvin reveals his preoccupations concerning the sale of his book, a question arises about a Bible which, at Daniel's request, Calvin had purchased with much difficulty.[34] Nothing prevents us from thinking that it was a copy of Lefèvre's French Bible, so suspect by the Sorbonne that the booksellers had refused to sell it publicly. But it would be hazardous to deduce from the simple fact of this purchase that

Calvin and Daniel belonged to the evangelical party. Young humanists with Fabrist leanings may well have been interested in a translation by Lefèvre.[35]

During the last half of May 1532, Calvin again left for Orléans in order to complete his law studies and to obtain his license in law. This most recent visit probably lasted an entire year.[36] Doumergue, following Herminjard, correctly observed that for this period—more precisely from 15 May 1532 to 27 October 1533—we do not possess a single testimony or witness.[37] We only know, thanks to the research of J. Doinel,[38] that in May and June of 1533 Calvin was serving at Orléans as the "deputy bursar" *(substitut du procureur)* of the "Picard Nation," an office he no doubt had already held for several months, since the duty of the deputy was generally conferred for an entire academic year.

This lack of documents complicates the task of scholars who seek to retrace the religious evolution of the future reformer. Is it not the period, immediately preceding the autumn of 1533, in which most historians think the decisive turning point in Calvin's reformist attitude should have occurred? Numerous difficulties that still seem insurmountable would disappear if we knew what new contacts Calvin made during his second stay in Orléans, what influences he experienced, and, above all, what biblical or Lutheran readings he undertook.

The last point is of major importance. Each time we have attempted to find the sources of one of Calvin's writings, we have been struck by the profound influence that his readings made upon him just before he prepared himself to write. Calvin was certainly not a reader like others. What he read he assimilated very rapidly, and *he was immediately inspired to write.*

Calvin's eagerness to appropriate the ideas from the works he devoured and to put his thoughts on paper is particularly well illustrated in the *De Clementia.* In June 1531, Calvin arrived in Paris and immediately began his humanist studies. He studied Greek and Hebrew, and above all he broadened his classical readings, which he no doubt had already begun in Bourges and Orléans. He read or reread as well Augustine's *City of God.* Then in April of 1532, hardly ten months after beginning his humanist studies, the ever-wakeful young jurist was already selling the firstfruits of his literary powers. An impressive number of authors are quoted: Seneca, Homer, Ovid, Pliny, Cicero, Plutarch, Virgil, Juvenal, Horace, Lucian, Terence, and still others, including Augustine, Gregory the Great, and Erasmus. There are learned etymologies of Greek words, along with explanations of Latin expressions. Much material was absorbed, digested, pondered, and written about in so little time! We will witness a similar phenomenon in the first edition of the *Institutes,* which reveals what Calvin read in 1534.

But is there a work by Calvin whose contents would shed light on what the future reformer was reading between 1532 and 1533? In fact there is: the *Psychopannychia,* [39] a study of the immortality of the soul, which Calvin wrote during his second stay at Orléans in the beginning of 1534. This work is distinguished by an astonishing knowledge of Holy Scripture—277 quotes in this little book of fifty-one folios!—and also of several treatises of Augustine,[40] Tertullian, and Irenaeus. We can be confident that while preparing for his final examinations in law at Orléans, Calvin was reading the Bible and the Fathers. This affirmation is quite logical: the Fabrist royal readers, Danès and Vatable, surely invited their student to scrutinize the Bible. Here again, we feel it is not at all necessary to invoke any direct Lutheran influence. The followers of the German reformer were not the only ones to read the Scriptures. Daniel and his entire circle of friends at Orléans were assiduous readers of the holy books.

On 23 August 1533, the future reformer was in Noyon. The city's archives, which were researched by Lefranc,[41] inform us that Calvin attended a meeting of the Chapter where they ordained secular priests and where, no doubt, a mass and a procession were held to implore God to stop the plague that was then creating havoc in the Picard capital. I disagree completely with K. Müller's hypothesis that witnessing these ceremonies, or more exactly Calvin's awareness that he did not belong there, would have produced the shock of conversion.[42]

CHAPTER FIVE
The Events of Autumn 1533
and the Stay in Saintonge

Returning to Paris, our humanist found the intellectual milieu there in full flower. The reformists had just won a victory: in May, the King asked Noël Bédier to leave the capital. Bédier had begun once again to harass the biblical scholars. First, he presented a memorandum to the sovereign, which was designed to defend the Vulgate against the *Textus Receptus* of Erasmus and the attacks from Wittenberg,[1] and then he took to task Gérard Roussel, the preacher of the Queen of Navarre. Roussel had been invited to preach the Lenten sermons of 1533 at the palace of the Louvre itself, in the presence of the King and of the Queen of Navarre and a very large entourage. His daily sermons, which were clearly reformist, were an enormous success. The Sorbonne reacted. On 12 May, Bédier had drawn up a list of Roussel's propositions that he judged to be heretical. At first, Francis I turned a deaf ear; then he lost his patience and on the advice of the Bishop of Paris, Jean du Bellay,[2] exiled Bédier along with several of his followers. But other traditionalists continued their undermining efforts.

Calvin was in Paris on 1 October, when students of the Collège de Navarre presented a comedy filled with allusions harmful to Marguerite and her chaplain, Gérard Roussel. Almost at the same time, the Faculty of

Theology placed on the Index a work of the Queen of Navarre, *Le miroir de l'âme pécheresse,* recently reedited by Simon Dubois.[3] The reformists did not respond, but thanks to the courageous intervention of Nicolas Cop, newly named rector of the university, the plotters were once again defeated.

Calvin provided an account of these exciting events for his friend Daniel in a letter sent to him in Orléans at the end of October.[4] This document, as well as a letter that announces his next epistle, reveals Calvin's state of mind during these incidents.

The letter is divided into two parts. The first contains the following salutation: "To my *brother* and good friend, Monsieur Daniel, lawyer of Orléans." And it is dated as follows: "Lutetiae, pridie Simonis," that is, the eve of the Feast of the Apostle St. Simon, which is celebrated on the twenty-eighth of October. The signature is simple: "Your Calvin." The second part, obviously a postscript, is longer and ends with the phrase: "Farewell, *brother* and virtuous friend. Your *brother,* Calvin." Some have wished to deduce from this triple mention of the word "brother" (which we note does not appear in any earlier letters addressed to Daniel) that Calvin was now involved in the fraternity of the radical, evangelical reformist party. Such a thesis is not impossible. However, it loses much of its likelihood when we consider that this letter is the earliest autograph we possess.[5] Earlier letters were copies where the original salutation and signature were omitted. The fact that we find the term "brother" in greetings and salutations of this autograph does not allow us to affirm that Calvin had not used the term earlier. Also, this detail could hardly be considered a sign that Calvin was already "converted." Besides, Calvin uses the feast day of a saint in order to date his epistle. Would a new evangelical convert do this? In any case, he will no longer do so when he really does become a part of the evangelical party.[6]

Now let us examine the important sections of the letter. In its first part, Calvin announces to his friend a forthcoming letter filled with details of the latest news: "Now I am writing a letter filled with many things." In the second he asks Daniel to communicate the contents to other friends in Orléans: "I am sending to you a collection of new matters, but with the understanding that they pass on to our friends through your hands in accord with your trust and duty." Then, farther on, Calvin adds: "I am sending the second abridgment of *our G.,* to which I decided to add those things[7] which had been dropped from earlier commentaries, except I ran out of time." Finally, after the signature we read again: "I shall not call these things disorderly; the things speak for themselves. Beware that you don't divulge this summary carelessly."

Here, as in the preceding sentence, we are dealing with the same "epitome," that is, "extract" or "abridgment" of the works or sermons of the mysterious "G." And it is a summary that François Daniel dare not reveal to anyone; given the presence of antireformist elements in Orléans, this would be dangerous. The context does not tell us anything about the content of the appendix that Calvin wants to add to the summary of "G." However, the very fact that he allows himself to make such a wish makes us think that there were common ideas and personal ties between "G" and himself that gave him such liberty. This impression is further reinforced by the adjective "our"; "G" seems to be part of a circle to which both Calvin and Daniel belong.

Who was this mysterious person whose name Calvin would not even spell? Most historians think it is Gérard Roussel, concerning whom there is a question in the correspondence that follows this letter and who is designated by the initials "M.G."—undoubtedly representing "Master Gérard."[8] I have no difficulty in accepting this interpretation. Along with K. Müller, I consider it certain that in the autumn of 1533, Daniel and Calvin were among the admirers of the Fabrist Roussel,[9] who should not be called "a complete Protestant as far as dogma is concerned."[10]

We will now examine the long account that follows this letter.[11] From the start, we have the impression that the young Calvin is passionately interested in the events he relates. He states that if he were to mention everything he has to say, he would need to write a volume. Then he relates the scandal of the comedy played at the Collège de Navarre, which he treats as a "bilious and acidic tale." The play has two prominent characters, a queen discreetly busy sewing in her bedroom and one of the three Furies of mythology, Megaera—an obvious allusion to "Master Gérard." Megaera begins to pressure the queen to try to get her to read the Gospels. The queen gives in, reads the book, and suddenly abandons all her good habits to oppress the poor and the innocent.

The Queen of Navarre was informed ahead of time and prevented the play from taking place. Calvin adds: "The worst possible example for the wanton desires of *those who gape at new things* has appeared to be established, if impunity is granted to this impropriety." Contrary to some authors,[12] we think that the expression "those who gape at new things" refers to those who were eagerly waiting for any new attack against the reformists and does not refer to those who were involved in the struggle for religious renewal. It would, in fact, be absurd that Calvin, who according to the entire context warmly supported Roussel's party, would here come out against him by using such pejorative language. For the Christian humanist of that time and for the reformer of tomorrow, the word "innovators" had a negative sense, conforming to the general understanding of the reformists who in no way wanted to be innovators; on the contrary they wanted to reestablish the ancient truth in its purity. The idea contained in the text would therefore be the following: at the intervention of the Queen the play was suppressed, for it was understood that if such an effrontery remained unpunished, it would encourage the unbridled desires of those who would applaud in advance any sensational blow against the party of Roussel and the reformists.[13]

After telling about the scandal of the comedy, Calvin goes on to describe another act of the adversaries. The plotters uncovered in Paris libraries the work of the Queen of Navarre, *Le miroir de l'âme pécheresse,* and placed it on the Index of prohibited books. We note here the first appearance in Calvin's writings of a contemptuous reference to some doctors of the Sorbonne: "certain factious theologians." Let us also underline the ironical way in which he speaks of the Index, the list of books that the theologians in question *wanted* to prohibit: "They listed a number of books that they wanted to prohibit from being read."

How did Marguerite react? She went to find her brother, the King, and asked him to intervene. The King invited the Sorbonne to give an explanation. Nicolas Cop, the recently elected rector, was given the task of conducting the inquest. He convened the four Faculties and lectured them sternly, blaming the audacious members who dared attack the Queen and initiate action in the name of "the Academy" without having received a mandate from them. He also threatened them with the anger of the King. The faculties of the arts, theology, canon law, and medicine submitted almost slavishly to Cop's rebukes. But toward the end of the meeting, Nicolas Le Clerc, rector of Saint-André and a doctor of the Sorbonne, arose to express several reservations in the name of the Faculty of Theology. Calvin remarks of this man: "It is upon him that the reproach fell, because he caused others to go astray." Le Clerc said in substance that in matters of faith, the King was beyond reproach; but there were some "sinister men" who were trying to pervert this excellent and noble soul, and they were the very same men who made plans to disgrace the sacred Faculty. He did not have anything against the Queen of Navarre, but because he had received the mandate of the Faculty, it was incumbent upon him to seize the books that had been published without ecclesiastical approval. He had only done his duty. Finally, Calvin also notes the intervention of the Bishop of Senlis, Guillaume Petit, who declared that having read the work of the Queen he did not see anything reprehensible in it, unless he had entirely forgotten his theology. The meeting ended with a statement by Cop: the Academy did not recognize the validity of any censure against *Le miroir.*

What does this document reveal about the religious evolution of the future reformer? One thing seems certain: Calvin clearly appears to be aligned with the party of Marguerite, Roussel, and Cop. This is why he speaks ironically regarding certain doctors of the Faculty, the antireformists of the Collège de Navarre, and the rector, Le Clerc, who wished to defend the King against the "sinister" supporters of Erasmus and Lefèvre. But in all of this, one does not see a single indication of anticlericalism or anti-Roman sentiment. The Bishop of Senlis is presented sympathetically.

Neither is there any indication of Lutheran radicalism, even though Calvin by this time had surely read several texts of the German reformer.

I do think that there are several traces of Lutheran heterodoxy in this document. The authority on which the young man of letters concentrates is actually that of the biblical scholars, who, like Gérard Roussel, did not make a clear distinction between the ideas of Lefèvre or Erasmus on the one hand and Luther and Melanchthon on the other. For them it was not safeguarding orthodoxy that was important but progress in evangelical renewal—in the original sense of the word. However, the authority for whom orthodoxy alone was important—the Faculty of Theology—from this time on was no longer taken for granted by Calvin. The "purely negative" function of theology for the Sorbonne made no impression on Calvin. The intolerance, the massive argumentation, and the police methods of Bédier's men filled him with indignation. The history of the Church contains many examples that prove that nothing pushes noble souls toward heterodoxy more than an orthodoxy that lacks soul and heart and that forgets the essentials.

For the time being, the fiery syndic of the Faculty was in exile, and the reformist party seemed to triumph in Paris. The new rector of the Sorbonne, the young medical doctor Nicolas Cop, seemed ready to conquer the furious, conservative forces that terrorized the university circle at that time. Appearances deceive! Soon Cop himself would awake from his illusions.

On 1 November 1533, the rector presented, according to custom, a discourse at the opening of the academic year. It was actually a sermon. Cop, who was not a theologian, used the discourse as an opportunity to comment on Erasmus' *Paraclesis*[14] and particularly on Luther's *Kirchenpostillen,* translated into Latin by Bucer in 1530.[15] The eight beatitudes of the Gospel According to Matthew were the theme of the address.

Calvin made in his own hand a copy of this speech, of which a fragment remains. On the basis of this text, many historians have thought that this speech, the *concio academica,* was written by Calvin himself.[16] But along with other authors,[17] we think that the textual criticism undertaken so well by K. Müller has definitely disproved this hypothesis. The learned scholar from Tübingen closely examined this fragment found at Geneva as well as another manuscript of the discourse, which is in Cop's hand and preserved at Strasbourg.[18] He has concluded that Calvin could not have been the author of the *concio.* [19] He has also shown that nothing supports the opinion that this text expresses the state of mind of a "convert."[20] By the end of the study, Müller is of the opinion that the best solution is to acknowledge that the speech of Cop is simply that, a speech by Cop![21] Let us add that in later sermons where the reformer comments on this passage in Matthew, he gives an interpretation opposed to that of Cop.[22]

All that one can conclude about this is as follows: As a friend of the young rector of the university, as well as for other reasons that one can easily imagine, Calvin was interested in this speech and copied it by hand, at least in part.[23] Thus, the content of the speech sheds light on ideas that were current in the Paris circles frequented in 1533 by the future reformer, but nothing more can be inferred.

First of all, we find in this discourse a clear allusion to the Erasmian conception of a "Christian philosophy"; this refers, in the language of the followers of the great Flemish humanist, to a clear, faithful, and loving understanding of the entire plan of salvation centered on Jesus Christ. This Christian philosophy was based on the conviction that "sins are forgiven by the grace of God alone" and that Christ is "the one intercessor before the Father."[24] However, this Christ-centered emphasis did not exclude but rather included the possibility of venerating and praising the most perfect created being, Mary, mother of the Lord. Thus, the introduction concludes with the usual formula—later erased from the manuscript in Geneva: "Because I expect we will succeed, if we greet the most blessed Virgin with that solemn praise: 'Hail, Mary, full of grace.' "[25]

Some Lutheran ideas are briefly developed in the speech, sometimes even in the language of Luther: the Gospel as opposed to the Law; the Christian should not serve Christ out of fear or self-interest, but only out of pure love. God in turn rewards the faithful "by grace alone" and not "because of our merits"; hardened theologians, those "corrupt sophists," do not truly proclaim the Gospel ("nothing of faith, nothing of the love of God").[26]

The speaker then comes to his commentary on the eight beatitudes. "Blessed are the poor in spirit" is interpreted as a condemnation of idolatry: "For silver and gold are the images of the people." The Christian should not take pleasure in the creature, but "with a pure and free heart" in God alone, according to the Gospel. Those who weep are declared happy, for they despair of their own strength and hope only in the righteousness of God. They who hunger and thirst after righteousness are also blessed. God reassures their consciences that they are "accepted by God," their sins are freely forgiven without any merit of their own. Nicolas Cop takes up the theme of Paul according to Luther: "We believe that man is justified by faith apart from works of the law."[27] Those who deny the free gift of the act of redemption are the ones who "overturn the Gospel, completely bury Christ, and abolish all true worship of God; for God cannot be worshiped with a doubting heart."[28]

"Blessed are the peacemakers" gave the speaker a chance to protest the methods used by adversaries who thought they could persuade by threats, sword, and torture. On the contrary, happy are they who, following the teachings of Jesus to the Jews, used only the Word—"by the Word rather than the sword"—to spread the faith and to stop dissension within the heart of the Church.[29]

Then we read the most moving part: "Truly, blessed are those who suffer persecution for righteousness' sake." The world and the ungodly surely considered these seekers after justice quite differently: "Heretics, seducers, impostors, slanderers: these are the names the world and wicked men are accustomed to giving to those who honestly and sincerely seek to plant the Gospel in the hearts of the faithful and who consider themselves obedient to God." Then this inspiring speech ends in an appeal to believe in the Gospel that all might be partakers of the peace and joy of faith.[30]

To the Catholic theologian of today, nothing would appear heterodox about this proclamation. The author certainly quotes entire passages from Luther, but the passages contain what is essentially Catholic doctrine. J. Lortz, L. Bouyer, and Hans Küng have shown that "by faith alone" and above all "by grace alone" are not in themselves anti-Catholic principles; on the contrary, they can express authentic Catholic doctrine. Only the negative statements presented in the ideas of "forensic justification" and of "faith formed without love" could deprive them of their orthodox character.[31] But in Cop's discourse, not one of these negative statements is to be found. Because of these regrettable circumstances which were so characteristic of the doctrinal confusion of the period around 1533, the speech set off a massive reaction by the Faculty, who were charged with defending Catholic dogma. Following his profession of reformist faith, an indictment for heresy was issued against Cop, and some of his friends were arrested.

Calvin was one of Cop's friends. No doubt he would have been willing to subscribe to Cop's discourse, even if at this time he was not familiar with all of the Lutheran literature. For Calvin, it was not a matter of taking a doctrinal position but of advancing the reform movement of the Gospel. It is in this sense that the words of his friend would have made a profound impression on him. In fact, we believe that Cop's discourse played an important role in Calvin's religious evolution: without having been its author, he nevertheless was influenced by it. At this time, Cop no doubt was still the "active factor," while Calvin was the one who was receiving; but in receiving he was reacting.

He reacted in a way that must have been determined by the following circumstances. Shortly after Cop's discourse, two Franciscan monks issued a complaint against him for heresy. Parlement followed suit. The rector of the university counterattacked by convening the representatives of the four Faculties on 19 November and declaring to them that only the university was competent to judge the supposed or real heresy of one of its members. The representatives of medicine and the arts upheld this position, but the theologians and the jurists were opposed.[32] By the end of the month, the police arrested Gérard Roussel and another preacher, Elie Couraud.[33] Soon other reformists were apprehended. Cop fled to Basle, and Parlement put a price on his head.[34]

This offensive of the traditionalist party occurred during the King's absence, from which the antireformists wished to profit as much as possible.

By letters and emissaries they tried to convince the sovereign of the necessity of dealing harshly with those whom they accused of heresy. The enterprise succeeded. Dated at Lyon, 10 December 1533, a royal letter was addressed to Parlement that gave the order to bring the "accursed Lutheran sect" to an end.[35] It should be noted that the victors applied this designation to the followers of Lefèvre as well as to those who were actually "Lutherans." Colladon relates that as a friend of Cop, Calvin was also sought out. Calvin was warned of the danger in time and fled from his Paris dwelling. They searched his room and confiscated his papers and correspondence.[36]

It was the first time that the future reformer learned at his own expense the cost of persecution. No doubt his sensitive personality received a violent shock. All of a sudden the forces that defended orthodoxy seemed to be not just repugnant but hostile. We must not forget this if we wish to understand how his evolution from this time moved quickly toward radical reform. At the very moment when our young humanist first experienced for himself brutal religious constraints, he must have wondered whether some of the vehement accusations of the German reformer were not fully justified.[37]

CHAPTER SIX
The Year of Wandering, 1534

After several moves that are difficult to trace and that may have included a short stay in Paris at the end of 1533, Calvin left for Saintonge, where one of his friends, Louis du Tillet, canon of Angoulême and rector of Claix, offered him hospitality.

Their correspondence, of which we possess six letters dated from 1538,[1] proves that they were bound by a deep friendship which probably went back as far as the years when Calvin was studying philosophy at Montaigu. We shall examine these letters in detail in chapter 27. There is also a letter from 1538, in which the reformer tells Farel of du Tillet's defection and of his attempts to bring Calvin back to the Roman communion.[2] Moreover, the agreement of several documents of unequal value, in particular the accounts of Beza and of Florimond de Raemond, allows us to maintain with certainty that the letter *Ex Acropoli,* addressed by Calvin to his friend Daniel and bearing no date, describes nothing more than the cautious reception that du Tillet gave his exiled friend in his home in Angoulême.[3] Herminjard and the editors of the *Opera* place this letter at the beginning of 1534. Its tone is joyful and confident. Its author has placed himself in the hands of God, "who, if we commit ourselves to him, will care for us," "who, by his providence, will provide all things very well." We also read of praise for the canon's hospitality: "The humanity of my patron is so great that I understand it to be bestowed for the benefit of learning, not me." This generosity obliges the recipient: "Even more must I try and seriously endeavor, lest I be overwhelmed by such kindness which presses and, as it were, prompts me." The time of exile spent in this "tranquil nest" must have been devoted to serious study.

Colladon never names du Tillet but speaks of a "young man" or a "friend" of Calvin who, in view of the evidence provided by other sources, must have been the canon of Angoulême.[4] Beza speaks only of a "certain friend."[5] On the other hand, Florimond de Raemond gives many details about him. He notes that the father of the young priest had been vice-president of the office of accounts in Paris, that two of his brothers had served as court clerks in Parlement, and that a third brother was a priest, like Louis, and since 1562 served as bishop of Meaux. He also reports that du Tillet's entire family was interested in the humanities and owned a library of several thousand volumes in Angoulême.[6] According to the same source, Calvin must have contributed to the humanist background of the young priest of Claix by teaching him Greek. Thus the people of the parish named him "the Greek of Claix."[7] Finally, Florimond de Raemond gives us a list of the people who belonged to the gracious monk's intimate circle, with whom the future reformer would have had frequent contact: Antoine Chaillon, prior of Bouteville who was called "the pope of the Lutherans"; the Abbot of Bassac, a man of letters as was Chaillon; the lord of Torsac and his brother, Pierre de la Place.[8] The latter had become a fervent follower of the reform and about 1550 wrote a letter to Calvin in which we find a clear reference to their friendly relationship at the time that the future reformer resided in Angoulême: "For I am not forgetful of how much you have made me better by your companionship and your erudition when we were at Angoulême, and how much more I owe you every day." The same letter mentions Louis du Tillet, who returned once again "to the palpable darkness" (to the papacy) after having seen the light.[9] We know that Pierre de la Place was among the most famous victims of the St. Bartholomew's Day Massacre. What Florimond de Raemond says concerning Calvin's exile in Angoulême interests us in two ways. First, this account reinforces the affirmation of Colladon and Beza that the young exile had preached in the parish; second, in spite of his polemical tendencies, he does not attribute to Calvin at this time an open break with the worship of the established Church.[10]

Here we have John Calvin surrounded by new reformist friends in a place far from persecution. No doubt he did not forget the shock and anxiety that the events in Paris of November 1533 had caused him. But while his friends and he bore this painful wound in their hearts and minds, Calvin threw himself into his readings and studies with the fervor of the intellectual and the courage of the believer. His new friends advised him, no doubt, in his choice of readings, but he also chose them himself in relationship to the problems about the Church's poor state, which he could no longer ignore. If we try to guess which works Calvin was able to read at Angoulême on the basis of the quotations in the *Psychopannychia* which appeared at the end of this period, we can assert that he continued to meditate on the Bible and the Fathers. The biblical text he used was the Vulgate, which he compared with Erasmus' Latin version. We assume our author used several collections of patristic texts.

Examining the *Psychopannychia* suggests that at Angoulême the future reformer did not increase his knowledge of the works of either Luther, Melanchthon, or Bucer. However, at this time Calvin was able to consult the German reformers in preparation for his later theological work, the *Institutes.* The editors of the *Opera* and other Calvin specialists are surely of this opinion.[11] In the vast library of the du Tillet family, there were certainly a number of writings by different reformers. But Calvin did not have the time to take advantage of these, for—we must not forget—1534 was for him a year of wandering. In all probability, our exile remained in the region of Angoulême for four or five months at most.

According to Beza and Colladon and the historians who follow them,[12] in April 1534 Calvin left his oasis of study to pay a visit to Lefèvre d'Etaples at the chateau of Nérac, where the famous scholar enjoyed the hospitality of the Queen of Navarre. From there, probably on horseback, Calvin crossed the 650–700 kilometers that separated him from Noyon in order to resign his ecclesiastical benefices. In the Noyon archives a document dated 4 May 1534 attests to the fact that on this day the chaplaincy of John Calvin was given to a new beneficiary.[13] Shortly afterward, according to Lefranc, the future reformer was imprisoned two times by the Chapter. This incident resulted from an inquiry made against his brother Charles, who was suspected of heresy.[14] Until recently, historians have attributed considerable importance to this matter.[15] But some of the most recent authors have reservations.[16] Dankbaar even affirms that the hypothesis of imprisonment rests on an erroneous interpretation of the documents at Noyon.[17]

Only the renunciation itself remains an indisputable fact. Yet we must note that neither Calvin himself, nor Beza, nor Colladon mentions it. This does not deny its truth but simply makes it problematic to affirm that this act is important enough to mark Calvin's conversion.[18]

In my opinion this resignation can be explained in two different ways. The first hypothesis: A very serious matter inspired this act, because Calvin did not hesitate to cross all of France to carry it out. Moreover, such a gesture shows true greatness of soul, for it deprived him of an important source of revenue. He no longer wanted to profit from the system of ecclesiastical benefices that were based on a purely fictitious ministry and that were unanimously condemned by the reformists. One could go even farther and say that by this sacrifice Calvin wished to express his deliberate attachment to the party of the Gospel. But to see it as a sign of a true conversion seems to exaggerate its importance.

The second hypothesis: Nothing proves that Calvin undertook this long trip with the specific intention of renouncing these benefices. There could certainly have been other reasons. For example, one could conjecture that Calvin went to Noyon to receive his revenues and that because of the suspicions surrounding the Calvin family, the Chapter forced him to renounce the benefice. And besides, even if the renunciation was voluntary and accomplished in a purely idealistic moment, did it really represent for Calvin a heroic sacrifice? His wealthy reformist friends might have been well disposed to cover the loss of his ecclesiastical income. The future reformer always accepted without suspicion the hospitality and material help offered by men such as Coiffart, Nicolas Duchemin, and Louis du Tillet. In any case, Calvin was now in possession of diplomas and knowledge that would permit him to find easily a teaching post or a position as a legal counselor outside ecclesiastical circles. If it was not possible to find a position in France, at least it was possible abroad, where the two friends intended to go anyway.

I do not accept entirely either the first or the second hypothesis, but only what is likely in both: the fact of the renunciation and its religious motivation.

We know nothing for certain about the exact length of Calvin's stay at Noyon or about the chronology of his movements which followed. All we have are a few indications from Colladon about a stay in Paris and then in Orléans[19] and a note by Beza in regard to the Placards affair.[20] These have a documentary value superior to that usually given to the three editions of the *Vita Calvini,* because they contain plausible details that are partially verifiable by comparison with other sources. Colladon relates in detail an abortive meeting between Calvin and Michael Servetus. This account substantially agrees with what the reformer himself wrote in 1554: "I was completely prepared in Paris to lose my life in order to gain him for our Lord, if it were possible."[21] His stay in Orléans is confirmed by the dating of the preface of the *Psychopannychia.* The incident of the Placards is treated in detail by all contemporary historians.

To use the language of W. Walker, "it *seems probable*" that at the time of his trip to Paris, Calvin stayed with Etienne de la Forge, the magnanimous patron of numerous biblical and Lutheran publications, who died as a martyr in February 1535.[22] One might also suppose that at this time our traveler became fully acquainted with the very serious problem of the introduction of anabaptism into France. In any case, Calvin will affirm in 1545 that "more than ten years ago" he met in his own country one of the leaders of the sect, the Flemish preacher Quintin.[23] The appearance of these mystics, some of whom were quietists and others enthusiasts, unsettled the Sorbonne and disconcerted the reform party. But a few reformist leaders, such as the Queen of Navarre, showed some sympathy for this new tendency, in spite of the repeated warnings of those who very quickly discerned in them many dangerous deviations in doctrine. One of the new apostles of the sect, Pocque, had already cast doubt on the immortality of the soul by preaching the idea of soul sleep.

At the request of his friends, Calvin wrote the *Psychopannychia* against this doctrine during his short stay at Orléans; its subtitle contained these words: "The souls of the saints who die in the faith of Christ do not sleep but live in the presence of Christ."[24] I have already emphasized that this work evidences a profound knowledge of the Bible and the Fathers. Here I especially highlight what it contains of importance for our inquiry.

In reading this little book, one is struck by the fact that it does not contain any anti-Roman references or even allusions. In the sentence in which Pope John XXII is mentioned among the famous representatives of the error of soul sleep, the tone remains quite moderate. But a few lines farther on, the contemporary defenders of the same error are described in very offensive terms as "the dregs of the anabaptists."[25] In the preface of Calvin's composition, the anabaptist partisans are severely criticized. When they are reproached for their eagerness to accept and profit from such fantastic doctrines, they begin to complain about the lack of charity toward them and that by rejecting them, the unity of the Church is torn. But they should understand once and for all that there is legitimate unity and true charity only in Christ and the integrity of the Christian faith.[26] In the body of the work the author refutes at length his adversaries' points with numerous impressive scriptural and traditional arguments. Certainly Calvin's thought—influenced no doubt by the Neoplatonism of the *devotio moderna*—does not always succeed in reconciling the immortality of the soul and the resurrection of the flesh.[27] But his language is filled with the assurance of a man who is henceforth conscious of his duty to speak, if he does not wish to be an accomplice to the corruption of Christian dogma. This is a remarkable advance since the *De Clementia*!

It is in the same antisectarian context that one can best situate a letter from Calvin to Martin Bucer concerning a man who was persecuted for his convictions and forced to seek refuge in Strasbourg.[28] The letter's place of origin and date are indicated: "*Noviod.* pridie nonas septembres," that is, Noyon, the fourth of September. The year is not indicated, which leaves the field open for a variety of hypotheses. The editors of the *Opera* put 1532, although they note that other specialists are of a different opinion. Emil Doumergue also opts for 1532, but A. L. Herminjard and A. Lefranc prefer 1534, a date also held as possible by H. Eells. A. Lang and W. Walker affirm that the letter was definitely not written before 1534, and that it is even doubtful that it was written in 1534. Finally, K. Müller puts the year of origin even later, between 1537 and 1547.[29]

In my opinion, 1534 is the most likely date for four reasons. First, the letter's content reflects a state of mind entirely dominated by religious concerns that are not evident to this degree in any of Calvin's earlier letters. Second, on the basis of this first point and of Noyon as the place of origin of the letter, it seems natural to date it during the last trip that Calvin made to his native city. That was in 1534. After this time, he never returned. Third, nothing prevents the future reformer from once again returning to Noyon from Paris at the beginning of September, after 4 May 1534, the day that he had renounced his benefices. Fourth, the "anabaptist context" of the writing fits right in with what we know of the time when the *Psychopannychia* was written, that is, the year 1534.

Now let us see what important features this letter contains. The address is worded: "To Bucer, Lord Bishop of Strasbourg." Then Calvin uses a salutation that has a very biblical tone: "May the grace and peace of our Lord be with you, through the mercy of God and the victory of Christ." In none of his later letters does the reformer call Bucer "Bishop," but rather "pastor," "father," and "fellow initiate." One is justified in believing that this was the first letter that Calvin addressed to the head of the church in Strasbourg.[30] One has the impression that Calvin knew Bucer only by reputation; he considered him as a great evangelical *bishop*,[31] whom it is appropriate to address with a solemn greeting in an almost Pauline style. In the rest of the letter there is no indication of exaggerated obsequiousness. On the contrary, with a dignified modesty the writer indicates the reason that led him to trouble his illustrious reader. He is addressing the religious leader of the capital of Alsace to solicit his intervention on behalf of a French exile whose reputation was unfortunately compromised by one of Bucer's followers. This resident of Strasbourg, or of Alsace, spread the rumor that the refugee was suspected of anabaptism. In order to be fair and accurate, Calvin checked this statement and found that it had no basis in fact; therefore he wished to defend the man who was unjustly suspected and slandered.

Calvin declares from the beginning that this is the only reason that led him to write; otherwise he would not have dared to trouble a person as busy as Bucer: "I do not have time to write, nor do I have an argument to make or advice to offer, but it seemed right to inform you in a few words of the deplorable and miserable condition of this excellent brother. His lot was made known to me by a letter from some friends whose trustworthiness and reputation are unquestionable. . . . I could restrain myself only by writing to you." It seems then that Calvin had been informed of the unfortunate state of this "excellent brother" by letters that had been sent from worthy and faithful friends. He was so informed either at Noyon, from where he had written, or at Paris, where he had previously stayed. Note that the term "brother"—which is found only once in the entire letter—may have an evangelical meaning. (One might object that strictly speaking the author of the letter uses this word only to conform to the language of its evangelical recipient.)

The text continues: "I knew the character and the values of the man, since up to now he was active in our native France. He thus conducted himself in a way agreeable to the men of our order." A man of intelligence and integrity, he was well esteemed by men of the same rank to which Calvin himself belonged, probably the Christian humanists. It was also in favorable times that the future reformer met his protégé when the latter was still in France. But at the time of the letter he was no longer there. Why? The rest of the letter gives us an explanation: "Nevertheless, when he was no longer able to risk his life *in that voluntary servitude which we bear even now,* he emigrated to you, with no hope of returning." One can easily guess the circumstances to which he alludes. For some time, but especially since Cop's discourse and the imprisonment of Gérard Roussel, the Fabrisian reformists and the Lutherans groaned under the pressure of their adversaries, who had a very powerful and repressive apparatus at their disposal. The partisans of Church reform were no longer able to speak freely. It was certainly a bondage for them, but a voluntary bondage, for if they wanted, they could be free by leaving for another country. For the moment, Calvin is one of those who firmly stood up against the opposition. But this does not prevent him from being very understanding toward those who chose to emigrate after they endured all they could. This was also the decision of his protégé; he left for Strasbourg.

But exile did not bring peace to the poor man. He could not even settle in the city, and now he was forced to run here and there like an unfortunate character in a classic comedy: "Now, contrary to his expectations, it turned out that he played a part in a 'lively tale'[32] and did not find a stable place where he could settle." They say that the exile came up to Noyon to solicit the help of his old friends and protégés. All his troubles came upon him only because of the slander hurled at him by a man belonging to Bucer's church: "Now look how much more powerful is calumny than truth. Some harsh person among you . . . so filled the ears of all with his denunciations that they were closed to any defense. And thus there was no one from whom he could get a cent." Instead of finding in Strasbourg a safe refuge and fraternal protection, the unfortunate man encountered distrust and suspicion resulting in a cruel experience: no one wanted to help him. The slander had closed all doors to him in Strasbourg and elsewhere.

Of what crime was he suspect? "But, as they say, this slander was hurled at him because he had been suspected of being an *anabaptist.*" We have seen the severe language the author of the *Psychopannychia* used to stigmatize these sectarians. According to the partisans of the evangelical movement as well as their adversaries, the anabaptists represented the gravest danger to the unity of the Church. Those who insisted on conserving the traditions of the past and those who wanted reform questioned these enlightened ones who, from all appearances, were trying to suppress the past. Above all, they wanted to suppress the sacramental structure of the Church, which they had declared dead, in order to create an entirely new and completely spiritual church by rebaptizing the faithful. Moreover, after the bloody throes of the recent peasant revolts, especially in Alsace, it became common to suspect the anabaptists of subversive intentions.[33] Thus we can understand why the evangelicals of Strasbourg refused to help a refugee suspected of belonging to that sect.

Calvin wished to defend his protégé against these suspicions. He had the opportunity to examine in depth the opinions of this man on the subject of baptism. The result was positive; his beliefs proved to be orthodox. Calvin writes: "On the basis of what he professed, I led him into a discussion of this sacrament. . . . Although we used such different words, we came to agreement, so that I have not yet seen anyone who professed the truth more sincerely on this matter." The letter does not specify where or when the interrogation took place; perhaps it was before the man had left for Strasbourg, or when he returned to Noyon to solicit the help of his friends. In any case, the episode reveals that by this time Calvin possessed sufficient theological knowledge on the subject of baptism to judge such a man's orthodoxy or heterodoxy.

The letter ends with an appeal to Bucer's generosity to show favor to the exile. It quotes (according to the Vulgate) Ps. 10:14: "The poor man commits himself to you; you shall be a helper of the orphan." It is obvious that the author of the *Psychopannychia* is already very familiar with the Bible.

This is the essential content of the future reformer's letter to Bucer. If this letter is really from 1534, it gives us a good indication of Calvin's state of mind following his biblical studies and his reformist contacts in Saintonge and prior to his departure for abroad. The letter appears to us to be a synthesis of all that an excellent lawyer, a good Christian humanist, and a generous reformist was capable of doing under the circumstances. At the same time, this document seems to indicate a new step in the religious evolution that we are studying. Calvin defends an exile just before experiencing exile himself. He defends "a brother" against the suspicion of anabaptism, and he will soon write his celebrated Dedicatory Epistle to the King to defend all the evangelicals against the accusation of making common cause with this seditious sect. Already the biblical humanist is beginning to be transformed—without knowing it—into an evangelical reformer.

No doubt this change was accelerated by external events. During Calvin's last trip to Noyon and Paris a new burning took place in the capital; the preacher Canus de la Croix was burned alive at Maubert Square on 18 June

1534, after heroically testifying to his faith. We would surely like to know what new impact this scene, or at least the account of it, might have produced on our humanist's very sensitive mind.

In autumn of the same year, Calvin left Paris for Orléans, where he completed his composition on the "sleep of the soul."[34] Then he probably went once more to Claix, the home of his good friend du Tillet. In the meantime, a new crisis broke out in Paris: the famous Placards affair. The crude and awkward attacks of the preacher Antoine Marcourt of Neuchâtel against the sacrifice of the Mass which were posted everywhere in the capital and the principal cities of the kingdom on the night of 17 and 18 October compromised the cause of the reformists more than any preceding incident.[35] The doctors of the Sorbonne and the men of Parlement no longer had to find reasons to convince the sovereign. This time Francis I, who was even encouraged by a humanist like Budé, gave free rein to his anger. A wave of arrests rolled forth upon the city and new executions took place.[36]

Then Calvin and du Tillet decided to leave France for Basle, a free center of humanist culture and a sure refuge for persecuted reformists, among whom was their courageous friend, Nicolas Cop. The cost of the trip caused them no concern. Du Tillet was wealthy and Calvin graciously accepted the financial aid of his friend. After several incidents on their way to Strasbourg, which are described by Colladon and Beza,[37] they arrived in Basle about January 1535. It was probably in Basle that Calvin learned the news of the execution of his dear friend and protector, Etienne de la Forge, who was burned alive in Paris on the sixteenth of February.

CHAPTER SEVEN
Calvin in Basle, 1535–1536

What was the intellectual and religious milieu that Calvin found in Basle?[1] From the intellectual point of view, in 1535 this city was dominated by the mind of the great Erasmus; but from the religious point of view, it was dominated by an eclectic type of radical reform.[2] The elderly prince of the humanists returned to Basle in June of that year, only to die there a year later on 12 July 1536. He spent his last days in almost complete retirement, having little contact with the outside world. We do not know whether during this period there was a personal meeting with his admirer, Calvin.

The reform of the church in Basle—prepared by Bishop Christophe d'Uttenheim, Capito, Hédion, and Farel—was the work of a humanist monk who became a Lutheran, John Oecolampadius; from 1523 to the time of his death in 1531, he progressively transformed the religious life of the city. Moving ahead of the other reformers, he created an ecclesiastical disciplinary power that was independent of the civil power and was entrusted to the "elders," together with the right to excommunicate.[3] Oswald Myconius succeeded him. This elderly schoolmaster was a friend and for a time a collaborator of Zwingli. After the death of the Zurich reformer, Myconius wrote the first biography of Zwingli. In 1534, he also wrote the first Confession of Faith of the Basle church. Myconius was not specifically a theologian, but above all a man of action and a fervent apostle of concord between different evangelical groups.[4]

It would be most interesting to know with what figures, other than Myconius, Calvin associated at Basle. Nicolas Cop? Olivétan? It is possible. Simon Grynaeus? Wolfgang Capito? Henri Bullinger? Pierre Viret? Guillaume Farel? It is probable. In any case we have this reference from Beza: "There he had as his best friends several men such as Simon Grynaeus and Wolfgang Capito."[5]

Grynaeus was professor of Greek at the University of Heidelberg from 1524 to 1529. In 1529, having been invited by Oecolampadius and attracted by the presence of Erasmus, he moved to the University at Basle, where he taught Greek until 1534. During this time he frequently corresponded with Bucer and Zwingli. In 1534 he went back to Swabia in order to reorganize the University of Heidelberg; but in autumn of the following year, he returned to Basle to teach dialectics and comment on the Pauline epistles. At that time he met Calvin. According to the dedication that Calvin wrote for his *Commentary on the Epistle to the Romans,*[6] a friendly collaboration was established between these two men. Together they tried to develop a valid method of interpreting Scripture. The German was a philologist of international reputation and no doubt contributed to Calvin's progress in the science of exegesis. But he was not, properly speaking, a theologian. He had opinions on only several doctrinal points, which he borrowed from Bucer and other representatives of a spiritualist tendency, such as Zwingli and Oecolampadius.[7] He was also a proponent of evangelical concord.

Capito was one of Martin Bucer's collaborators in Strasbourg. A disciple of Erasmus, he also followed the theological line of the humanist Zwingli rather than that of Luther. Among his most notable works are an edition of the Hebrew Psalter and a translation of Erasmus' work *De sarcienda ecclesiae concordia.* Calvin must have met him during his brief stay in Strasbourg. In any case, it is certain that he submitted to him his composition on the immortality of the soul. In fact, we have a letter of 1535 from Capito addressed to Calvin which treats this subject.[8] It should be added that Capito, even more than Myconius and Grynaeus, was intensely active in supporting Christian unity.

Henri Bullinger, the successor of Zwingli as the head of the Zurich church, was well known in Basle. His intellectual and theological journey led him first from Erasmus to Luther and Melanchthon and then to Zwingli. Above all a pastor of souls, he accomplished a magnificent work of charity in visiting the sick and corresponding with the afflicted. In 1535, Bullinger began to correspond with Myconius,[9] and it is probable that subsequently during his stay in Basle, Calvin had the opportunity to meet him.[10]

Farel and Viret, these two former students of theology in Paris, had collaborated very closely since 1530 on the reform in the French-speaking cantons of Switzerland. They were well known and highly regarded in Basle, where Calvin came to know them or renewed his relationship with them. Farel, the bold missionary and practical reformer, was the first of Lefèvre's disciples to choose Lutheranism without any compromise.[11] The gentle Viret was above all a man of evangelical charity, always prepared to serve where and when he was needed.[12] Among the other French refugees who found asylum in Basle, we should mention Pierre Caroli, formerly of Meaux and later an adversary of Calvin; the Augustinian monk Elie Couraud and Claude de Feray, future collaborators with Calvin, in Geneva and in Strasbourg respectively; and finally Pierre Toussaint, who was to become the reformer of Montbéliard.[13]

This is about all we know concerning the men in Basle who could have exercised some influence on our studious exile. As this brief summary indicates, the dominant theological tendency there was more Zwinglian than Lutheran. The aging Erasmus was not an important part of the scene. The intellectual elite of the city certainly respected him, but they criticized him both for his attachment to traditional doctrines such as the sacramental priesthood[14] and for his refusal to give wholehearted support to "the party of the Gospel."[15] Thus it was the militant reform inspired by Ulrich Zwingli that more and more set the tone at Basle; this reform movement was also of humanist origin, but it was willing to go beyond the many compromises of Erasmus. If, as good humanists, these men of Basle were seeking harmony in the midst of their different evangelical tendencies, they could find it only by uniting against the common enemy, papism.

Knowing this situation, one can properly ask whether Calvin became imbued with Zwinglianism at Basle. An examination of the sources of the first edition of the *Institutes,* the subject of Part Two, shows that an affirmative reply is unjustified. In Basle our young author no doubt became less distrustful of Zwingli's and Oecolampadius' theology than he had been earlier.[16] It is quite certain that at this time he read the *Commentary on True and False Religion* of the great Zurich leader, but he did not become a follower of Zwingli as a result. Proving his great independence of thought, he chose Martin Luther as the master to introduce him to the theological teachings of the reform. It was only to complement and verify his thinking that he turned to Melanchthon, Zwingli, and Bucer.

And so in January 1535, at the age of twenty-five and a half, Calvin arrived in Basle. He lived there under the pseudonym of Martinus Lucianus. For the first time he was in a foreign country whose language he did not know. Without the presence of Louis du Tillet and the French refugees of the city he would surely be aware of being a foreigner. But he was not seeking companionship; he had come to a German territory to live according to the demands of his conscience and to find the peace that was necessary for his very demanding studies. What he wanted above all was to deepen his knowledge of the Scriptures. By opening up the Bible to Calvin, Christian humanism had taught him that the sacred books were to be read and explicated according to the original text. Therefore he wanted to perfect his Hebrew and to continue to develop his knowledge of Greek.[17] (It was also at Basle, no doubt, that he hoped to find a publisher for the work that he planned to write.)

But the science of exegesis was not, for Calvin, an end in itself. Calvin wished to study carefully the Word of God, in order to find a salutary solution to the problems raised by the religious discord of his time and country. On the peaceful banks of the Rhine the young French intellectual thought about and meditated on his various memories of Noyon, Paris, Orléans, Bourges, and Saintonge. The Montaigu of Bédier, the struggles between the Sorbonne and Lefèvre's circle, the hopes of the young de Hangest, Cop, Daniel, and Duchemin, the intolerance of the canons of Noyon, the sermons of Gérard Roussel, Cop's discourse, the flight from the police and the retreat to Angoulême, his readings in the Bible, Erasmus, Lefèvre, and Luther, and the execution of martyrs whom he had seen burned[18]—all this now worked within him and called forth a response. With these thoughts of his persecuted countrymen and their persecutors, he began to study theology with intensity. To advance more rapidly in his research, he turned to guides whom he found more competent and resolute, for he began to believe that only radical reform could save the Church in its distress.

As I have already emphasized, it was Calvin's nature to express without delay in his own writings the ideas that he had assimilated from his readings. His prodigious memory allowed him to review, organize, and synthesize vast and often disparate material. His lively intellect and extraordinary ability to find just the right word assured him of a literary creativity absolutely without equal. Thus at the end of a very short gestation the first edition of the *Institutes* was born. Calvin arrived in Basle at the beginning of 1535 and the manuscript of his work was ready before September! Only the delays of the printer prevented it from appearing before March 1536.

During this time the young writer found the leisure necessary to write two prefaces for the French Bible of Olivétan.[19] These documents seem to us very instructive about Calvin's religious evolution. In fact, these are the first of his writings in which we encounter language that is openly hostile to the papacy or, more precisely, to papism.

The beginning of the first preface already reveals a very firm assurance: "Greetings, from John Calvin to all emperors, kings, princes, and men subject to the rule of Christ."[20] Then we read that since the Bible is the oracle and eternal truth of the very One who reigns above all kings, it does not need to be commended by human testimony, not even by some "privilege of kings." The dialectical opposition of the human and the divine seen in these lines already announces one of the principal characteristics of Calvin's entire theology.

The author then begins to criticize certain "wicked voices" who claim that it is dangerous to place translations of the Scriptures in the hands of the unsophisticated faithful. Here one senses that the Sorbonne is intended and charged with impiety in a way that foreshadows the terminology of the *Institutes,* where radical reformers and their adversaries are called respectively the "pious" and the "impious." To deprive the common people of the Word of God, or at least direct contact with it, is assuredly contrary both to true piety and to the intentions of the Lord, who always takes pleasure in "revealing himself to the poor" and chooses his prophets and apostles from shepherds and fishermen. Besides, had not God expressly commanded that the Gospel be preached above all to the poor? And did not the great Chrysostom say that reading the Holy Scriptures was more necessary for the masses than for monks? Tossed about by the floods of the world, they were more exposed to shipwreck and had no other anchor of salvation.

What follows is extremely important: "Not only during that purer age but for many years afterward this *freedom* flourished until the corrupt multitude, immersed in their own desires, cast aside this kind of commitment through their own wickedness and *laziness.* "[21] Here appears for the first time in Calvin's writings the opposition between the purity of the primitive Church and the corruption of the present Church. The corruption in question included not only an almost complete religious ignorance but also a lack of true Christian freedom in the relationship between the children of God and their heavenly Father. For such decadence, the priests and bishops were doubly responsible.

First of all, these so-called pastors—"for they wish to be called pastors and esteemed as such"—take from the mouths of the lambs the only food that is salutary and profitable for them, the *vitae patibulum,* the Word of the Lord. They commit this crime under the pretext of avoiding any serious disturbance that a misunderstanding of some biblical texts might provoke among uneducated minds. But this is simply to ignore that Christ is inevitably a "stumbling block" for many and to lack faith in the Holy Spirit, who is always able to grant readers the gift of interpreting the Word properly.

In addition—and this is the second part of the accusation—after taking the good food away from the lambs, these evil pastors give them corrupt food. They declare that all those who do not receive their human inventions and their arbitrary decisions as divine, honorable, and irrevocable oracles are filled with pride: "But they call it prideful, not to cling to whatever comes from their mouths and not to adore whatever springs forth from their caldron, or whatever they have imagined in their dreams."

And Calvin does not hesitate to name explicitly those whom he holds guilty of this adulteration: *"The Roman pontiff and his priestlings."*[22] It is the pope and his priests who today, as they have for a long time, put the light of the Scriptures under a bushel in order to sell "their own smelly merchandise" in reassuring darkness. Here is the first indisputable antipapist and antisacerdotal statement by Calvin. This is a direct attack against the host of abuses attributed to a corrupt hierarchy, but one already senses the emergence of a deeper criticism directed against the institution itself of the priesthood and the papacy—a criticism that will be expressed quite soon and more fully in the pages of Calvin's first theological manual. The preface itself describes the author's transition between the condemnation of behavior and the rejection of Church structures. We read here: "For these things are not said by me in the sense that I would remove *the order of teaching and learning* from the Church. The Church ought to acknowledge the splendid kindness of God, while it is properly instructed by *prophets,* teachers, and interpreters who have been sent by him. But I demand this much, that the faithful people be allowed to hear their *God* speaking and to learn from God's own teaching."[23] This means that our young reformist who is on the path to radicalism asserts that it is necessary that there be a teaching function in the Church; moreover, he does not yet affirm explicitly that the traditional ministers and ministries are definitely unfit for this function. However, in citing examples, he does not name these men, but the "prophets, teachers, and interpreters" of a biblical type, directly sent by the Lord himself. The context is clearly that of transition.

The second preface written for Olivétan's Bible was not included at the beginning of the volume but serves as an introduction to the New Testament. It is in French and begins with the following words: "To all who love Jesus Christ and his Gospel, greetings."[24] One must admit that the preface is a masterpiece of literary clarity and at the same time a magnificent testimony of a positive and enthusiastic evangelical spirit. One cannot read it without emotion. Contrary to the almost harsh tone of the Latin preface, its tone could be called "doxological." Without any critical or polemical allusions, the author recounts in language accessible to the simplest of the faithful the history of salvation accomplished in Jesus Christ. One has the impression that Calvin used no other source than the Bible itself and—let us willingly add—the responses that his readings of the Scriptures inspired in his own heart. The preface exhibits Lutheran thought in only a few statements about the seed of Adam as "vile, perverse, corrupted, empty, and deprived of all good,"[25] and the law which "can lead none to perfection,"[26] and the "constitutions of men"[27] which supplant those of God. But the text as a whole primarily praises Christ in elegant terms as the only mediator of the New Testament and as the end and fulfillment of the entire ancient law. Let us cite an example: "All these things are made known to us in this Testament through proclamations, demonstrations, writings, and sacraments, by which Jesus Christ makes us his heirs in the kingdom of God his Father." The appeal to receive this inheritance is universal; we should all participate in it "without respect to person, male or female, small or great, servant or lord, master or disciple, clergy or laity," that is, all men and women who recognize Christ "as the one sent from the Father." Then bursts forth the heart-felt cry of the Bible scholar soon to be a reformer: "And yet can any man or woman who hears the name Christian allow someone to seize, hide, or corrupt this Testament which so rightly belongs to us?" Without the Gospel, we "do not know what God requires of us or forbids us to do; we cannot distinguish good from evil, light from darkness, or the commandments of God from the institutions of men. Without the Gospel we are all helpless and ineffectual; without the Gospel we are not Christians."[28]

One thing is certain: for Calvin from this time on, the Gospel is Christ and Christ is the Gospel. He also paraphrased the famous passage from Paul, "Who can separate us from the love of Christ?" (Rom. 8:35), with these elegant words: "What might there be that could estrange us and alienate us from this holy Gospel? Will there be insults, curses, shame, or loss of worldly honor? But we know well that Jesus Christ traveled this same road which we must follow if we wish to be his disciples. . . . Will there be banishments, proscriptions, loss of goods and riches? But we know that if we are banished from a country, the earth is the Lord's. . . . Will there be tribulations, prisons, tortures, and affliction? But we know by Christ's example that this is the way to glory. Will there finally be death? But it will not take from us the life for which we long."[29] These are the inspired words of an exile who certainly did not flee his country with the single aim of finding tranquillity but of one who accepted the sacrifice imposed by his love of the Gospel. Moreover, by writing a preface to a Bible translated for the French people, Calvin wished to demonstrate his unity with his persecuted fellow countrymen. No doubt it was with Etienne de la Forge in mind that he added: "Let us not despair (as having lost all hope) when we see the true servants of God die and perish before our eyes. For it was truly said by Tertullian . . . that the blood of martyrs is the seed of the Church."

It is noteworthy that the word "Church" is capitalized, just as is "Gospel." This does not mean "other" or "new" or even "reformed," but simply "Church." The entire context shows that in our author's mind the martyrs of Paris and Meaux belonged to the same Church as the martyrs of whom Tertullian spoke and that together they formed the same seed and thereby the same people of God. They are the good wheat in the midst of the tares, and both the wheat and the tares are found in the same earth. Only divine judgment will separate them at the last day. Those who have confessed Christ will be "crowned with him eternally. But the depraved, rebellious, and reprobate who have condemned and rejected this holy Gospel; and likewise those who in order to maintain their honors, riches, and high station were unwilling to humble and lower themselves with Jesus Christ; and those who for fear of men have abandoned the fear of God, as bastard and disobedient children of their Father—all these will be on the left side (that is to say, on the left hand of the Judge, together with the damned)."[30]

It is probable that the exile of Basle was thinking here not only of Bédier's men or the inquisitors of the Sorbonne but also of Briçonnet, Roussel, Daniel, Duchemin, Budé, Vatable, Danès, and of his humanist friends, the Bible scholars and moderate reformers who would not do anything that would lead them to the stake or to exile. Carried away at this time by a torrent of emotions from being persecuted for the Gospel, Calvin no longer seemed to see these humanist friends as patient artisans of a peaceful reformation but only as frightened men who were not generous but self-centered and who deserved to be reprimanded.

But the author does not linger over this rather somber view of matters. The doxological emphasis continues and before ending with a final "Amen" he pours forth a fervent but gentle appeal to the pastors responsible for the Church: "O all who call yourselves bishops and pastors of the poor, take care that the lambs of Jesus Christ are not deprived of their proper food. Let no one be prohibited or forbidden, but may each Christian be free to read, study, and understand this holy Gospel in his own language, for God wishes it and Jesus Christ commands it." For this reason alone did the Lord send his apostles: "Surely, if you are true vicars, successors, and followers of them, your duty is to do as they did, watching over the flock and seeking by every means possible that all may be instructed in the faith of Jesus Christ by the pure word of God."[31]

The tone and content of the second preface to Olivétan's Bible is that of a deeply committed layman speaking to ecclesiastical leaders who have forgotten their duty. I consider it a document of capital importance for understanding Calvin's evolution, even if the vast majority of historians of Calvin pay no attention to it. For this writing appears to us to be a fervent *profession of faith,* bursting with the impetuosity of a volcanic eruption. Calvin read the Bible with increasing enthusiasm, and he testifies to us what this reading has brought to him personally: *an encounter with the living God* who speaks to humanity. In other words, a personal and life-giving encounter with Jesus Christ. Here he does not analyze a doctrine in order to weigh its dogmatic accuracy or the possibility of deviation, but he gives himself wholeheartedly to a new love that has conquered him and invites his brothers to open themselves to it as well.

While fervently entering into the knowledge of the things of God, Calvin, as I have already said, in no way loses touch with the events of his time. His retreat was an observatory. From there he paid very close attention to the events of France and the works that appeared there. More than any other writing, the statement of Francis I addressed to the Protestant princes in Germany on 1 February 1535 caught his attention.[32] In this document, written by his ambassador Guillaume du Bellay, the sovereign tried to justify before his outraged allies the antievangelical persecutions that he had ordered following the Placards affair. In substance he said that this affair clearly constituted an act of anarchy and rebellion against the established order of the kingdom. The government not only had the right but the duty to react with severity. The French evangelicals, unlike the German, were seditious and no different from the anabaptists. Were not the anabaptists put to death—and rightfully so—in German countries where the reform was taking place?[33]

Such a generalization was deeply revolting to our exile. He had just written an entire treatise against the anabaptists, and he knew that his friends rejected these sectarian tendencies as severely as the provocative affair of the Placards. Therefore he found the accusation intolerable. He decided then to reply, especially because the royal letter was not the only document to spread similar slanderous accusations. In 1534, a brochure of Cochlaeus had already appeared entitled *XXI Articles of the Anabaptist Monasteries . . . , to which is added an exposé of the origins from which they have flowed.* This document aimed to show that anabaptism is only the practical extension and necessary consequence of Luther's doctrines.[34] At the royal court of Paris, the confessor and preacher of the Queen Mother, Bishop Robert Ceneau, whom Calvin later called that "old theologizer of the Sorbonne,"[35] had written discourses against the seditious evangelicals purely to justify their "execution."[36]

But Calvin was not deceived when some humanists who were sincere reformists, such as Guillaume Budé and Cardinal Jacques Sadolet, also declared themselves opposed to the evangelicals and on the side of the theologizers. Budé did so in his *Transitus,* and Sadolet in his *Commentarius in Epistolam S. Pauli ad Romanos.* These illustrious men described the partisans or followers of the Gospel as an "ignorant multitude" who misunderstood the ideas of the cultured reformists and hereby created this "frightening sect" which the King rightly wished to exterminate.[37] Against all these different positions which seemed to him woefully undiscerning and unjust, the refugee felt obliged to establish the truth. He himself will say twenty-two years later: "It seemed to me that if I had not opposed these things with all the strength within me, I would not have forgiven myself; for in keeping silent I would have been cowardly and disloyal. This was the cause that inspired me to publish my *Institutes of the Christian Religion.*"[38]

According to its author, the *Institutes* were meant only to teach its readers to "correctly understand the holy Scripture." According to its title, it also had the goal of presenting a "summary of piety" for all who wished to know the doctrine of salvation. Finally, in view of the special circumstances in which it was brought to light, this work was destined to serve as a confession of faith before the "most Christian King" of France, to whom the preface was dedicated.

I shall devote a large portion of Part Two to the sources and content of the *Institutes* of 1536. Here I only want to point out what this long preface, probably finished around August 1535, and therefore shortly after the two biblical prefaces, reveals about the religious evolution of its author.

From the beginning of his letter to the King, Calvin declares that his primary intention had been essentially catechetic. He wanted to provide the indispensable fundamentals of the holy doctrine of the Gospel to his fellow countrymen who were seeking true piety and hungering and thirsting after Christer.[39] But having learned of the new persecutions unleashed in the kingdom of France, he decided to address his book to the sovereign; the King had been woefully deceived by iniquitous accusers, and Calvin wanted to prove to him the innocence of those who were being persecuted.

After this introduction, the strong hand of the brilliant lawyer, trained in juridical arguments, guides the evangelical catechist. With a sharp jab to the body, he attacks the weak point of the accusers and the judges: "Those who sit in judgment are seized with this desire [to conspire against us] and offer as judgments the *prejudices* they bring from home."[40] This was an appeal to the misinformed King to become well informed, so that the accused party could have its side heard as well.

The counsel's plea then takes on ecclesiastical dimensions. It is no longer a matter of a "private defense" or even the justification of a particular group of Christians, but of the entire "poor little Church" which has been decimated by executions and banishment or condemned to be only a "Church of silence."

What does Calvin mean by this "poor little Church"? Is it a new Church opposed to the old? At first glance, one might think so. Let us reread the entire sentence: "The wicked have achieved so much that even if the truth of Christ—persecuted and weakened—did not perish, it is certainly hidden as if buried and ignobly treated. Truly this poor little Church has been so ruined by cruel blows, or banished in exile, or so beaten down by terrors, that it dare not say a word."[41] The entire second part of the sentence seems to refer to the French evangelicals who are being pursued by the authorities of the established Church. Extending this thought a little farther, one might say that the text opposes Church to Church, a dominant Church to a "poor" Church.

In spite of appearances, I am convinced that such an interpretation is contrary to our theologian's thoughts about the Church. It is clear that there is a parallel between the fate inflicted upon the "truth of Christ" and that of the "poor little Church." The first is "hidden and buried as shameful," and the second is "destroyed," "pursued," and "overcome with threats and terror."[42] Although a false theology veils the truth of Christ, it does not at all follow that one truth is opposed to another truth. The same is true for the Church: because false brethren persecute the true sons of the Church, it does not follow that they are establishing themselves as one Church against another. The entire context of his ecclesiology proves that the Church is one and indefectible through the will and power of God. For Calvin there can be only one Church, just as there can be only one truth. What he suggests here and states more precisely in the *Institutes* is that the true state or form of the Church does not consist in its external structure but in the faithful and Christ-centered life of the elect of God. Not all are elect, not all persons belong to the Church just because they are baptized and bear the name of Christian. Thus it is possible that the persecutors are outside the community of the elect which, for the moment, has been reduced to those who are ready to serve the Lord at any cost. The "little Church" is then identified with the one and only Church of God. Like divine truth, it can be clouded over or ravaged for a time, but it can never cease to exist or be divided.

The cause of the Church in distress is the same as the cause of Christ. To defend this "kingdom of Christ" is to battle for the Lord. In fact, Calvin affirms that the doctrine that he upholds is not a human doctrine: "It is not ours, but that of the living God and his Christ."[43] This teaching rests on the "rule of faith" which does not at all consist of earthly reasons but only of the Word of God. Adversaries from the priestly order, "the order of sacrificers," neglect this word and misunderstand true religion "which is given in the Scriptures." They replace it with human inventions upon which they base the Mass, purgatory, and their pilgrimages. This is nothing but opposition to the "glory of God."[44]

The glory of God! Here is a leitmotiv that will be found in all of Calvin's theological, apologetical, and pastoral works. Calvin will exalt the glory of God at the expense of human glory; and he will seek to establish God's glory in the catholic Church re-formed according to the ancient ideal.

Next our author takes up one by one the six points of accusation advanced by the adversaries: that the evangelicals preach a "new Gospel," that they do not have a single miracle to confirm the correctness of their doctrines, that they scorn the authority of the Fathers, that they fight the time-honored customs of the Church, that they provoke schism, and finally that they give birth to seditious sects such as the "catabaptists."[45] Among these criticisms—and this is significant—Calvin is especially sensitive to the accusation of schism and sectarian deviation. We shall study his responses to this subject in Part Three. Here I emphasize only the extraordinary energy that he employs to prove his complete attachment to the *unity of the Church in Christ.* He declares: "Surely the Church of Christ has lived and will live as long as Christ reigns at the right hand of the Father, . . . [and] *against it we have no quarrel;* for in consent with all the faithful we worship and adore the one God and Christ the Lord, as he has always been adored by all the pious. . . . 'For God is not the author of division but of peace.' "[46]

In reacting against the unfaithfulness of some popes, bishops, and priests, as well as against several curial and juridical theories of the visible Church, our theologian loses sight of a good part of the institutional aspect of the Church and particularly its fundamental, sacramental structure. But is this surprising for someone who received most of his theological training from Luther and, to a lesser extent, from the spiritualist Zwingli?

Let us recapitulate the elements in this document that I believe are significant for the religious evolution of Calvin. Living in exile in Basle, influenced by the events of his new surroundings and particularly by his new readings, he made remarkably rapid progress in developing the basic points of his own theology. These views alone conformed to the truth. His thought is not abstract but is dominated by both a living devotion to Christ and an apostolic desire to proclaim the Gospel. Moreover, it is intensely aware of the glory of God, strongly Christ-centered, and solidly based on the Bible. We discover in his thought a profound ecclesiastical sensitivity, along with a genuine concern for justice and order. There is also a certain "lay spirit" or secular attitude, which is easily explained by Calvin's legal studies,[47] and a vital interest in the pastoral ministry. This interest continues to develop into an awareness of a true calling to the evangelical ministry.

To follow this line of development, we do not stop our historical inquiry at an analysis of the first edition of the *Institutes,* but we go on to the events of 1538, which mark the reformer's first "pastoral" crisis. Of course the *Institutes* may be justly considered as a doctrinal synthesis of all the essential elements of the young Calvin's religious evolution. One can even affirm that this synthesis possesses a "vital" character because it was developed in his mind under the influence of his experiences, trials, studies, and contacts with friends. However, we must admit that the first edition of the *Institutes* is still not an entirely adequate expression of Calvin's great transformation. The author still lacks a crucial experience before he becomes a reformer in the full sense of the word, namely, the enriching experience of pastoral ministry. We shall see how he acquires this in Geneva, where he was to live after a short period of travel.

CHAPTER EIGHT
Travels Between Basle, Ferrara, and Paris, 1536

Even while immersed in the reading of original sources and the writing of his compendium, our theologian kept in touch with religious developments in France as well as in the surrounding Swiss cities.

Thus he began to correspond with Christophe Fabri, called Libertet, a companion of Farel in the struggle, who had become a priest at Bole and then at Thonon. Calvin called him "best brother" and "minister of the Word of God" and sent him the manuscript of his *Psychopannychia;* he also discussed with him the text of Olivétan's New Testament and reacted to several incidents that took place in the community of Bole. He reacted to these events not only by expressing his personal opinion but by generously offering his correspondent specific advice and enthusiastic exhortations. We read in the postscript of his letter of 3 September 1535: "I do not know how I forget while writing what I was determined not to overlook. That is, that I would *urge* you and the other brothers, with few words but with all my heart, to seek peace. . . . You can hardly imagine with what indignation I heard about that tumult."[1]

It is certain that from his vantage point in Basle, Calvin also observed the troubles in the church in Geneva, namely, the poisoning of Viret and several other ministers,[2] the theological disputation organized by Farel which ended in an easy victory for the evangelicals against the representatives of the Roman clergy,[3] the occupation of the churches and the destruction of sacred images by the followers of Farel, and finally the prohibition of the Mass by vote of the Council of Two Hundred on 10 August 1535.[4] He also followed with great anguish the campaign undertaken by the Duke of Savoy to conquer Geneva and to reinstate the exiled bishop. The campaign failed and in January 1536 ended with victory for the troops of Berne, who came to help the besieged city.[5]

During this time, our young scholar remained preoccupied with the anabaptist problem. He had clearly recognized the difficulty of denying the original, more or less direct relationship between the Lutheran movement and sectarian deviation. (It is a fact that the *Schwärmer* quoted a number of statements by Luther to justify their views, even though Luther protested such use of his ideas.)[6] Gifted with penetrating judgment, Calvin understood that there was a serious danger of compromising the entire evangelical movement, which must be averted at all costs. His sense of order and his bourgeois, urbane mentality detested this unleashing of mystical enthusiasm.[7] Also, he continued to revise his *Psychopannychia*[8] in view of its imminent publication and added a second preface in which he attempted to analyze more deeply the dangers of enthusiasm.

The battle, Calvin writes, is essentially being waged over the Word of God. On the one hand, there are those who cry heresy as soon as pious men try to reestablish the honorable position of the Scriptures. They accuse the Bible scholars of being innovators and teaching dangerous ideas. To these hardened conservatives, one must give a firm reply: "There is one word of life: that which comes from the mouth of the Lord. . . . *That . . . word is not new;* it was from the beginning, is now, and ever shall be." But on the other hand, one has to deal with those who, like reeds shaken by the wind, bend with every fantastic teaching. Such men indiscriminately gather truth and lies, both solid and empty doctrines. Even worse, in spite of their ignorance, these "unlearned men" set themselves up as doctors of theology and teach as it were "ex cathedra." Is it astonishing that the result is a multitude of errors and dissensions? "And when one of them is ashamed that he does not know something, they respond most confidently about everything, as if they were oracles of the gods. From this source again arise all the schisms, errors, and scandals of our faith." Of course, these unfortunate people always refer to a biblical text. But that is precisely the "source of the evil"! What these people make the Bible say! Look at what they corrupt by their arbitrary interpretations! Surely this is not the way in which God intended teaching to take place. "Is this the way of learning? to twist and distort the Scriptures so that they serve our desires? so that they are subject to our notions?" That is the dreadful evil that gives rise to various sects among the evangelicals: "And now we wonder whence arise *all those sects* among those who have given first place to the Gospel and the renewed Word?" Two things are clear here: Calvin is conscious of the progressive disintegration which threatens the integrity and unity of the reform, and he does not hesitate to identify those guilty of this evil as "that worthless bunch of anabaptists."

One may ask whether the young reformer is content to diagnose the illness or whether he goes so far as to propose remedies. In fact, he does indicate one: "Let us always wait before the face of the Lord; and let us add nothing to his wisdom or mix with it anything of our own." In order to be content with what the Word of God actually reveals, one must cultivate spiritual simplicity and poverty and reject any rash curiosity and all dangerous inquiry of "esoteric" matters.[9] That is all. Calvin proposes no remedies other than this inner and personal attitude. It is significant that the need for a living Teacher of doctrine does not even enter his mind. The necessarily visible, institutional, and pastoral aspect of the Church escapes him for the most part. Did his negative experiences with the inquisitorial authority of the Sorbonne make him once and for all distrustful of this aspect?

After fifteen of the most intellectually stimulating months of his life—Hebrew studies, reading original sources, writing prefaces for the Bible, his epistle to the King, the *Institutes,* reediting the *Psychopannychia,* and correcting the proofs for these publications—Calvin left Basle for Ferrara in Italy around March 1536.[10] Louis du Tillet accompanied him. In all probability it was the evangelical reputation of Renée of France, daughter of Louis XII and by marriage Duchess of Ferrara, that attracted him to this famous center of culture. While living abroad, Renée was certainly worthy, one can say, of her native France. French reformists who were forced into exile could count on her warm welcome. With her humanist training and her interest in religious questions, she resembled closely her cousin, Marguerite, the Queen of Navarre. Just as Marguerite did, Renée continued to participate in traditional worship, while at the same time favoring the representatives of all the movements looking to reform the Church, including the Lutheran movement. Her uncertain mind needed both the security of tradition and the enthusiasm inspired by religious revolution.

The Duchess, who was probably the same age as Calvin, granted him hospitality and her deepest esteem, as witnessed by the later correspondence between these two noble souls.[11] At the court of Ferrara our traveler also met the duchy's physician, the German Johannes Sinapius and his future wife, Françoise Bussiron; they were most impressed by Calvin's religious ideas and corresponded with him from that time on.[12]

These friendships, and no doubt there were others, Calvin made in a very short time. But an unforeseen event forced Calvin to leave Ferrara quickly and to return to Basle. On 14 April, Holy Friday, the entire court and its guests were assembled in the chapel. Among them was a French refugee named Jehannet who had come to Ferrara in the company of the poet Clément Marot. This man Jehannet created a scandal during the ceremony by conspicuously leaving the chapel at the moment of the veneration of the cross.[13] After he was arrested and questioned, the unfortunate man revealed to his inquisitors that the Duchess was harboring other evangelicals who believed as he did. One can guess what followed; Calvin had to flee with several others. Du Tillet, his faithful friend, left with him. The story that the young author of the *Institutes* was incarcerated by the Inquisition as he crossed the Val d'Aoste and charged with preaching in the region has still not been confirmed by a single historical document.[14]

Returning to Basle, Calvin left his friend du Tillet and continued his journey to Paris to put his personal affairs in order and to bring his brother Antoine with him to Basle or to Strasbourg. All of this is reported by Colladon, who this time is given credence by the majority of historians because of the numerous plausible details in his story.[15] Let us add that Colladon's laudatory account has also been collaborated by A. Lefranc, who discovered in the archives of Noyon a notice of power of attorney signed in Paris on 2 June 1536, by John Calvin, which enabled his brothers, Charles and Antoine, to sell the lands that the family still possessed in Picardy.[16] Because of this, Calvin did not return at that time to his native city.

Our exile was already known for his publication of the *Institutes,* and he could make this trip only because of the religious détente in France following the royal edict of Coucy which authorized exiles to return under the condition of renouncing their heresy within six months.[17] Even if Calvin had no intention of obeying the demands of the decree, he was nevertheless able to take advantage of the reprieve in order to arrange his affairs.

Taking Antoine and his sister Marie with him, he set off on 15 July for

Strasbourg. But as the hostilities between the French and the imperial forces made a direct route impractical, the little group had to make a detour through the center of France and by way of Geneva.[18] Upon their arrival in the city, an event occurred that gave Calvin's life a totally new direction.

CHAPTER NINE
Calvin in Geneva, 1536–1538

In 1536, Geneva carried the old scars and the new wounds of the battles that had taken place between the civil and the ecclesiastical powers, on the one hand, and between the Roman clergy and the supporters of the reform on the other. Since 1387, when the bourgeois of the city wrested their franchises from Bishop Adhémar Fabri, a large part of the legislative, executive, judicial, and administrative powers was exercised by the Council General and the Little Council of citizens. The remaining powers were kept by the bishop, who was theoretically the sovereign of the city, and by the *vidomne,* the delegate of the bishop for temporal affairs. A good number of the titularies of the see of Geneva had never been consecrated or even ordained. The offices were often bestowed by secular lords, and most recently they were bestowed by a foreign political power, the Duke of Savoy. Between the Councils, the bishop, the *vidomne,* and the duke, each with its own authority and ambitions, there was continuous contention which often led to tragic consequences.

Thus, in 1519, Philibert Berthelier, one of the leaders of the bourgeois opposition who sought to free the city from the control of the bishop and the Savoyards, was led to the gallows. Undiscouraged, the Councils pursued the struggle, and on 1 October 1534, the citizens drove out the last bishop, Pierre de la Baume, a pawn of the Duke of Savoy.[1] As in other Swiss cities, it was in the context of a patriotic struggle for independence and civic freedom that the religious reformation took place in Geneva. In seeking political support outside the city, the bishops had gradually compromised the authority of the established Church. Unfortunately there were not enough lower clergy in the diocese who were sufficiently fervent and committed to be able to make up for the inadequacies of these pathetic representatives of the episcopacy.[2] In the majority of the cases, ignorance and moral mediocrity paralyzed both the secular and the regular clergy. In 1536 the situation was such that the civil power, that is, the Councils, believed it was authorized to direct the higher affairs of the Church and for all practical purposes took control of episcopal power.[3]

When Guillaume Farel,[4] the most fervent Lutheran preacher of France, appeared in the city in October 1532, there was no organized resistance to the rapid success of his undertaking. His acts of violence, taking over churches and breaking statues, were tolerated by the magistrate and passively endured by the clergy. In addition, since the entry into Geneva of the allies from Berne in 1530, there were a large number of supporters of the reform and adversaries of the clergy who were prepared from the start to be Farel's congregation and shock troops.

If we consult the *Register of the Council* of Geneva concerning the events that occurred shortly before the arrival of Calvin, we find of special interest a series of decisions taken by the authorities against the "papal" Mass and in favor of the "evangelical" doctrine. To cite several examples: on 3 April 1536, one of the syndics addressed an admonition to several priests inviting them to "live according to evangelical doctrine" and forbidding them to say the Mass or to celebrate "any other papal sacrament." The priests submitted, and after hearing an exhortation from "Master Guillaume Farel" they promised to study the Gospel and no longer "to say Mass, to baptize, confess, marry, or to offer or administer the sacrament, even if by papal order and direction."[5] On 12 May everyone was talking about the imprisonment of some malefactors: "Here we are speaking of those priests who are detained for saying the Mass against instructions; they were arrested, and it was resolved to take them to Riva, where, during the next Sunday's sermon, they will confess their deed in public and by such confession obtain their pardon."[6] On 19 May, after an admonition from Farel and other "preachers," the Little Council decided to convene "a great general council to ask if people wished to live *according to the new reformation of the faith.*"[7] Two days later appeared a general proclamation of the Council enjoining everyone from now on to live "according to the Gospel and the Word of God" and no longer "to seek after Masses, images, idols, or other papal abuses."[8] From then on, offenders were called "the heretical faction of the Mass."[9] Finally, on 24 July, about two weeks before Calvin's arrival, a new act of intolerance—very similar to the acts of the Inquisition or the Sorbonne—was reported by the *Register.* An inhabitant of the city of Léman, Jean Balard, was brought before the Council to explain why he did not want to attend the sermons of the preachers. The man replied by appealing to freedom of conscience: "He responded that he believed in God, who teaches through his very own Spirit, and that he was not able to accept our preaching. He said that we could not compel him to attend a sermon *against his conscience.*" Then they quote his own words: "I want to live according to the Gospel of God; but I do not wish to do so according to individual interpretations, but according to the interpretation of the Holy Spirit, according to the Holy Mother Church universal, in which I believe." Finally the sentence is pronounced: the man and his family are to be banished in ten days if they persist in their obstinacy.[10]

This document clearly shows that alongside the weak and easily submissive clergy, there existed in Geneva after four years of "evangelical" domination, courageous laymen who were prepared to submit to banishment rather than to abandon the traditions of the universal holy Church.

If we keep in mind all the details noted so far, we see that the religious atmosphere of Geneva at the time of Calvin's arrival was still very difficult and tense. The reformer himself will declare on his deathbed twenty-eight years later: "When I first came to this church there was practically nothing. They preached, and that's all. They searched for idols and destroyed them, but there was not the slightest reformation. Everything was in disarray."[11] It is certain that the destruction of the traditional structures had not yet been followed by the installation of positive "re-formed" structures. In place of the ruins, they still had not raised any habitable edifice. Farel and the preachers were well aware of the gravity of the situation, but they felt incapable of remedying it.

According to Calvin's statement made in 1557,[12] on which Beza and Colladon's accounts are based,[13] the reformer only intended to pass through Geneva before returning to Strasbourg, where he wished to concentrate on "some particular studies." He was in such a hurry that he had not even thought of visiting Farel, who learned of the presence of the author of the *Institutes* only through an indiscretion of Louis du Tillet. Calvin's friend could not contain his joy at seeing him again and immediately spoke about him to the ministers of the city. Then Farel, who "burned with a marvelous zeal to advance the Gospel," went to find him and made "every effort" to retain him. Faced with the reticence of the young scholar, the passionate preacher resorted to a "frightening adjuration" and began to threaten him with the thunderbolts of heaven if he was not willing to stay. And Calvin notes: "He went so far as to invoke a curse, that it would please God to curse my rest and the tranquillity of my studies that I sought if, *in such a great need,* I retired and refused to give help and aid. His words so shook me and frightened me that I desisted from the voyage which I was about to undertake."

Besides these documents written more than twenty years after the events, we have no other sources concerning these dramatic events. But there is no reason to doubt the essential truth of these testimonies. After all that we have said about how the future reformer was more an intellectual than an activist, we can understand that changing from a life of study to a public life represented a great sacrifice for him. No doubt he thought it absurd to assume a function for which he sincerely thought he lacked the necessary qualities.

Therefore Calvin did not give in to Farel until he realized the urgency of the situation in Geneva and until he had presented his conditions. In fact, he was not willing to serve as a pastor or preacher—a ministry for which he felt unprepared—but only as a "doctor" or "reader of the holy Scriptures,"[14] a task for which he felt he had the competence and the necessary experience. After a short trip to Basle at the beginning of September 1536 to take care of several matters, Calvin began his reading courses on the Pauline epistles. These lessons took place regularly at the Cathedral of Saint-Pierre. One can imagine that this first encounter with an audience of laity larger than any he had known so far made a very deep impression upon him. But his zeal to spread the Gospel, which he had expressed so strongly in his Bible prefaces, proved to be greater than his natural timidity. Thus a new perspective which was completely oriented to the concrete life of the people opened before him, and he took an important new step in his religious evolution. Very early, Farel and the other preachers recognized their new companion's exceptional qualities in oratory and organization as well as his sound judgment in controversial matters. The author of the *Institutes* did not let them down in any way. They also willingly brought him into the work of the "congregations" of pastors, established in November of 1536, and even encouraged him to express his opinion on the conduct of the congregations or of a brother who was under scrutiny.[15] When the inhabitants of Bern organized a public dispute in Lausanne, their new fief,[16] they invited Farel and Viret, who in turn brought their valuable new recruit.[17]

The Lausanne disputation, held during the first two weeks of October 1536, opposed the evangelical preachers to the orators of the local clergy on ten articles concerning justification, the unique mediation of Christ, the nature of the Church, the ministry, and the sacraments.[18] Calvin entered the debates at only two points, but each time with considerable success. He proved himself to be superior to his adversaries not only by the force of his convictions and the brilliance of his arguments but also by the great extent of his biblical and theological knowledge.

On 5 October, in the course of a discussion on the presence of the glorified Christ under the eucharistic elements, a speaker imprudently accused the evangelicals of despising and rejecting the authority of the Fathers. Calvin arose and protested.[19] It is false, he said in substance, that "we condemn and completely reject them." On the contrary, we know them better than our accusers, and we know that they are in agreement with everything that we teach. And here is the proof: Tertullian was certainly of the opinion that in the Supper it is not the "material body of Christ" which is given but "his figure by representation." In the same way, the commentary on Matthew attributed to Chrysostom presents a view "opposed to all your doctrine. . . . [It] obviously supports our view, saying clearly that we must not seek the natural body of Jesus Christ; but it is the mystery of communion which we have in his body." Augustine also speaks in a specific passage from his epistles in favor of a theory of representation. And in his writing against Adimantus, he specifically states that when the Lord said, "Here is my body," he gave in reality "the sign of his body." Moreover, the greatest doctor of the Church teaches that the "carnal sacrifices" of the Old Covenant have a prefigurative character and are now surpassed. The "sacrifice of the New Testament[20] is an act of grace and a commemoration of the flesh of Christ which he offered and of the blood which he shed for the remission of our sins." And Calvin adds: "Weigh every word and syllable (if you wish) to see if it in any way favors your error."[21] Then, setting aside his patristic quotations and addressing himself to one of the opposing orators, he began to prove the impossibility of the corporeal presence of Christ under the eucharistic elements. Finally, he presents his completely "dynamic" conception of the holy Supper: "It is a spiritual communion by which *in power and effectiveness* he makes us participants in all that we can receive by grace of his body and blood [and again] . . . by which he truly makes us participants in his body and blood, but entirely in a spiritual way, that is to say, through the bond of his Spirit."[22]

The more one reads this brilliant contribution of the young theologian, the more one is struck by its force as an argument *ad hominem* and by its insufficiency as a theological proof *ad rem*. The champion of the formal dialectics of Montaigu and the lawyer who was an expert in juridical discussions are combined here in a demonstration of scholastic method. Although the thesis is not put at the beginning of the argument but cleverly placed at the end, it keeps its fundamentally a priori character. The quotations from the Fathers are sentences detached from their context, removed from the counterexpressions that one could find in the same author, and quite arbitrarily chosen to serve the given thesis more than to solve a problem. The fact that it is an improvisation rather than a prepared discourse in no way excuses the procedure.

In spite of the weakness of his argument, Calvin does not seem to have met anyone at Lausanne capable of contradicting him. His adversaries continued to yield before the technically brilliant reasoning of this young man gifted with an unequaled memory and also, let us emphasize, with ardent faith.[23] We also think that this easy victory, coupled with the success of his *Institutes,* greatly contributed to developing his awareness of being a sort of "mouthpiece of God," called to overcome the enemies of the Gospel with only "the sword of the Word" and to establish authoritatively the "holy doctrine" of Christ. Neither in Lausanne nor in any other place later on did Calvin confront a truly worthy representative of traditional theology, or at least a theologian capable of resisting him and proving to him the solid foundation of the essential doctrines of the Catholic tradition.[24] The absence of a worthy opponent who was at least equal if not superior to Calvin was to play an important role in the reformer's rapid and unhindered turn toward positions that were objectively heterodox.

A letter that Calvin sent from Lausanne on 13 October 1536 to his friend from Orléans, François Daniel, attests to the sincerity and assurance with which from then on he committed himself to the way of radicalism.[25] He spoke with satisfaction of the favorable outcome of the dispute. The "opponents of true religion" finally displayed their "ignorance." *God* has wondrously destroyed the reign of idolatry in their hearts. This disputation was assuredly an event of great importance, whose documents are worthy of publication. But the harvest is plentiful and the laborers are few. "You can hardly be persuaded," writes Calvin, "how great is the scarcity of ministers, considering the multitude of churches *who need pastors.*" Ah, if all the so-called partisans of the reform who, like Daniel's colleagues, have a lot to say in the shadow and do so little in the open, would finally decide to dedicate themselves to the effective service of the Gospel! And the letter ends with this pressing invitation: "Oh, if those among you who are at least one with us in heart, when you see the *visible need of the Church* would put forth some effort to help." These are clearly the words of a Christian who recognized the importance of the missionary and pastoral aspects of the reform and of a reformer who appeals for help as he becomes aware of his responsibility.

From this time on, several great first-generation artisans of the reform considered the young Calvin as their equal. Martin Bucer himself now saw in Calvin a brother in the ministry of the Gospel. A letter that he wrote to Calvin on 1 November 1536 carries this salutation: "May grace and peace be added unto you, brother and fellow initiate *(symmista)* in the worship of the one Lord."[26] "Fellow initiate" translates a word that literally means "initiated in the same mysteries"; it is a title that the reformers and the first evangelical ministers were pleased to give themselves. Then the letter notes in a very respectful tone the great usefulness of Calvin's activity for all the evangelical communities: "It seems good to us to acknowledge that the Lord has ordained to use you in a most fruitful way for the benefit of his churches, and to generously grant his blessing to your ministry." Bucer, who was Calvin's elder by eighteen years, then displays extreme politeness: "And thus, freely we will come to an agreement where you wish, in such a way that we defer to the Lord in our great concern for the truth of Christ, and grant to you the ministry of teaching Christ. . . . Therefore, brother esteemed in the Lord, agree to a place with us." It seems quite evident to us that such language would flatter the self-esteem of the young reformer and strengthen his conviction of actually being called of God.[27]

At the end of 1536, Calvin was called to be an ordinary preacher, a pastor of the church of Geneva. This time he accepted without hesitation.[28] His promotion was in all probability an act of the Council, and it was not accompanied with any ceremony of ordination with the laying on of hands or any other liturgical rite.[29] The reformer never attached any importance to this lack of pastoral ordination. The certitude of being chosen by God was sufficient in itself. It made no difference to him whether one came to the reform from the ranks of the laity or the priesthood. The only thing that counted was being a good servant of the Word and a good pastor of the flock.

An instrument of the Lord should speak with authority. The author of the *Institutes,* now invested with an official pastoral call, was well aware of this need. Therefore, before the new year he finished writing two epistles on present problems,[30] one against accepting ordination to the papal priesthood (an interesting coincidence with his promotion to the pastorate without ordination!) and the other against participating in the Mass or other religious practices under the papacy. These works are entitled respectively *The Christian Duty of a Man Either to Administer or Cast Aside the Priestly Offices of the Papal Church*[31] and *On Fleeing the Illicit Rites of the Wicked, and Observing in Piety the Christian Religion.*[32]

The first is addressed to an "old friend, now prelate," whom the majority of Calvin scholars recognize as Gérard Roussel, who had recently been ordained Bishop of Oléron in Béarn.[33] In Part Four we shall study this letter in detail. Here we note only those things which inform us about the religious evolution of our reformer. Its theme is primarily pastoral. In a very positive first part, the author outlines the ideal of the episcopate which he calls a "ministry of the Lord." In their relationship to the faithful, bishops are "pastors," "guardians," "watchmen," and "stewards" in the Lord. They are set apart "for the good and benefit of all" and for the demanding ministry to souls. In the second part, Calvin begins to criticize the dominating spirit of the high papal clergy, their negligence in proclaiming the Word, and their cynical temporal ambitions. He does not hesitate on occasion to engage in very damaging personal attacks against his elder in the reformist struggle and his former guide toward the Gospel—whom he called, even in 1533, "our Gérard." For example: "Why did you stop? Why are you lethargic? Why do you sleep? . . . O unhappy man, you are responsible to God for so many deaths; you are so many times a murderer and a shedder of blood. The Lord will hold you responsible for every drop!" And after another severe indictment of village priests, monasteries, and the "Roman arch-pirate," the letter ends with a call to radicalism. There can be no more watching from the middle of the road, no compromise, and no acceptance of delays. God surely spits out the lukewarm. A truly prophetic oracle is proclaimed from the mouth of the young pastor.

The other epistle was directed against Roman worship and intended, no doubt, for Nicolas Duchemin, the good friend and benefactor of Calvin during his student years at Orléans who had since become an ecclesiastical official. Here Calvin's tone is less violent, but he is just as opposed to any compromise with papism. Nothing can justify even passive or pretended participation by the true Christian in the acts of idolatry and superstition practiced by the churches directed by Rome. The Mass is simply the "main source of abominations."

But much other work awaited this man who could think of nothing except the great renovation of the Church of God. Now the issue was to work together to write a code of ecclesiastical discipline, a confession of faith, and a catechism for the community of Geneva.

The first appeared as a modest project of rules entitled *Articles Presented by the Preachers.* Various paragraphs dealt with the organization of the Church, worship, and religious instruction. The document is dated 16 January 1536.[34] The editors of the *Opera Calvini* comment that the "writing, as far as we can tell by the style, is not directly attributable to Calvin, but one would not be incorrect to say that Calvin was its real author."[35] In any case, many of the essential ideas of the *Institutes* are clearly expressed and summarized there, especially frequent communion.

It is certainly one of the characteristics of the young reformer's thought that he envisions the Church in its concrete reality as a community assembled *around the eucharistic table.* "It is certain," we read at the beginning of the *Articles,* "that a church cannot be called well ordered and regulated unless the holy Supper of our Lord is often celebrated and frequented by the people." From this premise it follows that the unworthy should be excluded from communion by means of excommunication. But who are the unworthy? Those who "do not wish to align themselves in love and in complete obedience to the holy Word of God." Moreover, to worship properly, one must chant the psalms; to form the people according to evangelical doctrine, one must catechize the children in their youth; and to control the moral life of the faithful, it is necessary to elect overseers in each quarter of the city. And because it is in the interest of the Church to have as members only those who are openly and completely attached to the Gospel, it is desirable that each citizen, beginning with every member of the magistracy, publicly declare whether he accepts or refuses the confession of faith approved at Geneva.[36] Those who "prefer the kingdom of the pope to the kingdom of Jesus Christ" should leave the city without delay. If it is necessary to excommunicate impenitent sinners, how much more reason is there for the necessity of removing those "who are completely opposed to us in religion."

Calvin chose the way of radical reform, and he wanted to establish his program quickly and without delay. No one can serve two masters. Farel's zealous associate had become a man entirely different from the Fabrist humanist, the admirer of Roussel which he had been only a short time before. Fear no longer restrained the uncompromising and impatient aspects of Calvin's character as he continued to fulfill his true calling to be a reformer.

To put into practice the last proposition of the *Articles,* Calvin formulated a confession of faith "which all citizens and inhabitants of Geneva and subjects of the area should swear to keep and uphold."[37] To furnish a precise plan for religious education he composed *The Instruction,* an outline of future catechisms.[38] It summarizes quite abstractly the essential content of

the *Institutes,* while the *Confession* condensed still more the same doctrine.[39]

These were the principles of Calvin's reform. How were they applied to
life? As always, at the cost of many difficulties. First of all, the Council
rejected several points proposed in the *Articles,* notably the monthly celebration of the Supper and the institution of an ecclesiastical disciplinary
tribunal that was independent of the civil tribunals.[40] A considerable number of citizens were recalcitrant about the public confession of faith.[41] In
addition, considerable passive resistance emerged, which at the political
level later resulted in the triumph of those who were hostile to the dominating influence of the pastors.

The zeal of Calvin the neophyte encountered unforeseen obstacles which
greatly mortified his prophetic impatience.

There were much worse problems. Pierre Caroli, the former preacher of
Briçonnet at Meaux, was now a refugee in Switzerland following the Placards affair where he became the principal pastor in the church of Lausanne. His influence in the city developed to the detriment of Viret, even
though Viret was more responsible for the progress of the reform in the
area. The ministers of Geneva who were friends of Viret protested against
this state of affairs.[42] Their indignation increased even more when they
learned that Caroli had recommended that the faithful offer prayers for the
dead. Calvin wrote to this colleague to condemn his conduct; but Caroli,
during a confrontation that took place at Lausanne, replied by accusing
Viret, Farel, and Calvin of spreading the Arian heresy. According to the
account of the ministers of Geneva written to the citizens of Bern: "He
pronounced our entire company guilty of Arian falsehoods."[43] According
to the same source, Calvin then quoted a passage from the recently written
Catechism of Geneva, where faith in the Trinity was clearly affirmed, in
order to show the error of this statement. But Caroli was not satisfied. He
demanded an explicit adherence of all the ministers present to the traditional confessions of the faith, including the so-called Athanasian Creed:
"Let them, it is said, create *new confessions,* but let us instead adhere to the
three creeds." This demand was unacceptable to Calvin, who opposed it
with an argument that seems double-edged to us today: "To these, Calvin
responds that we swear by faith in the one God, not by the faith of
Athanasius, whose creed was *never approved by any legitimate church.*"

Here clearly appears the double standard to which the reformer willingly
turns in his discussions. In the statement quoted, the quality of a "legitimate
church" seems for all practical purposes to be denied to the Eastern and
Western Churches which, by the universal liturgical custom of almost a
thousand years, conferred on the Athanasian Creed an authority equal or
at least similar to that of other creeds.[44] On the other hand, this authority
is implicitly accorded to the evangelical church of Geneva,[45] whose minis-

ters agreed to a trinitarian formula inspired by the recent, first treatise of a young theologian. Whatever may have been the human, intellectual, and moral worth of Caroli, he rightfully noted in this specific case the "novelty" of Calvin's text concerning the so-called Athanasian Creed. But to our young reformer, this charge appeared intolerable. Let us try to understand this.

During the course of the preceding four years and under the influence of the German reformers, Calvin weighed the little that he knew of medieval scholastic theology against his massive knowledge of the Bible and the Fathers. He came to the firm conviction that the Church of the Middle Ages was "innovative" in comparison to the doctrine of the first centuries. Therefore, those who through a renewal movement sought to reestablish the "simplicity of Scripture" and the structures of the "primitive Church" did not deserve the name of innovator. Calvin had read the Bible and the Fathers and on their doctrine he built his *Catechism* and his *Confession*.[46] Moreover, the assurance of God was in his favor, since it was God who had chosen him and had placed his Word in Calvin's mouth and in his pen. Had not God blessed the *Institutes* and accorded it great success? Therefore, what Calvin had written was nothing less than the expression and explication of an authentic, revealed faith ("we swear by faith in the one God"). Before the authority of this faith, the authority of the so-called Athanasian Creed—with its obscure origin—could not have much weight.

Caroli's background shows that he was the epitome of the Fabrist reformist who was seduced by the dynamism of the Lutherans.[47] He had belonged to the circle of Meaux, preached against the abuses of the Church, experienced the vexations of the Sorbonne, and was forced to flee from the police during the Placards affair. But in spite of everything, he never approved in his heart all the anti-Roman and antitraditional negations of the German and Swiss reformers. Furthermore, his natural instability did not allow him to follow consistently a single and clearly defined line. In this he was quite the opposite of Calvin. After the polemics of Lausanne, he changed camps frequently, each time going in an opposite direction. His awkward behavior toward the devout pastor Viret earned him Calvin's deep dislike, especially when he accused the Genevans of Arianism. This half-evangelical—the reformer no doubt thought—who was preaching against papism and urging people to pray for the dead, this ambitious[48] man who did not hesitate to remove a preacher more worthy than himself, this creator of factions with his ready accusations had no right to criticize the orthodoxy of others and even less right to impose upon them conditions of agreement! Besides, one replies only to sincere and objective people. But while Calvin was willing to serve without payment,[49] Caroli was never known to scorn money.[50] All these things certainly influenced the reformer's response and gave it a passionate and biased tone.[51]

In the documents dealing with these confrontations we note another characteristic of Calvin's attitude toward the Church. One senses a constant fear of the danger of disunity and fragmentation that such quarrels entail. Under the pressure of this real nightmare, he exclaims: "For you see that the malice of a few arises so that the Church is miserably wounded by discord and contention."[52] The people, the simple people, are already making fun of ministers when they see that there is so little unity among them: "Thus the peasants are insisting that we agree among ourselves before we labor to lead others into our way of thinking."[53] Against these evils the only remedy that Calvin proposes is the following: the ministers of the churches of each region should assemble and agree on the doctrine to be taught. The controversial points can be resolved only in this conciliatory way: "And there are several other things, all of which can be settled in no other way except in an assembly."[54] "Synod," "convention," "collegium," "senate"— these terms all appear constantly in the documents of the Caroli affair to designate the different collegial groups charged with promoting "consensus" and "unity of doctrine." Of course, the doctrine could only be the evangelical doctrine.

The Lausanne affair dragged on. The inhabitants of Bern to whom they had appealed for arbitration showed an equal distrust of both parties. Megander, one of the ministers of Bern, did not hesitate to inform Bullinger in the following language: "Some of the French in recently occupied positions of authority are suspected by us of believing incorrectly about Christ and the persons of the Trinity. For this reason, Calvin came to Bern to petition strenuously for a synod to be convened which had been denied to *that man* until after Easter."[55] The tone is anything but cordial. Calvin, who had gone to Bern to speed up the meeting of the synod, is not even called "a brother," but simply "that man." Furthermore, he is considered as a newly arrived Frenchman who is suspicious and unstable.[56]

Was this distrust of the doctrinal plan at all justified? To be sure, Farel did not use the term "Trinity" in his *Sommaire* nor did Calvin in his *Instruction* and *Confession;*[57] and of course Calvin's trinitarian theology always retained a "slight modalist tendency."[58] But we think that the accusation of Arianism had not the slightest foundation in the work of the two Genevan reformers.

Whatever the case may be, the Bernese—as well as other evangelical leaders[59]—remained in a state of expectation. The frequently requested synod did not meet in Lausanne until 14 May 1538. It was presided over by the Bernese civil and ecclesiastical authorities and ended in a victory for Calvin and his friends. They removed Caroli from his position as minister. Farel pursued Caroli further by criticizing his private life, until it was impossible for him to live in any of the territories under Bern's control. On the other hand, the orthodoxy of the Genevans was acknowledged on two occasions: first, at this same synod,[60] then at the one that took place in Bern beginning on 31 May.[61] Megander, so distrustful and unfriendly in his relationships with them before the colloquies, now wrote to Bullinger: "It is agreed that the Genevans . . . believe concerning God, Christ, and the Holy Spirit in a holy and catholic manner."[62]

In spite of the suffering that this crisis may have caused Calvin, the dispute's happy outcome confirmed his feeling that he was on the right path and that he was sustained by providence.

At the same time as the Caroli affair, the reformer had to deal one more time with the anabaptist problem. The *Register of the Council,* in its notes of 9 to 19 March 1538,[63] speaks of the arrival in the city of two Dutch representatives of the sect. A theological disputation was organized by the local pastors in order to unveil publicly the error of the newcomers; but this method proved to be fruitless, and the two were banished from the city under pain of death. The *Register* makes Farel the star and does not even mention the role played by Calvin. But Colladon attributes this "success" to Calvin alone and does not even mention Farel.[64] It is probable that both were involved. A theological disputation was first accepted and even desired, but then refused by the ministers of Geneva; this can be cited as a new example of the double standard to which we have already alluded. The evangelicals always demanded the right to discuss publicly all matters that dealt with checking the papists and their adversaries who had little ability to resist them. But as soon as this means threatened trouble in their own ranks—and this was exactly the case with the two anabaptists—they preferred to cut short all discussion and banish the unwelcome visitors. Referring to the episode in question, the *Register*'s note of 16 March also says: "Here they disputed with the two catabaptists all day long"; but on 18 March it tells us that it is a very bad thing "to give rise to different and diverse opinions rather than union" and thereby risk "shaking the faith" of many. Therefore they must separate themselves from those who obstinately hold to doctrines that "stray from the truth"; they can no longer call them brothers, for they "are disturbers of our church" and they "do not wish to pray with us." And here is the decree of the Council of Two Hundred, dated 19 March: "An arrangement with the catabaptists was proposed according to which it was advised that these and all others of their sect be perpetually banished from this city and these lands under pain of death."[65]

With Caroli defeated and the anabaptists banished, Calvin and Farel were still not at the end of their troubles. The opposition of rebellious Genevans to the public confession of faith increased to the extent that the ministers had to constrain them. The Little Council upheld the pastors, but the protectors of Bern exhibited more understanding for the opposition.[66] This affair had been dragging on for a long time. From July to December 1537, there were numerous confrontations between the antagonists, which were complicated further by political interference. In the end, on 4 January 1538, the Council of Two Hundred had recourse to a compromise: they exhorted the reactionaries to act "according to common custom," but they simultaneously forbade the ministers from excommunicating those who did not eventually submit.[67] This was a serious failure for Calvin, who had worked with all his strength to establish an ecclesiastical jurisdiction independent of civil power. Even worse, the elections organized on 3 February carried into power the party opposed to Calvin and Farel's religious politics, in spite of an "admonition" from the reformers.[68]

This unfavorable situation in Geneva was offset by the success of a doctrinal agreement with the theologians of the other area churches. The colloquy that took place on 22 and 23 September 1537, in Bern,[69] reunited Capito, Bucer, Myconius, Grynaeus, Farel, Viret, and Calvin. To the general satisfaction of all, they quickly succeeded in coming to an understanding on the doctrine of the Trinity and the Eucharist.[70] The whole first part of the *Confessio fidei de Eucharistia,* which was signed by the representatives from Strasbourg and Geneva, reflects Calvin's thought on the spiritual and dynamic presence of the body and blood of Christ, who physically dwells in heaven. Bucer's corollary contained a formal rejection of the theory of the "bare symbol" and an affirmation of the "true communion with the body and the blood." The entire document clearly resembled Luther's position more than it did Zwinglian symbolism.

The realization of this agreement could be attributed to Bucer's conciliatory wisdom as well as to the precision of Calvin's thought. Moreover, this first personal encounter between the two men began what would eventually become an extremely fruitful dialogue for clarifying the question of the Supper and elaborating a reformed ecclesiology. In the letter that Calvin addressed to his Strasbourg colleague on 12 January 1538, one is struck by the tone of assurance and the way in which he treats as equals the most eminent personalities of the evangelical camp—including Luther, of whom our reformer goes as far as to say: "He is not the only one in the Church of God who is to be respected."[71]

In the midst of these important events Calvin learned that his brother Charles had died unexpectedly on 1 October 1537. Charles was a priest in the village of Roupy, but for unknown reasons he had been accused of heresy and excommunicated. On his deathbed, absolution and the last rites were offered him, but the proud Picard, who no doubt had come under the influence of his brother Jean, resolutely refused them. He was buried in the cemetery reserved for criminals and victims of the stake.

Another distressing event soon occurred: the departure of Louis du Tillet from Geneva. Du Tillet was a priest sincerely committed to the ministry and a person of delicate conscience. For at least five years he remained faithfully at Calvin's side, helping him with money and accompanying him on trips. We possess three letters of du Tillet that prove that he was also a good theologian and a sincere reformist. Nonetheless, none of the documents relative to the reformer's stay in Basle and his activity in Geneva gives any evidence of his participation in his friend's theological or pastoral work. Had Calvin kept him at a distance? Or had du Tillet preferred to abstain? The latter is more probable, for everything leads us to believe that du Tillet was tormented by doubts and scruples ever since Calvin's rapid rise. The subsequent epistolary controversy that developed between the two men, which we shall study in detail in Part Four, reveals the particular reasons for this agitation. Du Tillet, the priest, was especially shocked by how easily Calvin, an educated layman with no pastoral experience, had accepted, after only a few months of being a lecturer, a ministry that was properly ecclesiastical and thereby entailed the charge of souls and the commission to preach and to administer the sacraments. To see his unordained friend officiate at the holy table, teach with authority, and lead the church of Geneva with the same assurance as a true bishop made him very uneasy. Du Tillet in fact remained committed to the idea of apostolic succession and the hierarchical constitution of the Church, and he could not understand how his friend had received this extraordinary vocation to a prophetic mission. In spite of his sincere reformism and his proven generosity—had he not voluntarily chosen exile and abandoned his benefices for the Gospel?—du Tillet remained a man of tradition, opposed in the end to all revolutionary radicalism. But what was he observing on a day-to-day basis in Geneva? His former protégé, author of the polemical pages of the *Institutes* and letters against the priesthood and the Mass, was moving more and more in this radical direction. Besides, who knows whether du Tillet did not experience a degree of sympathy for and even solidarity with Caroli at the same time that he criticized his faults? Was not the former missionary of Meaux also a priest, humanist, and Fabrist? We know that Myconius, the leader responsible for the evangelical church at Basle, hesitated to condemn Caroli.[72] By the same token, could we not assume a similar attitude with du Tillet, who was less involved than Myconius?

Whatever the case may be, after reflecting carefully on what his conscience dictated, this patient and discreet friend of Calvin decided to leave Geneva, first for Strasbourg and then for France, where he intended to be reconciled with the authorities of the established Church. As he wished to spare Calvin the pain of an open break, he began to prepare the way at the beginning of April 1537 by speaking to him about a trip that he intended to make to France.[73] Then he continued to attend all the debates of the quarrel with Caroli and did not take leave until the beginning of the following year. Even in departing, he said his farewells only by leaving a note. The reformer reacted very bitterly. In his first letter to du Tillet, Calvin accused himself of impoliteness and rudeness, faults that may well have alienated his faithful companion. He also expressed his sadness at being deprived of his companionship and of no longer being able to enjoy conversations with him. But above all he stressed his astonishment at the reasons that du Tillet had given. In all sincerity, Calvin never thought that his friend had wavered in his evangelical convictions.[74] The inordinate length of this epistle and the painful tone of the letters following are proof of the deep wound that this defection inflicted on the reformer.

CHAPTER TEN
Crisis in Geneva and Exile to Strasbourg, 1538

Calvin was always able to overcome his grief and to remain firmly on the path that he had set for himself. Thus, when new internal problems arose in Geneva a little after du Tillet's departure, he firmly faced them. What had happened?

As we have seen, the elections in Geneva of 3 February 1538 gave the majority to the opposition party. The new syndics were politically dependent on Bern, which actually controlled all the territory surrounding Geneva, and they were hostile to the forceful methods advocated by Farel and Calvin. Beginning in March, the tension became stronger when the pastors decided to become involved in an incident concerning the competence of the Council of Two Hundred. As a result, the pastors were reprimanded and forbidden to "interfere with the magistrate" or, in other words, to interfere in political matters.[1] There was another humiliating incident: the authorities decided to make an inquiry into the exact content of one of Calvin's sermons in which the orator had compared their meetings to "councils of the devil."[2] But the real test of strength came when the Council—which did not hesitate to interfere in religious matters—took the initiative in adopting the ritual of Bern.[3] In contrast to Genevan customs, this ritual retained the baptismal font, unleavened bread for the Eucharist, and the observation of several traditional feasts. In Calvin's eyes, these differences in detail did not represent a valid reason for discord. But since this matter really dealt with the independence of the religious authority vis-à-vis the civil power, he was uncompromising.

The outcome came quickly. On 12 and 20 March, the Senate of Bern expressed its desire to invite Farel and Calvin to a synod that would meet at Lausanne, but on the preliminary condition that they accept the ritual of Bern.[4] The two guests came to the meeting but agreed not to make any commitment concerning the rituals. On 8 April, Couraud, one of the preachers of Geneva, decided to accuse the syndics of the city from the pulpit and was called before the Council.[5] On the fifteenth of the same month, the authorities of Bern wrote to the Genevans: "We beg you and admonish you in brotherly love to accept the same form" in religious ceremonies.[6] At the same time, Calvin and Farel received another letter from Bern (where for the first time Calvin is named before the older Farel) in which they are once again urged to conform to the decisions of Lausanne regarding ritual.[7] On the nineteenth, the two pastors were called before the Council. They stated that they wished to defer their answer until Pentecost. Then the authorities forbade Couraud, under penalty of imprisonment, to continue preaching. Calvin and Farel replied that they were in solid agreement with their brother, and they refused to distribute the sacrament according to the demands of Bern.[8] In defiance of the restraining order, the following day Couraud went to the pulpit. He was immediately arrested. Calvin and Farel, supported by their friends, demanded the immediate release of the incarcerated preacher. The tension mounted. To the compromise proposed by the Council, the two reformers replied that they would do nothing "except according to what God had commanded them." Then their right to preach was also withdrawn.[9] On 21 April, Easter Day, ignoring the constraints against them, Calvin and Farel completed their sermons as usual. But in view of the tense atmosphere, they refrained from distributing communion. In the following days, the three Councils of the city voted for the banishment of the incriminated ministers. Calvin then declared: "If we had served men, we would have been poorly compensated; but we serve a great Master who will compensate us."[10]

These words, riddled with phrases reminiscent of the prophets and the apostles, demonstrate to what extent Calvin identified his personal cause with the cause of God, for whom he was ready to make any sacrifice. These are the words of a man who *believes* in the divine origin of his calling.

After their expulsion, Calvin and Farel went to Bern, where the authorities were prepared to attempt a reconciliation. But the attempt failed. On 22 May, the Little Council of Geneva replied to the delegation from Bern who had led the two exiles to the walls of the city, saying that the two would never again set foot in the city.[11] They also rejected the fourteen articles that Calvin and Farel drew up as propositions for the reestablishment of peace.[12]

Realizing that there was no longer any hope, Calvin went to Basle, probably with the intention of devoting himself once again to theological studies.[13] His soul, strong but sensitive, now experienced great perplexity; we might even say that he began to doubt his pastoral vocation. His self-assurance was not the same as it had been a month earlier when he had so calmly appealed to the "great Master" who was powerful enough to overcome the injustice of men. He no longer saw things clearly. Had he not hoped against all hope? Had he not written to his friend Bullinger before returning to Geneva: "Now therefore we hastily make a journey, which, we pray, Christ may prosper. For as we look to him in our actions, so we commit our success to his providence"?[14] The eagerly awaited outcome had not materialized. Had God abandoned his servant?

The most poignant confessions of doubt regarding his call to public ministry are found in the letters that Calvin wrote at that time to du Tillet. In a letter of 10 July 1538, we read: "Above all, I fear taking on the responsibilities that have been given me, considering the great perplexity I had at the time that I was involved with them. For as I once felt the call of God . . . , now, on the contrary, I am afraid to try God in taking up again such a burden which I realize I cannot carry."[15] And on 20 October, Calvin spoke again to his friend of his "extreme perplexity," adding: "It is true that I have been greatly afflicted."[16] Bucer himself was aware of his young colleague's temporary discouragement. After welcoming him to Strasbourg, Bucer observed: "It indeed seemed that his soul was so weakened by the wound he received that he could not endure those daily blows."[17]

The young reformer, thrown out by the very ones whom he wished to evangelize, sought retreat and peace for the time being. He would ask those who wished to have him serve in another ministerial position to make no decisions without consulting him: "In the name of the Lord I beseech you not to determine anything concerning me without some prior warning."[18] Did they reproach him for maintaining silence in the midst of a multitude hungering for the Word? He replied that public preaching was not everything and that a small congregation could be just as worthy of his efforts.[19] And when some became uneasy about his future plans, he replied: "I have deliberately tried to earn a living *privately.* "[20] Moreover, his companion in exile, Farel, at least for some time felt the same way. He too wanted no more than peace and rest.[21]

There is no doubt that one of the main reasons that Calvin withdrew into himself was his awareness of having committed considerable errors in his ministry at Geneva. He in fact wrote to Farel: "Before God and his people let us confess that partly by our inexperience, carelessness, negligence, and error the Church committed to us has so sadly declined."[22] He was prepared to make the same confession not only before the Lord and before his intimate collaborator but also before the people who had witnessed their failure. In a letter addressed to "the faithful of Geneva during the decline of the church," he declared: "When it is a matter of appearing before God, I have no doubt that he has humbled us in this way to teach us to recognize our ignorance, imprudence, and other weaknesses which, for my part, I have felt within me and which I found not difficult to confess before the Church of the Lord."[23]

We must note particularly that this public examination of conscience in no way degenerates into unworthy lamentations or an excessive *mea culpa.* While recognizing his imperfections, his errors, and his lack of tact, Calvin still refuses to consider himself guilty of any positively reprehensible act. "It is true," he declared, "that with our adversaries I have always maintained my innocence in such a way that I could testify of it before God."[24] And he adds as well: "I know that not only is our conscience pure before God but we can also clear our consciences before the whole world."[25]

We must recognize that no matter how deep the humbled reformer's perplexity concerning his call to the public ministry and in spite of his preoccupation with being judged with equity, his fundamentally theological disposition and his faith in providence remained intact and unshakable. Although he was put to the test and despised by his enemies, the will of God never ceased to appear to him with clarity. This benevolent and instructive will could even turn evil to the advantage of his elect: "But if we understand that they do not slander us except by the will of God, we do not doubt to what end this will of God tends. Therefore we will be humbled unless we are willing to struggle with God, who reaches out to us when we are brought low."[26] The tests become a blessing! Besides, God is merciful and his clemency is infinite.[27] He is truly the one who heals all evil. Calvin's solid faith expresses itself thus: "When I consider my state, my difficulties seem to be beyond human help. However, all I have to do is commend the outcome to the great Healer who alone can provide and give order."[28]

Depending on God, Calvin remained very close to his companion in exile, Guillaume Farel. One reads with admiration the letters the two deposed pastors wrote together during that time and signed: "Your most loving brothers, Farel and Calvin."[29] This beautiful expression of Christian solidarity by Calvin goes hand in hand with several acts of charity that without exaggeration one can call heroic. For example, in August 1538, the reformer learned at Basle that a member of Farel's family[30] was ill with the plague and had just been transported there. Calvin himself was ill at the time. However, as soon as he could, he came to the bedside of the dying man and, disregarding the danger of contagion, prepared him for a Christian death. The unfortunate victim did not have a cent, but Calvin, who possessed very little himself, paid the expenses out of his own pocket.[31] This act of a good minister proves that Calvin was far from being overwhelmed by his own problems and that he remained prepared to respond to the call of charity.

I must stress one other fact. From their respective places of refuge, the two exiles kept in contact with the community of Geneva and also with the pastors Viret and Couraud, from whom they continually demanded news: "It is incredible how much we are excited by our desire for your letter, whereby we learn what has happened since our departure."[32] They were grieved to discover that their successors had been so poorly chosen[33] and that a slow decline was ruining everything they had built at Geneva.[34] Also, Farel did not hesitate to send what could be called "pastoral letters" to the community in distress.[35] But Calvin preferred not to sign them. Was this another indication that he doubted his pastoral vocation?

But this state of perplexity was not to last. Surrounded in Basle by friends (among whom we must mention especially Simon Grynaeus[36]) who esteemed his talents as a theologian, orator, and organizer, as well as his moral qualities, and encouraged by reformers at Strasbourg, Calvin gradually regained his self-assurance. Finally, he even accepted the offer of a new ministerial position.

Calvin in Strasbourg

From the first act of the drama, Martin Bucer[37] displayed a special concern to remedy the injustice that his Genevan brothers had experienced. On this subject we can read in a letter from Calvin dated 14 June 1538: "For before our letters were received, Bucer appealed to Grynaeus after learning about the matter, that they not fail to extend to the church certain extreme remedies."[38] The Strasbourg reformer, who bore no grudge against his young colleague from Geneva for the polite but severe criticism that the latter had written in January,[39] did everything possible to give him a position worthy of his talents. He did not encourage him to return to Geneva. But on the other hand, he made him understand clearly that such a gifted man would be committing a grave sin if he persisted in trying to escape from pastoral activity: "For you can never think this way without offense to God, namely, that you might withdraw from the ministry for a brief time while some other place of ministry is offered to you." And he continued along these lines: Certainly you may object that it is your fault that the church of Geneva has been shaken. But in any case, it would not be right to do penance by refusing to place at the service of a church the talents that you did not receive for yourself. To speak more clearly: if you do not find a more important pastoral service, we are ready to give you such at Strasbourg: "At this time we determine that you ought to come to us."[40]

This appeal to his obligation to develop his talents for the glory of God and the service of the Church was no doubt convincing in the eyes of the author of the *Institutes.*[41] If Calvin still hesitated for a time, it was because his mistrust of the theology and the overly conciliatory nature of Bucer remained acute. But the minister of Strasbourg insisted[42] and proposed a relatively autonomous field of service for him: he was placed in charge of the spiritual welfare of the city's French community.[43] How strong was Bucer's insistence? According to a statement that Calvin made at the time of the events, and according to the testimony of his Preface to the *Commentary on the Psalms* edited in 1557, Bucer had not hesitated to threaten him by alluding to the Lord's thrashing of the rebellious prophet Jonah.[44]

What Bucer obtained by his persevering firmness, du Tillet provoked by his well-intentioned but clumsy attempts to dissuade his friend from returning to the ministry. For when Calvin was in the midst of the crisis, du Tillet found it opportune to write to him: "I doubt that your vocation is of God, who only calls men to whom he has given a responsibility." Then, after suggesting that Calvin remain in Basle and no longer be involved in pastoral activity, du Tillet proposed to help him financially.[45] This letter startled its recipient. After several days of reflection, Calvin began his reply firmly and curtly: "As far as the question of *my vocation* is concerned, I believe that you do not have sufficient reason to impugn it, for the Lord has given me stronger reasons to *convince me* of its validity." There is no longer any trace of doubt here. What the unfortunate events had shaken for a time is here confirmed and reestablished. The problem of Calvin's vocation was submitted to the judgment of the famous servants of God, whose authority was equaled only by their moderation. By their mouth the Lord has declared once again that John Calvin is still called to the ministry of the Gospel. Du Tillet, the former friend now returned to papism, should keep his "completely human reasons" to himself! He suggested to his former companion in the struggle that he desert with him. Such an idea could have come only from the devil. Indeed Calvin adds: "I take everything that you say in this matter as coming from a sincere heart, but I attribute it to *another spirit* than that of God. Concerning my retreat, I confess to you that I find your first word on the matter very strange. I should try to 'return' or is it in 'hell I shall burn'? . . . But I beg you to allow me to follow the rule of my conscience, which I know to be more sure than yours." Calvin thanks his correspondent for the offer of financial aid, but he does not wish to take advantage of it. He prefers selling some volumes that remain at his disposal: "The money from the books will provide for necessities other than food.[46] For I hope that our Lord will provide me with more according to my need."[47]

By the beginning of September 1538, Calvin was settled in Strasbourg.[48] Once again he was in a pastoral position. His first sermons were favorably received by the French of Strasbourg. Bucer and his collaborators had already thought about establishing their community as an independent parish, having the right to administer the Eucharist. Not without some pride, Calvin provided for Farel an account of this favorable turn of events: "I held a discourse on the Lord's Day; and since it was commended to the people by the praises of all the brethren, it had many listeners and viewers. The brethren agreed to grant the ministry of the Supper, if they see that some form of a church is manifest."[49] As we have seen, for Calvin each church is essentially a eucharistic community. One therefore senses his satisfaction at learning that Bucer planned to transform his modest flock into a "little church," where they could distribute the bread of life. Calvin was assured that the Strasbourg reformer possessed a proper "understanding of the Church"; and as he became aware of this, he opened himself with confidence to all that Bucer's ecclesiastical views could offer him.

Once more involved in the service of a cell of the "true Church," the reformer thought again about his followers in Geneva. Now he felt less embarrassed before them, and nothing stopped him from sending them, as

Farel had done, "pastoral letters." The tone and form of these letters recall the epistles of Paul. Here is the opening of the first: "To my beloved brothers in our Lord who are the remnant of the scattered church of Geneva." The bonds that the Lord had created between the Genevans and their pastor were sufficient reason for the latter to write: "For our confidence is certain before God, for it was *by his vocation* that we were at one time joined with you. Therefore it should not be within the power of man to break such a bond." This biblical analogy leads the author to identify the cause of the church in Geneva with the cause of Christ, and the cause of Christ with his own. His adversaries are therefore the adversaries of the Lord, and they are inspired only by the "prince of darkness." But they shall not be victorious. God allows them to dominate for a time in order to punish the Genevans for their sloth and their negligence in obeying the Word. The faithful of Geneva should follow the example of the banished ministers and humble themselves under the powerful hand of God, and he who alone is just will surely be kind to his own. The letter is signed: "Your brother and servant in our Lord, J. Calvin."[50]

The same faithfulness of the pastor to his flock to which God had bound him will soon inspire another of Calvin's letters: his famous *Reply to Sadolet.*[51]

The occasion of this letter was the attempt in March 1539 of Cardinal Jacques Sadolet (1477–1547), the famous humanist and a true pastor and bishop,[52] to bring Geneva back into line with Rome. The letter he sent to the Little Council of Geneva was placed in the hands of the Bern authorities, who in turn had it brought to Calvin and asked him to reply to it. The reformer accepted, and in September 1539 the printed copies of his text left Strasbourg.

I shall analyze this most important document in Part Four. But for now, we can emphasize the outstanding *ecclesiastical* spirit which enlivens it from beginning to end. It is at the same time a brilliant defense of the exiled ministers, a justification of the call to the evangelical ministry, a summary of a genuine ecclesiology, and a forceful rebuttal of the Roman notion concerning the schismatic character of the reform. This writing may be considered the definitive expression of the religious evolution that the young Calvin had experienced so far. The firm conviction of being right and the clear awareness of an urgent duty which emerge from these lines are those of a reformer who as such has reached full maturity.

The Calvin of the *Reply to Sadolet* was thirty years old. He had emerged strengthened from his first and last crisis over his vocation. Now he no longer doubted. With complete peace of conscience and in good faith he confirmed his existential choice and without a backward glance was on the way to realizing the vocation that he perceived to be of divine origin.

The city of Strasbourg supported him, and the reformers of Strasbourg encouraged him. They willingly communicated to their guest the fruits of their experiences, which he knew to be more extensive than his own. But if Calvin accepted the insights of Bucer, Capito, Sturm, and Hédion, he did so freely and with a sense of his complete equality with them.

While accompanying the principal pastors of Strasbourg to colloquies at Worms and Ratisbon, seeing in Germany champions of the pontifical party such as Contarini and Eck, and becoming acquainted with evangelical theologians such as Melanchthon, he observed and listened. But he also spoke out and made judgments. He was no longer a student but a colleague. The Germans too considered him as such.

His French parish in Strasbourg provided him with an ideal place to gain experience. What he could not obtain in Geneva because of his youthful haste and the resistance of the people, he could prudently realize here with the faithful elect. In this community, communion was held every month, church discipline was independent of civil power, and there was regular religious training and singing of the psalms. An entirely new French liturgy was worked out by Calvin based on the local model.[53] And in addition to all this activity, the reformer enjoyed again the leisure he needed in order to study, teach, and explain the Scriptures and to write new treatises or theological works. In all these fields he flourished in the Alsacian capital.

CHAPTER ELEVEN
Conclusion to Part One

At the end of this historical inquiry into the facts and context of the religious evolution of young Calvin, several observations must be made.

First, we have learned that during his childhood and period of study, Calvin lived in more or less direct and continual contact with men of the Church. At Noyon were the canons whom his father served as notary; at Paris, the regents and the religious professors at the schools of la Marche and Montaigu; at Orléans, the vicar-general Pierre de l'Estoile; among the Paris humanists, Fabrist priests such as Gérard Roussel; and in Saintonge, du Tillet and his circle of friends. Among the close friends of the future reformer, many, such as Claude de Hangest, entered into orders, and others, such as Daniel and Duchemin, had become secular officials of the ecclesiastical administration. There is nothing astonishing about all of this, for in the sixteenth century the clergy still dominated the fields of education and studies. Calvin, who received the tonsure at age twelve and for a long time was the titulary of the benefits of a parish and a chaplaincy and who was initially destined to be a priest, not only profited from this situation but also was imbued with a certain "spirit of the Church" and became familiar with a number of concrete problems of the ecclesiastical community.

A second general conclusion that we can make is that the future reformer passed his entire youth—because of his ecclesiastical connections, not in spite of them—in a reformist atmosphere. The de Hangest family of Noyon, whom Calvin visited while very young, was filled with the spirit of the great Christian renewal. Cordier, the pedagogue enlightened by Christ-centered piety; Olivétan, the future translator of the Bible; the protagonists of Erasmus and Lefèvre in the great controversies concerning the Scriptures; the entire family of Nicolas Cop; the people surrounding the Queen of Navarre; and finally, the eminent men and women whom Calvin met in the course of his journeys to Nérac, Strasbourg, Basle, and Ferrara—all were there to fan the flames of reform within him.

And third, the burning at the stake of the martyred French Lutherans may also have left an impression upon the reformer in his early years. To mention only the most well known: Jean Vallière in 1523; Jean Chastellain, Jacques Pavannes, and Jean Guibert in 1526; Denis de Rieux in 1528; Louis de Berquin in 1529; Canus de la Croix in 1534; and Etienne de la Forge in 1535. All were victims of the intolerance of the "sacred Faculty" and the "most Christian King"; all were witnesses to a faith which, if not orthodox, was at least vital and heroic and which provided the young Calvin with abundant material for his reflections on the "poor state of the Church."[1] His thinking may well have been stimulated by his personal experiences with clerical harshness: the attitude of the canons of Noyon at the time of his excommunicated father's death, the attempt to arrest him after the discourse of Cop, and the equally serious and intense accusations hurled at him and his companions in the struggle by the theologians of the Sorbonne.

These three general factors indicate the condition and direction in which Calvin's evolution had to develop. And all the specific facts that we are going to summarize make this clear.

The most important facts dealing with this religious evolution may be divided into two distinct periods: the first, in which the absence of documents from Calvin himself leaves considerable room for hypotheses; and the second, in which the correspondence of the young Calvin and his first works permit us to reach a greater degree of certainty.

The first goes up to 1532. For this period there have been conjectures relating to the evangelical influence that Olivétan and Wolmar may have exerted on the future reformer. Certainly these conjectures have some foundation, but in themselves they are not sufficient to prove that a true conversion had taken place before 1532. In fact, one could always object that, parallel to the supposed Lutheran influence of Olivétan, our young student was enthusiastically accepting the teaching of an anti-Lutheran as famous as Pierre de l'Estoile; and at the same time that Wolmar was supposedly exerting an evangelical influence upon him, Calvin was regularly visiting Daniel, Duchemin, and de Connan, who were all moderate reformists and humanists far removed from any form of radicalism.

The letter relating Calvin's visit to a young novice, Daniel's sister, takes us across the threshold of the second period. As we have seen, this document contains nothing that shows a break with the traditional structures and doctrines of the Church. It seems more likely that this might be the first written testimony of the young Calvin's adherence to some views of Lefèvre, who was in sympathy with some of Luther's ideas. Lefèvre was even suspected of being a Lutheran, but in reality he always proved himself to be opposed to the negations and extreme criticisms of the German reformer. Lefèvre was an avid reader of Luther, but he never became a Lutheran. Neither did most of Lefèvre's admirers. Only a minority moved in that direction. And Calvin was one of them. But this did not occur for some time.

A whole series of documents from 1532 to 1535 present us with a Calvin who is obviously a "Fabrist" or, if one wants a more comprehensive description, a Christian humanist devoted to moderate reform. During this period, nothing is more characteristic of the future reformer than his growing love of Scripture and his admiration for men such as Gérard Roussel. The notes dealing with the comedy at the Collège de Navarre and the placing of the *Miroir* on the Index, the various references to Cop's discourse and the discourse itself, the fragmentary pieces of information dealing with his stay with du Tillet and the renunciation of his benefices—all these documents are clearly written from a Fabrist perspective. There is no need to explain them as resulting from an exclusively Lutheran influence, and they do not indicate a true conversion.

The sources immediately preceding and following the *Psychopannychia* do present a new element. No doubt through his friends who were followers of Lefèvre, Calvin became acquainted with the anabaptist problem. Even without recourse to later statements that relate Calvin's encounter with Flemish anabaptists in Paris and the failure of his plan to meet with Michael Servetus, we need only refer to Calvin's first letter to Bucer concerning the "unjustly suspected refugee" and to the *Psychopannychia* in order to establish to what extent Calvin was at the time opposed to this sectarian movement. However paradoxical this may seem, we believe that Calvin's taking this position against the anabaptists contributed to his estrangement from the supporters of Lefèvre and brought him closer to the Lutherans. Calvin was definitely a passionate partisan of Church reform but also of order and clarity. As a reformist, he no longer tolerated the negative, confusing, and intolerant orthodoxy of the Sorbonne; as a man of order, he irrevocably condemned sectarian anarchy. With a mind thirsting for clarity and opposing any "confusion" in doctrinal matters, he more and more lost confidence in the majority of moderate reformists who proved to be indecisive. Among these were the Queen of Navarre and many others who warmly welcomed representatives of anabaptist mysticism. What else remained for him but to align himself with the only man who, in his eyes, truly wrote "reform" with a capital "R," who made the Bible the only basis for faith, and who allowed no compromise with deviations to the right or the left: Martin Luther?

Our historical inquiry also shows that Calvin's stay in Basle played a major role in his evolution. Putting aside his short stay in Strasbourg, we can assert that it was at Basle that he saw for the first time an evangelical community organized as a church. Coming from France, where no such thing could exist and where the differences between the reformist movements were far from being overcome, he no doubt experienced a kind of "spiritual catalyst" in this new contact. The clearly evangelical discipline and doctrine of this city certainly impressed him.

However, Calvin did not give himself wholeheartedly to the theological teaching of his hosts. Those in Basle preferred to follow Zwinglian tendencies, while the future reformer, faithful to his original choice, was drawn above all to the study of Luther. In all good faith, he adopted the principal *Lutheran ideas;* the instincts acquired during his years as a follower of Lefèvre would prevent him from noting any slight heretical deviation in these ideas. In any case, the fragmentary theological knowledge that he acquired at the Sorbonne would not have prompted any doubts in him about the Catholic orthodoxy of Luther. The first time that Calvin became thoroughly convinced of a theological perspective, it was Luther's perspective that triumphed.

Calvin's first writings in Basle included the two prefaces to Olivétan's Bible. The one written in Latin contains Calvin's first explicitly antipapist statement. The other, in French, is a magnificent testimony of Christ-centered piety and fervent Bible scholarship. The *Institutes* and the Dedicatory Epistle to the King of France are not only a manifestation of the Lutheran views which he affirmed from that time on but also an expression of how his thought was expanding more and more in its ecclesiastical dimensions. Calvin's love for his native country certainly did not stop him from thinking in a "Catholic" manner. To summarize in one sentence the program advocated by his first theological compendium, we would say that he wanted to *re-form the one, holy catholic Church, in and by Christ, according to the Gospel, for the greater glory of God.*

Geneva was a new stage: that of putting into practice the program defined in the *Institutes.* In this city, where the breakdown of the traditional structures had not yet given way to a positive "re-forming" construction and where civil power had practically monopolized the vacant episcopate, a man of the Church was needed who was endowed with notable pastoral talents. Calvin, a young lay theologian, did not think that he possessed any of these qualities. Thus, his initial reservation. But then he decided to act when he realized that the urgent state of the church of Geneva would require at least for a time an extraordinary ministry. Calvin was encouraged by his victory in the polemics of the dispute of Lausanne and the considerable success of his *Institutes,* which he accepted as signs of providence. Therefore he accepted this appointment. All of a sudden his vocation as a reformer took on a pastoral direction.

The constructive work could begin. The *Articles,* the *Confession of Faith,* and the *Catechism* were the first stones of the new edifice founded on evangelical discipline and "sound doctrine." All these works carried Calvin to power, but this power brought opposition with it.

The vicissitudes of the Caroli affair, the opposition of the rebels of Geneva, and the abortive dispute with the anabaptists had a double consequence. On the one hand, these things revealed the incurably impatient character of Calvin—a former humanist champion of the virtue of clemency. On the other hand, they strengthened his conviction that he was a chosen servant of God, an "instrument of the Spirit" thrust into the great reform combat, and that he was sustained by the Lord's powerful hand.

The crisis that resulted in his expulsion from Geneva no doubt temporarily disturbed his conviction of actually being called to the pastoral ministry, if not his faith. But the intervention of Martin Bucer, his wise and respectful elder, revived his former self-assurance by encouraging him to accept a new pastoral responsibility. Thus Bucer played an important role in completing the religious evolution of Calvin. In this new ministry to the French church of Strasbourg, the reformer appears to have attained full maturity.

These are the main aspects of young Calvin's religious evolution which are established by the historical documents. We have drawn all that we can from them. But we still have reservations about the hypothesis of young Calvin's so-called conversion, for none of the contemporary documents that we studied speak either directly or indirectly of conversion. None of them verify a sudden passage of the future reformer from a state of religious indifference to a living faith. From childhood on, his piety was deep. Still less can we conclude that there was an abrupt turnaround from "Catholic fanaticism" to Calvin's "evangelical docility." At the end of our inquiry, the problems of Calvin's conversion and schism remain open. Only the problem of his vocation seems somewhat clearer. In the rest of our work, we shall continue to try to find a solution to these three problems.

In Part Two we shall closely scrutinize the 1536 *Institutes* in order to discover its primary sources. Then we shall proceed systematically to draw out its primary theological ideas, which are indispensable for understanding in depth the great religious transformation that we are studying.

PART TWO
The Sources of the First Edition
of the *Institutes*

Our historical investigation has enabled us to discover the circumstances in which Calvin became acquainted with the different reformist movements, the moderate group directly inspired by Lefèvre d'Etaples, and then the radical group principally inspired by Luther. In this process the future reformer of Geneva was influenced more by his readings than by various personalities with whom he had contact. His friends, his teachers, and the great protagonists of the French biblical movement certainly aroused in him a profound and, in general, a lasting sympathy; but it seems that none of them played a determining role in the development of his religious and theological thought. On the contrary, it is certain that the ideas that he assimilated through reading influenced him more strongly and enriched his mind rapidly.

In large part, Calvin was a self-taught, independent thinker who made judgments for himself. He was more a passionate seeker for truth than the disciple of a man or a school. In this search, the written word and ideas expressed with conviction exercised an unusually strong power over him. Calvin was more or less directly involved in the reform movements, and he retained memories of many shocking events; but it was the works he read which moved him to integrate his ideas into a powerful synthesis.

What were these readings? Is it possible to identify with any precision the books and authors that influenced Calvin's mind? And above all, can we establish with certainty the direct sources of his first theological compendium? Can we find the material the young reformist used to write his *Institutes,* in which he expressed himself for the first time as a reformer?

To give an adequate reply to all these questions is an arduous task. In fact, Calvin did not deem it necessary to cite all his sources. In the first *Institutes,* only the references to the Bible, the Fathers, and his adversaries are indicated with any great precision. On the other hand, none of the evangelical theologians used is named, and no explicit references to their works are made. Perhaps Calvin's resolute desire to emphasize only the teaching of Scripture explains this procedure. In his view it was legitimate not to name the great evangelical commentators of the Bible who preceded him, since they worked toward the same goal.

Moreover, we can suppose that none of these theologians entirely satisfied Calvin, for he used them without completely following any of them; he adopted only those ideas which stood up under his criticism. This superior eclecticism reveals not only an independent mind but a profoundly religious man who sought to base his ideas only on what he discovered in the Word of God itself, not on human authority.

In spite of the difficulties that Calvin's procedure raises, the tracking down of Calvin's sources is not impossible. Calvin scholars such as A. Lang,[1] the editors of the *Opera Omnia*[2] and the *Opera Selecta,*[3] or the historians of dogma such as R. Seeberg[4] have already indicated several writings of Luther, Melanchthon, Zwingli, and Bucer. They include Luther's *Small Catechism,* the treatises *The Babylonian Captivity of the Church* and *The Freedom of the Christian Man,* the *Sermon von dem Sakrament des Leibes und Blutes Christi wider die Schwarmgeister* and the *Sermon von dem hochwürdigen Sakrament des heiligen wahren Leichnams Christi;* and Melanchthon's works, the *Loci Communes* of 1521 or 1522; Zwingli's *Commentary on True and False Religion;* and the second edition of Bucer's *Enarrationes perpetuae in sacra quatuor evangelia.* Among scholastic sources, scholars note the *Decretals* of Gratian and the *Sentences* of Lombard.

Having read all these works in detail and compared them to the first *Institutes,* I have noticed a great number of similarities, not only in the plan and in the ideas but sometimes even in the expressions and theological arguments. The majority of these are not indicated by the editors of the *Opera Selecta.* For those which have been indicated, references are provided in the notes.

The framework of my study obviously does not allow me to present all points of similarity. Consequently I shall restrict myself to giving several striking examples that illustrate *the fact* of the young Calvin's dependence—and also his independence—vis-à-vis these sources. This is the object of my considerations in Part Two. In Part Three, I shall deal with the *content* itself of the work in view of Calvin's strictly critical and reformist position which he adopted concerning piety, doctrine, and the ecclesiastical structures of his time.

This should allow us to see a new dimension of the origin and evolution of Calvin's vocation as a reformer, a dimension that the documents studied in Part One were able to reveal only in a very limited way.

One of the principal preoccupations of the young Calvin was to understand as thoroughly as possible the word of God in Scripture. To reach his goal, he followed the method adopted by the great Christian humanists: he took the Church Fathers as guides, among whom he preferred Augustine.[5] But from the beginning and with growing intensity after the events of autumn 1533, he also consulted several works written in or translated into Latin by the reformers and German evangelical theologians. Here he clearly prefers the Augustinian monk and theologian Martin Luther.[6] This preference is not surprising if one considers the extraordinary influence that the personality and the writings of the Saxon reformer exerted on the intellectual circles frequented by Calvin. Also, the men of the Sorbonne unanimously designated the partisans of the different reform movements by the name "Lutheran."

The thoroughly Latin mind of the future reformer, trained in dialectical and juridical disciplines, demanded not only living and convincing explanations of various biblical texts but also systematic formulations of revealed truth. Thus, when the occasion arose, he studied with interest the systematic works of Melanchthon or Zwingli, while continuing to read the homilies and treatises of Luther and then the commentaries of Bucer. He recorded them in his prodigious memory rather than in notes, and he compared them with each other and with texts gleaned from the scholastics—while seeking above all the doctrine that conformed to the Scripture. During this comparative study which he accomplished with extraordinary rapidity, Calvin used these authors only to understand the Bible. When Calvin understood the Bible's teaching, he then used the Bible to judge the works he was reading. At the end of this time of reflection, Calvin's fruitful mind gave birth to the first edition of the *Institutes.*

In the chapters of Part Two, I shall attempt several "soundings" to illuminate the respective roles that Luther, Melanchthon, Zwingli, Bucer, and several representatives of traditional scholasticism played in Calvin's notable summation of his study. I shall add an excursus on the influence of Erasmus and Lefèvre.

CHAPTER TWELVE
Luther

Even the outline of the *Institutes* reveals Luther's influence. Just as Luther's *Small Catechism* treats Christian doctrine in the order of law, faith, prayer, and sacraments, the four first chapters of Calvin's compendium are entitled "Law," "Faith," "Prayer," and "The Sacraments."[1] According to W. Walker, this division was also that of classic religious instruction as given in the schools of the Middle Ages.[2] However, a whole series of similarities lead us to believe that in writing the *Institutes* our author actually took as his model the *Small Catechism* of Wittenberg[3] and not the catechism of his childhood.

In the chapter entitled "Law," which contains his exposition of the Decalogue, Calvin closely follows the model of Luther, even though he includes his own personal reflections and his own scriptural quotes. In the same way that Luther introduces the explanation of each commandment by the expression, "We ought to *fear and love*[4] God," Calvin continually takes up the refrain: "It is fitting that God be feared and *loved* by us."[5]

In addition, we find that both authors expound each commandment by dividing it into two parts: one part stresses the divine prohibition to be observed and the sin to be avoided, and the other emphasizes the corresponding positive duty. The movement from one part to another is marked with a conjunction: a "but" with Luther and a "truly" or "but rather" with Calvin.

But the most striking resemblance is shown in the commentary on "You shall not bear false witness," which Calvin considers as the ninth and Luther as the eighth commandment.

Luther	Calvin
What does *this mean?* Response: We ought to *fear* and *love God* so that we do not involve our neighbor in lying *falsehoods,* betray him, dishonor him, or bring against him any *evil report.* But let us excuse him and speak something good of him, *interpreting* all things the *best way* we can.[6]	*This means:* since *God* is to be *feared and loved* by us, let us press *false* accusations against no one, nor impugn the *reputation* of anyone, nor yield our tongue or ears to cursing and bitter sarcasm, nor suspect or imagine anything evil about someone. But if there is any *fear* or *love* of God in us, let us speak honorably and think honestly of all, as far as possible; so that as fair *interpreters* of all, we may accept what others say and do *in the best way* we can.[7]

In the second chapter, entitled "Faith," both Calvin and the German reformer follow the exposition of the Apostles' Creed. It is obvious that Calvin explains the creed more fully, in particular adding a large number of quotations from the Scriptures, while Luther, restricted by the narrow limits of a catechism, treats the creed quite succinctly. Another difference is that Luther divides the creed into three articles—creation, redemption, and sanctification—and mentions the Church only in passing. To these three paragraphs dedicated respectively to the work of the Father, the Son, and the Holy Ghost, Calvin adds a long fourth paragraph on the Church. In this paragraph he is inspired not by Luther but by Bucer.

In spite of these differences, Calvin's commentary on the creed develops substantially along the same lines as that of the Saxon reformer. In particular, in the passage dealing with the generous fatherly blessings of God and the gratitude due him, we find striking similarities:

Luther	Calvin
. . . that . . . he abundantly and daily bestows *all* good *things,* with all the necessities of life, that he protects me against all dangers and frees me and guards me from all evils. All of this comes *merely* from his *fatherly* and divine *goodness* and mercy, without any *merits* or worthiness of my own. I ought justly to *give thanks* with a strong voice, to offer *praise,* to serve and *obey* him. This is *most certainly true.*[8]	But *all things* are done for us by him, not because of some *worthiness* of our own, not because of some *merit,* for which this is owed, not because we are able to pay back his beneficence by a mutual exchange. Rather, it is through his *fatherly kindness* and clemency that he deals with us, the *sole* cause of which is his *goodness* (Romans 11). For this reason, let us be sure to *give thanks* for such goodness, which we should ponder in our hearts, proclaim with our tongues, and extol with such *praises* as we can. Let us worship such a Father in pious gratitude and ardent love, so that we devote ourselves completely to *obeying* him. . . . For it is *most certain* and *true* that this is the right faith.[9]

Another likeness that is not based primarily on verbal similarities is the way the two reformers treat Jesus Christ. There is first of all the powerful Christ-centered orientation of the entire exposition of the creed which strikes the reader in first the one and then the other. Luther mentions Christ five times—having the word "Lord" printed in capital letters—while he mentions the Father and the Holy Spirit only once. In a similar manner, Calvin devotes four times as much space to Christ as to the Father and the Holy Spirit. Even more significant is the soteriological perspective of the two commentators. Neither pauses to analyze the *being* of the eternal Son of God made man, that is, to describe the hypostatic union; but they proceed directly to the exposition of his *work* of redemption. Calvin develops his teaching on the economy of redemption inaugurated and accomplished by the crucified Savior, just as Luther did.[10]

The third chapter of the *Institutes,* "Prayer," reflects many influences from Bucer,[11] but it is not without elements that remind us of Luther. Referring to the second petition of the Lord's Prayer, the German reformer notes: "The name of God is sanctified *in itself, but* we pray in this *petition* that it would be *sanctified* in us."[12] The French reformer echoes him in these words: "Therefore *we ask* that this majesty *be sanctified* in such virtues as these, not in God himself, to whom *in himself* nothing can be added or taken away, *but* that it be held as sanctified by all; that is, that it be truly acknowledged and magnified."[13] Calvin differs from his source of inspiration only by emphasizing the objective glory of God more than Luther did.

Referring to the petition "Thy will be done," Calvin develops the very same ideas as his predecessor. He especially stresses that although the will of God does not need our prayers to be accomplished, we must nevertheless pray, so that God's will is ratified and accomplished in us, by and through our lives.[14]

On the petition for the forgiveness of sins, Calvin's text contains the same insistence found in Luther's catechism on the absolutely free gift of God's pardon, the radical indebtedness of man, and the need for mutual forgiveness (both use *condonare*) between brothers.[15] There is one slight difference: Calvin explains that God's forgiveness "in Christ" satisfies all the demands of his own justice; Luther, at least in this passage, does not mention this.

In commenting on the final "Amen," the text of the *Institutes* seems to take up again—except for a few subtle differences in terms—the formula of the *Small Catechism,* which says: "That I may be *certain* that *petitions* of this kind which come from us are *accepted* and *heard* in heaven. Because he himself commanded us, that we pray this way; and he *promised* that he would hear us."[16] Here is Calvin's text: "Amen: by which is expressed the ardor of our desire to obtain those things which are *petitioned* of God, by which our hope is confirmed that all such things have already been obtained and will *certainly* be granted to us; for they have been *promised* by God, who cannot deceive us."[17]

In moving to the chapter on "The Sacraments," Calvin abandons Luther's catechism only to delve into other writings of Luther which he decided to complement with several texts of Melanchthon and to compare these with several ideas developed by Zwingli. In fact, given the circumstances of 1535, when the *Institutes* were written, the doctrine of the sacraments contained in Luther's popular manual of 1529 proved to be clearly inadequate. With the disputes over the sacraments reaching full tilt in the evangelical ranks—with the papists over the seven sacraments, with the anabaptists over baptism, and with the Zwinglians over the Supper—we can understand why our young theologian was not content with a source whose three articles on the sacraments were respectively entitled "the sacrament of baptism," "confession," and "the sacrament of the altar." This is no doubt why he turned to more radical and explicit Lutheran writings, especially the *Babylonian Captivity,* which appeared in 1520, and to the two *Sermons* on the Supper published in Latin, in 1524 and 1527 respectively.

The ideas and even the language of the *Babylonian Captivity* appear first in Calvin's paragraph dedicated to the doctrine of the sacraments in general, where we also find several definitions borrowed from the *Loci Communes* of Melanchthon. Here it is especially clear that Calvin only summarizes and rearranges Luther's thought.

Luther's treatise equally condemns what he considers two extremes, the doctrine of the papists and the Zwinglian spiritualists: "There are very many who think that there is *some hidden* spiritual *power* in the word and water, which works the grace of God in the souls of those who receive the sacrament. Others contradict these and affirm that *there is no power* in the sacraments."[18] Calvin writes likewise: "On the contrary, we must be admonished that just as these men diminish the *power of the sacraments* and directly overturn their usefulness, so *others* on the opposite side attribute *secret powers* (I know not what) to the sacraments."[19]

Then, just as Luther followed this consideration by attacking the theory of the "impediment," Calvin adds this rejection with exactly the same argument. Luther affirms: "And thus they are impelled to attribute so much to *the sacraments of the new law* that they affirm these are effective even for those who are in mortal sin and they *do not require faith* or grace. But it is enough *not to have placed an impediment,* that is, the actual intention of sinning again."[20] A little later he adds: "Therefore, to seek the *efficacy* of the sacrament *apart from* the promise and *faith* is to strive in vain and to meet with *damnation.*"[21] Calvin echoes him faithfully: "The first [group] teaches that the *sacraments of the new law* . . . justify and confer grace, as long as we do not place an impediment of mortal sin. Such a notion, . . . while promising *righteousness apart from faith,* drives souls headlong into confusion and *judgment.*"[22]

The impression of direct dependence between the two texts is further reinforced by reading what follows. The issue is the difference between the sacraments of the Old and New Covenants. The *Babylonian Captivity* denies any fundamental difference: "For it is an error that the sacraments of the new law differ from the sacraments of the *old law;* concerning the efficacy of the signs, they are equally significant. For the same God . . ."[23] The *Institutes* introduces three texts of Augustine, but it essentially reproduces the Lutheran position that we have just quoted. "But those immoderate praises of the sacraments, which are read in the older authors, deceived them. . . . For the sacraments of the *old law* only promised salvation, while ours truly give it." Thus Calvin replies to the question raised: "The sacraments of the Jews were diverse in their signs but *equal in the reality which they signified.* "[24] Finally, corresponding to Luther's phrase "for the same God," Calvin briefly develops the idea that both the old and new sacraments signify, offer, and present the one and the same Jesus Christ.

We also see a striking correspondence between the descriptions of the sacrament of baptism. For example, where Calvin affirms that baptism "is to be accepted as from the hand of God,"[25] and that all sacraments "are not to be accepted from the hand of the one who administers it, but as if from the very hand of God,"[26] we easily discover traces of a statement from the *Babylonian Captivity:* "whence it is necessary that we receive baptism *from the hand of man* in no other way than if it were Christ himself, indeed *God* himself, who baptized us by his very own hands."[27]

We can also cite a similar example concerning the Mass. Luther's treatise condemns the eucharistic sacrifice as an impious and widespread abuse. We read: "The third captivity of this same sacrament is *by far that most impious abuse,* by which it has happened that there is almost nothing more accepted and more persuasive in the Church today than the belief that the *Mass* is a good work and a *sacrifice.* "[28] It is likely that this sentence, or at least the idea contained in it, was in the memory of the young and ardent reader of Luther when he in turn attributed the invention of the Mass to the devil: "But the *extreme of this horrendous abomination* was reached . . . when he [the devil] blinded almost the whole world with this *most pestilential error,* that it would believe that the Mass is a sacrifice and offering to obtain the remission of sins."[29] Here are the same superlatives, the same allusion to an abuse that has become universal, and the same rejection of meritorious human work. We note that in what follows Calvin seems to abandon his Lutheran source to gain inspiration from a Zwinglian text that contains stronger and clearer arguments against the sacrificial nature of the Mass.

However, the *Babylonian Captivity* also inspires the two chapters that follow the discussion of the Eucharist: "The False Sacraments" and "Christian Freedom." Here again Calvin is quite faithful to his source; first he illustrates the confession of sins "before God" by the example of the repentant sinners before John the Baptist, according to Matthew 3;[30] then he rejects the theory according to which auricular confession is the second plank of salvation, the "second plank after shipwreck";[31] and finally he affirms that the true "sacrament of penance" is none other than baptism.[32] The same conformity is found in the commentary on the sacrament of ordination, where Calvin combats the theory of its "indelible character"[33] and declares himself in favor of reestablishing the diaconate as a "ministry to the poor."[34] In considering marriage and explaining the "great sacrament" of Ephesians 5, Calvin refers to 1 Timothy 3 as does the corresponding passage of his source.[35] He advocates the marriage of priests with the same insistence as Luther;[36] and he opposes the Roman discipline of "impediments" with the same arguments from Moses' writings that Luther used.[37] One has the impression that the entire chapter devoted to the "false sacraments" is Calvin's own summary, with only minor modifications, of Luther's famous treatise on the "captivity" of the seven sacraments.

In the chapter that deals with Christian freedom, Calvin criticizes the Roman claim to promulgate dogma, "the *right* to declare *new* dogmas and *compose articles of faith,* "[38] in language that reminds us of the *Babylonian Captivity* which affirms that the church "has no authority to *compose new articles of faith.* "[39] Thus Calvin rejects the arbitrary reduction of the Church to the clergy alone[40] and condemns the "tyranny of human traditions."[41]

This last chapter of Calvin's compendium seems to be inspired mainly by Luther's *On Christian Liberty,* which appeared in 1520.

Calvin had already used this treatise to write the previous chapters. In fact, the first chapter contains a statement on the principal use of the law, which seems to come directly from *On Christian Liberty.* Luther's treatise says: "The precepts *teach . . . what* we must *do,* but they do not give the power to do it; it is the same with the ordinances, in that they show man to himself, and through them he knows *his own powerlessness* to do good, and *he despairs of his own ability.* " The goal of these divine precepts is to convince us of our miserable state ("by which we are convinced that all are sinners") and to prepare us thereby to place all our confidence in God's mercy.[42] Calvin describes this first "use of the law" in the following language: "First, while setting forth God's righteousness, that is, what God *demands* of us, it admonishes each one about his own unrighteousness and *convicts him of sin.* For thus it is necessary that . . . once they have set aside the stubborn *opinions of their own virtue,* men acknowledge that they stand and abide by the hand of God alone. And then, . . . that naked and empty they flee *to the mercy* of God."[43]

The chapter on "The False Sacraments" contains other recollections of Luther's *On Christian Liberty.* On the priests' usurpation of clerical and religious titles to the detriment of the people, Calvin notes: "But it was a sacrilege to usurp for themselves this title which belonged to the *whole church.* . . . And Peter did not, as they improperly imagine, call a few shaven men *clerics,* but the entire people of God."[44] Here is what we read in Luther's treatise: "Harm has been done to the words 'priest' and 'cleric' . . . when they are transferred from all Christians to those *few* who are now described, according to a noxious custom, as 'Ecclesiastics.' "[45] Later in the chapter, we find Calvin writing: "In [Christ] we are all priests";[46] and in Luther: "Thus in Christ we are all priests."[47]

Approaching the question of Christian liberty, Calvin first of all stigmatizes the error of those who, under the pretext of enjoying liberty, fall into the abuse of liberty and provoke disorder. Of those who have gone astray, he writes, "On the pretext of this liberty they cast off all obedience to God and rush forth in *unbridled license.*"[48] This reminds us of the sentence from *On Christian Liberty:* "So there are many who, when they hear of this freedom in the faith, immediately turn it into an occasion of the flesh and instantly judge that all things are allowed."[49] Both authors advocate safeguarding public order and condemn anarchy, in that they say true liberty in Christ means freedom to obey God; in other words, it leads to a spontaneous and joyful fulfillment of the will of the Lord. Just as the German reformer's treatise insists that the Christian should promptly exercise his "obedience to God" with "joyful zeal" and "grateful love,"[50] Calvin emphasizes the need to devote oneself to "obeying God" without restraint, but with "ready cheerfulness," "joyfully and with great delight."[51]

To solve the problem posed by Acts 16, which relates how the apostle agreed to circumcise Timothy even though the Jewish observance had been set aside, Calvin once again obviously followed the arguments of *On Christian Liberty.* Just as Luther did, he sees in Paul's action an example that illustrates to what extent "our freedom ought to be moderated, or curbed for the sake of those offended," at the moment we find ourselves in the presence of the "weak" who are easily offended. Continuing to agree with his source, Calvin quotes Galatians 2 to show that as soon as the same apostle Paul was no longer surrounded by "superstitious Jews" as in the case of Titus, he did not hesitate to declare his freedom from the Mosaic law.[52]

Finally, I quote from the last chapter of the *Institutes* where the criticism of "human laws" in the Church clearly takes on the same form as the corresponding text of *On Christian Liberty.*

Luther	Calvin
Therefore, if one holds the view that he can easily move without danger among that *infinite number* of mandates and precepts . . . which those foolish *pastors* urge on them, *as if they were necessary for* righteousness and *salvation* . . .[53]	On the contrary, the constitutions *can scarcely be numbered,* which they [those who wish to be seen as *pastors* of the Church] gravely sanction with great severity, *as if they were necessary for salvation* . . .[54]

It is evident that such parallels—especially if taken individually—do not allow us to affirm that Calvin had before his eyes the various texts of the German reformer when he worked on his compendium. But taken as a whole, they allow us to establish with a high degree of probability that Calvin had read these texts and was inspired by them in his personal reflections.

Since our young theologian was living in a reformist milieu (in France and especially Basle) that was severely agitated by disputes concerning the sacrament of the Supper, it is understandable that he sought to form his own views on the question. He wished to know the truth concerning the way in which Christ is present in the sacrament of the Supper or, more exactly, to establish with clarity what the Scripture teaches and what it does not teach on this subject. To this end he probably read several texts published by different evangelical theologians engaged in the dispute, particularly Luther, Bucer, and Zwingli; and in comparing them, he concluded that Luther was nearest to the truth. In this connection, it is interesting to examine how Luther's two celebrated *Sermons* on the Eucharist are reflected in the text of the *Institutes.*

The first, the *Sermon von dem hochwürdigen Sakrament des heiligen wahren Leichnams Christi und von den Bruderschaften,* [55] which appeared in 1519 and was translated into Latin in 1524, seems to have been used by Calvin only as a secondary source. On the other hand, the second, the *Sermon von dem Sakrament des Leibes und Blutes Christi wider die Schwarmgeister,* [56] published in German in 1526 and in Latin in 1527, has left more traces in Calvin's work. The explanation of this fact, in our opinion, may be found in the nature of the events of 1533–1535. The second sermon was written against the partisans of Zwinglian theories, and in the Latin version was published with an epistle "against Bucer, refuting a new error concerning the sacrament." [57] The concerns of Luther's second sermon were still relevant during this period when Calvin was gathering material on the question of the sacraments.

First, the author of the *Institutes* expresses his regret at the "horrible dissensions" that divide the evangelicals as soon as they approach the theological problems of the Supper; but at the same time he hastens to reject the Zwinglian interpretation of "This is my body." [58] In this way he implicitly declares himself a follower of Luther's theory, at least to the degree that Luther held that the body and blood of Christ are truly present in the sacrament and actually received by the communicant. We note that this basic acceptance does not prevent Calvin from criticizing several expressions of the Saxon reformer, some of which are found in the two sermons in question. It is notable that Calvin rejects the phrases "The bread itself is the body" and "the body under the bread," [59] as well as the "glorified body" *(verklerten Leib)* [60] and the "true and natural body of Christ" *(wahrhaftig natürlich Fleisch).* [61] He also declares himself in disagreement with Luther's idea of the ubiquity of the glorious body. [62]

In the rest of the text, Calvin uses quite a few ideas from the two sermons. For example, there is the idea borrowed from Augustine according to which the unity of communicants is compared to a single loaf of bread, which has been kneaded together from numerous grains. Luther said, "Just as a *single grain* loses its form and becomes a general, single form with the other grains so that *you cannot distinguish one from the other* . . . , so should Christendom be *one.* "[63] Calvin also notes: "The bread represents that *unity* which is exhibited in the sacrament. As it is made of *many grains* which are thus mixed and combined so that one cannot be distinguished from the other, it is fitting that we are joined and connected together in this manner."[64]

As the German reformer declares that the bread of life is for the spiritually ill, for those to whom "sin cleaves in front and behind,"[65] Calvin writes that "this sacred feast is medicine for the sick, solace for sinners."[66] To Luther's protest against the habit of depriving the people of communion of both kinds ("The pope has restricted us to one form"[67]) corresponds Calvin's criticism of the "constitution which has stolen or snatched away half of the Supper from the majority of the people of God."[68] The master of Wittenberg rejected the sacrifice of the Mass because he saw it as a "work" that one pretends to *give* to God, whereas one should rather *receive* in all humility the body and blood of the Lord, which is "given" *(geschenkt)* to us.[69] Calvin expresses this same idea in a brief and striking expression: "The difference between a sacrifice and a sacrament is as great as the difference between giving and receiving."[70] Finally, just as the Augustinian monk stigmatizes the monastic practice of private Masses which are celebrated "alone in a corner" and destroy the sense of community,[71] our lay theologian writes: "The sacrifice of the Mass destroys and dissolves this community." And he adds: "An opening was made for *private Masses,* which refer to a kind of excommunication rather than that community instituted by the Lord."[72]

In my opinion, these "soundings" are sufficient to establish the fact that Luther's writings exerted a profound influence on the young author of the *Institutes.* It is difficult to measure with certainty the exact extent of this influence. We only know that it was limited by the fact that Calvin did not understand German[73] and had access only to the Latin works or Latin translations of the works of his famous predecessor. But that did not stop him from becoming a "Lutheran" in the sense that Luther influenced him more than any other evangelical theologian.[74]

We have also established that having chosen Luther, Calvin made his choice *in* Luther, that is, he did not follow him on all points but only when he found him in agreement with the Scriptures. Let us repeat: what counted for Calvin was the absolute sovereignty of the message of the one Lord, of whom the great Saxon reformer was, in the final analysis, one of the best interpreters. Also, Calvin did not hesitate to extend the process of his formation by reading other theologians, especially Philip Melanchthon.

CHAPTER THIRTEEN
Melanchthon

Calvin's Latin mind developed finesse and clarity because of his philosophical, legal, and humanist studies, but it still lacked order and structure. Thus he joyfully discovered the writings of Melanchthon, a self-taught man like himself. At first a biblical humanist, Melanchthon transformed himself into a systematic theologian, without sacrificing to theology all he received from humanism.[1] The sense of balance which we encounter in this man, his clear and pleasant style, his rejection of subtle and scholastic abstractions, his gift for definitions, and his distaste for using outrageous or violent expressions—all these qualities obviously aroused deep sympathy in Calvin. Furthermore, on several points of doctrine, especially the Christian and evangelical reevaluation of the law, our young theologian seemed to have had a greater intellectual affinity for Melanchthon than for Luther. Thus Calvin saw in Melanchthon a useful complement to Luther.

Hardly three years after the first *Institutes* appeared, Calvin met Melanchthon in Germany and established a deep friendship with him. Their relationship was to continue for quite a long time; and it is paradoxical that in the painful Servetus affair, Melanchthon was one of the few evangelicals to approve unreservedly Calvin's inflexible attitude.[2]

When Calvin was preparing his compendium, the work of systematic theology that enjoyed the greatest authority among the evangelicals was without doubt Melanchthon's *Loci Communes.* In France, the fame of the "Preceptor of Germany" was widespread. He was known as well as, if not better than, Luther since he was actively interested in the affairs of France. The Sorbonne judged it necessary to place his works on the Index as soon as they appeared.[3] Given these circumstances, we can understand why many historians of Calvin think it is probable or even certain that the *Loci* influenced the first edition of the *Institutes.*[4] I have no doubt about this influence and shall illustrate it by several examples taken from the first edition (1521) of the *Loci.*[5]

The first traces of Melanchthon's influence appear in the opening chapter of the *Institutes* ("Law"). As the theologian from Wittenberg saw the first three commandments of the Decalogue summarized in the single commandment of love,[6] our author explains "the first table" of the law according to the precept that ordains that "we love God with all our heart, with all our mind, and with all our strength."[7]

On sanctifying the day of the Lord, the two works set forth the same idea: we should refrain from all activity on this day, for God alone desires to work within us. The *Loci* affirms that we are obligated to "sustain the work of God in us," to renounce "works" every day, and to be open to the life-giving influence of the Holy Spirit. Moreover, these attitudes should characterize a "perpetual Sabbath," that is, the entire life of the Christian.[8] The *Institutes* declares: "All *works* of this sort are servile; and the law of the Sabbath commands us to cease from them, *that God may dwell in us, work* what is good, and rule us by the leading of his Holy Spirit. . . . By this we are taught: a *perpetual Sabbath* has been commanded by God for us, and no end has been established for it."[9]

When Calvin describes the spirit with which the faithful are obligated to observe the divine precepts, he follows his source by criticizing an observance that is purely external and negative and affirming an ideal attitude that is inward and positive: "But this is not to be passed over lightly: *not only external works* are prescribed or prohibited by the *law* of God but also thoughts themselves and the inner *affections of the heart.* Let no one think the law is satisfied when the hand only refrains from acting." It is not sufficient to refrain from doing evil, to obey passively "You shall not kill" and "You shall not commit adultery"; it is necessary to intend to do good and to be pure "in heart before God."[10] Melanchthon speaks in the same way: "But the sophists of the law teach these precepts in terms of *external works alone,* as if the law were fulfilled if you do not kill or fornicate openly, and so on. On the contrary, Christ expounds the law *in terms of the affections* and does so positively." Simply respecting "You shall not kill" and "You shall not commit adultery" does not satisfy the divine demands. One must obey "from the heart"; one must acquire "purity of heart."[11]

Calvin continues: "Those who do not understand these things fashion Christ into another Moses, one who brings the law of the Gospel which supplies what is lacking in that of Moses. This is completely false."[12] Melanchthon reacts in the same way against the error of the "sophists" who believe that "Christ was the successor of Moses and the giver of a new law."[13]

The two theologians obviously use the same expressions to show to what extent the old law is of value in Christian economy.

Melanchthon	**Calvin**
I am pleased to have taught that the Decalogue belongs to antiquity; *not that it ought not to be done, but that it does not damn* us if we have failed in something.[14]	Many, when they wish to express this freedom from the curse of the law, have said that the *law has been set aside* for the faithful; *not that it no longer commands them* what is right, but merely . . . that *it does not damn* and destroy.[15]

In the chapter on "Faith," Calvin distinguishes between two types of faith. The first consists only of holding as true all that is affirmed about God and Jesus Christ: "If one believes that God exists, let him judge that the story which is told about Christ is true." In Calvin's view, this faith "is not worthy of the name 'faith,' " for it does not contain any personal commitment, and as such it could exist among the most impious: "it is held *in common with the devils.*" True faith is entirely different. It is the movement of one's entire being toward God and a confident and personal giving of oneself to him who alone is able to save: "The other [type] is that by which we not only believe that God and Christ exist, but we also believe *in God* and Christ. . . . This is truly . . . to place all hope and *trust* in the one God and Christ." This is really the "*substance* of things hoped for," the *hypostasis* on which we lean to have "a *certain* and secure possession of those things which God has *promised* us."[16] The first kind of faith also may have its seat "in a deceitful, perverted, and hypocritical heart"; the second, the true "confidence," can dwell only within souls who sincerely believe.[17]

If we read what the *Loci* teaches on this subject, we shall find the same distinction. The first species of faith is only a "frigid opinion," a "historical faith" which does not go beyond the abstract acceptance of Christ's historical existence. In truth, it is "no faith at all" but "deceit and hypocrisy."[18] This semblance of faith is typical of the impious: "It is commonly accepted that the multitude of sophists calls it faith when they assent to those things set forth in Scripture; but that is also the faith of the wicked."[19] On the contrary, the second requires one to "believe from the heart"[20] and consists of a "most lively knowledge of both the power and the goodness of God."[21] This is truly a trusting faith: "And thus faith is nothing other than confidence in the divine mercy, promised in Christ and indeed in whatever sign [God has ordained]."[22] It is the "*substance* of things hoped for, it is the expectation and *certitude* of what does not appear." Melanchthon insists again that in faith we must "believe the *promises.*" Otherwise we simply do not have faith: "Therefore those who do not wait for the *promised* salvation do not believe."[23]

Calvin does not seem to have consulted the *Loci Communes* to explain the Lord's Prayer, but his analysis in chapter four, on the nature of the sacraments, reveals quite a few traces of Melanchthon's influence.

Melanchthon describes the sacramental sign in these terms: "For in the Scriptures, *signs are added to the promises,* as if they were seals; while they remind us of the promise, they also are certain *testimonies* of the divine *will toward us.* They testify that we shall certainly receive what God has promised."[24] This idea that God reveals his saving will by a sign and a seal leads the author to quote the term *sphragis* ("seal") which Paul used to show the relationship between the old and the new sacraments (Rom. 4:11): "*Circumcision* is nothing, *baptism* is nothing, and participating in the Lord's *table* is nothing, but they are witnesses and seals of the divine will toward you."[25] Finally, two examples from the Old Testament illustrate how God willingly confirms with signs the vacillating faith of the faithful:

"The Lord extended the life of *Hezekiah* through the prophecy of Isaiah. So that the king might know what would surely take place, God confirmed the *promise* with an added sign, that the *shadow of the sundial* would be turned back ten steps (4 Kings 20). *Gideon,* lest he doubt what was to be, namely, that Israel would be led forth in liberty by his leadership, was convinced by two signs (Judges 6)."[26]

Calvin treats the same subject in very similar terms and in much the same order. Here is his definition of the sacrament: "It is an external sign by which God represents and *testifies* to us his *goodwill toward us,* in order to sustain the weakness of our faith." He also believes that the sacrament is a seal that is added and affixed to the divine promise: "By this we also understand that a sacrament is never without a preceding *promise;* but rather it is *joined* to it as a kind of *addition,* so as to confirm or seal the promise itself."[27] Then to respond to an objection of his adversaries, Calvin also uses Paul's term *sphragis:* "They cannot boast that this comparison was recently invented by us, for Paul himself used it (Rom. 4:11), calling *circumcision* a *seal* ($\sigma\varphi\rho\alpha\gamma\hat{\iota}\delta\alpha$)."[28] As God used this teaching under the ancient economy, so he uses it in the new: "To Abraham and his posterity circumcision was commanded (Genesis 17), to which later purifications and sacrifices of the Mosaic law were added. These were sacraments of the Jews until the advent of Christ; by which the former were set aside, and two other sacraments were instituted, which the Christian Church now uses: *baptism* and *the Lord's Supper.*"[29] Finally, it is most revealing that to support his idea Calvin quotes exactly the same Old Testament examples as Melanchthon: "Examples of the second kind [miracles] were when he watered the fleece with dew, and the earth was dry, and then he watered the earth with dew and left the fleece untouched in order to promise Gideon victory; when he turned back the *shadow of the sundial ten steps in order to promise Hezekiah freedom from harm"* (Judges 6; 2 Kings 20; Isaiah 38).[30]

In what follows, Calvin agrees with his source in affirming that the true sacrament of penance is baptism, and when one lapses into sin it is only necessary to remember this sacrament: "The memory of our baptism ought to be called to mind."[31] He varies from Melanchthon only in denying that the Jews who were baptized by John the Baptist would have to be rebaptized in order to become Christians.[32]

In defining original sin, Calvin seems to have adopted the terminology of Melanchthon, who comments on this doctrine from the Epistle to the Romans: "Original sin is a natural propensity and a congenital impetus and *energy* by which we are drawn into sin."[33] And farther on: "Original sin is a kind of *vigorous energy* which bears in all our parts and in all times *fruit,* namely, vices."[34] Here is Calvin's passage: "This perversity never ceases in us, but constantly bears new *fruits* (Romans 7). . . . Therefore those who defined original sin as the 'lack of original righteousness' have not adequately expressed its vigor and *energy.*"[35]

The last similarity we note is in the chapter on the false sacraments. We can establish in particular how Calvin uses not only the ideas but also certain references from the Scriptures and the Fathers which are furnished by his source.

On the subject of auricular confession, Calvin first notes: "But I marvel with what effrontery they [our opponents] dare to contend that the confession of which they speak *is by divine law.*"[36] Then a little farther on, he reproves the papist custom that constrains the faithful to offer a detailed account of their sins: "to review the catalog of sins."[37] Melanchthon expressed his views on this point in a similar way: "The divine law does not demand a review of what has been done," and it is not necessary "to review the whole catalog of sins."[38] The section that follows is even more revealing. To combat the practice of private confession, Calvin cites the same passage from the *Historia tripartita* (bk. 9, ch. 35) which the author of the *Loci* quoted in the same context.

Calvin writes: "Sozomen relates (*Tripart. hist.,* bk. 9) that this constitution of the bishops was diligently observed by the Western churches, above all at Rome. Thereby he indicates it was not universally instituted by all the churches. He also says that one of the presbyters was specially designated to have charge of this office." Several lines later he notes: "Then he adds: this was also the custom in *Constantinople,* until a certain *matron,* pretending to confess, was found to have covered up under the appearance of confession an affair that she was having with a deacon. Because of this outrage, Nectarius, . . . the bishop of that church, *abrogated* the rite of confession."[39]

Is this not an adaptation, pure and simple, of what Melanchthon said? "The most ancient custom was that public crimes were brought before the entire congregation. . . . This custom was *abrogated* sometime ago, and a *certain one from the number of presbyters* was designated, before whom even public crimes were privately prosecuted." At this point, the *Historia tripartita* is quoted with this comment: "To this day this [custom] is *diligently observed in the Western churches and chiefly in Rome,* where there is even a certain place for the penitents." Finally, the scandalous incident of Constantinople is mentioned to show why Bishop Nectarius had to suppress private confession.[40]

In the same passage, after using the patristic materials furnished by his source, Calvin also adopts biblical references from Melanchthon, notably 1 John 1:9; Psalm 51; and Psalm 32.[41] He does this to establish the admonition that Melanchthon offered, that is, the believer needs to confess "before God." As Melanchthon declared that "confession is nothing other than acknowledging our sin and condemning ourselves before God,"[42] Calvin affirms that "since it is the Lord who forgives, forgets, and wipes out sins, it is to him that we confess our sins in order to obtain pardon."[43]

These general similarities, as well as the number of agreements in detail,[44] permit us to conclude with a high degree of probability that there was a literary dependence between the *Institutes* and the *Loci.* Certainly Calvin did not copy Melanchthon any more than he did Luther. He only drew from him what he could not find in Luther and benefited from the advantages of Melanchthon's systematic thinking.

CHAPTER FOURTEEN
Zwingli

It is often said that Calvin always had a negative attitude toward the Zurich reformer, whom he had considered a destroyer of the reality of the sacraments. Such a statement, I believe, should be qualified. It is true that we possess a document from 1539 in which our young theologian defines Zwingli's theology of the Last Supper as a "false and pernicious opinion,"[1] as well as two texts of 1540 in which he explicitly places Luther above Zwingli,[2] and a fourth of 1542 in which he states that not all of Zwingli's works are worth reading.[3] However, it does not seem justified to conclude that a "very close rapport" between Calvin and Zwingli could not exist because of Calvin's "almost limitless approval" of Luther.[4] With A. Lang[5] and the editors of the *Opera Selecta,*[6] we believe that in spite of his initial— and even continuing—distrust of the most humanistic and spiritualistic of the reformers, our young author did not hesitate to consult, indeed to use, Zwingli's great systematic treatise, the *Commentary on True and False Religion,* which was written in 1525 at the demand of several Frenchmen and dedicated to Francis I.[7] Within the circle of Lefèvre d'Etaples and Gérard Roussel, with which Calvin was associated, this book was certainly known and read.[8]

The first evidence of Zwingli's thought may be found in Calvin's Dedicatory Epistle. To prove that the truth is not necessarily found with a majority and with tradition but often with a misunderstood minority suspected of dissidence, Calvin cites the examples of Elijah, Moses, and Micaiah which are also found in the *Commentary.*[9]

Later, in the chapter on "Law," Calvin takes a position very similar to that of Zwingli on the subject of the worship of statues. Using the same arguments, but in reverse order, both Calvin and Zwingli insist upon the invisibility of God, reject the favorite argument of their adversaries, and cast doubts on the usefulness of the "books of the poor." Here are the three points of Calvin's argument, compared with Zwingli's three points. (The original order of the text is indicated by Roman numerals in parentheses.)

Zwingli	Calvin
(III) We *worship* God, who is *invisible,* and who forbids us to *portray* him by any visible *figure.* . . . Therefore, when they say that Christ as God can be *portrayed,* they are deceived.[10]	(I) "You shall not make for yourself a graven image. . . ." By this is meant that all *worship* and adoration is due the one God. Since he is incomprehensible, incorporeal, *invisible,* and thus contains all things so that he cannot be enclosed in any place, let us not imagine that he can be *portrayed* by any *figure.*[13]
(II) But then the argument is raised: *images are not worshiped,* but those beings of which they are images. We respond: *none of the Gentiles* was ever so *stupid* as to worship *stone,* bronze, and *wooden* statues in and of themselves. But they venerated their Joves and Apollos *in them.* Whence, although the sacred writings frequently deride the worship of *likenesses* as if the worshipers worshiped *stones* or *wood,* no one was so ignorant to believe that they worshiped the images to any degree. Rather, they worshiped those beings *in them,* whom they considered to be Gods.[11]	(II) *Images,* they reply, *are not taken for gods.* . . . Neither are these Gentiles to be esteemed *so stupid* that they did not understand God to be other than *wood* or *stones.* . . . But since they judged that they contemplated God *in those [images],* they worshiped him in them as well. . . . They reply, we do not call them our gods. *Neither* did Jews or *Gentiles* so call them, but they called them merely signs and *likenesses* of the gods.[14]
(I) But some of them say: *"Man is taught* and piety is aroused *by images";* they are effective of themselves. For Christ *never* taught *this manner of teaching.* . . . We ought to be taught by the *Word of God.*[12]	(III) The ultimate evasion is that they call them *"books of the uneducated."* Let us concede this . . . ; nonetheless I do not see that images are able to provide any benefit to the uneducated. . . . But then we will also respond: *this is not the manner of teaching* the people of God, whom the Lord wants instructed in doctrines far different from these tales. He declares the preaching of *his Word* to be the common teaching for all.[15]

Furthermore, note that to describe the worship of images, the author uses the word "carnal," an adjective typical of Zwingli.[16]

It is obvious that these similarities do not deny the fact that when the occasion arose, Calvin severely criticized the Swiss reformer's concept of faith and sacramental symbolism. In the third division of the chapter on "The Sacraments," we even find a direct quote—unique in the entire work—from the *Commentary.* The passage is quoted as the foundation for a negative judgment on Zwingli's idea of faith: "Others say: our faith cannot become better if it is good; for it is not faith unless it is firmly supported by the mercy of God, unshaken and without distraction."[17] Calvin refuses to subscribe to this opinion which he places among the "exceedingly frivolous and weak reasons"; he affirms that faith may be increased by everything that places the soul in contact with the divine power, especially receiving the sacraments.

Calvin's criticism of Zwingli's tendency to spiritualize the sacraments follows the etymology of the word *sacramentum.* Calvin says it is an error to reduce the word to its military meaning—"by which it signifies that solemn oath which a soldier offered to the commander when he was initiated into the military"—and to assert that our sacraments are no more than "signs" or "symbols" by which "we profess Christ to be our commander and testify that we serve as soldiers under his standard."[18] The allusion is obvious. The trained reader knows that Zwingli compared the sacraments to a military "oath" *(iusiurandum)*,[19] and that he considered them a simple "initiation":[20] "Therefore the sacraments are signs or ceremonies . . . , by which a man of the Church proves himself to be a candidate or *soldier of Christ.* "[21]

Zwingli and Calvin also agreed on baptism by John the Baptist. Contrary to Luther and Melanchthon—whom he does not name explicitly—Calvin subscribes to the following opinion: "By this it is also most certain that the ministry of John is absolutely the same as that which was later given to the apostles."[22] This opinion agrees with the Zurich reformer's words: "The distinction that they make between the baptism of John and Christ is altogether void, because both baptisms relate to the same cause and goal."[23]

Calvin's essay on the Supper is ambiguous. On the one hand, our theologian occasionally prefers Zwingli's terminology to Luther's. For example, he does not entitle this part of his work "The Mass" or "The Sacrament of the Altar" as Luther did in the *Babylonian Captivity* and the *Small Catechism* respectively; instead, he chooses the title "The Supper of Our Lord," which corresponds to Zwingli's "The Lord's Supper."[24] The two authors completely agree in deliberately using the term "Eucharist."[25]

But although the words are often the same, the meanings given them by each author often differ. It is well known that Calvin especially rejects the symbolism with which Zwingli explains the sign of the sacrament: "only a sign and figure of the body."[26]

Calvin's insistence on taking from his source only what he finds in harmony with "holy doctrine" is apparent in a whole series of detailed parallels, and most notably in the discussion of the eucharistic sacrifice.

The most interesting, detailed agreements are the following: just as Zwingli cites the attitude of the Twelve during the Last Supper to refute the adoration of the eucharistic elements, Calvin uses the "example of the apostles" to reject what he calls "carnal adoration."[27] Calvin's emphasis of the commemorative nature of the sacrament—"that he might exercise us in the *memory* of Christ's death"—and the life-giving character of this commemoration—"namely, that the *death* of Christ is *our life*"[28]—recalls a passage from Zwingli in which he discusses the "commemoration, by which those who firmly believe they are reconciled to the Father by Christ's death and blood make known this *life-giving death.*"[29]

Finally, writing on 1 Cor. 11:28 ("Let a man examine himself"), Calvin seems to establish the same connection that Zwingli noted between the brotherly love of the members of Christ and the disposition necessary to avoid receiving communion unworthily. Zwingli says: "Let a man examine himself, etc. For whoever eats of this symbol *proves himself to be a member* of the Church of Christ."[30] Later: "They testify by doing, so that they themselves are *members of the one body;* they partake of one bread."[31] In turn, Calvin asserts: "For this reason Paul teaches that a man should examine himself. . . . As he himself is possessed by Christ, so in turn he holds all the brethren *to be members of his body.*" He adds that there is a correlation between "eating worthily" and the "duties of love."[32]

When he confronts the problem posed by the sacrificial nature of the eucharistic celebration, Calvin first of all declares, in agreement with Luther, that the Mass is the "epitome of these horrid abominations"; but to prove that this statement is well founded he resorts to Zwingli's arguments. This is understandable, for none of the reformers stressed as strongly as Zwingli *the unique character of Christ's priesthood and sacrifice* in order to reject the sacrifice of the altar. Luther claimed that the Mass was a "good work," Melanchthon emphasized the impossibility of offering Christ, and Bucer especially stressed the "memorial" aspect of the Supper but was not opposed to its sacrificial nature. Before Calvin wrote, only the Zurich reformer had produced a unified statement of the essential arguments on which the evangelicals' important denials were founded.

Zwingli's clear-cut position emerged in controversy. By 1523, in his *De Canone missae epichiresis,* the Swiss reformer, whose humanistic erudition was considerable, had submitted the prayers of the Canon to rigorous criticism in the name of *sola Scriptura.*[33] In this strongly Christ-centered text, the phrases "was offered once," "was sacrificed once," and "the one Christ and Christ alone once made"[34] are a constantly repeated refrain. The logic of Zwingli's thought is simple. The offering and the sacrifice are inseparable. Christ offers himself only one time. It is therefore blasphemous to claim to offer him in every celebration of the Eucharist. This is equivalent to wanting to put him to death in each Mass. Moreover, all the texts of the Canon which speak of offering and sacrifice are improper additions to the simple and pure doctrine of the Scriptures.

A German humanist and specialist in the art of controversy, Hieronymus Emser (1478–1527), who was the chaplain and secretary of Duke George of Saxony, took it upon himself to reply to Zwingli's book.[35] Emser's reply, entitled *A Defense of the Mass Against Huldrich Zwingli,* appeared in 1524.[36] We doubt that it was an adequate refutation of Zwingli's utterances. Emser loses himself in details trying to prove—which he does quite effectively—that this adversary has committed many errors of history and etymology.[37] In several crucial places he loses sight of the main problem, the meaning of "offered once."[38] Regarding the phrase "Therefore this offering," he stresses the mystical and representative character of the eucharistic offering rather than its literal, "bloody" understanding. He also concedes the validity of the phrase "died once,"[39] but not one of his replies is entirely satisfactory. He does not attain to the notion formulated by the Council of Trent that "the one making the offering is the same as the victim."[40]

According to Emser, the victim on the altar is the same as the one on the cross. The only difference is that his suffering state has been transformed into a glorious one. But the one who makes the offering is not the same: at the cross it is Christ, while in the Mass it is the priest.[41] Therefore, along with many theologians of the period,[42] Emser distinguishes between the offering made by Christ and the offering made by the priest in the name of the Church. This could only increase the uneasiness of the evangelicals for whom the Christ-centered nature of the sacrament was a question of life and death, as it was in every doctrinal statement. Needless to say, the ironic tone of the *Defense,* the circumstances of its publication,[43] and its essentially apologetic character[44] greatly decreased its chances of being considered seriously by Zwingli and his followers.

The reply of the Zurich reformer was not long in coming. It appeared under the title *Adversus Hieronymum Emserum antibolon* and was dated 20 August 1524.[45] In addition to its refutations concerning the Church, the intercession of the saints, merits, and purgatory, its principal aim was to justify the irrevocable rejection of the sacrificial nature of the Eucharist. Zwingli was dissatisfied with Emser's distinction between the offering of Christ and the offering of the priest, for this distinction leads to the alternative of a unique sacrifice or a multiple sacrifice. Zwingli maintains his criticism that sacrifice is equivalent to putting to death.[46] The essential arguments of this last point were afterward inserted in the *Commentary* which, I believe, served in turn as a source for Calvin.

Thus, in my opinion the origin of Zwingli's position on the Mass brings to light the origin of Calvin's interpretation of the same subject. Examination of the text leads me to assert that Calvin borrows this part of his eucharistic doctrine from Zwingli. This means that in addition to Zwingli, Emser is also responsible for the caricature that our young theologian has of the Mass. If this theory is correct, we understand why Calvin so hotly attacks the "immolation" or "mystical destruction" theory, according to which the priest sacrifices once again the victim, Jesus Christ. It is true to say that this theory was supported by only a few post-Tridentine theologians.[47] Emser did not value sufficiently the notion that the "one who makes the offering" and the victim are the same, and he distinguished the sacrificial act of Christ and that of the Church in a "nominalist" fashion. These two aspects of Emser's thought were transmitted in a deformed way through Zwingli's polemics, with the result that Calvin took for the doctrine of the Church a view that was a lamentable caricature. Let us now look at the texts.

The part of the *Institutes* that treats the Supper is filled with quotes from the Fathers and allusions to the doctrines of scholastic opponents and evangelical authors. At the exact place where Calvin approaches the question of the Mass, all of these quotations cease and the parallels with Zwingli's *Commentary* begin.

Calvin's first objection to the Mass is that it blasphemes and offends the unique priesthood of Christ. He uses the same expression as Zwingli: "an insult against Christ."[48] Then he summarizes and explains the doctrine contained in Hebrews 5; 7; 9; and 10, obviously following the framework and emphases of his source. Let us compare the texts.

Zwingli

Many explained many things about the priesthood of Christ, but in such a way that they take into *themselves his priesthood*. . . . Therefore, when you come to the saying of Hebrews 5, you find plainly that Paul explains the priesthood of Christ through the analogy of the ancient high priest. This is not the ordination of *sacrificers* as *substitutes,* or replacing those who have died. For how could Christ be a *priest forever,* according to the saying of the prophet, if someone *succeeds* to his place? . . . But when *he sits at the right hand of the Father* in eternity and wipes away our sins by the one offering made on the cross forever, he does not need someone to act as his *substitute.*[49]

Calvin

But, for Christ, who is immortal, a *substitute is not at all necessary.* And thus he has been designated by the Father a priest forever. . . . But those who sacrifice daily must appoint priests for their offerings, which they put in place of Christ as *successors* and *substitutes.* By this substitution they not only deprive Christ of his honor . . . but they try to drive him *from the right hand of the Father,* where he cannot be seated as immortal without at the same time remaining *priest forever.* And let them not contend that their *sacrificers* are not substituted for Christ as if he were dead, but that they only share in his eternal priesthood which does not cease to be. . . . Christ . . . is one and needs no partners.[50]

Although the two texts develop in reverse order, it is quite clear that both authors emphasize, on the one hand, the impossibility of priests being "vicars" and "successors" of Christ and, on the other hand, the eternal nature of Christ's priesthood. The resemblance is especially obvious in the use of the same term "sacrificers."

In my opinion these similarities cannot be explained simply by the fact that the two authors are commenting on the same scriptural text. In fact, the scriptural text contains many other ideas (the holiness of the eternal high priest, his solidarity with men in their weakness, etc.) which neither Zwingli nor Calvin attempt to discuss; but they do stress with equal insistence an idea to which the epistle alludes only indirectly: the impossibility of attributing successors or vicars to the one high priest.

In addition, to indicate the eternal nature of Christ's priesthood, Calvin and Zwingli agree in using the expression "sits at the right hand of the Father," and not the expression of the epistle itself: "He sits at the right hand of majesty in the highest" (Heb. 8:1). Therefore we doubt that the two depended equally and directly on the scriptural text, but it is likely that Calvin was directly dependent on Zwingli.

This dependence is further supported by examining the second argument with which our theologian combats the Mass: "Another power of the Mass was proposed: it conceals and suppresses the cross and passion of Christ."[51] The papist idea of sacrifice is contrary not only to the unique priesthood but also to the unique sacrifice of Christ. It is offered every day for sins, whereas the Lord offered himself one time for all, making satisfaction for the sins of the world once and for all.

Calvin develops this thought in a long passage marked by several instances of opposing "once" and "daily"; the first evokes the idea of perfect efficacy and the second the idea of radical inadequacy. The pretension of the papists who wish to "duplicate often," to "repeat often," and to "carry out every single day" the offering of the body and blood of Christ casts doubt upon the complete efficacy of Christ's sacrifice on the cross: "Therefore it will be said either that Christ's sacrifice, which was fulfilled on the cross, lacks the power to cleanse eternally or that Christ carried out his task by the one sacrifice, offered once for all ages." There is no hesitation on this point: the cross is unique because of its sovereign efficacy. Therefore one must not add to it: "For in the entire disputation the apostle contends not only that there are no other sacrifices but also that the one sacrifice was *offered once* and is not to be repeated anymore."[52]

This reasoning reflects that of the *Commentary* and reveals throughout the ambiguous position represented by the phrases ("We err daily—we offer daily the mystical body of Christ") of Hieronymus Emser.[53] Here is Zwingli's text: "For if it is necessary that Christ *be offered daily,* then it becomes necessary that *what was offered once* on the cross does not suffice forever." But the sacrifice accomplished *"once on the cross"* does suffice, and no one has the right to demand "that it be offered *anew.*"[54]

Calvin seems to produce yet another idea developed in Zwingli's argument against Emser, that of the equivalence between offering and sacrifice.

The Zurich reformer declares: "Thus, an offering is complete when that which is offered is *slain.*" Now, "Christ cannot die again. . . . Therefore, Christ cannot be offered *again.*"[55] Calvin affirms that "the offering which is *brought to the altar* must be *slain* and sacrificed." Consequently, if the Mass is based on the fact that "we offer . . . Christ to the Father," we must say that "the Mass looks directly to this [end], that *once again,* if it were possible, Christ is slaughtered."[56]

I believe that these textual similarities and the dependence that they imply explain how a gap in Emser's theology (or even in scholastic theology), which was exposed and trivialized in Zwingli's criticisms, might have been the origin of Calvin's opposition to the sacrifice of the Mass. Surely Emser and the other pontifical controversialists would have rejected the "sacrificial" theory that Calvin attacked, and they would never have accepted Calvin and Zwingli's interpretation of "Christ is offered." It is all the more tragic to find that Calvin thought it was necessary during his whole life to combat the claim that the Lord was put to death in each Mass: "At a single moment, he is cruelly slain in a thousand places."[57] Would he have done this had the doctrine of "the same Christ offers" been clearly and universally taught in the Church of his time?

CHAPTER FIFTEEN
Bucer

When one speaks of Bucer's important influence on Calvin, one most often thinks of Calvin's stay in Strasbourg between 1539 and 1541, after having been expelled from Geneva, and the second edition of his *Institutes,* which he wrote during that time. This way of thinking is correct to the extent that the first prolonged personal contact between the two men and the most significant exchange of ideas took place during this period. But it would be incorrect to go so far as to pay no attention to the influence that the writings of the reformer of Alsace exerted on the writing of the first *Institutes.*

One could certainly object that before 1536 and a long time afterward, Calvin regarded with mistrust—if not worse—Bucer's position in the controversy over the sacraments.[1] But the validity of this objection does not oblige us to reject the possibility of Bucer's influencing Calvin prior to 1536. Zwingli's example proves that our young author was quite capable of using portions of the writings of a theologian whose theories he did not accept as a whole.

In developing an essentially biblical theology, Calvin no doubt would consult evangelical commentators who were most familiar with the sacred text. Therefore everything leads to the belief that he knew Bucer's *Enarrationes perpetuae in sacra quatuor evangelia* which appeared in 1530.[2] This was the second edition, revised and enlarged, of a work first published in 1527 under the same title.

According to A. Lang,[3] several ideas and passages in the first *Institutes* bear a "strong resemblance" to the *Enarrationes*. R. Seeberg[4] also points out several doctrinal similarities between the two books. Although J. Courvoisier speaks of Bucer's influence only in terms of Calvin's stay in Strasbourg, he emphasizes the considerable influence that the *Enarrationes* exerted in French-speaking countries. As a result of this influence the work was soon translated into French, and in less than four years after the appearance of Calvin's compendium it was published in Geneva.[5]

Having carefully compared different texts of the *Enarrationes* and the *Institutes*, I have found several striking similarities that can be explained only by the dependence of the second work on the first. This assertion is not contradicted by the historical evidence. Calvin knew by reputation the *episcopus Argentoratensis* before 1534; and given the frequent contacts between the circles of Lefèvre in France and evangelical Alsace, it can be assumed that Bucer's writings were found in the libraries that Calvin visited.[6]

The most interesting traces of Bucer's thought are found in passages of the *Institutes* that deal with the Church (the community of the elect and the kingdom of God), the Lord's Prayer, and the power of the keys.

In the Dedicatory Epistle, the young Calvin outlines his ecclesiology. He defines the Church in terms of the earthly reign of the heavenly Christ: "Indeed, the Church of Christ has lived and will live as long as Christ reigns at the right hand of the Father. . . . It should not be doubted that Christ has always reigned on earth, from the time when he ascended into heaven." Then he adds that this Church of the heavenly King should not be reduced to its visible forms alone: "But they are far from the truth when they do not acknowledge the Church, unless they see it with their very eyes, and they try to confine it by those limits in which it is not at all enclosed. . . . They contend that the form of the Church is always apparent and visible." Contrary to what the adversaries may think, the reign of Christ has no need at all of "external splendor" or even an "external mark." The Church is where God recognizes "his own"; it matters little whether they possess a visible organization or not.[7] The Church is an object of faith: "For those things are believed which cannot be seen by the eye alone. From this it is plain, that [the Church] is not a carnal thing that ought to be subject to our sense, or circumscribed to a certain space, or fixed in some spot."[8]

This idea that the Church is not necessarily visible and consists of the dynamic influx of the reign of the heavenly Christ rather than an earthly organization reminds us of several statements from the *Enarrationes*. These statements affirm that Christ is "our true King" in order to conclude that the "Republic of Christians" is the "heavenly government of God."[9] Concerning the "false Christs" of Matthew 24, these statements offer the same objection as Calvin: "Since even now some turn to this place, against the deceptions of the Romans and Mohammedans, . . . they do so rightly; because when Christ testified here that the kingdom of God stands by faith, that it is not limited to a particular place in this world, and that it does not know immediate happiness, those nevertheless taught that the kingdom of God was to be sought in external things. . . . The kingdom of God is not limited to a place or to visible things."[10] Furthermore: "The kingdom of Christ is not of this world, that is, based on external domination; therefore it is destitute of the glory of riches and external power, both in Christ, its head, and its members."[11]

Another summary of Bucer's ideas can be found in the chapter on "Faith." The Church presented as the reign of the heavenly Christ upon the earth is here defined as the "entire number of the elect," men of all origins "in whatever lands they make their way, or wherever in the world they are scattered." This "entire number of the elect" is identified with the body of Christ, "to be one Church and society, and one people of God, whose Christ, our Lord, is its leader and ruler, and as it were head of one body. Just as they have been elected in him through the divine goodness before the foundation of the world, so they are all gathered together in the kingdom of God." How do the "elect" form the body of Christ? By living "in one faith" and by being filled with "the same Spirit of God."[12] The role of the Holy Spirit is of primary importance; he works within the elect who are "led by the Spirit of God."[13] "Through the Holy Spirit," God justifies and sanctifies us,[14] and "through the blessings of his Holy Spirit" he regenerates us from day to day.[15] In sum, by the divine Spirit, God reveals himself among his elect: "The Lord offers and manifests his election in this manner."[16]

The election of God which constitutes the Church is absolutely infallible: "And thus this order of God's mercy is described for us by Paul, that those whom he elects from men, he calls, those whom he called, he justifies; those whom he justified, he glorifies."[17] Thus: "It cannot be that . . . they perish. . . . First, [their salvation] stands with God's election, and it cannot vary or fail, unless that eternal wisdom fail as well. Therefore, they can stagger and waver, or even fall; but they will not be shattered, because God supports them by his hand. . . . Therefore, those whom God elects he places in the trust and care of Christ his son, so that he loses none of them but raises up all of them in the last day (John 6). Under such good care they can wander and fall, but they certainly cannot perish."[18]

Other scholars also sense a strong influence from Bucer when Calvin defines the mystery of the Church in terms of election and God's eternal predestination.[19] In his reference to the gathering of the elect "from the four winds" described in Matthew 24, Bucer also opposes their geographical dispersion to the Roman claim that the elect are within the limits of the visible Church: "The elect are to be gathered from all parts of the earth; therefore, not only those who are under Roman power are Christians."[20] For Bucer too, the elect are the body of Christ,[21] and they are such because of the influence of the Holy Spirit: "Therefore let it be enough for someone to be in the body of Christ and to live by his Spirit; and let this be so in any place whatsoever."[22] Their unity is a unity "in Christ and the Spirit." God has willed "that they all be one body."[23] Thus, "one sheepfold has been made, that is, one Church gathered from Gentiles and Jews, under one pastor, the head of this Church, Christ."[24] The elect "have the Spirit of God," and it is through him that they are unified: "For they are one with him: the Lord is in them, and they are in the Lord."[25] Bucer constantly stressed the primary role of the Spirit in the Church. He expressly said that God "gave the Spirit first, for nothing can be done in the kingdom of God apart from him."[26] And he especially showed the importance of the Spirit's activity in the revelation of God's eternal plan; the "manifestation of election" is brought about "through the blessing of the Holy Spirit."[27]

In the *Enarrationes,* Bucer truly affirmed the infallible nature of election or predestination before Calvin wrote his *Institutes.* As Calvin would do later on, Bucer highlights the importance of Romans 8: "They are not glorified unless they have been justified; they are not justified unless they have been called; they are not called unless they have been predestined." And he says of the elect: "They cannot be lost in contradiction of God's decree."[28] The divine plan does not vary. In every case we must suppose "the immutable power of God's election."[29] We read this point in Bucer's comments on John 6, and referring to the parable of the good shepherd Bucer writes: "In these things he clearly teaches that all things depend on divine election, and those to whom it has been granted to be his sheep can never be lost." And a little farther on: "Therefore, just as none of the elect can be seized from the hand of the Father, so they cannot be taken from the hand of Christ."[30]

In these passages we find that for both authors election is the reality that constitutes the universal community of the Church. The differences are minimal: while Bucer adheres to the biblical text on which he is commenting and proceeds analytically, Calvin does so systematically. While Bucer brings out both the positive aspect of election and the negative aspect of reprobation,[31] Calvin is content to emphasize the positive role and the ecclesiastical perspective of the eternal plan of God. Finally, the *Enarrationes* expressly deals with the "external society of the Church"—in which the proclamation of the "external Word," the administration of the sacraments, and the discipline of "admonitions"[32] constitute the visible and pastoral complement to the invisible nature. The first edition of the *Institutes* prefers to consider the Church in its invisible aspect. Later, Calvin's doctrine of predestination and the Church was to evolve and be more in line with Bucer's thought.[33]

Bucer's influence on young Calvin's theology is verified in yet another important text: the chapter on "Prayer." It seems certain that to write this chapter Calvin used not only Luther's *Small Catechism* but also Bucer's exposition of the Lord's Prayer in Matthew 6.[34]

The introduction to the ideal way to pray seems to follow the ideas developed in the corresponding passage of the *Enarrationes.* Therefore Calvin presents prayer as a dialogue between man, who is immersed in misery, and God, who manifests his endless mercy in Christ.[35] Calvin stresses that we should implore the Lord with confidence, that is, "with certain faith"[36] and always "in the name of Christ."[37]

When Calvin discusses the principal object of our prayers, he severely condemns anyone "who assigns to [the saints] a prayer other than that by which he asks God's kingdom to come."[38] This recalls Bucer's text: "For in all our prayers this ought to be foremost: 'Hallowed be thy name; thy kingdom come,' which certainly ought to be sought by all."[39] Even more important, this statement is made by the two authors in exactly the same context of rejecting prayers addressed to the saints and prayers for the deceased. Both authors are of the opinion that the intercession of the living for the dead has no scriptural foundation and cannot occur apart from a rash desire to comprehend God's impenetrable designs.[40]

Bucer described prayer as a conversation with God in which "we give thanks to him for benefits received, [and] we pray as well for his blessing."[41] Later, Calvin states that "prayer . . . has two parts: petition and thanksgiving."[42] Both Bucer and Calvin fail to mention the two other classical purposes of prayer: adoration and the request for forgiveness.

To the question of how much time to devote to prayer, Calvin replies with the same quote from 1 Thessalonians that Bucer used, stressing the command to "pray without ceasing."[43] Calvin opposes the notion that not following obligatory times for the exercises of piety is a sin, and his words recall this sentence from Bucer: "And it is clear that it is an intolerable madness to prescribe, yes, to command a *certain time,* manner, and place of prayer for everyone, so that to omit something would be considered a deadly offense."[44] For both authors, liturgical rules are necessary for the human community, but they are "matters of indifference to God."[45]

Let us also note that both use the same New Testament texts—Matthew 6; 1 Corinthians 14; and 1 Timothy 2—to determine the correct balance between the prayer of personal meditation and public, communal worship.

Bucer wrote: "But in commanding one to enter his room and close the door to pray to the Father, he wished to say nothing more than that ostentation ought to be avoided in all ways." The formula "in a room" signifies a spiritual attitude of inner silence rather than an actual place.

Bucer believes that public prayer is also necessary: "For it is not a new custom to pray in the gathering of the Church . . . 1 Corinthians 14 and 1 Timothy 2. . . . For as the benefits of God are, above all, commemorated in the gatherings of the Church, it is proper that the souls of all are enflamed to render thanks to him and to ask the Spirit about his judgments on life."[46] "In a room" is not opposed to "in a gathering": one may very well pray without ostentation in the midst of a crowd given to praising God. What is condemned is a hypocritical formalism and the absence of true contemplation: "Certainly contempt of God is enormous when you either pour out words to him mindlessly; that is, you do not pray at all, but you simulate a prayer and thereby deride God; or you go beyond words with vague imaginations . . . and are caught up with things of the flesh. Thus it is necessary that as much as possible the mind be empty of human things when prayer is offered to God." Instead of hindering this devotion of the spirit so essential to meditation, a fervent assembly only promotes it: "For in the gathering of the Church, preaching of the Word of God and equally the example of those praying take the place of solitude, as long as it is concerned with calling the mind away from human affairs."[47] Therefore there is nothing more favorable to personal prayer than an assembly that "prays by reading or singing."[48]

Calvin develops the same ideas in the following way. He first notes the inward nature of true prayer: "Its primary parts are placed in the mind and heart. Or rather, prayer itself is properly an emotion of the inner heart."[49] That was the point, and that alone, which the Lord wished to state in recommending retreat: "Therefore when our Lord Christ wished to offer the best rule for praying, he commanded [us] to enter the bedroom, and there with closed door to pray to our Father in secret, so that our Father, who is in secret, may hear us (Matthew 6). For when he draws us away from the example of hypocrites, who secure the favor of men by self-seeking and ostentatious prayers, he adds at the same time what is better: namely, to enter our bedroom and to pray there with closed door."[50] Several lines farther on he says: "And he did not wish to deny that it is expedient to pray in other places also, but to show that prayer is something secret, which is best located in the heart, and it especially requires its tranquillity, away from all the disruptions of our cares."[51] God detests prayer that is offered mechanically, without feeling: "They [voice and song] provoke his wrath against us if they come only from the lips and throat, inasmuch as that is to abuse his holy name and to deride his majesty." God desires one who prays to gather together the faculties of his mind, which otherwise "are drawn in various directions." The Lord wishes to rule as sovereign over the body as well as the soul of man in prayer, and, in particular, over his speech: "It is especially proper that the tongue has been consecrated and devoted to this ministry, both in singing and speaking. The tongue was made especially for telling and proclaiming the praise of God." The spoken or chanted word stimulates in a salutary way the prayers of all: "But the best use of the tongue is in public prayers, which are made in the gathering of the faithful, by which with one voice and, as it were, with the same mouth, we all glorify [God] together—and do it publicly, so that all in turn, each one by his own brother, receive confession of faith and are invited [to pray] by his example."[52]

Before we move to the commentary on the Lord's Prayer, let us examine another parallel in the same passage. Bucer noted that this prayer, above all others, consists of two parts: "But the heart will not order these [prayers] otherwise, and Christ's model *(formula)* will prescribe that we pray primarily for those things which are done for God's glory and that we not pray for those things opposed to God's glory. And then in the second place, [we pray for] those things which pertain to the present life."[53] Calvin takes up the same ideas. He remarks that the Son of God has furnished us with a form or a model *(formula)* that consists of six requests; then he adds: "But in all these things, even though consideration of God's glory is to be held primary, and although . . . all things are our concern; nevertheless, the first three [petitions] are especially devoted to God's glory, which alone ought to concern us in these petitions. . . . The remaining three deal with our cares, and properly deal with those things which are for our use and for which we are to pray."[54]

Next comes the explanation proper of the Lord's Prayer. Just as Bucer did, Calvin approaches the "Our Father" by drawing attention to our adoption as sons in Christ,[55] the direct source of our fraternal feelings toward the other elect. Let us compare the texts.

Bucer	Calvin
And finally, when he teaches us to say *our* Father, he commends the mutual love of the *brotherhood. . . .* And finally, just as we hold our *Father,* who is the greatest of our goods, somehow in *common,* so all the more should we hold all other things in *common.* [56]	But we are not so instructed that each one should individually name him his own Father, but rather we all in common would call him *our* Father. By this we are admonished about how great *a feeling of brotherly love* ought to exist *among us,* who are the common children of such a Father. For if one *Father is common* to us all, . . . nothing ought to be divided among us which we are not prepared with great alacrity of heart *to share* with one another, as much as need prescribes.[57]

The two expositions resemble each other in their interpretation of "who art in heaven"; they both see it as an invitation to consider God as a father who is infinitely superior to our earthly fathers and to seek only heavenly things.[58]

But it is in Calvin's explanation of "Thy kingdom come" that the influence of the *Enarrationes* predominates. The idea that the "kingdom" is established on earth through the Holy Spirit, who reveals the division of humanity into the elect and the reprobate, and the insistence upon glorifying God and loving one another follow so closely the lines of Bucer's thought that there is no question about his influence.

Here is what we read in Bucer. First, there is a "manifestation of election through the blessing of the Holy Spirit,"[59] while the "reprobate" are "led by the power of the Holy Spirit in such a way that they have absolutely nothing" to open themselves to the truth.[60] This idea is also underlined in what follows: "The same thing in the first petition is what is asked here, namely, that the Lord's name be adored, that the father would be acknowledged and adored everywhere; that *he would reign in us through his Spirit.* . . . For when the Lord reigns over us, . . . we thus confess and *glorify* his holy and illustrious name; he reigns over us while *he leads us by his Spirit,* so that we all commit ourselves to him and serve our brothers with all our strength in gratitude to him." The passage ends with an appeal that, "free and blessed," we would live "under Christ our King, in complete faith and active love" until the reign of God is completed within us and "he is all in all (1 Corinthians 15)."[61]

Here is the corresponding text of Calvin: "The kingdom of God is to lead and rule *his own by his Holy Spirit, by which he makes clearly known* in all their works the riches of his goodness and mercy. On the other hand, the *reprobate* . . . are destroyed, cast aside, and their sacrilegious arrogance is overthrown; whereby it is made *manifest* that there is no power which is able to resist his power." And several lines later he says: "And thus we pray that this kingdom of God may come; that is, that the Lord daily would add new people to the faithful, who celebrate his glory in all ways." And the text also ends with the quotation from 1 Corinthians 15: "And he will be all in all."[62]

Setting aside other, less striking parallels,[63] we note only the last section that Calvin adds to the Lord's Prayer. The line "For thine is the kingdom and the power and the glory forever" seems to have been taken from Bucer,[64] because the other possible source, Luther's *Small Catechism,* does not contain it.

In the chapter on "The False Sacraments," Calvin discusses penance and the power of the keys in terms that also recall the *Enarrationes.*

The context is the same for both Calvin and Bucer, the criticism of the Roman practice of penance; and both authors use the same scriptural material: Matthew 16 and John 20 for the first point, and Matthew 18 for the second.

Bucer's exegesis of Matthew 16 and John 20 stresses that the power to bind and to loose was first promised to and conferred on Peter because he represented the entire community. And subsequently the same power was granted to the other apostles without distinction to show that it actually belonged to the entire Church: "That absolution of sins . . . for public admission into the Church was promised and granted first to Peter, in the name of the Church, and then equally to the others."[65] And elsewhere he says: "And indeed according to John 20 the Lord said to all the disciples: . . . Receive the Holy Spirit."[66] To the question about exactly what this power includes, Bucer replies that it is identified with the ministry of the Word: "But that is nothing other than the Word of God."[67] The forgiveness of sins, which is equivalent to entry into the Church, and the withholding of this forgiveness, which signifies being put out of the Church, are brought about "through the same Word."[68] The power of the keys can come only from Christ and as such is identified with the Spirit, acting in and through the minister: "This power in preaching is the Holy Spirit, but it is made effective in listeners through the Word."[69]

In exegeting Matthew 18, Bucer brings out more of the disciplinary aspect of the power of the keys, namely, excommunication.[70] The "power" of "excluding from the Church or receiving into the Church" fundamentally belongs to the community of the faithful. "But it is clearly indicated here that this power belongs to all who come together in the name of Christ, that is, all who come to him in faith. This power is the keys of the kingdom of heaven, because the Spirit of God and his Word belong to such people."[71] Excommunication, whether it is carried out publicly or only by a small group of faithful "among themselves," is a "most holy . . . and beneficial institution of Christ."[72] For all practical purposes, it is the exclusion of the unrepentant sinner from participating in the holy table.[73] Its only goal is to safeguard the honor of God and the salvation of the faithful. When "some are proscribed by the Church and pronounced to be sinners, . . . it is the glory of God and the salvation of the brethren which are sought."[74] It is the spiritual welfare of the person excommunicated which must be sought: "Therefore the [excommunicant] is not at all damned. Whatever judgment love exercises while it inquires about the vices of the brethren, it makes a judgment that he may be healed."[75] Finally, to pronounce a judgment of exclusion is in reality to declare the divine sentence, just as readmitting the penitents "is nothing other than pronouncing them absolved by God."[76] In every ecclesiastical sentence or absolution, one should see a translation in human language of a decision by the Holy Spirit. The Church only functions as a herald and spokesman in the service of the heavenly Judge: "For the Church has no other power of remitting sins than the Holy Spirit; he merely absolves from sin and pronounces those who believe in Christ to be free. Therefore the Church will not be able to remit sins other than by acknowledging and testifying that sins have been remitted for those who believe in Christ."[77]

If we now examine Calvin's text, we find that he also divides his exposition into two parts: he explains John 20 and Matthew 16, identifying the power of the keys with preaching; then he comments on Matthew 18 about the meaning of excommunication.

In the first part, Calvin first pauses over the question of the relationship between Peter and the apostles as a group: "The keys of the kingdom of heaven, which were previously promised to Peter (Matthew 16), are now presented to him and to the other apostles; for whatever was promised to him, he receives equally with all the others." Then he declares that the exercise of the power of the keys is nothing other than the act of preaching: "This command about remitting and retaining sins and that promise made to Peter concerning binding and loosing refer to nothing other than the ministry of the Word."[78] Finally: "We contend that the power of the keys is simply the preaching of the Gospel; if we consider men, it is not so much power as it is ministry. For Christ did not actually give this power to men, but to *his Word,* of which he made men ministers."[79]

In the second part, Calvin explains that he sees a difference in meaning between Matthew 16 and Matthew 18: "They differ in this regard, that the first passage deals particularly with preaching in which ministers of the Word are engaged. The second pertains to the discipline of excommunication, which is granted to the Church." For both Calvin and Bucer, the right to excommunicate belongs fundamentally to the community: "Therefore, let no one obstinately despise the judgment of the Church, or esteem it a minor thing to be damned by the decision of the faithful."[80] Excommunication is divinely instituted: "And they are not able to err or to dissent from God's judgment, because they judge only in accord with God's law, which is not an uncertain or earthly opinion but the holy will of God and a heavenly oracle."[81] As such, a judgment of exclusion has a healing purpose; it is not given to throw the excommunicated party "into perpetual ruin or despair."[82] It is always dictated by the Spirit: "Therefore I deny that the power of the keys is appropriate to any who have not received the Holy Spirit. I deny that someone can use the keys unless the Holy Spirit has first come to him and taught him and told him what to do." The Spirit is the "judge and ruler of the keys."[83] Finally, Calvin asserts that excommunication is a declaration and a witness of the divine sentence: "Such a judgment of the faithful is nothing other than the promulgation of his judgment."[84]

I believe these examples constitute a sufficient reason to place Bucer along side Melanchthon and Zwingli (after Luther) among the men who gave young Calvin the theological initiation that he desired.

But were these the only men to introduce Calvin to theology? And, more important, were they the first?

Based on the present state of research, one may first reply to these questions that Calvin probably did not acquire his knowledge from any other evangelical theologian of the first order. When we say "of the first order," we exclude Farel, Oecolampadius, Simon Grynaeus, Myconius, Capito, Bullinger, and others, even though Calvin no doubt read their works and was personally influenced by them. We can, with some difficulty, determine a few specific points of influence, but these men were not sufficiently influential to say that Calvin followed them as his masters in expounding revealed truth.

It is also not easy to reply to questions about the theological initiation Calvin received before becoming acquainted with Luther and the other reformers. The Christian humanism which Erasmus and Lefèvre contributed to Calvin certainly constituted an important heritage, but this was much more—or so it seems—on the level of biblical knowledge and the formation of a reformist mentality than on the level of theology. I shall return to this point in the excursus.

Several Calvin scholars have formulated hypotheses and developed arguments that affirm or contest the scholastic imprint on Calvin's thought. We must closely examine this question about the scholastic theological formation that young Calvin received at the Collège de Montaigu.

CHAPTER SIXTEEN
Scholastic Theology

In reading the fifth chapter of the *Institutes,* "The False Sacraments," one is struck by the frequent references to two classical sources of traditional scholasticism: the *Decretals* of Gratian and the *Sentences* of Peter Lombard.[1] Calvin not only fails to cite his evangelical sources but—with only four exceptions[2]—he does not refer to scholastic authors in any of his five other chapters. Why does he break this pattern precisely in the most polemical chapter of his work? The response to this question may illuminate the young author's attitude toward scholastic theology and his intellectual and religious evolution in general.

For the moment, let us limit ourselves to factual matters. Calvin refers 34 times to Gratian and 35 times to Lombard. Some of the references are allusions: 10 times for Gratian and 17 times for Lombard; and some are references to explicit passages: 24 times for Gratian and 18 for Lombard. Of the 24 explicit references to the *Decretals,* 15 reproduce the meaning of the passage, while 9 quote the text directly. For the *Sentences,* the proportion is the following: there are 18 references to explicit passages, of which 10 give the meaning and 8 quote the text.

All these references—a total of 69—naturally reflect only a very small part of Gratian's and Lombard's teaching, namely, several statements about the sacraments. To give an idea about the proportion of material involved, we note that of the 1,870 columns in the Migne edition of the *Decretals,* Calvin uses at most the equivalent of 50 columns;[3] and of the *Sentences,* which includes 440 columns in the same edition, he uses only the equivalent of 70.[4]

We also note that all the passages quoted from the *Sentences* are taken from the fourth book; Calvin has no interest whatsoever in the first three books which deal respectively with the Trinity, creation, and the incarnation.

In spite of his limited use of these two sources, the author of the *Institutes* considers them the most authoritative representatives of his adversaries' official doctrine. If we consider only the *Institutes,* we may even say that, for Calvin, scholasticism is simply Gratian and Lombard. When he introduces a quote from either author, he deliberately uses a comprehensive term such as "scholastic theologians"[5] or "scholastic sophists."[6]

To identify the Master of the Sentences this way is justified, for even at the beginning of the sixteenth century Lombard was actually considered at the Sorbonne as the "Magister scholae" par excellence.[7] Commentary on the *Sentences* constituted the content of dogmatic theology at the Sorbonne.[8] Therefore, when Calvin said of scholastic theologians that "Lombard [was] their leader [*coryphaeus*],"[9] he was simply telling the truth.

On the other hand, no author today considers Gratian a theologian in the true sense of the word. His *Decretals* were actually a collection of texts from the Fathers, popes, and councils which are of unequal authority and doctrinal value, and not a work of systematic theology. This vast compilation, which originally (and with good reason) bore the title *A Concordance of Discordant Canons,* is a classical source of canon law. Calvin must have studied it with the faculty of law in Orléans and in Bourges.[10] However, if one considers that this collection and the personal commentaries that the monk Gratian added to it enjoyed considerable authority even among scholastic theologians, and that at the beginning of the sixteenth century the theological and juridical fields overlapped to the point of confusion, one can understand how Calvin could see in the *Decretals* a basic work of scholastic theology on a par with the *Sentences.*

Besides these two sources, the author of the *Institutes* appeals or alludes to only a few texts and ideas which he attributes to the *Decretals* of Gregory IX,[11] to Hugh of Saint-Victor,[12] to Theophylact,[13] to Guillaume of Paris,[14] to Isidore of Seville,[15] and to Bartholomeus Platina.[16]

However, none of the great names of Thomist, Scotist, or nominalist scholasticism are mentioned. Thomas Aquinas, Bonaventure, Duns Scotus, William of Ockham, Gregory of Rimini, Thomas Bradwardine, Pierre d'Ailly, Gabriel Biel, and Jean Gerson seem to be ignored.[17]

If one now asks about Calvin's intentions and uses of these materials, the reply is easy. Of the 69 direct and indirect references that we have enumerated, 66 serve to illustrate "the Roman error," or the abuse of "human inventions," or the falsehood of "sophist speculations." Even the three texts that our author uses in a positive sense (one affirms the priority of truth over customs,[18] another affirms collegiality among bishops and presbyters,[19] and the third illustrates true repentance)[20] are presented in such a way that the reader may easily conclude: "There even the sophists have to recognize that . . ."[21]

Calvin's resolutely polemical intention naturally influences the way he uses his quotations. I have compared, one by one, all of Calvin's citations with their form and context in the original sources, while allowing for the imprecision that might result from using an imperfect edition. I have arrived at the following conclusions: Of the 15 references to the *Decretals* where Calvin provides the meaning of the passage, 11 are precise and 4 are either distorted or arbitrarily strengthened; of the 9 times when Calvin quotes a passage, 5 are entirely correct, 1 is quite out of place, and 3 are distorted.[22] There are 10 passages from the *Sentences* cited according to their meaning, of which 6 are precise and 4 have a misplaced emphasis or a distorted meaning; of the 8 direct quotes, 6 are precise and 2 are distorted.[23] Here are some examples of distortion.[24]

Referring to priestly ordination, Calvin writes: "We shall begin with the order of presbyters or priests. For by these two names they signify the same reality; and so they name those to whom they say it pertains to carry out the *sacrifice* of Christ's body and blood on the altar, to say prayers, and to bless the gifts of God (Isidorus c. perlectis, 25. dist.—Lib. 4. sent. dist. 24. c. 8)."[25] The first reference is to the *Decretals,* the second to the *Sentences.* Since the two sources reproduce in almost identical fashion the same text of Isidore, we see that Calvin has brought them together into one quote. But he goes farther, and where both use the term "sacrament,"[26] he writes "sacrifice." It is obvious that he does this for emphasis in his polemical passage on the sacrificial character of the priesthood!

In another place, our author criticizes what he understands to be the Roman doctrine of confirmation. He cites two texts of Gratian: one is an excerpt from a papal letter and the other is from the canons of a particular council. Both stress the necessity of receiving this sacrament to become a true Christian. But in his criticism, Calvin uses the process of montage: he cuts each text in two, and he combines the beginning of the first with the end of the second. The result is that the inexperienced reader finds the papal thesis formulated in a much more inadmissible way than it appeared in the original sources. These sources reproduce actual directives that stress ecclesiastical discipline and law. By themselves they have no dogmatic authority, and detached as they are from their historic context, they are very difficult to interpret. This is especially true of the second text, which in Gratian already appears to be corrupt and ambiguous. Taken out of context, cut up and rearranged to appear as a proper doctrinal statement, this defective material appears in Calvin's text as a caricature of the original. Here are the original passage and our author's reproduction of it.

Gratian	Calvin
(Canon 1) All the faithful ought to receive the Holy Spirit after baptism through the laying on of hands by the bishops, so that they would become complete Christians; for when the Holy Spirit is poured out, the faithful heart is opened to prudence and conscientiousness.[27]	They add further: All the faithful ought to receive the Holy Spirit through the laying on of hands, after baptism, so that they become complete Christians, because
(Canon 6) Let the humble come to confirmation when they come of age and let them be admonished first to make confession so that cleansed they are able to receive the gift of the	
Holy Spirit. For he will never be a Christian unless he has been anointed by episcopal confirmation.[28]	he will never be a Christian who has not been anointed by episcopal confirmation. *This is what they literally say.* (Verba c. 1. De consecrat. dist. 5. In concil. Aurelian. c. Ut ieiuni. De consecrat. dist. 5.)[29]

Considering the way the material is presented, the phrase "This is what they literally say" seems unjustified. Also, it seems tendentious to interpret literally the last statement of Canon 6 ("because he will never be a Christian . . ."), if one regards this statement as an obviously alien element in the text in view of its relationship to what precedes it. We must assume that Calvin lacked patience and scientific objectivity. He uses this statement to draw the most absurd interpretation possible, that his adversaries claim that a person who is simply baptized is not a Christian in the full sense of the word, or even that they attribute to the anointing of confirmation the power to make Christians of those who were not truly such beforehand.[30]

The same polemical exploitation of a doctrinal weakness, a grammatical barbarism, or the juridical inflexibility of several texts of the *Decretals,* as well as the forced symbolism and complicated speculations of the *Sentences,* is also seen in other passages on confirmation.

For example, the *Decretals* give an excerpt of a letter from Pope Melchiade, which describes in a positive way the sacramental graces appropriate to baptism and confirmation. Calvin appears to quote the passage directly, but he gives the original statement a negative turn: what confirmation confers is not at all given in baptism!

We read in Gratian: "The Holy Spirit, who descends upon the waters of baptism filling [all] with healing, offers complete innocence in the font and presents an increase of grace in confirmation. And because we who are to conquer throughout our lives in this world must advance in the midst of invisible enemies and dangers, we are regenerated to life in baptism, and after baptism we are *confirmed* for the struggle. In baptism, we are washed; after baptism we are strengthened. And although the benefits of regeneration are immediately sufficient for those who experience it, nevertheless the aid of confirmation is necessary for those who would conquer. *Regeneration itself saves* those soon to be received into the peace of the blessed age to come; *confirmation arms* and prepares *for the struggles* and battles of this world those who are to be preserved."[31]

Here is how Calvin presents this passage in a negative way: "The Word of God is (Galatians 3): All who have been baptized in Christ have put on Christ with his gifts. The word of the anointers: no promise has been received in baptism *by which we are prepared for struggles* (De consecrat. dist. 5. c. Spirit)."[32]

The canon quoted next by Gratian contains a reply from the same Pope Melchiade to a rather trifling question raised by his correspondents: Which of the two sacraments is the greater? The pontiff admits no real difference in grandeur between baptism and confirmation; he declares: "Let it be known that each sacrament is great"; but he agrees that one might bestow "greater veneration" on the celebration of confirmation because of the presence of the bishop who administers it: "It is done by the greater ones, that is, by the highest priests." But he concludes by stressing once again that one must neither oppose nor separate these two means of grace: "But these two sacraments are conjoined, so that in no way (unless prevented by death) can they be separated from each other; and one rite cannot be complete without the other."[33]

Calvin, who no doubt became angry at the phrase "more worthy" in the title Gratian had given to this canon, did not want to consider the expression "each is great" or the term "conjoined." On the contrary, he detached the second sentence of the canon from the others. Calvin forgets that the canon dealt only with a disciplinary and liturgical directive, and he uses this fragment as if it were a doctrinal statement of the apostolic see. Here is what he writes: "Finally, they decide: (C. spir. eadem dist.) this holy anointing is to be held *in greater honor* than baptism, because the former is administered only by the hands of the highest priests. Baptism is distributed by all priests in common." Then, without paying any attention to what the source says ("in no way can they be separated"), he becomes angry with those who oppose this anointing invented by men to the baptism instituted by God: "O sacrilegious mouth, do you dare to oppose to Christ's sacrament the oil so befouled by the stench of your breath and enchanted by your mumbled words, and to compare it with water sanctified by the Word of God?

. . . These are the responses of the Holy See; these are the oracles of the apostolic caldron."[34]

We can note still other examples of distortion. Our author disapproves of a text attributed by the *Decretals* to Augustine on the necessity of satisfaction in the sacrament of repentance. However, Calvin does so without noting the attribution and implies instead that the passage is taken from his adversaries.[35] He also changes the emphasis of a remark by Lombard to suit his own purposes and has him say that the subdiaconate and the minor orders "were unknown in the primitive Church and were devised only many years later."[36] However, in reality the Master of the Sentences was merely stressing the excellence of the presbytery and the diaconate with this remark: "The primitive Church is said to have had these alone." Lombard adds: "The Church established for itself subdeacons and acolytes in later times."[37] In another place, the two canons of Gratian and Lombard offer a definition of the clergy and a description of the ideal of clerical sanctification (the latter symbolized by the tonsure). Calvin strips them of all positive implications and then uses them to illustrate a long polemical passage.[38]

This collection of quotations—some precise and others distorted, some rearranged and others with changed emphases—gives the impression that the author of the *Institutes* used two basic works of scholastic theology only as targets for his antischolastic polemics. It seems certain that the Calvin who writes in this way had already made up his mind about the "sophists." We may even conjecture that he did this under the direct inspiration of Luther, who found great pleasure in ridiculing the weaknesses of scholasticism. In any case, we have found several passages in Calvin's compendium where the traces of the *Babylonian Captivity* curiously coincide with the quotations from Gratian or Lombard.[39] It is as if our young author had placed the famous Lutheran treatise on his desk alongside the two works of traditional theology with the deliberate intention of condemning the latter in the name and with the help of the former.

This analysis leads us to ask what importance one should attribute to the scholastic formation that the future reformer received during his four years at the Collège de Montaigu.

Part One summarized all that the historical documents (which among other things are of unequal value) allow us to affirm about this period—which is to say, very little. In addition to grammar, we know that the young student of Noyon studied logic, metaphysics, ethics, mathematics, physics, astronomy, and psychology. We conjecture, along with Beza, that Calvin worked there under the tutelage of a Spanish professor of grammar who could be none other than the logician Antonio Coronel. I have good reason to believe that of the various divisions within scholastic thought, terminism alone predominated in this Collège.[40]

According to the historical documents, it is quite likely that Calvin studied only scholastic philosophy at Montaigu and that he had no real contact with theology as such. It is true that at first his father planned on Calvin's studying theology, but we also know that when his son was about to undertake this study, he withdrew him from the famous Collège to enroll him in the faculty of law.

However, one might object that in studying metaphysics and ethics— subjects that were often taught by the same masters who taught theology— young Calvin became aware of several ideas of Peter Lombard and other scholastics, notably those of the existence of God and free will.

Before we accept or reject this idea, let us recognize that its underlying hypothesis has eminent proponents in the ranks of contemporary Calvin scholars. For example, F. Wendel points out that Coronel "must have made a definite impression on the young man from Picardy by his philosophical teaching," and then comments about "the famous nominalist theologian," John Major (or Mair): "It is probable that he also exercised a more profound influence on the future reformer than one generally admits." And a little farther on, the same author asserts in an absolute way: "In any case, J. Major introduced him to the intricacies of the *Sentences* of Peter Lombard and the Ockhamist interpretation which he gave them."[41]

W. F. Dankbaar does not completely reject this hypothesis, but he has several reservations. While affirming that Calvin was actually a student of Major, he attributes to this master only an initiation of the future reformer into philosophical and patristic studies.[42] He also points out that Calvin acquired the greater part of his theological knowledge as a self-taught man, for apart from a few lessons on scholastic thinkers and the Fathers, he was never a student in a theological school.[43]

On the contrary, K. Reuter treats this hypothesis as if it were an established fact, when he affirms that the theological training received from Major determined a whole series of doctrinal positions with Calvin. Let us examine the most important points of Reuter's position.

Its fundamental element is obviously the conviction that the future reformer was in fact a student of Major.[44] Upon this basis, Reuter asserts that Calvin received from the Scottish professor a *Scotist* training with an anti-Pelagian and Augustinian slant,[45] presented in the categories of Ockhamist terminism.[46] In this way, Calvin was connected with the scholastic current chiefly represented by Gregory of Rimini and Thomas Bradwardine.[47] What did he inherit from these masters? Above all, an "anti-Pelagian doctrine of God," as taught in the Scotist-Augustinian metaphysics of the late Middle Ages,[48] and moral teachings derived from Aristotelian ethics.[49] In addition, Calvin also assimilated the theory of providence held by Bradwardine[50] and the doctrine of sin and justification elaborated by Gregory of Rimini.[51] Finally, in theological method Major taught his student a "positivistic biblicism,"[52] while awakening within him an interest in the texts of the

Fathers.[53] And all of this was offered within a violently anti-Lutheran perspective![54] This is surely giving a lot of credit to the Scottish master!

I must note that these general points of Reuter's thesis rely principally on a comparison of ideas found almost exclusively in Calvin's works which *follow* the first *Institutes* and very little on strictly historical documents.[55]

I have made it a point to examine several important works by Major, which were published in Paris and Noyon between 1513 and 1521 and likely were used in this theologian's courses at the Collège de Montaigu. This examination will help us learn whether the teaching contained in these works actually left any traces in the first edition of the *Institutes.*

I am especially interested in a volume that bears the title *Books on the illustrious arts and the sacred page by the most learned Scottish teacher and master, John Major; which he published while teaching on the arts faculty of the Collège de Montaigu in Paris.*[56] This title is enough to prove that Major, at least up to 1513, had taught arts at the famous college. Moreover, a letter of Antonio Coronel addressed to Ludovicus Coronel is found in this volume and contains the following praise of Major: ". . . whom they commended by virtue of his most sublime and mysterious teaching in *philosophy and theology,* not only for posterity but for eternity." This reinforces the idea that Major taught both theology and philosophy. However, the content of the work is rather disappointing. It is a collection of short treatises on logic written from a strongly terminist point of view. First, we find a "Quaestio de complexo significabili," then a first and second "Liber terminorum cum figura," followed by explanations of *praedicabilia, praedicamenta, syllogismi, exponibilia, insolubilia,* and *argumenta sophistica.*

I have also examined two commentaries by Major on the fourth book of the *Sentences,* the only one that Calvin quotes in his compendium. One is entitled *John Major's Commentary on the Fourth Book of the Sentences, edited by him and reprinted.*[57] The preface is dated at Montaigu in 1508 and leads us to believe that the commentary was used as a text for theology courses. A letter "To the Readers," signed by Petrus Tempestas, is inserted next. The text itself of the commentary does not follow the *Sentences* very closely. He grants certain questions—for example, that of the real presence[58]—a disproportionately larger place than others that are just as important, if not more so. Finally, he deals with so many subtleties that he loses sight of what is essential.[59] The principal authorities quoted are Pierre d'Ailly, Gabriel Biel, William of Ockham, Durand, Thomas Aquinas, Alexander of Hales, Hugh of St.-Victor. (Note that not one of these authors, except for Hugh of St.-Victor, is mentioned in Calvin's compendium of 1536!)

The other commentary, which bears the title *Most Useful Investigations in the Fourth Book of Sentences, by John Major, Doctor of Theology,*[60] is dated 1516, has the same characteristics, and in general treats the same questions as the preceding one.

Finally, I have examined an exegetical work of the famous Scotsman in order to see how he eventually influenced the young Calvin, the future Bible scholar. I chose his *Commentary on Matthew,* written at Glasgow and edited at Paris in 1518.[61] I must say that the book is more a collection of scholastic speculations in reference to passages from Matthew than a clearly exegetical work. Thus, on the subject of Jesus' fast in the desert, the author raises the question: "Whether God can feed a man without giving him anything to eat?"; and then this topic: "To seek in what way an incorporeal demon could move the body of Christ." On the Beatitudes he says: "It is doubtful whether a good prelate who becomes senile or ill . . . should be deposed." The reader who seeks primarily to understand the biblical text itself will not find it discussed.

However, we need to recognize that the commentary actually includes some of the ideas that, according to Reuter, correspond to certain statements by Calvin. The passage that affirms that "God alone remits sin . . . by his own authority" because "it belongs to him alone not to impute a penalty for sin on his own authority," and that the priest remits sins only "instrumentally and by command,"[62] does in fact recall several statements of the 1559 *Institutes.* One may say the same thing about a long section that upholds the principle of "council over pope" by means of frequent quotations from Augustine[63] and another that declares in an antipapal tone: "Christ, who is the head of the true Church, . . . is over the whole body, including the pontiff."[64] And another: "The Church is said to be one on the basis of the unity of its true head, that is, Christ."[65]

But the explanation of the granting of the keys to Peter especially shows a striking resemblance to the corresponding text of the *Institutes* of 1543 and 1559. Major emphasizes that in the person of Peter the entire Church received the keys: "Not one man has these keys; it is the unity of the Church which accepts them," since Peter only represented the entire Church ("figuratively he played the part of the Church").[66] In the same way, Calvin will speak of Peter as "representing the ecclesiastical unity."[67]

What conclusion can we draw concerning these parallels? At most, that Calvin was able to read several theological and exegetical works of Major during the years 1540 and 1559. But certainly not before 1536! Let us repeat: the first edition of the *Institutes* bears no trace of any theological influence from Major. There is even less possibility of concluding that Calvin took theological courses from this professor at Montaigu between the ages of fourteen and eighteen.

Let us summarize our findings. The first *Institutes* reveals only a very limited and superficial knowledge of scholastic theologians. Calvin alludes to none of the great names of the Thomist, Scotist, and Ockhamist schools, and he identifies scholastic theology purely and simply with Gratian and Lombard. And even with these, he quotes only a very small number of texts, which appear to him to illustrate best the Roman teaching of "the false sacraments." These quotations are chosen from among the weakest passages, or they are cut up, enlarged upon, or interpolated in such a way as to present them in an absurd light. We also have evidence that leads us to believe that Calvin adopted this way of treating scholasticism as a result of reading Luther, especially the *Babylonian Captivity.*

I believe that Calvin reduced scholasticism to two twelfth-century authors and used them for polemical purposes for the following reason: he became familiar with traditional theology only *after* he had read, appreciated, and assimilated the thought of the German reformer. We can see that after comparing Luther's profoundly religious, vital, dynamic, biblical, and Christ-centered thought to the dryness of the scholastics, Calvin judged Luther to be far superior to the learned compilations and speculations of Gratian and Lombard. Thus we can understand why he experienced no scruples about partially distorting them. Besides, during this time, such practices were generally accepted among all controversialists, evangelical as well as Roman.

Whatever may be the case, I do not believe that it is possible to suppose that during the years 1535 to 1536 the self-taught theologian had a profound understanding of true scholastic theology or even the books of the *Sentences.* If he had known them well, he would not have ignored the greater part to use only some very limited excerpts. Moreover, if he had known them according to a Scotist or nominalist interpretation which John Major offered at Montaigu, one would have necessarily found traces of this interpretation in the first *Institutes.*

Major himself is never directly or indirectly mentioned. Even more, not a single allusion is made to the authorities upon which Major drew, neither Scotus, Ockham, Gregory of Rimini, Bradwardine, nor Pierre d'Ailly. Several of these theologians appear in the work of Calvin only *after* 1536. Before this date, during the period of his religious evolution, we find no significant allusions to any of them.

Thus we cannot accept the hypothesis that Calvin had a proper initiation in theology at the Collège de Montaigu. Such a hypothesis is not confirmed by any historical document and is difficult to reconcile with what we know of the program for students of the arts at this college. To accept this conjecture, we would have to prove that Calvin, between fourteen and seventeen years of age, departed from the ordinary regimen of the strictest Parisian school to take the courses reserved for older students of the Faculty of Theology, instead of—or in addition to—lessons in grammar, philosophy, and science. Or else we must establish that the masters of Montaigu did not follow the program, or at least from time to time commented on the *Sentences* for the younger students instead of or in addition to the treatises of Aristotle and other manuals of the "liberal arts."

Could this really be the case with John Major, who taught both arts and theology? It is possible, but not proven.

To remain in the realm of what is likely, we must assume instead that at Montaigu the young Calvin, like everyone else, learned the various disciplines taught by his faculty. Thus he was introduced to a scholastic philosophy that included a technique of dialectical reasoning, a metaphysics that systematically opposed (in nominalist fashion) the divine and the human, and an Aristotelian ethics that was no doubt impregnated with scholastic casuistry. It is quite likely that all of this contributed to the dialectical structure of Calvin's thought and indirectly to the elaboration of his theological doctrine.

Like Luther, his principal tutor in theology, Calvin saw in scholasticism as a whole a dead and evil idol which must be overthrown. Nonetheless, just as the German reformer was formed by the masters of the *via moderna* and the thought of Gabriel Biel, Calvin also was influenced by scholasticism. But whereas Luther received this influence through his early studies in philosophy *and* theology, Calvin seems to have assimilated scholastic thought only through the philosophical teaching he received and then through his personal reading after the year 1536. One could also say that while taking up Luther's thought, Calvin assimilated—without knowing it—diverse elements of the scholastic system. But his conscious position was characterized from the start by an indignant refusal to accept this "theology of sophists."

CHAPTER SEVENTEEN
Calvin and Humanist Thought

Our historical inquiry has shown that for several years Calvin lived in an environment imbued with Christian humanism. He visited several friends (the de Hangest family, Olivétan, Cop, Daniel, Duchemin, and Wolmar) and was taught by several masters (Cordier, Alciati, Danès, Vatable) who were—at least in the beginning—followers of Erasmus and Lefèvre. Through contact with them he himself became a "biblical" humanist, an advocate of the inner renewal of the Church by a return to its original sources. Just as they did, Calvin came under the spiritual influence of the "modern devotion."

One may therefore raise the question: What traces of this humanism in general and the works of Lefèvre and Erasmus in particular can be found in the writings of the young Calvin?

To answer this we shall recall several results of the inquiry we have just completed regarding Calvin's early letters, the *De Clementia,* the *Psychopannychia,* and the first *Institutes,* and we shall add to them some new observations.

The letters are written in a typical humanist style which is elegant, pleasant, witty, and reminiscent of classical models. They are dated according to the custom of ancient Rome. They reveal the mentality of the best Christian humanists, which is free, flexible, optimistic, but takes seriously matters of faith. The letters dealing with his conversation with a novice, the events of October 1533, and the misadventures of the refugee suspected of anabaptism are the most striking examples of these traits.

His commentary on the *De Clementia* is the epitome of a humanist study of an ancient document. Seneca's treatise on the virtue par excellence for a monarch concerned about justice is explained by constant reference to other classical authors, including fifty-five Latin and twenty-two Greek.[1] The etymological method is used a great deal by Calvin. The ethics of Seneca the Stoic and the philosophical statements of Aristotle and especially of Plato sometimes receive due praise and sometimes criticism which a convinced Christian should address to them. We encounter in this work the perspectives of the Christian moralist, a disciple of Paul and Augustine. The views developed in the Bishop of Hippo's *City of God* help to complement the teaching of Plato's *Laws* and *Republic.* In addition, the influence of Erasmus is obvious. Just like the great man of Holland, Calvin knows how to dwell in the serene heights of the scholar; he does not like "the profane crowd," and he does not descend into the arena of the burning issues of the day. While extolling the clemency of the good prince, he refrains from making any recommendations, even by allusion, to his king, Francis I. This does not mean, however, that the commentary on the *De Clementia* gives no witness to solid social and political thought on the part of its author, at least on the level of principles.

With the *Psychopannychia,* the tone, the method, and the perspectives change. Unfortunately we do not possess the first two versions (1534 and 1535), only the corrected text published in 1542, six years after the appearance of the first *Institutes.* However, we can legitimately suppose that the difference between the first and the last version was not very great. Thus we may affirm that with this study Calvin presents himself for the first time as a true "biblical" humanist, from this time on engaged in contemporary controversies. He was no longer detached, above the fray, but involved in defending a scriptural doctrine, the immortality of the soul, against the heterodox idea of soul sleep. The ancient philosophers, especially Plato, were still used to define "body," "soul," or "spirit," but these heterodox judgments were being made in the name of the prophets, the apostles, and the evangelists. Therefore absolute priority must be given to the Scriptures.

I have tried to get an idea about which version of the Bible and what commentaries Calvin used to write his study. To do this, I have examined thirty quotations in the *Psychopannychia,* taken from various epistles of Paul. (We know the importance that both humanists and reformists attached to the study of Paul.) I have compared these passages in the different

Latin editions of the period and arrived at the following conclusions: 20 of them clearly and simply reproduce the Vulgate; 5 are entirely or in part taken from Erasmus' version, published in 1516 "according to the reading of the Greeks";[2] only 1 seems to follow the text of Lefèvre;[3] and 4 appear to be Calvin's own translation.[4] This eclectic use of different translations illustrates perfectly the independent mind of the young Bible scholar. In spite of Erasmus' and Lefèvre's distrust of the traditional Vulgate, which the Sorbonne so vigorously defended, Calvin thought it good to keep it as the basic text! He corrected it according to the versions of the two humanists only when he found he had no choice.

To explicate the texts quoted, Calvin does not appear to have used commentaries based on the Fathers, on the mystical views of Lefèvre, or the moralizing *Paraphrases* of Erasmus. In the thirty quotations examined, I have not found one clear example of exegesis in the style of Lefèvre or Erasmus. I must believe that the young Calvin took the trouble to reflect for himself on the sacred text, comparing passages with each other. He followed the Augustinian principle of interpreting the Bible by the Bible,[5] a principle that Erasmus' *Ratio verae theologiae*[6] and Lefèvre's *Commentaires*[7] were also careful to respect.

The first *Institutes* obviously follows the same method, although at the doctrinal level it proceeds in an entirely new direction.

It is paradoxical that this thoroughly evangelical work has a larger proportion of Scripture passages drawn from the Vulgate—so criticized by the humanists and the reformers—than does the *Psychopannychia.* Of the 30 quotations selected according to the principle explained above, 28 agree with the Vulgate, while only 1 follows the translation of Erasmus[8] and 1 that of Lefèvre![9]

The only biblical commentary whose influence on Calvin's compendium can be established with certainty is Bucer's *Enarrationes.* This fact demonstrates clearly the resolutely theological and evangelical orientation of the work. Certainly several of the guiding ideas of the first *Institutes,* such as its Christocentrism, its affirmation of the Scriptures as the supreme norm for all doctrine and ecclesiastical constitutions, justification by faith and *sola gratia,* as well as its criticisms of monasticism, the worship of saints, customs, and scholasticism, were dear to Erasmus and Lefèvre[10] as well as to Luther, Zwingli, and Bucer. But the important thing here is that the *Institutes* presents these ideas in a fundamentally Lutheran spirit and brings them together into a theological system that is entirely subordinate to the demands of the radical reform.

The two great masters of Christian humanism in France only served to introduce Calvin to an intellectual and religious current, which made it easier for him later on to choose a direction quite different from theirs. As a result of this change, humanism ceased to be an end in itself for Calvin, and simply helped to support the reform. From that time on, his principal guide, as we have seen, was Luther.[11] It is in the name of Lutheran ideas that Calvin, starting with the Preface of his *Institutes,* criticized those who first influenced him, and categorized them as "Nicodemites."[12] Calvin thought that they did not have the courage to break with papism and devote themselves entirely to the Gospel. The somewhat paradoxical fact that Calvin often preferred the Vulgate to the translations of Erasmus and Lefèvre shows how much he maintained his intellectual independence. The events we have described show how it became easier for Calvin to be independent of their intellectual and spiritual example.

In spite of everything, the break was not complete. Although the commentaries of Lefèvre and Erasmus do not figure among the established sources of the *Institutes,* we can assert that a good portion of the humanist heritage passed into Calvin's theology. We think especially of his method of exegesis, the importance attached to the study of the Fathers, the acceptance of a kind of "Christian philosophy," the respect for several thinkers of pagan antiquity, and the strongly ethical character of his teaching on the Christian life.

Even after he became a reformer and a severe judge of men like Sadolet, Budé, and Rabelais, Calvin could not help retaining several aspects of his humanist background.[13]

After this investigation of the probable or confirmed sources of the first *Institutes,* the figure of Calvin, this young, resolutely evangelical theologian, appears to have two sides. He is both a seeker who rejoices in every discovery and a master who is supremely free in dealing with his sources. As a seeker of truth, he certainly follows Luther most fervently; but this does not stop him from also turning to Melanchthon, Zwingli, and Bucer. As a master, he rethinks, reformulates, and reorganizes the material drawn from his sources, and he submits all of it to the supreme judgment of the Scriptures. The result is a doctrinal synthesis which, in spite of its incomplete development and its lacunae, was able to serve as the foundation of a program to criticize and reform the life and teaching of the contemporary Church.

It is this reformist criticism, so distinctive of Calvin's evolution, which still must be examined.

PART THREE
The Content of the First Edition
of the *Institutes*

In Part Three, we must limit ourselves to what is essential. I shall try to set forth only the basic doctrinal themes of Calvin's compendium that clarify and explain the reformed position that he maintained on the Church.

But first, in chapter 18, I shall discuss the specific structure of Calvin's theological thought. This will give us a better grasp of the way he formulated his fundamental principles, criticisms and ideals, as well as his reasons for doing so.

Then, in chapters 19 through 22, I shall deal with the main principles of Calvin's thought as well as several negative and positive views in the *Institutes* on piety, doctrine, and ecclesiastical structure.

Finally, in chapter 23, I shall clarify Calvin's idea of reformation and shall offer as a conclusion several considerations on the validity of Calvin's attitude toward the life and teachings of the Church of his time.

CHAPTER EIGHTEEN
The Dialectical Structure
of Calvin's Thought

Anyone who reads Calvin's work is struck by a tension that characterizes not only the method but also the substance of his theology. It is as if there are two kinds of dialectic. The first is the art of reasoning according to the demands of formal logic, which gives great clarity and strength to statements; the second is a habit of systematically placing the divine and the human elements in opposition to each other and then resolving the tension with the help of a principle that synthesizes the opposites.

We can explain the origin of Calvin's dialectical method not only by his thoroughly Latin intellectual temperament but also by his entire philosophical training, which was influenced by nominalism. Just the title of Major's *Books on the Illustrious Arts,* already mentioned,[1] gives us an idea of the accomplished skills of analyzing, making distinctions, arguing, reasoning, and discussing that the professors of Montaigu instilled in their students.

After this training, the analytical abilities of our young student must have developed further through the legal training he received at Orléans and Bourges, where the famous masters trained learned jurists and clever lawyers. One cannot overemphasize the importance of the years spent among the two faculties of law. Calvin left them armed for battle. Even in his attacks against Roman legalism and "human laws," he carried the victory, thanks to his ability to interpret and apply laws.

The humanist influence completed the development of the dialectical faculties of our young thinker. The reader of Erasmus and of the classic Greek and Roman authors learned not only to construct but also to love clear, logical, and well-balanced sentences. As one reads the truly masterful pages of the Dedicatory Epistle, one surely has the feeling that in spite of his pure intentions, sincere zeal, and distrust of literary glory, Calvin feels real satisfaction in writing. Discussing, accusing, defending, refuting, demonstrating—he obviously does all of this with the pleasure that a gifted artist feels in his work.

In addition, the historical situation in which the mind of the future reformer evolved was conditioned by constant antagonisms and intermittent persecutions. It is therefore easy to understand that his dialectical art soon became a weapon. He struggled to defend truths and save human lives.

Sometimes it even seemed more important to score a polemical victory against a dangerous adversary than to distinguish objectively between error and truth.

Under these conditions, we can perceive that the dialectical structure of his thought was not simply limited to purely technical matters but was constitutive of a system. The confrontations between men, parties, and currents of thought which all appeal, with equal conviction, to the same Author of truth necessarily involve the systematic bringing together of the human and the divine, of the sin of man and the thrice holy grandeur of God.

A profound bipolarity, a true inner dualism marks Calvin's thinking from the time of the 1536 *Institutes.* Here again we must recall Luther's influence. The forceful protest of the German reformer, often conceived in terms of hyperbole and paradox, and his fervent appeals in favor of reestablishing the ideas of "grace alone," "Scripture alone," and "the crucified Christ alone" must have made a deep impression on our young reader. Therefore the origin of several elements of Calvin's dialectical theology is to be found in the dialectical thought of Martin Luther.

Let us add that the way in which our theologian placed the Bible at the foundation and the center of his entire doctrinal synthesis, or rather the way in which he placed his theological work at the service of the Bible, certainly reinforced this characteristic of his thought. How did he read the Bible? No doubt at first as a follower of Lefèvre, that is to say, in a spirit of goodwill. But soon he read it as a Lutheran, in a spirit of uncompromising radicalism. In other words, Calvin's biblical reading rapidly conformed to that of the second generation of the reform: it approached the sacred texts from a perspective strongly conditioned by several ideas and events.

The future reformer assimilated the written Word of God in all of its complex variety: its alternate stresses, its paradoxes, its hyperbole, and its apparent contradictions. Now, these "dialectical" elements in the very source of revelation were not always unified or synthesized, because the harmonizing function of the Church's living tradition was often lacking. Therefore Calvin deliberately brought from the Scriptures partial statements that could illustrate certain oppositions that he held as important: the opposition between transcendence and immanence, between the thrice holy God and completely corrupt man, between Christian freedom and papal tyranny. When this tendency becomes excessive, it results in a polemical use of scriptural texts.

Lastly, there is a peculiarity of Calvin's thought which makes his systematic dialectic even more profound, what one might call his conceptual and existential dynamism. By this is meant that the author of the first *Institutes* manifests little sympathy for static and abstract constructions; on the contrary, he reasons in a dynamic way and in terms of concrete existence. For him, faith is a way of life which expresses itself more in action than in thought. Grace is a divine act which works upon man more than it works with him. The ministry is much more an instrument of the Spirit to pro-claim the Word than a sacred and sacramental position in a hierarchical order. In the first edition of Calvin's dogmatics, the "event" aspect certainly predominates over the "institutional" aspect. Its style, concepts, argument, and doctrinal content are all essentially dynamic.

On the other hand, Calvin clearly prefers concrete considerations to speculations. In this he proves to be in opposition to the nominalist tradition on which he was still dependent in other areas. Thus he devotes his attention almost exclusively to religious truths relating to the glory of God and the salvation of man. Even in considering God, it is not the essence, the attrib-utes, or the inner life of the Trinity that interests Calvin, but providence, revelation, redemption, justification, and God's glory which every creature is called upon to make known. One could say that Calvin almost always speaks of God in terms of God's relations with the salvation of elect human-ity and that he deals with man only in terms of his relations with God. Before the ineffable mystery of the divine being, Calvin respectfully pauses—he even defines religion by this restraint—to scrutinize only the life, the way, and the truth revealed "in Christ," in the hope of bringing about the reign of God on earth as it is in heaven. Calvin's theological thought, from its first systematic expression, is entirely dynamic and con-crete and—by this very fact—kerygmatic.

Given the abyss and complete difference which he recognizes between God and man, this vital and dynamic conception of things reinforces the bipolar and dialectical character of his theology. Once the relationship between the divine and the human is conceived more in terms of opposition than union, the intellectual expression of these matters cannot have a per-fectly unified structure.

In concluding these thoughts about the dialectical structure of Calvin's thought, let us stress two consequences: the one positive and the other negative.

First, it is indisputable that in the confusion that characterized the dog-matic teaching and religious practice of the period, this clear, critical, and concrete way of thinking was very helpful. To the precise extent that it protested against dangerous abuses and compromises incompatible with authentic Christianity, and to the degree that it forcefully recalled the forgotten rights of God, it constituted a necessary and salutary work of reform.

Second, to the extent that this dialectic stifled dialogue and destroyed the discernment necessary for comprehending the issues involved, it carried its own seeds of destruction. In studying several disputes and several quota-tions, we have seen that our young theologian often lacked objectivity and the spirit of dialogue. Even more serious: his dialectical theology, which was so vital and vivifying for many Christians, was destined by its very structure to fail to attain a divine-human synthesis. Even in Calvin's Christology, human nature remained to some degree juxtaposed to the divine nature.[2] For fear of confusing the two natures, the reformer refused to recognize the profound union between the divine and the human. In his doctrine of the sacraments and ministry,[3] several similar lacunae appear; one consequence was the failure to recognize the "sacramental" nature of the inner life of the Church and with it the refusal to recognize all the consequences of the incarnation.[4] Having said this, let us turn our attention to what is positive and bring out Calvin's early, fundamental insights which allowed him to formulate his criticisms as well as his program of reform in piety, doctrine, and Church structure.

CHAPTER NINETEEN
The Major Constructive Principles
of Calvin's Thought

After what has been said, it is not surprising that Calvin's fundamental principles in doctrine and practice, his basic intuitions, presuppose opposition between the divine and the human. These are principles that are expressed consistently with the help of the adjective "alone," which stresses the one and only in contrast to the many. And this is precisely the intention of our theologian: to bring out, to free the divine, who alone is worthy of worship, from the grasp of the human many, which is outrageously possessive and usurping. He ardently wishes to reestablish the primitive order of the Church where God alone is king and where the multitude of sinners necessarily occupy the position of servants and worshipers.

The Principle of "Glory to God Alone"

Although the formula "glory to God alone" is not found in the first *Institutes,*[1] it is indisputable that the idea underlies the entire treatise and is expressed many times and in many ways.[2]

Calvin does not analyze the concept of the glory of God and refrains from providing a theoretical definition. Instead, in conformity with his catechetical purposes and the biblical example, he explains that the entire world was created for the glory of God and that this glory should be manifest in creation by every person and by the entire Church as an exclusive, total, and absolute sovereignty.[3] This affirmation is made in terms that recall the ideas of Roman jurists and Roman law on royal or imperial monarchy.[4]

The very first sentences of the *Institutes* invite us to recognize this basic truth: God alone is God, and all that is not God ought to serve his glory: "Almost all of sacred doctrine consists of these two parts: the knowledge of God and ourselves. But these things of God ought to be learned by us for the present: first, that with sure faith we hold it as established that God is infinite wisdom, righteousness, goodness, mercy, truth, power, and life; and that there is no other [source of] wisdom, righteousness, goodness, mercy, truth, power, and life (Baruch 3; James 1). And whatever of these things is seen anywhere is from him (Proverbs 16). Then, all things in heaven and on earth were created for his glory (Psalm 148; Daniel 3). All this is due him by right, so that every single thing serves him for his nature's sake, recognizes his rule, honors his majesty, and in obedience acknowledges him as Lord and King (Romans 1)."[5]

God is the king of the universe, and he has the rights which only the sovereign of the world can have. God possesses "rule" or "dominion" in the fullest sense.[6] The glory of God is described by Calvin, just as in the Scriptures, in terms of royalty.

To God's right corresponds man's obligation to glorify him ("due him by right"). But what is it to glorify him if not to live and act in such a manner that "God's glory shines . . . more brightly";[7] that is to say, that his rule be recognized and manifested more and more widely. This is also the main purpose of our prayers: "Thus, let us pray that this kingdom of God would come; that is, that God would daily multiply for himself a new group of the faithful, who would celebrate his glory in all ways."[8]

Calvin especially stresses two ways of celebrating the glory of God: service and praise. Every creature must serve the Lord: "that every single thing serve him because of his nature";[9] and every earthly king "serve God's glory."[10] Every mouth must praise the Lord of Glory and sing for him alone. In setting forth the second commandment of the Decalogue, our theologian declares: "This means that all worship and adoration is owed to the one God."[11] And in reference to the first precept: "By this we are prohibited from directing to another our confidence, which ought to be placed completely in him, or turning to another to seek for help, or transferring to another praise for whatever is good and virtuous, for this is due him alone (Isaiah 30; 31; Jeremiah 2)."[12] The right of God to be glorified is exclusive and total. The worst of sins consists of "transferring" or "dividing" his glory and his praise.

"Whatever God does, let all his works appear glorious, as they are."[13] Everything that God does is glorious; may the entire universe, therefore, reflect his magnificence: "In short, let there be absolutely nothing in which the imprint of his glory does not shine; and thus in every heart and from every tongue, let his praises sound forth."[14] Salvation and damnation, happiness and misery, good and evil—everything should proclaim his eternal glory: "In everything, either prosperous or adverse, let us give him glory."[15]

One may assert without hesitation that for Calvin "glory to God alone" is the foremost and most basic principle, under whose aegis he undertakes his entire reform program. Thus, in the preface we read: "A great matter is at issue, namely, how God's glory may remain secure on earth, how the truth of God may retain its dignity, how the kingdom of Christ may remain safe and sound among us."[16]

The Principle of "Christ Alone"

The glory of God is manifested in an unequaled manner in and by Christ. Thus "the kingdom of God" and "the kingdom of Christ" are synonymous in the *Institutes.* The Son of God made man manifests the divine glory in a way quite different from ordinary creatures. He does so in an entirely unique manner, inasmuch as he is "wholly God" and "wholly man," and the "only Mediator."[17]

Christ is the only Mediator. This is the central dogmatic affirmation of Calvin's theology from its opening statements. Therefore we may qualify this theology as essentially Christ-centered.[18]

The name "Christ" and the expression "in Christ" appear hundreds of times, and the chapter that treats the Creed devotes eight times more space to Christ than to the Father or to the Holy Spirit.[19] This conforms with the kerygmatic intention of the author, who seeks above all to proclaim Christ as the only means and the unique path to God; to know Jesus Christ "who is the only way by which one comes to the Father."[20]

Christ is the Mediator between God and man from the moment of eternal election: "in him we are elected from eternity, before the formation of the world"; he is also the Mediator of our adoption: "in him we are adopted by the Father to be sons and heirs." But above all he is the Mediator of our redemption: we are "reconciled to the Father through his blood."[21] Nothing is more strongly emphasized than the idea that our salvation is rooted in the Lord, who is crucified, risen, and ascended to heaven.

Christ's coming has been awaited since the Fall, and especially since the promise that Abraham received concerning his "blessed seed, in whom all the nations of the earth will be blessed." Christ came to fulfill this promise and to wash away the stains of humanity: "And this cleansing was Christ, by whose blood we are washed, and by whose wounds we are healed."[22] Christ accomplished the great "exchange": "that taking up our weakness, he has strengthened us by his power; that receiving our mortality, he has given us his immortality."[23] Thus his death has become our life.[24]

In dying to redeem sinners, Christ was much more than a victim. In his death he fulfilled the priestly work par excellence: "This high priest was Christ; he poured out his own blood; he himself was the victim."[25] In him we may recognize the "priest who by his own sacrifice placated the Father for us."[26]

But the work of the Redeemer as mediator and priest certainly did not end at the cross. The mystery of the ascension reveals the royal, heavenly, and permanent character of the Redeemer, who will reign until the end of the world. In a long and beautiful passage in his explanation of the Creed, Calvin describes how Christ's priestly anointing and royal investiture are accomplished through the fullness of the Holy Spirit.[27] Then, on the following page, he expresses the mystery of the ascension: "Likewise, we believe that as he was manifested in the flesh, he sits at the right hand of the Father. This means that he has been constituted and declared king, judge, and Lord over all. All creatures without exception have been subject to his lordship." Calvin adds that the heavenly Christ is "forever our advocate and mediator."[28]

As royal priest and heavenly advocate until the end of the world, the Lord does not tolerate anyone seeking "other means of reconciliation" or "another satisfaction." Here Calvin underlines the theme of "only": "Behold, he who takes away the sins of the world. He himself takes away, it says, not another. That is, since he alone is the lamb of God, he is also the offering for sins; he alone is the expiation; he alone is the satisfaction."[29] To the end of the age he is the unique, heavenly intercessor; there is no other to whom we should address our prayers. Calvin states: "Thus we are ordered to invoke God in the name of Christ alone"; he adds: "It is clear that those who invoke God in a name other than that of Christ stubbornly contend against his commands." The special promises that God makes can be accomplished only "in Christ." This idea leads our author to speak of the one and only way: "Moreover, since he is the only way, or the one access, by which it is given us to come before God (John 14), those who depart from this way and abandon this access have no other way, and no access to God remains." To address oneself to a "private patron" is to commit the serious crime of *lèse-majesté*.[30] It is an empty and vain dream to think that there is "another way to be sought."[31]

As the heavenly king, Christ not only rules individual souls, he is also the sovereign head of the Church. The Church is justly called the "kingdom of Christ"[32] or the "Church of Christ"[33] or even the "mystical body of Christ."[34]

This powerful Christocentrism, the central principle of his theology, led Calvin to repeat continually the refrain "Christ alone" in opposition to all idolatry and usurpation of Christ's authority.

Against those who are "not content with Christ, and endeavor to penetrate higher," he declares that "we have found in Christ alone [*uno*] the goodwill of God the Father toward us, his life, salvation, and, in brief, the kingdom of heaven itself. He alone ought to be more than sufficient for us."[35] Against those who seek another doctrine than that of the Gospel, Calvin recalls with gravity: "Paul said (1 Corinthians 3), in the building of Christian doctrine the foundation which he laid must be retained, beyond which no other can be laid, which is Jesus Christ."[36] Finally, in opposition to those who believe they may find their salvation elsewhere, he proclaims: "And thus when we see the whole sum of our salvation and all its parts comprehended in Christ, let us beware not to judge that even the smallest portion of our salvation reposes elsewhere. For in him alone all the treasures of heaven have been hidden."[37]

To make his point clear, Calvin says again that to cleave to Christ without reservation is to anticipate the great and definitive manifestation of divine glory: "It is necessary for us to hunger for, to seek, to look for, to learn and study only Christ alone, until that great day dawns when the Lord will manifest fully the glory of his kingdom and show himself to us as he is."[38]

Note in conclusion that several other principles to which the evangelicals (following Luther) added the adjective "alone," especially "faith alone" and "grace alone," are found in the first *Institutes*. However, they are closely tied and subordinated to the theme of "Christ alone." I will not deal with any of them in detail, except for the "Word alone" because of its importance for Calvin's reform program.

The Principle of the "Word of God"

The expression "Scripture alone" is not found in the 1536 *Institutes*. But when Calvin speaks of the "Word of God," the context indicates that he almost always means the written Word of God, the only norm in doctrinal matters.[39] At the outset of this short discussion, it may be useful to bring out the nuance of meaning that this preference for the term "Word of God" represents. Better than any other, this phrase expresses the idea that the written Word is not to be considered as an entity in itself or as a group of lifeless texts. It is essentially the word of someone: a permanent revelation of the living God. Since this revelation is made known in Christ, the incarnate Word of God and King of the Church, Calvin does not hesitate to identify the "Word of God" in both its Old and New Testament forms with the "Word of Christ."

Calvin writes that the "Word of Christ" is the royal scepter of the glorified Lord. Referring to the passage in John 8:47, "He who is of God hears the words of God," Calvin notes: "In sum: since the Church is the kingdom of Christ, and he reigns only through his Word, will it not be clear to everyone that those words are lies, according to which it is imagined that Christ's kingdom exists apart from his sceptre, that is, his most sacred Word?"[40]

As the scepter of the king of the universe, the Word of God is perpetually exercised. It alone serves as the judge of truth and justice. Every action, every work, and especially every human teaching must be submitted to its judgment. To express this idea, Calvin uses several obviously dialectical expressions.

Calvin does not criticize "tradition" as much as "customs"[41] and "constitutions"[42] which are based only on their antiquity or on a human "consensus." The reformer demands that they be carefully examined to learn if they conform to the Word of God or not.[43] This rule is valid for all doctrines and all ecclesiastical authorities; neither councils, pastors, nor popes are exempt from it.[44]

Calvin especially wished to apply the critique of the Word, the true touchstone which can differentiate between falsehood and authenticity, to the sacraments. His principle is clear: "The Word of God must precede, because it makes a sacrament a sacrament."[45] If he mercilessly denies that the sacrifice of the Mass is a sacrament, it is because he does not find it "clearly confirmed by the Word of God."[46] What the Word affirms is the absolute uniqueness of the sacrifice of the cross: "The most sacred Word of God not only affirms but also proclaims and attests that this sacrifice was carried out once."[47] It is not very important if the error of the Mass is rooted deeply in Christian antiquity; the sword of the Word cuts through it in one blow.[48]

Preaching must also conform to the criteria of the Word of God and be judged by it. The pastors of the Church are only servants of the Word: "ministers of the Word of God."[49] In reality, their authority comes only from the authority of the divine message which they transmit: "Whatever authority or dignity Scripture attributes to prophets, priests, apostles, or the successors of the apostles is given completely, not to the men themselves, but to the ministry to which they have been appointed; or to speak more to the point, to the Word of God, in whose service they have been called."[50]

Every man is invited to obey the Word of God, and those who spend their entire life in this obedience will one day judge the angels and the world.[51]

One could give many more examples to show what tremendous respect the young Calvin had for the Word of God, how he forbade anything to be added to it, deleted from it, or mixed with it,[52] and how the Word of God represented for him the only source and the unique criterion of the truth.

The foundation of the reformer's attitude is surely his basic Christocentrism. In Calvin's view, the Word is truly the "Word of life" of the "good Shepherd" and the "one Teacher." He writes: "Christ alone should speak, while all others are silent; Christ alone should be heard, while all others are neglected and set aside."[53]

"Glory to God alone, in Christ the Lord alone, through his Word alone." Such a motto would summarize Calvin's three great constructive principles, according to which he conceived his criticisms and programs of reform.

Any impartial reader of the first *Institutes* realizes that, in spite of the numerous polemical passages, the aim of this work is basically constructive. It is constructive in the sense that the author does not wish in any way to destroy the present order, as would a pessimist or an anarchist; rather, as a true reformer, he wishes to remedy a disorder that he finds more and more pervasive. In other words, even in his verbal attacks Calvin is only attempting to signal a danger that he thinks constitutes a threat to the Church. His purpose is not to destroy but to describe a state of ruin in order to bring about the reconstruction of the fallen edifice. His most ardent desire is not to suppress but to purify, heal, and save. Even when he demands that something be suppressed, it seems that he is acting as a surgeon who operates only to remove a tumor or fatal growth.

With these characteristics in mind, I would prefer to examine first the positive message of Calvin's compendium and only later treat its specific critical content. However, the demands of a historical study oblige me to take the opposite approach.

Given the fact that Calvin formulated his ideas after having perceived distortions and abuses in the Church and after having experienced persecution for advocating moderate reform, the historian is obligated to examine the negative aspects of Calvin's work before the positive.

Therefore I will briefly examine in a critical and then in a constructive manner what Calvin said concerning piety, doctrine, and ecclesiastical structure.

CHAPTER TWENTY
Critique and Ideal of Piety

We take the term "piety" in a pragmatic rather than a strictly theological sense; and we understand it to refer to the concrete religious life with its different practices and devotions that center on the sacraments. It is this religious life of his contemporaries that Calvin wished to criticize and redress.

But when Calvin undertakes this evaluation, he has in mind an ideal that is much more theological and spiritual than pragmatic. For him, piety, which is the opposite of impiety, does not mean principally a group of practices or exercises; it means an inward and fundamental disposition of the soul which lives in contact with God. The author of the first *Institutes* gives neither a detailed description of piety, as he will in 1539,[1] nor a clear and precise definition, as he will in 1559;[2] but the idea is the same as that which he will describe and define later. It already underlies all that is said about the religious life of Christians in general and in particular. One sees it appear in numerous contexts as an essentially theological attitude brought about by affection for and filial fear of God, which results[3] in a knowledge of the living God and Christ, that is direct, faithful, and confident.

This filial piety is a fundamental virtue which serves as a support for other virtues, especially the virtue of religion, which for Calvin consists of a careful respect for the limits that mark off the inviolable realm of the Creator from that of the creature. Calvin presents religion as conformity or obedience to the grand divine laws that govern the human condition. Religion and piety together animate the true worship of God, which is an individual or common expression of the adoration due to the Lord and which in practical terms is identified with glorifying the heavenly Father "in spirit and in truth."

From another point of view, Calvin's view of piety is radically opposed to all that encumbers or alters the filial relationships of love and reverence for God. It cannot be reconciled with what Luther called "works righteousness," a spirituality based on human meritorious works. This servile and mercenary spirit that characterizes works righteousness and inspires the so-called satisfactions is diametrically opposed to the spirit of trusting faith, which is the very source of piety.

Calvin wants to contrast various superstitions and idolatries with piety as well as with the virtue of religion and the pure and legitimate worship of God.

It is obvious that Calvin does not present these contrasts consistently anymore than the terms "piety," "religion," and "worship" are always used with an absolutely clear and identical meaning. Calvin does not seek to determine the meaning of these words and concepts, nor does he seek to distinguish and classify them according to a definitive plan. This is understandable. The *Institutes* is his first attempt in systematic theology, and he merely wishes to proclaim in a contemporary and concrete way the complexity of the doctrine of salvation contained in the written Word of God.

In the paragraphs that follow, I shall therefore avoid any excessive simplification or schematization. I shall point out the basic meaning of various passages that criticize the practice of piety in the name of the fundamental virtue of piety. Then I shall retrace Calvin's ideal of piety, religion, and worship in his initial systematic work.

Calvin's Evaluation of Piety

Calvin makes a three-pronged attack against the practices of piety that were widespread in the Church of his time. He accuses the Church of multiplying satisfactions, superstitions, and idolatry.

Calvin's Criticism of Satisfactions

In condemning "satisfactions," Calvin directs his attack against the bastions of works of merit, the lists of penalties for penance, and the sale of indulgences.[4]

He deems that the custom of imposing on the penitent a certain number of prayers or good actions as an indispensable condition of absolution is incompatible with true piety. Calvin offers three reasons.

First, it is inconsistent with man's radical inability to correct his sin and it denies that justification is an absolutely free gift. He writes: "Therefore the ability to make satisfaction was taken away. Those who flatter themselves with this ability certainly will never satisfy God. . . . Therefore our sins must be taken away and covered up before God will respect any of our works. From this it follows that remission of sins is gracious, which those who assail us with their satisfactions obscure and blaspheme."[5] To God alone belongs the glory of justification. Those who seek to justify themselves blaspheme against the glory of God.

Second, the practice of satisfactions and indulgences implies that one doubts the supreme sufficiency of the expiation accomplished once and for all by Christ. Not to protest against such an error would be dangerous: "When the expiation of sins is sought elsewhere than in the blood of Christ, when satisfaction is transferred to another, it is dangerous to be silent." For the same reason, one must strenuously disapprove the belief in purgatory which underlies the practice of indulgences: "Therefore it must be shouted, not only by the straining of our voices but our throats and lungs, that purgatory is a deadly invention of Satan which empties the cross of Christ."[6] All of this is to be condemned in the name of "Christ alone."

Third, one would search the Scriptures in vain for a text to justify satisfactions: "To such lies," Calvin writes, "I oppose the gracious remission of sins; nothing is proclaimed more clearly in Scripture."[7] Here as elsewhere, only the Word of God is normative.

Our theologian is harsh toward those whom he calls *satisfactionarii,*[8] and their trafficking in indulgences provokes in him a feeling of bitter irony. The pope and his "bull bearers" pretend that "the price of salvation is set at a few coins; nothing is offered gratis."[9] In fact, these indulgences are only "pious frauds," "impostors, deceits, deeds of greed," and a horrible "profanation of the blood of Christ."[10] It is criminal to make people believe that it is necessary or even possible to redeem suffering due to the sins of anyone living or dead by fasts, offerings, and alms. Calvin asks: "Is this the penalty, which is to be redeemed by satisfactions?"[11] Cannot one see that such a belief introduces a commercial relationship between man and God in place of filial piety?

The same spirit inspires the theory of "supererogatory" works, or "works of supererogation." This theory affirms that after doing our required duties to God, we can still offer him a kind of additional payment which is highly meritorious. Calvin proclaims this theory to be contrary to the theme of "unworthy servants" found in the Gospel; he adds: "And thus the Lord orders us to sincerely determine and consider within ourselves that we take upon ourselves no unrequired duties, but we offer the obedience we owe." Woe to those who "nevertheless dare to glorify themselves by adding a puff of something to the just measure" and who "wish to sell works of supererogation to God."[12]

"To sell" something to God! The reformer finds this intolerable! Piety is completely destroyed where the filial spirit of love and reverence is supplanted by a servile, self-seeking, and commercial mentality.

Calvin's Criticism of Superstitions

The background of Calvin's criticisms of superstitions includes the prolif-eration of several semipagan practices of the time[13] as well as the polemics that Gerson[14] and the Christian humanists Erasmus, Lefèvre, Briçonnet, Roussel, and de Berquin[15] directed against these practices. Our author certainly took up and continued these polemics, which were reinforced by the contributions of Luther and Zwingli. We also must recognize that Calvin did so with extraordinary vigor.

Calvin does not define superstition until the 1559 edition of the *Insti-tutes.*[16] For the moment, his aim is to attack customs widespread within Christianity that he judges incompatible with true Christianity which con-forms to Scripture.

He frequently describes these customs by opposing them to true "reli-gion" and sometimes to "piety" and "true worship." Of the Roman sacra-mental rites, he declares: "They call this containing the people by religion, when the people who are dulled and infatuated by superstition are drawn every which way."[17] He refers to the increase of religious observances invented by man: "It has been done in this way for several centuries earlier and within our memory, and it is also done today in those places where the authority of the creature is greater than that of the creator. Religion (if it still deserves to be called religion) has been defiled by more (and more absurd) superstitions than any paganism ever was."[18] A little farther above, he identifies "religion" with "heavenly wisdom," which consists of "de-pending only on prayer to God." Its opposite is the whole collection of "perverse observances."[19]

A little farther on in the same context, Calvin carefully distinguishes legitimate religious observances that are necessary for good order and proper celebration of the liturgy from those which are tainted with supersti-tion and which are imposed on the faithful as necessary for salvation: "Nevertheless, with these observances it is always to be stipulated that they are not to be believed as necessary for salvation so that they bind con-sciences by religion; nor are they to be referred to the worship of God, as if piety reposed in them. . . . But when a law is understood to be made for the sake of the public good, there is taken away the superstition into which those fall who measure the worship of God by human inventions."[20]

Elsewhere, Calvin again stresses that lack of respect for Christian free-dom brings about a multiplicity of superstitions which, in turn, condemn souls to scruples and constant anxiety: "And the knowledge of this freedom is absolutely necessary for us. If it vanishes, there will be no quiet for our consciences and no end to superstitions."[21] Moreover, "if some superstitious opinion throws us into doubt, those things which were pure by nature are contaminated for us."[22]

What elements can we draw from these passages to establish Calvin's concept of superstition? The most striking and significant fact is that the reformer does not criticize the different uses of popular magic, such as incantations, conjurations, and the wearing of amulets, as much as the rites or ceremonies of traditional worship and ecclesiastical observances or institutions. It is the five "nondominical" sacraments and the sacramentals[23] that he most vehemently stigmatizes as a perversion of the order determined by the authority of the Creator over the creature. He discovers in regulations regarding fasts, abstinences, vows, prescribed feasts, and obligatory penances a blasphemous and reprehensible incursion of the human into the divine realm. When one realizes that for Calvin the virtue of religion consists principally in submitting to the divine will and accepting the rules or limits imposed by the Lord,[24] one can understand why Calvin considers superstition to be principally and diametrically opposed to "religion."

Sometimes superstition is presented as a remnant of pagan magic and sometimes as a residue or trace of Jewish law; but it is always a carnal attitude which degrades and brutalizes the people. As an example, we quote this description of the Roman observance of the Lord's Day: "For those who adhere to their constitutions exceed the Jews threefold in their crass and carnal superstitions about the sabbath."[25] Such a deviation from genuine religious feeling cannot coexist with worship "in spirit and in truth."

It is significant that the only list enumerating the different kinds of superstition is found in Calvin's comments on the commandment "You shall not take the name of God in vain." From this point of view, the sin of superstition appears as a revolt against the supreme law of "glory to God alone." The name of God is holy, says Calvin, and it must not be pronounced either in the administration of the sacraments or in oath "unless the glory of God or the benefit of the brethren makes it necessary." The Roman or papist ceremonies do not respect this rule, and here Calvin inserts his enumeration about "those who make [his name] serve necromancy, incantations, horrible devotions, illicit exorcisms, and other impious superstitions."[26]

By necromancy Calvin probably means the invoking of saints, by whom he means the dead who now live with the Lord;[27] incantations are no doubt numerous blessings pronounced in a language incomprehensible to the people;[28] "horrible devotions" are probably some public practices of penitence; finally, by illicit exorcisms he probably means rites accompanying the administration of baptism and sprinklings with blessed water.

These severe criticisms, except for what is clearly legitimate, seem to reveal Calvin's invincible distrust of a largely sacramental and "incarnational" understanding of the Christian religion. It is as if he constantly feared that material, carnal, corrupt humanity might cover, restrict, or "hold captive" the divine power which is supremely free and essentially spiritual. In fact, only with great caution and in reserved language will he admit the use of "holy signs" in Christian worship. He will accept, of course, the use of water, bread, and wine for the dominical sacraments, for the Scriptures prescribe it; but he will prove to be hesitant and indecisive about the laying on of hands.

These protests against superstition provide the background for one of Calvin's reasons for abrogating the Mass. He places the celebration of the eucharistic sacrifice on the same level as other ceremonies he considers magical and superstitious.[29] It is with good reason that after he ends his discussion of the Eucharist and proposes a sort of "order of the Supper" carefully purified of human inventions, he again comes to the Roman "order of the Mass" and claims that it is filled with "trifling histrionics, which have no other use than deceiving the understanding of the stupefied people." He adds: "They call this containing the people by religion, when the people who are dulled and infatuated are drawn every which way by superstition."[30] A text that is nearly contemporary with the one just quoted states: ". . . that no vain opinion about the transition of the bread into God, or any of their superstitions which they fashion about the impious Mass itself, may be established in our minds."[31] If we compare the two texts, we see even more clearly that in condemning superstitions, Calvin surely intended to reject the celebration of the Eucharist as practiced under the papacy.[32]

Calvin's Criticism of Idolatry

Calvin's criticism of idolatry focuses on three points: the worship of images, the worship of saints, and especially the adoration of the holy sacrament. Here the reformer seems to conform more than anywhere else to the spiritualizing tendency in Zwingli's theology. Just as did the leader from Zurich, Calvin contrasts the "true worship" prescribed by the Scriptures and the various practices and acts of devotion within the Roman Church.

While explaining the second commandment, Calvin attacks the veneration of images and in particular what the Middle Ages called "the Bible of the poor."[33] In chapter 14 we compared the principal sections of this passage to several statements of Zwingli's *Commentary on True and False Religion,* on which Calvin probably relied.[34] Without repeating them, I wish to point out the most characteristic critical ideas.

Since God is by nature spiritual and invisible, it is not only forbidden but absurd to express or represent him by material images. It is just and necessary to conform our worship to the divine nature and to adore him "in spirit and in truth." Therefore it is vain to justify the "execrable idolatries" of the papists by arguing that frescoes, paintings, and statues are not divine, but simply representations of the true God, Jesus Christ, the Virgin, and the saints. Nonsense! The Scriptures clearly state, "You shall not make for yourselves images or likenesses." There is nothing to quibble about. Every "likeness" is a concession to man's carnality and inevitably provokes a lapse into idolatry. Finally, the human mind will not believe in the presence of God "unless it is exhibited before him carnally." He no longer can see the invisible with the eyes of faith if he cannot perceive him "with his fleshly eyes." Soon man prostrates himself before the images themselves, adorns them with flowers, and expects miracles from them. To claim that images are necessary for the simple—"books of the unlearned"—is even more ridiculous. Simple people are much more sensitive to the pure preaching of the Word of God than one might think. Does not the Bible call them "taught by God"? We must not be afraid to treat them like all other Christians, according to this principle of the Lord: "He declares the preaching of his Word to be the common doctrine for all."[35]

For Calvin, the second form of idolatry probably consists in the veneration and invocation of patron saints represented by images and statues.[36] But we must recognize that he does not designate this practice specifically by the term "idolatry," although he seldom refrains from vilifying it. He calls it a "carnal" attitude which is impossible to reconcile with the exclusive adoration of God. Moreover, he remarks that treating the saints this way offends the saints themselves who do not wish to receive the devotion of mortals but want it offered entirely to the Lord. We read in the *Institutes:* "Those who choose or select for themselves particular patrons from the saints . . . are just as abusive to them. For they draw them away from that one will which they hold to be established . . . in God, that his kingdom would come, when they attribute carnal affections to the saints to make them more inclined to one or another of their worshipers." Calvin argues that there is profound harm in this attitude: "But thus they make them mediators for themselves, as if Christ had failed or was too severe for them. They dishonor him and deprive him of the title of the only mediator."[37]

In our theologian's view the third and the most outrageous form of idolatry is assuredly the adoration of the Eucharist. In dealing with this subject, Calvin gives free rein to his repugnance at granting too much importance to the reality of the sacrament. In no sacrament should we allow "the glory of God to be turned aside to the creatures." Trusting faith should never be placed in that which is only an instrument of grace: "And it is up to us to place no trust . . . in other creatures, nor to admire or speak of them as if they were the causes of our good. Thus neither should our trust be placed in the sacraments nor should God's glory be transferred to them."[38]

There is an even stronger reason why we are forbidden to adore a sacrament. Once again using ideas and even expressions that resemble those of Zwingli,[39] Calvin joins the Zurich spiritualist in battle against the eucharistic worship of his time. Just as did the great Zwingli, Calvin calls it "carnal adoration" and notes that Christ "commanded the sacrament to be received, not adored"; he appeals to the example of the apostles: "We do not read that they prostrated themselves and worshiped, but they were lying down, and received it and ate it."[40]

Calvin then mentions the practices described in Acts 2 and 1 Corinthians 11: "Those who adore [the sacrament] rely on conjectures alone and I know not what kind of arguments which arise from their own minds. They are not able to bring forth one syllable from the Word of God." The origin of adoration is simply "outside of Scripture." What does the Bible say about the adoration that we are supposed to offer to Christ? In reply to this question, our author stresses that the Scripture brings to the fore the mystery of the ascension: "by which it [Scripture] drove from us all carnal understanding of him (Colossians 3); and as often as it reminds us of Christ, it urges us to raise up our minds and to seek him in heaven, where he is seated at the right hand of the Father. He is to be adored spiritually in the glory of heaven, instead of inventing that dangerous adoration which is filled with a carnal and gross opinion of God and Christ." The papists have dared to fabricate an artificial God in place of the "living God" who alone is to be worshiped and glorified. In doing so, they have sinned twice: "For honor has been seized from God and given to the creature; and God himself has also been dishonored in that his gift has been polluted and profaned, while an execrable idol has been made from his holy sacrament."[41]

Therefore papists deserve to be called "idolaters,"[42] and their Mass, where they prostrate themselves before the host, the "head of horrible abominations."[43]

If one compares these passages with the epistle *On Fleeing the Illicit Rites of the Wicked,* published less than a year after the first *Institutes,* one realizes even better how much the young Calvin was convinced of the fundamentally idolatrous nature of the Roman sacrament of the Mass. The entire papal community is compared to Egypt "in which all the portents of idols and idolatry are observed."[44] Using the language of the prophets, Calvin compares participation in the Mass to fornication with idols;[45] and the celebration of the Eucharist is considered the epitome of all sacrilege, superstition, and idolatry.[46] This epistle offers its supreme condemnation of the eucharistic sacrifice, in these words: "Therefore the Mass is for us a fitting example, with which . . . one can compare whatever is recounted by the Scriptures or can be said concerning idolatry."[47]

The extreme limit of Calvin's criticism is to equate the heart of the Church's sacramental worship and the grave sin of idolatry which the prophets constantly condemned. Calvin believed he was right to criticize the practice of Christian piety in his time according to the great principles of "glory to God alone," "Christ alone," and "the Word of God alone." It remains to see what he wanted to establish in its place.

Calvin's Positive Definition of Piety

As I have already noted above, piety for Calvin refers only indirectly to what is generally called a "pious life." Calvin uses piety merely as a standard by which to judge pious acts. For the reformer, piety is essentially an inward and spiritual disposition, without which no act of devotion, no form of prayer or penance, no partaking of the sacrament can be in harmony with the divine will.

Piety

As with many other concepts, Calvin does not seek to define piety. Nevertheless, there is no doubt that this concept played a very important role in the first *Institutes.*

The term appears in the opening lines of the Dedicatory Epistle where the author indicates his reason for writing: "My desire was only to transmit certain rudiments, by which those who are touched by some desire for religion might be formed in accord with true piety. And I engaged in this labor especially for our French people, many of whom I see hungering and thirsting for Christ, but very few have been imbued with even a little understanding of him."[48]

In this passage, "piety" is clearly in a context dominated by the idea of the knowledge of God. One might even say that Calvin establishes an equivalence between initiation into true piety ("the rudiments . . . by which they might be formed") and a knowledge of the Redeemer.

It is obvious that Calvin is not thinking of a purely theoretical knowledge of revealed truths but of a vital devotion of all the faculties of the soul to the One who reveals these truths. Therefore he invites the reader to acquire wisdom by which one experiences God[49] rather than knowledge which only deals with God.

The vital nature of this "knowledge" is stressed again in passages on the living God, faith, and our filial relationship with the heavenly Father.

In his preface, the reformer declares that the doctrine that his evangelical brothers and he proclaim is not their own: "It is not ours but that of the living God and his Christ."[50] Then a little farther on he adds that this doctrine is inseparably bound to hope: "We place our hope in the living God, because we believe this is life eternal: to know the one true God and the one whom he sent, Jesus Christ."[51] (We note that God and Christ are constantly mentioned simultaneously, which is typical of Calvin's Christocentric approach.)

This vital knowledge of the "living God," without which there is no "true piety," is obviously the same as the knowledge of faith. To believe in God and to show piety toward him constitute two aspects of one and the same attitude. Our duty is "to worship God in true faith and piety."[52] If piety enables us to experience God, it is because of faith. In this sense Calvin readily speaks of "that faith which offers to us a taste of the divine goodness and mercy."[53]

In the same context of ideas, piety appears as an essentially filial concept.

God is our Father, we are his adopted sons, and thus it is only right that "we worship such a Father with grateful piety and ardent love, so that we might be totally devoted to his obedience."[54] As our Father, God promises us salvation which is unmerited and gracious: "The promises of the Gospel are graciously offered to us by the merciful Lord, not by reason of our dignity or good deeds, but by reason of his fatherly goodness."[55] Following this affirmation, Calvin returns several times to our duty as children of God to combat any attitude that would disrupt the divine-human relationship with the quid pro quo of meritorious works.[56] Then Calvin also stresses that our Father wishes "to be loved freely"[57] and that he desires to be served spontaneously and disinterestedly, not in a servile and self-seeking way.[58] Finally, Calvin declares that in view of our relationship as adopted children, eternal life will be granted us not as a "stipend" but as an "inheritance."[59]

In this chain of thought, it appears that piety is what one may call a theological virtue in the sense that it has God as its sole object. Commenting on the Decalogue, Calvin remarks that the "first table" enumerates our duties to God and teaches us piety, which is the correct manner of "fearing and loving God": "In the first table we are especially instructed in piety."[60] Inspired by faith, we are not directed by piety to men or angels but exclusively to the Lord. God alone will reply to our homage of faith and love and grant us his paternal piety for our filial piety. Our theologian uses several beautiful expressions to exalt the piety of God toward mankind: his "heart of piety"[61] and his "piety toward his children."[62]

Once again we note Calvin's idea that the virtue of piety is acquired only at the price of sustained effort. It is a love that is learned. It is learned by listening in a teachable spirit to the Word and the Law "by which we are instructed . . . in piety."[63] No individual, community, prince, or council should make an abstraction of the "desire for piety."[64] Quite the contrary, the entire life of every Christian must be a continual exercise in piety: "The entire life of all Christians should be a kind of meditation on piety, for they are called to a life of sanctification."[65]

In these last passages, the use of "piety" is an extension of its first meaning. The "desire for piety" may signify a preoccupation about doing nothing against God's will—which is close to the idea of "religion"—rather than deepening our filial relationship with the heavenly Father. The phrase "meditation on piety" may express more the attempt to live in a regenerated and sanctified way than reflecting on the deeper meaning of piety. Calvin would surely permit such broad interpretations, because he does not feel bound to a rigid definition. Besides, these broader definitions are connected with one another: piety as an effort to respect the divine will and as a desire for sanctification are based on and are an extension of the fundamental and strictly theological virtue of piety. In any case, this example illustrates very well a characteristic of Calvin's thought: in spite of its clarity, unity, and systematic structure, [it] never loses its fluidity and variations.

One may observe this more easily by examining passages in which Calvin uses the noun "impiety" or the adjective "impious."

In most cases these terms clearly mean an attitude diametrically opposed to piety which is directed to God. In other words, "impiety" describes all that is profoundly sacrilegious. Instead of loving and revering the living God and his Christ, it offends and dishonors them. Thus "all impiety ... profanes and pollutes this holy name,"[66] and therefore some papist laws are "manifestly impious before God."[67] Communion taken in an unworthy manner is an "impious sacrilege" against the body and blood of the Lord,[68] and the Roman priesthood constitutes an "impious sacrilege," a blasphemy against the unique priesthood of Christ.[69]

But in the examples cited, and even more so in others, the opposition between "piety" and "impiety" is incomplete. "Impiety" is applied more often to abuses of a collective and ecclesiastical nature than to a personal disposition contrary to the wise, vital, and trusting knowledge of God and Christ. This seems to reveal a particularly interesting aspect of Calvin's thought: in the first *Institutes,* Calvin's criticisms clearly have ecclesiastical implications, while the ideal he proposes generally appeals to the individual soul. Thus, certain customs, doctrines, and "human inventions" which enjoy the "consensus" of several centuries and play a dominant role in almost all Churches are declared to be "impieties."[70] In the same way, the papacy is called an "impious power,"[71] several ecclesiastical laws are called a "thousand forms of impiety,"[72] and a commonly taught scholastic view of confirmation is also labeled as "impiety."[73]

Among the variations on the theme of impiety we again stress that those which deal with satisfactions, superstitions, and idolatry are especially important. For Calvin, one of the most serious betrayals of true piety is without doubt the doctrine of indulgences. It is called the "fountain of impiety," in that it is the source of the practical abuses committed by the "sellers of indulgences." But what is most grave is that the doctrine of indulgences constitutes a "profanation of the blood of Christ and a mockery by Satan, by which he leads Christian people astray from the grace of God, from the life which is in Christ." By appealing to individual satisfactions, this doctrine denies that the blood of Christ is supremely sufficient "to achieve reconciliation, to make satisfaction."[74] Superstitions and idolatry also make love and reverence for the heavenly Father impossible, and therefore they too are identified with the sin of impiety.[75]

We must admit that the virtue of piety was truly basic for Calvin, for he frequently presented men as divided into two categories: the "pious" and the "impious." In agreement with the first meaning of piety, the reformer considers as pious the true worshipers of all times[76] and those who are able to maintain their confidence in God, even if the visible form of the institutional Church does not sustain them.[77] He especially attributes this name to all the "disciples of Christ"[78] and to the true sons of the Church, the "society of the pious."[79] To the "pious" are opposed the "impious" of all times, whether they be of the Old[80] or the New Covenant.[81]

By extension, Calvin applies the same terms to the evangelicals and their papist adversaries. In the Dedicatory Epistle, he declares his solidarity with the cause of the persecuted pious who are identified with the cause of Christ: "But I embrace the common good of all the pious, which is the cause of Christ himself."[82] Elsewhere, he challenges the pious to bear witness against scholastic impiety.[83] Calvin depicts the multitude of "adversaries" or "impious" as opposed to the little flock of true Christians. In the passage from the Dedicatory Epistle just quoted, Calvin affirms: "For the impious have succeeded thus far, that the truth of Christ, if it has not perished from having been purged and dissipated, certainly lies hidden, buried, and wretched."[84] On another page, he protests against the "impudence of the impious" who viciously slander the evangelicals' doctrine of justification;[85] and farther on, he does not hesitate to describe papal power as basically impious.[86]

To demonstrate that "papist" and "impious" are synonymous, we would have to complete this brief inquiry by reading the treatise *On Fleeing the Illicit Rites of the Wicked.* [87]

If we are not mistaken, we can now affirm that piety is the fundamental virtue of Calvin's spirituality. It springs from a personal knowledge of the living God and Christ. It constitutes a special attitude of the soul that believes in God, not with a theoretical and passive "historical faith," but with a faith that is truly trusting. Its principal characteristic is its childlike trust which is animated by feelings of love for and fear of the heavenly Father. It is surely not an accumulation of prayers, good works, or satisfactions that one offers to God in a servile and mercenary spirit; rather, it is a free and spontaneous desire to live according to God's will. Piety is also a distinctive sign to distinguish the faithful and the unfaithful, the evangelical and the papists. The first, with few exceptions, live according to a piety which the second, in general, do not possess.

As this fundamental virtue, "piety" for Calvin also supports "true religion" and "pure worship." According to its basic or extended meaning, piety appears to be sometimes associated with "religion,"[88] sometimes with "worship,"[89] or both at the same time.[90]

True Religion

Let us return briefly to what we said about Calvin's concept of religion in relationship to the superstitions which he opposed.[91] We have seen that superstition appears to Calvin as a dispersion of religious energies, as the "vain presumption" of a soul that wanders beyond the limits of what is essential and truly necessary, while the virtue of religion is characterized by a concentration of all the forces of the soul upon the one true Lord, by a strict respect for the limits of the relationship between Creator and creature, and by observance of the limits and the demands imposed by God.

One may gain a better idea of "religion," which at times seems to be a norm for action and sometimes a personal ethical attitude, by studying more closely the passages in which Calvin treats this subject.

Here is something quite surprising: without saying it directly, as he will much later,[92] our author follows Cicero in deriving the word "religion" from the verb *relegere* ("to gather once again" or "to reread")[93] rather than Augustine, who defines it by *religare* ("to bind" or "to bind again").[94] Calvin readily uses such expressions as "bound before God by religion,"[95] "to be held by religion,"[96] or "to bind consciences by religion."[97] A concept that upholds a kind of spiritual continence or modesty as an ideal may seem strange to us and quite unattractive, if we do not remember the historical situation in which it was elaborated and if we forget that it is closely related to the more comprehensive concept of piety.

During the first half of the sixteenth century, the religious life of Western Christianity often suffered from an excess of complicated practices, a proliferation of unbiblical approaches, an excessive number of ecclesiastical precepts, and other "vain presumptions." These were developed according to the model of pagan antiquity by several humanists. These practices of the late Middle Ages and the early Renaissance covered up the essentials in religion and emphasized the peripheral. For all reformists, and especially for all reformers who preached and wrote before Calvin, this religiosity appeared "false." All of them had attempted to cut back the excesses that they judged evil and incompatible with the Gospel; all wished to "gather together again" *(relegere),* that is, to return the Christian life to the limits determined by the Word of God. Zwingli's *Commentary on True and False Religion,* where religion is systematically contrasted with and opposed to superstition,[98] is perhaps the best example of the purification and simplification that was undertaken by the reformers.

Calvin reacted in the same way. It is very significant that in the first *Institutes* he also speaks of "religion" and quite frequently adds the adjective "true" in order to distinguish it from the superstitious religiosity of his contemporaries.[99]

Our theologian wishes to establish at the individual and collective levels, a spiritual and ethical disposition of "gathering together" again in accord with Scripture. In other words, he wants to establish "the true religion which is handed on in Scripture and which ought to be established among everyone."[100] With the prophet Jeremiah, he declares: "The Lord acknowledges nothing anywhere to be his, except where his Word is heard and religiously observed."[101] Also Calvin ridicules several ecclesiastical directives that are not based on any scriptural text: "Now, as I see it, the true form of religion is to be sought and learned from a source other than Scripture."[102]

The true form of religion, however, Calvin discovered with enthusiasm in the apostolic Church, that ideal form of the Church in which the "whole power of religion flourished."[103] On the other hand, he felt obligated to remark that the Church of his time "frolics about and luxuriates, going beyond the limits of God's word, bringing forth new laws, and dreaming up a new species of religion."[104] Calvin's plan for upholding "true religion" is quite clear. Both the faithful individual and the community should obediently submit to the "rules" of the Bible, return to and remain within its limits, content themselves with what is essential, and renounce all superfluous and superstitious extras in order to give themselves with fear and love to the worship of God in spirit and in truth.

"Worship in Spirit and in Truth"

Having declared that papal religion is not only superstitious but also idolatrous, Calvin turns to presenting the ideal form of worship. He does so first in his explanation of the Second Commandment, which forbids any representation of God in images.

Immediately after the quotation from the Decalogue, we read: "Which means, that all worship and adoration is owed to the one God." And several lines later: "Let us adore God, who is spirit, in spirit and truth."[105]

Worship for Calvin, then, is essentially adoration and should be addressed only to God. And since God is spirit, his worship should also be spiritual, that is, stripped of all carnal elements, images, and rituals that tend to be magical or excessively ceremonious. Thus the value of worship does not depend on special times or places. To imagine it does would be to lapse into the "carnal" customs of Judaism and paganism. The true seat of worship is "in the mind and heart"; the actual temple in which it takes place is of only secondary importance. "Those who think," Calvin writes, "that the ear of God is moved closer to them in a temple, or consider their prayer to be more sacred in a holy place, are acting according to the crassness of the Jews or Gentiles who adore God carnally. Against this it has been prescribed that we are to adore God in spirit and in truth, without any distinction between places."[106]

"It has been prescribed . . ." The proper way to worship the Lord is prescribed by the Lord himself. It is forbidden to invent anything concerning this matter. The sacred texts teach us everything that is truly necessary. God is offended "whenever he is worshiped according to laws of human invention, since he himself alone wishes to be regarded as the lawgiver of his own worship."[107]

True worship should possess the fundamental characteristic of the entire economy of salvation: it depends in no way upon the work of man, but only upon grace through faith. Calvin declares: "This confidence is necessary for us in no little way, for without it everything we attempt is in vain. For God considers himself to be worshiped by no work of ours, unless we truly do it in worship of him. But who is able to do this in the midst of these terrors, when it is doubted whether God is offended or worshiped by our works?" So-called good works have such uncertain value that one can never know whether they glorify or offend the divine majesty. For this reason the author of Hebrews places no value on works unless they are inspired by faith in the mercy of the Lord; "he refers to faith and judges them solely on the basis of faith."[108] Thus Calvin condemns the "ecclesiastical constitutions . . . which they heap upon us as necessary for the true worship of God"[109] and the observances invented by men which contaminate the pure worship of God.[110] He also warns against the danger of approving an act of worship only because of the splendor of its external rites: "Let us not judge the worship of God to be preferable because of a multitude of ceremonies."[111]

As we have seen, the reformer strongly insists upon the role of personal faith in worship which is truly spiritual and inward. But Calvin in no way rejects communal and public worship. On the contrary, he desires that all true worshipers participate together in the great celebration of the act of grace, the Eucharist. The Supper for Calvin is the act of worship par excellence. It "contains all our prayers, our praise, our thanksgiving, and whatever else we do in worshiping God."[112] It is here that we as a community spiritually offer ourselves as living sacrifices, thus giving to our Lord our "reasonable worship." This "sacrifice of praise" has nothing "carnal," nothing Jewish. It is part of the spiritual economy of the New Testament: "Paul has certainly spoken clearly when he called it 'worship.' For he understood the spiritual rite of worshiping God, which he tacitly opposed to the carnal sacrifices of the Mosaic law. Sacrifice of this kind cannot be lacking from the Supper of the Lord, in which, while we proclaim his death and render thanks, we offer nothing other than a sacrifice of praise."[113]

It is impressive to note the force with which Calvin insists upon the necessity of prayer "in the congregation" or "in the gathering of the faithful," and the care with which he describes the essential rites of eucharistic worship. He notes that since the Creator has given us a body, it is necessary that the body express the adoration that is due him: "Furthermore, since the glory of God ought to shine in some degree in the parts of the body of each of us, it is especially appropriate that the tongue be dedicated and devoted to this ministry, both in singing and in speaking. . . . But the best use of the tongue is in public prayers that are held in the gathering of the faithful, among whom it happens that we worship God in one spirit and with the same faith, in one common voice, and we all glorify him, as it were, with the same mouth."[114]

In spite of possible excesses, the spirituality of the young Calvin is far from being individualistic. As personal faith is inseparable from the "one faith," so every soul is invited to worship with "one spirit" and every mouth to pray in the spiritual chorus with "one voice." Calvin explains why the last three requests of the Lord's Prayer are in the first person plural: "The prayers of Christians ought to be public and look to the public edification of the Church and the perfection of the communion of the faithful."[115] If public worship should always be inspired by personal faith, it is also necessary that every personal prayer be imbued with the spirit of the community.

At the end of his chapter on the sacraments, Calvin gives a long description of the required ceremonies and the optional rites for the administration of baptism and the Supper. No ceremony is indispensable if it is not "established by God's authority."[116] This authority and this alone should never be overlooked. Calvin stresses that the Supper must be administered "most properly" and that the only essential rites are the opening public prayers, the sermon, the pronouncement of Christ's words over the bread and the wine, the recollection of the promises contained in Christ's words, the dismissal of the excommunicated, the distribution of the elements preceded and accompanied by prayers and psalms, and finally some words of admonition and prayers of thanks.[117] This form of public worship contains no superstitions. All these rites are based on Scripture and directly nourish the faith of the participants.

This is Calvin's ideal of "worship in spirit and in truth," as we understand it. This worship is the language that gives concrete expression to the inner feelings that come from the virtues of religion and piety. It establishes a practice and a life of piety that conform to the Gospel. We note again that the terms "piety" and "religion" are used endlessly in the passages that describe "worship." These three notions are mutually related and in a great many instances are interchangeable.[118]

However, young Calvin's criticisms and proposals for reform are not only applied to the external forms of his contemporaries' religious life. Beyond these deviations in practice, Calvin's proposals criticized an even more serious evil: doctrinal corruption. The self-taught theologian of Basle was not content to contribute to the reestablishment of "true religion"; he also wanted to undertake the restoration of "sound doctrine."

CHAPTER TWENTY-ONE
Critique and Ideal of Doctrine

From our examination of the scholastic sources of the first *Institutes*,[1] we learned that Calvin's criticisms were aimed at scholastic theology as a whole and made no distinctions between the various teachings offered in the schools of the period. We also saw that Calvin rejected scholasticism in the name of the "Word of God," the only criterion of doctrinal authenticity.

A preliminary comment is necessary. A careful reading of Calvin's *Institutes* clearly shows that "Word of God" and "Word of Christ" for all practical purposes indicate the Scriptures and for the most part are synonymous with "Scripture." However, as these phrases denote the dynamic and vital, the real and personal aspects of saving revelation, our theologian usually prefers them to the term "Scripture" (or "Scriptures"), whose meaning is not as rich and profound. "Word of God" and "Word of Christ" have a more spiritual and kerygmatic sound for him, while the word "Scripture" has a more technical theological meaning. Therefore, "Scripture" is preferred in passages where evangelical doctrines are opposed to scholastic ideas.

Calvin's Criticisms of Scholastic Theology

In the opening section of his preface, Calvin pronounces a terrible judgment upon men who, in the name of traditional learning, dared to persecute those who held evangelical ideas: "For the impious have accomplished this: that the truth of Christ, if it has not been destroyed after having been purged and dissipated, certainly lies hidden as if it were buried and ignoble."[2]

The expressions are striking: the truth of Christ, without being eliminated—which would be impossible—is "buried alive." Buried under what? The polemical passages of Calvin's compendium state the answer clearly: under an inextricable array of complicated ideas that have no foundation in the Scriptures; in other words, under an inert mass of artificial reasonings that are useless for the work of salvation.[3] This doctrinal system hides the truth instead of transmitting it, because it is entirely under the sway of formal logic and syllogisms. Calvin never stops attacking the representatives of this logic, whom he delights in calling "sophists," "scholastic sophists," and "inventors of ratiocinations."

These theologians are incorrigibly curious men who are not content with what God has willed to reveal but seek to explain the inexplicable and to define the undefinable. Thus they trouble souls and cause rival factions within the Church. To cite an example: "The Church is miserably vexed, while curious men wish to define in what way Christ's body is present in the bread." These impudent men have claimed to perfect the simple and clear doctrine of the Scriptures by their own fuzzy thinking: "They added to the simplicity of Scripture."[4] Acting this way shows a complete lack of humility and docility before the Author of truth: "But if in humility (which is proper) the inventors of such ratiocinations kept all these understandings of their imaginations under the Word of God, they would certainly have heeded what he himself said."[5] Such theology has no respect for mystery!

Babbling scholars like these men do not know how to listen to the Lord, and they constantly interrupt his word! For example, those who invented the adoration of the holy sacrament prove that they lack all docility before Scripture: "Those who thought up the adoration of the sacrament have dreamed it by themselves, apart from Scripture. . . . By this they despised God, who does not allow anything to be added to his Scripture or anything to be taken from it."[6]

When our author comments on the traditional interpretation of John 20 and Matthew 18 about the power of absolution, he notes: "From these two [passages] . . . these mad men, carried away by their own dizziness, try without any discrimination to establish confession, then excommunication, then jurisdiction, then the right to present laws, and then indulgences."[7] These "madmen" make the Bible say what they wish. They violate it and cut it up, they rearrange and falsify its texts—they use the Bible without any discernment. Calvin severely condemns the scholastic attempt to justify communion in one kind: "I certainly know that these ministers of Satan, as their custom is to hold the Scriptures in contempt, ridicule this and treat it cavalierly."[8]

Without making any distinctions, the young reformer condemns in one sweep the unscriptural—or even antiscriptural—theology of his time as a world apart from patristic theology. "All the Fathers," Calvin writes, "with one heart decried and with one voice detested the fact that the holy Word of God was contaminated by the arguments of the sophists and entwined by the squabbles of dialecticians. Do they keep themselves within limits, when they do nothing in their whole life other than ensnare and enwrap the simplicity of Scripture in their endless contentions and worse than sophisticated quarrels? If the Fathers were revived and they heard this kind of quarreling (which they call speculative theology), they would not at all believe that they were disputing about God."[9] Calvin holds the supporters of this theology in such contempt that he often refuses to acknowledge them as theologians. He sees them as sophists, prisoners of their syllogisms,[10] miserable people to whom the true "philosophy of Christ" (which is communicated directly by God) remains incomprehensible: "This indeed is that secret and hidden philosophy which cannot be derived from syllogisms."[11]

What has just been said shows how Calvin viewed the relationship between the doctrinal system which he criticized and the doctrinal tradition of the Church. By opposing the Fathers, the privileged witnesses of this tradition, to the scholastics, Calvin implicitly recognized the validity of tradition in dogma that was content to explain and clarify the Word of God. But in accepting this tradition, Calvin had as his criterion conformity with the Scriptures. Antiquity alone was not enough. Nor was universality. Thus Calvin rejects much traditional doctrine, because he judged that it lacked foundation in the sacred texts. He scornfully labels as "novelties" those doctrines which contradict the source of revelation and the teaching of the Fathers which are faithful to the Scriptures. Statements concerning the five "false sacraments" especially fall into this category. "But this has been taken away from men, that they cannot establish new sacraments in the Church of God; thus it is to be desired that those which are from God be mixed with those things of human invention as little as possible."[12] Of confirmation our author states: "If only we had retained the custom, which I suspect was found among the ancients before this abortive mask of a sacrament was born."[13] Because these sacraments seem to be instituted "without the Word of God," he rejects them as "new and strange dogmas"[14] or "new doctrines."[15]

Obviously Calvin's adversaries would reply that their doctrine on the seven sacraments goes back to the primitive Church. Calvin does not try to contest this fact. Yes, he responds, this opinion is of very ancient origin and universally recognized: "That opinion about the seven sacraments, a trite opinion of almost everyone which has flourished in all the schools and congregations, has put down roots from antiquity and even now has implanted itself in the minds of men."[16] Calvin also recognizes that certain nonscriptural rites associated with baptism and the Last Supper go back to the times immediately following the apostles: "If someone wishes to maintain these sorts of inventions by their antiquity, I myself am not ignorant of the fact that the use of the chrism and exsufflation is ancient, and that not long after the age of the apostles the Supper of the Lord was tainted by mold."[17] But he refuses to recognize this ancient origin as a reason to legitimize these doctrines and practices, for all "human inventions" that come after the definitive promulgation of essential truths in Christ can only be superfluous and harmful.[18]

The first *Institutes* presents scholastic theology as complicated, sterile, unscriptural, too human and syncretistic.[19] To understand Calvin's criticisms properly, we must notice first that he does not distinguish between dogmatic teaching and theological opinions. Second, his criticisms refer almost exclusively to the doctrine of the sacraments or the sacramental structure of the Church. All the passages that I have quoted relate more or less directly to a sacramental context. This fact strongly reinforces the conclusions that I have drawn from my examination of the scholastic sources of the *Institutes* and from Calvin's statements on superstition and idolatry: for the young Calvin the most intolerable scandal of the Church is that for centuries responsible doctors have insisted upon humanizing the divine and making grace material. The multiplying of sacraments clearly indicates this tendency, and the notion that the Church is the medium of salvation demonstrates it even more. There is only one way to eliminate these tendencies once and for all: return to the holy and pure original doctrine of the Scriptures.

True Doctrine Founded Upon the "Simplicity of Scripture"

In contrast to the complicated and artificial nature of scholastic theology, Calvin emphasizes the simple and "natural" character of doctrine contained in Scripture. He enthusiastically speaks of the "true and simple purity of God's Word."[20]

To understand what Calvin meant by "the simplicity of Scripture," we must recall what he asserted about the divine and Christlike essence of the "Word." Behind the idea of the simplicity of Scripture, there is the absolute simplicity of the One who reveals himself in Scripture. It is probable that Calvin has in mind the pedagogical aspect of revelation which he already stressed in his first preface to Olivétan's Bible[21] and in the *Institutes* on the subject of the "books of the ignorant."[22] Calvin thinks that the Lord always prefers to reveal himself to the poor, to the simple, to the humble; it is therefore logical that his message be written in a language accessible to all. Therefore the Scripture written in the language of the people can and should be placed in everyone's hands. It contains "the common doctrine" which "the ignorant"—these people illumined by the Spirit and "taught by God" par excellence—can understand as well as, if not better than, the most erudite and learned.

Finally, we note that this insistence upon the simplicity of Scripture is entirely appropriate for a compendium whose declared aim is to furnish the "rudiments," a sort of ABC,[23] for those who desire to know Christ and to be initiated "in true piety." In the very first line of his preface Calvin says: "The book itself, framed according to a simple and, as it were, rudimentary form of teaching, declares that this was my proposed purpose."[24]

Let us examine the text. In a passage that brings out the difference between the theology of the Fathers and that of the scholastics, our author praises Augustine: "It was a Father . . . who pointed out the temerity of defining in any way an obscure matter without the clear and obvious testimonies of Scripture."[25] A few lines farther on, he protests against procedures that "cover up" or obscure the clarity of the sacred text. Why complicate things when the language chosen by God is itself so clear and obvious?[26]

When dealing with the real presence of the Eucharist, we must also be content with the "simplicity of Scripture."[27] In trying to define Christian penance, one must proceed "simply according to the rule of Scripture."[28] In trying to determine the words that best express the unity of essence and the diversity of persons in the Trinity, one should mistrust everything that "draws one away from the simplicity of the Word of God." The general rule for preparing valid theological terms is the following: "The rules of speaking and thinking are certainly to be sought from the Scriptures; all the thoughts of the mind and the words of the mouth are to be examined according to this standard."

At this point, Calvin recognizes that even Scripture can sometimes appear obscure to our limited intelligence. In such a case, he admits that one could legitimately explain and interpret Scripture by using concepts that are not strictly scriptural, on the condition that one never lose sight of the general truth of Scripture.[29]

The best exegetical method is always to clarify partial and relative obscurities in Scripture by those passages of Scripture whose meaning is clear. This is the method of the analogy of faith already recommended by Paul: "When Paul (Romans 12) wanted all prophecy to be formed according to the analogy of faith, he put forth a most certain standard by which any interpretation of Scripture ought to be tested."[30] This is a case in which the exception really confirms the rule: in the final analysis, a passage of the Bible that seems complicated and obscure only draws attention to the clarity of the other passages to which we turn to explain it.[31]

God is simple. His Word is straightforward and accessible to the most simple people. Consequently, valid dogmatic pronouncements should also be expressed in an elegant simplicity which in no way detracts from their profundity. Thus Calvin introduces his explanation of the Creed with this concise sentence: "Now let us hear the simple confession of truth."[32]

Every text in which our theologian describes the ideal form of Christian doctrine falls within this perspective. For instance, this statement: "All things that pertain to Christianity are comprehended and prescribed in the Scriptures."[33] Therefore Calvin desires to formulate, teach, and defend what he calls "sound doctrine" that accords with Scripture.[34] This is in no way a "new theology" set forth by a new school. Those who uphold it may declare with assurance: "But our doctrine must stand victorious over all the sublime glory and power of the world; because it is not our doctrine, but the doctrine of the living God and his Christ, whom the Father has established as king, . . . so that he might smash the whole earth with his iron and brazen strength, with his golden and silver splendor, and strike it by the rod of his mouth, as if it were a potter's vessel."[35] The word of Christ, his scepter of government, is also a rod that strikes. Through the words of evangelical theologians it strikes the wretched earthen vessel of scholastic theology which by its "novelties" has perverted the original Christian dogma. In the face of these novelties Calvin declares: "Therefore, content with the perfection of Christ's doctrine, let us learn to fashion nothing new for ourselves and admit nothing devised by others."[36]

Calvin wishes to spread sacred doctrine, the doctrine of Jesus Christ set forth in the simplicity of Scripture, to glorify God and to reestablish his Church.

CHAPTER TWENTY-TWO
Critique and Ideal
of the Ecclesiastical Structures

We have had several opportunities to stress that, beginning with the first *Institutes,* where ecclesiology is still found less developed than in subsequent editions, Calvin demonstrates a true "ecclesiastical sense." He is probably indebted to Bucer on the theological level for the basic elements of his concept of the Church.[1] But it is certainly his legal studies that gave him the means of expressing with clarity a critical and reformist attitude toward the practical organization of the Christian community, that is, ecclesiastical structures. It should be said again that he seems to have borrowed his critical ideas from Luther, specifically from the *Babylonian Captivity.*[2]

However, Calvin's competence as a lawyer never pushed him to excessive legalism. When he spoke of Church structure as a lawyer, he never forgot that this Church was, above all, an object of faith. The legal form of his indictments and his reform projects was only a means of emphasizing the spiritual reality of the Church, "the universal number of the elect," the people and the reign of God, the communion of the saints and the mystical body of Christ. His knowledge of civil and canon law helped him to react against Roman legalism which made the Church resemble a kingdom of this world and which prevented the Church from seeing itself in terms of mystical and Christ-centered communion.

Calvin's Criticism of the "Papal Kingdom"

On the strength of his very rudimentary but scriptural and Christ-centered ecclesiology, Calvin addresses a merciless indictment against papalism, clericalism, and the corruption of the ministry.

At the time when he was writing his book, the papacy no longer enjoyed indisputable authority. Since Gregory VII, the pontifical power had attempted to impose its supremacy on the Holy Roman Empire, and thereby it had become secularized to the extreme. Rome's spiritual authority had been universally respected a short time ago, but it became a prisoner of its political and financial dealings and began to be more and more like an Italian principality. The evils of simony and nepotism began to undermine it. Antipapal criticisms aimed at individuals as well as the institution itself became commonplace in Western Christianity. These criticisms were brought about and intensified by many factors: the struggles between Philip the Fair and Boniface VIII (1302–1303); the period of the Avignon papacy

(1309–1377) and Wyclif's writings; the Great Schism of the West (1378–1429) and the protests of Hus; conciliarist ideas; the abuses under the pontificates of Alexander VI, Julius II, and Leo X; and finally the great protest of Martin Luther.[3] Calvin only had to take up the arguments of his many predecessors.

Starting with the preface of his work, Calvin protests against the practical identification of the Church with the papacy.[4] He opposes the excessively temporal character of the Church and emphasizes forcefully that the people of God do not need visible appearances, for the kingdom of Christ is primarily spiritual. "Our controversy," Calvin writes, "turns on these hinges: first, they contend that the form of the Church must always be apparent and visible; and then they establish that same form in the see of Rome and its order of leadership."[5] No, the Church of Christ cannot be reduced to the "external splendor" of the Roman see. Even less should one identify it purely and simply with the hierarchy. "The pope . . . of Rome, who holds the apostolic see, and the other bishops represent the Church; and they ought to be considered as the Church. Therefore they cannot err."[6] Such pretension is intolerable.

Following the logic of his premises, Calvin is careful not to attribute the title of "Catholic Church" to the papacy or the papists. Instead, he calls them the "papal kingdom"[7] or even the "church of the Antichrist."[8] This is an important distinction, for it indicates that the young reformer does not think of rebelling against the one, holy, catholic and apostolic Church, but only against its distortions. Since nothing is more unjust than to desire to defend these distortions under the pretext that they belong to the Church, he cries out: "And we still cover up such abominations with the name of the Church and defend them under this pretext!"[9] The cancer is in the body; it is not the body itself. The "church" of the Antichrist claims to supplant the Church, but it is not the Church.

We read the most severe judgment of pontifical power in the chapter on "Christian Freedom": "There is no reason why anyone would doubt that the spiritual power, on which the pope with his whole kingdom prides himself, is a wicked tyranny opposed to the Word of God and an unjust tyranny against the people of God." The abuses of "new doctrines," "new laws," and universal jurisdiction are obviously all contrary to the Scriptures. A power that is responsible for such misdeeds no longer has anything in common with Christ but is merely an immense enterprise of outrageous dominion which has usurped the exclusive reign of the Lord. The reformer proclaims: "If we allowed Christ to rule among us, all that kind of domination would be overturned easily and cast down."[10]

If Calvin had studied theology with the conciliarist John Major or other doctors of the same persuasion, he would have asserted here or elsewhere the principle of "council over the pope." But he does nothing of the kind. In the Dedicatory Epistle where he first speaks of a council, Calvin stresses its "external" nature and its inability to lead to clear and irrevocable decisions. He cites the Council of Basle which, in spite of its external guarantees of legitimacy ("to which nothing in external majesty was lacking"), could not enforce its decision to depose Pope Eugenius IV as a schismatic. Calvin, a clever lawyer, notes the dilemma this caused for posterity. He concludes that it is better not to seek a guarantee of legitimacy in purely human criteria: "The Church is not bound to external pomp." Immediately before the example of Basle, another quite respectable and very official council is mentioned, the Sanhedrin that condemned Jesus: "Did not such splendor shine forth in that council which the priests, scribes, and Pharisees called, to take counsel together about killing Christ?"[11] This severe judgment concerning the "external masks" of the councils seems to prove clearly that young Calvin was not influenced by the conciliarism of John Major or of anyone else.[12]

In another place, the reformer attempts to show that even in dogmatic matters the validity of conciliar decisions is completely relative. He writes: "Therefore, let them name the councils of bishops a thousand times; they accomplish little. For they will not succeed in making us believe what they contend, namely, that a council is ruled by the Holy Spirit, before they establish with confidence that it is gathered in Christ's name. Impious and improper bishops can conspire against Christ, just as much as good and proper bishops can gather in his name." These councils are not necessarily infallible, and sometimes even "oracles of Satan" are uttered "through the service of councils"! Calvin also mentions the "councils that are in conflict with councils"[13] and the synods that contradict Catholic teaching: "Indeed, doctrinal [decisions] sometimes have been seen to be strongly at variances with each other." Only after he has forcefully demonstrated the weakness of councils does our theologian admit that there are some positive exceptions: "But I am not arguing . . . here that all councils are to be damned or the acts of all are to be rescinded. For I see a true desire for piety shine forth in some of them, especially in the ancient ones."

All these considerations are strongly characterized by distrust. I think that the basic reason for this is once again Calvin's denial of the Church's "sacramental" nature, in the traditional sense of the word. At least this is what appears in the final observation of Calvin's treatment of councils: "Now let them go and boast, as their custom is, that the Holy Spirit is affixed and fettered to their councils."[14]

Having rejected papal claims and questioned the disciplinary and doctrinal value of councils, Calvin also criticized the arbitrary division of the people of God into clergy and laity. For Calvin, all Christians are basically equal.[15] None should be able to take advantage of a special consecration to dominate others. All are equally under the guidance of the Holy Spirit, who, through its various gifts, raises up different ministries wherever it wills.

Calvin accepts the word "clergy" but rejects "laity." To his way of

thinking, the word "clergy" maintains its etymological sense of "inheritance" which he applies to all the faithful who together constitute without
distinction the inheritance that the Father gave to his incarnate Son. By this
very fact, the word "laity" becomes useless and superfluous.

Calvin writes: "They are called clergy because of the lot, or because they
are chosen by the Lord, or because of the lot of the Lord, or because they
have God as their portion. But it was a sacrilege to usurp this title for
themselves, which belonged to the whole Church. For it is that inheritance
of Christ given to him by the Father. For Peter did not call a few shaved
men 'clergy' (as they improperly imagine) but the whole people of God (1
Peter 5)."[16]

On the other hand, the "shaved" or "tonsured" men—nicknames dear
to Calvin[17]—are false clerics whose hair is tonsured in the form of a crown
to symbolize their vocation to a supposedly royal government: "because
clerics ought to be kings, that they might rule themselves and others." This
interpretation of the "royal priesthood," which is found both in Gratian and
in Peter Lombard, provokes Calvin's anger. "See! Once again," Calvin cries,
"I prove them false. Peter speaks to the whole Church, but those men
distort it to refer to a few, as if it were spoken to them alone: 'Be holy'; as
if they alone were won by the blood of Christ; as if they alone were made
a kingdom and priesthood before God through Christ."[18]

In several other passages of the *Institutes,* this dialectic between the
"few" and the "whole Church" explicitly denounces the minority "consecrated" to a "state of perfection," because they have usurped the vocation
to holiness or to the royal priesthood which by right belongs to all Christians. The "few" are most often identified with the priests, the "little
priests" or "sacrificers," but sometimes also with the monks.

All the texts that will be quoted protest, more or less directly, the arbitrary division of the Church into a dominating priesthood and worldly
laymen who are subject to them.

Regarding the sentence of excommunication that should be pronounced
"by the judgment of the faithful" or the "votes of the faithful," Calvin
stresses what God, who has inspired the Scriptures, understands as
"Church": "But he calls the Church the gathering of the whole people of
God, united in his [Christ's] name—not a few tonsured, razored men
clothed in linen."[19] To allow disciplinary judgment to become a monopoly
of the clergy is an abuse that cries out for correction.

On the subject of communion under both species, Calvin criticizes the
"constitution which has stolen or seized half of the Supper from the greater
number of the people of God: that is, the symbol of the blood, which has
been forbidden to the laity and profane people (by these titles they designate
the inheritance of God!) and has been conceded to a few razored and
anointed men as a private possession."[20]

The custom of private masses (the *Winkelmessen* of Luther) gives rise to a similar remark: "For after the error grew strong that there ought to be priests who would sacrifice for the people, as if the Supper had been relegated to them, it ceased to be communicated to the faithful of the Church in accordance with the mandate of the Lord. Then an opportunity for private masses opened up, which refers more to a kind of excommunication than that communion instituted by the Lord. The priestling, when he is about to devour his victim apart from the others, separates himself from the whole company of the faithful."[21] Here is a striking picture of this deplorable division, this "clerical segregation," which divides the Church! The priest isolates himself from the people to receive privately a sacrament that should be the epitome of unity and fraternity! This is comparable to the beast who jealously retires with his prey to devour it alone. Calvin's indignation increases even more in the passage that deals with the question of payments for the Mass, these "sordid gains" which the "priestlings" make by "their own Mass-makings."[22]

Finally, the reformer has a word of criticism to offer on auricular confession, in which the priest has a very important role. Commenting on James 5:16, "Therefore confess your sins to one another," Calvin contests the traditional ideas according to which one "must confess to priestlings alone." Along with Luther, Bucer, and Zwingli,[23] Calvin believes that the Scriptures demand only "that we cast our infirmities on one another's heart."[24]

He is equally severe toward monks who claim that they alone follow the evangelical "counsels" and live in the "state of perfection." These prideful men gravely sin against the unifying spirit of Christianity. Commenting on the Beatitudes, Calvin writes: "Therefore, who are sons of the heavenly Father? Monks? It would go well for us if monks alone dared to call God 'Father.' And thus, those who so licentiously shake off the common yoke of the sons of God truly show themselves to be sons of Satan!"[25]

This serious distortion of ecclesiastical structures in the papacy and clergy brings with it a profound corruption in the exercise and competency of the various ministries as well as in the life of the ministers themselves.

How does one become a minister under the papacy? By ordination to a "title," which in principle means that a minister takes spiritual charge of a community and the community takes charge of the minister's material needs. But Calvin notes that in practice these "titles" no longer have any pastoral meaning: "I do not accept as legitimate those titles which they put forth. Are not most of their titles dignitaries, personages, canonries, prebendaries, chaplaincies, priories, and even monasteries, which are acquired partly from cathedral churches, partly from colleges, partly from deserted sanctuaries, and partly from cloisters? I confidently affirm and determine that they are all brothels of Satan."[26] When speaking of the "brothels of Satan," our author is not thinking especially of the possible immorality of the titularies but of the deceitful, mercenary, and sacrilegious character of allocating fictitious functions to fictitious titles.[27]

Of course, Calvin recognizes that the bishop functions as moderator in ordination. But at the same time, he is forced to observe that too often this role degenerates into arbitrary and tyrannical dealings. "These horned prelates,"[28] Calvin writes, "certainly have completely corrupted proper ordination by their rights of collations, presentations, representations, patronages, and other kinds of tyrannical domination."[29] In addition, the selection of candidates is made according to unacceptable criteria: "It has been accepted according to public customs that for practical purposes only barbers, cooks, mule drivers,[30] and spurious men of such dregs are created pastors of churches. I do not say enough! Episcopal dignity is the reward for panderings and adulteries." The lower clergy are recruited among the vulgar and bastards, and the higher clergy among the libertines! Calvin relentlessly criticizes this elevation of unworthy and unqualified people to offices that should be assumed by true pastors of souls. They ordain "ignorant people"[31] when they should ordain men who know the Scriptures thoroughly. The episcopate, the highest pastoral responsibility, is bestowed on courtiers or lords who have absolutely no intention of caring for their diocese and consider it exclusively as a possession, a supplementary source of prestige and income.[32] Calvin offers a whole list of major criticisms, including the spirit of domination, simony, and nepotism.

Even if a bishop effectively cares for his church, the exercise of his ministry is still subject to criticism. Thus our young theologian enters into the fray "against the power which they, who wish to be seen as pastors of the Church, usurp for themselves. In reality they are the most savage murderers." Alas, such people often behave more like butchers than shepherds toward their flock. They promulgate "spiritual laws" and "constitutions" by which they claim to ordain or forbid whatever they want under the pain of mortal sin. Thereby they violate Christian freedom and become involved in the area of conscience which is reserved for the Lord: "And thus the kingdom of Christ is invaded; thus, freedom given by Christ to the consciences of the faithful is completely oppressed and destroyed."[33] These bishops do not exercise the true power which belongs to ministers of the Word of God. There is as much distance between the exercise of authentic spiritual power and the despotism of these "mitered priests" as there is between Christ and the prince of demons: "But surely if that power [inherent in God's Word] is compared with that power by which those spiritual tyrants have so far ingratiated themselves with the people of God—those who pretend to be bishops and directors of souls—there will be no more agreement than there is between Christ and Belial."[34]

Yet they dare to call themselves successors of the apostles! "But," Calvin says, "since they are not ashamed to pride themselves on being the successors of the apostles, it is worthwhile to see with what trust they carry out their duties."[35] The apostles spent their lives in proclaiming the Gospel, administering the sacraments, serving as good pastors the various churches founded or visited by them. But these unworthy bishops, who do not carry out a single one of these apostolic duties, make for themselves titles of glory and dominion out of their positions as consecrated "high priests."

If so little is needed to claim spiritual descent from the apostles, one understands why simple priests and even monks want to join with bishops in the glory of this title. "Now," our author writes, "bishops, begging monks, and little sacrificers fight with hostility over the apostolic succession."[36] Each one points out the many ways, which are all purely exterior and incidental, he resembles the first heralds of the Gospel. The monks, for example, stress their itinerant ministry, and each one wishes to take advantage of his priestly function. But not one of them does what the apostles did. Thus Calvin the jurist arrogantly retorts: "Therefore those who do not apply themselves to the preaching of the Gospel or the administration of the sacraments falsely impersonate the apostles. Once again, those who sacrifice falsely claim a common ministry with the apostles."[37] And elsewhere he says: "[These] little sacrificers are neither the vicars nor the successors of the apostles."[38]

It is noteworthy that Calvin refuses to make facile arguments based on the unedifying morals of a good number of the "sacrificers" and "horned bishops." Certainly he speaks of these occasionally, but he does not call them the worst of evils. He discusses this subject with ironic magnanimity: "I do not speak of their morals and their tragic misdeeds, which gush forth from their lives, since they claim to be Pharisees, who are to be heard but not imitated."[39] What interests Calvin is not the "private vices of men" but the "common crimes of the whole order."[40] His criticism is therefore aimed at the structures and doctrines themselves[41] which he believes are the cause of these vices.

Calvin's criticism of ecclesiastical structures, from the papacy to the organization of individual churches, appears to be the witness of a profoundly religious layman who is rebelling against the inner schism of the Christian community which is artificially divided into clergy and laity. He is rebelling against clerical domination and consequently against the sacramental priesthood itself. The real reasons for this attitude are complex. Besides Luther's influence, Calvin's inability to understand in a positive way the sacramental reality of the Church and the painful situation in which he had to develop his ecclesiological thought must certainly be taken into account.

A parenthesis in the Dedicatory Epistle says much about Calvin's views on this matter: "Now consider our adversaries (I speak of the order of sacrificers, by whose command and judgment others exercise such hostility toward us) and reflect with me awhile on the zeal by which they are carried along."[42] It is most likely that the intense hostility, persecution, and intolerance of some theologians of the Sorbonne and other priests created in Calvin a negative reflex against the clergy and the priesthood in general; and in spite of several painful experiences, he was not aware of this attitude during his youth.

The Ideal of the "Kingdom of Christ"

Calvin criticized the decadent structures of the Church under the title of the "papal kingdom," and then he described the ideal under the title of the "kingdom of Christ." The reformer is very careful to bring together the Church's legal structure and doctrine in his constructive statements. Thus he demands that every element in the practical organization of the life of the Church be in harmony with Scripture and manifest the absolute and total dominion of Christ over his people.

To the papacy of his time, Calvin directly opposes the royalty of Jesus Christ; to the rigid distinction between clergy and laity, the basic equality of the universal priesthood; and to the "tyranny" of the prelates, an essentially pastoral ministry.

We have already encountered the theme of the "kingdom of Christ" in the principles of "Christ alone"[43] and the "Word of God," the scepter of the heavenly king.[44] Here we limit ourselves to emphasizing a special aspect of this theme: the manifestation of the "kingdom." For Calvin it is not enough to believe that the Savior is king, the unique and absolute Lord of his people; the entire concrete life of the Church must be ruled so as to express and make known—to make visible and palpable, as it were—that it is entirely dominated and governed by him. Each individual community should bear the "marks" that prove that it really belongs to the "true Church."

This visible manifestation of Christ's rule is realized first in that all other dominion is declared to be decadent. Especially the "papal power" of the so-called "sovereign pontiff" must vanish: "For if we permit Christ to rule among us, that entire kind of domination will be easily overturned and cast down."[45]

The manifestation of Christ's "kingdom" goes hand in hand with ending all division between a privileged caste and a mass of thwarted laymen. Every Christian without distinction belongs to this great universal "clergy," to this "universal people of God" who form the "inheritance of Christ."[46] Therefore, all may be called a "chosen race, a royal priesthood, a chosen nation, a people of [his] possession,"[47] and all may exercise the priestly and royal functions that Christ wished to give to his faithful followers, the members of his body. As a community they may offer the "sacrifice of praise": "In this office of sacrificing, we all as Christians are called to the royal priesthood, because through Christ we offer the sacrifice of praise to God: the fruit of our lips, the confession of his name."[48] As a community they also have the right to make judgments concerning ecclesiastical discipline. Since the head of the Church gave the right to bind and to loose to his people, he who receives such a judgment should consider himself struck by a divine sentence: "Therefore let no one haughtily despise the judgment of the Church or consider it insignificant to be condemned by the votes of the faithful. The Lord has testified that such judgments of the faithful are none other than promulgations of his own sentences, that what they have done on earth has been ratified in heaven."[49] This disciplinary jurisdiction belongs to small local communities as well as large ones, or even to the universal Church: "Christ has made it fully known that he speaks of each Christian congregation, so that churches can be constituted in individual places or provinces. 'Wherever,' he says, 'two or three have gathered in my name, there I am in the midst of them.' "[50]

The fundamental equality of the members of the body in Christ's kingdom is nevertheless not equivalent to an anarchical egalitarianism. The young reformer favors an institutionally organized ministry to which he attributes the dominant role in preaching, administration of the sacraments, and ecclesiastical government. Even if all Christians have the right to exercise the role of the "royal priesthood," they are not all "ministers of the Word of God." A special calling is necessary to become a "minister."

Calvin's comments allow us to glance at two of the fundamental elements in his conception of the ministry that are opposed to the papal hierarchy. First, ordination to the ministry does not confer a sacramental priesthood which is essentially superior to the royal priesthood of the faithful; rather, it is a call to a higher and more demanding service of God and the Church. Second, this ministry is basically a ministry of the spoken word, which is the organ and instrument of the "Word of God." Calvin's views are based on the great biblical themes of preaching by the Levites and the prophets and are meant to correct the distortions of the "papal priesthood." Turning to the biblical sources allows Calvin to give a new orientation to the search for a "re-formed" structure of the Church.

In the first *Institutes,* the episcopate is still considered normative.[51] The reformer distinguishes only between a sacerdotal episcopate which seeks to dominate and an episcopate which is willing to serve through the pastoral proclamation of the Word: "Bishops and ministers of the churches should apply themselves faithfully to the ministry of the Word, so that they do not adulterate the doctrine of salvation but deliver it to God's people in its pure and simple form. They should instruct the people not only by doctrine but also by the example of their lives. In brief, let them preside as good pastors of their sheep."[52] In another passage, Calvin presents a clear and positive definition of the bishop as one who dispenses the Word and the sacraments. Elsewhere Calvin denies that the bishop is radically distinct from a presbyter: "A bishop is one who has been called to the ministry of the Word and sacraments and who executes his duties in good faith. I call both bishops and presbyters ministers of the Church, without distinction."[53] It seems certain that if the reformer is thinking of a change in structure, he has in mind the papal episcopate, which he believes is corrupt, and not the episcopate itself.

This position is expressed again in a passage in which Calvin describes authentic pastors as opposed to those who "pretend to be bishops and directors of souls": "Here is the plainly and clearly defined power, with which it is proper that pastors of the Church, by whatever name they may be called, be endowed: namely, that they confidently undertake all things by the Word of God, whose ministers and stewards they have been appointed to be."[54] To such pastors one may justly attribute apostolic succession: "Here is the holy, inviolable, and perpetual law imposed on those who succeed the apostles, in accord with which they receive the mandate of preaching the Gospel and administering the sacraments."[55] Thus Calvin thinks that the existence of such ministers agrees entirely with what Scripture teaches about the original structure of the Christian Church. The "truth of Scripture," he says, "acknowledges no other minister of the Church than the preacher of God's Word who is called to rule the Church; sometimes he is called bishop, then presbyter, and sometimes even pastor."[56]

Whatever the ideal name may be that one should give to the true minister, one thing is absolutely certain: from the first edition of his compendium, Calvin considers the ministry to be indispensable to the existence of the Church. As we would say today, the minister is essential not only for the "well-being" of the Church but for its very "existence." In fact, the "marks" that manifest the presence of the "kingdom of Christ" in a given community and its relationship to the "true Church" depend on the minister. This is the idea that emerges from the following passage, which opposes papal claims: "We assert on the contrary that the Church is able to exist without a visible form and that its form is not contained in that external splendor which they foolishly admire; but rather it is contained in other marks, namely, in the pure preaching of the Word of God and the legitimate administration of the sacraments."[57] The distinctive marks of the true Church are constituted by these two principal functions of a properly exercised ministry.

The Church is the "kingdom of Christ," the inheritance of the Son of God who is King and High Priest, which is manifested in a general way by the "collegiality" of the Christian people who are called to the royal priesthood. It is manifested in a special way by a properly exercised pastoral ministry. This is the ideal which the young Calvin has in mind when he considers the reformation of ecclesiastical structures. Later on, this ideal will receive a more concrete and more developed formulation, when Calvin attempts to describe more explicitly the "visible Church" and the "four ministries." But the foundation remains the same. Without being sacramental, sacerdotal, or priestly, the visible manifestation of the Church will always have the same characteristics.

We come to the end of our inquiry about the young Calvin's criticisms and ideals regarding piety, doctrine, and ecclesiastical structure. It remains for us to establish how our theologian actually wished to accomplish the great work of reformation.

CHAPTER TWENTY-THREE
The Outline of Calvin's Plan
for Reformation

This chapter poses the following question: Calvin has diagnosed the disease and proposed remedies, but does he give in the *Institutes* exact prescriptions for healing? In other words, in his criticisms and in the announcement of his program, does he propose a relevant plan of action?

It is difficult to reply simply in the affirmative. Nowhere in the first *Institutes*—unless I am in error—is either the noun "reformation" or the verb "reform" used in the technical sense. I find only "to be deformed," "deformed," and several considerations of the "form" of the Church.

In the preface, for example, one reads that Calvin's adversaries are wrong when "they contend that the form of the Church is always apparent and visible, and then they constitute the form itself in the seat of the Church of Rome and the order of its leaders." Calvin adds: "We assert on the contrary that the Church is able to exist without a visible form and that its form is not contained . . . in that external splendor." The corruption of the Church is then compared to that of the Old Testament community: "They grumble unless the Church is always pointed out with a finger. But among the Jewish people, how often did it happen that it was so deformed that no appearance stood out? What form do we contend showed forth when Elijah deplored the fact that he alone remained (1 Kings 19)? How long from the advent of Christ was it hidden and deformed?" Finally, this loss of outward form is interpreted as the chastisement of God, who sometimes permits unfaithful men to be plunged temporarily into darkness: "He allowed it to be plunged into deep darkness, so that no countenance of the true Church stood forth."[1] In another passage, the same idea of disfigurement is directly applied to the contemporary Church, and in sorrow the reformer cries out: "Those who can look with dry eyes at this countenance of the Church which is seen in our age are cruel and impious, for when they could heal it, they neglected it and thus exceed the limits of inhumanity."[2]

The corrupt form of the Church is condemned, the absence of a true form is considered a grave misfortune, and there is even an allusion to a desirable remedy. But in the entire context the term "reformation" never appears, and the idea is not directly developed.

Again we find that in spite of his basically positive intention, Calvin expresses his criticism more completely and concretely than the corresponding ideal. But is this so surprising? We must not forget that no matter how ingenious the *Institutes* may be, it is the work of the *young* Calvin. As I have said, this work was written principally under the inspiration of his readings and not under the impulse of any experience as a reformer or pastor. It is to be expected that Calvin's criticisms and ideals are not viewed from the perspective of a precise and practical plan of action. Moreover, the primary aim of the compendium is catechetic and kerygmatic. Calvin wanted to elucidate and proclaim the Gospel in all its simplicity in a contemporary way. That is why he included numerous prophetic protests and exhortations that are inspired by a sincere desire for renewal; but we seek in vain from the reformer a "code of reform" and a call to "follow me."

Given these reservations, we must nonetheless admit that we find in the first *Institutes* important outlines of a plan of action. These deal mostly with the spirit and general orientation of the reform as well as with the question of knowing who is called to bring it about.

For the Christian humanists and earlier reformers, as well as for Calvin, it is the spirit of the Gospel that should give life to this great work. Today as yesterday, salvation comes from Christ. In the Gospel, "Christ is offered to us with all the outpouring of heavenly blessings."[3] To proclaim Christ is to proclaim the Gospel. To reestablish the kingdom of Christ is to devote oneself to proclaiming the good news. Therefore, nothing new is being done unless Christ himself is considered "new."[4] Certainly this doctrine has been buried for a long time, but the time has come to rediscover it in all of its ancient purity: "That it lay buried and unknown for a long time is a crime of human impiety; now when it is restored to us by God's kindness, its antiquity ought to be accepted, at least by right of restoration."[5]

The same dialectic of "long buried, now restored"[6] is found in another passage whose importance, in view of the general orientation of Calvin's reform, cannot be exaggerated. It deals with the divine promise contained in baptism, which retains its validity and efficacy even when the sacrament is administered "under the papacy." In contrast to the anabaptists who desire to rebaptize all those baptized in the Roman communion, Calvin states: "No matter how contemptuous or ignorant they were of God, those who baptized us did not immerse us into the community of their ignorance or sacrilege but into faith in Jesus Christ; for they did not invoke their own names but the name of God—and in no other name did they baptize us." The promise of God inevitably comes to pass, even if those who transmit it or receive it lack true faith. An "unfaithful" administration or reception does not benefit the individual—it is "buried." But as soon as the individual awakens to a faith worthy of the name, all the power of the promise holds sway over him. The text ends: "This promise was offered to us in baptism; therefore let us embrace [it] by faith. Indeed, for a long time it lay buried to us because of our lack of faith; therefore now let us receive it through faith."[7]

We see that Calvin recognized the validity of Roman baptism. This is a fact of supreme importance for his doctrine of the Church. It means that the continuity and the fundamental unity of the Church remain secure and that the reformation has no other aim than to restore what had been buried alive.

Although reform efforts should be determined by an awareness of continuity and a refusal of innovation, knowing who is responsible to bring about this work raises considerable difficulties. Calvin is well aware of this; he prepares his reply very cautiously.

Who should reform? Or to use an expression more in harmony with the language of the first *Institutes,* Who should bring out the "buried truth"? From the passages we have studied, it is clear that Calvin no longer expects any help from the pope, from the "horned bishops," or even from a general council convened by the pontiff and composed of only his partisans.[8] But does he think, as Luther did,[9] that the laity, the lords, the kings and magistrates—in a word, the civil power—should be called to reform the Church?

The first *Institutes* does not seem to contend that the obligation of purifying the Church falls principally to the civil authority.[10] Of course, the work is dedicated to Francis I, and in the dedicatory letter the sovereign is designated as a "minister of God in the administration of his kingdom." There are other appeals as well: "But it will be up to you, most serene King, not to turn aside your eyes or mind from such a just defense; especially when such a great matter is at issue, namely, how the security of God's glory may be established in the earth, how the truth of God may retain its dignity, and how the kingdom of Christ may remain in good order among us. This is a matter worthy of your attention, worthy of your examination, and worthy of your tribunal."[11] But it would be an exaggeration to see in this a direct appeal to take the initiative in reform. What does Calvin mean? He certainly wishes to plead the cause of the evangelicals persecuted by the King's officials. He appeals on their behalf before the King's tribunal to obtain a judgment based on a more complete understanding of the facts, which would acquit them of the accusation of sedition. Finally, he urges the King to protect the great work of the reformers, but he does not ask him to bring it about himself.

A similar conclusion is drawn from the last twenty pages of the book that Calvin devotes to the civil power. There too the princes are called "ministers of God" and the magistrates "representatives" or "legates of God."[12] According to the divine order, citizens are obligated to submit to them: "All are to be acknowledged by us according to the ordinances of God," for otherwise they would fall into anarchy, "from popular rule into sedition."[13] But in matters of religion, the monarch or the magistrate is only called on to exercise the role of protector, comparable to its role as the protector of public order and welfare. Thus Calvin lists them together. The "political function," he says, consists not only of watching over the material welfare and security of the citizens but also "that neither idolatry, nor sacrilege against the name of God, nor blasphemies against his truth, nor any other public offenses against religion emerge from or spread among the people; that the public peace not be disturbed, and that what belongs to each one be safe and sound, and that men carry on blameless exchanges between themselves. In sum: that the public countenance of religion may exist among Christians and that humanity be established among men."[14] The author adds that although the political power has no right to forge human laws "concerning religion and the worship of God," it does have the duty to do all it can so that "true religion, which is contained in the law of God, not be violated and defiled with impunity and openly with public sacrilege."[15] We see that while Calvin invites the magistrate to protect, favor, and defend "true religion," he does not ask him to undertake the actual work of reform.

Who, then, should lead this absolutely essential enterprise? Because of the way in which he disqualifies the hierarchy, it does not seem that a solution will come from on high. On the contrary, it seems that Calvin is thinking more or less explicitly of a solution through new leadership, that is, that God would raise up from among all Christians, ministers as well as laymen, those who would take up the task neglected by the irresponsible ecclesiastical authorities.

I lean toward this hypothesis because of the frequent allusions in the first *Institutes* to the mission of the prophets, which seems analogous to the ministry of the reformers. The two parts that are most "reformist" in tone, "The Epistle to the King" and the chapter "On Christian Freedom," are filled with quotations, examples, and allusions to the prophets.[16] Numerous passages recall the great men whom God made his direct spokesmen, his "special envoys" to proclaim his message in all its purity and with all its demands.[17]

To act as a "watchman" of God's people and to transmit to them the Word which comes directly "from the mouth of God," the prophet has two principal objectives: to proclaim the "kingdom of Christ" which is to come or which has already come[18] and to rid the community of abuses and the distortions. To the prophet, idolatry or spiritual fornication necessarily appears as the most abominable sin. In stressing this, Calvin clearly shows that he is thinking not only of the past but especially of the present, where those who "wish to be considered Christians" nevertheless offer to God an entirely "carnal" veneration.[19]

The desire to apply the prophetic message to his time is in the sentence where our author declares to Francis I: "Moreover, he is deceived who expects lasting prosperity in his kingdom which is not ruled by God's holy Word, that is, the scepter of God. For that heavenly oracle cannot fail which declares: 'Where there is no prophecy the people cast off restraint (Prov. 29:18).' "[20] All people, the whole Church, are destined to internal decay if the critical and inspiring voice of the heralds of the Lord are silenced in their midst. This is precisely the case of the Church under the sway of the papacy.

Calvin again refers to the example of the prophets in a passage that combats the pretense of the pope and his bishops that they alone represent the entire Church because they possess priestly consecration. "And Aaron," we read, "and other leaders of Israel were pastors. Aaron (Exodus 31 and 32) and his sons, although designated priests, nevertheless erred when they made the calf." The reformer also cites the case of the prophet Micaiah; before four hundred false prophets who claimed to be representatives of the ecclesiastical institution, Micaiah alone represented the true Church of God: "But the Church was on the side of Micaiah, who was alone and contemptible; but out of his mouth came forth the truth." Then the similar circumstances of Jeremiah are called to mind: "Jeremiah alone was sent against the whole tribe of prophets, threatening from the Lord that the law would perish from the priest, counsel from the wise, the word from the prophet (Jer. 18:18)." Finally, after showing how Christ himself stood alone before the priests who were going to condemn him, Calvin alludes to the burning issue of the day: "Now let them go and cling to outward masks, and thereby make schismatics of Christ and all the prophets of the living God, and make ministers of Satan into organs of the Holy Spirit."[21]

The parallel between the calling of the prophets and the reformers seems well marked. Each stands alone before an institution or a caste of the "consecrated" who alone claim to represent the Church and to teach dogma. Each is rejected, anathematized, and persecuted. But, in spite of everything, each is on the side of the true Church.

It is necessary to see that this same analogy applies to Calvin's statements that reflect his distrust of those who misunderstand the prophetic stance, take it to an extreme, and thereby become perpetrators of disorder. These are rebellious sectarians—in a word, pseudoprophets. If we understand Calvin's position on the anabaptists, we know who the young theologian has in mind when he refers to the *pseudoapostoli* (2 Cor. 11:13; translated by Calvin as "false prophets"),[22] "who tear the Church asunder"[23] or those who "seized the freedom of the Spirit as an excuse for fleshly license."[24] Moreover, on the preceding page Calvin expressly says: Satan "incited dissent and contentions over dogmas through his catabaptists and other monsters of darkness."[25]

The excesses of the sectarians proved to be particularly serious given the circumstances, because they discredited the evangelicals as a whole and furnished their adversaries with an easy pretext for accusing them of subversion. However, Calvin thinks—and here the analogy with the prophets reappears—that the danger presented by these arrogant men should in no way stop the efforts of authentic reformation. In fact, the prophets were familiar with this risk. All, including Christ himself, came to a moment in their missions when their enemies labeled them rebels: "This is . . . not a new example. Elijah was asked (1 Kings 18) whether he was the one troubling Israel; to the Jews, Christ was seditious (Luke 23; John 19); the crime of public rioting was brought against the apostles (Acts 24). What else are they doing today when they charge us with all the disruptions, tumults, and contentions that are rising up in our midst? But Elijah taught us how to respond to such changes."[26]

When one wishes to reestablish the order of God on earth, it is normal for the evil one to interfere in order to sabotage the undertaking. When one proclaims Christ, the "stone of offense," a "stumbling block," and a "sign of contradiction," opposition is inevitable. It would be wrong to recoil from the risk: "Should [the apostles] have dissembled for the time, or completely set aside the Gospel . . . [because it was] the cause of so many dangers and the occasion of so many scandals?"[27] No. Enough excuses. The work of reform has too often been set aside or put off until tomorrow. The Gospel has been kept under a bushel long enough. Now it is necessary to follow the prophets' examples and proclaim the divine demands once again, "in season and out of season."

This is all one can say about Calvin's plan for reformation as outlined in the first *Institutes*. Without using the word "reformation," Calvin urgently preaches a return to Christ through the Gospel. This preaching presupposes the continuity of the Church and opposes all "novelty." However, without treating the question directly, he makes it clear that the reform is only an interim work led by Christians who have been specially called for this task in place of the faltering ecclesiastical authorities. As surrogates, the architects of this renewal act in a situation similar to the prophets. It does not matter whether they are "laymen" or pastors; they do not work as representatives of an ecclesiastical or civil institution but as the direct spokesmen of the Lord. The hierarchical power is guilty of omission and should listen to them; the civil power by divine mandate is obligated to support and protect them. But the beginning of the reform work, properly speaking, is theirs and theirs alone, for they are in fact the chosen instruments of God.

CHAPTER TWENTY-FOUR
Conclusion to Part Three

For an overview of the points made so far, let us first briefly recall the essential conclusions of Part One.

The young Calvin lived in the milieu of the Church without being part of the ecclesiastical hierarchy. He often associated with reformers without falling into radicalism, and he witnessed the martyrdom of many Lutherans without joining their ranks. Therefore he slowly proceeded toward an awareness of his calling as a reformer. The events of 1533–1534 accelerated the movement. The brutal intervention of the defenders of orthodoxy drove the young humanist out of his circle of moderate reformist friends. During a period of exile he was introduced to Lutheran theology. At Basle, he began to read and reflect. The problems that he wished to solve were those of the Church of his time, and from that time on, his personal questions appear to be inextricably bound to the problems of the Church. For solutions and replies, he waited upon the Word of God, whose meaning he no longer sought only among the humanists and the Church Fathers but more and more from the reformers.

Calvin's writings at Basle, in particular the *Institutes,* reveal that the humanist reformer of yesterday was quickly transformed into an evangelical theologian. Then, actions followed ideas. At Geneva, Calvin became an active reformer and had his first experience as a pastor. From the crisis that followed, he emerged more confident of his call.

To determine more precisely the initial and fundamental orientation of Calvin's calling, we tried in Parts Two and Three to discover the sources and to interpret the content of the first *Institutes.*

Our examination revealed first that the refugee of Basle possessed an independent mind that did not give in to the Zwinglian tendencies of his hosts. Instead, Calvin selected Martin Luther as his principal mentor.

But this affirmation of Luther's influence should not be understood quantitatively or absolutely. In the *Institutes,* the expressions taken directly from Luther's vocabulary are no more numerous than those which originated with Erasmus, Melanchthon, Zwingli, or Bucer. However, the doctrinal substance underlying these expressions corresponds primarily to the principal ideas of the Saxon reformer. The framework of our study has not allowed us to demonstrate this systematically and exhaustively. We had to be content with comparing a few significant texts of the *Institutes* with their sources, and then to point out briefly several parallels between Calvin and his principal teacher.

I do not wish to portray Calvin simply as an imitator of Luther who was limited to repeating and adapting him. Any attentive reader of the *Institutes* would quickly agree that for Calvin the one, supreme authority in doctrinal matters was the Bible. He certainly knew the Bible before reading the works of Luther. Later he made abundant use of these writings in his theological interpretation of Scripture, but he never followed them blindly or without reservation. For his exegesis of biblical passages, he took as his basic text the Vulgate, correcting it on occasion by Erasmus' version or by referring directly to the original Greek. To comment on the text, he quite often preferred the *Enarrationes* of Bucer. Finally, it is indisputable that Calvin was from the start superior to Luther in his careful biblical and patristic documentation.

We find dependence and teachability on the one hand but independence and originality on the other. As a young theologian, Calvin cannot be compared to a musical performer or to an orchestra conductor whose task is limited to interpreting faithfully a piece of music; rather, he is like a composer who borrows several themes and then orchestrates them according to his personal inspiration. Calvin makes the themes of Luther, Melanchthon, Zwingli, and Bucer resound at times *forte* and at other times *piano* and integrates them into a composition that is his own.

It would be an abusive oversimplification to assert absolutely that Calvin's work amounts to a "Latin" reformulation of German thought or a jurist's expression of prophetic ideas. We can say that many fundamentally biblical statements of Calvin carry the imprint of his Latin genius and that some of his arguments reveal at times the mind of the jurist, or the humanist, and even the terminist dialectician. They are clear, orderly, logical, and suited to distinguishing the essential from the superfluous.

The Calvin of the first *Institutes* is a man who wishes to obey without reservation the authority of the divine Word; he is respectful of but not intimidated by the authority of the reformers. We should add that he is strongly critical of the scholastic defenders of orthodoxy.

In Part Three we summarized Calvin's criticisms and redefinitions of piety, doctrine, and ecclesiastical structures. We demonstrated that Calvin went quite far in rejecting several dogmas and traditional institutions of the Church of his time. Why? Was he an enthusiast, a new convert, who saw only good on the side of the evangelicals and only bad on the side of the Roman Catholics? The strong impression that the events of 1533–1534 and his reading of Luther had on him could lead to this conclusion. But is that sufficient to explain the widespread audience that the first *Institutes,* a modest compendium written in Latin, found among reform circles? The work's literary qualities, its passionate and convincing tone, and the favorable circumstances in which it appeared do not adequately explain its smashing success.

To answer this problem satisfactorily, let us first recall what was said in chapter 1 on the direct and indirect reasons for the penetration of Luther's ideas into France.[1] It is obvious that the reasons for the success of Luther's writings at the beginning of 1520 and the rapid diffusion of the *Institutes* in 1536 are the same.[2] In fifteen years the representatives of the established Church could not stop the abuses that aroused the discontent of the French elite, nor bring about the internal, widespread reform that alone may have neutralized the revolutionary danger from beyond the Rhine. Neither prohibitions, condemnations, executions, nor partial reforms undertaken by some enlightened bishops were enough to silence the criticisms and the protests. A general council, of which the moderate reformers and even the radicals—at least in the beginning—expected so much, still had not been called in 1536, more than fifteen years after the Lutheran revolt. An ill-fated delay among all the delays of the Church! The qualified authorities insisted on finding a political solution to a fundamentally religious problem. This was a fatal mistake by ecclesiastical authorities unable to disengage themselves from the patterns of the past!

Faced with this situation, Calvin used stern language to stigmatize the piety of his contemporaries with its self-seeking religiosity, superstition, and idolatry. We have not reached a judgment about whether Calvin was right in wishing to suppress indulgences, images, sacramentals, and even some sacraments because of the way they were abused. But we can ask whether the abuses existed or not, and whether they were so widespread that they cast doubt upon the legitimacy of the customs.

For indulgences the answer seems clear. There must have been a reason why several authors from the fifteenth century onward referred to the widespread selling of pardons as a sign of the coming of the Antichrist. There were good reasons that the Council of Trent suppressed the institution of the *quaestores,* preachers and collectors of alms for indulgences. Since these criticisms could not keep the faithful from placing undue confidence in their own works of satisfaction rather than in Christ's redemptive sacrifice, we should not be surprised that Calvin, following Luther's example, was not willing to tolerate "satisfactions" of any kind. Should not Luther and Calvin's rejection of purgatory be understood in terms of the crass role that it played in Tetzel's preaching and that of many other priests seeking offerings and fees? In an era obsessed by the thought of death, in a time that had a strongly materialistic concept of the afterlife[3] and sought to buy celestial happiness with earthly goods, was it not expected that many elite minds would emphasize, perhaps too strongly, the scriptural themes of free salvation and "unworthy servants"?

It is an indisputable fact that in 1536 superstitions were still widespread. The sarcasm of Erasmus and the heavy-handed mockery of Rabelais against the practices of a devious, morbid, and "inconsistent"[4] piety were meant to be taken seriously. They echoed the sober criticisms of a Gerson and were inspired by a sincere Christianity which desired to "free the faithful, the simple believers, from infantile terrors and gross superstitions."[5] We should recall, for example, the popular custom of attributing an illness to the vengeance of some outraged saint, magical uses of the consecrated host, belief in the automatically beneficial effect of sacred places or special times, or the widespread use of semierotic and semireligious practices concerning the sacraments. These were all largely tolerated by the ecclesiastical authorities. Then we are less surprised to hear Calvin speak of "perverse observances" or of "carnal," "Jewish," or "pagan practices." When one knows that the sacraments were often administered and received in a similar spirit, one can understand at least the psychological motivation of Calvin's reaction against the substance of several traditional sacraments.

Superstition and idolatrous tendencies always go together. The need to "materialize" and "domesticate" the supernatural is also seen in the excessive worship of images. This excess is contrary to the original use of images and creates a barrier between the one, true God and the believer. We think of the statues of the Virgin in whose belly is enclosed the image of the Trinity, the relics that the priest raised up in the so-called "dry mass" instead of the body of the Lord, the statues of plump saints, and the flowery legends which deterred people from contemplating Christ and reading the Scriptures, the vows and offerings to patron saints on whom people relied more than prayers addressed to God himself. All these are closely related to the practices of ancient polytheism. The iconoclastic stance, the proposals and actions of Zwingli, Farel, and Calvin are understandable only if we take this situation into account. To prefer the mediation of a saint to the Redeemer is really to "divert the glory of God to creatures." To forget that Scripture declares that God is spirit and demands to be worshiped in spirit and in truth is surely to fall back into a kind of paganism. We can understand the well-founded basis of Calvin's criticisms, even if we cannot accept his antisacramental radicalism.

Calvin's ideals of piety, religion, and worship raise no difficulties. In fact, they are merely a straightforward and vigorous recollection of the basic principles of Scripture. There is first a humble knowledge and filial love of the living God, characterized by faith and trust ("piety"); second, a solemn and thoughtful collection of religious energy into a clear vision of what is essential ("religion"); and third, prayer in the Church of God which is both internal and external, personal and communal ("worship"). It is striking to note that, while Calvin's critical attacks are aimed at concrete attitudes and often call into question the essential points of Catholic tradition, his constructive statements on reform remain at the level of principles that do not deviate from Catholic teaching. This observation will be useful when we comment on the profound significance of Calvin's calling as a reformer.

Doctrine follows piety. We have seen how passionately the young reformer stigmatizes the theological teaching of his time, more precisely, scholastic theology. No doubt he accepted completely Luther's severe judgments against the "sophists," who are disciples of Aristotle rather than the Holy Spirit. He seems to have adopted this a priori negative attitude all the more easily because he had been directly influenced by the example of the great Erasmus and indirectly by the intolerance of the Sorbonne. In preparing his *Institutes,* he certainly did not go to the trouble of making an in-depth study of the *Sentences* or their contemporary commentators. His introduction to scholasticism at Montaigu stopped at philosophy. The bits and pieces of the fourth book of Lombard and Gratian's *Decretals* that are found in Calvin's compendium were hastily assembled with the obvious aim of caricaturizing the "Roman" doctrine of the sacraments. Besides, this doctrine is presented in such a way that one cannot perceive where canonical and ritual arrangements end and where the strictly dogmatic statements begin. Can this be attributed solely to the intellectual impatience, incompetence, and animosity of our young author, this victim of the Sorbonne's persecution? Or is the scholastic theology of the period equally responsible? If one can prove that it actually was decadent and distorted, it is no longer possible to make Calvin totally responsible for understanding it so poorly and caring for it so little.

In chapter 16 we surveyed several books of John Major.[6] His commentaries on selected themes of the *Sentences* seem very abstract, hardly scriptural, and extremely disorganized. The complicated method, the excessive use of logical exercises on the mysteries of faith, and the tiresome subtlety of his arguments inevitably make reading them unbearable for any humanist Bible scholar. But such works of "theology" were not exceptional at that time. If such a commentary introduced young Calvin to the *Sentences,* we can understand his reaction.

In consulting the doctrinal decrees of the regional synod of Sens, we realized that the theology of the bishops was worth no more than that of the Sorbonne. It was no more clear or certain. In these decrees we noted the same confusion between the dogmatic and canonical realms as in Calvin's caricature. In the part devoted to the "decrees of the faith,"[7] the unity and infallibility of the Church are defended under the same heading as the celibacy of priests; the sacrifice of the Mass is treated under the same heading as the obligation to fast. Opponents of these doctrines and laws are lumped together as heretics without any distinctions. The exposition in various chapters possesses a form that one may call "materially" scriptural: it is a mass of biblical texts which are really paraphrases that are often not related in an exegetically justifiable way. Finally, the doctrinal position expressed at the end of each chapter does not always logically follow from the preceding arguments. The threat of condemnation makes up for the weak proofs.[8]

Let us add that the teaching of the popes and the councils during the time of Calvin's development was far removed from the clarity of Trent. And for good reason: the supporters of a council and the champions of the pope, the national episcopates and the Roman Curia, the circle of Christian humanists and the faculties of theology, quarreled endlessly. No single ecclesiastical authority was universally recognized. Thus, superior minds that were deeply attached to the Catholic Church, such as Lefèvre d'Etaples, could accept the essential orthodoxy of Luther, even well after 1521. We note in passing that while the theology of the Christian humanists was assuredly more vital and based more on the Bible and the Fathers than was scholasticism, it was nonetheless no more clear or certain as to the essential content of Christian dogma.

Is this astonishing? Let us not forget that we had to wait until Trent for the doctrines of justification, the Mass, and the seven sacraments to be defined dogmatically,[9] and several centuries more before papal infallibility, the immaculate conception, and the assumption were formulated.

Under these circumstances we can understand how the young Calvin in his first effort as an evangelical theologian could condemn the scholastics and several traditional doctrines without thinking of himself as a heretic. It cannot be denied that numerous truths that are clearly affirmed in the Bible and the Fathers were at that time "buried" under the learned ratiocinations of the theologians. It would also be absurd to assert that at the beginning of the sixteenth century, scholasticism in general and that of the Parisian School in particular possessed a clearly Christ-centered and positively biblical character. Of course, scholastic theology did not teach anything truly heretical. To use an expression of J. Lortz, it took pride in its "negative correctness." But it was too "wordy" to "listen" in humility and yield to the Word of God, too encyclopedic to lead seekers of truth with certainty. Yet this was the kind of learning Noël Bédier taught and defended, and it was according to his criteria that the Sorbonne censored Bible scholars and condemned the evangelicals. Who would still argue that this "orthodox" system was not partially responsible for heresy?

The ideal that Calvin opposed to scholasticism was a catechism and a theology constructed according to the "simplicity of Scripture." I must emphasize again that his biblical principle conforms substantially to Catholic doctrine. His appeal to "Scripture alone" does not exclude frequent recourse to tradition, especially the Fathers.

Calvin's criticism of church structure is without doubt the least difficult to explain in terms of the contemporary situation. "Papism" naturally gave birth to antipapism. The "external splendor" of Rome scandalized pilgrims thirsting for spiritual life. The spirit of domination characterized the hierarchy at virtually all levels. An unbridled search for wealth was present as well. There was a factual basis for the verses of the *Antithesis figurata,* illustrated by Lucas Cranach, which were extraordinarily popular in France: "Jesus flees the earthly kingdom. But the pope by force makes it his own. Jesus is pitifully crowned with thorns. The pope is sumptuously crowned with gold and precious stones. Jesus gladly washed the feet of his disciples. The slippers of the pope are kissed by kings."[10]

Calvin was neither the first nor the only one to express his pessimism about a council. The councils of Constance, Basle, and the Fifth Lateran did not result in a "reformation of the head and its members." What could one expect of a new council whose convening was constantly postponed?

The clericalism of the period certainly no longer represented a peaceful possession of traditional privileges. The Renaissance, which Lortz calls "an essentially lay movement,"[11] progressively led to the emancipation of the laity and tended more and more to secularize the different areas of society. But many members of the high clergy found a means of regaining lost ground by becoming secularized themselves, that is to say, by becoming involved in politics, diplomacy, and commerce. Thus a new clericalism was born, probably worse than the preceding, for it was based on the exploitation of ecclesiastical "titles" for profane and temporal ends. It is this kind of clericalism that Calvin attacks when speaking of the "empty titles" of so-called pastors and of the tyrannical spirit of the "horned prelates." But his criticism went to the heart of the matter when, following Luther, he contested the legitimacy of the rigid division of the people of God into the priestly clergy and the profane laity. Although Calvin did not fully develop the idea of the royal priesthood of the faithful, it was basic to this criticism and to the protest over communion in both species, the power of the keys, and the call to holiness common to all members of the Church.

Apart from its purely polemical characteristics, Calvin's vision of the "kingdom of Christ" as opposed to the "kingdom of the pope" is a beautiful profession of faith which is entirely in harmony with the ancient Catholic tradition of the unique kingship of Christ and his unique priesthood, as well as the essentially ministerial or "diaconal" character of all ecclesiastical functions. The authentic bishop is merely a servant of God and the community, who serves by preaching the Word and by administering the sacraments and discipline. Calvin does not stray from traditional teaching except in his denial of the priestly ministry and its sacramental character. Here we again touch upon a critical divergence in doctrine: the young Calvin did not have the Catholic understanding of the sacrament. His prophetic protest led him to separate the divine and the human to an excessive degree and to experience an implacable aversion to anything that seemed to bind grace to "carnal elements." But do not the seriousness and the extent of the spiritual abuses committed for grossly temporal reasons by so many of the hierarchy make this excessive reaction understandable?

Calvin was born and raised in, and then contemplated and wrote about, a Christianity that suffered from an inability to reform itself.[12] A fervent and generous soul, he sought a rallying point that would allow him to hasten reform. He knew the men of the Sorbonne. He met moderate reformists. But the complicated interplay of ideological influences and dramatic events made him finally choose the Gospel of those who were willing to die for reform. He then accepted on his own the criticisms and ideals that the evangelical martyrs proclaimed even in the flames of the stake.[13]

These conclusions from our inquiry about events and ideas permit us to approach the three problems that, I believe, determined the spiritual transformation of the young Calvin: the problems of conversion, schism, and vocation.

PART FOUR
The Problems of Conversion, Schism, and Vocation

CHAPTER TWENTY-FIVE
The Problem of the Conversion

Of the great transformation we are studying, only the word itself is clear: Calvin did become an evangelical reformer. But the origins, development, and significance—both subjectively and objectively—of Calvin's transformation have been and still remain an object of investigation.

The investigation that I have undertaken in length and breadth, I shall now continue in depth.

The essential question that I now pose to Calvin may be stated as follows: "What do you say about yourself?" What did Calvin's youthful movement toward the Gospel and his deliberate choice of radical reform mean for the reformer himself?

It has become commonplace to say that Calvin spoke of himself infrequently, in contrast to Luther who readily spoke of himself and frequently made his doctrinal statements in the first person singular (in German one would say that he was "Ich-betont"). The French reformer only rarely referred to details of his personal history.[1]

Another problem is that the small number of autobiographical fragments that we encounter have been interpreted by most historians in order to justify or defend Calvin. As I said in the beginning of my study, people have often sought to explain the young Calvin by the elder Calvin, or Calvin's whole being and thought by Calvinism. Confessional concerns have held an important place especially in the description of the spiritual transformation of the reformer.

A glance at the earlier literature clearly shows to what extent various authors are divided on the dating, motivation, and definition of what they almost unanimously call Calvin's "conversion." Far be it from me to complain about the disagreements of these many qualified scholars. I am aware of the extremely delicate nature of the task. Thus I claim no more than to present a new hypothesis, or rather a judgment on the whole matter, which appears to me more probable than the others. What I formulate will obviously take into account, with gratitude, the solid results attained by earlier studies.

"What do you say about yourself?" The reformer's reply appears quite brief if we seek it only in the few texts where he consents to unveil the secrets of his development. Because of this fact, I intend to expand the field of investigation to passages that merely allude to such secrets and then to other specifically "reformist" developments that have a personal tone. For I am persuaded that the "I" of Calvin is inseparably tied to his doctrine. This is not the same as with Luther, where the subjective element often "transfigures" the objective element of a statement. Quite the opposite. With Calvin, the objective dominates the subjective. But in dominating the subjective, the objective preserves the reality of the subjective. It brings out the hidden dimensions of the subjective in such a way that sometimes in what appears to be a theoretical statement, we encounter an authentic expression of Calvin's personality or experience.

To answer this question, I shall refer not only to several passages of the *Institutes* but to other texts that were briefly explored or not used at all so far in my study, such as the letter to Sadolet, the correspondence with du Tillet, the two "open letters" on the Mass and the priesthood, and several documents after 1539. I shall seek to resolve the following problem in particular: How did the young Calvin view his transformation as it was developing? Did he see it as a "conversion" in the usual sense of the word today which entails a break with a particular church? Or was it, rather, a gradual awareness of a calling to be a reformer? In conclusion, I shall offer several thoughts on the significance this transformation has for the history of the universal Church.

Emil Doumergue quite properly directed the attention of historians to an essential aspect of the problem when he wrote: "We cannot really know what the word 'conversion' meant"[2] as it came from the pen of sixteenth-century authors. P. Sprenger tried to fill this gap by determining the exact meaning of the word in Calvin's writings.[3] But he inquired almost exclusively into relatively late texts, especially the *Commentary on the Acts of the Apostles* (1554) and the final Latin edition of the *Institutes* (1559). His stated intention was to clarify the famous expression of the Preface to the *Commentary on the Psalms* (1557): *"subita conversione."* Considering the goal, this process seems entirely correct. However, it is quite inexplicable that Sprenger did not think it useful to analyze the term and the concept of "conversion" in the texts of the Psalms commentary itself.

We are mainly interested in the actual period of Calvin's spiritual transformation. Therefore we shall try first to establish whether the earliest writings of Calvin, written at or near the time of the transformation, contain the term "conversion" and what meaning or sense they attribute to it.

To give a broader historical dimension to our study, I shall begin by pointing out what "conversion" means in the Latin Bible, for some of the Fathers and theologians, for the Christian humanists, and finally—and above all—for Luther.

Only after this inquiry which focuses on the actual period of Calvin's transformation shall we examine later documents, from about 1557.

After we have done all we can to clarify Calvin's concept of conversion, we will be able to appreciate more fully to what extent and in what sense the reformer used this concept to describe his own spiritual evolution.

The Term and the Concept of Conversion

In the Old Testament, especially in the psalms, we find the term *šûb* and its derivatives translated by the Vulgate as *convertere* and *conversio. Šûb* signifies a turning around followed by reconciliation, the movement of one who *returns* or is made to return.[4] It is sometimes used in a profane sense and sometimes in a religious sense. In the latter sense, it means the turning (return) of God to man or of man to God.[5]

In the New Testament, the verb ἐπιστρέφειν corresponds to the Hebrew *šûb* and is translated by the Vulgate as *convertere.* The noun ἐπιστροφή is found only once, in Acts 15:3, where it designates the conversion of the Gentiles.[6] The secular use of the verb is rare.[7] It almost always refers to a change in religious orientation, sometimes in the transitive ("to convert someone") and sometimes in the passive ("to be converted"). Most often it is accompanied by a complementary phrase indicating the *terminus ad quem* ("to God"—Acts 15:19; 1 Thess. 1:9; "to the living God"—Acts 14:15; "to the Lord"—Luke 1:16; Acts 11:21; "to light"—Acts 26:18), or the *terminus a quo* ("from deception"—1 Thess. 1:9; "from the error of his ways"—James 5:20; "from darkness"—Acts 26:18). But the most important religious use of the word is in passages where it has no complement ("unless you turn and become like little children"—Matt. 18:3; "when you have turned, strengthen your brothers"—Luke 22:32; cf. James 5:19), and especially in passages where it is accompanied by a form of μετανοεῖν, which expresses the specifically New Testament idea of repentance ("therefore repent and turn again"—Acts 3:19; "that they do repent and be converted to God, doing works worthy of repentance"—Acts 26:20). As far as we can tell, there is only one text in the New Testament where ἐπιστρέφειν expresses the opposite idea of apostasy (Gal. 4:9).

These texts show us, first, that according to the apostles and the evangelists, conversion has a twofold theological meaning: it was directed to God and accomplished by God.[8] Moreover, we see that the Hellenistic author of Acts saw in it a reality strongly connected to repentance as *metanoia.* Therefore conversion was not basically detachment (disgust, refusal, break) but attachment (a higher love, acceptance, commitment).[9] Often the role of the minister whose mission was to "convert" pagans or sinners is equally emphasized.[10]

For Augustine, himself a convert, the concept of conversion is inseparably linked to the tension between sin and grace or to the relationship between the will and grace. The teacher of North Africa strongly emphasizes the fathomless misery of sinful man and the irresistible force of divine intervention. Conversion occurs against a mysterious background of original sin and predestination.[11]

Medieval scholasticism used the terms *convertere* and *conversio* as often in a secular or philosophical sense as in a strictly religious way. Commentators on Lombard frequently insist that the will cooperates with "assisting grace," indicating a Semi-Pelagian tendency. In this perspective, the subjective conditions of conversion are a "right will," humility, and fidelity to grace; its objective conditions include believing certain truths, observing moral precepts, receiving the sacraments, and obeying ecclesiastical authority. This view, in which the work of the convert is stressed more than the work of God, and in which the juridical and ecclesiastical aspects are stressed more than the spiritual and biblical elements, characterizes not only most of the sixteenth-century scholastics[12] but also certain modern works on spirituality.[13]

The Christian humanists, in returning exegesis to a place of honor, contribute only indirectly to the spiritual and biblical reevaluation of the concept, for they hardly pause to analyze it theologically.[14] For example, Erasmus opposed some scholastics who wanted to find in some way the sacramental triad of contrition, confession, and satisfaction in the biblical idea of μετάνοια. For this reason, Erasmus preferred to translate μετάνοια by "repentance" rather than "penitence."[15]

Luther's position is quite different. He eagerly takes up the biblical theme of conversion and gives it an Augustinian interpretation. For him, conversion comes about through the experience of one's own evil and by trusting faith in the infinite mercy of God.[16] In *The Bondage of the Will,* Luther rejects Erasmus' attempt to prove the existence of free will on the basis of Zech. 1:3: "Turn to me, . . . and I will turn to you." In the same way that man "by his own power" is incapable of loving God above everything else, he can do nothing to convert himself. The passage from Zechariah contains two things: the harsh demand of the law which requires of the sinner an impossible conversion and the consoling promise of the Gospel which grants absolutely free forgiveness.[17] In other words, the turning of man to God presupposes the turning of God to man; and the true "conversion of peace" can only be the work of the Holy Spirit.[18] Here human efforts and merits are powerless or nonexistent; the miracle, the *wunderwerck,* of grace triumphs.[19] To be brought to life by the work of God,[20] the sinner need only recognize his corrupt nature and impious acts in the spiritual experience of mortification.[21] With Luther, repentance and conversion are inseparable, for they are foci of one spiritual process that is conditioned by the encounter of faith and grace. The fruits of repentance, good works, follow and manifest the conversion.[22]

Now let us examine Calvin's early writings.

In the *De Clementia,* the verb *convertere* is used six times, but always in a secular way.[23] It is true that this treatise contains only a few religious considerations, and it is evidently earlier than Calvin's conversion as most historians date it.

The *Psychopannychia,* especially in its definitive version, comes after the conversion, but one seeks in vain for the slightest allusion to the author's religious transformation. Although the work is addressed to sectarians accused of schism and doctrinal deviations, it does not invite them to abandon their errors or to be converted to the truth. The term *convertere* is found four times, but always with the profane meaning of "to turn" or "to return."[24]

In the *Institutes* of 1536 we find for the first time the verb *convertere,* and indeed even the noun *conversio,* used in a clearly religious sense. In the section on "Penance" in the chapter "The False Sacraments," Calvin first takes up Luther's distinction between "repentance of the law" and "repentance of the Gospel." Then he closely follows the German reformer by using the themes of sin and mercy, terror of judgment and confidence in grace, the vow of mortification and the pardon which brings life.[25] To express the "legal" aspect of repentance, he goes so far as to borrow Luther's image of the descent into hell.[26]

It is in the context of repentance that we find the first mention of conversion in the religious sense of the word: "We see Gospel repentance in all those who, wounded by the sting of sin but raised up and renewed by trust in God's mercy, are turned to the Lord." A reference to the story of Hezekiah (2 Kings 20) follows, and then another to the inhabitants of Nineveh (Jonah 3) where the "conversion" of God toward the repentant sinners is mentioned ("hoping that the Lord might be turned to them"). After four other biblical references, of which the last two are from Acts, Calvin refers to the prophets and the apostles: "For they were striving for this, that confused by their sins and pierced by the fear of God, they might fall down and humble themselves before God and return to the way and revive. Therefore they use these [words] interchangeably, signifying the same thing: "to be converted" or "return to the Lord" and "do penance." And John said, "Bear fruit worthy of repentance"; "lead a life which is worthy of this kind of repentance and conversion (Matt. 3:8)."[27]

All that Luther drew from Scripture, especially from the prophets and Acts, is condensed as accurately as possible in Calvin's text. We find a direct connection between, indeed an identification of, ἐπιστρέφειν *(convertere)* and μετανοεῖν *(resipiscere)*; then we see the idea of the "way of conversion" or "repentance," and finally the Johannine theme of the "fruits of repentance."

It would truly be forcing the text to draw from it a "confessional" concept of conversion or to discern in it a reminiscence of a conversion recently experienced by the author himself.

Besides, we cannot find a religious meaning of the term *convertere* in any other page of the first *Institutes*—not even on the topic of repentance where we would expect it.[28]

What do we find in Calvin's two epistles of 1537 which deal explicitly with the abandonment of "papal superstitions," the greatest of which is the Mass? Neither the epistle *On Abandoning the Papal Priesthood* nor the epistle *On Fleeing the Illicit Rites of the Wicked* uses "turn" or "conversion" in a religious sense, much less a "confessional" sense. Calvin speaks of "confession" as an act of confessing one's faith, piety, and indeed his religion in a way purified of superstitions.[29] But there is not a single reference to a spiritual turning that would lead a man from one "confessional" community to another.

The word "conversion" is not used in this latter sense, except in a passage from the *Reply to Sadolet*. Here is the context: along with the other evangelical ministers of Geneva, Calvin feels himself to be the object of the Cardinal's "sinister suspicions." In fact, the Cardinal insinuated that Farel, Calvin, Viret, and other preachers were motivated only by ambition and greed when they led the citizens of Geneva to dissent.[30] Because they felt unjustly deprived of the honors and riches that the Church should have offered them for their knowledge and work, they broke from the Church.[31] Calvin replied to these insinuations: "Do you think that they were forced by hunger to depart from you, and that despairing of material goods they fled to this *conversion* or to these 'new accounts'?"[32]

What does Calvin mean by "conversion"? First, we must note that in using the phrase "Do you think" Calvin attributes to his adversary the opinion that follows. Then, in view of the fact that Calvin regularly uses the word in a profane sense and only occasionally in the religious and penitential sense, one may properly suppose that "conversion" here means simply "change." A change of group or party, if you will, but not necessarily a change of "confession" or Church. Besides, the anonymous translator of the document[33] felt a need to diminish slightly the density of the Latin; he writes: "Do you think that hunger constrained them to depart from you; and that despairing of goods they became separated and reduced to *this change and new conversion,* as if going bankrupt, or as in a complete cancellation of old debts?"[34] Only with great difficulty could either the text, its context, or translation lead us to see here the idea of conversion in the modern and confessional sense of the word. Moreover, the word is used nowhere else in the *Reply.*

Since our goal is to understand the religious transformation of the young Calvin, we could stop here in our conceptual and linguistic investigations concerning Calvin's use of "conversion." But since many historians refer to the later writings of the reformer to explain his "sudden conversion," we must extend our inquiry beyond 1539 before we can appreciate the value of their hypotheses.

The *Institutes* of 1539 basically reproduces the biblical and Lutheran notion of conversion-repentance which was succinctly expressed in 1536. Calvin first notes that even for the sacred authors of the Old Testament the "results of our conversion"—that is, our obedience to the divine will, justification, sanctification, and piety—were essentially a gift of God. Having said this, he quotes Zech. 1:3 ("Turn to me, . . . and I will turn to you") and interprets it as Luther did.[35] Commenting on Jer. 31:18, he adds that no one can escape the slavery of sin and experience the "movement of conversion to God" if it were not for the grace of God.[36]

Referring to the "false sacrament" of penance, Calvin stresses that the process of repentance, which the Jews call "conversion" and the Greeks a "change of mind and purpose" (μετάνοια), is inseparable from faith. He continues: "Thus *repentance* could be defined as a true *conversion* of our life to God, which is brought about by a sincere and serious fear of God, and which consists of the mortification of our flesh and the old man and the vivification of the Spirit."[37]

In 1551, we encounter a new development. Every experience that the sinner has undergone is considered a "preparation for conversion," that is, "for repentance." Even Egypt, addicted to impiety, superstitions, and idolatry—which Calvin gladly compares to the "papal kingdom"—after submitting to salutary chastisement, may know the mercy of the Lord.[38]

Writing the *Commentary on the Acts,* published from 1552 to 1554, allows the reformer to reflect on conversion more from the point of view of its cause than its effect. He emphasizes that it is the Word of God which effects conversion and enables the sinner to pass from death into life.[39]

But it is especially Paul's conversion that holds Calvin's attention. Here he sees the work of divine grace in all its irresistible and truly creative power: "Here Luke refers to the well-known and especially memorable story of Paul's conversion: not only how the Lord subdued him under his power when he was raging like an uncontrollable beast but how he immediately made him into a new and different man."[40] The resistance of the "uncontrollable beast," the persecutor of Christians and enemy of the Church, was extraordinarily strong.[41] But it vanished in a twinkling of an eye when the hand of God seized him. In the end, Saul's ferocity only served to manifest the wonder of God's almighty power: "But it was even more incredible how *suddenly* he was able to be subdued. Moreover, a cruel wolf was not only turned into a sheep, but he assumed the character of a pastor!

In this the *wonderworking hand of God* was openly stretched forth."[42] A little farther on, Calvin takes up the same idea: *"Suddenly,* in an unusual way, he was changed into a new man; for not only was a wolf turned into a sheep but he assumed the character of a pastor."[43] The "old man" followed his own passions and will. He became an entirely "new man" only by divine constraint: "he willingly struggled against Christ; now he is involuntarily led to obedience." The "old man," proud and insensitive to divine promptings, was broken; the "new man," humble and ready to receive the Word, began to exist: "But in Paul this was the beginning of humility, that he might be teachable before the voice of Christ."[44]

Several ideas are brought out here. First there is the dialectical opposition between the human will which is rebellious but powerless and the divine will which is sovereign and compelling. Next there is the sudden nature of God's triumphant and transforming intervention. Then there is the affirmation that the convert begins an entirely new existence, which is marked by docility, or teachableness. Finally conversion develops into a pastoral calling.[45]

If we must express the specific kind of conversion described here, we would say: "conversion as miracle." It is the miracle of the road to Damascus that Calvin wants to emphasize. In a later part of the commentary, he does not hesitate to state that all conversion takes place "contrary to nature," "according to the wonderful and secret power of God."[46] Farther on, he explicitly speaks of "miracle" on two occasions.[47]

But is this a conversion radically different from *"conversion as repentance"*? I do not think so. Although Calvin places the theme of repentance in the background, he in no way eliminates it. He clearly states that Paul is urged by Christ to a true *metanoia:* "Christ pushed him nearer to repentance."[48] Therefore it is my opinion that for Calvin "conversion as miracle" is a particular kind, a higher form of "conversion as repentance." What follows in the text specifically confirms this opinion, for it is said that Paul's spiritual turning typically illustrates the grace of our daily conversions. "Moreover," Calvin writes, "we have in this story a universal example or type of the grace that God manifests daily in calling all of us." Of course, we are not all persecutors like Saul, and God does not work a miracle for each of us. But, except for this difference, we all must recognize our sin, believe in the promise of forgiveness, and with docility follow the road of the new man exactly the same way that Saul became Paul. "Certainly not all exalt themselves against the Gospel with such violence; nevertheless pride and rebellion against God are innate in all; we are all depraved and cruel by nature. Therefore, when we are converted to God, it occurs contrary to nature and by the wonderful and secret power of God. . . . But when God mortifies our flesh, he subdues us no differently than he did Paul; our will is not one bit more inclined to obedience than was Paul's. Not until the pride of our hearts is broken are we in any way flexible. But he renders us willing to follow him. Therefore such is the beginning of our conversion, that God . . . changes the affections of our heart, whereby he makes us teachable before him."[49] On this road of docility, God obviously does not abandon us to our own strength. He knows that, just as we were unable to begin our conversion, so we cannot advance alone. Therefore he still takes us by the hand and "leads us gradually to the goal."[50]

Referring to Acts 22:6ff., Calvin again returns to the miraculous context of the apostle's conversion[51] and to the necessity of teachableness in every authentic experience of repentance. He notes: "And there is no doubt that Ananias faithfully initiated Paul in the rudiments of piety."[52] (We shall find this expression again in reference to Calvin's *"subita conversione."*)

From 1556 on, it is again "conversion as repentance" which appears to be dominant. For Calvin, the miracle on the road to Damascus seems to highlight the idea that each conversion has divine grace as its unique and sovereign cause.

Nevertheless it is interesting to note that several important elements in the idea of "conversion as miracle," such as the dialectical tension between man's obstinate malice and God's efficacious mercy, or the themes of docility and obedience, are integrated harmoniously in the reformer's later thoughts on repentance.

This beautiful passage from a sermon dated in 1556 illustrates our point: "The nature of man is such that in general we are apostates as we leave our mother's womb. We are enemies of God, and there is nothing in us but perversity and rebellion. God must therefore change us from the very root. . . . Now this word 'conversion' means that man, instead of turning his back to God, turns his face toward him. It is as if Scripture is speaking of a change, as it also says that we must be renewed. Let us therefore learn that if we submit to being taught by our God, it is a sign that we are reaching out for him and that we wish to manifest the fear, obedience, and submission that we owe to his law. But we must reach this point to be converted."[53]

In the same series of sermons, the reformer states that the conversion that is truly a sincere and continual "repentance" brings us to life and inclines us to devoted service of our Lord.[54]

The Preface to the *Commentary on the Psalms* (1557) has become so famous that many historians seem to forget the rest of the work. But the autobiographical section of the Preface is not the only place where Calvin speaks of conversion. Calvin notes all the verses where the terms "to turn" and "conversion" are used, seeking to establish whether they are to be interpreted in the sense of repentance.

This leads him to compare the Latin version with the original Hebrew, and after this examination to eliminate almost all uses of "to turn" by the Vulgate, which could suggest the idea of repentance where the sacred authors had no intention whatsoever of doing so. Therefore several times Calvin replaces "to turn" with "restore" or "renew," meaning "to bring comfort," "to do again," "to reinvigorate," and "to restore."[55] To maintain his identification of repentance and conversion, Calvin sometimes stresses precision to the point of subtle nuances. Speaking of Ps. 7:12 (Vulgate 7:13; "Unless he turns, he will sharpen his sword"), Calvin remarks: "Conversion here should not be taken to mean repentance, but only a change of will."[56] It goes without saying that in these numerous instances, Calvin uses *convertere* with its original meaning of "to turn," "to return," "to change," "to come back," and "to cause to come back."[57]

Two passages of the *Commentary on the Psalms* are particularly significant. The first describes the conversion of a people who have been unfaithful and impenitent for a long time. It is a typical example of "conversion as repentance," but with a singular emphasis on divine causality. Calvin comments on Ps. 22:27: "The ends of the earth will remember and be converted to the Lord." The commentary is: "The conversion or return mentioned here refers to (I grant) those who earlier had been alienated from God through impious defection; but remembrance [cf. *metanoia*] means nothing other than that the Gentiles, awakened by the miraculous signs of God, would again devote themselves to true religion, from which they had fallen away." There follows a messianic application of the text to the preaching of the Gospel, where the unconquered people are directed back to God, "led by Christ."[58] We note the clearly "reformist" coloring of the passage: the people are not to be destroyed, or even torn apart, but only led back to the pure religion of former times. The only break that may be imposed upon the people does not oppose one community to another but opposes only the corrupt community to its own sins, its own defection. Here we are dealing with an inner reform under the aegis of the Gospel.

The second significant passage is related to the mission or communal vocation of one who has just experienced repentance. Here the role of the Word is especially emphasized. Calvin reads verse 13 of Psalm 51: "I will teach sinners your ways, and the wicked will be converted unto you." Calvin explains the verse: "Here he (namely, David, contrite and forgiven) promises to give thanks to God . . . and to work so that *others would repent* because of his example." It is not just brotherly love which urges the forgiven penitent to help others to return to God but also filial love for the Lord and the desire to glorify him: "desire for piety and zeal for God's glory." The preaching of the "Word of the Lord" is obviously the chief instrument of this apostleship. Only through the Word can the preacher effectively touch souls: "Thus joining the accomplishment of conversion to his teaching, he shows that he hopes to complete his work." And what is the goal of this apostleship? Not to remove sinners from their imperfect community in order to integrate them into a new society of saints, but simply to set them on the right path. Applying this principle to himself, Calvin declares: "We seek to call back those who have wandered away."[59] The one who repents should preach repentance.

Finally, we observe that throughout the *Commentary on the Psalms*—which begins with an allusion to his own "sudden conversion"—the reformer never refers to a sudden or miraculous element in spiritual transformation.

Only in the *Institutes* of 1559 does Calvin come back to the "sudden and unexpected change" of the apostle,[60] as he frequently develops different variations of the theme "conversion as repentance."[61]

During the last years of his life, Calvin seemed to be preoccupied with relating the conversion of the sinner to God's eternal election and rejecting the role of free will in order to emphasize that of the Holy Spirit.

In the text of the *Treatise on Eternal Election* (1562), we read: "Referring to repentance, it is said, 'Let the sinner be converted and live'; this means . . . that God invites everyone to repentance. . . . But this gift of repentance is not common to everyone. It is not within our power to convert ourselves from our evil life, unless God changes us and cleanses us by his Holy Spirit."[62]

And in the *Lectures on Jeremiah* (1563), Calvin asserts that the elect do not turn to God by their own strength: "He was converted not by his own will but by the secret work and inspiration of the Holy Spirit."[63] It is the same for all Christians: "Certainly we do not turn, unless we are turned. It is not willingly or by our efforts that we turn; but it is the work of the Holy Spirit."[64] To believe that free will plays the slightest role in "conversion as repentance" would be to lapse into Pelagianism: "*Repentance* is the gift of God. . . . This is the view that Augustine accepts, against Pelagians, when he proves that it is not in man's power to be *converted* or to pray."[65]

Finally, I quote a passage that is very characteristic of the last phase of the evolution we are studying. It sums up quite well Calvin's thought on repentance, while placing new emphasis on the progressive nature of conversion. The sinner is converted only little by little, precisely because he drags with him the burden of persistent moral depravity. God grants a sudden and miraculous "beginning" only in exceptional cases. Similarly, he snatches from perdition only a few members of a religious community at a time. As a general rule, individual conversion and collective restoration occur in a progressive manner.

Here are the essential thoughts of the passage: "For we are renewed from day to day, and gradually we renounce the desires of our flesh; we do not put off the old man in a day." After referring to the miracle by which God brought back from captivity a part of his elect people, Calvin writes: "The same thing happens in spiritual conversion with respect to the whole body as well as each member. As I have already said, we are converted gradually to God, and by several steps, for repentance has its own stages of progress."[66]

What conclusions can we reach from this study of terminology? First of all, Calvin takes up and brings together in a single idea the Old Testament and New Testament themes of conversion, while giving them a noticeably Lutheran interpretation. Furthermore, we possess practically no written evidence from before 1539 of Calvin's theological reflections on this topic. The works dating from the period of the presumed conversion of Calvin furnish us with only a single passage where "to convert" possesses a clearly religious meaning that includes the idea of repentance. This is found in the *Institutes* of 1536. The theme of the "sudden conversion" appears only between 1552 and 1554 and has the specific purpose of shedding light on the miraculous nature of the transformation of the apostle Paul. Although this transformation was an extraordinary event, it is considered as a type of our conversions. "Conversion as miracle" and "conversion as repentance" do not differ on the essential point: both are equally the exclusive work of God.

We have not found one reference that clearly shows that conversion, this experience of repentance, ever necessitates a break of an ecclesiastical or "confessional" nature, in the modern sense of the word. The only break that it demands (and that is also brought about by grace) concerns sin in general and impiety, idolatry, and superstitions in particular. In this view, even Egypt—the stereotype of the "papal kingdom"—may know the mercy of God. Finally, Calvin never tries to suggest that conversion may be dated or located, as the pietists will do later.

I have intentionally set aside for the present Calvin's remark about his "sudden conversion." I shall analyze it later, taking into account its context. For the moment, we have to examine again the earlier documents from 1536 to 1539, where Calvin does not speak of conversion in general but where he alludes (or seems to allude) to his own transformation.

Calvin's Conversion

Let us grant in principle that several texts of the reformer describe, or at least reflect, his conversion, even if they do not use the word. Life generally precedes the letter, and experience the expression. Calvin was able to become conscious of his progressive, rapid, or even sudden transformation without publicly declaring: "Look! I am converted!" For this transformation really to have constituted a conversion, it is sufficient that what he experienced at that moment he will later designate by this word. In other words, he need only have undergone a personal experience of repentance. The essential question to ask is whether Calvin thinks that this passage from the state of an obstinate sinner to the state of a forgiven sinner requires the ruptures that the majority of historians see in it.

A first observation: In spite of its explicitly evangelical character and severe criticisms of the papacy, the first *Institutes* is not preoccupied with the road to repentance that Calvin and his companions needed to travel in order to depart from typically "papist" sins. How, when, in what circumstances, and especially with what precise intention they abandoned the Mass, auricular confession, prayers to the saints, and fasts, Calvin does not tell us. We do not find such a description even in the most personal part of his work, the Dedicatory Epistle, which is a brilliant apology for the "evangelical party." The author does not seem to be concerned with his immediate past; his attention is entirely fixed on the present and the future of his Church, within which the "pious" and the "impious" confront the questions of reformation. And when he says reformation, he means renewal of the community. From the first sentences of the Epistle, it is a man of the community who is arguing. What he desires is to lead French Christians and, above all, their "very Christian King" to "sound doctrine" and "true piety." Let us note well: the adjectives "sound" and "true" in this context allude more to a "healing" of defective doctrine and to a correction of wayward piety than to the adoption of another credo and another ethic. What was buried alive should be brought forth; those who were unjustly persecuted should be set free. These statements are made on behalf of the "truth" and also on behalf of the "poor little Church." We do not have the impression that we are listening to a "convert" who is recalling personal memories, but a reformer who announces and defends his program of reform.

Although the compendium as a whole reflects the same positive, reformist orientation, there is a passage that may deal with the movement toward repentance which led Calvin and his companions out of the "darkness of the papacy" into the light of the Gospel.

The passage deals with an argument in which Calvin rejects the position of the anabaptists on baptism. In practice, the sectarians think the same way as the donatists: they make the effectiveness of the sacrament depend on the dignity or the faith of the minister: "Today, such are our anabaptists; they completely deny that we were properly baptized, because we were baptized in the papal kingdom by impious and idolatrous men. Therefore they furiously urge rebaptism."[67] An obvious error! The value of baptism depends only on the Holy Trinity in whose name it is administered. But the papist ministers—while being "most ignorant and contemptuous of God"—did baptize them "in the name of the Father, Son, and Holy Spirit." In spite of their ignorance or their apostasy, they baptized them "in faith in Jesus Christ."

Of course, Calvin admits that being baptized in the faith of Christ does not necessarily mean that one possesses a personal faith that is pure and perfect. Although they are now evangelicals, Calvin and his friends were in fact blind and unbelieving for a very long time. But that matters little, for God remains faithful, even when his sons live apart from faith: "Even if all men are liars and faithless, God does not cease to be true. Even if all are lost, Christ remains our salvation."[68] This is why a minister devoid of "sound doctrine" or one baptized into a dormant faith does not compromise the validity of the promise granted by the sacrament. Faith need only be revived for the promise to take its full salutary effect.

At this precise point Calvin introduces what we can consider an allusion to the repentance that he and his friends experienced. He writes: "Therefore we confess that baptism did not benefit us one bit before that time, since the promise offered us in it, without which baptism is nothing, lay neglected. Now, when by God's grace we begin to repent, we blame our hardness of heart and blindness. For a long time we were ungrateful toward his great goodness. But we believe that the promise itself did not vanish. . . . Indeed, for a long time it was buried to us because of our lack of faith; therefore, let us now receive it in faith."[69]

There is no doubt that the entire context deals with repentance. Calvin considers that men like him (the "we" is obviously collective) were blind, hardened, ungrateful; they conformed to the life of those who were ignorant and contemptuous of God and who had—validly—baptized them. But the times have changed and the state of impiety has passed away. The grace of God led them to the beginning of repentance which brought about an entirely new life of repentance, marked by a living dialogue between faith and promise.

All of this change in life and spirit, this revitalization of what was buried, occurs basically in the subjective realm. It never reaches the objective realm of the sacrament, which is unchangeable because it is guaranteed by God. In this view, the continuity between a deformed state and a re-formed state of the Christian community is implicitly affirmed. Moreover, any idea of founding a new Church by means of a new baptism is categorically rejected.

In brief, I think this passage of the first *Institutes* expresses, at least indirectly, the "conversion as repentance" experienced by young Calvin, even though the personal and collective parts are not very easily distinguished and the terms "conversion" and "repentance" are not used.

The strange thing is that this passage is not used, as far as is known, by any of the historians who are especially interested in the reformer's conversion. On the contrary, their attention is drawn to the two famous sections of the *Reply to Sadolet,* in which the author attempts to justify the position of the evangelical minister and follower.

To understand these texts thoroughly, one needs to remember that the *Reply to Sadolet* not only deals with the themes of the Cardinal's letter but also borrows from it several literary characteristics. Sadolet presented two fictional characters publicly examining their consciences before the tribunal of God; the first personifies one of the simple faithful and the other a dissident minister.[70] In the same way Calvin has a minister speak first and then a faithful follower of the evangelical group. There is therefore a parallel: in both cases there are persons who express what any knowledgeable member of the community in question might assert.

Doumergue, relying on other authors,[71] thinks that the "personal accent" is so strong in the testimony of Calvin's two characters that they certainly express more than a "type" of conversion; they describe the conversion of Calvin himself.[72]

Without entering into a discussion of this thesis, I merely point out that A. Lang, K. Müller, and P. Sprenger have reservations—to say the least—on this matter.[73] I will immediately approach the task that none of the authors quoted deemed necessary: a detailed analysis of the text itself.

Calvin first of all asserts his intention to respond to Sadolet by using the technique of dramatic fiction: "But at the end [of your plea] a person was brought in who would uphold our cause,[74] and then you cited us as if we were criminals before God's tribunal. Therefore I summon you in turn, without hesitation, to that place."[75] It is the lawyer experienced in legal contests who responds to the challenge. The cause that he wants to defend is "our cause." The significant "I" is Calvin's last clearly personal note; then the lawyer hastens to step aside in order to allow his principal witness to speak, the fictional evangelical minister. He also indicates the reason for stepping aside: the collective apology which follows does not aim to defend individuals, including Calvin himself, but the ministry with which they are charged: "I do not speak of persons . . . ; but as far as it concerns the cause of the ministry, there is not one of us who could not speak thus on his own behalf."[76] The good pastor never justifies himself as a private individual but only as a man of the Church.

"O Lord, I have experienced," the minister's testimony begins, "how difficult and burdensome it is to bear the ill will of this accusation, by which I am oppressed on earth." An obvious allusion to the harsh words of Sadolet on the misdeeds imputed to the heretics. But the conscience of the accused is at peace; he acted in accord with God's will within the Church of God: "whatever was done by me in *your* Church." The indivisibility of the Church which is implicit in the passage is stressed several times in what follows. It is to the Church, not *a church,* that the minister preached the Word;[77] within the Church are found the enemies of God[78] and the doctrinal errors that have arisen from human speculations.[79] The thought that one might divide the Church by a schism, even a salutary one, is emphatically and explicitly rejected.[80] This is the theme of the entire passage. We shall return to it.

Sadolet's accusations were aimed at heresy and schism. The minister replies: "But the heresy to them was that I dared to contradict the dogmas accepted among them."[81] For "dogmas" the French translation puts "constitutions." Moreover, the entire immediate context of the passage dissuades us from attributing to the term "dogma" its proper sense of revealed truth defined by the Magisterium.

What are the "dogmas" in question? They are the "doctrines born in men's brains" which are presented as "words of God."[82] But the witnessing minister knows what is truly the Word of God. He learned it from the very mouth of the Lord: "I heard from your mouth that there is no other light of truth directing our souls in the way of truth than what is kindled by your Word." As for doctrines or constitutions not founded upon the Scriptures: "I heard that whatever they conceived by their own human minds concerning your majesty, the worship of your divinity, and the mysteries of your religion is vanity."[83]

After opposing the Word of God to "human inventions," the fictitious orator gives a veritable summary of Luther's criticism of evil pastors, superstitions, the improper worship of saints, the sacrifice of the Mass, the sacrificial priesthood, and especially justification by works. The criticism of merits and satisfactions appears in a form that may be called classic or stereotypical. Calvin's originality perhaps comes through only in this allusion to the glory of God: "so that the glory of your justice and goodness, dispelling the clouds by which it was previously concealed, might shine forth conspicuously."[84]

Calvin's response to the accusation of schism also recalls Luther's statements about Roman responsibility for all "dissent" and the evangelicals' basic goal of reform. Since the hierarchy neglected or refused to bring about reform, the partisans of the complete Gospel had to compensate for them, just as the prophets of the Old Testament had done for certain omissions of which the Levitical priesthood was guilty. The evangelicals are persecuted because they obeyed God rather than man: "Then they attacked me. Those who ought to keep others in line led them astray into errors. And when I completely refused to desist, they violently resisted."[85] Therefore, if anyone is guilty of causing tumult in the Church, it is not the persecuted but the persecutors.

This is the essence of the evangelical minister's testimony before the tribunal of God. I do not think there is much that describes the conversion of Calvin himself. Personal recollections may be mixed with statements of a rather typical nature, but they are not obvious. Besides, in accord with Calvin's initial statement, the subject at hand is much more the reform of the Church by the so-called "prophetic" ministry of the reformers than the spiritual journey of any one of them.

Do these conclusions apply to the testimony placed in the mouth of another fictitious character, the representative of evangelical laymen? Calvin presents this character, similar to the "common man" of Sadolet, in the following manner: "And indeed, those who have been taught by our preaching and have joined with us in the same cause will not be at a loss about what to say for themselves, since this defense will be prepared for each one."[86]

Thus the new witness summoned to the stand is supposed to be one of those who were drawn to the Gospel by the preaching of Calvin or another minister. Nothing in principle precludes this from being at the same time a representation of the young Calvin himself.

He is also described as speaking "for himself," as making an apology for all the evangelical faithful. But is this the apology he will actually make? Or is he, rather, going to justify those who evangelized him? Examining the text will give us the answer.

The first sentences bring together in a significant way the assertion of ecclesiastical continuity and criticism of deviations within the Church. Baptized and raised "under the papacy," the witness has never professed any other faith than that of Christianity: "O Lord, as I was educated from my childhood, I have always professed the Christian faith. But in the beginning I had no other understanding of the faith than that which was found everywhere at the time."[87] Unfortunately this "understanding of the faith" (or according to the French text this "knowledge" of the Christian faith) was quite imperfect. Because of educators who were forgetful of the "Scriptures," this knowledge provided an inadequate initiation into the true worship of God, the sure hope of salvation, and the Christian life in general: "But the rudiments in which I was initiated were such that they did not satisfactorily instruct me in the legitimate worship of your majesty. And they did not set me on the way to a certain hope of salvation or train me well in the duties of the Christian life."[88] The emphasis is on the insufficiency of the teaching, not on its absence or that it was absolutely contrary to the truth. Consequently, the assertions of some continuity and criticism go together. What follows continues along the same lines: the witness recounts what he received and did not receive from his education "under the papacy," and in so doing follows the same design taken from the Lutheran criticisms of the preceding testimony.

At the end, one even hears statements that remind one especially of the monk of Wittenberg's crisis of conscience. The papal preachers, says the witness, insisted that he must confess all his sins and carry out numerous expiatory works. This threw him into complete spiritual confusion: "Then, because you were a strict judge and a stern punisher of iniquity, they showed how dreadful your presence must be." Where can one hide before the terrible Judge? "In the intercession of the saints," said these priests! The faithful follower obeyed, but praying to the saints gave him no peace at all: "Still I was far from true tranquillity of conscience." It was constant torture: "For as often as I descended into myself or offered my soul to you, extreme horror seized me, which no expiations or satisfactions could remedy." Deliverance came to him only by the doctrine proclaimed by the evangelical preachers: "When in the meantime a far different form of doctrine was raised up, not one that led us away from the Christian profession but one that returned it to its source and, as it were, restored it to its purity, purged of refuse."[89]

The witness was first of all shocked by this preaching. It seemed to him entirely new and contrary to traditional teaching: "But I was offended by the novelty, and with difficulty I opened my ears. And in the beginning, I confess, I strenuously and passionately resisted." It is hard for an adult to recognize that for a long time he lived in error without realizing it. It is not easy for a good son of the Church all of a sudden to stop respecting a part of the teachings, laws, and customs of the established Church, as well as its clergy. This is the context for understanding the following statement: "One thing above all turned my soul away from them, reverence for the Church."[90]

What follows seems to confirm this interpretation: "But when I opened my ears and was willing to be taught, I understood that the fear that this would detract from the majesty of the Church was unnecessary."[91] As long as the believer was incapable of distinguishing between the human elements capable of reform and the sacrosanct divine institutions, he could be truly paralyzed by reverence for everything that bore an ecclesiastical name or association. But from the time that he learned to distinguish between the essential and the unessential, he no longer had to fear disparaging the true majesty of the Church.

It is the evangelical preachers who brought him this illuminating instruction. They explained to him that there is a great difference between wishing to reform the Church and to separate from it. Moreover, they highlighted the fact that simply bearing the title of "successor of the apostles" or "vicar of Christ" does not necessarily mean that it is so in fact. They also demonstrated that their doctrine contained nothing new but was in keeping with the message of early Christianity. The rest of the discourse indirectly praises the ministers of the Gospel by criticizing the papacy. The believer only has to listen to them to understand clearly the true situation regarding sin and salvation: "Now when my mind was prepared for serious consideration, I realized, as if the light had dawned, in what a dung heap of errors I was mired and therefore how much I was defiled by filth and stains."[92]

Here again the theme of repentance arises. In fact, according to the preachers, the faithful person should consider himself guilty even if he had lived in these errors in good faith. They declare: "Indeed, one who was led astray through mere ignorance does not err with impunity." Consequently, the testimony ends with an appeal to the mercy of God: "And now, O Lord, what else remains for a miserable man like me, other than to offer to you for my defense a plea that you not call me to judgment for that horrible defection from your Word, from which you delivered me once and for all by your wonderful kindness."[93]

This allusion to the marvelous grace of the Lord makes us think of the commentary on Paul's conversion where it was a matter of the "wonderful hand of God."[94] There too, Paul's initial resistance and his subsequent teachability were mentioned.[95] It is especially interesting to note that the testimony of the faithful Christian says nothing about a sudden, indeed miraculous, transformation. Quite the contrary, what is emphasized is the role of human means, the teaching of the preachers.

The spiritual journey schematically retraced by this testimony is much more like "conversion as repentance" than "conversion as miracle." The latter, which Calvin calls in his *Commentary on the Acts* the "type of our daily conversions," here lends some of its elements to the former but is not identical with it.

This observation is helpful if one considers that twenty years later it is "conversion as miracle" that Calvin associates with his own "sudden conversion," making no allusion to an impetus prior to the event.

We come to the essential question: Can the testimony of the faithful evangelical in the *Reply to Sadolet* be considered, even partially, the story of Calvin's own conversion? In my view, only with great difficulty. Aside from the fact that Calvin explicitly ranks himself among the ministers rather than the faithful, several important details of the testimony do not correspond to what we know of his youth. To start with, the attitude characterized by the expressions "offended by its novelty," "I opened my ears with difficulty," and "I resisted strenuously and passionately" is hardly discernible in the documents concerning young Calvin. His correspondence and early writings testify instead of his great curiosity and intellectual concerns, his passionate interest in the ideas of the Christian humanists and the reformists, as well as his gradual, deliberate movement to the radical evangelical party. If there was any resistance, it came from the outside, from the persecuting representatives of orthodoxy; and according to the reaction it caused, it only accelerated Calvin's spiritual evolution.

Another discordant note: In Calvin's early writings there is not a single indication that the young jurist felt "extreme horror" or torment caused by the terror of judgment or by moral scruples. Calvin's balance and peaceful dedication to his work indicate quite the contrary. Let me add that the testimony of the faithful believer makes no allusion to an intellectual journey, to readings or studies. This man appears as a "common man," a "simple learner," who has none of the traits of an erudite humanist. In spite of what has just been said, I do not believe that this story is "purely literary" and only describes "an abstraction of a typical conversion of a man of the people" (Doumergue). The Calvin of the *Reply to Sadolet* was a pastor of souls who was already experienced enough to be able to sketch the drama that most of the faithful had experienced before coming to a fully assured evangelical faith.

The Preface to the *Commentary on the Psalms* is the document to which historians of Calvin most often refer to prove the fact of his conversion and to elucidate its significance. Therefore we must study the text in more detail.

In examining this text, we shall try to respond to three questions: To what extent can we consider it historical, strictly speaking? What is the exact meaning of the expression *"subita conversio"*? Is the dominant idea the personal conversion of Calvin?

The historian's attention is drawn in particular to the last third of the Preface, where allusions to relatively recent events abound. (The reformer uses verbs in the present tense several times.) But these allusions are made without much concern for chronological precision. Twice Calvin notes that he is speaking of a period of five years,[96] but he does not specify either the beginning or the end. In the French text, the imprecision is even more apparent. After a general statement referring to his frequent difficulties, the author begins a new sentence with the following expression: "Then, afterward for a period of five years."[97] If we suppose that this statement refers to the last concrete detail mentioned in the text, Calvin's return to Geneva after his exile in Strasbourg, we are led to understand the "five years" as 1541 to 1546. Now, we know that the vicissitudes to which the reformer alludes began especially after 1546.

If one tries to establish the meaning of this "five years" by an internal analysis of the text, one runs into other difficulties. Calvin's reference to those who opposed his understanding of predestination[98] could make us think of the Bolsec affair (1551) or the persistent refusal of Castellio and the residents of Bern and Basle to accept this doctrine (1552–1555). The allusions to the "internal struggles" stirred up by certain "internal enemies of the Church" who were trying to destroy the discipline established by the reformer[99] could refer to the revolt of the "libertines" of Geneva who, under the direction of Ami Perrin, Philibert Berthelier, and Pierre Vandel, emerged from time to time between 1546 and 1555. From the mention of criticisms and threats against Calvin's life,[100] one could just as well conclude that these may have been the attacks of Pierre Ameaux (1546), the bitter utterances of Jacques Gruet (1547), Jerome Bolsec (1551), Zeraphin Trolliet (1552), or even the passionate quarrels that took place during and after the trial of Michael Servetus (1553–1555). Moreover, the text names no actors and describes no particular event in all these conflicts, so that one cannot truly know from what date one should count the five years in question. We know that the reformer had to struggle from 1546 to 1555, nearly ten years, not five, to establish his power. It is also important to note that the year 1555 brought about his definitive victory over his opponents; and this prevents us from supposing that while writing his Preface in 1557, he could have been alluding to present antagonisms.[101]

Now let us examine, from a chronological point of view, the earlier part of the Preface where Calvin relates his *"subita conversio."* There too no date is indicated, and a period of several years seems to disappear behind a *quum* ("then afterward"), or at least it is extremely condensed. Let us look at the essential portion of this passage.

"While I was still a young child, [my father] destined me for theology. But when [then afterward] he saw that knowledge of the law everywhere advanced its devotees to riches, that hope suddenly [immediately] impelled him to change his plan. Thus it came about that I was recalled from the study of philosophy and drawn to studying law. And although I tried to devote myself faithfully to this work in obedience to my father's will, nevertheless in the end God turned my course in another direction through the hidden bridle of his providence." Then Calvin mentions his attachment to the "superstitions of the papacy," which was broken by the "sudden conversion." This statement follows: "And thus having received some taste of true piety, I was enflamed by such a great desire to advance that I pursued my other studies indifferently (even though I did not cast them aside). When not even a year had elapsed, all who desired a purer doctrine kept coming to me in order to learn, even though I was still a beginner and a novice." After a short note on his repugnance at appearing in public—a vow that the Lord undertook to overturn—Calvin concludes his story: "With this plan, I left my homeland and withdrew into Germany, so that while hidden away in some obscure corner I might enjoy the quiet so long denied me."[102]

These few concise sentences sum up a period of twelve years (1523–1535), which were filled with decisive events. As formulated, they could lead an uninformed reader to believe that before the conversion, there was a very short lapse of time marked by a rapid change of studies; and then following the conversion, there was a single year ("When not even a year had elapsed") after which disciples begin to flow toward the convert who had withdrawn into Germany. If Calvin wished to provide a historical account, he would certainly not have taken the risk of leading his readers into such an error. On the contrary, he would have suggested that his studies of philosophy had lasted several years, that he had received a complete training as a lawyer, that his reformist friends had brought him to discover the Bible and the evangelical doctrines, that the events of 1533 had completely unsettled his life, and that it was in fleeing persecution that he finally went to Basle.

As P. Wernle quite correctly remarks, Theodore Beza, Calvin's first biographer, already had felt the need to correct some statements in the Preface, which he used as a source for his *Life of Calvin.*[103] According to Beza, it was not only to obey his father that Calvin devoted himself to ecclesiastical studies, but he did so of his own accord: "His heart was completely absorbed in theology." Then Beza asserts that it was through Olivétan that Calvin "tasted something of pure religion" and that he went through a process of development before resolving "to dedicate himself entirely to God."[104] Moreover, Beza does not speak of a "conversion" or "a sudden conversion," and he does not hesitate to complement his source with other testimonies: contemporary oral traditions, personal recollections concerning Wolmar, and information about Olivétan. Here we see the effort of someone who is trying to do the work of a historian in placing his master's venerable "logion" in a chronological context and the actual course of events. This means that the logion in itself is not, in Beza's view, a historical narrative in the proper and complete sense of the word. What is it then? Wernle replies that it is a "reflection of his faith," an expression of Calvin's belief concerning his own development.[105] It is a "judgment of faith," or a "theological judgment" which transcends chronological precision, according to Sprenger.[106]

I willingly accept the opinion of these two authors and on this basis seek to resolve the second question: What is the exact meaning of the expression *"subita conversione"*? More precisely, what did Calvin himself mean by this expression?

Let us first quote the entire sentence that contains this expression: "And first, when I was so obstinately addicted to the superstitions of the papacy, it would not have been easy to draw me out of such deep mire.[107] But, by a sudden *(subita)* conversion to docility,[108] God subdued my soul, which was too hardened for my age." The subject of the sentence, as in the preceding one, is God, who acts "by the hidden bridle of his providence."

If we set aside a strictly historical interpretation and accept as a hypothesis that this is a theological statement, we can analyze this sentence by referring to the results of our study on Calvin's understanding of "conversion."

We have seen that in the reformer's theology, as in the Scriptures and in Luther, conversion essentially means repentance: recognition of sin as one abandons oneself in faith to the divine mercy. This turning around is entirely the work of the Lord, not of the subject himself. The ordinary work of God, "conversion as repentance," often comes about in an extraordinary, divine way, "conversion as miracle," of which the most typical example is the miracle on the road to Damascus.

As Sprenger has shown,[109] the similarity between our text and the commentary on Paul's conversion is obvious.[110] In both cases, it is the all-powerful God who is at work. With Calvin it is "God . . . by the hidden bridle of his providence," and with Paul it is the "marvelous and hidden power of God." In each case, God does the work of the "subduer"; he "subdues and renders teachable" the obstinately superstitious young Calvin, in the same way that he has "subdued" Paul, the "indomitable beast."[111] In both instances, everything happens suddenly: Calvin is transformed by a *"subita conversione"*; Saul is brought back "suddenly," "unexpectedly." The effect is the same: the disposition to listen to the Word. Paul was humbled "so that he would be teachable before the voice of Christ." Calvin was converted "to teachableness."

The obvious similarity between these two accounts—which clearly does not exclude differences of detail[112]—leads us to believe that Calvin at age fifty intentionally compares the miraculous change in Paul to the beginning of his own transformation in order to emphasize its divine origin. The fact that in the *Reply to Sadolet* he said that even involuntary attachment to superstitions was sinful allows us to think that after a quarter of a century of reflection, he saw his opening up to "pure doctrine" to be the essence of repentance.

Calvin's desire to offer an impressive example of God's power makes the use of the adjective *"subita"* plausible. If one is not telling a story but is highlighting the "theological" aspect of an event (or, if one prefers, the point of impact of the divine invasion into human existence), one may legitimately reduce matters to their essential content.[113]

One has all the more right to do this because Scripture itself often proceeds in this way. Especially in the books of the prophets, sometimes the past, the present, and the future are condensed and joined together to an extreme in order to furnish the basis for a theological statement.

In my opinion the entire Preface to the *Commentary on the Psalms* belongs to this prophetic genre. Calvin considers the psalmists as prophets: "But here the prophets themselves are speaking with God,"[114] proclaiming the "heavenly teaching."[115] Calvin considers David to be the most important of the prophets ("since David was the chief among them"),[116] and he does not hesitate to compare his own unsettled existence to David's: "It was great solace for me . . . to conform myself to such an excellent example."[117] He gladly turns to prophetic themes such as the hand of God stretched forth upon his servant;[118] the repeated escapes of God's messenger from the heavenly call, as with Jonah;[119] the calling of the humble to the prophetic ministry;[120] and the hatred of fellow countrymen toward the spokesman of the Lord.[121] He applies all these themes to himself or his ministry. It is therefore not surprising that he uses, at least from time to time, several literary genres from the prophets.

It seems clear that the exact meaning of *"subita conversione"* should therefore be sought in a theological-prophetic context and not in a purely historical point of view. This is the only means of correctly dealing with the "insurmountable difficulties" of which Doumergue speaks,[122] over which all the historians stumble who try to establish a chronological order in our passage and take literally the adjective *"subita."*[123] K. Müller stresses that this interpretation is also the best way to avoid the contradiction between the slow evolution attested by the earliest documents and the spontaneous transformation affirmed by our text.[124]

If Calvin had wanted to give an autobiographical summary, we may reproach him for the chronological imprecision of the word *"subita,"* just as for the phrase "five years" or for condensing matters with a word like "unexpectedly." But the author of the *Commentary on the Psalms* stands above the perspective of a simple chronicler. He wishes to proclaim force-fully the eternally valid theological truth that the grace of God is stronger than man's resistance. He wishes to do so as the prophets did by fleshing out his statement with examples taken from his personal experience as a messenger of the Lord. The story of his first penitence in the light of the Gospel is only one of these examples. We shall see that he refers to at least five other examples that illustrate exactly the same truth and that are expressed schematically. Just as the prophets did not wish to offer a chronicle but to bear witness, Calvin does not speak of his experiences in order to give an exact account of his life but to edify, in the profound sense of the word, his readers and his Church. Can we reproach him for contemplating these events from on high and seeing them with the eyes of faith, that is, from the point of view of the Lord, for whom "a thousand years are as one day (Ps. 90:4; 2 Peter 3:8)"? Who can blame him for condensing facts that, from a mundane point of view, extend for several years and presenting them as if they had occurred rapidly or suddenly?

This Preface is much too rich to examine only the passage dealing with the *"subita conversio."* It seems quite clear that this passage is secondary in importance to the comparison of the reformer's calling with that of David and the apostle Paul. It is significant that after referring to his conversion, he "suddenly" mentions his plans to enter the active ministry of teaching. Underlying this statement is a new analogy with Paul. In the same way that Paul was "not only a wolf converted into a sheep, but he also put on the character of a pastor,"[125] so the superstitious, hardened, and obstinate Calvin was changed into a teachable soul and soon into an evangelical pastor.[126] To speak of the pastorate is to speak of service to the Church. Thus the reformer devotes the major part of his text to illustrating the grace of God, who initiated and then nurtured Calvin's ecclesiastical vocation: "as the beginning of my vocation, so the continuing course of my charge."[127] At the very beginning he stated that in publishing his *Commentary on the Psalms* he had in view their usefulness to the Church.[128] Then in the course of his development, he reaffirms in many instances his ecclesiastical preoccupations: it is the internal afflictions of the Church which unsettle him, it is for the salvation of the Church that he is ready to give his life, it is the discipline of the Church which he wishes to safeguard, it is the ruin of the Church which he is attempting to prevent, and it is the Church's enemies whom he has decided to combat.[129]

Thus our reply to the third question is ready: In the Preface to the *Commentary on the Psalms,* the personal conversion of Calvin is not the dominant subject but the triumph of the divine power over every human obstacle, accomplished through the ministry of his servant in order to restore the Church.

However, it would be a misunderstanding of our conclusions to see in them a tendency to minimize the significance of the *"subita conversio."*

First, in all that has emerged from our examination of the *Institutes,* the *Reply to Sadolet,* and the Preface to the *Commentary on the Psalms,* I in no way wish to deny that there was a conversion for Calvin. I only stress the indisputable fact that it was at a mature age that Calvin described his own spiritual transformation as "conversion" and that he did so clearly only once, and that was from a theological perspective. It appears obvious to us that this a posteriori interpretation of an early event was expressed according to Calvin's concept of "conversion as repentance" which was developed by a lengthy study of the Scriptures. The adjective *"subita"* was not introduced by a chronicler's concern for precision but by a theologian's desire to emphasize the divine origin of the event. This procedure seems to conform to the prophetic literature and to be justified by it. The concept of "conversion as miracle," developed in reflection on the story of Paul, furnished an analogy for it. Finally, we think that the idea of conversion applied by the elderly Calvin to the religious transformation of his youth is inseparable from his idea of vocation; it is even subordinate to it.

There is an essential, heartfelt element in every vocation, and this is true with Calvin's "conversion." The life-giving power of grace and the faithful response of the person are more important than mortification, contrition, and breaking with the past.

Therefore, in my view many historians have incorrectly emphasized the negative aspect of Calvin's conversion, seeing it as a break with the "superstitions of the papacy" and the "Roman Church" rather than as a response to a call to reform the Church. For example, H. Lecoultre is of the opinion that Calvin was converted to "Protestantism" when he understood that it was necessary to "combat" and "replace" the Church of his fathers "rather than amend it."[130] A. Lang sees in the *"subita conversio"* a sudden break by Calvin with his former aspirations and ideals or with the errors of the "old Church"; this break is followed by the adoption of a "new concept of life" and commitment to the true God.[131] K. Müller advances the hypothesis that Calvin may have been converted during his last participation in public prayers ("certain sacred ceremonies") at the Cathedral of Noyon,[132] for in so doing he discovered the falsehood of Roman worship. J. Pannier describes the conversion in these terms: "Openly, in some official sense, Calvin broke the ties that held him within the framework of the Roman Church, on 4 May 1534, the day when he resigned his benefices."[133] F. Wendel also does not hesitate to speak of Calvin's break with the Church and Christian humanism; this occurred after a long period of stubbornness "which for some time held him within the bosom of the Roman Church."[134] Finally, P. Sprenger first makes of Calvin a "fanatical" adversary of the "new doctrine"[135] and then presents him as having broken with the mother Church.[136]

Certainly these authors do not consider Calvin's conversion uniquely or exclusively in terms of a break, but I believe they tend to emphasize this aspect more than the documents allow. Some of them overemphasize the motif of detachment from the ecclesiastical order and underestimate Calvin's attachment to the Church. In so doing, they succumb to preoccupations that perhaps are more apologetic than strictly historical. To the extent that these authors give in to this tendency, they risk separating themselves from the Bible's and Calvin's notion of conversion, which essentially means "repentance" and has nothing to do with a confessional change. Furthermore, they seem at times to be influenced by a pietistic view of conversion when they attach so much importance to determining its date, place, and setting.[137]

Several reasons prevent me from accepting this way of viewing Calvin's "conversion." First, we grant absolute priority to the early documents, which are contemporaneous with these events, rather than the later documents, which are of a retrospective nature and strongly "theological." Second, I wish to respect as much as possible the diversity in genre between the earlier and the later documents. I do not try to reconcile them where that proves to be difficult. Finally, I wish to adhere to a major point on which both the earlier and the later documents notably agree: the conversion is understood as penitential and not as confessional. We encounter this fundamental idea everywhere: In being converted, the convert abandons himself to God and consequently breaks with sin in general and with "papal superstitions" in particular. But he does not break with the Church. Quite the contrary, in being converted one contributes to the purification of the Church in which one was baptized. The convert battles mercilessly against his personal sin as well as against all the sins that disfigure the true face of the great assembly of the sons of God.

If Calvin necessarily associated conversion with a break in ecclesiastical order, he would have had to accept the idea of schism as just and salutary. But did he really do this? This is the question we must now address.

CHAPTER TWENTY-SIX
The Problem of Schism

In early sixteenth-century France, people were very sensitive to questions concerning the unity of the Church. This was, no doubt, one of the results of the long confrontation between Gallican and papal theologians, which culminated in the conciliar controversy. These questions were far from being fully clarified. The influx of Luther's ideas and anabaptist mysticism made it easy to rekindle the discussions. Definitions of the true nature of the Church multiplied. Attempts were made to determine the relationship between the visible and the invisible aspects of the Church. Some wondered to what extent the papacy and the Roman Curia authentically represented the universal Church, the Church of Christ. And there was little agreement about how far one could oppose the hierarchy and criticize traditional ecclesiastical structures before separating from the body of the Church, properly speaking.

The humanist followers of Lefèvre, who were avid readers of Luther, went quite far in their reformist criticisms, just as much as the faculty of the Sorbonne, while minimizing their Gallicanism, fiercely combated the intellectual audacity of the humanists. But both were preoccupied with the problem of schism: the humanists supported the German reformer, or at least excused him, while the others condemned him. The humanists distinguished between Lutherans and anabaptist sectarians, while the others confused them. The humanists saw in the evangelical ideas a grand attempt, however risky, to return the Church to its original purity, while the others rejected them as heresies.

It was in the midst of these antagonisms that the young Calvin articulated his thoughts on the Church. More and more attentive to the Lutheran ideas which he assimilated through personal contacts and especially from his reading, Calvin felt a need to think through these ideas in order to define his own position concerning the unity and continuity—or the division—of the Church.

Therefore it will be useful to summarize the German reformer's thoughts on this point before we examine Calvin's statements on schism in general and his replies to particular accusations of schism.

Luther on the Unity of the Church and Schism

More interested in questions of justification and personal salvation than in problems of ecclesiology, Luther expressed infrequently, in occasional writings, his opinion on the identity of the Church and ways in which one belonged to it or separated from it.

In 1519, for example, while discussing pontifical power, Luther was led to distinguish between the catholic Church and the Roman church. After noting that the Christian community of Jerusalem and other primitive assemblies already formed the Church of God in the full sense of the word, well before the faith and power of the Roman church were established, he declares: "Therefore, the Church is built not upon the 'rock,' that is, the power of the Roman church, as certain decretals expound, but upon the faith confessed by Peter representing the entire Church. For the universal, *catholic* Church existed long before the *Roman* church."[1]

This is a strong protest against Sylvester Prierias and other papal theologians who incessantly stressed the "power" aspect of ecclesiastical reality in thoroughly legalistic, Roman terms. Luther, the "prophet," reacted against this legalism and emphasized the aspect of "faith." For him, the catholic Church is the community of all those justified "by faith alone," "by grace alone." The Church is the body of Christ.[2] Therefore the Church may not be defined by what it possesses of an external, legal, or human nature. The Church exists where faith lives, or where souls who believe in Christ are found. Moreover, faith and ecclesiastical structure, believers and bearers of hierarchical power, are not necessarily found in the same places or persons. Luther later expressed the opinion that Rome and pontifical power are not to be identified purely and simply with the catholic Church. He will say explicitly[3] that they are part of the Church only to the extent that they rest upon the one foundation of faith in the redeemer.

But does the papacy still possess this faith? Does the Roman church still find its unity in its commitment to the Word that alone establishes the community of the children of God?[4] Alas, no! It has become the "papist" Church; it seeks its unity in communion with "external idols," with those tyrants who have become the Roman pontiffs.[5] To the extent that popes and papist bishops have lost faith in the Lord, the Son of the living God, and have neglected to preach that faith, they have also ceased to be successors of Peter and the apostles.[6] From the contrast between "faith" and "power," Luther goes on to distinguish between the "true Church" and the "false Church."[7] The first mystically descends from the line of Abel, the true believer; the second, which is the Church only in name, comes from the line of Cain, the proud builder of cities. Thus, the second attempts to oppress the first.[8] By what means? By spiritual and material weapons.[9] She who teaches false doctrine and takes part in impious worship does not hesitate to decree that true believers are heretics, to excommunicate them, to terrorize them, and to kill them. Is it surprising that the true Church must be hidden *(abscondita)* and scattered *(dispersa)*?[10]

Here we touch upon the problem, properly speaking, of the break, as the German reformer conceived it: It is not that the true believers separate themselves from the "false Church" but that the false Church chases them and throws them out.

In this way, it is the Church in title only, the *nichtige Kirche,*[11] which alone bears the responsibility for separation.

However, we would misunderstand Luther's thought, which is complex and changing, filled with variations and exaggerations and deliberately paradoxical, if we believed that the opposition of the "false" and the "true" Church implies a total separation. Although Luther speaks of the *nichtige Kirche,* in reality the false and the true do not contradict each other in his way of thinking, just as being does not contradict nonbeing. Except for a few differences, one may say that Luther applies to the Church his affirmation that the individual believer is "simultaneously sinful and justified." Truth and falsehood are found together within the one and only "Church of God." The confrontations and the ruptures between truth and falsehood are in the end internal conflicts.

For Luther, the two great factors of ecclesiastical continuity are the Gospel and baptism. In the tremendous battle that the evangelicals were forced to wage against the papists who treated them as heretics and schismatics, they never thought of denying that there were authentic Christians among their adversaries. Those who are baptized, follow the Gospel, and correctly make use of the sacrament are "genuine Christians" and are integrated *"into* the Christian churches," whether they submit to the papacy or not.[12] These are men of good faith.

But what of those who attach more importance to works and human constitutions than to the Word of God? Are they no longer members of the Church? Here Luther's thought becomes subtle. Such people are *in* the Church, but they are not true members *(rechte Glieder);* strictly speaking, they do not belong to it. They are inside *(drinnen),* but not properly as they should be *(nicht rechtschaffen).*[13] They are scoundrels *(Schelcke),* who are Christians only in appearance. They mix with the people of God like pepper with salt.[14] Several lines later, Luther explains that by scoundrels he means especially the clerics of the "false Church," who have no living and authentic faith and yet take for themselves a legitimate ministry.[15]

In 1541, Luther explains the same idea by affirming that this type of false follower may well arise from within the true Church *(aus);* he may even live and act within *(in)* the "Temple of God" in the manner of the Antichrist; but he is nonetheless not *of (von)* the Church.[16]

In summary, the German reformer wishes to have it both ways: he firmly believes in the fundamental indefectibility of the Church, in that he recognizes a miracle of God, who in the midst of Satanic corruptions safeguards the integrity of the Word and faith, the constitutive elements of the Church.[17] But he is very harsh with what he calls the prostitution (the *Hurerei*) of the papists and especially the clerics. This spiritual fornication, which is the work of man and his self-proclaimed power, tends to eliminate the pure and simple obedience of faith.

In this respect, it is interesting to quote this passage in which Luther succeeds in maintaining simultaneously the holiness and the corruption of the Roman church: "Today we speak of the Holy Roman Church. Even though all its bishops were impious and subversive, nevertheless God rules in the midst of hostile men. . . . Although the city of Rome may be worse than Sodom, there remains in it baptism, the call of the Gospel, the texts, the sacred Scripture, the ministry, the names of Christ and God. . . . Therefore the Roman Church is holy, because it has the holy name of God, baptism, the Word, and so forth. If these are found among the people, they are sanctified."[18]

In this passage we can see an excellent application of the *simul peccator et iustus* idea to the Church.[19] In this text the "Roman Church" is portrayed according to the flesh as sinful and culpable, but according to the Spirit and by the grace of God it is just. In reality, the Lord is not reluctant to reign even in the midst of his enemies. On the other hand, according to Luther, faith continually erases sin. As long as there remains a bit of living faith within the papist assembly, even its sins may be forgiven. It is precisely within the bosom of the Church that there exist the means of grace that continually give rise to faith, namely, baptism and the Gospel.

These fundamental ideas of the German reformer explain his extreme verbal violence against the papacy as well as his refusal to consider schism. In his treatise *Wider Hans Worst* (1541), where we once more find all these ideas, Luther opposes the "true Church" to the "false Church"; but he also maintains his thesis about the essential continuity of the one Christian Church. You accuse us, he replies to his adversaries, of having defected from the holy Church and having founded a new Church.[20] This is absolutely false. For we only separated ourselves from the papists who are in no way identified with the Church. It is we who are the Church of Christ, and they are the church of the devil.[21] Novelties were not invented by us but by them. We are in complete agreement with the ancient Church, while they deny it.[22] They are the schismatics.

Obviously Luther spent little effort in defining his point in terms of actual circumstances in the visible Church. His thought is dominated by the idea of the invisible nature of the people of God. For him the Church is a higher reality, profound and hidden (cf. "the hiddenness of the Church"). No one may see it or recognize it with the eyes of the flesh. It is by baptism, the sacrament, and the Word that one grasps it and believes it. The Church is an object of faith. External organization and human doctrine only hinder this act of faith. Clerical domination merely constitutes an obstacle for those who wish to believe that the Church is made up of all the faithful without exception.[23]

Luther's emphasis on the invisible aspect of the Church explains, I believe, how he could simultaneously exalt the indivisibility of the catholic Church and accept the break with Rome. We might suppose that he saw the unity in terms of the inward nature of faith and the break in terms of the external nature of human institutions which could be reformed. (I say "might," for, as we have seen, there are quite a few points where the two dimensions touch and even overlap.)

I do not intend to affirm that young Calvin could have assimilated all the elements of Luther's thinking on the problem of unity and schism. Several of the passages that we have just quoted are dated after the first *Institutes*. Some of Luther's earlier writings were circulated only in German. But since the essential meaning of these writings logically flows from the *Responsio Lutheri de potestate papae (1519)*, and given that similar ideas were current in the circles of Lefèvre out of which a Farel emerged very early, I believe that Calvin could easily have benefited from Luther's heritage.

The Problem of Schism in the Writings of the Young Calvin
(1534–1539)

It would not be very beneficial to devote ourselves to a study of the concept of schism in Calvin as we did for conversion. The word "schism" meant exactly the same thing for the young reformer and his adversaries that it means for us today: the culpable act of separating from the unity of the Church.

Calvin mentions schism for the first time in the foreword, written in 1536, of his *Psychopannychia*. In condemning the thoughtless way in which the anabaptists haphazardly "dogmatize," he states: "From this source [arise] again and again so many schisms, errors, and scandals in our faith."[24] Then he criticizes the dissidents' arbitrary and unsystematic interpretation of the Bible: "And must we still wonder from what source [arise] so many sects among those who would give first place to the Gospel and to the renewing Word?"[25] Whoever reads these lines without any preconceived ideas should recognize that they come from a man who is strongly committed to Christian unity. The mention of the sects that have cropped up among those who have chosen to follow the renewal of the Gospel implies that the young Calvin looked with an evil eye upon any attempt, even by evangelicals, to form separate ecclesiastical communities.

The same preoccupation with unity already appeared, although indirectly, as "something negative" in the first preface, dated 1534, of the *Psychopannychia*. Calvin notes that the anabaptists complain that their rejection by other Christians reveals a lack of love and disrupts Christian harmony: "They mournfully deplore the rending of the unity of the Church and the violation of love." The ironic tone shows that the author finds this complaint not only illogical but hypocritical. As if the sectarians were so concerned about remaining in the Catholic communion! Thus his reply eliminates all discussion: "This is my response to them: first, we acknowledge no unity except in Christ; and no charity except that of which Christ himself is the bond. Therefore, let this be the chief means of maintaining love, that the faith remains sacred and whole among us."[26] The reasoning is clear. There is certainly no unity without love. But love in turn is not authentic if it is not founded upon Christ and a faith that is completely established in him. The anabaptists, therefore, are wrong in demanding a love that would bargain away doctrinal integrity.

In the Dedicatory Epistle, the preoccupation with unity and its Christocentric definition remain the same, but the discussion has another setting. This time it is the evangelicals who are accused of schism and consequently persecuted. As a lawyer, Calvin attempts to demonstrate the injustice of this accusation. The "faction of adversaries," those evil advisers of the King, are mistaken when they link the evangelical party to the sectarians. No, the doctrine preached by the evangelicals does not differ from the doctrine of

Christ: "It is not our doctrine, but that of the living God and his Christ."[27] It is not new: "For we are not forging some recent gospel."[28]

It is also incorrect to insinuate that they would establish a new Church, as if the Church of Christ had disappeared. No, the evangelicals also believe that the Church is indefectible: "The Church of Christ has lived and will live well, as long as Christ reigns at the right hand of the Father." The promise of the Lord to remain with his own until the end of the age cannot fail to be fulfilled. Against this immortal Church of Christ, Calvin and his friends have no war to wage: "Against this [Church] we have no struggle, for with one accord, with all the faithful, we worship and adore the one God and Christ the Lord, as he always has been adored by all the pious."[29] But it is still necessary to agree on the identity of this Church!

Here arises a reminder of Luther's idea about the invisible essence of the Church. Calvin first rejects the claim that the Church consists exclusively of its visible, exterior, legal, and hierarchical structures: "Our controversy hinges on these cardinal points: first, they contend that the form of the Church is always apparent and visible; and second, they constitute the form itself in the seat of the Roman church and in the order of [its] prelates." To this concept of the "Church as power" the reformer opposes that of the "Church as faith," always stressing—even more than Luther did—the aspect of ministry. Calvin draws his inspiration from the definition of the Augsburg Confession: "On the contrary, we assert that the Church is constituted not by any apparent form, and its form is not contained in that external splendor which they foolishly admire. But it is constituted by quite different marks, namely, the pure preaching of the Word of God and the proper administration of the sacraments."[30]

In what follows, Calvin applies this definition to the problem of the authentic representation of the Church. He believes that the pope, the bishops, and the priests alone do not represent the Church adequately. The Bible clearly shows that the priestly class always needs to be corrected by prophecy. Consequently, one must admit that even messengers of God who are not consecrated by the institutional Church can represent the people of God. Their corrective function often occurred in opposition to representatives of the institution. This was the case with Micaiah, who alone represented the Church of God on one occasion: "The Church stood on the side of Micaiah, who was alone and contemptible; but from his mouth the truth came forth." This was also Jeremiah's situation before the priests who believed that their control of the law could not be taken from them. Calvin concludes: "Now let them go and grasp this outward mask, so that they make Christ and all the prophets of the living God to be schismatics, while they make the ministers of Satan into instruments of the Holy Spirit."[31]

If the evangelicals were schismatics, they would be ministers of Satan. But they are not schismatics any more than were the prophets or Christ himself. The evangelicals are true believers who proclaim the Word in all its purity and who only wish to correct the vices of a decadent and domineering priesthood. If one must at any cost find schismatics, one should look instead among partisans of anabaptism or even among certain popes! The sectarians are obviously progeny of Satan. It is the prince of darkness who raised up these enemies of unity to compromise the triumph of the renewed Gospel: "He stirred up dissent and contention over dogmas through his catabaptists and other monsters of darkness, by whom he might obscure and finally extinguish the [truth]."[32] One does not have to go back very far to find a schismatic among the popes. Was not Pope Eugenius IV condemned as a schismatic at the Council of Basle? "There Eugenius was condemned as schismatic, rebellious, and pertinacious, along with the whole company of cardinals and bishops who plotted with him the dissolution of the Council."[33] Carried away by his zeal, Calvin indulges in a counterattack that appears to be an argument *ad hominem.* Preoccupied with the idea of succession so often invoked by his adversaries, Calvin first states that this pontiff was established in his position only by the favor of princes, that is to say, illegitimately. Then as a thorough schismatic he ordained—or had ordained by his accomplices in the schism—a whole group of clergy whose successors are still in power today. Finally, Calvin places this dilemma before his adversaries: "Will they confess that Eugenius and all his cohorts, by whom they were all sanctified, were schismatics? Therefore, let them either define the form of the Church in other ways or, regardless of their number, they will be held by us as schismatics."[34]

Let us note how Calvin turns the accusations against his adversaries but does not call them the "false Church." Thus he agrees with Luther's position. Even in the beginning of the epistle when he is speaking of the "poor little Church" which for centuries was mishandled and ruined by evil pastors, Calvin is careful not to oppose the "true Church" and the "false Church." He is content to speak of the confrontation between the "pious" and the "impious" which, after all, occurs within the Church.[35]

This way of seeing things corresponds well to what Calvin said in the first *Institutes* concerning the unity and the indivisibility of the catholic Church, the mystical body of Christ,[36] the antagonism between the "kingdom of Christ" and the "papal kingdom,"[37] and the Church's continuity which is assured by the incorruptible sacrament of baptism.[38] In only one place does he use the expression "the church of the Antichrist" to stigmatize those who "in the name of the Church" introduced communion in one kind; Calvin opposes them to the "apostolic Church." But even here the context shows that he intended to compare two states, the one corrupt and the other ideal, of the same catholic Church.[39]

All of this leads us to think that for Calvin, as well as for his master Luther, even the Antichrist, his abominations, and the divisions caused by him are within the Church. We note that elsewhere Calvin speaks expressly of the internal schism of the Church: "diabolical division . . . *in* the Church."[40]

In his "open letter," *On Fleeing the Illicit Rites of the Wicked,* Calvin invites his readers to flee papist ceremonies, especially the Mass, which he considered idolatrous, superstitious, and sacrilegious.[41] However, he does not issue an appeal to break with the Roman Catholic Church. What he wants is to eliminate the distortions existing within the Church, which are due to its subjugation to the "kingdom of the pope." He specifically speaks of corruptions from which the Church must be purified and the disciplinary provisions that must be enacted to correct the Church from top to bottom.[42] However, we should recognize that according to his comparisons the reformer gives the impression that he considers the superstitions and idolatries of the papacy as external to the Church. In fact, he likens them sometimes to those of Egypt[43] or Babylon[44] and sometimes to those of the synagogue[45] or pagan Rome.[46] Do these three comparisons indicate that Calvin intended, even implicitly, to oppose "Church" to "Church"? We do not think so. A comparison is not necessarily the same as an identification.

It would also be forcing the matter if one would draw a similar conclusion from the fact that Calvin requires of his correspondent that "nothing alien to the integrity of our religion be said or done by us,"[47] or because he mentions a "wife who dissented in religion."[48] We saw in Part One that in Calvin's vocabulary "religion" does not possess a confessional meaning, as it does today when one says "Catholic religion" or "Protestant religion"; it essentially meant respect for divine rules by each believer or community. When Calvin notes that the enemies of the Word of God make participation in the Mass "a symbol of denying true religion,"[49] he gives as his reason the view that all "superstitious" acts are grave offenses against the integrity of religion.

In his epistle *On Abandoning the Papal Priesthood,* written at the same time as the preceding one, the young reformer addresses a few pointed criticisms to an old friend who has been ordained a bishop. He reproaches him with most of the classical errors of the prelates "under the papacy," but he does not ask him to consider his episcopal ministry as an intrinsically evil institution. Quite the contrary, he exalts it as a divine institution established in Scriptures,[50] he sees in good bishops authentic ministers of the Church of God,[51] and he implicitly recognizes the validity of their consecration by the "papal kingdom."[52]

The entire first part of this writing is a vibrant appeal to the new bishop, which invites him not to be content with his title but to take very seriously his pastoral office.[53] We may summarize Calvin's exhortation as follows: "Presently you are not a true bishop. Therefore you must not delay in achieving that to which you committed yourself by oath before God and man. You bear the dignity of the episcopate. Not to fulfill its corresponding responsibility would be sacrilege. Do not forget that the title of bishop has been sanctified by the very mouth of God, for the holy service of his people. Therefore, become what you are called to be. Become a selfless leader and an impartial ruler of the faithful in your charge.[54] Feed your sheep in the good pasture of the Word, defend them against the attacks of Satan, show them the way by the example of your irreproachable life."[55]

In all these passages, as well as in the rest of the epistle, the reformer always speaks simply of "the Church." He never adds "true" or "false" or any other epithet. (The only exception to this general rule is in the full title, where we read "the Papal Church.") Elsewhere, on several occasions he clearly shows that the "Church" in question is the Church of God: "His own Church." It is in this Church that the reformer places his correspondent, a most reprehensible papist bishop. Therefore we must admit that although Calvin severely criticized the deformed episcopate, he does not disassociate it from the "one, holy Church."

This observation is particularly reinforced by passages in which Calvin touches upon the idea of *reform* itself: personal reform of the deficient pastor and general reform of his diocese. God is great and magnanimous. Thanks to him, no falling away is irreversible. Strengthened by this conviction, the reformer challenges his old friend with these words: "Therefore, let us realize that with you as well as with other men not yet completely blind the truth of God is powerful. This is what is desired foremost by the Lord himself: he prefers to correct both you and others by his castigations rather than crush you."[56] Even Egypt was brought to repentance by such beneficial testing! Yes, God desires to correct his unfaithful servants rather than to crush them. It is the same with dioceses that have fallen into spiritual ruin; they must be rebuilt and not simply left to perish.[57] Thus Calvin jolts his friend out of his torpor and invites him to settle down to the task of reform: "Let the watchman take his post; let the shepherd take up arms. Why do you delay? Why are you lazy? Why are you asleep?"[58]

In another place, Calvin presents his friend with an alternative: Either become a real pastor of souls or resign.[59] But he clearly prefers the first solution: "It is certainly preferable and far more desirable that you not let slip through your hands such a great opportunity to manifest the glory of God. For you have the means to do many things, which, if they are done in complete obedience to God and in great faith, can offer many occasions for advancing the Gospel."[60]

These are surely the sounds, not of an instigator of division who incites his readers to desertion, but of a reformer who possesses a sense of the Church's continuity and who is prepared to use all the elements of the Church that are still salvageable for the grand work of reconstruction.

This work cannot be achieved as long as two kinds of adversaries continue to undermine it. The first are adherents of the "Roman Pluto" or "archpirate,"[61] who destroy the holy institution of the Lord by their human constitutions. The others are the false prophets, active agents of dissension.[62] Calvin urges his correspondent to lead a war against both groups and thus to carry out one of the principal functions of a pastor worthy of the name.

After all is said, in spite of the polemical tone of the epistle the guiding idea is the portrait of the ideal pastor. Let us add that the letter's content is better expressed by its complete title than by the abridged title of the modern editors. The complete title still leaves a choice between a positive solution and a negative one: *The Christian Duty of a Man* Either *to Administer* or *to Abandon the Priestly Duties of the Papal Church.* However, the abridged title, *On Abandoning the Papal Priesthood,* does not allow any alternative.

We should note that this writing speaks often about the episcopate and very little about the priesthood. More precisely, it flatly rejects the sacramental-priestly character of the episcopate[63] and explains at length its pastoral-ministerial dimension.

We may conclude that the epistle reveals exactly the opposite of a schismatic attitude. There is no opposition of one Church to another. Calvin does not invite his correspondent—some critics say it is Gérard Roussel—to desert and to rejoin the ranks of the evangelicals in order to help them establish a Church destined to replace the old one. There is not a single allusion to the possibility of a salutary schism! The bishop is begged to fulfill his duties, to reform himself, and to reform his diocese. More concerned to correct than to tear down, the young Calvin urges his friend to become one of the good prelates, whose existence he recognizes even under the papist regime.[64]

In January 1538, as a result of a very painful event Calvin formulated this rather subtle position more clearly. The canon Louis du Tillet, Calvin's faithful companion during his wanderings, left him to return to the Roman Church. Deeply moved, Calvin wrote a long letter to him in which he explicitly takes up the problem of schism.

The starting point of Calvin's reasoning is the following: If du Tillet, recently "so set and resolute" in his intent to participate in evangelical renewal, abandons it at the present time, it must be due to his feeling that his friend, Calvin, has gone too far in his criticisms of the Church. But this is false; Calvin knows that his firmness is entirely justified, for the Lord "does not wish to be served halfway!" Accepting corrupt papal communities as authentic Christian churches would be giving in to a confused understanding of charity. Du Tillet gave in. But whether he knew it or not, he implicitly accused his former evangelical colleagues of schism: "If you recognize as churches of God those which we loathe, I take your word for it; but we would be in a bad way if this were the case, for surely you can give them this title only if you consider us to be schismatics."[65]

It ought to be noted that Calvin does not speak of the Church but of churches, that is, individual local churches under the papal regime. To the extent that these churches are an integral part of the universal Church of Christ, those who separate from them deserve the name of "schismatic." These congregations would be right in condemning the evangelicals, and the evangelicals are wrong not to recognize the validity of their excommunication.[66]

But Calvin refuses to be treated as a dissident, for he no longer considers these communities as churches of God. At best he finds in them some remnants of the Church: "If you understand that there are always some remnants of the blessing of God, as Paul affirms of the Israelites, you may understand that I agree with you, seeing that I have declared to you that such is my judgment, indeed including the Greek churches."[67]

An interesting and rare mention of the Eastern churches! Calvin implies that he sees the remnants of authentic elements of the Church in the Eastern churches generally held to be schismatic. According to his comparison, it is clear that he places the congregations controlled by the papacy in the same category, thus accusing them of responsibility for separation.

But he wants to affirm above all that forming a religious community around "vestiges" alone is not sufficient to constitute a living part of the Church of God: "But it does not follow that one must recognize the Church in the congregation. And if we recognize it as such, that is our doing, not that of Jesus Christ, who marks or indicates his own according to other signs when he says, 'My sheep hear my voice.' "[68] A community that refuses the demands of the divine Word cannot be Christ's!

Here is the criterion for denying that the papist churches are part of the Church of God. They only appear to listen to the divine Master. Of course, they invoke "the name of Christ" but immediately cast aside "its power." Their leaders are always ready to "flatter themselves with the title of the Church and strongly condemn all those which are not like them." But this is a completely unfounded claim. Their abominations have made them worse than the "synagogues of the Jews" or the "people of Israel under Jeroboam, or even Ahab." Separating from such gatherings is not schism. On the contrary—and this is surely aimed at du Tillet—"to some extent one separates from the Church of God when joining with that which is contrary to it."[69]

The essential tenor of this letter comes out more clearly if we consider du Tillet's reply.[70]

Composed three months later, du Tillet's reply is basically a long discussion of the subjects raised by Calvin. Its tone, ideas, and thrust are evangelical and—we could even say—"ecumenical." Du Tillet takes up one by one the arguments of his friend and uses them to justify his position. He always speaks in the plural of the churches to which he has returned,[71] referring to them explicitly as "individual churches" to distinguish them from the "catholic Church."[72] He submits them to the judgment of Scriptures[73] and in the end concludes that they do not possess merely some vestiges of the Church of God but that they are still truly part of the Church of God.[74]

Du Tillet believes that the religious situation of these communities cannot be compared fairly to that of the synagogues, unless one minimizes to the extreme the importance of baptism. He refuses to do so and hopes that Calvin will not contradict him on this point. Then from the validity of the baptism received in "these churches" he deduces the validity of their ministry.[75] Finally, he returns to his principal thesis: "And if there was and still is a true ministry of God in these churches, it follows that they were and are true churches of God."[76] Even if one admits—and it would be difficult to deny the evidence—that corruption has not only affected customs and discipline but also doctrine and the sacraments, an impartial application of the Augsburg Confession allows us to recognize that these churches are still living cells of the great and universal Christian body. Certainly their deformities are extremely grave. "But all of that does not mean that they are not churches of God, since in spite of all this the name of God and Jesus is truly and publicly invoked, his Word proclaimed, his sacraments administered."[77] Of course, preaching and the administration of the sacraments are not always done here and everywhere "correctly." However, the number of sincere and upright ministers and laity is large enough that one may apply to them the word of the Lord: "Where two or three are gathered in my name, there am I in the midst of them (Matt. 18:20)." These congregations "may in part constitute themselves in the name of the Lord" and in part "in another name."[78]

Consequently, no one need "withdraw from the communion of these churches as from the churches of Satan," no one need "establish other new additional churches which may be of Christ."[79] Had Calvin become too extreme? Is he therefore a schismatic? Du Tillet replies that these churches "have reason to believe that you separated from them, when you should have remained united with all that God had done." And farther on he says: "Thus I cannot see how you can be entirely free from schism or any blame."[80]

This letter is a very valuable testimony of how the reformer's intimate friend, who was imbued with reformist and Lutheran ideas[81] right to the bone, resolved for himself the problem of separation. We regret that this letter probably never reached its destination[82] and that we will never know how Calvin would have reacted. In their subsequent correspondence, the two friends will discuss another subject: the legitimate calling to the pastoral ministry. However, we may presume that Calvin's reply would have contained a rejection of the charge of schism. In his very last letter to du

Tillet, we in fact find a sentence in which he appeals to the tribunal of God in these terms: "May the angels of God bear witness as to *who are the schismatics.*"[83]

The same good conscience characterizes the *Reply to Sadolet*. We have seen with what assurance Calvin defends the evangelical ministers accused of dissidence.

A man of honesty and good intentions,[84] the Bishop of Carpentras wished to bring the Genevans back to Roman governance, outside of which there could, in his eyes, be no catholic unity. But misinformed and awkward, he hurled grave accusations against Calvin and his colleagues who were expelled from Geneva.

Let us look at Sadolet's *Letter to the Genevans*. At the very beginning, he confesses frankly that he knows of the situation only from hearsay: "Indeed . . . it has come to my attention that certain crafty men, enemies of peace and Christian unity, . . . have sown seeds of evil discord among you and your city and have turned the faithful people of Christ aside from the way of the fathers and their elders and from the traditional teachings of the catholic Church and filled everyone with dissent and sedition."[85] Later on, he calls the reformers "innovators [who want to transform] old and well-established matters"[86] and "inventors of new things."[87] Such expressions could only make Calvin angry.

A second blunder was that although Sadolet was a good bishop, he forgot that the Genevans for centuries had known only bad bishops. They chased the last one out by force of arms! Yet he praises without distinction all the decrees claiming ecclesiastical authority and invites the people to submit to them in humility and obedience, as if they had been dictated by the Holy Spirit.[88]

Subsequently, Sadolet gives a definition of the Church that we find very incomplete, for he practically reduces the Church to a "consensus."[89] He depicts schism as an abscess that insidiously gnaws away inside the body and destroys its substance.[90] Then, he imagines that one of those creators of division is called before the tribunal of God and says: "I was not able to destroy all authority within the Church, but I was the author of great sedition and schism within it."[91] Finally, Sadolet puts him in the company of his peers in hell, where he must expiate his crime of attempting to dismember the Bride of Christ, tear her gown, and shatter the catholic community.[92]

Under these conditions, we understand why Calvin's reply was filled with indignation. But as outraged as he was, Calvin did not give way to an entirely personal apology. On the contrary, his thought takes up ecclesiastical issues. Pleading not guilty to the accusations of innovation and dissidence, he thoroughly deals with the question of true catholic continuity.

To Sadolet's definition, which he judges to be insufficient,[93] he opposes his own: "Now if you can bear to receive a definition of the Church more accurate than your own, say from now on that it is a community of all the sanctified, which is spread throughout the whole world and scattered abroad throughout the ages. Nevertheless, it is bound together by the doctrine of Christ and the one Spirit, and it observes and cherishes unity of faith and fraternal concord."[94] The Church is thus defined mainly by divine doctrine which gives rise to faith and by the Spirit which inspires charity. Taking into account the context allows us to be more precise: the "Word of the Lord," which cannot be separated from the "Spirit," is the constitutive element of the Church. The Word is the Church's "most evident mark" and the "touchstone" of its teachings.[95] All the prophets, all the apostles, all the truly orthodox Fathers agree in giving first place to the Word in Christian life.[96] Thus Calvin allows no other continuity than that which binds us through centuries of corruption to the Church of the apostles[97] and in general to the ancient Church.[98]

The Bishop of Carpentras is gravely mistaken, therefore, concerning the "schism" of Calvin and his companions and their desire to separate and to draw people away from the true catholic fellowship: "Your opinion is false, when you say that we wish to lead people away from that manner of worshiping God which the catholic Church has always observed."[99] Quite the contrary; they wish only to remain in its maternal bosom: "We deny that we have any disagreements with this [Church]. On the contrary, since we revere her as our mother, we desire to remain in her bosom."[100] What Calvin categorically rejects is Sadolet's statement that the evangelicals have declared war on the Church.[101] Calvin places a marvelous declaration of unity in the mouth of the fictitious evangelical minister called before the tribunal of the Lord.

Here in essence is what Calvin has him say: "Lord, you have placed your Word before me like a torch, so that I may see the true nature of the Church and its doctrine. I have embraced this doctrine, and I have never wished to go beyond its limits. I in no way feel guilty of having separated from the Church, unless one considers as a deserter a soldier who, to bring back order into the general confusion, raises the standard that the captains have allowed to fall. If faltering leaders try to prevent him, should he not resist them? And if the result is a momentary tumult, or even a temporary loss of unity, whose responsibility is it? Lord, you know how much I am devoted to Christian unity, for you are its beginning and its end. Your truth created it. It would therefore be criminal to wish to purchase peace at the price of truth. No, in taking up the struggle against evil pastors, I have not separated from your people. I have only followed the example of the prophets who resisted the priests who became enemies within and who attempted to amend the religion corrupted by the priests.

"In so doing, the prophets remained within the true communion; no one would dare call them schismatic. The same with me; I have done everything to mitigate controversy and reconcile people, so that the two parties may work together (lit. "joined in spirit") to build up your kingdom. But alas, our opponents reacted by taking up sword, fire, and gallows! Now, Lord, it is up to you to judge who are schismatics."[102]

Calvin rejects with equal force the complaint that the evangelical preachers are innovators, "inventors of new dogmas."[103] No, he insists, innovations come from his "adversaries." It is they, not the evangelicals, who have invented dogmas foreign to Scripture and who have violated the chastity of the virgin Bride of Christ.[104] They, not the partisans of the Gospel, have formed a sect comparable to the anabaptists when they divorced the Spirit from the Word.[105] Calvin is very careful not to designate these "adversaries" as the Church. He usually refers to them as the "kingdom of the pope,"[106] "the faction of the Roman pontiffs,"[107] "your kingdom,"[108] "your faction,"[109] and "your community."[110] Only once, in an ironic context, he lets slip the phrase "your Church" (singular),[111] and in another place "your churches" (plural).[112] But he never gives the impression that he is opposing one "Church" to another. He is careful to distinguish between the "papal faction," which without being the Church oppresses churches, and these churches themselves, which in spite of being oppressed and nearly ruined do not cease being the Church. In this sense he declares: "However, Sadolet, we do not deny that those churches over which you preside are churches of Christ. But we say that the Roman pontiff, with the whole company of false bishops who occupy the positions of pastors, are savage wolves. Thus, they have only one desire: to destroy and scatter the kingdom of Christ until they disfigure it by dissolution and ruin."[113]

Although they are ruined, deformed, and buried, these churches contain, by the grace of God, vestiges of their ancient integrity which allow us to still call them the Church of God.[114] What are these vestiges? Calvin does not spell this out here. But since the first *Institutes* accepts the validity of Roman baptism[115] and even alludes to a ministry,[116] indeed to an ecclesiastical jurisdiction capable of once again becoming legitimate,[117] we may conclude that Calvin understands "vestiges" much the same way as Luther. In any case, he clearly agrees with Luther when he sees the Antichrist within the Church.[118]

This theory permits Calvin to insist that the evangelicals wish only to correct, reconstruct, and to fill in with authentic elements the gaping void around these scattered vestiges.[119]

I could stop our investigation here if it were not for several Calvin scholars who, based upon later writings of the reformer, assert that although Calvin denied the accusation of schism, he systematically contrasted the "false church" to the "true Church." Moreover, they assert that Calvin did so after his "conversion." If this is correct, I would have to admit that Calvin was led at some point in his religious evolution to accept a break with the Church as being necessary for reform. To clarify this question, I must prolong our examination to include several important texts dated after 1539.

The Problem of Schism in Calvin After 1539

In his article on the unity of the Church in Calvin, O. Weber states that there are several crucial questions for the reformer: Why and to what extent is the "Roman Church" the "false Church"? Why and to what extent is the "Church of the Gospel" the "true Church"? And how is it that the existence of this "Church of the Gospel" does not represent a separation from the one true Church but rather its reestablishment?[120] Weber notes further that Calvin is faced with the "terrible reality" of the "false Church" relentlessly cursing the "true Church."[121] Weber is always very careful about documentation, but we note that here he does not cite a single passage from Calvin that contains the expression "false Church." The reason for this omission, I believe, is simple: the expression is not in Calvin's vocabulary. The reformer did not conceive of any ecclesiastical "reality" outside of one, indivisible and true Church of God.

This is true, as we have seen, for the works written prior to 1539. Is it also true of the later works? The *Index Theologicus* of the *Opera,* vol. 22, lists under the heading "Church" and the subheading "True and False"[122] a passage from the 1543 *Institutes* (which includes passages from the 1539 edition); but this listing is incorrect, for the passage does not speak of a "false Church" in either the 1543 or the 1539 edition. In the 1539 passage, "Church" is used without an epithet, and in the 1543 edition we read: "Then, if the true Church is the column or support of the truth (1 Tim. 3:15), it is certain that there is no church where falsehood and lying have seized power."[123] It is clear that there is only one "Church," the "true Church." Its opposite is not a "Church" or even a "false Church," but only a reign of deceit and falsehood.

In the 1559 *Institutes,* IV.ii. is entitled "A Comparison of the False Church with the True."[124] Unless I am wrong, it is the first and only mention of the "false Church." The chapter itself—except for a paragraph on the alternative of "succession of persons" or "succession in doctrine" added in 1559—reproduces substantially the texts of 1539 and 1543. There is an interesting detail: while the passages of 1539 examine the communities subject to the papacy in order to establish whether they are "churches,"[125] the relevant sections in 1543 refer to these communities on four occasions in the singular as "their Church" or "their own Church."[126] These passages also deal more intensely with the problem of schism. Must we see in these passages a sign that Calvin's views were becoming more rigid? By 1543 did he come to the point of opposing one "Church" to another "Church"; and then by 1559, was he calling the fallen Church "false"? I reject this interpretation for four reasons.

First, in the four passages in question, it is not Calvin who is the subject of the statements but the papists. In fact, these statements are indirect quotations introduced by expressions such as "they commend," "they cry out," or "they wish."

Second, another passage from 1543 explicitly refuses to consider the "appearances" of the Church or the "masks," which have no obvious relationship to the Word of God, as the "Church."[127]

Third, the paragraph that deals with the idea of vestiges, principally developed in 1539, remains an integral part of the chapter. According to this theory, the "papacy" and the "papists" are not the Church of God, even though "among them," within the communities subject to their tyranny, there remain several incorruptible elements: baptism and "certain other remnants."[128]

Fourth, the content of the chapter, which furnishes the only plausible interpretation of the title, leads us to conclude that this *hapax* does not oppose the "Church of the Gospel" (the "true Church") to the "Roman Church" (the "false Church"). Instead, Calvin maintains the absolute oneness of the true Church of God, whose name the "papacy" falsely bears. To this one Church, this one true Church, Calvin wishes to compare—and not to oppose—the "outward masks," which have no ecclesiastical reality but which can cover up the authentic vestiges of the Church. From the perspective of the Church's reality, the adjective "false" here signifies "nonexistent." These churches only possess this "terrible reality," of which Weber speaks, because of the power of the Antichrist, who arises from this corrupt world.

Now let us examine the passages in this chapter that deal with the problem of schism. First of all, we find this definition: "Those who disrupt the communion of the Church by creating dissent are called heretics and schismatics."[129] This communion consists of a harmony in faith and charity, which is established "in Christ" and "according to Christ." Any harmony that is not founded upon the one faith in the one Lord can only produce a "faction of wicked men."[130] This Christocentric idea of unity clearly appears in Cyprian, who "proclaims that heresies and schisms arise because one does not return to the source of truth or seek out its origin, and when the teaching of the heavenly teacher is not preserved."[131]

Looking to his own time, Calvin concludes that it is his adversaries who have turned away from the Master and his "sound doctrine." One need only examine the theology, preaching, and sacramental life of these adversaries to see how much they disagree with Christ. These false pastors and false Christians are a very powerful group who falsely claim the Lord for themselves. By claiming to be the Church, it actually abuses the name! In truth, they are the heretics and the schismatics. Calvin declares: "Now they go about and cry out that we who have withdrawn from their Church are heretics, even when the only cause of alienation is this: that they in no way are able to uphold a pure profession of the truth." Then, as a parenthesis, Calvin adds: "And I say nothing about the anathemas and the curses with which they expel us."[132] Vain accusations, a vain condemnation! The choice of Calvin's friends was correct: "For it is abundantly clear to me that it was necessary for us to depart from them in order to come to Christ."[133]

Calvin's conception of unity, his concern to do nothing that would risk damaging this unity, then his description of the "true Church" and that which is irrelevant to the "Church," and finally his theory of "vestiges" are all described in the very same way as in the writings prior to 1539.

What is new in the text of 1543 is an increased concern with the problem of schism, the relationship between schism and heresy, statements that explicitly attribute the responsibility for the break to the papists, and finally the idea that the evangelicals were rejected by the papists and not the other way around.

It is not difficult to find in historical circumstances the causes of this considerable change in emphasis. We know that after having participated in 1540 in the colloquies of Hagenau and Worms, Calvin also attended the diet of Ratisbon in 1541, as a representative of the city of Strasbourg.[134] There he assisted Bucer and his new friend, Melanchthon, in their attempts to reestablish doctrinal harmony with the papal party. Some authors think that Calvin's influence only made the reformists more rigid.[135] It seems more probable that Calvin was, at least in the beginning, among those who sincerely wished to avoid a breakup of the dialogue.[136] This opinion is based primarily on a letter that Calvin addressed from Ratisbon on 11 May 1541 to his friend Farel. He expresses his satisfaction with his adversaries' unexpected concession on justification and invites his correspondent to realize that the evangelicals have obtained the maximum possible on this point, given the circumstances.[137] He also notes that they had been able to agree on the definition of the Church but not on ecclesiastical power. There was even less agreement on the Supper.[138] We should note that in relating these failures and the deception of Bucer and Melanchthon, Calvin manifests no secret pleasure; nor does he manifest the feelings of one who had been a pessimist from the beginning.

Everything leads to the belief that the conferences of Ratisbon, with their highs and lows and with the atmosphere marked at times by mutual distrust and at other times by hope of union, made Calvin more sensitive than ever to the problems of unity. Their ineffectiveness terrified him, no doubt, but it also convinced him more than ever that he was on the right track. Thus, without delay he published a French version of the *Acts of Ratisbon* and added to it an "Epistle to the Reader," along with some personal commentaries.

Calvin tells his readers that he wishes to inform them how "doctrine, which should reconcile us to God and bring peace and harmony among all men on earth, is now debated with such extraordinary contention that the Church is miserably wasted and half destroyed because of it." It is good, he adds, that true Christians be informed of what happened at Ratisbon, so that from now on they may have "peace of conscience" and no longer doubt the soundness of their religious position: "For it is a poor state of affairs always to wander and stagger."[139] At the end of the volume, where he reproduces several letters of the pontifical legate, Contarini, we read Calvin's bitter commentaries on the attitude of Rome. He writes: "No man of good judgment can doubt that the pope is hardly trying to find a solution to the desolation which is presently in the Church. And in trying to find excuses, as is his custom, he causes more delay and clearly condemns the cause of the Church." Then Calvin asks himself: "What can one hope from such company?"[140]

Calvin benefited more from this publication than did his readers. Numerous texts in the 1543 *Institutes* reproduced the ideas contained in the documents of Ratisbon. For example, there is Cyprian's conception of the unique episcopacy of Christ in which earthly bishops only participate. Cyprian illustrated this episcopacy by comparing the sun to its many rays. This conception probably comes from the *Articles* proposed by the pontifical delegates.[141] From this source Calvin also seems to have borrowed his definition of both schism and heresy.[142]

To repulse the insinuations that he was guilty of schism, Calvin seems to have turned to the *Response of the Protestant Princes and States*, written at Ratisbon by Melanchthon. In this document, the speech for the defense concludes: "But our churches have been rejected and divided by others, primarily by the unjust condemnation of the pope, and then by the cruelty of the bishops. How many of us have been murdered for this doctrine? From this we may judge from what source this separation has come and who is responsible for it."[143] In the same way, the 1543 *Institutes* places the responsibility for the separation on the papists, and it states that "by anathemas and curses they expelled us."[144]

The hypothesis that this passage bears the imprint of Melanchthon is confirmed by a text of *The Response Against Pighius Concerning Free Will*, also written in 1543 by Calvin and dedicated to Melanchthon.[145] The reformer first states: "Indeed, we deny that the beginning of separation was caused by us." Then he affirms: "It was . . . this Church, because the Roman Antichrist by violent and tyrannical means expelled all of us who dared to take the Word as truth and to embrace it. And thus the Romans made us guilty of defection, when they had earlier rejected us from their own so-called communion by violent and bloody edicts."[146]

From the same year, we have Calvin's *Supplex exhortatio*, one of whose principal goals was to prove to Charles V that the evangelicals were not and never would be enemies of Christian concord.[147] Again we find the definition of schism and heresy according to the *Articles* of Ratisbon,[148] as well as several ideas expressed in the 1543 *Institutes;* for example, that Christ is the one true bishop and source of all unity,[149] that holy doctrine is the only criterion for authentic unity,[150] that one must sacrifice all to remain united with the Church,[151] and that "prophetic" resistance to a deficient priesthood is legitimate.[152]

Among Calvin's later writings that deal with the problem of disunity is the treatise *De Scandalis,* which appeared in 1550.[153] Nothing new is added to the themes expressed in 1543.

As we have seen, the years 1541–1543 mark an important step in Calvin's reflection upon the mystery and the correct "form" of the Church. Under Bucer's influence, this reflection became more and more directed to the visible aspect of ecclesiastical reality, but it was no doubt the conferences of Ratisbon which exercised the most stimulating influence on Calvin's thought. There Calvin was able to comprehend the tragedy of the situation: the two parties easily agreed on the definition of the Church—here was an opportunity from which they had to benefit!—but they did not budge on the question of ecclesiastical power. Calvin wrote: "On definitions their views agreed; but on power they began to dissent."[154] His participation in the conferences as a delegate of a local church and as a friend of the "great" Melanchthon and Bucer, as well as his statements on ecclesiology made before and after the diet, lead to the belief that Calvin subscribed to the common declaration on the Church, as he had done on the agreement concerning the doctrine of justification. This makes all the more debatable Th. Werdermann's statement which claims that Calvin had elaborated an ecclesiology that was "essentially" opposed to the Catholic concept of the Church.[155]

On the contrary, all the documents prove that both the Calvin of Ratisbon and the Calvin of the first *Institutes* never intended to break with what was most essential in the Catholic doctrine of the Church.[156] Moreover, Calvin never thought that it was necessary to oppose a new Church to the old by making a "beneficial amputation." Several modern Calvin scholars recognize this without any hesitation. Thus, J. Koopmans, relying particularly on *The Response Against Pighius,* stresses the organic continuity between Catholic dogma and Calvin's doctrine of the Church;[157] and W. F. Dankbaar is clearly of the opinion that Calvin did not seek to break with the Roman Church but to reform it;[158] and P. Sprenger is persuaded that for both Calvin and Luther there is only one Christian Church, and outside it are all the sects.[159]

Our study has shown to what extent Calvin's ecclesiological thought follows Luther. Calvin's faith in the continuity of the Church and his demand for a prophetic type of reformation are the same. Although he took up the essentials of Luther's heritage, Calvin left the imprint of his own personality. First, he shows greater care in his choice of words and avoids speaking of the "false Church." Then, he clearly defines what the Church is not, what it is, and what vestiges remain under the nonecclesiastical "mask" of the "papacy." Finally, his clear definitions and distinctions make it unnecessary to have recourse, even implicitly, to the analogy of *simul peccator et iustus.* Thus, it seems that the essential sanctity of the Church is stressed more by Calvin than by Luther.

When he embraced the Gospel, Calvin did not think of himself as separating from the one, holy, catholic Church. The idea of a "beneficial break" never entered his mind. What was the powerful impetus that pushed him to fight against the Roman distortions and to proclaim "another form of doctrine" from that proclaimed in the established Church? As we have already suggested, it was his awareness of being called by God to a ministry of reformation.

CHAPTER TWENTY-SEVEN
Calvin's Consciousness of a Divine Call

At the end of Part One we considered the events and circumstances in which the young Calvin was led to discover his life's task.

It remains for us to examine several documents that could pinpoint to what extent this discovery determined his entire spiritual transformation and what specific significance he attributed to his work.

Thus we shall attempt to establish as clearly as possible what Calvin himself thought of his calling and to show what we as historians may infer from this.

This chapter is divided into two sections: the first deals with documents from 1534 to 1539, and the second analyzes some important texts that, although they were not written by the *young* Calvin, will help us understand better the development of his vocation.

Calvin's Calling in His Writings of 1534–1539

No true vocation is contrary to nature. Even if a supernatural call gives rise to it and determines it, there are natural qualities and inclinations that predispose one, as well as human and social influences that condition it.

What do the earliest writings of Calvin reveal to us in this regard? Letters of his youth betray a sensitive, virtuous, and fundamentally religious person who was committed to treating matters fairly and open-mindedly in all fields. His commentary on Seneca's *De Clementia* reveals the acuity of his intelligence, the prodigious capacity of his memory, and especially his interest in the human community, which should be well ordered according to clear and unchangeable principles. Inspired by Stoic wisdom (whose limits he knew well), Calvin clearly takes a position in favor of the normative role of ethics in politics and stresses the value of authentic religion as opposed to superstition. Imbued with the spirit of Erasmus, Calvin does not miss any opportunity to show his distrust of the irrational, turbulent, and seditious "profane crowd."

These qualities of the young humanist, which suggest several positions he will take as a reformer, may be seen even more clearly in the *Psychopannychia*. We have already seen the imperious scorn with which he treats the "flock" of anabaptists, those primitive, confused, and arrogant people who compromise the purity of religion and the order of society by abusing the Bible. We have already noted Calvin's extraordinary use of scriptural and patristic documentation to defend a doctrine of the Catholic tradition.

The Scriptures and the Fathers are the sources in which Calvin seeks objective rules that will allow him to keep his distance from the subjective mysticism of the anabaptists, the revolutionary reform, and then, more and more, from the "established disorder" of the contemporary Church. It is obvious that only the first source is absolutely normative for him. The Fathers are to be followed only to the extent that their interpretations faithfully conform to the principles of Scripture. This was already—with few exceptions—the position of the reformists, who were followers of either Luther or Lefèvre and who had directly or indirectly influenced Calvin's thinking.

The more clearly Calvin discerned the objective norms contained in the Bible, the more he felt armed to criticize and prepared to establish the ideal. Given his passionately intellectual temperament and also his experiences of persecution, he could no longer maintain a calculating passivity and tolerate the evil that he saw besetting him, his friends, and what he appreciated most within the Church. Moreover, his legal mind and even more his acute sense of justice rebelled against this flagrant injustice: some Christians, who were powerful but who (in Calvin's view) were out of step with the Gospel, were persecuting other Christians who were sincerely and passionately devoted to the Gospel. This gifted lawyer then took up the arms of biblical, patristic, and Lutheran theology to protest this oppression and to justify the oppressed.

At Basle, Calvin questioned what God wanted of his Church and of himself in his Church, and there he observed church discipline organized entirely according to the principles of the reform. In Basle he could follow the struggles of the reformists living in France. There he wrote the work that made him an accomplished evangelical theologian. In the beginning, he may have felt, as others before him, the confusion of a layman standing

at the threshold of the sanctuary of sacred knowledge. But he had Melanchthon's example to reassure him.

Let us read again the Dedicatory Epistle and the 1536 *Institutes,* the first
systematic expressions of Calvin's thought and his evangelical meditations,
and see to what extent we find revealed there his awareness of being called
to be a reformer.

From the very first lines of the epistle, his sense of community is expressed. He does not intend to write a "private defense" but to embrace the
common cause of all those who are in Christ.[1] It is the universal Christian
family which is in extremely grave danger. It is being reduced to no more
than a "poor little Church" as a result of secular abuses and present repres-
sions. It must be delivered from its miserable state, and its original order
must be established, that is, the sovereign reign of Christ, sound doctrine,
and true devotion to the complete glory of God.

In this masterful plea, the lawyer fades before his cause. He seems to wish
to say nothing about himself or even his calling. All his efforts are devoted
to advocating the true program of the evangelical party for the monarch's
consideration, so that he will understand how slanderous are the accusations hurled against them. No, it is not correct to say that they are seditious.
In reality they attempt to reestablish the old order, not according to their
own thinking, but according to the teaching of the holy books as professed,
explicated, and understood by the Fathers.[2]

In expressing this ideal, Calvin, the lay jurist and novice theologian,
indulges in several attacks against the "order of priests"[3] and their so-called
speculative theology.[4] Later on, he does not hesitate to imply that the clergy,
or at least those who are hostile to radical renewal, are comparable to the
Levites of the Old Testament. They claimed they were the only legitimate
representatives of the Church and the only authorized interpreters of the
law, and then they built golden calves and had to be called back in line by
the prophets.[5] But not by just any group of prophets; not by the "official
prophets" who could be bought by the powerful and not by those enthusiasts who had no valid call. Only the direct spokesmen of the Almighty
could carry out this task. Calvin conceived the work of the legitimate
instruments of reform according to the prophetic analogy, and therefore he
resolutely rejected the propagandists of a subversive sectarianism.

We have already set forth the reformist criticisms and ideals of the first
Institutes as well as the plan for reformation outlined in it. We recall here
two important themes: the explicit rejection of dividing the people of God
into a dominant clergy and a servile, obedient laity;[6] and the implicit idea
that conscientious Christians should make up for the serious omissions of
a lethargic hierarchy.[7] These ideals are based on the royal priesthood of
believers and its active role in the life of the Christian people.

The two "open letters" that Calvin addressed in 1537 to a lay friend who
was forced to live "under the papacy" and to an old friend who had become

a prelate (therefore to a representative and to an official beneficiary of the papal regime) show that Calvin himself did not hesitate to take this active role when circumstances demanded it.

In his opening words he speaks of authority, but he seeks to justify his intervention only by referring to the will of God. He remarks that he makes no excuses for using a preemptory tone, for he is only repeating the exhortations of the eternal God, whose name is formidable and whose judgment is terrible. Thus, God intends to be heard with docility, for the only proper attitude to the Word is immediate obedience. Finally—and this is a very significant detail—he cites this passage from Ezekiel: "They throng towards you; my people sit down in front of you and listen to your words, but they do not act on them. They cannot tell the truth and their hearts are set on dishonest gain. As far as they are concerned, you are like a love song beautifully sung to music. They listen to your words, but no one puts them into practice. When the thing takes place—and it is beginning now—they will learn that there has been a prophet among them" (Ezek. 33:31–33).[8]

The first epistle, *On Fleeing the Illicit Rites of the Wicked,* maintains this prophetic tone throughout. The rebukes and urgent appeals of the books of Isaiah,[9] Daniel,[10] Micah,[11] and Zechariah[12] are quoted and commented on with great approval. The dominant themes of their proclamation, such as Yahweh's exclusive right to be glorified[13] and the rejection of all idolatry and superstition,[14] give constant support to Calvin's admonitions. The readers' situation is compared to that of the pious Jews in captivity in Egypt or Babylon.[15] The definition of the prophetic task as the "ministry of the Word of God"[16] and the stated intention of the epistle lead us to suppose that in writing it Calvin saw himself in line with the servants of Yahweh who were sent to purify the defilements of Israel. Finally, we mention a particular emphasis. In using the image of the "sound of the trumpet" for his definition of the "ministry of the Word," he implicitly refers to Isa. 58:1[17] and suggests that the true ambassador of the jealous God must distrust human respect and not be afraid to shake up his sleepy listeners. Just as the horn of the temple of Jerusalem does not emit any entertaining music but calls people together for the obligatory celebrations and announces the beginning of fasts, so the messenger of the Lord must speak clearly, openly, and austerely in order to arouse sluggish souls from their torpor.

Nowhere else does this "sound of the trumpet" resonate more strongly than in the second epistle, *On Abandoning the Papal Priesthood.* We have seen how vigorously Calvin reminds us of what God demands of his prelates. In the chorus of congratulations lavished on the newly consecrated bishop, Calvin does not hesitate at all to raise his dissenting voice.[18] As in his first epistle,[19] he does not address only his correspondent but all bishops and priests in general.[20] Although there are fewer quotations from the prophets than in the first epistle,[21] one can consider the entire letter as a proclamation similar to the admonitions of an Isaiah or an Ezekiel to derelict priests. This appears very clearly in the passage in which Calvin gives the rest of the text of Ezekiel that he had quoted in the opening lines: "Trouble for the shepherds of Israel who feed themselves! Shepherds ought to feed their flock, yet you have fed on milk, you have dressed yourselves in wool, you have sacrificed the fattest sheep, but failed to feed the flock. You have failed to make weak sheep strong, or to care for the sick ones, or bandage the wounded ones. You have failed to bring back strays or look for the lost. On the contrary, you have ruled them cruelly and violently. For lack of a shepherd they have scattered, to become the prey of any wild animal; they are scattered far. . . . The Lord Yahweh says this: I am going to call the shepherds to account. I am going to take my flock back from them. . . . I shall rescue my sheep from their mouths; they will not prey on them any more."[22]

A passage of unusual relevance. Calvin remarks that this passage accurately reflects the attitude of the servile high clergy who forget their pastoral obligations but not their rights and benefices. They are quick to punish the poor who have gone astray, but neglect to protect them against greedy priests or the propagandists of aberrant beliefs. However, we note that this "prophetic" criticism of the clergy,[23] in spite of its conspicuously anticlerical statements, never hardens into a systematic opposition of prophets to priests. Quite the contrary, in this epistle[24] as in later writings Calvin ends up demanding the same qualities of both pastors and prophets. It is therefore more exact to say that he considers the two as complementary, and at times he even combines them.[25]

This writing is distinguished by its insistence on the need for revitalizing the sick structures rather than destroying them. Calvin does not ask his readers to resign their episcopal charges but to fulfill them in an irreproachable manner and to purify their dioceses of abuses[26] and errors.[27] Calvin has no illusions; humanly speaking, he would consider it Utopian to expect the hardened papal prelates to suddenly transform themselves into good pastors. But on the other hand, Calvin has endless confidence in the miraculous power of the Word: "Surely the power of the Word of the Lord is great, and more powerful than anyone can easily imagine, unless he has experienced it. And its power is very effective in both ways, so that whoever is touched by it, no matter how hard or strong he may be, is immediately softened or crushed."[28]

The writings that we have examined so far show that the young lay theologian was preoccupied with reform from the beginning. His concerns are not so much the reflection of an individual religious experience, comparable to a conversion in the pietistic sense, but a determination to formulate in a profound and understandable way the critical and constructive objectives of a renewed universal, catholic community. Calvin is revealed as an ardent theoretician of the reform, a "committed" writer with a prophetic message. However, these works do not give the impression that he thought that by writing them he was dedicating himself to public action in the interest of an effective reformation.

In this regard, his correspondence with du Tillet and his *Reply to Sadolet* bring new insights. Here Calvin expressly speaks of the pastoral and therefore public vocation in the service of the renewed Gospel. And even more important, for the first time he specifically considers his own calling. From then on he is prepared to defend the legitimacy of his call. We know that between the writing of the first two works and the latter two, there was the forceful intervention of Guillaume Farel which obliged Calvin to abandon his initial plan of dedicating himself completely to theological research. At that time Calvin actually began to open himself up to the calling of a reformer, in the strict sense of the word. In Farel's appeal and afterward in his own personal success in Geneva and Lausanne, Calvin saw more and more the signs of God.

First, we will examine how this awareness is expressed in Calvin's replies to du Tillet. Having exchanged their ideas on the problem of schism and then remaining silent for several months, the two friends began an active correspondence during the second half of 1538. (This exchange of letters was to be the last.) Calvin broke the silence. Without knowing that du Tillet had sent him a long discourse on the problems of Christian unity, Calvin once again wrote to inform him of his activities following his expulsion from Geneva. Calvin had already informed du Tillet of the circumstances of this distressing event through Jean du Tillet, his brother.

Although this letter reveals the confusion of a pastor rejected by his flock, it is even more a wonderful testimony of his confidence in God. We read: "Nevertheless, I hope that our Lord will lead me in this very ambiguous deliberation in such a way that I shall regard what he would reveal to me rather than what my own judgment determines. Since my own judgment is drawing me inordinately in a contrary direction, it ought to be suspect." As surely as Calvin saw that his ministry in Geneva corresponded to a "calling from God," he was persuaded that God would again undertake to put him where he could serve him. Besides, in spite of his temporary disappointment, Calvin remained vitally interested in the cause of the reform. He alludes to his hope that the truce concluded in June of 1538 between the King of France and the Emperor of Germany will favor reform: "Presently he is undertaking a matter of marvelous consequence not without knowledge of Augustus and Caesar. . . . It is very doubtful that one would attempt such a crossing without intending to proceed."[29]

From Paris, du Tillet replied to this letter without much delay. He took up the theme of his earlier letter, which had never reached Calvin, and applied it to Calvin's new situation. He first invites Calvin to take advantage of the situation by seriously examining his conscience.[30] Is he truly certain that he has not erred by taking his own will for the will of God? Has he not deceived himself concerning his true calling?[31] Du Tillet thinks that his friend has made a twofold error. First, Calvin responded to a human call from people without Church authority—an obvious allusion to Farel and the Genevans—as if he had acted upon a divine call.[32] Second, Calvin has denied that the churches in which he had been baptized, raised, and trained were the Church of God only because of their numerous deficiencies and errors.[33] Was not this attitude more typical of the "carnal" and impatient man than the spiritual man who knows how to contemplate higher things? Was this call not suggested by "the one who knows how to transform himself into an angel of light"? These criticisms are quite extreme, but du Tillet seems to have decided to conceal none of his thoughts. He further insinuates that his lay friend has arrogated to himself a ministry reserved for the priestly order. "For our concupiscence," he writes, "often moves us to despise or even to abandon our own state and the calling that we have from God and to desire to undertake that which is beyond the capacity he has given us and to involve us in what has nothing to do with our true state and calling."[34] What a misunderstanding of the diversity of God's gifts! Calvin should recognize his fault as soon as possible, renounce completely the pastoral ministry, and return to Roman obedience.[35] Then du Tillet offers Calvin financial help which, to say the least, comes at an awkward moment.

These lines reached Calvin when he had just been officially confirmed in his new pastoral charge at Strasbourg and was enjoying the warm approval of his new parishioners.[36] He also confessed in a letter to the Genevans that his faith in the divine origin of his calling was reaffirmed.[37] Thus his reply to du Tillet was imbued with a thinly disguised sense of irritation. "Sir," he begins, and then in essence says, "I thank you for your exhortations, but I have no need of them to recognize my faults, to the extent that I have any." He adds: "Those which you note are not mine. If it is a question of disputing my calling, I do not believe that you have any reason to impugn it, for the Lord has given me strong reasons to confirm myself in it. If you have any doubt about this, it is enough for me to be sure of it; and not only that, but I can also prove it to those who would wish to submit their censures to the truth."[38]

The young reformer has regained his prophetic tone. He does not need to search for arguments to refute the opinion of his opponent. The Lord will deal with that directly. God's infallible truth will decide if the censures of his servant are right or wrong. It is his tribunal which will condemn the true dissidents and absolve the true Christians.[39]

Note, however, that Calvin does not claim to have a well-formed conscience based only on his own direct perception of the divine will. It is the Lord who called him to pastoral service, but his calling is equally confirmed by the representatives of the Church. "I have discussed this matter," Calvin declares, "with someone whom you know." Farther on he writes: "In such perplexity I found it necessary to follow what I believed that the servants of God were showing me." Not just any servants, but "the most moderate." A clear allusion to M. Bucer and the Strasbourg ministers.[40]

Strengthened by these assurances, Calvin categorically rejects the invitation to remain a layman and to rejoin the community he abandoned. In turn, Calvin counsels du Tillet not to judge "in a closet" those "who daily uphold their doctrine before the whole world" and to examine his own conscience: "I wish that you would apply some of these exhortations to yourself. For in calling darkness light throughout your letter, you condemn those who stick more closely to the path than any of you."[41] In other words, "Physician, heal thyself."

In conclusion, the reformer once again alludes to the source of his renewed assurance when he declares: "But inasmuch as you reject the truth of God and his servants, I need reply to you in only a few words so that it does not seem that I concede anything to you."[42]

Du Tillet replies once again, and this was in all probability the last piece of this moving correspondence. With dignity he restates his doubts about Calvin's "vocation to the ministry of the Church," adding that only the sacrament of ordination conferred by legitimate successors of the apostles can establish such a ministry. In the history of the Church there are certainly cases where lay ministers, such as Ambrose, were called "by some miracle or extraordinary revelation," but even they had to receive priestly ordination before assuming their duties. But simply to be nominated by "the servants of God" such as Bucer or other priests who have broken with the legitimate hierarchy can in no way replace the sacrament.[43] I do not know how Calvin read these lines. The care that he later takes to define ordinary and extraordinary ministries leads me to conjecture that du Tillet's words gave birth to fruitful reflection.

Calvin's activities in Strasbourg occupied all his time. He preached, baptized, administered the Lord's Supper, all the while working to clarify the principles of the reformation in matters of doctrine, discipline, and liturgy. This peaceful labor was interrupted only by the Sadolet affair and by participation in religious conferences in Germany.

Once again we take up the *Reply to Sadolet*. From the very first lines, Calvin presents his calling as a reformer. Certainly he does not consider himself the first reformer of Geneva. He recognizes that at the time when he was called ("to that place I was called"), the church of Geneva already possessed a "corrected form" and already lived according to the "true religion" ("already constituted according to religion, or the corrected form of the Church"). But he immediately adds (and not without some pride) that he participated quite actively in the work begun by Farel and Viret. Not content with supporting them as a theologian, he did all within his power to consolidate the half-finished edifice. Thus he considers his mission, like his cause, to be identified with those of the two other reformers.[44]

What follows is an eloquent confession of faith in the divine origin of his calling, which is not only a personal matter but a matter for the Church. (I shall reproduce here the complete text according to the contemporary French translation, in order to bring out its persuasive force. Then I shall comment on it, using the key words of the original.)

"If you had accused me in particular, I would have doubtlessly given in because of your knowledge and in honor of your learning. But when I see my ministry (which I know to be founded upon and confirmed by the calling of the Lord) wounded and broken by the affliction you have caused, it would be disloyalty, not patience, to keep quiet and hide my views on this matter. At the outset, my first duty in this church was the office of reader, and then later minister and pastor. As far as what I undertook as my second charge, I maintain as my right that I did it legitimately and as a proper calling. I do not need many words to demonstrate how assiduous and religious I was in administering it. I would not attribute to myself any subtlety of intellect, erudition, prudence, or dexterity. Not even diligence. But at the same time I certainly know that, before Christ my judge and all his angels, I have proceeded in this church with such purity and sincerity that it was the work of the Lord. To this all the faithful bear good and ample testimony. After one recognizes that my ministry is from God (which is certainly clear after hearing the deduction based on this matter), who would not judge my silence to be pretense and dissimulation and accuse me of prevarication, if I were silent and allowed myself to be defamed and slandered? Therefore there is no one who does not recognize that by great necessity I am not only constrained but also unable to escape (if I do not wish to traitorously abandon the task that the Lord has placed in my hands) from opposing and contradicting your reproaches and accusations. Although at the present I am discharged from the administration of the church of Geneva, this cannot and ought not stop me from maintaining paternal love and charity toward it. I say that I am obliged to be bound always in faith and loyalty to that to which God has ordained me. Therefore I now see traps laid for the church for which the Lord wants me to take care and solicitude, and I know the great and imminent perils and dangers that, if one does not prevent them by proper action and diligence, will promptly befall it. Who, then, is this who would advise me to wait in safety and patience for the end and outcome of such dangers? What stupidity would it be, I ask you, to remain dumb and astonished, not to acknowledge the ruin of this church for whose protection one must be on watch day and night?"[45]

This last sentence clearly reminds us of the exhortation from *On Abandoning the Papal Priesthood:* "Watchman, sound the trumpet; pastor, take up arms. Why do you hesitate? Why do you languish? Why do you sleep?"[46]

It is among the principal duties of a good bishop to watch the sleeping flock and to be prepared to defend it against any enemy. One certainly has the impression that even though he was exiled from and rejected by Geneva, Calvin considers himself as charged with an "episcopal" duty and responsibility in regard to the Genevans. This impression is confirmed by what he said earlier: If it is God who has "ordained" him as pastor of this church, he is bound to it forever by a "promise" which is, so to speak, conjugal. What God has thus joined together, let no man put asunder! Is this only a reminiscence of the "mystical marriage" between the bishop and his diocese which is so often evoked in Catholic tradition?

The other dominant notes of the *Reply to Sadolet* include both a clear distinction between the personal interests of the minister and the interests of his ministry, and the profound bond between the office of the ministry and the Lord himself. Emphasizing that he does not possess extraordinary human qualities at either the intellectual or the moral level, Calvin wishes to show that his apology does not have his personal justification as its goal. Since he has "made his way" into the local church of Geneva in "purity and sincerity," it follows that he does not wish to glorify himself. What he has done, he has done with God and for God, as the Lord's instrument. The work accomplished was "the work of the Lord." Who dares to attack him attacks Christ himself. And if he, Calvin, maintained some kind of false and confused humility and kept silent before such attacks, he would be a traitor and a prevaricator. Such an attitude would be simply disloyal. Therefore, since Calvin considers everything that deals with him "personally" to be negligible, he feels obliged to raise his voice to defend his ministry.

Calvin is so certain that this pastoral, reformed, and quasi-episcopal ministry is founded upon a legitimate vocation from God that later on he declares himself ready to defend it at the price of his life.[47] This is not the assurance of a young layman before an illustrious cardinal! There is not the slightest trace of a feeling of inferiority. Just as he treated his friend, du Tillet, as an equal, he speaks to his accuser, the Bishop of Carpentras and member of the Sacred College, as a man of the Church who has no more authority than he.

In the rest of the reply, Calvin again explicitly states that his duties in Geneva were truly pastoral[48] and that he and his companions had the basic task of reforming the churches that the Lord had given them.[49] But when a building has fallen into ruin, it is not enough to clean it out; one must rebuild it according to its original plans. The important thing is to know where these plans are found. With false plans one can do nothing. Let us listen to Calvin: "You know very well, Sadolet, and if you deny it I shall tell everyone that you have maliciously and cunningly hidden the fact, that not only do we agree more clearly with antiquity than all of you, but we ask for nothing else than that the ancient face of the Church may sometime be restored. Moreover, we want to reestablish completely that which was deformed and stained by unlearned men, after which it has been miserably torn apart and almost destroyed by the pope and his faction. I do not wish to contradict you or to press you so hard that I would recall, reform, and reinstate the Church in its original state as first constituted by the apostles. (That state is always a singular example of the true Church, which we must follow if we do not wish to fall into grave error and failure.) But to spare you a little, I beg you to consider and place before your eyes the ancient state of the Church as it was among the Greeks at the time of Chrysostom and Basil, and among the Latins at the time of Cyprian, Ambrose, and Augustine, as fully described in their writings. Then contemplate the ruins that remain about you."[50] It is quite clear: "The pope and his faction," which includes Sadolet, hesitate to compare the present ruins with the integrity of the Church of the first four or five centuries, because they are themselves responsible for having ruined and "almost destroyed" it. Christians like Calvin not only have the courage to restore this integrity but they are dedicated to the task of reconstructing the fallen edifice according to its original plans. Thus they were able to say that they were in complete harmony with antiquity and that they were attempting with all their might to re-form "the ancient face of the Church." It is to the exalted task of reestablishing—he says: "to correct in order to improve"—that Calvin feels called. Let them stop demeaning him as an innovator![51]

If anyone asks Calvin by what right he undertakes this eminent ecclesiastical task, he will refuse to enter into fruitless discussions on sacramental ordination or canonical mission. Necessity makes the law. When the invited guests refuse to appear, the king sends for those along the side of the road. When the captains let their standards fall, the ordinary soldiers have to pick them up.[52] When those responsible are asleep and fail to confront mortal danger, others must take their place.[53] Is not this the way the prophets have always acted? Once again it is their example which inspires the ministers of the Gospel.[54]

This is the thirty-year-old Calvin as he appears to us at the end of his spiritual transformation, when he becomes fully aware of his pastoral and reformist calling. It remains for us to see to what extent several texts after 1539 reflect this awareness and develop the essential characteristics of his calling.

Calvin's Calling in Several Texts After 1539

The letters that Calvin addressed from 1540 to 1541 to the Senate of Geneva clearly show that in spite of his "prophetic" awareness, he conceived of his reform mission in an essentially pastoral or even "episcopal" sense. We cite only two illuminating passages.

On 13 October 1540, Calvin replied to his friends in Geneva who were pressing him to return as soon as possible from his exile in Strasbourg: "I cannot lightly set aside the charge to which the Lord has called me here, unless he frees me from it in a proper and legitimate manner. I have always believed and taught, and I still cannot be persuaded otherwise, that when our Lord places a man as pastor in a church to teach his Word, he should think of himself as being responsible for its government to the extent that he cannot easily withdraw, unless he knows for certain in his heart and testifies before the faithful that the Lord has released him from his duty."[55]

And on 19 February 1541, having already determined to return to Geneva, Calvin wrote to the Senate in these words: "Because I belong to God and not to myself, I am always ready to be used where it seems good to him to call me. And since it has pleased you to have so much confidence in me, I feel obliged to fulfill whatever you desire of me, not to mention the perpetual obligation that I have to your church, to which our Lord once dedicated me."[56]

"I belong to God," says Calvin, which means that he no longer belongs to himself or to men. God uses him where he wills, and he goes where he is sent. Only the Lord can make him a pastor, dedicate him to the service of a local church, or relieve him of it "in a proper and legitimate manner." To change his position for human reasons, or at least without having the certitude that God desires this change, would be most reprehensible.

A person who speaks this way implicitly reveals his reaction to the abuse, which had become widespread among papist clergy, of changing positions according to personal desires and temporal interests. On the other hand, the reformer was not a traveling prophet. He possessed a sense of stability, which was an essential value of ancient discipline. He desired to throw himself wholeheartedly into the battle of reformation, but he was convinced that this battle should be regulated and ordered, if one wished it to result in a peaceful reconstruction. Liberated from an evil and paralyzing conformity, he wished to be united with a "form" of the Church whose constitution was healthy and efficient. He believed that once the hardened ranks of the "papacy" were rejected, it was essential to reestablish and maintain the ecclesiastical ranks according to the Gospel. Any attempt to create an unstructured ministry which lacks a solid local foundation and which may be removed at the whims of uncontrolled inspirations would be to fall into the ill-fated anarchy of the "spiritualists."

In the years following his final return to Geneva, Calvin continued to reflect on his calling. His experiences in Strasbourg, as well as the influence of the great man of the Church, Martin Bucer, helped him immensely. One of the most interesting aspects of Calvin's reflections is his attempt to relate the prophetic and pastoral ministries. The reformer continues to maintain the analogy between the pioneers of the reform and the prophets of the Old and New Testaments, but at the same time he wishes to avoid the idea that one can take an analogy for a pure and simple identification.

In his *Supplex exhortatio* of 1543, he first declares: "Concerning doctrine,

I say that here we have common cause with the prophets." Just as the ancient messengers of Yahweh had a mission to the Jews to demonstrate forcefully the emptiness of ceremonies without living faith and the necessity of worshiping in spirit and truth, Calvin sees himself as obliged to fight against certain deep-rooted habits of worship in contemporary Christianity.[57] However, he is careful to be precise: "In this matter, we confess that there are some differences between us and the prophets."[58] The similarity of their tasks does not eliminate important specific differences.

The same concern to make a broad but careful use of the analogy between the past and the present is also expressed in other passages of the *Supplex exhortatio.* It is absolutely necessary, Calvin remarks, that Christians who have heard the call of reform not let themselves be intimidated by an inconsistent ecclesiastical authority and that they not fear to take over those ministries neglected by that authority. One must show in this area the same courage and initiative as an Isaiah or a Jeremiah: "Do not immediately be frightened when you hear the name of the Church; but remember that a struggle such as you see today between us and the Roman pontiff and his whole cohort occurred between the prophets and the apostles and the masked church of their own age." Just like the ancients, the modern "prophets" were raised up "by the command of God" to oppose the "lazy and dull priesthood."[59]

In another text from 1543, Calvin compares the frightening passivity of the contemporary hierarchy to a refusal to assist someone in mortal danger, and he exclaims: "What would have become of the imperiled Church if we too had kept quiet?"[60] He replies in the *Supplex exhortatio,* "Certainly, our adversaries would never stop reproaching us for our audacity in undertaking reforms as 'private men' and without the authorization of the pope.[61] But what should we have done when the human appeals kept us waiting indefinitely and the call from God became more and more urgent?"[62]

However, in spite of this insistence on the prophetic and extraordinary aspect of his calling, Calvin endlessly stresses the need to respect, as a general principle, the ordinary ecclesiastical power: "Certainly, I profess that respect must be given to the priests, and there is great danger in despising the duly instituted power. Therefore, if they say that duly instituted power should not be resisted easily, we subscribe to that statement without difficulty."[63]

There is the same attitude of both wisdom and radicalism in the *Institutes* of 1543. The reformer states that in reforming the Church, the example of Christ, the apostles, and the prophets must be followed.[64] Then he adds: Isaiah, Jeremiah, Joel, and Habakkuk stigmatized the corruptions of Jerusalem with extraordinary severity, but they did not go so far as to break with the corrupt community: "Nevertheless, the prophets therefore did not erect new churches for themselves or construct a new altar on which they should offer separate sacrifices. But even though they were merely men, they

believed that the Lord had set forth his Word among them and instituted
ceremonies by which he was worshiped, and they raised up pure hands to
him in the midst of the company of the wicked." The heralds of Yahweh
had a sense of divine appointment and consequently a "desire to preserve
unity."[65]

All these considerations—which may have been inspired indirectly by
certain remarks from the last letter of du Tillet—led the reformer to establish the idea of ordinary and extraordinary ministries. Quoting Eph. 4:11,
"And he also gave some to be apostles and others to be prophets, and some
evangelists and still others pastors and teachers," Calvin comments: "Of
these, only two finally remain in the ordinary service of the Church. Three
others God raised up at the beginning of his kingdom, and he revives them
occasionally, as the necessity of the times demands." Only pastors and
teachers, therefore, were part of the ordinary institutional ministry. Be they
perfect or imperfect, their function should be permanent among the people
of God. It is not the same with apostles, prophets, and evangelists. They
are raised up by the Lord only from time to time. Their function essentially
consists of responding to the needs of the times and serving the Church
during its periods of regeneration and renewal. Calvin considers his own
period as such a time. He also admits that there may be prophets, although
"less conspicuous" than in the ancient Church, and that there certainly are
apostles and evangelists "in our time." "It was necessary that there be such
people who would restore the Church from its defection to the Antichrist."
Then he becomes more precise: "Nevertheless, I call the office itself extraordinary which has no place in properly constituted churches."[66] The immediate and extended contexts allow us to affirm that Calvin, to some extent,
places Martin Luther, the other reformers of the first generation, and himself in this category.[67] We say "to some extent," for he considers himself also
a pastor, an ordinary minister of a specific local community.

These thoughts on the ministry are quite characteristic of Calvin's ecclesiology. A man of the second generation of the reform, Calvin was not
content to call for and announce the great renewal; he felt the need to
organize and to express the doctrines of "re-formed" Christianity. In other
words, he felt it necessary to stress both the charismatic and the institutional elements in the ministry as parallel and complementary to each other.
His fervent faith and qualities as a systematic thinker and a practical lawyer
joined together to predestine him to this task and eminently qualified him
for this dual ministry.

It is significant that in the *Institutes* of 1543, the description of the call
to the evangelical ministry begins with a note about the need for order in
everything that concerns "government."[68] The pastor is the servant not only
of God but also of the community that he is in charge of governing.
Therefore it is necessary that he be called both inwardly by the Lord and
outwardly by the legitimate ecclesiastical authority: "It is necessary that he

be properly called." And here is a passage that amounts to a definition: "I speak of the external and solemn calling which pertains to the public order of the Church; I omit that secret calling, of which each minister is conscious before God and which does not have the testimony of the Church. It is the good testimony of our heart; because we do not receive the ministry offered to us with a spirit of ambition or avarice, nor any other desire, but by a genuine fear of God and a desire to upbuild the Church."[69] Surely, long before having thus defined his calling, Calvin knew himself called both "secretly" by God and "publicly" by a church of God.

The certainty of being divinely elected and predestined to the noble mission of the rebuilding and edifying of the Church remained with Calvin until the last moment of his life. This permitted him to face all his "domestic enemies." But, alas, it also pushed him to acts of religious intolerance comparable to those of the Inquisition of the Sorbonne. A psychological analysis of this phenomenon would be most interesting: the more Calvin was criticized as a pastor, the more he turned to prophetic themes to defend his pastorate. After the execution of the Comparet brothers (1555), when Calvin was accused of no longer being a good shepherd of the flock but a cruel and bloody dictator, he cried out from the pulpit: "But such blasphemy is addressed to God, not to men!"[70] And several days later he stated: "If I wished to do all that God has commanded me, everybody will hate me."[71] Blamed even more strongly after the torture and execution of François-Daniel Berthelier (1554), Calvin retorted to his attackers: "We have a Master who will not suffer anyone to scorn him. I am not here in my own name; I wish to do nothing to advance myself or to bring forth anything of my own. But when I speak, it is in the name of God."[72]

To speak, to judge, to condemn, to place seditious and heretical people under secular jurisdiction were for the Genevan reformer all ways of edifying the Church in the name and at the command of the eternal God. At the time of the tragic and shameful Servetus affair, as well as during the repression of the Perrinists, Calvin had the peaceful conscience of one who was scrupulously fulfilling his duty—his duty as a good "student" of the jealous God who does not suffer anyone to scorn him. With the Old Testament in hand,[73] Calvin never stopped repeating that if he spoke in the name of God, it was because he knew well how to listen to God; and if he proclaimed the divine demands, he would first of all apply them to himself. He is both the instrument and the disciple of the Spirit: "I speak, but I must also listen, since I am taught by the Spirit of God."[74] Thus, his listeners must obey him as promptly as he himself complies with the preached Word: "When I speak here in the name of God, may they listen to the doctrine in order to follow it and pay homage to it. It is more than all the laws and edicts of kings and emperors."[75] His preaching is like the "trumpet sound" of Isaiah: God "desired that I be like a trumpet so that his people would come to him and obey him."[76]

It is most instructive to note how Calvin reacted to adversaries who condemned his prophetic stance. In a sermon on Ezekiel in 1552, he upbraids his congregation: "There are those who will say today: 'Calvin is making a prophet of himself when Ezekiel says that we will recognize that there was a prophet among us! Calvin applies this to himself. Is he a prophet?' Now since it is the doctrine of God that I proclaim, I must use this language."[77] A very forceful and suggestive reply. The reformer does not refuse the title of prophet, but he does have reservations. Calvin reasons: "It is of little importance if I am a prophet or not. The main thing is that I accomplish the same function and use the same language as the ancient messengers of God. The person of the minister and the name that one gives him are only secondary in relationship to his acts, the service that he effectively accomplishes." Here is an essential distinction in Calvin's thought on the ministry, where everything is conceived in dynamic terms.[78] In this the French reformer is superior to Luther, who sometimes refused the title of prophet; it seems that Luther never succeeded in discerning the exact limits of the analogy.[79]

These few texts from after 1539 show that the leader of Geneva saw his calling then just as he did when he was a young pastor in Strasbourg. The only difference is that Calvin's definition has become clearer and more precise.

To conclude, we will examine the famous Preface to the *Commentary on the Psalms* (1557), which is most frequently quoted as the supreme testimony concerning Calvin's conversion. We have already discussed what one may call the strictly historical and biographical value of the passage on the *"subita conversio."* Now we will reread the entire Preface to see what variations it contains on the theme of vocation.[80]

The first sentence itself indicates the eminently ecclesiastical scope of the work, while suggesting that this time the author will share some personal, confidential matters: "If the reading of my commentaries brings as much advancement to the Church of God as I have gained in writing them, I shall never have occasion to repent of having undertaken this labor."[81] We note that the entire last sentence of the Preface obviously takes up the same idea: "I know of nothing more important than to consider the edification of the Church. God has given me this desire, and it is so by his grace."[82]

To advance and build the Church of God are the specific objectives of Calvin's calling as a pastor of the reform. It is surely through the minister's preaching that souls are "raised up to God"[83] and as living stones become part of the temple of the Lord.[84]

But to be raised up to God and to edify the Church are not within the ability of man weighed down by the flesh. Even one who gathers all his strength to speak the language of faith and prayer must recognize the abyss "between the companionship of God and the hindrances of the flesh." Great is the "infirmity of the flesh" which is tenaciously opposed to "the virtue of faith."[85] Who is able to pass from this dialectical tension to the peace of complete integrity and wholeness?

The psalms, Calvin replies, show us the way. One must recognize that "there is no other book that teaches us more perfectly the way to praise God" and to pursue piety. And not just in a general fashion: "Moreover, I know that this book is filled with all the teachings that can serve to reform our life to all holiness, uprightness, and justice. But principally it will teach and prepare us to bear the cross, which is a true sign of our obedience. We must renounce our own affections, so that we submit ourselves entirely to God and permit him to govern and ordain our lives, so that the most shocking and bitter miseries of our lives become sweet for us, especially since they proceed from him."

Here Calvin comes to the point. He is not content to explain the psalms in an academic way, but he adds the witness of his own life: "I want them to know that the experience I gained by the struggles in which the Lord has exercised me" has "greatly benefited [me]."

What were these struggles or combats? How did they teach Calvin to free himself from the "hindrances of the flesh" and to respond to the "companionship of God" and submit himself totally to his direction? They were similar to those of David and caused Calvin to undergo the same experiences as the prophet-king of Israel, the most eminent of the psalmists: "And because among all those David is the chief, it has greatly benefited me to listen more carefully to the complaints that he made of the afflictions that the Church had to suffer within itself and the afflictions from those who claimed to be its members. I have suffered the same or similar things from the domestic enemies of the Church."[86]

This is a very significant passage. After the short ecclesiastical comment of the first sentence, Calvin speaks at such length of "the anatomy of all the parts of the soul"—that is, of individual infirmities, faith, prayer, struggle, and obedience—that the unsuspecting reader is surprised by this abrupt return to the communal theme. Calvin as an individual seems to withdraw suddenly into the background in order to discuss only his experiences as a man of the Church. Whether one interprets the "domestic enemies" as the papists or—which is quite probable[87]—as the Genevan adversaries of Calvin, the allusion is clearly to his mission as a reformer. In any case, the rest of the text speaks only of the different stages of his calling.

Calvin knows that he is quite different from David and inferior to him in many respects, but he finds in their respective duties enough resemblance to allow him to compare himself to David, or at least to take him as a model. Thus he declares: "It was most useful to contemplate in him, as in a mirror, both the beginning of my calling and the course and continuation of my duty. Thus I clearly recognize that everything that this excellent king and prophet[88] suffered and experienced was given to me by God as an example to imitate."[89]

The analogy begins with the way in which the divine call was made. Just as David was raised from his humble condition as a shepherd "taking care of his animals" to "the supreme height of royal dignity," the young Calvin was "advanced" from his "small and low beginnings" and promoted to the "most honorable duty of a minister and preacher of the Gospel." This comparison recalls Luther's words: "God raised us up from the dung and mire and placed us with the leaders of his people."[90] Moreover, the word "advanced" suggests the victory of divine interventions over human hindrances of which Calvin will speak later in his account.

Any careful reader can recognize that each sketch of the significant moments of the reformer's career contains a dialectical opposition between the tenacious resistance of man and the all-powerful grace of God.

Let us look at the first. Here is the human obstacle: "Since I was a young child, my father had destined me to theology; but a little afterward, when he considered how the knowledge of law usually enriches those who serve it, this hope caused him to change his mind abruptly. This was the reason that I withdrew from the study of philosophy and set forth to study law." Then comes the irresistible intervention of grace: "Nevertheless, God, in his secret providence, finally pulled my bridle in another direction." Calvin does not get lost in details; he does not mention a word about his four years at Montaigu but stresses that his father's change of mind occurred "suddenly." He is careful not to mention his father's death, in order to attribute the outcome entirely to providence. As in an abstract painting, the subject and its contrasts are reduced to essentials.

The second example of this dialectical opposition, the obstinate and obdurate attachment of the young Calvin to "the superstitions of the papacy" and the *"subita conversione"* to evangelical docility or teachability, is well known. Human resistance is illustrated by the unconventional image of the "mire" from which one "extricates" oneself with great difficulty, and the force of grace is illustrated by the comparison with an animal trainer. It is not important if these things did not actually occur so swiftly or so simply. An outline is not a complete story. Describing his turnabout according to the model of the "conversion as miracle" of Paul, Calvin notes that he was "suddenly inflamed" with a great desire to progress along his new path and that very rapidly ("a year had not yet elapsed") all those who were interested in "pure doctrine" began to flow to him. Here is a brief sketch of the first phase of his calling: the "teachable one" rapidly became the "teacher."[91]

The second phase will occur only at the end of two new confrontations between his pitiful human resistance and the grand divine design. "As far as I am concerned," he continues, "as much as I am by nature somewhat retiring and shy, I have always loved peace and quiet. I began to seek some hiding place and a way to withdraw from people." All in vain! God had ordained something else: "But although I was intent on achieving my own desires, all retreats and places of refuge were for me like public schools." One may not flee from the Lord: "In spite of my natural inclination, he brought me forth into light."[92] Obviously God had not inflamed this elect man in order to let him hide under a bushel. He drew him out of his "meager and low beginnings," he "brought him forth" from the "deep mire" in order to "lead him forth" into public service.[93] He "reduced him" to total docility in order to "lead him through" many detours into the evangelical adventure.

But obviously the inertia of his nature was great. Calvin again becomes obstinate: "Leaving France, I deliberately came to Germany so that I might live in peace in some unknown corner, as I had always wished." Again we have no details. The reformer even fails to mention the important incidents of October 1533, and the affair of the Placards, when he had to flee Paris and then France. But he stresses a new intervention of the Almighty; an irresistible call led him to react against the persecution of the evangelicals, who were slandered by the evil counselors of the King: "But while staying in Basle, where I was almost hidden and known by only a few persons, they burned at the stake several of the faithful and holy people in France." They accused them of being "seditious people." Now "it seemed to me that if I did not courageously oppose them with all that is within me, I could never forgive myself, and in remaining silent I would have been cowardly and disloyal. And this was the cause that aroused me to publish my *Institutes of the Christian religion*."[94] Here is the private teacher who sees himself as constrained to write a public defense. Here we have the novice theologian who feels obliged to spread the ideas that he has just made his own.

However, Calvin wishes to go no farther. Having fulfilled the dictates of his conscience, he resumes his freedom as a scholar: "Now, since it was not at all my purpose to assert myself and attract attention, I let everyone know this by at once withdrawing from there." But the Lord's plans were entirely different, and this time he revealed them in angry tones to his servant who tried to slip away again. He used the most testy of his ambassadors. Calvin confessed: "Finally, master Guillaume Farel brought me to Geneva, not so much by advice and exhortation as by a dreadful adjuration, as if God on high had stretched forth his hand upon me to stop me. . . . And after hearing that I had several particular studies for which I wanted to preserve my freedom, and when he saw that he was getting nowhere by begging, he went so far as to utter an imprecation that it would please God to curse my rest and the tranquillity of the studies that I sought, if in such great need I were to withdraw myself and refuse to give help and aid."[95] The context of this passage is clearly prophetic. The mention of the hand of God is not only a recollection of the "wonderworking hand of God" of the *Commentary on the Acts,*[96] which transformed Saul from a wolf to a shepherd, but it is also an implicit reference to the books of Isaiah, Jeremiah, and the Psalms where this gesture is a symbol of divine anger.[97]

Is this the last confrontation between the hesitation of the flesh and the unrelenting grace of God? Not at all. Continuing his testimony, the reformer speaks of his expulsion from Geneva and how he believed that he had again found tranquillity: "When free as a result of this [expulsion] and discharged from my vocation, I was determined to live in peace without taking up any public charge." Another illusory attempt to withdraw, inevitably destined to failure. For "the excellent servant of Christ, Martin Bucer, using admonitions and protests similar to those Farel used earlier, called me to another place. Thus, having been frightened by the example of Jonah, which he pointed out to me, I once more began to fulfill my responsibility to teach."[98] Another intervention of the One who sees all, to trap the "prophet" who is intent on slipping away. From this moment the power of the Lord will always sustain him when human obstacles stand in the way of fulfilling the vocation of his elect. The Lord's power will confront Calvin's timidity and personal weaknesses as much as the plots of his enemies.

From Strasbourg, the Lord sent Calvin "as if by force" to the imperial diets of Worms and Ratisbon. By "his wonderful strength," the Lord dissipated the efforts of the opposition in Geneva and brought back the reformer against his "desire and inclination" to his first post. Then he exercised him in "various struggles," without ever allowing him to succumb. Calvin discovered in these experiences proof of the "secret providence of God" and his "eternal predestination," before which one's so-called free will is absolutely powerless.[99]

At the end of his Preface, Calvin compares himself several times more to the prophet David, who had to confront both external and "domestic" enemies of the Church in order to accomplish his mission in Israel.[100]

The conclusion that seems to emerge at the end of this study is the following: the dominant theme of the Preface to the *Commentary on the Psalms* is not Calvin's conversion but his vocation. Seven years before his death, the reformer—having conquered the resistance of his adversaries, sometimes by means of harsh measures that were incompatible with the spirit of the Gospel—glances back at his eventful past. He does not do so as a historian or an autobiographer, but as a theologian concerned to prove the infallible predestination of God and the supernatural origin of his calling. Thus he greatly condenses the real course of events and describes his transformation in dialectical terms, with several scriptural examples. He makes it clear that he was called to the evangelical ministry in the same way that Paul was called to be an apostle,[101] and he explicitly compares himself to David, the perfect man of the Church, a prophet and psalmist of the eternal God. In all of this, Calvin expresses very forcefully the deep conviction of being a legitimate minister, which he acquired from his first activity in Geneva and which he would maintain steadfastly until his death.[102]

I think that the Preface, along with other documents after 1539, explicitly confirms the testimony of the earliest texts: Calvin's religious transformation was essentially a response which at first was hesitating and then became more and more resolute. He responded to a call to work toward the "reformation" of the Christian Church. His conversion occupied him only secondarily, and he understood it in a fundamentally penitential sense: in response to the divine call, Calvin unceasingly sought a trusting faith in God's mercy which delivers his elect from all "fleshly" attachments. The problem of schism resolved itself. He never stopped claiming his unshakable attachment to the unity of the Catholic Church which he did not want to replace, but to restore.

CHAPTER TWENTY-EIGHT
Summary and Conclusions

After Calvin's death, Theodore Beza and Nicolas Colladon were the first to affirm that Calvin had been "like a true instrument of the Spirit of God"[1] and a "prophet of the Lord" to his companions in the struggle.[2] Several modern Calvin scholars also place him in line with the prophets.[3] L. Bouyer stresses that "the only legitimate totalitarianism" for Calvin was that which demanded "glory to God alone" and then declares: "What we have been able to say of Calvin and his various disciples does not seem to us to be understood seriously unless we recognize an echo not only of Mosaic revelation and the great Hebrew prophetic tradition but also (and not least of all) of evangelical preaching."[4] And Y. M.-J. Congar writes: "The reformers, inasmuch as they are truly of God, are in their own way men of the Spirit, whose function is similar to that of the prophets."[5]

It is not up to historians to judge to what extent Calvin was actually a man of God. But they can recognize—an objective examination of the documents forces them to do so—that from the first time that Calvin determined his lifelong task, he was persuaded of his mission's divine origin. Anyone who does not try to force and distort the texts cannot doubt Calvin's good faith.

If we consider Calvin's "prophetic call" in a similar fashion, we see that this call was not only a protest.[6] Quite the contrary. Everything leads us to believe that his primary intention was positive and constructive, or, to use a word dear to Y. M.-J. Congar, "edifying" *(structurante).*[7] Of course, this is not true for Calvin in the same sense as for the inspired heralds of God; as privileged instruments of revelation, they helped determine the essential and normative form of the faith. Calvin's task was to reestablish this faith by "returning to the sources." Calvin's grand attempt to integrate his "prophetic call" into ordinary pastoral work and to construct an ecclesiology that takes into account the royal priesthood of believers testifies to this basically positive intention.

Of course, Calvin was not an ordained clergyman. All his life he remained a simple Christian, but a Christian whose memory of his baptism was enough to make him fully a man "of the Church," who was prepared to assume his community responsibilities and to respond to an extraordinary call of the Lord. He never sought pastoral ordination; both his inner call and its ecclesiastical confirmation appeared adequate to legitimize his ministry. One might say that he felt moved in an extraordinary way to take up an ordinary ecclesiastical responsibility.

From the first stirrings of his call, he conscientiously applied himself to acquiring the knowledge and abilities necessary to fulfill it. He did not wish to treat lightly the dogmas and structures of the Church of his time. Of course, he dedicated little, far too little, time for reflection, but when he did so, it was with extraordinary intensity and concentration. As a disciple of biblical humanism, who became more and more "engaged" in reformist university circles, he was naturally drawn toward minds like Luther and Melanchthon. On the other hand, the scholastic representatives of orthodoxy, who were intellectually inferior to the reformists and prisoners of their inquisitorial methods, had no appeal for him. In view of the circumstances in which the young Calvin had to choose his path in life, it would have been contrary to all the laws of psychology for him to choose the party of the Sorbonne. Thus, in his exile at Saintonge and especially at Basle, he studied intensely in the school of the great German "prophet" and his direct or indirect disciples in order to prepare himself quickly and thoroughly for the task awaiting him. Turning against Rome, he also separated himself from several essential doctrines of the Catholic tradition without being aware of it. Nothing allows us to assert that this change meant for him an abandonment of Catholicism, a break with the *Una Sancta,* or even a conversion in the contemporary, confessional sense of the word. Calvin never called himself a Protestant. On the contrary, he often confessed that his Church was called catholic.

These statements are all valid at the subjective level in that they answer the question: What did Calvin say of himself in his soul and conscience? But we can go even farther and at least sketch a historian's reply to another question: What is the significance of Calvin's calling as a reformer for the history of the universal Church?

First, there is an indisputable fact about the Roman papacy, which from the Gregorian period claimed to be the sole representative for all practical purposes of the Christian Church: at the beginning of the sixteenth century the papacy experienced what we would characterize as an "evangelical decline" without precedence. We mean that it was no longer able to offer a witness that was clear and worthy of the Gospel.

The Magisterium did not teach anything formally opposed to the doctrines of Christ or the apostles; but did the Magisterium offer a clear witness when it emphasized or allowed to be emphasized secondary or "derived" aspects of these doctrines and left the essentials in the shadows? Anyone who goes through the documents of the councils from Constance (1414–1418) to the Fifth Lateran (1512–1517), and the pontifical documents of Gregory XII (d. 1415) to Leo X (d. 1521), frequently finds statements concerning the spiritual and temporal power of the Roman pontiff, his primacy, the relationship of his authority to a general council, the legitimacy of canonical penalties, the form and matter of the sacraments, the substance and accidents of the Eucharist, communion under one kind, indulgences, purgatory, the filioque and the immaculate conception, alongside directives relating to scholastic problems such as "future contingents" or ethical questions such as usury.[8] None of these documents possesses the Christ-centered character of the texts of the Council of Trent. By treating minor points and subordinate dogmas of the Catholic faith, none of the documents gives the impression that the Magisterium was concerned with stressing the fundamental principles of Christianity: the absolute transcendence and exclusive glory of God, the unique mediation of Christ, the free gift of justification, the primacy of Scripture, the relationship between the Word and faith, the sacraments as acts of the living Christ among his people, and the hierarchical ministry as "servanthood" under the one glorified Head of the Church. Numerous contemporary testimonies also prove that the teaching of the majority of theologians and preachers was no more centered on the essentials than that of the Magisterium. Hence there was a fatal lack of clarity that permitted much confusion and deviation.

But if the testimony of the official representatives of the Church as a whole lacked evangelical clarity, it lacked compelling conviction even more. One must be very credulous or have arrived at a high degree of holiness in order to assent to the arguments of preachers who do the opposite of what they proclaim. Just when there were too many vicars of Christ, too many bishops, too many priests or monks who failed to support their words by the good example of their lives, people ceased being credulous and saints became critics during this dawning of modern times. One cannot help charging even so excellent a pastor as Sadolet with great naïveté when we hear him declare to the Genevans: "Perhaps you dislike our persons, if in some way they diverge from the Gospel. But you certainly ought not to hold doctrine and the faith in contempt. For it is written: 'Do what they say.' "[9] There is no doubt that the Gospel teaches that one should not knowingly allow one's assent to revealed truth to depend on the dignity of those who proclaim it. But it would be illusory to think that hypocritical messengers would not compromise the credibility of the message in the long run. The spiritual and moral demands of the Gospel are so great that people try constantly to dispense with them, especially when the bad examples of their pastors encourage them to do so.

According to authentic, traditional Catholic theology, the unity, holiness, catholicity, and apostolicity of the Church not only exist in principle and theory, but they are to be manifested concretely. Only as these traits are lived do they become "incentives of credibility." This is the only way that the Church can function as a "light to the nations" to gather together all the peoples of the earth.[10] To the exact degree that its "marks" become unclear and confused, the Church appears less and less as a "sign," and people have greater difficulty in believing it and believing in Jesus Christ through the Church. What historian would dare assert that at the time of the Renaissance the majority of official representatives of the Catholic Church were concerned about manifesting in their lives the substantial unity, holiness, catholicity, and apostolicity of the Church? Certainly Luther had no difficulty in providing concrete, daily examples of their lack of harmony, charity, and piety, their "works righteousness" *(Werkheiligkeit),* private rivalries, and practical scorn of apostolic life and action.

All these circumstances greatly influenced the spiritual transformation of the young Calvin. If in his master, Luther, we have the demanding priest who rebelled against the confused and unworthy testimony of faith in what he sweepingly called *Papsttum,* in Calvin we have the believing layman who becomes "mature" and conscious of his ecclesiastical role and who then refused to accept the deficiencies of his Church. He expresses himself in his passionate, rational, unyielding, critical, impatient, and intellectual temperament. But his acute sense of social and community realities, which was further developed through his legal training, also allowed him to propose a "form of the Church" that was much more structured and in conformity with the ancient Catholic tradition than that of Luther. It is true that his distrust of the enduring sacramental structures and his insufficient emphasis on the unity of the human and the divine prevented him from agreeing with all the essential elements of this tradition. But I believe these deviations would have been minimized if the responsible ecclesiastical authority had had the courage and patience to turn an attentive ear to all the positive elements to be found in the "form of the Church" proposed by Calvin.

The authorities missed the opportunity of taking responsibility for Luther by accepting that part of his message which accorded with Scripture and tradition, and then they refused to "integrate" Calvin by admitting the positive principles of his Christ-centered ecclesiology. If a modern historian were to render a very abstract judgment on this extraordinarily complex period, he would be tempted to say that the Catholic hierarchy reacted as an old man to these young and ardent reformist sons of the Church. Sometimes indolent, the hierarchy let itself be surpassed by events; sometimes incensed, it intervened with extreme inflexibility. A document such as

Sadolet's letter to the Genevans could lead us to think that for the established ecclesiastical authority, only the faithful who were humble, passive, and submissive were good Christians and that it found it unthinkable that Luther, Calvin, and their disciples who constituted a moral and intellectual elite could also be good Christians. It is a fact, at least in matters concerning Calvin, that it showed no flexibility to the blows justly or unjustly received, that it had no orthodox theologian who could oppose Calvin or who was at least his equal in scriptural and patristic knowledge as well as in courage, imagination, and piety. The Sorbonne of Bédier chased him from France, the priests of Lausanne acknowledged that they were conquered by his arguments, the excellent Sadolet attacked him without knowing him and tried to apply to Geneva the diplomacy of "divide and conquer." Finally, the troops of Savoy besieged the rebellious city in order to reinstate the "lord-bishop," who was the legitimate ruler but pitifully inferior to the task. Only those friends who remained in the Roman church or who returned to it, such as a du Tillet, represented the party prepared for dialogue in a world of polemics, burnings at the stake, and wars of religion.

It seems to me that for the history of the universal Church the primary significance of Calvin's calling as a reformer is negative. Although Calvin neither wanted a break nor felt responsible for it, his positions in fact separated him from the rest of the Church. And this separation continued to widen. Rejected and separated from the influences and the men who might have kept him within the Roman Catholic communion which would eventually be reformed, Calvin (thanks to himself in part) enclosed himself in a local church. Although he was initially "open," he became the "Calvin of Geneva," always "prophetic" and pastoral, but also more and more intolerant. Thus, Calvinism was born. This militant Protestantism, with its rigorous organization, austere morality, and conquering dynamism in spiritual and temporal affairs, was to cause much concern for the Counter-Reformation and the Roman Catholic reform. Thus, two intolerant positions rivaled each other and inevitably led to the wars of religion.

But in spite of these developments, I am persuaded that Calvin's calling as a reformer had a positive meaning for the history of the Church. First of all, to the extent that it represented a recollection and a living witness of the transcendence of God, of the absolute sovereignty of the Word, of the unique priesthood of Christ and his place as the one Mediator, of the nature of the ministry as service, of its Christ-centered collegiality,[11] and of the role of the laity which is at the heart of the idea of the priesthood of the people of God (to take but a few major examples), it introduced and still maintains in Christianity a ferment nourished by the complete Gospel. In principle, nothing prevents the Roman Catholic Church today from recognizing and assimilating this ferment in order to profit from it in its own perpetual, contemporary inner reform.[12]

Finally, I believe that even those aspects of Calvin's thought in his earliest works which clearly diverge from the Catholic tradition are able to stimulate theological reflection whose goal is the best possible formulation of revealed truth. This would not be a posthumous and arbitrary "integration" of Calvin into a system that he probably would refuse even at the present time; but this would perhaps at least respond to one of his deepest intentions.

To speak of history is to speak of evolution. The universal Church does not stop evolving. Several statements of Vatican II agree in an astonishing way with ideas that were decisive for Calvin's call as a reformer (a Christ-centered ecclesiology, constitutional pluralism, a return to biblical and patristic sources, liturgical reforms, eucharistic renewal, the mission of the laity, etc.). Whether we want to or not, we must recognize Calvin as a forerunner on these points. In a similar way, the churches separated from Rome do not stop evolving. At times these churches ignore Calvin's positions which remained "catholic," and at other times they explain some of Calvin's positions in a way that goes far beyond what Calvin intended. I think especially of the reevaluation of the sacrament, both in general and specific terms, by several groups within contemporary Protestantism[13] who no longer fear an excessive "Roman sacramentalism."

Thanks to the fortunate law of evolution and the various evolutions that are now converging, Calvin's calling as a reformer, a factor in division for the past four centuries, may in some way now become a factor in reunion.

NOTES

Foreword

1. Léopold Schummer, *Le ministère pastoral dans l'Institution Chrétienne de Calvin à la lumière du troisième sacrement,* Veröffentlichungen des Instituts für Europäische Geschichte, Mainz (Wiesbaden: Franz Steiner Verlag, 1965), vol. 39.

2. In spite of the radical difference, one also finds remarkable analogies with the crisis of conscience of Luther in the monastery (p. 261): "I was enflamed by such a desire to advance that I pursued my other studies indifferently . . ." (Preface to the *Commentary on the Psalms*).

3. Cf. n. 2.

4. Furthermore, we have in no way forgotten that his evolution always leads the man of the Church, largely open to Catholicism, to an aggressive intolerance and antagonism toward Rome.

5. A. Ganoczy, *Calvin, théologien de l'église et du ministère.*

6. Ganoczy, *Calvin, théologien,* 1. c. 431.

7. We must recognize that this negative side is intentionally less stressed than the other (we can only applaud this fact): "Let us concentrate our attention on the positive" (p. 188).

8. According to the opinion of V. Conzemius in an announcement of the 4th edition of J. Lortz, *Die Reformation in Deutschland* (Freiburg, 1962) in *Revue d'Histoire ecclésiastique* 59 (1964), p. 989.

9. On this subject, see Ganoczy, *Calvin, théologien.*

10. Ganoczy, *Calvin, théologien,* p. 13.

11. Permit me to remind the reader that the name of the department is a solution imposed by fortune and circumstances. The original title envisaged was Department of Historical and Ecumenical Research.

Introduction

1. See the cover of the book by W. F. Dankbaar, *Calvin, sein Weg und sein Werk.*

2. Frontispiece to the French translation (Geneva, 1909) of W. Walker, *John Calvin: The Organiser of Reformed Protestantism 1509–1564.* This engraving is probably by René Boyvin and belongs to the Tronchin Collection in Geneva.

3. Cf. E. G. Léonard, *Histoire générale du protestantisme,* vol. 1: *La Réformation,*

p. 258. The seventh chapter carries the significant title "Calvin, Founder of a Civilization."

4. J. D. Benoit, *Institution de la Religion Chrétienne,* vol. 1, Introduction, p. 9.

5. J. Cadier, *Institution chrétienne,* vol. 1, Preface, p. x.

6. We are preparing an article that summarizes the most recent errors and inaccuracies in various Catholic publications.

7. Cf. Léonard, *La Réformation,* pp. 8–9, where the author cites "moral," "political," "economic and social," "geographical and psychological" explanations as "false solutions." Also see L. Febvre, "Les origines de la réforme française et le problème des causes générales de la réforme," *RH,* 1929.

8. J. Lortz, "Die Leipziger Disputation 1519," *BZThS* 3 (1926), pp. 12–37; idem, *Wie kam es zur Reformation?* 2d ed.; idem, *Die Reformation in Deutschland* (hereafter cited as *RD*), vol. 1, pp. 193ff.; idem, *"Luthers Vorlesung über den Römerbrief,"* *TThZ* 71 (1962); cf. H. Böhmer, *Der junge Luther* (Gotha, 1925).

9. OC 21, 22–171.

10. OC 21, 17–18. E. Doumergue, *Jean Calvin, les hommes et les choses de son temps,* vol. 1: *La jeunesse de Calvin,* p. 190: "We know that Beza wrote some thirty years after the events. We know that the records of this period do not display precision and exactitude and that Beza in particular committed more than one error in detail."

11. OC 31, 22.

12. E. Staehelin, *Johannes Calvin, Leben und ausgewählte Schriften.*

13. Ibid., p. 7.

14. Ibid., p. 21.

15. Ibid., p. 31.

16. F. W. Kampschulte, *Johannes Calvin, seine Kirche und sein Staat in Genf,* vol. 1.

17. Ibid., p. 233.

18. Ibid., p. 241.

19. A. Pierson, *Studien over Johannes Kalvijn,* pp. 58–109.

20. A. Lefranc, *La jeunesse de Calvin;* on Calvin's father and his brother Charles, see pp. 15–22; on Olivétan, see pp. 39–40, 81, 99: "It is he who brought Calvin to the new faith."

21. Ibid., pp. 74ff.

22. Ibid., p. 97. "The definitive conversion of Calvin was, above all, a question of logic and reflection in which feeling did not play a role. The scandals of the clergy had shocked him very little. Matters of doctrine were his only preoccupation." P. 98: "This change must have taken place in the second half of the year 1532."

23. Ibid., pp. 38, 112–113.

24. H. Lecoultre, "La conversion de Calvin," *RThPh,* 1890, pp. 5–30.

25. Ibid., pp. 27–28.

26. Ibid., p. 27.

27. Ibid., p. 14.

28. Ibid., p. 24.

29. Lecoultre, "La conversion de Calvin," says, first, "In 1528, during the time that Calvin began to take part in the reform movement, the churches of Germany *did not yet have a clearly defined, uniform doctrine"* (p. 21); then he says, "In France, the work of reform was even less advanced and *doctrine much less well*

defined" (p. 22). Thus "the most ignorant Protestants" could arrogate for themselves the "right to dogmatize however they wished" (p. 23). In spite of that, the author affirms without fear of contradicting himself that Gérard Roussel was *"thoroughly Protestant as far as dogma was concerned"* (p. 20) and that Calvin possessed, even before his conversion, *"convictions on the subject of Protestant dogma"* (p. 27). (Emphasis mine.)

30. A. Lang, "Die Bekehrung Johannes Calvins," *StGThK,* 1897, vol. 2, fasc. 1, pp. 1–56.

31. Ibid., p. 21.

32. Ibid., p. 36.

33. Ibid., pp. 38–39.

34. Ibid., p. 41.

35. Doumergue, *La jeunesse de Calvin.*

36. Ibid., p. 299.

37. Ibid., p. 338.

38. K. Müller, "Calvins Bekehrung," *NGG,* 1905, pp. 188–255. Cf. F. Büsser, *Calvins Urteil über sich selbst,* pp. 23–34. Büsser states that he only desires to make an "extension of Müller's theory" (p. 26).

39. K. Müller, "Calvins Bekehrung," p. 202.

40. Ibid., pp. 204, 211–212.

41. Ibid., p. 208: "This 'sudden conversion' is therefore something entirely different from the development which we have been able to pursue to this point. Neither in its beginning nor in its continuation has this development presented itself as a sudden transformation or break. Rather, it seems to have been a slow and, as far as we can see, peaceful growth of his interests in the thoughts and concerns of a greater circle."

42. Ibid., pp. 213–214.

43. Ibid., pp. 224–242.

44. P. Wernle, "Noch einmal die Bekehrung Calvins," *ZKG* 27 (1906), cahier 1, pp. 84–95; idem, "Zu Calvins Bekehrung," *ZKG* 31 (1910), cahier 4, pp. 556–583. (Hereafter cited as Wernle I and Wernle II, respectively.)

45. Wernle I, pp. 85–86: "It is immediately clear: this is not a historical reference; Calvin wishes to give the reader his interpretation based on his faith."

46. Wernle II, p. 572: "I shall never draw . . . the conclusion from this evidence that the completely sudden conversion is to be attributed simply to the reckoning of Calvin's later, retrospective view, which stamped a gradual process with the character of a supernatural miracle."

47. W. Walker, *John Calvin: The Organiser of Reformed Protestantism 1509–1564.* I shall use the French translation, which, with some modifications and adaptations authorized by the author, was done by N. Weiss: *Jean Calvin, l'homme et l'oeuvre.*

48. Ibid., p. 98.

49. Ibid., p. 103.

50. Ibid., p. 105.

51. Th. Werdermann, "Calvins Lehre von der Kirche in ihrer geschichtlichen Entwicklung," *Calvinstudien,* 1909, pp. 246–338.

52. Ibid., p. 257.

53. Ibid., p. 258.

54. J. Pannier, "Recherches sur l'évolution religieuse de Calvin jusqu'à sa conversion," cahier 8 of *RHPhR* (1924).

55. Ibid., p. 43.

56. P. Imbart de la Tour, *Les origines de la réforme,* vol. 4: *Calvin et l'Institution Chrétienne;* cf. p. 30: "The conversion of Calvin occurred only slowly, by degrees."

57. F. Wendel, *Calvin, sources et évolution de sa pensée religieuse.* (E.T. *Calvin, Origins and Development of His Religious Thought;* 1963.)

58. W. F. Dankbaar, *Calvijn, zijn Weg en Werk.* I quote this work according to the German version of H. Quistorp, adapted and approved by the author: *Calvin, sein Weg und sein Werk.*

59. K. Reuter, *Das Grundverständnis der Theologie Calvins.*

60. P. Sprenger, *Das Rätsel um die Bekehrung Calvins* (Neukirchen, 1960).

61. Ibid., p. 4.

62. Ibid., p. 23: "a fanatical adherent of the old beliefs" (cf. p. 28); p. 16: "he was cured of his zealous commitment to the papal faith"; p. 14: "according to his own description, a fanatical opponent of the new teaching."

63. Ibid., p. 61: "a conversion . . . of a self-assured, deluded, fanatical champion of the so-called true faith to the gentle and mild nature of a scholar eager to learn."

64. Ibid., p. 45: "Moreover, in many places Calvin speaks of *superstitio* in various contexts. Thus it is very surprising that in a chapter in which one would especially expect to find it, the word does not occur even once—nor does its adjectival form. This chapter is that dealing with the papal Mass."

65. For example in his *On Fleeing the Illicit Rites of the Wicked,* edited in 1537, a period very near to his presumed "conversion," Calvin writes: "lest a vain opinion about the transition of the bread into God, lest any opinion of their superstitions which they make about the impious Mass itself find a place in our minds" (OC 5, 260).

66. Sprenger, *Das Rätsel,* p. 80.

67. Ibid., p. 86: "For them [namely, Luther and Calvin], there is simply the one Church, and groups outside this Church are merely sects. For them, the plural 'Churches' must be understood as an entirely impossible idea." P. 87: "Therefore it must be more surprising that Calvin resigned his benefices by 1534 than that he had not done so earlier. I might add that this action by Calvin should still not be understood as indicating his 'break' with his Mother Church."

68. Lecoultre, "La conversion de Calvin," p. 14 (for the use of the term, see also pp. 6, 9, 11, 14, 15, 19, 20, 22); Doumergue, *La jeunesse de Calvin,* p. 337 et passim; Lang, "Die Bekehrung," pp. 20–21.

69. Walker, *Jean Calvin,* p. 96.

70. Lang, "Die Bekehrung," pp. 12–13; Sprenger, *Das Rätsel,* p. 29.

71. Werdermann, "Calvins Lehre von der Kirche," pp. 256, 269–274.

72. Dankbaar, *Calvin, sein Weg und sein Werk,* p. 80.

73. Lefranc, *La jeunesse de Calvin,* p. 41. Cf. O. Bloch and W. v. Wartburg, *Dictionnaire étymologique de la langue française,* p. 326: "*Huguenot,* 1552, in the sense of 'protestant.' A word that comes from Geneva, where it was used in the form of *eyguenot* from 1520 to refer to the partisans of the political party who fought against the annexation attempts of the Duke of Savoy. It was borrowed from the German and the German-influenced Swiss *Eidgenosse(n),* 'confederate(s).' . . . The form *huguenot* comes from France, because, as contemporary historians tell us, the

reformers from the city of Tours used to gather to worship at night near the gate of the city known as 'Roi-Hugon.' "

74. Lang, "Die Bekehrung," p. 12; Walker, *Jean Calvin,* p. 91; Sprenger, *Das Rätsel,* p. 24.

75. Lang, "Die Bekehrung," pp. 20, 37; K. Müller, "Calvins Bekehrung," p. 209.

76. Lecoultre, "La conversion de Calvin," p. 24.

77. Doumergue, *La jeunesse de Calvin,* p. 172.

78. See pp. 274 and 280 of our study.

79. OC 5, 470, *Concilium Pauli III* (1540): notes relating to the discussions at Augsburg. OC 5, 484: The "protestants" are opposed to the "followers of the pope" who favor the imperial forces "in Germany." OC 5, 503, 505, where Calvin describes the German "protestant" party. OC 5, 645, 647, *Actes de Ratisbonne* (1541): The German "protestants" express their desires (text attributed to Calvin). OC 7, 667–668, *Interim adulterogermanum* (1549–1550). Cf. OC 28, 304 and 53, 553. See also Beza's *Life of Calvin* (1564), OC 21, 30, where the name "protestant" is applied to German princes hostile to the politics of the emperor.

80. Bloch and Wartburg, *Dictionnaire étymologique,* pp. 516–517: "In French, the word was used from 1546 to refer to the protestants of France, but it was rare until the seventeenth century. In 1623, we find the word 'protestantism.' " On the origin of the word "protestant," also see J. Lindeboom, *Oorsprong en geschiednis van de naam Protestant; RGG,* vol. 5, cols. 649–650.

81. See p. 281 of our study; cf. pp. 103 and 204.

82. Quoted by Doumergue from the *Colloques* of Mathurin Cordier, *La jeunesse de Calvin,* p. 62. Cf. Beza, OC 21, 31; Sibiville quoted by W. G. Moore, *La réforme allemande et la littérature française,* p. 184.

83. OC 21, 198, *Annales de Genève* (1536).

84. IRC (1536), OS, 253–254.

85. Ibid., OS 1, 43.

86. Ibid., OS 1, 22.

87. Ibid., OS 1, 21.

88. Ibid., OS 1, 86, 134, 250.

89. Ibid., OS 1, 22, 31; cf. OC 6, 520.

90. Texts of the Parlement of Paris, 1525 and 1530, quoted by Moore, *La réforme allemande,* p. 248.

91. Letter of Parlement to King Frances I, 1533, quoted by Dankbaar, *Calvin, sein Weg und sein Werk,* p. 21.

92. OC 5, 371, 374, *Lettre de Sadolet aux Genevois* (1539).

Chapter 1. Paris and Reformism in France
Around 1523

1. On the Parlement of Paris, the supreme tribunal of the kingdom, see P. Imbart de la Tour, *La France moderne,* pp. 42ff., 113ff.

2. V. L. Bourilly (ed.), *Le journal d'un bourgeois de Paris sous le règne de François I,* p. 397. Condemnation decree AN Y⁶, 4. Cf. R.-J. Lovy, *Les origines de la réforme française,* pp. 87–88. According to P. Imbart de la Tour, *L'évangélisme,* p. 210, n. 1, there is no evidence that Vallière was an Augustinian monk or a Lutheran.

3. Moore, *La réforme allemande,* pp. 46ff.; Imbart de la Tour, *L'évangélisme,* p.

169; P. Taverney, *Doctrines réformatrices et influences luthériennes à Paris et à Meaux;* J. Cadier, "Luther et les débuts de la réforme française," *Positions luthériennes,* 1958.

4. WA Br 1, 332, a letter from the Basle printer John Froben to Luther on 14 February 1519: "Various books well written by you and approved by the judgment of all learned men, I have directly published in my own type. We sent six hundred into Gaul and Spain, and they are selling. In Paris, they are even read and approved at the Sorbonne." Cf. Beatus Rhenanus, *Briefwechsel,* ed. A. Horawitz and K. Hartfelder, p. 157: Tschudi to B. Rhenanus, 17 May 1519: "Luther's works . . . are being snatched up . . . by all erudite men."

5. Text in WA 2, 254–383. Luther especially denied the infallibility of councils and the primacy of the pope. Cf. Lortz, "Die Leipziger Disputation 1519," pp. 12–37; N. Weiss, "Martin Luther, Jean Eck et l'Université de Paris, d'après une lettre inédite, 11 septembre 1519," *BHPF,* 1917.

6. Moore, *La réforme allemande,* p. 51.

7. Lortz, *RD,* vol. 1, p. 223: "Both the fact that none of the theological faculties placed Luther unequivocally in the wrong and not even Eck's university, Ingolstadt, ventured to condemn him show the indecision and confusion of the Church party and the vagueness of their position. Moreover, in 1521 the theological faculty of Vienna appealed to the silence of the Paris faculty in order to avoid making a decision." On this "theological confusion," see pp. 137, 207ff.

8. Represented by such men as Jean Gerson, Jacques Almain, and John Major. In 1508, the Faculty still condemned the opinion that denied the superiority of the synod over the pope. Cf. the Register of Conclusions of the Faculty of Theology, BN Lat. N. Acq., 1782 fol. 9.

9. Denz 1492 (781): "We condemn, reject, and completely cast aside each and every one of the articles listed above as erroneous in one or more of the following ways, as premised: they are either heretical or scandalous, or false, or offensive to pious ears, or seductive of simple minds; and they are contrary to Catholic truth."

10. See Allen in particular, vol. 4, Erasmus' letter to Compeggio, 6 December 1520, p. 403: "In these [writings of Luther], which in truth I have sampled rather than read, I seem to discern rare natural gifts and a genius wonderfully fitted for interpreting mystical writings according to the ancient manner, and fitted too for stirring up the spark of evangelical learning. . . . Moreover, his way of life is praised even by those who cannot abide his teachings." P. 407: "Whatever sort of person Luther was, certainly it was more humane to cure him than to do away with him." P. 408: "Those who are pleased to see Luther condemned are not happy to see him condemned in this way." P. 409: "A frightful bull has come out under the authority of the Roman pontiff. Books were burned. The people are up in arms. A more hateful act could hardly have been performed. Everyone thought that the bull was more lacking in clemency than is characteristic of our Pope Leo; yet those who carried out the act added no small measure of cruelty to that of the pope." Erasmus' letter to Leo X, 13 September 1520, p. 345: "I have admired the good in him, not the bad; I have admired only the glory of Christ in him." P. 346: "Free and generous natures rejoice in being taught but do not want to be compelled."

11. On Bédier, see P. Féret, *Histoire de la Faculté de Théologie de Paris et de ses docteurs les plus célèbres;* V. Carrière, "La Sorbonne et l'évangélisme au XVIe siècle," in *Aspects de l'Université de Paris,* pp. 159–186; A. Renaudet, "L'huma-

nisme et l'enseignement de l'Université de Paris au temps de la Renaissance," in *Aspects de l'Université de Paris,* pp. 133–155.

12. Text in CR 1, 366–388.

13. Jean Visagier, *Epigrammes* (Paris, 1536), vol. 2, p. 149: "Bédier, while your trivial opinions vex the upright, this language harms you more than them."

14. Reuter, *Grundverständnis,* p. 67: "Calvin became a witness of how Bédier, with unrelenting force, entered into that struggle in which he beheld an opponent of the Church hierarchy and orthodox doctrine. It was probably Erasmus, Luther, or Faber Stapulensis."

15. Lovy, *Les origines,* p. 57: "In searching the voluminous registers of the Faculty of Theology of Paris, we found 850 judgments on matters of religion for the ten years preceding the beginning of the reform."

16. Cf. M. Mann, *Erasme et les débuts de la réforme française;* A. Renaudet, *Erasme, sa pensée religieuse et son action d'après sa correspondance (1518–1521).*

17. K. H. Graf, *Essai sur la vie et les écrits de Jacques Lefèvre d'Etaples;* idem, "Faber Stapulensis," *ZHTh* 22 (1852), pp. 1–86 and 165–237; J. Barnaud, *Jacques Lefèvre d'Etaples, son influence sur les origines de la Réformation française;* P. Imbart de la Tour, *L'Eglise catholique,* pp. 383–396.

18. Cf. Ph. A. Becker, "Les idées religieuses de Guillaume Briçonnet, évêque de Meaux," *RThQR,* 1900; M. Mousseaux, *Briçonnet et le mouvement de Meaux;* L. Febvre, "Le cas Briçonnet," *AEPHE,* 5th section, 1946.

19. On the "circle of Meaux": D. Toussaint du Plessis, *Histoire de l'église de Meaux;* Ch. Schmidt, *Gérard Roussel, prédicateur de la reine Marguerite de Navarre;* idem, "Gérard Roussel, inculpé d'hérésie à Meaux, 1525," *BHPF,* 1861; H. M. Bower, *The Fourteen of Meaux;* Léonard, *La Réformation,* p. 203.

20. Lovy, *Les origines,* pp. 74–76.

21. Cf. A. Lefranc, "Les idées religieuses de Marguerite de Navarre d'après son oeuvre poétique," *BHPF,* 1897; Ph. A. Becker, "Marguerite, duchesse d'Alençon et Guillaume Briçonnet, évêque de Meaux, d'après leur correspondance manuscrite, 1521–1524," *BHPF,* 1900; P. Jourda, *Marguerite d'Angoulême, duchesse d'Alençon, reine de Navarre, 1492–1549;* idem, *Correspondance de Marguerite d'Angoulême, duchesse d'Alençon, reine de Navarre, 1492–1549.*

22. Lovy, *Les origines,* p. 226.

23. According to Doumergue, *La jeunesse de Calvin,* pp. 93, 242, 245, and Reuter, *Grundverständnis,* p. 67. On the origin and content of the *Betbüchlein,* see WA 10/II, 343ff.

24. Moore, *La réforme allemande,* pp. 67–81; cf. W. Maurer, "Franz Lambert von Avignon und das Verfassungsideal der 'Reformatio Ecclesiarum Hassiae,'" *ZKG,* 1929, pp. 208–260; A. Moser, "Franz Lamberts Reise durch die Schweiz im Jahre 1522," *Zwingliana,* 1957, pp. 467–471; G. Müller, *Franz Lambert von Avignon und die Reformation in Hessen.*

25. Moore, *La réforme allemande,* p. 171.

26. Ibid., pp. 242–278.

27. Lovy, *Les origines,* p. 95.

28. Cf. L. Febvre, *Le problème de l'incroyance au XVIe siècle, le siècle de Rabelais.*

29. The situation of the Church at the beginning of the reform has been adequately brought to light by historians. For a more detailed examination, see J.

Huizinga, *Herbst des Mittelalters* (E.T. *The Waning of the Middle Ages;* 1949); Imbart de la Tour, *La France moderne; L'Eglise catholique;* and *L'évangélisme;* A. Renaudet, *Préréforme et humanisme à Paris pendant les premières guerres d'Italie (1494–1517);* L. Febvre, *Au coeur religieux du XVIe siècle;* J. Lortz, *Geschichte der Kirche* (hereafter cited as *GK*), vol. 2, pp. 1–78.

Chapter 2. Calvin at the Collège de Montaigu, 1523–1527

1. Cf. M. Reulos, "Les attaches de Calvin dans la région de Noyon," *BHPF,* 1964, pp. 193–201. The author brings to light an interesting detail. Charles de Hangest, bishop of Noyon, had four nephews. Jean and Claude were fellow students of Calvin, but they entered religious orders and remained within the Roman community. The two other nephews, François and Jean, with whom Calvin had little contact, joined the reform and ultimately fought in the army of Condé.

2. Cf. E. A. Berthault, *Mathurin Cordier et l'enseignement chez les premiers calvinistes;* J. Le Coultre, "Mathurin Cordier et les origines de la pédagogie protestante dans les pays de langue française," *Mémoires de l'Université de Neuchâtel,* vol. 5; P. Mesnard, "Mathurin Cordier (1479–1564)," *Foi et Education,* April–June, 1959, pp. 76–94.

3. Reuter, *Grundverständnis,* p. 57. For the close relationship between biblical humanism and the *devotio moderna,* see J. Hashagen, "Die Devotio moderna und ihre Einwirkung auf Humanismus, Reformation, Gegenreformation und spätere Richtungen," *ZKG* 55 (1936), pp. 523ff.; L. Bouyer, *Autour d'Erasme,* pp. 112, 142, 156.

4. Reuter, *Grundverständnis,* p. 58.

5. The reformer will welcome Cordier in Geneva to entrust him with the organization of teaching and in 1550 will dedicate to him his commentary on 1 Thessalonians. Cf. OC 13, 525–526, for the text of the dedication.

6. Erasmus, *Colloquia,* Ichtyophagia, Er Op 1, col. 806; Rabelais, *Gargantua et Pantagruel,* bk. 1, ch. 37; bk. 4, ch. 22.

7. M. Godet, "Le collège de Montaigu," *Revue des Etudes rabelaisiennes* 7; idem, *La congrégation de Montaigu (1490–1580).* (Hereafter cited as Godet I and Godet II respectively.)

8. Godet II, p. 11; cf. A. Renaudet, "Jean Standonck, un réformateur catholique avant la réforme," *BHPF,* 1908, pp. 5–81; A. Hyma, *Renaissance to Reformation,* pp. 337–354.

9. Godet I, p. 11.

10. On the *devotio moderna,* see the bibliography in *LThK* 3, 314, and in *RGG,* vol. 6, col. 864. General studies: F. W. Wentzlaff-Eggebert, *Deutsche Mystik zwischen Mittelalter und Neuzeit,* pp. 139ff.; Leclercq-Vandenbroucke-Bouyer, *La spiritualité du Moyen Age,* pp. 512ff.; M. A. Lücker, *Meister Eckhart und die Devotio Moderna.* Concerning the *Imitation:* F. Kern, *Die Nachfolge Christi.* On the spread of the *devotio moderna,* see A. Hyma, *The Christian Renaissance: A History of the "Devotio moderna";* idem, *The Brethren of the Common Life;* see also Hashagen, "Die Devotio moderna."

11. M. J. Pohl, *Thomas à Kempis, Opera Omnia,* vol. 3 (Freiburg im Breisgau, 1904), pp. 500–510. There are 1,159 direct or indirect biblical quotations in the *Imitation.*

12. Is it purely coincidence that the first work of Calvin is a commentary on Seneca?

13. Calvin's second work, the *Psychopannychia,* will be heavily influenced by this dualistic philosophy.

14. J. Huizinga, *Herbst des Mittelalters,* p. 186: "In the *devotio moderna* of the Fraterhouses and Windesheim, pietistic circles in fact separated themselves from worldly life." On devotees' distrust of "the world," science, and "human knowledge," see W. James, *The Varieties of Religious Experience,* p. 348: "a simplified world."

15. Cf. E. Iserloh, "Die Kirchenfrömmigkeit in der 'Imitatio Christi,' " in *Sentire Ecclesiam,* ed. J. Daniélou and H. Vorgrimmler, pp. 251–267; K. Pellens, "Kirchendenken in der 'Imitatio Christi,' " in *Nachfolge Christi in Bibel, Liturgie und Spiritualität,* ed. Th. Bogler and Maria Laach, pp. 41–67.

16. Cf. Renaudet, *Préréforme,* p. 26; cf. pp. 466–467: the statutes written by Noël Bédier in 1508 (Bibliothèque de l'Arsenal, MS. 1168, fols. 82r–85r).

17. According to the list established by Cardinal d'Estouteville in 1452. Cf. Renaudet, *Préréforme,* p. 28.

18. Ibid., p. 27.

19. Godet II, pp. 62–64.

20. Godet I, p. 12.

21. Godet I, pp. 7, 15; Godet II, pp. 62–65.

22. OC 21, 54.

23. OC 21, 121: "Then after being moved to the gymnasium named after Montaigu, he had a learned teacher who was a Spaniard. When his own genius, which was already quite sharp, had been refined by this teacher, he advanced, so that . . . he was promoted to the study of dialectic and other subjects, which they call the study of the arts."

24. Cf. Reuter, *Grundverständnis,* pp. 31, 41; Wendel, *Calvin, sources et évolution,* p. 6.

25. Reuter, *Grundverständnis,* passim; cf. T. G. Law, "John Major, Scottish Scholastic," *Scottish Review,* 1892, pp. 344–376.

26. Wendel, *Calvin, sources et évolution,* p. 6; Renaudet, *Préréforme,* pp. 366, 464ff.

27. Pp. 174ff. of our study. On John Major, see also K. Prantl, *Geschichte der Logik im Abendlande,* vol. 4, pp. 247–251; A. J. G. Mackay, "A Biography of the Author," in *A History of Greater Britain,* by John Major, ed. A. Constable; Féret, *Histoire de la Faculté de Théologie de Paris,* Epoque moderne, vol. 2, pp. 78–96; *Dictionary of National Biography,* vol. 12 (1961), art. "John Major," pp. 830–832.

28. OC 21, 29.

29. Beza affirms in his text of 1564: "He was, from that time on, of a singular spirit and very conscientious, an enemy of vice and devoted to the service of God, as they then said." It seems to us that here *laudatio* is not far from the truth.

30. The coexistence of the *devotio moderna,* open to certain major ideas of reform, with "traditional" scholasticism, may seem paradoxical at first. But it becomes plausible when one considers that the *devotio* was a school of spirituality without a specific theological program. If its antischolastic tendencies were removed, it could very well lend itself to the spirit of Montaigu.

31. Cf. Lefranc, *La jeunesse de Calvin,* pp. 67–71; Doumergue, *La jeunesse de Calvin,* pp. 75–77.

32. Cf. E. and E. Haag, *La France protestante,* vol. 4, pp. 615–617; A. L. Herminjard, *Correspondance des réformateurs dans les pays de langue française,* vol. 2, p. 346. (Hereafter cited as Herminjard.)

33. K. Müller, "Calvins Bekehrung," pp. 211–212.

34. Wendel, *Calvin, sources et évolution,* pp. 6–7: "In this environment, which was open to every new idea, Calvin no doubt learned of the writings of Lefèvre d'Etaples, Luther, and Melanchthon. At least he must have frequently heard of them. But we must not conclude from this that at the time he was inclined to align himself with the partisans of Lefèvre's reforms. It is certain that he was not ready to embrace Luther's ideas." Wendel is referring to the time that Calvin was at the Collège de Montaigu.

35. Contrary to Sprenger, *Das Rätsel,* pp. 14, 16, 23, 28, 61, etc.

36. Cf. Moore, *La réforme allemande,* p. 184.

37. H. Eells, "Martin Bucer and the Conversion of John Calvin," *Princeton Theological Review* 22 (July 1924), p. 403; Herminjard, vol. 1, pp. 318–320.

38. Moore, *La réforme allemande,* pp. 249ff.; Lovy, *Les origines,* p. 142.

39. Cf. S. Berger, *Le procès de Guillaume Briçonnet au Parlement de Paris en 1525.*

40. Lovy, *Les origines,* p. 142; Moore, *La réforme allemande,* p. 177.

41. Imbart de la Tour, *L'évangélisme,* p. 250; Lovy, *Les origines,* pp. 137–146.

42. Lovy, *Les origines,* pp. 146–147.

43. On the controversy between Erasmus and Bédier, see A. Renaudet, *Etudes érasmiennes, 1521–1529,* pp. 237–304.

44. Imbart de la Tour, *L'évangélisme,* pp. 251–252; cf. Actes du Parlement de Paris, AN X^{1a} 1529, fol. 107.

45. Cf. J. Crespin, *Histoire des martyrs persecutez et mis a mort pour la verité de l'Evangile, depuis le temps des apostres jusques à present* (1619), ed. D. Benoit in 3 vols.; Imbart de la Tour, *L'évangélisme,* p. 253; Lovy, *Les origines,* pp. 90–92, 113–124, 127–129.

Chapter 3. Calvin in Orléans and Bourges, 1528–1531

1. Cf. Beza in OC 21, 29, 54, 121; Calvin himself in OC 31, 22.

2. OC 21, 29.

3. OC 21, 54.

4. OC 21, 121.

5. Doumergue, *La jeunesse de Calvin,* p. 117.

6. OC 9, 790.

7. Lang, "Die Bekehrung," p. 18, maintains in opposition to Lefranc that neither the influence of the environment of Noyon nor that of Olivétan is proven decisively.

8. OC 10/b, 1: "I have with me a young man from Noyon who migrated here when persecutions erupted in Orléans, where he was studying literature. . . . He decided to learn languages, above all Greek and Hebrew, in which up to now he is quite unskilled."

9. Herminjard, vol. 2, p. 451, vol. 3, p. 44, and no. 20; K. Müller, "Calvins Bekehrung," p. 205.

10. Eells, "Martin Bucer," p. 406: "Whoever he was, the 'youth of Noyon' was not Calvin. Herminjard has suggested that it was Olivétan, and this probably is as good a guess as can be made."

11. OC 10/b, 1, n. 7.

12. Wendel, *Calvin, sources et évolution,* p. 7: "The influence in his religious development which he must have felt from his cousin, Olivétan, the future translator of the Bible, did not leave any direct traces." Imbart de la Tour, *Calvin et l'Institution Chrétienne,* p. 21: "An assertion of Beza which no other document justifies."

13. OC 9, 790; cf. 826; 10/b, 51f., 315, 333f., 342, 371f.

14. OC 10/b, 364f. Among others are found the Greek grammar of Melanchthon, the commentaries of Capito on Habakkuk and of Zwingli on the Psalms, the German Bibles of Zwingli and Luther, along with other works by Cajetan and Rabelais.

15. The first mention of Calvin as a master of arts is found in a document from Noyon dated 30 April 1529. Cf. Lefranc, *La jeunesse de Calvin,* p. 197.

16. Wendel, *Calvin, sources et évolution,* p. 8, cites for support J. Broussard, "L'Université d'Orléans au XVIe siècle," in *Humanisme et Renaissance* 5 (1939), pp. 223ff., and G. Beyerhaus, *Studien zur Staatsanschauung Calvins,* pp. 27ff.

17. Walker, *Jean Calvin,* p. 53.

18. Doumergue, *La jeunesse de Calvin,* pp. 130, 175–177; cf. Lefranc, *La jeunesse de Calvin,* p. 72.

19. Cf. Pannier, *Recherches,* p. 12.

20. Cf. Imbart de la Tour, *L'évangélisme,* p. 263; Lovy, *Les origines,* pp. 186–189.

21. The decrees are in Mansi 32, 1149–1202. The provincial Council of Bourges, which met on 21 March 1528, voted on similar decrees. Ibid., cols. 1141–1148.

22. On the local reform undertaken by certain "Erasmian" bishops, see Léonard, *La Réformation,* pp. 202–203, n. 3: "Only the province of Normandy at that time was familiar with the reform statutes of the archbishop of Rouen, Georges d'Amboise (1494–1510), of the bishop of Lisieux, Jean le Veneur (1505–1539), of the bishops of Bayeux, René de Prie (1498–1516) and Louis Canossa (1516–1539), and of the bishop of Sées, Jacques de Silly (1511–1539). Under Canossa's influence, Caen and Basse-Normandie became one of the most lively centers of humanism and reform. The prelate was a follower of Erasmus, and the Caen edition of the *Adages* assures us that he had 'changed, transformed, and modified everything for the best.'" Imbart de la Tour, *L'évangélisme,* pp. 324–331, mentions the bishops of Paris, Poucher and Jean du Bellay; the bishop of Carpentras, Jacques Sadolet; the archbishop of Bourges, François de Tournon; and the bishop of Lavaur, Georges de Selve. He notes that the majority of them were patrons of Christian humanism rather than pastors of souls.

23. OC 9, 785, where we read a little before the text quoted above: "But let no one think he was lacking support, or interpret his silence as a confession . . . ; but let it be understood that the man was occupied with serious business, relying in this matter on his confidence in the truth, and that he did not want to waste his efforts on trifles, since the matter adequately spoke for itself."

24. OC 21, 29 and 54; cf. OC 10/b, 29, where, in a document dated 1533, Calvin himself alludes without any hostility to l'Estoile's position, which the latter had assumed in 1532. Cf. also OC 10/b, 12, n. 2.

25. OC 21, 121–122.

26. Lovy, *Les origines,* pp. 158–159, reports that the condemned was tied to a rack and beaten by the monks of Cordeliers. He was then lifted above the flames three times to prolong the agony of his suffering.

27. Ibid., p. 159; Pannier, *Recherches,* p. 15.

28. Moore, *La réforme allemande,* pp. 102ff.; Pannier, *Recherches,* p. 40.

29. Moore, *La réforme allemande,* pp. 127ff.; Pannier, *Recherches,* p. 40.

30. Cf. R. Rolland, "Le dernier procès de Louis de Berquin," in *Mélanges de l'Ecole française de Rome*; N. Weiss, "Louis de Berquin, son premier procès et sa retractation, d'après quelques documents inédits," *BHPF,* 1918.

31. G. Goyau, *Histoire religieuse de la nation française* (Paris, 1923), pp. 343ff.

32. According to a letter from Bucer, WA 5, 566ff.

33. Moore, *La réforme allemande,* p. 127.

34. Pannier, *Recherches,* p. 24.

35. OC 21, 29, where Beza says emphatically: "He made such great progress in such little time that they did not consider him a student but rather one of the ordinary doctors. Since he was more often a teacher than a listener, he could have become a doctor without doing anything more. Nevertheless, he refused." On Calvin's austere regimen of study at Orléans which compromised his health, see Colladon's account: OC 21, 55.

36. Cf. Herminjard, vol. 2, pp. 280–281, note; E. J. de Groot, "Melchior Wolmar, ses rapports avec les protestants français et suisses," *BHPF,* 1934.

37. C. E. Bulaeus, *Historia universitatis parisiensis,* vol. 6, p. 963.

38. Doumergue, *La jeunesse de Calvin,* p. 181.

39. Ibid., pp. 181ff.; K. Müller, "Calvins Bekehrung," p. 194; Pannier, *Recherches,* p. 14.

40. Florimond de Raemond, *Histoire de la naissance, progrès et décadence de l'hérésie de ce siècle,* p. 882; cf. J. Desmay, "Remarques sur la vie de Jean Calvin hérésiarque, tirées des registres de Noyon, Rouen, 1621 and 1657," *Archives curieuses de l'histoire de France,* Paris, vol. 5, p. 393, cited by Doumergue, *La jeunesse de Calvin,* p. 188.

41. Lefranc, *La jeunesse de Calvin,* pp. 39ff.

42. Lang, "Die Bekehrung," p. 18.

43. From 1530, Calvin referred to Wolmar in his correspondence by his first name. Cf. OC 10/b, 4. In 1546, he dedicated his commentary on 2 Corinthians to him: OC 12, 365. This dedication mentions only Calvin's friendship and "monumental gratitude" for the "rudiments" of Greek which Wolmar taught him. See also several pieces of correspondence between the two friends: OC 13, 403; 14, 360; 15, 642; for Calvin's allusions to Wolmar in his letters addressed to other people, see OC 13, 458; 15, 196, 677; etc.

44. Wendel, *Calvin, sources et évolution,* p. 9.

45. Walker, *Jean Calvin,* p. 56; Wendel, *Calvin, sources et évolution,* p. 9.

46. OC 21, 29–30 (cf. 55 and 122): "There was an excellent gentleman from Germany, a professor of Greek letters, named Melchior Wolmar. . . . This good man saw that Calvin was lacking in Greek letters and did all he could to teach him such, an act that was a great service to him."

47. See in particular Wolmar's letter of 1552, addressed to "Calvin, overseer of the Genevan church . . . incomparable friend" (OC 14, 360). Wolmar makes it clear that he is a partisan of reform.

48. H. Clouzot, "Les amitiés de Rabelais en Orléans," *Revue des Etudes rabelaisiennes* 3, pp. 174ff.

49. Walker, *Jean Calvin,* p. 56.

50. Cf. P. E. Viard, *André Alciat, 1492–1550.*

51. Imbart de la Tour, *Calvin et l'Institution Chrétienne,* p. 11. From 1521 to 1531, Erasmus repeatedly expressed his admiration to Alciati in several letters: Allen, nos. 1250, 1261, 1278, 1288, 1706, 2051, 2276, 2329, 2394, 2468.

52. Cf. OC 10/b, 3–4, nn. 1 and 8 by the editors.

53. Cf. OC 10/b, 7, notes by the editors; Herminjard, vol. 2, pp. 315ff.

54. OC 9, 786.

55. Note that Beza also praises the Italian professor: OC 21, 29 and 55: "the excellent lawyer Andreas Alciati"; OC 21, 122: "There was at that time a great celebration of the Bourges Academy, because Andreas Alciati, who was called there from Italy as easily the leading lawyer of his age, had come."

56. Doumergue, *La jeunesse de Calvin,* pp. 202–205.

57. A. Lefranc, *Histoire du Collège de France,* p. 122.

58. Cf. W. Köhler, *Erasmus von Rotterdam, Briefe,* vol. 2, p. 449.

59. OC 10/b, 3–6.

60. OC 21, 55: "At the same period he preached several times in a little city in the region of Berry, named Lignières, and entered the house of the man who ruled that place; he . . . said . . . that it seemed to him that Mr. John Calvin preached better than the monks."

61. OC 21, 122: "Therefore, well versed in these studies, he nevertheless passed the time constantly studying the sacred writings; and thus in the meantime, in the region of Bourges, in a little town they called Linerias, he held several discourses, the Lord remaining with him and approving him."

62. Doumergue, *La jeunesse de Calvin,* p. 191, cites Gilles le Duc (1662) and J. B. Dupré (1786), *Mémoires inédits pour servir à l'histoire de la ville et des seigneurs de Lignières-en-Berri,* published in 1890 by L. Jerry. In this book, p. 308, Gilles le Duc, the dean of the chapter of Lignières, relates that the lord of the place did not "permit himself to be taken in by Calvin's heresy which was not yet expressed openly"; and that, when Calvin preached "it was in the church or in an ordinary pulpit *like other Catholic preachers.*" (Emphasis mine.)

63. Contrary to Lecoultre, "La conversion de Calvin," p. 19, who speaks of "a quite exceptional breach of ecclesiastical authority."

64. Doumergue, *La jeunesse de Calvin,* p. 191.

65. Dankbaar, *Calvin, sein Weg und sein Werk,* pp. 9–10: "There, no doubt, he spoke in tones that sounded forth the new insights of the Christian humanists. But one could not yet speak of a fundamental criticism of Roman Catholic teaching."

Chapter 4. The Second Period in Paris and Orléans, 1531–1533

1. OC 10/b, 8–9; cf. Walker, *Jean Calvin,* p. 61; Kampschulte, *Johannes Calvin, sein Kirche und sein Staat in Genf,* p. 228.

2. Cf. Lortz, *GK,* vol. 2, p. 34: "A misuse of spiritual jurisdiction: the Ban and Interdict were decreed too frequently, often because of secular conflicts, frequently in a purely routine manner because of insignificant financial obligations."

3. Lefranc, *La jeunesse de Calvin,* pp. 17ff.

4. Pannier, *Recherches,* p. 26: "These painful circumstances where the Calvin brothers had to defend the memory of their father against the clergy did nothing to confirm the 'licentiate in law' in his ecclesiastical career." Cf. Wendel, *Calvin, sources et évolution,* p. 11.

5. For example, OC 45, 516, *Harm. ev. Matth.* 18, 18 (E.T. *Calvin's Commentaries: A Harmony of the Gospels;* 1972): "Thus it is also seen how absurdly the papists twist the present passage to disguise all kinds of tyranny. The right of excommunication is certainly to be granted to the Church, and all sane people profess this. But should someone created by a horned and masked beast let loose his empty clatterings about excommunication according to his own desires?" See also OC 1, 552, 637, 664. Cf. the action taken by the synod of Sens in 1528 against the abuses of excommunication, Mansi 32, 1197: "except for a serious reason, and one that is recognized according to legal form; . . . not . . . because of injurious words, except those which are extremely violent. These distinctions are left to the judgment of the officials. We admonish . . . them to be most cautious about multiplying such judgments."

6. According to the chronology established by K. Müller, "Calvins Bekehrung," pp. 189–195.

7. Doumergue, *La jeunesse de Calvin,* p. 197; Lefranc, *La jeunesse de Calvin,* p. 89.

8. Pannier, *Recherches,* p. 27: "Calvin may have met Gérard Roussel, the Queen of Navarre's confessor." Cf. Lang, "Die Bekehrung," pp. 38–39.

9. Pannier, *Recherches,* p. 27.

10. OC 21, 56: "Among others whom he knew in Paris, he always remembered a wealthy merchant, Estienne de la Forge, who feared God, and who was also burned at the stake on account of the Gospel. Calvin referred to him in ch. 4 of his book against the Libertines (cf. OC 7, 160). When he spoke of this person, it was always to testify of his great piety, simplicity, and sincerity." Cf. OC 21, 122–123.

11. I follow the date of 1531 indicated by OC 10/b, 11, n. 12, and adopted by Doumergue, *La jeunesse de Calvin,* p. 198. On the other hand, Pannier, *Recherches,* p. 36, and Th. Dufour, *Calviniana,* in *Mélanges offerts à M. Emile Picot* (Paris), vol. 2, pp. 51ff., date this letter in 1533.

12. F. Gaffiot, *Dictionnaire illustré Latin-Français* (Paris, 1937), p. 466: "Most often *voti damnari* = to see one's vows fulfilled"; p. 1695: "*voti damnatus* = condemned to fulfill his vow, (thus) grant." E. Georges, *Ausführliches lateinisch-deutsches Handwörterbuch,* 11th ed. (Hannover, 1962), vol. 2, col. 1878: "before God, to *condemn someone to a vow* . . . , to sentence one to the fulfilling of an offering (through granting of the stated wish) = allowing someone to fulfill *his* wish. . . . In the passive, *damnari voti* (or less often *voto*) = participate in *his* wish, to attain *his* wish." (Emphasis mine.)

13. OC 10/b, 10: "I questioned your sister's heart, whether she now was receiving that yoke agreeably, her neck broken rather than bent. I urged her again and again freely to disclose to me whatever might be troubling her. I have never seen her more eager and prepared, so that nothing completely unexpected could be ascribed to her wish. You would say she was 'playing with dolls' whenever she heard the word 'vow.' I did not wish to distract her from her views, because I did not come for that reason. But I admonished her in a few words that she not conduct herself by her own strength and not make to herself rash promises about her own ability. Rather, she should place all things in the power of God, in whom we abide and live."

14. Wernle II, pp. 559–560.

15. K. Müller, "Calvins Bekehrung," p. 202.

16. Contrary to Pannier, *Recherches,* p. 36, who shows that Calvin had already proven the "value of the right of freedom of examination." We are, rather, of the opinion of Imbart de la Tour, who declares: "But this awareness of the weakness of nature and the power of grace, this inward religion, is typical of the evangelicalism of Meaux" (*Calvin et l'Institution Chrétienne,* p. 25).

17. OC 10/b, 11: "You know that we have a bishop of your nation, whose arrival we expect daily. I wish that through the efforts of your friends you would be commended to him, so that he would adorn you with an official dignity of some kind or another."

18. Cf. H. Lecoultre, "Calvin d'après son commentaire sur le 'De Clementia' de Sénèque," *RThPh,* 1891, pp. 51–77; Q. Breen, *John Calvin: A Study in French Humanism,* pp. 67–99.

19. OC 5, 5: "John Calvin's preface to the most holy and wise prelate, Claude de Hangest, abbot of Saint Eloi of Noyon."

20. This work of Augustine is cited fifteen times in the *Commentary:* OC 5, 15, 45, 90, 95, 102, 120, 142, 154, 156, 157. L. Smits, *Saint Augustin dans l'oeuvre de Jean Calvin,* vol. 1, p. 16: "He also quotes figures of speech that come from the *De communi vita clericorum,* actually *Sermo* 355, and from *De spiritu et littera.*" Doumergue, *La jeunesse de Calvin,* p. 222, exaggerates a lot, it seems to me, when he declares that the content of the *Commentary* reveals a Calvin who is already completely Augustinian, and adds: "Now Augustinianism is the contrary of humanism."

21. Cf. L. Zanta, *La renaissance du stoïcisme au XVIe siècle;* A. M. Hugo, *Calvijn en Seneca, Een inleidende studie von Calvijns commentaar op Seneca "De Clementia," anno 1532.*

22. Imbart de la Tour, *La France moderne,* pp. 33–43, 199–209, 557–559, underlines the influence of the royal counselors on the contemporary society and points out traces of this influence in the *Institutio principis christiani* of Erasmus that Calvin probably knew. On Calvin's Platonism, see J. Boisset, *Sagesse et sainteté dans la pensée de Calvin: Essai sur l'humanisme du réformateur français.* Cf. Léonard, *La Réformation,* p. 269.

23. OC 5, 18.

24. OC 5, 49.

25. OC 5, 43.

26. Wendel, *Calvin, sources et évolution,* pp. 12–13: "Not a line can be interpreted in this sense unless one forces Calvin to say what he did not."

27. Ibid., p. 14.

28. OC 5, 27 and 155.

29. Smits, *Saint Augustin dans l'oeuvre de Jean Calvin,* p. 16: "In this commentary on the *De Clementia,* there are no reformist views."

30. OC 21, 122: "That commentary he wrote on Seneca's *De Clementia* was outstanding. It is known that Calvin was quite delighted by that most serious writer whose character was so agreeable to his own." Cf. OC 21, 56.

31. OC 10/b, 19–20. Cf. OC 10/b, 20–21 and 21–22.

32. OC 10/b, 16–17.

33. OC 10/b, 17–18.

34. OC 10/b, 20–21: "Concerning the Bibles, I have carried out your instructions to the letter; obtaining them took more effort than money."

35. For a similar view, with a slight variation, see Walker, *Jean Calvin,* p. 70, who quotes Herminjard, vol. 2, pp. 388, 418–421.

36. See the chronology of K. Müller, "Calvins Bekehrung," pp. 189–195.

37. Doumergue, *La jeunesse de Calvin,* p. 297.

38. J. Doinel, "Jean Calvin à Orléans," *BHPF* 26 (1877), pp. 174ff.

39. OC 5, 163–232. This title was not given to this work of Calvin's until the second edition, which appeared in 1545. The first title was *The Souls of the Saints Who Died in the Faith of Christ Live with Christ Rather than Sleep.*

40. Of the 277 biblical quotes, 148 are taken from the Old Testament and 129 from the New Testament. The most frequently quoted Old Testament books are: Psalms (59 times), Isaiah (21), Job (12), Genesis (12), and Ecclesiastes (9). New Testament: 1 Corinthians (18), John (16), Romans (13), Matthew (13), Acts (11), and Luke (9). Since the subject strongly influenced the choice of texts, we can hardly conclude that the numbers indicate young Calvin's preferences among the books of the Scriptures. However, the considerable number of quotes from the Psalms is notable. There are 31 quotes from the Church Fathers: Augustine (8 times); Tertullian (6); Irenaeus (3); Chrysostom, Hilary, and Ambrose (each 2 times); Jerome, Origen, Cyprian, Cyril, Eusebius, Basil, Gregory, and Bernard (each 1 time). On the quotes and references to Augustine, see Smits, *Saint Augustin dans l'oeuvre de Jean Calvin,* p. 19.

41. Lefranc, *La jeunesse de Calvin,* p. 200.

42. K. Müller, "Calvins Bekehrung," pp. 213–214.

Chapter 5. The Events of Autumn 1533 and the Stay in Saintonge

1. Reuter, *Grundverständnis,* p. 69, following A. Lang, "Die Quellen der Institutio von 1536," *EvTh* 3 (1936).

2. Cf. V. L. Bourrilly and N. Weiss, "Jean du Bellay, les protestants et la Sorbonne," *BHPF* 53 (1904), pp. 193–231.

3. Moore, *La réforme allemande,* p. 185.

4. OC 10/b, 25–26.

5. OC 10/b, 25. See the critical textual notes on the preceding letters. Cf. K. Müller, "Calvins Bekehrung," p. 199: "This report and the accompanying letter which came from Calvin are the earliest writings we have in Calvin's own hand."

6. See the following letters beginning with OC 10/b, 30. Contrary to Luther, who kept the custom of dating letters according to traditional saints' days (e.g., WA 52, 587, Hauspostillen 1544: "The Feast of St. Stephen"; 598: "The Slaughter of the Innocents"; 654: "The Feast of Sts. Peter and Paul"; 664: "The Feast of Mary Magdalene"; 725: "The Feast of Sts. Simon and Jude"; 715: "Michaelmas"; 673: "The Feast of St. James"; etc.), Calvin at that time used the old system of Roman dating adopted by the humanists (Calends, Nones, Ides).

7. The word *assuere* literally means "to sew on something." It is certain that we should not read *assuescere,* a similar Latin word which means "to become accustomed to something."

8. A. L. Herminjard, A. Lang, E. Doumergue, K. Müller, H. Lecoultre, and P. Wernle.

9. K. Müller, "Calvins Bekehrung," p. 199: "Calvin's friends in Orléans recognized him by these initial letters and acknowledged him as one of their own. These friends also belonged at that time to Lefèvre's circle."

10. Contrary to Lecoultre, "La conversion de Calvin," p. 20, who uses this expression to refer to Roussel.

11. OC 10/b, 27–30.

12. A. L. Herminjard, E. Staehelin, H. Lecoultre, E. Doumergue, etc.

13. See K. Müller, "Calvins Bekehrung," p. 198, and Walker, *Jean Calvin, l'homme et l'oeuvre*, p. 76.

14. Er Op 5, 137ff., *Paraclesis, id est adhortatio ad christianae philosophiae studium.* Mann, *Erasme et les débuts de la réforme française*, p. 165: "This discourse could serve as the 'party manifesto' of Lefèvre and Erasmus." Note that the discourse of Cop uses the Latin New Testament of Erasmus, whereas Calvin preferred the Vulgate in his earliest theological writings.

15. Lang, "Die Bekehrung," pp. 46, 49ff.

16. See Lecoultre, "La conversion de Calvin," pp. 6–7; Lang, "Die Bekehrung," pp. 10, 46; Doumergue, *La jeunesse de Calvin*, pp. 331–335; Pannier, *Recherches*, p. 40; Moore, *La réforme allemande*, p. 320; J. Rott, "Documents strasbourgeois concernant Calvin, I. Un manuscrit autographe: la harangue du recteur Nicolas Cop," *RHPhR* 44 (1964), no. 4, pp. 291–311. This author relies primarily upon the "better" manuscript of Geneva rather than that of Strasbourg to affirm Calvin's authorship of the speech. But his arguments on this point are not convincing. All historians rely on OC 21, 123, where Beza, in the definitive edition (1575) of his *Life of Calvin*, notes: "Calvin suggested it [Cop's oration]." In my opinion, "suggested it" does not necessarily mean "wrote it with him" (cf. OS 1, 2).

17. In this sense: Pierson, *Studien over Johannes Kalvijn*, pp. 58–109; Walker, *Jean Calvin*, p. 108; Werdermann, "Calvinslehre von der Kirche," p. 259; Wendel, *Calvin, sources et évolution*, pp. 22–23; Dankbaar, *Calvin, sein Weg und sein Werk*, pp. 21–22.

18. J. Rott, "La harangue du recteur Nicolas Cop," p. 291, has established that this document is written in Cop's hand.

19. K. Müller, "Calvins Bekehrung," p. 236: "Thus the same thing occurs repeatedly: sometimes the Genevan, sometimes the Strasbourg is correct. Therefore neither the one nor the other is original; both are copies. Calvin is not the author of the speech. In order to attribute it to him as such, one must—apart from everything else—accept the idea that he incorrectly copied his own rough draft." J. Rott, "La harangue du recteur Nicolas Cop," p. 294, also acknowledges "the existence of a lost source, common to the fragment in Geneva and to the rector's original copy, which has also disappeared and from which the Strasbourg text was copied."

20. K. Müller, "Calvins Bekehrung," p. 238: "This much is clear: if Calvin were the author of the speech, he would have maintained at the time the same views that he held before his 'conversion.' "

21. Ibid., p. 242.

22. E. Mülhaupt, *Die Predigt Calvins*, pp. 4ff.

23. Wendel, *Calvin, sources et évolution*, p. 23.

24. OS 1, 4–5. On the idea of a "Christian philosophy," see J. Bohatec, *Budé und Calvin*, pp. 241ff.

25. OS 1, 5. The manuscript of Geneva adds further: "We greet the Blessed

Virgin with that solemn praise, by far the most beautiful of all: 'Ave Maria, gratia plena.' " Here the recitation of the Ave Maria at the beginning of the sermon is all the more significant because the moderate reformers such as Roussel were already in the habit of leaving it out and replacing it with the Pater Noster. Cf. Imbart de la Tour, *L'évangélisme,* pp. 163–164, n. 3. J. Rott, "La harangue du recteur Nicolas Cop," p. 294: "In any case, when he was transcribing this text, the reformer could not have considered invoking the Virgin as completely incompatible with his convictions, since he reproduced this in rather large letters (although perhaps with some hesitation)." We also note: "It [this hesitation] may be expressed in the parenthetical remarks which Calvin himself seems to have placed at the beginning and the end of the invocation. After his death, his chief collaborator, who had Calvin's manuscript in hand, crossed it out, while noting in the margin: 'Because these [phrases] were used on such occasions, we think they should not be suppressed.' The second collaborator, who later wanted to eliminate the end of the exhortation along with the invocation, was mistaken about the extent of what was to be crossed out." ("To be crossed out": for what reason if not because of his apologetic concerns?)

26. OS 1, 5–6.

27. OS 1, 7–8. On the Pauline idea of justification by faith alone as understood by Lefèvre and Briçonnet, see several references in Imbart de la Tour, *L'évangélisme,* pp. 144–145.

28. OS 1, 8.

29. OS 1, 9.

30. OS 1, 9–10.

31. Lortz, *RD,* vol. 1, 183; L. Bouyer, *Du protestantisme à l'église,* pp. 18–61, 101–122; H. Küng, *Rechtfertigung. Die Lehre Karl Barths und eine katholische Besinnung,* pp. 243–266. Nothing would lead us to affirm that Cop's address is "the first evidence of French Protestantism, as the theses of Wittenberg [were of German Protestantism]" (J. Rott, "La harangue du recteur Nicolas Cop," p. 291).

32. Bulaeus, *Historia universitatis parisiensis,* vol. 6, p. 239.

33. Herminjard, vol. 3, p. 146, note.

34. Ibid., p. 130.

35. Ibid., p. 114.

36. OC 21, 56: "Because of his association with Cop, Calvin also was forced to leave Paris. The bailiff Morin even went to his room at the Collège de Fortet, where he resided, thinking to take him prisoner; but not finding him, he seized all he could of his books and papers, among which were several letters from his friends in Orléans." Cf. 21, 123.

37. Dankbaar, *Calvin, sein Weg und sein Werk,* p. 22: "The events surrounding Cop's lecture and its contents furnish no sufficient proof of a decisive turn or conversion in Calvin's spiritual life. It is only certain that from now on Calvin was one of those under suspicion."

Chapter 6. The Year of Wandering, 1534

1. OC 10/b, 146–151, 163–178, 220–222, 241–245, 269–272, 290–302.

2. OC 10/b, 340: "Louis had been lost to me. He was the only one who offered [me support]; but he also tried to sell his liberality at too high a price, since he did not just urge me to recant."

3. OC 10/b, 37–38.

4. OC 21, 56: "From Paris, Calvin then went to stay in Xantonge; there he stayed with a young man from a wealthy home who had a benefice there. This young man begged him to write several brief sermons and Christian admonitions, which he had certain priests recite in prose in those parts."

5. OC 21, 123.

6. Florimond de Raemond, *Histoire*, p. 885.

7. Ibid., pp. 883–885.

8. Ibid. Cf. Doumergue, *La jeunesse de Calvin*, pp. 372–374.

9. OC 13, 681.

10. Florimond de Raemond, *Histoire*, p. 889: "Calvin stayed for several years [*sic*] in the city of Angoulême, still wearing the mask of a Catholic, appearing at church, but as little as possible. He was used by the chapter to give Latin sermons as was the custom when the synod assembled for the Supper. He did this two or three times in the church of St. Peter. During his stay in Angoulême, he did not preach, pray, or worship in any way contrary to Catholic custom." On the relationship between Calvin and du Tillet, see the introduction by A. Crottet in his work, *Correspondance française de Calvin avec Louis du Tillet (1537–1538)*, pp. 4–15.

11. OC 3, Introduction, pp. xi–xiv; Doumergue, *La jeunesse de Calvin*, p. 372; Walker, *Jean Calvin*, p. 119.

12. See Doumergue, *La jeunesse de Calvin*, pp. 380–415; Walker, *Jean Calvin*, pp. 119–120; Wendel, *Calvin, sources et évolution*, pp. 23–24; Dankbaar, *Calvin, sein Weg und sein Werk*, p. 29. These authors follow Colladon, OC 21, 57: "While he was in Xantonge, he traveled to Nérac to see the esteemed Jacques Lefèvre d'Etaples. Lefèvre, who had taught the children of King Francis, was quite old, but he had been persecuted by the Sorbonne and therefore retired to that country. The elderly gentleman was pleased to welcome Calvin and to confer with him."

13. Lefranc, *La jeunesse de Calvin*, p. 201.

14. Ibid., p. 21.

15. Lang, "Die Bekehrung," p. 13; Doumergue, *La jeunesse de Calvin*, pp. 427–438; Walker, *Jean Calvin*, pp. 122–128.

16. In particular, Wendel, *Calvin, sources et évolution*, p. 24, who mentions the resignation of the benefice, but says nothing of an arrest.

17. Dankbaar, *Calvin, sein Weg und sein Werk*, p. 30: "Through an inaccurate reading some have come to accept the notion that Calvin was imprisoned there for a few days and thereafter set free. However, the report refers to someone else who, because he was also called 'Mudi,' should be distinguished from our Calvin." The author quotes as supporting evidence a letter from Calvin (1545) in which we read: "I praise the Lord . . . that he has *never* tested me by inquisition or *imprisonment*" (OC 12, 68).

18. Lecoultre, "La conversion de Calvin," p. 27: "The first public indication of this conversion, the first at least that we know of. . . . This act, along with its natural consequence of voluntary exile, necessarily made Calvin a true protestant." Pannier, *Recherches*, p. 43: "Openly and officially, Calvin severed the clerical ties that attached him to the Roman Church when he resigned his benefices on 4 May 1534." Imbart de la Tour, *Calvin et l'Institution Chrétienne*, p. 31: "Nothing more in common with the Church from which he had just separated himself. He went to

Noyon, resigned his benefices, and thereby testified to his definitive break with the Church."

19. OC 21, 57: "Sometime afterward, Calvin left Xantonge and returned to Paris. He rarely appeared in public, for it was not safe for him to do so. . . . He spent that year in Orléans, but before leaving France, he composed his book entitled *Psychopannychia.*"

20. OC 21, 124: "This year, 1534, was noteworthy for the horrible cruelty directed toward many pious people. . . . [T]he wrath of the deluded King Francis [was] inflamed because of some pages written against the Mass."

21. OC 8, 481.

22. Walker, *Jean Calvin,* p. 129.

23. OC 7, 160: On the appearance of anabaptism in France, see K. Müller, "Calvin und die 'Libertiner,' " *ZKG* 40 (1922), pp. 83–122; W. Niesel, "Calvin und die Libertiner," *ZKG* 48 (1929), pp. 58–74.

24. OC 5, 170–232.

25. Ibid., 169/170–171/172: "Since we read that certain Arabs had been the authors of this dogma. . . . And sometime after that [we read] that the school of Paris drove the Roman bishop John to recant. But though quieted for some centuries, it was recently stirred up by several people from the dregs of the anabaptists, and put forth some sparks once again."

26. Ibid., 171/172: "To these let the response be that we recognize no unity except in Christ, no love unless he is its bond. Therefore this is uppermost in preserving love, that faith remain holy and complete among us."

27. In the *Psychopannychia* one reads about man as the image of God that "the image itself is outside the flesh" (OC 5, 181), "only in the spirit" (182). The body is presented as "an earthly home" or "tabernacle" of the soul (182), as "the prison of the soul" (196), "a slave's prison" (195, 201). The "soul or spirit" is defined as a "substance distinct from the body" (184). "Flesh" is opposed to "spirit" in the same way that "death" is to "life" (186). Cf. R. W. Battenhouse, "The Doctrine of Man in Calvin and in Renaissance Platonism," *Journal of the History of Ideas* 9 (1948), pp. 447–471; Boisset, *Sagesse et sainteté dans la pensée de Calvin,* pp. 253–314. We again note an interesting peculiarity: Although the second book of Maccabees is first called a "book of uncertain faith," it is later used to prove that the souls of the dead are "awake": "when Jeremiah, who was dead, prays to God for his warring people." His plea to pray for the dead is cited without any polemical remark (232)!

28. OC 10/b, 22–24.

29. Doumergue, *La jeunesse de Calvin,* p. 299: Herminjard, vol. 3, p. 204; Lefranc, *La jeunesse de Calvin,* p. 46; Eells, "Martin Bucer," p. 412; Lang, "Die Bekehrung," pp. 16–17; Walker, *Jean Calvin,* p. 74; K. Müller, "Calvins Bekehrung," pp. 245–253.

30. Cf. Eells, "Martin Bucer," p. 409.

31. At this time neither Luther nor his disciples were absolutely opposed to the episcopate as a legitimate ministry. The Augsburg Confession (1530) devoted all of article 28 to episcopal power: BSLK 120–133. Cf. P. Brunner, *Nikolaus von Amsdorf als Bischof von Naumburg. Eine Untersuchung zur Gestalt des evangelischen*

Bischofsamtes in der Reformationszeit, SVRG 179 (1961); WA 53, 231ff.: "An instance of ordaining a proper Christian bishop occurred in Naumburg on 20 January 1542." See Luther's criticism of "bogus bishops": WA 38, 222ff.

32. F. Gaffiot, *Dictionnaire illustré Latin–Français* (Paris, 1937), p. 646: *fabula* in the sense of "a play." P. 997: *motoria* = "a lively and animated theatrical play, full of movement." Cf. OS 1, 309: "When that deceiver comes near the altar, he begins to act out his *fable,* sometimes *moving about* and sometimes standing still."

33. On the various tendencies of anabaptism, see F. Heyer, *Der Kirchenbegriff der Schwärmer,* SVRG 56 (1939).

34. OC 21, 57 and 124.

35. Imbart de la Tour, *L'évangélisme,* pp. 553ff.; N. Weiss and V. L. Bourrilly, "L'affaire des placards," *BHPF* 53 (1904), pp. 96–143; L. Febvre, "L'origine des placards de 1534," *Bibliothèque d'Humanisme et de Renaissance,* pp. 62–75; B. Hari, "Les placards de 1534," *Aspects de la propagande religieuse,* 1957, pp. 79–142.

36. OC 21, 124. Cf. Bohatec, *Budé and Calvin,* pp. 100–101, 121–141: Budé encouraged the King to deal severely with the heretics.

37. OC 21, 57 and 124.

Chapter 7. Calvin in Basle, 1535–1536

1. Cf. P. Wernle, *Calvin und Basel bis zum Tode des Myconius, 1535–1552;* E. Choisy, "Calvin und Basel," *Kirchenblatt für die reformierte Schweiz* 86 (1930), pp. 274–279.

2. On the reform in Basle: R. Wackernagel, *Humanismus und Reformation in Basel;* P. Roth, *Durchbruch und Festsetzung der Reformation in Basel;* P. Burckhardt, *Basel in den ersten Jahren nach der Reformation;* idem, *Geschichte der Stadt Basel von der Zeit der Reformation bis zur Gegenwart;* Léonard, *La Réformation,* pp. 133–137, 140–145.

3. J. J. Herzog, *Das Leben Johannes Oecolampads und die Reformation der Kirche zu Basel;* E. Staehelin, *Das Buch der Basler Reformation;* idem, *Das theologische Lebenswerk Johannes Oekolampads;* idem, *Briefe und Akten zum Leben Oekolampads;* A. Moser, "Die Anfänge der Freundschaft zwischen Zwingli und Oekolampad," *Zwingliana,* 1958, pp. 614–620.

4. O. E. Strasser, art. "Myconius," *RGG,* vol. 4, col. 1230; K. R. Hagenbach, *Oswald Myconius.*

5. OC 21, 124.

6. OC 10/b, 402. "I remember when three years ago we were informally commenting on the best way of interpreting the Scriptures, that the method you liked most was also the one I then approved above all others." This preface is dated "Strasbourg, 18 October 1539."

7. G. W. Locher, art. "Simon Grynaeus," *RGG,* vol. 2, col. 1898; J. V. Pollet, *Martin Bucer, études sur la correspondance,* vol. 2, pp. 389–394.

8. OC 10/b, 45–46.

9. OC 10/b, 47–49.

10. W. Kolfhaus, "Der Verkehr Calvins mit Bullinger," *Calvinstudien,* 1909, p. 28; A. Bouvier, *Henri Bullinger, réformateur et conseiller oecuménique,* p. 49.

11. Ch. Schmidt, *Etudes sur Guillaume Farel;* L. Junod, *Farel, réformateur de la Suisse romande et pasteur de l'église de Neuchâtel;* H. Heyer, *Guillaume Farel, Essai sur le developpement de ses idées théologiques; Biographie nouvelle de Guillaume Farel,* written by a group of historians, professors, and pastors, Neuchâtel-Paris, 1930; J. Staedtke, art. "Farel," *RGG,* vol. 2, col. 876.

12. H. Jacquemot, *Viret, réformateur de Lausanne;* J. Barnaud, *Pierre Viret, sa vie et son oeuvre (1511–1571);* R. Pfister, art. "Viret," *RGG,* vol. 6, col. 1407.

13. Wernle, *Calvin und Basel,* p. 4.

14. OC 10/b, 47: In a letter addressed to Bullinger in 1535, Myconius criticizes the following phrase of Erasmus: "How much dignity is proper for the ministers of the New Testament, who sacrifice that heavenly victim every day?" And he declares, "It does not seem right to permit such a thing to be printed in a Christian city."

15. OC 10/b, 48: Bullinger responds to Myconius' letter: "This man knows how to hold two positions and wear the insignia of each on either arm."

16. OC 9, 51, *Secunda defensio contra Westphalum* (1556): "When I was beginning to emerge from papal darkness with a slight taste of sound doctrine and I read in the works of Luther that nothing was left of the sacraments by Oecolampadius and Zwingli except bare and empty figures, I confess that I was so alienated from their books that I refused for a long time to read them. Later, when I began to write, I put away some of this former vehemence under the influence of the colloquia held at Marburg."

17. Doumergue, *La jeunesse de Calvin,* pp. 488–489, 505; A. Baumgartner, *Calvin hébraïsant et interprète de l'Ancien Testament,* p. 20.

18. At Basle, Calvin learned of the execution of his friend and protector, Etienne de la Forge, burned alive on 16 February 1535. He still remembered it twenty-two years later. See OC 31, 24, Preface to the *Commentary on the Psalms* (1557).

19. I follow the opinion of the OC editors on the date and place of the composition of the two prefaces: "We believe that they were written . . . at the same time that he was considering his first *Institutes* at Basle and concentrating on his biblical studies (9, lxii)."

20. OC 9, 787.

21. OC 9, 788.

22. OC 9, 789.

23. OC 9, 788.

24. OC 9, 791.

25. OC 9, 793.

26. OC 9, 801.

27. OC 9, 807.

28. Ibid.

29. OC 9, 809.

30. OC 9, 811.

31. OC 9, 819.

32. Herminjard, vol. 3, pp. 250–254.

33. After the terrible repression, approved by Luther, which followed the Peasants' Revolt (1524–1525), Zwingli himself gave the signal for a new persecution of the anabaptists in 1527. Between 1527 and 1535, hundreds of peaceful sectarians were tortured, burned alive, beheaded, or drowned. Melanchthon encouraged the repression. For more details, see Léonard, *La Réformation,* pp. 178–188.

34. Bohatec, *Budé und Calvin,* p. 140.

35. OC 7, 666, *Vera ecclesiae reformandae ratio* (1549).

36. These writings appeared in 1534 in the *Appendix ad coenam dominicam* by Father Robert, Bishop of Abrincensem.

37. Bohatec, *Budé und Calvin,* pp. 128–129.

38. OC 31, 24. Earlier, Calvin alluded to the writings of his adversaries: "These burnings were considered so evil by a large part of the Germans that they became deeply resentful of the authors of such tyranny. To appease them, they circulated several little malicious books filled with lies, in which they cruelly portrayed anabaptists and other seditious people." Cf. OC 21, 30, 124–125, and 57–58, where Beza and Colladon reproduced the reformer's statement. Colladon even explicitly names his source.

39. OS 1, 21: "I have expended this labor especially for our French people, many of whom I saw hungering and thirsting for Christ."

40. OS 1, 22.

41. Ibid.

42. BL 1, 10 (translation by Calvin himself).

43. OS 1, 23.

44. OS 1, 23–25.

45. OS 1, 25–35.

46. OS 1, 31 and 35.

47. By the end of the Middle Ages, the French lawyers who were theoreticians of absolute monarchy had created a powerful lay following whose influences were felt in the realms of ideas as well as practice. Cf. Imbart de la Tour, *La France moderne,* pp. 89–123.

Chapter 8. Travels Between Basle, Ferrara, and Paris, 1536

1. OC 10/b, 52.

2. OC 21, 194, *Annales Calviniani;* Kampschulte, *Johannes Calvin, seine Kirche und sein Staat in Genf,* p. 159; Doumergue, *Les premiers essais,* p. 131.

3. Th. Dufour, *Un opuscule inédit de Farel, Le résumé des actes de la Dispute de Rive, 1535.*

4. H. D. Forster, "Geneva Before Calvin, 1387–1536: The Antecedents of a Puritan State," *AHR* 8 (1903), p. 225. Cf. H. Naef, *Les origines de la réforme à Genève.*

5. Forster, "Geneva Before Calvin, 1387–1536," pp. 228–229; Walker, *Jean Calvin,* pp. 189–191.

6. Lortz, *RD,* vol. 1, p. 312: "These prophets took very seriously, in a naive way, Luther's demand that the entire life of the Christian should be placed under the Word." See also pp. 313–319.

7. Ibid., p. 314: "Anabaptism is a releasing of the spiritualist elements of reformation doctrine and at times a reaction against the firm restriction of reformation forces, which soon appeared in the varied, newly urbanized Christendom of the territories and cities." Cf. W. Köhler, *"Das Täufertum in Calvins Institutio von 1536,"* *Mennonitische Geschichtsblätter* 2, pp. 1–4.

8. OC 10/b, 52, Calvin to Libertet, 3 September 1535: "Know that the book itself has been completely redone by me."

9. OC 5, 173/174–175/176.

10. OC 21, 30, 58, 125. Beza and Colladon mention this trip without giving any details.

11. We possess three letters from the duchess to Calvin and eleven from Calvin to the duchess. The first of these, OC 11, 323–331, respectfully draws attention to the danger of the duchess's continual presence at the "papal" Mass.

12. Letters of Sinapius to Calvin: OC 10/b, 127, 363–364; 11, 655; 15, 688; 17, 374.

13. Doumergue, Les premiers essais, p. 52.

14. Walker, Jean Calvin, pp. 163, 166–167; Dankbaar, Calvin, sein Weg und sein Werk, pp. 42–43.

15. OC 21, 58: "Now sometime afterward he went from Basle to France, and his aforementioned companion [i.e., du Tillet] went from Neuchâtel to Geneva. But Calvin, after arranging his affairs, once again wished to retire to Basle and Strasbourg, and took his brother Antoine along with him."

16. Lefranc, "Les idées religieuses de Marguerite de Navarre," pp. 205–208.

17. OC 10/b, 55 and 58.

18. OC 31, 26: "Because the straightest road to Strasbourg, where I wanted to go, was closed because of war, I quickly decided to come here [i.e., to Geneva]."

Chapter 9. Calvin in Geneva, 1536–1538

1. Lortz, RD, vol. 1, p. 340, on the reform in Zurich: "A patriotic emphasis, a mark of the Swiss Reformation, was especially prominent in the Zurich reform: it opposed foreign rule and advocated freedom."

2. Kampschulte, Johannes Calvin, sein Kirche und sein Staat in Genf, pp. 90, 169, 171; Forster, "Geneva Before Calvin, 1387–1536," p. 223.

3. Walker, Jean Calvin, p. 191.

4. On the reform activity of Farel, see Ch. Borgeaud, L'adoption de la réforme par le peuple de Genève; H. Delarue, "La première offensive évangélique à Genève, 1532–1533, Bulletin de la Société d'Histoire et d'Archéologie de Genève 9 (1948), pp. 83–102.

5. OC 21, 198.

6. OC 21, 200.

7. OC 21, 200–201.

8. OC 21, 202.

9. Ibid.

10. OC 21, 203.

11. OC 9, 891–892, Discours d'adieu aux ministres (1564); OC 31, 26, Preface to the Commentary on the Psalms (1557): "Now a little beforehand, the papacy had been driven out by means of this good man whom I have named [i.e., Farel] and by Pierre Viret; but since everything was not in good order, there were terrible divisions and dangerous factions among the citizens."

12. OC 31, 26.

13. OC 21, 30, 58, 125–126.

14. OC 21, 30: "Then he agreed to stay, not in order to preach, but to read theology. . . . Having thus been declared a doctor in this church . . ." OC 21, 126: "chosen not only as a preacher (he first refused this) but as a teacher in the sacred writings, because they were accepting one."

15. Herminjard, vol. 4, pp. 107, 123; Walker, *Jean Calvin,* p. 198.

16. Cf. Ch. Guilliard, *La conquête du pays de Vaud par les Bernois.*

17. Ch. Subilia, *La dispute de Lausanne;* H. Meylan and R. Deluz, *La dispute de Lausanne;* A. Piaget (ed.), *Actes de la dispute de Lausanne 1536, publiés intégralement d'après le manuscrit de Berne,* in *Mémoires de l'Université de Neuchâtel,* vol. 6 (1928); G. Bavaud, *La dispute de Lausanne (1536): Une étape de l'évolution doctrinale des reformateurs romands.*

18. OC 9, 701–702, *Les articles de Lausanne.*

19. OC 9, 877–886: for the text of Calvin's comments.

20. OC 9, 881. Note that Calvin rarely uses the expression "sacrifice of the New Testament" to refer to the Eucharist.

21. Bavaud, *La dispute de Lausanne,* pp. 90–92, shows that the adversaries of the evangelicals presented a nominalist theory of the real presence; then, p. 106, he adds that they did not try "to show how the sacrifice of the Mass is substantially identical with that of the cross."

22. OC 9, 884.

23. Doumergue, *Les premiers essais,* pp. 180–218; Dankbaar, *Calvin, sein Weg und sein Werk,* pp. 48–49.

24. Bavaud, *La dispute de Lausanne,* mentions that two laymen contradicted the evangelicals: the doctor Blancherose, a confused individual trained in the doctrines of Joachim of Fiore, and Fernand Loys, head of the abbey of the Noble Children. Five priests also objected: Jean Michod, Jean Mimard, Jacques Drogy, Jean Berilly, and Dominique de Montbusson O.P. Montbusson gave an erroneous interpretation of the relationship between the Church and the Scripture (pp. 61–62). Mimard and Drogy were convinced and joined the evangelical camp. P. 36: "No defender of Catholicism was prepared to reply to the reformers' objections. The reformers presented their doctrines with *an assurance and firmness* that contrasted with the timidity and hesitation of a Jean Michod." (Emphasis mine.)

25. OC 10/b, 64.

26. OC 10/b, 67.

27. On the meaning of this letter for the relationship between Bucer and Calvin, see Eells, "Martin Bucer," pp. 412–419.

28. OC 5, 386, *Reply to Sadolet:* "In that church I first served in the office of teacher, then of pastor." OC 21, 58: Colladon reports that Calvin was named reader in theology in September 1536 and that "a little later he was also named pastor."

29. Dankbaar, *Calvin, sein Weg und sein Werk,* p. 49: "Toward the end of the year 1536 the *government* of Geneva appointed him pastor of the city. We learn nothing of an ordination by the laying on of hands or the like." (Emphasis mine.)

30. Wernle, *Calvin und Basel,* p. 8, thinks that Calvin began writing these two letters while he was in Italy.

31. OC 5, 279–312; OS 1, 329–362.

32. OC 5, 239–276; OS 1, 289–328.

33. OC 5, xxxix; cf. Lecoultre, "La conversion de Calvin," p. 27, note; Lang, "Die Bekehrung," p. 39; Walker, *Jean Calvin,* pp. 165–166.

34. OC 10/a, 5–14.

35. OC 10/a, 5, note; cf. Kampschulte, *Johannes Calvin, sein Kirche und sein Staat in Genf,* p. 289; OC 21, 206; the *Registres du Conseil* of Geneva noted on 16

January 1537: "Here were spoken and read the articles by Mr. G. Farel and the other ministers." See also Beza's and Colladon's account: OC 21, 30–31 and 31–59.

36. Wernle, *Calvin und Basel,* p. 10, thinks that the *Articles,* especially concerning the public profession of faith and excommunication, were inspired by the "Church Order" of Basle.

37. OC 22, 85–96.

38. OC 22, 33–74. Concerning Calvin's authorship of these two writings, see OC 22, 11/12–17/18; A. Rilliet and Th. Dufour, *Le Catéchisme français de Calvin publié en 1537.*

39. OC 22, xlii; Walker, *Jean Calvin,* p. 210; Wendel, *Calvin, sources et évolution,* p. 31.

40. OC 10/a, 5, note.

41. Wendel, *Calvin, sources et évolution,* p. 31.

42. Herminjard, vol. 4, pp. 107, 109.

43. OC 10/b, 83. A particularly dangerous accusation in view of the circumstances and precedents. From 1530, Servetus' heretical views on the Trinity caused particular concern for Swiss evangelicals. Cf. OC 8, 744, n. 1: Oecolampadius' attempts to bring Servetus back to the traditional faith.

44. Denz, p. 41, no. 75: "The opinion now prevails that the creed arose in the south of France, primarily from the province of Arles, between A.D. 430 and 500. Its author is not known. Gradually this creed took on so much authority in the Western as well as the Eastern Churches that in the Middle Ages it was made equal to the Apostles' Creed and the Nicene Creed and became part of the liturgy."

45. OC 10/b, 86: Calvin accuses his adversary of not being concerned about a decree coming from "the whole Church," meaning the evangelical communities of the region. He says: "But just as that fellow cared not a bit how much he might annoy the kingdom of Christ by his temerity, so he regarded a decree of the whole Church as a matter of indifference."

46. OC 10/b, 86: "I answered that I was not wont to approve anything as the Word of God unless it was properly considered."

47. For a favorable judgment on Caroli: E. Baehler, "Petrus Caroli und Johann Calvin," in *Jahrbuch für Schweizerische Geschichte,* vol. 29 (1904), pp. 41–169. For rather negative judgments: Doumergue, *Les premiers essais,* pp. 252–268; Lovy, *Les origines,* pp. 177–179. For ambivalent judgments: Walker, pp. 214–219; Wendel, *Calvin, sources et évolution,* pp. 32–33.

48. OC 10/b, 85, Calvin's letter to a minister in Bern: "An ambitious man wanted to recommend himself to the people by some novelty; he is not commendable to them otherwise." The reformer turns the charge of teaching novelties against his adversary.

49. OC 21, 208, *Registre du Conseil,* 15 February 1537: "Here it is said of Calvin that he had just been received and retained on the condition that he is paid six gold crowns."

50. Walker, *Jean Calvin,* p. 215: "Thanks to the credibility which he obtained with the government of Bern, he was named principal pastor of Lausanne with a good stipend."

51. To get an idea of the animosity with which Calvin treated Caroli, see his letter to a minister of Bern in which the offensive language is considerable (OC 10/b, 85–87). Cf. OC 7, 309, *Adversus P. Caroli calumnias* (1545).

52. OC 10/b, 84.

53. OC 10/b, 87. *Pagani* in the sense of "pagans" does not mesh with the context. The old English translation had rendered it by "the peasants." But we think that Calvin used this word according to classical Latin to describe the citizens in contrast to the pastors.

54. OC 10/b, 84.

55. OC 10/b, 89, letter of 8 March 1537. The tone changes after the synod of Lausanne: OC 10/b, 104, where the same Megander speaks of "Farel, Calvin, and many other *brethren,* pious and very learned men."

56. Walker, *Jean Calvin,* p. 219.

57. OC 22, 52: "When we name the Father, the Son, and the Holy Spirit, we do not imagine that there are three Gods; but the Scriptures and the very experience of piety show us the simple essence of God, the Father, his Son and his Spirit. Therefore, let us stop and fix the desire of our heart upon one single God; nevertheless, at the same time let us contemplate the Father with the Son and his Holy Spirit."

58. E. Wolf, *Deus Omniformis. Bemerkungen zur Christologie des Michael Servet,* in *Theologische Aufsätze K. Barth zum 50. Geburtstag* (1936), p. 448: "slightly modalistic understanding of the Trinity." L. Goumaz, *La doctrine du salut d'après les commentaires de Jean Calvin sur le Nouveau Testament,* p. 283: "The hypostases actually designate the 'modes' or the manifestations of God's activity" (quoted by W. Krusche, *Das Wirken des Heiligen Geistes nach Calvin,* p. 10).

59. Walker, *Jean Calvin,* p. 220: "It was necessary to dissipate the suspicions and doubts at Bern, Basle, Zurich, and Strasbourg, including those of Melanchthon." Cf. Doumergue, *Les premiers essais,* pp. 266–268.

60. OC 10/b, 104: Megander gives an account to the people of Zurich of the results acquired at Lausanne: "Farel [and] Calvin . . . have been unfairly stained and charged with the evil of this heresy."

61. OC 10/b, 105–106: Certification of the orthodoxy of Farel, Calvin, and Viret delivered by the Senate of Bern. Cf. OC 10/b, 112.

62. OC 10/b, 111.

63. OC 21, 208–210.

64. OC 21, 56: "As for the anabaptists, he knew them so well and handled them so adroitly that the magistrate did not have to lift a hand. From that point on, the contest was lost in this church." This statement by Colladon is a good example of his tendency to exaggerate. According to the *Registre du Conseil,* the magistrate certainly did intervene by banishing all adherents of the sect, under pain of death. Cf. Walker, *Jean Calvin,* p. 221.

65. OC 21, 209–210.

66. OC 10/b, 130–131 and 133–134, letters from the Senate of Bern to the Council of Geneva.

67. OC 21, 219–220, *Registre du Conseil,* 4 January 1538.

68. OC 21, 221.

69. OC 10/b, 124–125, letter from Capito to Calvin; 125–126, letter from the Senate of Bern to the Council of Geneva.

70. OC 9, 703–710, *Confessio de Trinitate;* 711–712, *Confessio fidei de Eucharistia.*

71. OC 10/b, 138.

72. OC 10/b, 113–114, letter from Myconius to Bullinger.

73. OC 10/b, 95, letter from Calvin to Viret, 23 April: "The master from Haut-mont [i.e., du Tillet] sought advice about traveling to France."

74. OC 10/b, 147ff., letter from Calvin to du Tillet, just after the latter's departure.

Chapter 10. Crisis in Geneva and Exile to Strasbourg, 1538

1. OC 21, 222, *Registre du Conseil,* 12 March 1538.

2. Ibid.

3. Ibid., note of 11 March: The Council of Two Hundred accepted "the ordinances of the Gentlemen of Berne."

4. OC 10/b, 178–179.

5. OC 21, 223.

6. OC 10/b, 185.

7. OC 10/b, 185–186.

8. OC 21, 224.

9. OC 21, 225.

10. OC 21, 226–227.

11. OC 21, 229.

12. OC 10/b, 206. Cf. OC 10/b, 190–192, *Articuli a Calvino et Farello propositi ad pacem Genevae restituendam.*

13. Wernle, *Calvin und Basel,* p. 21, thinks that during this new stay in Basle, Calvin prepared the second edition of his *Institutes.* The editors of OC (10/b, 261, n. 20) do not share this opinion.

14. OC 10/b, 201.

15. OC 10/b, 221.

16. OC 10/b, 272.

17. OC 10/b, 248.

18. OC 10/b, 229, letter from Calvin to Farel, 4 August 1538.

19. Ibid.: "Is it not a shame, he said, for you to remain silent in such a multitude? Or was there no temple open to you here? I answered that there were audiences also at home which suited well enough. He wanted nothing short of my preaching in public."

20. OC 10/b, 271, letter from Calvin to du Tillet, 20 October.

21. OC 10/b, 231, letter from Farel to the citizens of Geneva, 7 August 1538: "For my intention was to rely on the grace of God without taking over any office."

22. OC 10/b, 246, letter from Calvin to Farel, September 1538.

23. OC 10/b, 253, letter from Calvin to the citizens of Geneva, 1 October 1538.

24. OC 10/b, 269–270, letter from Calvin to du Tillet, 20 October 1538.

25. OC 10/b, 253.

26. OC 10/b, 229, letter from Calvin to Farel, 4 August 1538.

27. OC 10/b, 202, letter from Farel and Calvin to Viret and Couraud, May 1538.

28. OC 10/b, 221, letter from Calvin to du Tillet, 10 July 1538.

29. OC 10/b, 208; cf. 202 and 224.

30. The Latin is *nepos,* which may mean "nephew" here.

31. OC 10/b, 236–237, Calvin to Farel, 20 August 1538: "And when there were definite indications of death, I proffered comfort, more for the soul than for the

body. . . . I am certain that he did not have a penny when he died. And so it was necessary to spend something for the benefit of the living and the burial of the dead."

32. OC 10/b, 210, Calvin to Viret and Couraud, 14 June 1538.

33. OC 10/b, 208, Farel and Calvin to the ministers of Zurich, June 1538: "It were better now for the Church to be absolutely destitute of pastors than to be occupied by so-called 'pastors' concealed behind the mask of pastors."

34. OC 10/b, 208, 233, 250, etc.

35. OC 10/b, 210–213 and 230–232.

36. On the important role that he played in the resolution of the crisis, see OC 10/b, 202, 209, 210, 224, 228–230, 236–237, etc.

37. On Bucer and the reformation of Strasbourg: J. Adam, *Evangelische Kirchengeschichte der Stadt Strassburg;* H. G. Rott, *Forschungen und Arbeiten zur Geschichte des Protestantismus im Elsass,* AElsKG (1941), pp. 331–339; H. Strohl, *Le protestantisme en Alsace,* and the extensive bibliography given by him.

38. OC 10/b, 209, Calvin to Viret and Couraud.

39. OC 10/b, 137–144. In this long letter, Calvin criticizes Bucer in these terms: "Where has it been conceded that we can step outside the limits of God's Word with impunity? Nor do you do this in one matter alone, but wherever you appear to want some sort of kingdom to be divided between Christ and the pope" (col. 143). Then: "In this moderation you are so unlike Luther that I think he will be more gravely offended by the rationale of what you are doing, should he come upon it in your work, than he was earlier by the opinions of Zwingli and Oecolampadius."

40. OC 10/b, 219, Bucer to Calvin, June 1538.

41. Calvin will soon quote Bucer word for word, which shows to what extent he was impressed with him.

42. OC 10/b, 229, 236.

43. OC 10/b, 219.

44. OC 10/b, 271, Calvin to du Tillet, 20 October 1538: "It is my sincere hope that I will soon take charge of matters. . . . But when the most moderate threaten that the Lord finds me no more favorable than Jonah, and when they go so far as to speak of me in these terms, 'You who are endowed with those gifts, how could you in good conscience refuse the ministerial office offered to you, etc. . . . ,' I have thought it necessary in such perplexity to follow what I believe the servants of God have shown me."

45. OC 10/b, 242 and 244, du Tillet to Calvin, 7 September 1538.

46. Walker, *Jean Calvin,* p. 243: "It is improbable that he sold his books, as is often said, but that he got something for the sale of books that had belonged to Olivétan." Cf. Doumergue, *Les premiers essais,* pp. 454–458.

47. OC 10/b, 270–272, Calvin to du Tillet, 20 October 1538.

48. On Calvin's stay in Strasbourg, one may find the following books helpful: A. Erichson, *L'église française de Strasbourg au seizième siècle, d'après des documents inédits;* E. Stricker, *Johannes Calvin als erster Pfarrer der reformierten Gemeinde zu Strassburg;* J. Pannier, "Calvin à Strasbourg," Cahier 12 of *RHPhR* (1935); the study of J. B. Benoit and P. Scherding in the work *Calvin à Strasbourg* (Strasbourg, 1938); J. Courvoisier, "Bucer et l'oeuvre de Calvin," *RThPh* 21 (1936), pp. 66–77; M. B. van't Veer, *Catechese en catechetische stof bij Calvijn,* pp. 39–57, 265–278.

49. OC 10/b, 247.

50. OC 10/b, 251–255, Calvin to the citizens of Geneva, 1 October 1538.

51. OC 5, 385–416; OS 1, 457–489.

52. Cf. R. M. Douglas, *Jacopo Sadoleto, Humanist and Reformer;* Beekenkamp, "Calvijn en Sadoleto," *Veritatem in Caritate* 4 (1959), pp. 21–27.

53. Cf. A. Erichson, *Die calvinische und die altstrassburgische Gottesdienstordnung.*

Chapter 11. Conclusion to Part One

1. On the evangelical martyrs of France and their confessions of faith, see Crespin, *Histoire des martyrs.*

Part Two. The Sources of the First Edition of the *Institutes*

1. Lang, "Quellen," pp. 100–112.

2. OC 3, xi–xiv.

3. OS 1, 14–17.

4. R. Seeberg, *Lehrbuch der Dogmengeschichte,* vol. 4/2, pp. 554–559.

5. Cf. Smits, *Saint Augustin dans l'oeuvre de Calvin,* vol. 1.

6. Seeberg, *Lehrbuch der Dogmengeschichte,* vol. 4/2, p. 556: "Luther's thought *was decisive* for him as a theologian *in general and in particular.*" P. 559: "He grasped Luther's interpretation of the Gospel in its depth and uniqueness as no other reformer had done." Moore, *La réforme allemande,* pp. 321–322: "One must recognize in the formation of Calvin's theology that his reading of Luther played a very large role and that Luther's influence was strong and continuous." Léonard, *La Réformation,* p. 261: "The last of the great reformers in time, Calvin would have had great difficulty in creating a perfectly original theological work; thus the *Christian Institutes* in its first edition was *profoundly Lutheran.*" (Emphasis mine.) Cf. Lang, "Die Bekehrung Calvins," pp. 47ff.; idem, *Reformation und Gegenwart,* pp. 72–87, ch. "Luther und Calvin"; K. Holl, *Luther und Calvin;* D. Nauta, "Calvijn en Luther," *Free University Quarterly* 2 (1952), pp. 1–17; E. Mülhaupt, "Luther und Calvin," *Luther,* 1959, p. 113; A. D. R. Polman, "Calvijn en Luther," in *Vier redevoeringen over Calvijn.*

Chapter 12. Luther

1. On the way that Calvin could have become acquainted with Luther's *Small Catechism,* see Moore, *La réforme allemande,* pp. 321–322; P. Wernle, *Der evangelische Glaube nach den Hauptschriften der Reformatoren,* vol. 3: *Calvin,* p. 86; cf. pp. 38, 52, 55, 94, 165. In 1529, Luther's *Small Catechism* was translated into Latin and added to the Latin edition of the *Betbüchlein* published the same year under the title of *Enchiridion piarum precationum cum Calendario et passionali.* Cf. WA 10/II, 343.

2. Walker, *Jean Calvin,* p. 146: "Calvin follows the old order of popular religious instruction that had already served Luther in his *Small Catechism* of 1529. The order adopted is that of the elementary teachings which, for centuries, every Christian child was supposed to learn by heart." Note that recent research shows that it is doubtful that there was a regularly organized religious instruction in northern France at the beginning of the sixteenth century. Cf. J. Toussaert, *Le sentiment*

religieux en Flandre à la fin du Moyen Age, p. 574. However, everything leads us to believe that the school of Capettes at Noyon, where Calvin received his elementary education, used such teachings.

3. *Parvus Catechismus pro pueris in schola . . . ,* Wittenberg, 1529. I quote according to BSLK, pp. 507–527; cf. WA 30/I, 365–368.

4. BSLK 507–509.

5. OS 1, 42, 45, 49, 50 (bis), 52. In the 1539 edition, Calvin abandons this expression.

6. BSLK 509.

7. OS 1, 51.

8. BSLK 510–511.

9. OS 1, 76. Note the significant difference between Luther's singular and Calvin's plural verb. Cf. OS 3, 203, n. 1, and WA 30/I, 294.

10. BSLK 510–512; cf. OS 1, 75–86.

11. Wernle, *Der evangelische Glaube,* vol. 3, p. 81: "From a literary point of view, Calvin's exposition of the Lord's Prayer is most dependent on Martin Bucer, who prepared the way for Calvin in a whole series of points in his commentary on the Gospels."

12. BSLK 512–513.

13. OS 1, 108.

14. BSLK 513; cf. OS 1, 110.

15. BSLK 514; cf. OS 1, 112.

16. BSLK 515. Cf. OS 4, 364, n. 2.

17. OS 1, 115.

18. WA 6, 531.

19. OS 1, 123; cf. OS 1, 124: "some hidden power."

20. WA 6, 531–532.

21. WA 6, 533.

22. OS 1, 123.

23. WA 6, 532.

24. OS 1, 123.

25. OS 1, 132.

26. OS 1, 133.

27. WA 6, 530.

28. WA 6, 512.

29. OS 1, 152.

30. OS 1, 177; cf. WA 6, 546.

31. OS 1, 202; cf. WA 6, 527 and 529.

32. OS 1, 202; cf. WA 6, 527.

33. OS 1, 217; cf. WA 6, 567.

34. OS 1, 218; cf. WA 6, 567–568.

35. OS 1, 221; cf. WA 6, 551.

36. OS 1, 222; cf. WA 6, 557.

37. OS 1, 222–223; cf. WA 6, 553–555.

38. OS 1, 238.

39. WA 6, 508.

40. OS 1, 239 and 250; cf. WA 6, 509.

41. OS 1, 242; cf. WA 6, 536.

42. WA 7, 52–53.
43. OS 1, 61–62.
44. OS 1, 206–207.
45. WA 7, 58.
46. OS 1, 210.
47. WA 7, 56.
48. OS 1, 223.
49. WA 7, 69.
50. WA 7, 60.
51. OS 1, 225.
52. OS 1, 230–231; cf. WA 7, 67.
53. WA 7, 68.
54. OS 1, 233.
55. WA 2, 742–758.
56. WA 19, 482–523.
57. Cf. WA 19, 469.
58. OS 1, 139: "others, that only a sign and figure of the body is set forth"; cf. WA 19, 498 and 503. For "this is," Zwingli reads "this signifies" (CR 90, 795f.).
59. OS 1, 139; cf. WA 2, 749: "his flesh under the bread."
60. OS 1, 139; cf. WA 19, 489.
61. OS 1, 142; cf. WA 2, 749.
62. OS 1, 141; cf. WA 19, 491.
63. WA 19, 511; cf. WA 2, 743–744, 748, and OS 5, 402, n. 1.
64. OS 1, 145. Cf. Augustine, *Sermon* 272 on John 6, PL 38, 1247ff.
65. WA 19, 507; cf. WA 2, 744–747.
66. OS 1, 148.
67. WA 19, 501; cf. WA 2, 742.
68. OS 1, 150.
69. WA 19, 502; cf. WA 2, 751ff.
70. OS 1, 155.
71. WA 19, 505.
72. OS 1, 156.
73. Cf. J. Pannier, "Calvin savait-il l'allemand?" *BHPF* 78 (1929), pp. 344, 476; W. Niesel, "Verstand Calvin deutsch?" *ZKG* 49 (1930), pp. 343ff.
74. On the personal relationship between Calvin and Luther, see the text cited in the *Index historicus,* OC 22, 385–387. Calvin always held the German reformer in high esteem, even when Luther began to disapprove of him. For example, in 1544 he stated: "I have been accustomed to say frequently that, even if he called me a devil, I would offer this honor to him, that I recognize him as a remarkable servant of God. Although he was equipped with extraordinary virtues, he labored under many vices" (OC 11, 774). Note that the two reformers never met. Cf. A. Zahn, "Calvins Urteile über Luther," *Biblische Zeugnisse,* 1928; E. W. Zeeden, "Das Bild Luthers in den Briefen Calvins," *ARG* 49 (1958), pp. 177–195.

Chapter 13. Melanchthon

1. R. Seeberg, *Lehrbuch der Dogmengeschichte,* vol. 4/2, p. 558, found a good expression to characterize the role of humanism in the work of Calvin. "Calvin's

humanist training was not only the candlestick from which the light of the Gospel arose; but the humanist spirit, in spite of Calvin's strong biblicism, blended with the Gospel in a rather harmonious way." Cf. Bohatec, *Budé und Calvin;* Boisset, *Sagesse et sainteté dans la pensée de Calvin.*

2. OC 9, 463. For more details on the relationship between Calvin and Melanchthon, see the references of the *Index historicus* in OC 22, 396–397. Cf. Lang, *Reformation und Gegenwart,* pp. 88–135: "Melanchthon und Calvin"; A. Sperl, *Melanchthon zwischen Humanismus und Reformation.*

3. Moore, *La réforme allemande,* pp. 236–237: "Melanchthon's fame was almost greater than that of Luther himself. Known by the intellectuals and humanists of all countries, he had more relationships with France and French people than did his master. His fame as the *praeceptor Germaniae,* the emulator and successor to Erasmus, brought him to the attention of the French who cultivated and made famous the Renaissance of letters." Then, on Melanchthon's response to the *Determination* of the Sorbonne in 1521, the author notes: "His *Loci Communes* and other Latin works were censured by the Faculty of Theology during the same year."

4. The OC editors: 3, viii; the OS editors: 1, 17. Lang, *Quellen,* p. 106; Moore, *La réforme allemande,* p. 322.

5. Quotations are according to *Die Loci Communes Philipp Melanchthons in ihrer Urgestalt,* edited according to G. L. Plitt by D. Th. Kolde (Leipzig, 1900).

6. LC 117; cf. OS 3, 332, n. 1.

7. OS 1, 41–42.

8. LC 118.

9. OS 1, 47.

10. OS 1, 54.

11. LC 121.

12. OS 1, 54.

13. LC 145.

14. LC 213; cf. OS 3, 339, n. 2.

15. OS 1, 62–63. The context clearly shows that Calvin agrees with these "multi."

16. OS 1, 68–69.

17. OS 1, 70.

18. LC 166 and 168; cf. 170: "the faith of the scholastics," "deadly opinion"; 176: "frigid opinion"; 177: "historical opinion"; 194: "frigid opinion of the Parisians."

19. LC 165.

20. LC 167; cf. 166: "by the affection of the heart."

21. LC 176.

22. LC 168.

23. LC 174–175.

24. LC 224.

25. LC 226.

26. Ibid.

27. OS 1, 118.

28. OS 1, 118–119.

29. OS 1, 125.

30. Ibid.

31. OS 1, 128; cf. LC 231.

32. OS 1, 134–135; cf. LC 233.

33. LC 81.
34. LC 85; cf. OS 3, 238, n. 2.
35. OS 1, 131.
36. OS 1, 178.
37. OS 1, 182.
38. LC 239.
39. OS 1, 178.
40. LC 237–238; cf. OS 4, 94, n. 1.
41. OS 1, 179; cf. LC 236.
42. LC 236.
43. OS 1, 179.
44. Especially compare OS 1, 246–247 with LC 131–136.

Chapter 14. Zwingli

1. OC 10/b, 344–347.
2. OC 11, 24 and 36; cf. 12, 98.
3. OC 11, 438; cf. 9, 51. On Calvin's attitude toward Zwingli, see the passages cited in the *Index historicus* in OC 22, 484. Cf. B. Soós, "Zwingli und Calvin," *Zwingliana* 6 (1937), pp. 306–327; F. Blanke, "Calvins Urteile über Zwingli," *Zwingliana* 11 (1942), pp. 66–92.
4. Seeberg, *Lehrbuch der Dogmengeschichte,* vol. 4/2, pp. 556–557, where he notes: "The usual construction, which tries to establish a close relationship between Calvin and Zwingli, is historically untenable, as is evident both from Calvin's rejection of Zwingli and from his almost boundless acceptance of Luther."
5. Lang, "Quellen," p. 107: "That he did not emerge from the school of Zwingli . . . is certainly acknowledged generally. Yet the French reformer knew Zwingli's *Commentary on True and False Religion* before 1536, and his occasional references to it *are not entirely negative.*" (Emphasis mine.)
6. OS 1, 16: "But the *Institutes* published in 1536 *make it clear* that after he was alienated from Zwingli by reading Luther, he certainly read in the meantime the greatest of Zwingli's theological works, the *Commentary on True and False Religion,* written in 1525" (emphasis mine).
7. Cf. OC 3, viii–ix.
8. Cf. the introduction to the *Commentary* in the Corpus Reformatorum 90, 590–591.
9. OS 1, 31–32; cf. CR 90, 790.
10. CR 90, 901–902.
11. CR 90, 901.
12. CR 90, 900–901.
13. OS 1, 42–43.
14. OS 1, 43–44.
15. OS 1, 44.
16. OS 1, 43.
17. OS 1, 120; cf. CR 90, 761: "For it is faith by which we lean unshakably, firmly, and undistractedly upon the mercy of God, as Paul has it in many passages." This argument serves to prove that the sacraments cannot increase faith.
18. OS 1, 122; cf. OS 1, 127; OS 5, 286, n. 1.

19. CR 90, 758; cf. OS 5, 270, n. 1.
20. CR 90, 759.
21. CR 90, 761.
22. OS 1, 129.
23. CR 90, 765.
24. OS 1, 136; cf. CR 90, 775 and 807.
25. OS 1, 136; cf. CR 90, 775.
26. OS 1, 139; cf. CR 90, 795 and 801.
27. OS 1, 143–144; cf. CR 90, 808–809 and 817.
28. OS 1, 145.
29. CR 90, 807.
30. CR 90, 802.
31. CR 90, 807.
32. OS 1, 147; cf. 146.
33. CR 89, 552–608.
34. CR 89, 574, 583, 585, 592.

35. Cf. G. Kawerau, *Hieronymus Emser;* L. Enders, *Luther und Emser,* nos. 8 and 9 of *Flugschriften aus der Reformationszeit;* E. Iserloh, *Der Kampf um die Messe,* pp. 19–26.

36. CCath 28, 38–93.

37. For the etymology of the word "Mass," see CCath 28, 48–51.

38. CCath 28, 60. In reference to *pro se suisque* of the canon, Zwingli had raised the difficulty of the *Christus, unus semel.* Emser does not reply to this objection but limits himself to giving an interpretation of the preposition *pro.*

39. CCath 28, 74: "We offer a mystical representation of that bloody sacrifice and death of Christ. Therefore we concede to Zwingli that Christ died but once and was but once offered on the cross."

40. CCath 28, 74: "In spite of this perfection or redemption we slip and slip again daily; for this reason we seek again daily the mystery of this offering. Now we do not make an offering of blood, but we participate in the mystery of the offering of Christ's glorious body." Cf. Council of Trent, Denz 1743 (940).

41. CCath 28, 82: "As only Christ could make his offering by dying on the cross, so today only the priests before altars everywhere make an offering *sub mysterio,* in order to fulfill what the Lord said beforehand through Malachi." 28:75: "Just as at the altar an offering is made not so much of Christ as of ourselves, yet both are mystical." Cf. Iserloh, *Der Kampf um die Messe,* p. 21: "In spite of all the attacks by the reformers upon the Mass as our own work, Emser was not influenced by the idea that Christ is the real priest of the sacrifice at the Mass just as he was on the cross."

42. It seems that among the first controversialists only Kaspar Schatzgeyer (1463–1527) arrived at a clear and precise formulation of the identity of the priest, the victim, and the act of offering. Cf. Iserloh, *Der Kampf um die Messe,* p. 59. When Cajetan was later stimulated in his theological reflections by the objections of the evangelicals, he came to the same conclusions. Cf. E. Iserloh, "Der Wert der Messe in der Diskussion der Theologen vom Mittelalter bis zum 16. Jahrhundert," *ZKTh* 83 (1961), pp. 44–79. He cites the *De missae sacrificio et ritu adversus Lutheranos* (1531) by Cajetan (*Opuscula omnia,* Lyon, 1558), fol. 341 b: "unity of the victim" . . . "the immolation, that unique and all-sufficient pouring out of blood

on the cross, continues even now in the Eucharist." "It is said at the first concerning the unity of the priest, that in the New Testament Christ is the only priest, and he himself is the priest at the new altar. Every minister consecrates the body and blood of Christ not in his own person but in the person of Christ, as witness the words of consecration; and in this way they make the offering acting in place of Christ."

43. Cf. CR 90, 590ff.

44. Iserloh, *Der Kampf um die Messe,* p. 21: "In no place in his writings against the Reformation has he represented Catholic teaching in context. That is because of his method. His writings are *refutations,* and indeed in a literal sense they are only reflection of the relevant text of a reformer." (Emphasis mine.)

45. CR 90, 230–287.

46. According to F. Clark, *Eucharistic Sacrifice and the Reformation,* pp. 388ff., Zwingli is wrong, for no Catholic theologian of the time would have recognized as his own such an interpretation of the word "immolation." Clark writes, p. 394: "It was the fertile mind of the Swiss reformer Ulrich Zwingli that elaborated this argument (namely, sacrifice = new slaying) against the Mass." P. 395: "The Catholic apologists answered Zwingli by denying the validity of his principle that sacrifice is offered only when death is inflicted. It was misapplied to the Mass, they insisted, because that was a sacrifice of a special nature—commemorative, mystical, sacramental. Although it was indeed the death of Christ that gave meaning and efficacy to the eucharistic sacrifice, it was not a new death that did so but the one past death never to be repeated." He cites Cajetan for support, *De erroribus contingentibus in sacramento eucharistiae,* cap. 9. We add that it is unfortunate that Zwingli never encountered Cajetan, but only Emser!

47. It is true that Augustine had already applied the term *immolatio* to the Mass, adding each time the necessary clarifications (Ep. 98, 9, PL 33, 363): "Was not Christ sacrificed once for all in himself? And yet in the sacrament . . . he is sacrificed every day for the people." The scholastics only repeat these formulas in general terms and often lose the subtleties, which contributes to misunderstandings. Erasmus' position was as follows: "The sacred teachers of antiquity did not shy away from the term 'sacrifice and immolation.' I acknowledge that Christ died once and does not die again; but that unique Sacrifice is, as it were, renewed daily by the mystical rites, while we repeatedly draw from that inexhaustible fountain our own renewed grace. We sacrifice the victim for the living and the dead, while through the death of the Son we entreat the Father on their behalf" (*De amabili ecclesiae concordia,* Er Op 5, 503 D). Only the theologians of the late sixteenth century and the seventeenth century, such as Bellarmine, Suarez, Lessius, and de Lugo, begin to deviate from the tradition. Clark, *Eucharistic Sacrifice,* p. 440: "Not only Catholic writers (e.g., Renz, Lepin, de la Taille, Gaudel, Diekamp, Arnold, Halmer, Jungmann), . . . but also Protestant historians of dogma, such as Kattenbusch, Scheel, Seeberg, and Wiegand . . . , agree in assigning a post-Tridentine origin to the 'destruction theories' of the Mass, and in acquitting pre-Reformation theology of responsibility for them."

48. OS 1, 153; cf. CR 90, 805: "such a horrible affront to Christ."

49. CR 90, 806.

50. OS 1, 153.

51. Ibid.

52. OS 1, 154.

53. See above, n. 40.
54. CR 90, 805.
55. CR 90, 804–805.
56. OS 1, 155.
57. Ibid. In the *Institutes* of 1543, OC 1, 1086–1087, and up to that of 1560, OC 4, 1110–1111, Calvin persisted in stigmatizing the Roman priests, calling them "butchers, in order to make daily sacrifices."

Chapter 15. Bucer

1. Eells, "Martin Bucer," p. 419, at the end of his analysis of the early documents relating to the relationship between Calvin and Bucer, declares: "The conclusion is unavoidable that Bucer made no direct, personal contribution to the conversion of Calvin and, although Calvin may have read his books, his disagreement with their teaching on the Supper and other subjects indicates that they did not impress him altogether favorably."

2. *Enarrationes perpetuae in sacra quatuor evangelia, recognitae nuper et locis compluribus auctae. In quibus praeterea habes syncerioris Theologiae locos communes supra centum, ad scripturarum fidem simpliciter et nullius cum infectatione tractatos,* per Martinum Bucerum . . . Argentorati apud Georgium Ulricherum Andlanum, mense martio anno MDXXX. The volume is divided into two parts: I: *In evangelion Matthaei enarrationes,* fols. 1–204, completed in *In ev. Marci enarrationes,* fols. 205–213, and in *In ev. Lucae enarrationes,* fols. 213–236; II: *In evangelion Ioannis enarrationes,* new numbering: fols. 3–102. We quote the work according to the lettering EN I and EN II. On the doctrine contained in these commentaries, see A. Lang, *Der Evangelienkommentar Martin Butzers und die Grundzüge seiner Theologie.*

3. Lang, "Quellen," pp. 108–110.
4. Seeberg, *Lehrbuch der Dogmengeschichte,* vol. 4/2, p. 554.
5. J. Courvoisier, *La notion d'église chez Bucer dans son développement historique* (Paris, 1933), p. 136.
6. On the personal relationship between Calvin and Bucer, see the texts indicated by the *Index historicus* in OC 22, 274–276. Cf. W. Pauck, "Calvin und Butzer," *JR* 9 (1929), pp. 237–256; Courvoisier, "Bucer et l'oeuvre de Calvin," pp. 66–77; H. Strohl, "Bucer et Calvin," *BHPF* 87 (1938), pp. 354ff.; A. Wiedeburg, "Die Freundschaft zwischen Butzer und Calvin nach ihren Briefen," *HJ* 83 (1964), pp. 69–83.
7. OS 1, 31.
8. OS 1, 91.
9. EN I, 38b.
10. EN I, 180c and d.
11. EN I, 197c.
12. OS 1, 86.
13. OS 1, 87.
14. OS 1, 85.
15. Ibid.
16. OS 1, 87.
17. OS 1, 86.

18. OS 1, 87.
19. See Seeberg, *Lehrbuch der Dogmengeschichte,* vol. 4/2, p. 554, and Lang, "Quellen," pp. 108–110.
20. EN I, 181d.
21. EN I, 197c; II, 15d.
22. EN II, 20b; cf. EN I, 159a.
23. EN II, 89c, d.
24. EN II, 65a.
25. EN II, 23b.
26. EN I, 138c.
27. EN I, 184c; cf. EN I, 37b, and EN II, 71d.
28. EN II, 44c.
29. EN II, 44b.
30. EN II, 65c.
31. See EN I, 88b, 121d, 122a, b, 146b; EN II, 23a, 30a, 46a, 73d, 76d, 77a.
32. See EN II, 73a.
33. Cf. Ganoczy, *Calvin, théologien,* pp. 192–211.
34. EN I, 62c–67c. Cf. Wernle, *Der evangelische Glaube,* vol. 3, p. 81.
35. OS 1, 96; cf. EN I, 63b, c.
36. OS 1, 98; cf. EN I, 63d: "to pray in faith."
37. OS 1, 99; cf. EN I, 63d: "through Christ."
38. OS 1, 99.
39. EN I, 64a.
40. OS 1, 100; cf. EN I, 64a.
41. EN I, 62d.
42. OS 1, 101.
43. OS 1, 102; cf. EN I, 63b: "pray without ceasing."
44. EN I, 63b.
45. OS 1, 102.
46. EN I, 63c, d.
47. Ibid.
48. EN I, 63b; cf. OS 4, 339, n. 3.
49. OS 1, 102.
50. Ibid.
51. OS 1, 103.
52. Ibid.
53. EN I, 63a.
54. OS 1, 104.
55. OS 1, 105; cf. EN I, 64a.
56. EN I, 64a, b.
57. OS 1, 106.
58. OS 1, 105 and 108; cf. EN I, 64b.
59. EN I, 184c; cf. 37b, 44c: "to the elect, that is, to those given the Spirit of God," 122b.
60. EN I, 122a, b; cf. II, 23a: "He blinds and hardens the reprobate to whatever extent this Spirit leads," 73d, etc.
61. EN I, 64c, d.
62. OS 1, 109.

63. OS 1, 111 and 112; cf. EN I, 65b, c, d.

64. OS 1, 115; cf. EN I, 67c.

65. EN I, 23a.

66. EN I, 138c.

67. Ibid. Cf. Lefèvre d'Etaples, *Comm. in Matth.* 16, no. 158, fol. 74v: "Let no one say that Peter is the rock on which the Church is built. . . . Nor did Peter alone accept them [the keys] from the Lord, but also all the others who in faith have built up the Church upon Christ, according to the will of Christ the Lord. And the keys of the kingdom of heaven are to be understood as the doctrine of faith, the doctrine of Christ, and the Word of God."

68. EN I, 138d.

69. Ibid.

70. There is already an allusion to this in EN I, 23a, where he notes that there exist two kinds of "public admission into the Church," one at the time of baptism and the other at the restoration from excommunication.

71. EN I, 149c.

72. EN I, 149a.

73. EN I, 149b.

74. EN I, 75c.

75. EN I, 75b.

76. EN I, 23a.

77. EN II, 13a.

78. OS 1, 185.

79. OS 1, 186.

80. OS 1, 187; cf. ibid., below: "Christ makes it sufficiently clear that he speaks of all Christian *congregations,* as *churches* are able to be constituted in specific places and provinces. 'Wherever,' he says, 'two or three have gathered in my name, there am I in the midst of them.' " Bucer cites these same words of Jesus in relation to the right of excommunication, which can be legitimately exercised even by a small group of the faithful. Cf. EN I, 148d.

81. OS 1, 187.

82. Ibid.

83. OS 1, 188.

84. OS 1, 187.

Chapter 16. Scholastic Theology

1. According to my calculations there are 69 explicit or implicit quotes from these two sources in the 1536 *Institutes.*

2. OS 1, 30, 130, 150, 152.

3. PL 187: 46, 48, 115, 117, 133, 134, 136, 137, 141ff., 442, 447, 448, 884, 1392, 1397f., 1442f., 1469, 1520, 1532 (3 times), 1544, 1549, 1594, 1598, 1661ff., 1736ff., 1791, 1855.

4. PL 192: 841, 855f., 866f., 868, 877f., 879, 880f., 882, 885f., 887, 889, 892ff., 898, 899, 900, 901f., 903, 904, 905, 908, 909f., 918f., 922f., 931, 937f.

5. For example, OS 1, 175, where this expression introduces a quote from Lombard.

6. For example, OS 1, 172, where this expression is followed by a quotation from Lombard and from Gratian.

7. OS 1, 206.

8. Renaudet, *Préréforme,* p. 27.

9. OS 1, 199.

10. Smits, *Saint Augustin dans l'oeuvre de Calvin,* vol. 1, p. 206: "He must have studied the *Decretum Gratiani* in his legal studies at Orléans and Bourges, because this code was even followed on certain questions in the civil domain such as marriage." Cf. M. Reulos, "Le décret de Gratien chez les humanistes, les Gallicans et les réformés français au XVIe siècle," *StG,* vol. 2 (1954).

11. OS 1, 180; cf. 1, 213.

12. Named without any reference in OS 1, 181 and 206.

13. Cf. OS 1, 211.

14. Named without any reference in OS 1, 206.

15. Quoted according to the *Decretum Gratiani,* OS 1, 206 and 210.

16. OS 1, 178; cf. 1, 150.

17. The editors of the OS believe they see allusions to Thomas Aquinas in 1, 128, 131, 181, 194, 195 and to Scotus in 1, 123 and to Alexander of Hales in 1, 130, 181. In my view, these allusions cannot be proven.

18. OS 1, 30 cites *Decr. Grat.,* Pars I, Dist. VIII, can. 3 and 9; cf. PL 187, 46 and 48.

19. OS 1, 210 cites *Decr. Grat.,* Pars I, Dist. XCIII, can. 25, and Dist. XCV, can. 5; cf. PL 187, 442, 448.

20. OS 1, 197 alludes to *Decr. Grat.,* Pars II, Dist. I, can. 1; cf. PL 187, 1520.

21. The quote in OS 1, 210 is introduced by this expression: "But the reasoning [of the scholastics] is exceedingly weak, and clearly does not require a lengthy refutation. Indeed, they acknowledge this from their own writings."

22. In citing the *Decretals,* I indicate respectively the page from OS 1, and then in parentheses the column of PL 187. Of those which give the sense of a passage, 11 are exact: 30 (46 and 48), 168 (447), 192 (1549), 202 (1520), 206 (two times), 210 and 216 (115), 210 (442 and 448), 222 (1397f.), 222 (1469); 4 are distorted or have a different emphasis: 192 (1532), 206 (136), 207 (115), 211 (117). Of those which quote the passage, 5 are exact: 173 (1594), 173 (two times) (1532), 192 (1544), 208 (137); 1 is inappropriate: 206 (884); 3 are distorted: 166 and 167 (1855), 210 (141ff.).

23. In citing quotations from the *Sentences,* I indicate the page from OS 1 and the column from PL 192. Of those references which give the sense of a passage, 6 are exact: 180 (880ff.), 180 (885ff.), 192 (887f.), 206 (900), 222 (909f.); 4 are distorted or have a different emphasis: 205 (900), 209 (904), 211 (905), 222 (908f.) (uncertain meaning). Of those which quote the passage, 6 are exact: 167 (885), 173 (two times) (868), 200 (898ff.), 202 (868), 216 (904); 2 are distorted: 207 (900), 210 (904).

24. On the way in which Calvin treats the texts that he quotes, see Smits, *Saint Augustin dans l'oeuvre de Calvin,* vol. 1, pp. 244–248, where Smits refers to modifications by exaggerating, condensing, or summarizing. Cf. J. Owen, *Commentaries on the Twelve Minor Prophets by John Calvin,* vol. 1, p. ix: "In making quotations from Scripture, the author seems to have followed no version, but to have made one of his own; and they are often given paraphrastically, the meaning rather than the words being regarded." OC 6, 325, *Defensio doctrinae de servitute humani arbitrii*

(1543): Calvin replies to the accusation of changing the texts: "Do I not quote faithfully? Do I deliberately disregard those which contradict me . . . ? I can always amass very many from whatever sources . . . by little effort."

25. OS 1, 209–210.

26. PL 187, 143, *Decr. Grat.*, Pars I, Dist. XXV, c. 1: "It pertains to the presbyter to prepare the sacrament of the body and blood of the Lord on the altar, to say prayers and to bless the gifts of God." PL 92, 904, *Sent.*, Lib. IV, dist. XXIV, c. 9: "It pertains to the presbyter to prepare the sacrament of the body and blood of the Lord on the altar, to say prayers and to bless the gifts of God."

27. PL 187, 1855, *Decr. Grat.*, Pars III, De cons., dist. V, c. 1, entitled: "After baptism, the sacrament of confirmation is next in importance. Likewise *Pope Urban* [which one?] to all Christians, ep. I, c. 7."

28. Ibid., 1857–1858, c. 6, entitled: "Let only the humble come to confirmation. Likewise from *Concilio Aurelianensi*, c. 3."

29. OS 1, 166.

30. OS 1, 166–167: "anointed by holy oil, all complete their Christian responsibilities; or rather, they, who were not yet Christians, become such."

31. PL 187, 1855–1856, *Decr. Grat.*, Pars III, De cons., dist. V, c. 2, entitled: "What the Holy Spirit confers in baptism, He confers in confirmation. Likewise, *Pope Melchiades* in *ep. ad Episc. Hisp.*, c. 2."

32. OS 1, 166.

33. PL 187, 1856–1857, *Decr. Grat.*, Pars III, De cons., dist. V, c. 3, entitled by Gratian (improperly, in my view): "The sacrament of the laying on of hands is more worthy than the sacrament of baptism."

34. OS 1, 167.

35. OS 1, 192; cf. PL 187, 1532.

36. OS 1, 209.

37. PL 192, 904, *Sent.*, Lib. IV, dist. XXIV, c. 9.

38. OS 1, 206–207; cf. PL 187, 115 (dist. XXI, c. 1), 884 (causa XII, Q. I, c. 7) and PL 192, 900 (IV, dist. XXIV, cc. 1 and 2).

39. *For Gratian:* OS 1, 173, on satisfactions, cf. WA 6, 529 and 544, and PL 187, 1594; OS 1, 292, on the "second plank," cf. WA 6, 527 and 529, and PL 187, 1520; OS 1, 206–207, on the clergy, cf. WA 6, 563–564 (cf. WA 7, 58), and PL 187, 884; OS 1, 222, on the marriage of priests and canon law concerning marriage, cf. WA 6, 553, 555, 557, and PL 187, 1397f. *For Lombard:* OS 1, 173, on satisfaction, cf. WA 6, 529 and 544, and PL 192, 868; OS 1, 200, on the sacramental nature of penance, cf. WA 6, 530 (Luther's explicit reference to Lombard!), cf. PL 192, 898ff.; OS 1, 202, 207, on the clergy, cf. WA 6, 563–564, and PL 192, 900; OS 1, 222, on marriage, cf. WA 6, 553, 555, 557, and PL 192, 908, 909f., 931.

40. See pp. 59–62 of our study.

41. Wendel, *Calvin, sources et évolution*, p. 6; cf. p. 92: "It has been proven that he had studied the works of Anselm, Peter Lombard, and Thomas Aquinas. . . . But the instruction at Montaigu was strictly nominalist in its perspective, and because of this Calvin came into contact with the principal representatives of the Franciscan school, especially with Duns Scotus and Ockham, or at least with their disciples." Smits, *Saint Augustin dans l'oeuvre de Calvin*, vol. 1, p. 14: "In the upper level courses, John Major gave an Ockhamist commentary on the *Sentences* of Peter Lombard. *Calvin attended these courses* and thus had a new opportunity to have at

least indirect acquaintance with St. Augustine, since the writings of the African bishop and doctor constituted a significant portion of the *Sentences."* Cf. p. 206. (Emphasis mine.)

42. Dankbaar, *Calvin, sein Weg und sein Werk,* p. 5, notes that Calvin had unpleasant memories of the scholasticism represented by Noël Bédier, and then adds: "However, clearly opposed to this is the fact that he also was taught by the Scottish scholar, who familiarized him with medieval philosophy and the Church Fathers."

43. Ibid., p. 26: "It should also be noted that he acquired his very extensive theological knowledge *for the most part through self-study.* Apart from his readings in some works of the scholastics and Church Fathers, he *in fact neither* attended theological lectures *nor* attained an academic degree in that faculty." (Emphasis mine.)

44. Reuter, *Grundverständnis,* pp. 11, 14, 31, 37, etc.

45. Ibid., p. 21: "By the spring of 1528, Major had been Calvin's teacher for three years. He imparted to Calvin a new conception of anti-Pelagian and Scotist theology and a renewed Augustinianism." P. 36: "He had been guided, *without Lutheran influence,* through the school of John Major into an Augustinianism, which he himself developed more decisively" (emphasis mine).

46. Ibid., p. 37. "Major . . . Buridan. . . . Both men taught Ockhamist Terminism."

47. Ibid., pp. 21, 26, 36, 47, 158, 159, 180.

48. Ibid., p. 47: "He accepted the metaphysics of the late Medieval Scotist, Augustinian, and anti-Pelagian doctrine of God." Cf. pp. 144, 147.

49. Ibid., p. 49: "the Aristotelian [ethics] which, as a student of Coronel and Major, he must have absorbed."

50. Ibid., p. 158: "Calvin was indebted to the study of Thomas Bradwardine for the essential, fundamental understanding of his doctrine of providence."

51. Ibid., pp. 148ff., 180, 202. In these two last pages, the author states that it is from Major and from Gregory of Rimini—and *"independent of Luther"!*—that Calvin had received the "basic features of his doctrine of sin."

52. Ibid., pp. 129, 147.

53. Ibid., pp. 32, 35–36.

54. Ibid., pp. 67–68.

55. Reuter's references from the *Institutes* come almost exclusively from the last Latin edition (1559).

56. Published in Lyon in 1513, there is a copy at the National Library, Res. D 2035.

57. Published in Paris in 1512, there is a copy at the National Library, Res. D 2031.

58. Folios XXX and LXII treat the following questions: the real presence, transubstantiation, the adoration of the eucharistic elements, the obligation to celebrate the Mass and to recite the breviary, communion in both kinds observed by the heretics and the schismatics; but there is not a word, for instance, of the doctrine of the eucharistic sacrifice.

59. Here are some typical questions that are raised and "resolved": May a priest whose tongue has been cut off consecrate the elements (part VIII, q. 1)? Should one be allowed to take communion after a nocturnal emission (part IX, q. 1)? What is

the color of Christ's body (part X, q. 1)? Should one adore the body of Christ in the stomach of the communicant (part XI, q. 2)? Is it enough for a priest to celebrate only one Mass a day (part XII, q. 2)? (Response: yes, "because Christ suffered once"!)

60. Edited in Paris in 1521, there is a copy at the National Library, Res. D 2033.

61. National Library, Res. A 1188.

62. *In Matth.*, fol. XXVI va and vb.

63. Ibid., fols. LXVIII va–LXXII vb.

64. Ibid., fol. LXX vb.

65. Ibid., fol. LXXI vb.

66. Ibid., fol. LXIX ra; cf. IC (1543 and 1559) IV. 6. 4, OS 5, 92–93.

67. OC 2, 815. We should note that the similarity of these ideas does not prove any direct connection because it is a paraphrase from an Augustinian text that Calvin may well have taken from somewhere other than from Major.

Chapter 17. Calvin and Humanist Thought

1. Cf. Boisset, *Sagesse et sainteté dans la pensée de Calvin*, p. 248.

2. Er Op 5, *Novum Testamentum.* See Phil. 3:11; Heb. 10: 27; Rom. 8:1; 1 Cor. 15:56; and esp. 2 Cor. 5:1ff. in this version and in the *Psychopannychia* where they are quoted, respectively, in OC 5, 191, 213, 206, 206, 195.

3. *S. Paulus Epistolae XIV, Commentarius Jac. Fabri* (Paris, 1515): Rom. 8:10; cf. OC 5, 194.

4. Calvin seems to be very careful to find the Latin word that substantially gives the meaning of the original and effectively fits into the context of his own discourse. For example, OC 5, 196; for Phil. 3:20 he writes: "But our *dwelling place and state* is in heaven," while the Vulgate and Erasmus have "conversation" and Lefèvre "republic." In the same way, OC 5, 218, for Heb. 11:15: *"power* to return"; the Vulgate: "time"; Erasmus: "opportunity."

5. Augustine, *De doctrina christiana,* cap. 26 and 28, PL 34, 79–80: "Obscure [passages] are to be explained by the more obvious passages." "An uncertain passage is more likely to be explained accurately through other passages of Scripture than through reason."

6. Er Op 5, 131 B: "This is the best method of interpreting Scripture, not only according to Origen but also Augustine. If we make an obscure passage clear by comparison with other passages, then one mystical passage explains another, and one sacred passage explains another."

7. *Comm. in ep. cath.* (Basle, 1527), on 1 Peter 3, no. 26, fol. 30r: "If the understanding of the divine is to be rendered, nothing other than the divine can be used; so that when at times some word of God, that is, a specific term, is unclear to us, it is expressed very well, distinctly, and clearly through some other word of God."

8. OS 1, 103–104: 1 Cor. 14:16.

9. OS 1, 23: Rom. 16:6: "analogy of faith."

10. *Erasmus* on the monks: Er Op 4, 471ff., on the cult of the saints: 5, 501 A, D, F and 504 D, on superstitions: 5, 32 F–33 A, 34 D, 36 A, on indulgences: 4, 444 A and 482 E, on private Masses: 5, 503 A, on scholastic theologians: 4, 406 C, 461 C, 463 B, C, 464 C, 465 C–466 A, 469 A, 495 A, B, C, 5, 127 E, 136 F. Cf. M.

Schulze, *Calvins Jenseits-Christentum in seinem Verhältnisse zu den religiösen Schriften des Erasmus untersucht;* Léonard, *La Réformation,* pp. 26–28; cf. p. 124. *Lefèvre d'Etaples* on the primacy of the Scriptures: *Comm. init. in quatuor evang.,* preface, fol. a 2v; *Comm. in Matth.,* no. 10, fol. 16r; *Comm. in Iudae ep.,* no. 5, fol. 72v; on justification by faith: *Comm. in Rom. 3:1ff.,* nos. 25–28, fols. 71r–71v; *in Rom. 4, 1ff.,* nos. 29–37, fols. 73r–74v. On the differences between Lefèvre and Calvin, see H. Dörries, "Calvin und Lefèvre," *ZKG* 44 (1925), pp. 544–581.

11. Mann, *Erasme et les débuts de la réforme francaise,* p. 167: "It seems that Calvin has passed through each stage: formed by the humanism of Erasmus, he stopped awhile to savor the evangelicalism of Lefèvre before finding the road he was to follow all his life."

12. Cf. OC 6, 593–614, *Excuse à Messieurs les Nicodémites* (1544); OC 8, 6–84, *De scandalis* (1550) and the analysis given by Bohatec, *Budé und Calvin,* pp. 119–239.

13. For the influence of humanism on Calvin, see also K. Spies, *Der Gottesbegriff des J. Faber Stapulensis* (Marburg, 1930); D. Nauta, "Calvijn en Erasmus," *Alm. van het studentencorps an de Vr. Univ. Amsterdam,* 1937; B. Hall, *John Calvin, Humanist and Theologian* (London, 1956).

Chapter 18. The Dialectical Structure of Calvin's Thought

1. P. 175.

2. See Ganoczy, *Calvin, théologien,* pp. 87–94.

3. Ibid., pp. 110ff.

4. At the present time there is a considerable movement among Protestant theologians to interpret the word "sacramental" in the Catholic sense of the word. For example, P. Tillich, "Die bleibende Bedeutung der katholischen Kirche für den Protestantismus," *ThLZ* 9 (1962), cols. 643–644, writes: "Protestantism is the prophetic protest against the sacramental interpretation of the Gospel." Then: "But Protestantism must agree to the necessity for a new appreciation of the sacramental basis of the Church as it was always maintained in the entire Catholic tradition."

Chapter 19. The Major Constructive Principles of Calvin's Thought

1. OS 1, 110: "It is proper to hold only the glory of God before our eyes." We note that Lefèvre already insisted strongly on glorifying God. In his *Comm. in Rom.* 3, 21–26, no. 26, fol. 71r and v, he declares, for example: "And men ought to ascribe *glory to God alone.*"

2. See, e.g., OS 1, 101, 105, 108, 121, 145. Cf. O. Ritschl, *Dogmengeschichte des Protestantismus,* vol. 3, pp. 169, 178; U. Schmidt, "Calvins Bezeugung der Ehre Gottes," in *Festgabe für A. Schlatter.*

3. Cf. R. T. L. Liston, *John Calvin's Doctrine of the Sovereignty of God,* thesis, Edinburgh, 1930.

4. Cf. Beyerhaus, *Studien zur Staatsanschauung Calvins,* pp. 148ff.; Bohatec, *Budé und Calvin,* p. 326: "Calvin now applies . . . the categories taken from law and politics to God and his relationship to men. . . . More significant is the fact that he sees the true monarch in God the sovereign." See also pp. 327, 341, 345; Reuter, *Grundverständnis,* pp. 61–62.

5. OS 1, 37; cf. Er Op 5, *Handbook of the Christian Soldier,* 10 F: "Christ is our Commander"; 13 E: "He is our King because of the eternal law divinely engraved by him"; 46 E: "Christ is your Commander."

6. OS 1, 109, the passage on "Thy kingdom come."

7. OS 1, 161, the passage on the Eucharist.

8. OS 1, 109; cf. 108.

9. OS 1, 37.

10. OS 1, 23.

11. OS 1, 42.

12. Ibid.

13. OS 1, 108.

14. Ibid.

15. OS 1, 45; cf. 108.

16. OS 1, 23; cf. OS 1, 463: a beautiful passage from the *Reply to Sadolet* on the priority of the glory of God over the personal salvation of man.

17. OS 1, 78–82. On the phrase "Christ alone" in Luther, see, e.g., WA 1, 340; 6, 667; 33, 157; 39/I, 8: "We are nothing, Christ alone is everything." On the phrase "the only mediator": WA 10/III, 203; 11, 415; etc. Cf. H. Schroten, *Christus, de Middelaar bij Calvijn;* J. F. Jansen, *Calvin's Doctrine of the Work of Christ;* W. Niesel, *Die Theologie Calvins,* pp. 108–116.

18. The systematic Christ-centered approach to all issues is not original with Calvin. The theologians influenced by the *devotio moderna,* especially Erasmus, Lefèvre, and Luther, adopted it before him. Cf. Léonard, *La Réformation,* p. 124.

19. OS 1, 77–85.

20. OS 1, 41.

21. OS 1, 63. Cf. P. Jacobs, *Prädestination und Verantwortlichkeit bei Calvin,* p. 77: "Christ is election itself"; H. Otten, *Calvins theologische Anschauung von der Prädestination.*

22. OS 1, 126.

23. OS 1, 137.

24. OS 1, 145: "Our faith . . . has acknowledged that the death of Christ is our life."

25. OS 1, 126.

26. OS 1, 82.

27. Ibid.

28. OS 1, 84.

29. OS 1, 193.

30. OS 1, 99–100.

31. OS 1, 99.

32. OS 1, 240–241; cf. 23.

33. OS 1, 20; cf. 31: "The Church of Christ has indeed lived and shall live, as long as Christ shall reign at the right hand of the Father."

34. OS 1, 92; cf. 86ff. and 137: "those joined . . . with him."

35. OS 1, 88.

36. OS 1, 63.

37. OS 1, 84–85.

38. OS 1, 160.

39. Lefèvre, *Comm. init. in quatuor evang.,* preface, fol. a 2v: "The Word of God

is sufficient. It alone is enough for finding the life that knows no end. This one rule is the teacher of life eternal. Any others that are not illumined by the Word of God are not just unnecessary but altogether superfluous." Luther, WA 10/II, 215: "The Word of God is above all things. Here I stand, here I sit, here I glory, here I triumph." WA 6, 561: "The Word of God is incomparably greater than the Church." Cf. J. A. Cramer, *De heilige Schrift bij Calvijn*; R. S. Wallace, *Calvin's Doctrine of the Word and Sacrament;* Niesel, *Die Theologie Calvins,* pp. 23–38.

40. OS 1, 240–241; cf. 23: "Moreover, he is deceived who expects lasting prosperity in that kingdom which is not ruled by the scepter of God, that is, his holy Word."

41. OS 1, 30.

42. OS 1, 233–234.

43. OS 1, 25: "They prove none of these things from the Word of God."

44. Cf. OS 1, 250.

45. OS 1, 163.

46. OS 1, 153.

47. OS 1, 154.

48. OS 1, 153: "this most powerful ax, the Word."

49. OS 1, 187.

50. OS 1, 234. Lefèvre, *Comm. in Matth.* 16, no. 158, fol. 74v: "Even the keys of the kingdom of heaven are to be understood as the doctrine of faith, the doctrine of Christ, and the Word of God."

51. OS 1, 162: "But we shall remember that God holds obedience to his Word of such value that he wants us to judge his angels and the whole world in accord with it."

52. OS 1, 241: "What other than their own obstinacy do they declare when, after such prohibitions, they boast nevertheless that the additions and contaminations from their own [version of the] Word of God provide a handle on it? . . . There is nothing complicated in those words, nothing obscure, nothing ambiguous, and therefore it is forbidden by the universal Church to add to the Word of God or to take anything away from it." Lefèvre, *Comm. in Iudae ep.,* no. 5, fol. 72v: "The new law, the evangelical law, has been handed down once for all by Christ. . . . There was nothing to be added, nor to be subtracted, nor in any way altered." Luther, WA 6, 551: "Such means and human customs they brought into the Scriptures, transforming them in their dreams, fashioning whatever they wanted out of whatever they wanted." 561: "For the Word of God is above the Church. . . . In it there is no establishing, arranging, or creating; but only being established, arranged, or created, as in the creation."

53. OS 1, 237; cf. 236: "Hear him. . . . For it is as if he had established us for this one alone, having led us away from the teachings of all men, and had enjoined upon us to seek from him alone all doctrine of salvation, to depend upon him alone, and finally to cling to him alone, and to listen to him alone, because his words ring out."

Chapter 20. Critique and Ideal of Piety

1. OS 1, 285: "It must be explained in a few words of what sort is that unique knowledge of God which is instilled only in the hearts of the faithful, and of what sort is that affection of piety which follows."

2. OS 3, 35: "I call 'piety' a sense of reverence joined with the love of God which is brought about by the knowledge of his blessing."

3. We cannot accept the opinion of Sprenger (*Das Rätsel,* p. 68), who affirms that piety, for Calvin, is a condition anterior to the knowledge of God, "a condition and presupposition of the knowledge of God," for OS 1, 285 (cited above, n. 1) says clearly that it is piety which derives *(consequitur)* from the knowledge of God and not vice versa. Incidentally, the text that Sprenger cites for support, OS 3, 34, 9, does not contain the notion of an anterior condition but rather the idea of manifesting the knowledge of God. Here is the text: "For we shall say that God, properly speaking, is not known where there is no religion or piety." According to the French version of 1560, OC 3, 43: "For to speak rightly we shall not say that God is known where there is no religion or piety."

4. On the problem of indulgences, see the measures taken in 1563 by the Council of Trent against the abuses and the institution of the *quaestores:* Mansi 33, 193ff. and Denz 1820 (983), 1835 (989); Lortz, *GK,* vol. 2, p. 35: "A strong tendency toward the idea of merit and an unhealthy increase in the number of spiritual indulgences allowed." Toussaert, *Le sentiment religieux en Flandre,* pp. 118, 131, 149 and passim; G. LeBras, *Introduction à l'histoire de la pratique religieuse en France;* Imbart de la Tour, *L'Eglise catholique,* p. 266, emphasizes the "positive" aspect of the preaching of indulgences: "In the storm which lasted for more than half a century, in which everything had been destroyed, the Church had recourse to the great concept of works of satisfaction as the only way of once again benefiting the people." Nevertheless, he adds, pp. 266–267: "But it is precisely the success that created the abuse; and, justly so, protests arose against both the multiplicity of pardons or collections and against the abuses by the collectors." Finally, pp. 267ff., he quotes a series of contemporary documents that illustrate the abuses. Luther formulated his protest in theological terms chiefly in his *Resolutiones disputationum de indulgentiarum virtute* (1518), WA 1, 525–628, and in his *De Captivitate* (1520), WA 6, 521: "It is an impious error . . . to use the Mass to achieve remission of and make satisfaction for our sins." 527: "Those burdens of atonements, pilgrimages, indulgences, and orders are infinite"; 530: "going mad in their wretched souls by their contritions, anxious confessions, . . . satisfactions, works"; cf. 548.

5. OS 1, 57–58.

6. OS 1, 200; Lefèvre admitted, with some reservations, the existence of purgatory. *Comm. in Luc.* 12, no. 120, fol. 238r: "If someone can satisfy divine justice by undergoing punishments, there must be a place of expiation"; *in Luc.* 16, no. 141, fol. 250v: "From this passage one must concede that among the dead there is a place of expiation, which not a few call purgatory."

7. OS 1, 192.

8. OS 1, 199. Luther, WA 5, 319: "justifiers."

9. OS 1, 189. The use of the ironic diminutive ("little bull bearers," "a few trifling coins") is quite typical of Erasmus.

10. OS 1, 190.

11. OS 1, 192.

12. OS 1, 58. This entire passage is very Lutheran. Cf. WA 1, 606: "None of the saints in this life have sufficiently fulfilled the commands of God; therefore they have not at all done anything in superabundance. . . . When you have done what

has been written, say, 'We are useless servants.' . . . Every saint is a debtor in loving God." See also pp. 607–614.

13. Cf. the reactions of the provincial synod of Sens (1528), Mansi 32, 1190, and of the Council of Trent (1563), Mansi 33, 171 A and Denz 1825 (988), against superstitions; N. de Clemanges, *De novis festivitatibus non instituendis, Opera* (Leiden, 1613), p. 143; Huizinga, *Herbst des Mittelalters,* pp. 161ff.: the day of the Innocents (28 Dec.), the abuse of blessed water, numerous practices which, according to Gerson, come "merely from man's imagination and melancholy fancy"; p. 166: a mixture of the erotic and the religious; Febvre, *Le problème de l'incroyance au XVIe siècle,* pp. 478ff.: prayers to heal the sick, doctors believing in demons, belief in good and evil spirits, treatises on occultism; Toussaert, *Le sentiment religieux en Flandre,* pp. 102ff.: the magical use of the oil of baptism and confirmation; p. 200: the ministration of the consecrated host to sick animals, etc. On the superstitions relating to relics, see Calvin's *Traité des reliques* (1543): OC 409–452.

14. Cf. J. Gerson, *Contra superstitiosam dierum observationem praesertim Innocentium, Opera,* vol. 1, col. 608–612; idem, *De erroribus circa artem magicam,* ibid., col. 617–628.

15. Sprenger, *Das Rätsel,* p. 80, notes that Louis de Berquin, who was burned alive in 1529, had published a work entitled *Débat de piété et de superstition.*

16. OS 3, 105: "It seems to me to be called a superstition because it is not content with rational method and order, but amasses a pointless collection of unsubstantial things"; "from that it is clear how pure religion differs from superstition." We note that already in his *De Clementia,* Calvin is occupied with this problem. OC 5, 155: "Cicero in the second book *On the Nature of the Gods* says that not just the philosophers but our ancestors of old made a distinction between superstition and religion. . . . Those who diligently revise and as it were traverse again all things relevant to the worship of the gods are called religious." Cf. the analysis of Calvin's conception of *superstitio* by Sprenger, *Das Rätsel,* pp. 41–44.

17. OS 1, 161.

18. OS 1, 254.

19. OS 1, 253.

20. OS 1, 256.

21. OS 1, 226.

22. OS 1, 227.

23. Cf. Huizinga, *Herbst des Mittelalters,* p. 159: "And even if theology tries to make a sharp distinction between the sacraments and the sacramentals, what means is there to keep the people from basing their faith and hope on all the magical and flashy elements?"

24. This idea of "religion" underlies all of the first *Institutes.* Calvin will define it in 1559 by recourse to Cicero's explanation of the word as contemplation or restraint *(relegere)* rather than "bond" or "connection" *(religare);* OS 3, 105: "I rather think that this word is opposed to a wandering, unrestrained freedom, because most people in the world seize whatever comes their way, indeed rushing around here and there. But piety, to continue at a steady pace, restrains itself within its own limits." We note the significant reference to "piety." This fundamental virtue appears as the "basis" of all religion.

25. OS 1, 48.

26. OS 1, 45.

27. OS 1, 99: "Concerning the saints who have died and now live in Christ, let us not imagine for them any other way of seeking than Christ."

28. Cf. BL 1, 233: The French text has "sorcery" for "incantations."

29. We recognize that during Calvin's time many superstitions centered around the Mass. See J. Altensteig, *Vocabularius Theologiae,* art. *"Missa,"* fol. CLII va: "Moreover, it is superstitious, frivolous, imprudent, and vain—indeed, harmful—to assert that someone will acquire such and such temporal things through attending Mass, as Gerson writes." *Acta Concilii Tridentini* (ed. Freiburg im Breisgau, 1902), pp. 73ff., 916ff.; J. B. Thiers, *Traité des superstitions qui regardent les sacrements,* vol. 2, pp. 350–358; A. Franz, *Die Messe im deutschen Mittelalter,* see pp. 297–308 for the reactions of Gerson, Nicolas of Cusa, Biel, Tauler, etc.; Huizinga, *Herbst des Mittelalters,* pp. 161–163; on the day when one attends Mass, he will not grow older; a rushing sound at the moment of elevation; the expectation of actually seeing God; Clark, *Eucharistic Sacrifice,* pp. 56–68; Toussaert, *Le sentiment religieux en Flandre,* pp. 150–158: Masses "for escaping mortality" with "certain results," "dry masses" without consecration, the elevation of relics in place of the host, Masses for success in hunting, etc. P. 157: "The Mass has become a talisman. . . . This is far from supernatural faith in redemption, but is rather reliance upon a series of devotional exercises."

30. OS 1, 161. Luther also sees an incidence of superstition in the custom of pronouncing the words of consecration in a low voice; see WA 6, 516: "We revere these things with superstition more than we believe them." On the theory of the "fruits of the Mass," ibid., 519: "the little fruits of the Mass, which some superstitiously contrive."

31. OS 1, 289–328, *On Fleeing the Illicit Rites of the Wicked* (1537).

32. Consequently, we cannot accept Sprenger's statement that the Mass did not appear to be superstitious to young Calvin as he progressed in his understanding of the Gospel and that Calvin did not feel hypocritical in continuing to attend Mass. Sprenger, *Das Rätsel,* p. 45: "Whenever Calvin speaks of superstitions, one should always think in the first place of sins against the first and second commandments; that is, when a statement concerns the papacy, the issue is venerating the saints and worshiping images. Therefore a phrase like 'superstitions of the papacy' does not prompt us to think of the Mass!" Let us add that the author arrives at this conclusion after analyzing only one chapter on the Mass in the 1559 *Institutes.*

33. Cf. G. G. Coulton, *Art and the Reformation;* H. von Campenhausen, "Die Bilderfrage in der Reformation," *ZKG,* 1957, pp. 96–128. Huizinga, *Herbst des Mittelalters,* p. 158, rightfully underlines the danger inherent in excessive worship of images. "Through this propensity for images, everything holy is continually exposed to the danger of becoming rigid and superficial." P. 164: examples of abuse: a beer stein in the form of the Virgin; statues of the Virgin with the symbol of the Trinity on its stomach; etc. P. 174: "The one picture is as realistic and awe-inspiring as the other, and the fact that one is to pray to God and merely honor the saints is not taught by the picture itself. The Church in its teaching must constantly warn about this distinction."

34. See pp. 151–153 of our study.

35. OS 1, 42–44. Erasmus, *De amabili ecclesiae concordia* (1533), Er Op 5, 501 D, already argued that the Church authorize only those images with a biblical theme: "As it was decreed in the African Council, let nothing be proclaimed in the

sanctuaries except the canonical Scriptures; thus, let it be agreed that there be no pictures, unless support for it be contained in the canonical Scriptures." Cf. provincial synod of Sens (1523), Mansi 32, 1200: "because of lewd images inappropriate to the truth of Scripture."

36. Cf. Erasmus, Er Op 5, 501 A: "Superstition, which I confess is rampant in invoking the gods, should be refuted." Lefèvre, *Comm. in Ioh.* 12, no. 94, fol. 352r, invites us to place all our "confidence" in "Christ alone" and to ask of him rather than those saints, as if he would accept the support of the prayers and supplications of his saints on our behalf"; *in Ioh.* 2, no. 18, fol. 292r: "All prayers . . . ought to be poured out, not to any creature, but to the only Son and God"; *in Marc.* 16, no. 104, fol. 181r: "not to venerate so much the instruments of God . . . as the God who moves the instruments"; on the Virgin: *in Ioh.* 19, no. 140, fol. 398r: "He gave to us the Mother, not that we would worship her, but the Father of our Lord Jesus Christ and him who is the Son of both. . . . Hence praise and glory [may be given] to her; but worship, that is, *latriam,* is never offered to her." Luther, inspired by the Bible, did not hesitate to claim that the "perverse cult of the saints," devotion to a patron saint (WA 36, 388: "S. Hannah was my idol"), the veneration of images (WA 44, 176: the papal Church is compared to Egypt), and certain forms of devotion to Mary (WA 47, 257) were all "idolatry." But he did not enter into Zwingli's deliberations on the spiritual and carnal. Calvin seems to follow the humanists, Zwingli, and Luther all at the same time.

37. OS 1, 100. In the *Hortulus animae,* a very widely read book of prayers which was printed numerous times between 1500 and 1519 at Mainz, Strasbourg, Basle, and Lyon, Mary is portrayed as "Mediatrix," "Restorer," a protector against divine anger. According to the editors of the WA, 10/II, 334–337, Luther wrote his *Betbüchlein* to counteract the *Hortulus.*

38. OS 1, 121–122.

39. Cf. CR 90, 808–809, 817. Luther does not seem to insist on this point. He calls the priests idolaters "because of this ignorance, abuse, and ridicule of the Mass, the sacraments, or the promises of God" (WA 6, 517); but he does not establish the reasons for this.

40. OS 1, 143–144. Cf. Er Op 5, 503 F: "Christ is in this sacrament in the form of food and drink, that he may be received with the greatest purity of heart, not that he be displayed, or paraded about in pomp and public spectacles or carried about on a horse around the fields."

41. OS 1, 144.

42. OS 1, 134.

43. OS 1, 152 (two times) and 156: "abomination of the Mass." By this expression Calvin wanted to allude to the "abomination of desolation" in Dan. 9:27 and Matt. 24:15, which signifies the advent of the Antichrist. In fact, several lines earlier he speaks of the "abomination" in reference to the "church of the Antichrist." Cf. OS 1, 289, *On Fleeing the Illicit Rites of the Wicked,* "that greatest of abominations, the Mass."

44. OS 1, 289.

45. OS 1, 298.

46. OS 1, 305–322. We note 306: "the sacrileges of the Mass"; 307: "sacrilegious idolatry, when it is imagined that the bread assumes divinity, and it is exalted to be sublimely adored in God's place, and having been exalted it is worshiped by all";

309: "Behold at last that idol, a trifling idol of the appearance of a body, . . . exalted to impress by superstition the souls of the spectators."

47. OS 1, 306.

48. OS 1, 21.

49. Cf. OS 1, 37: "Almost all of sacred doctrine consists of these two parts: knowledge of God and ourselves." In 1541, Calvin translated this phrase, BL 1, 39: "The entire sum of our wisdom, which is worthy of being called true and certain, is as it were comprised of two parts: to have knowledge of God and ourselves."

50. OS 1, 23.

51. OS 1, 24.

52. OS 1, 268. This idea is essentially Lutheran. But the word "piety" is much less so. Whereas Luther makes abundant and varied use of the words "impiety" and "impious," he uses "piety" and "pious" much less frequently. *Frumkeyt,* which he sometimes translates as "righteousness" (WA 8, 560 and 8, 474), expresses fiducial faith (WA 6, 371: "All hold one faith and confidence. . . . A bit of perfection, that is, faith, will bring a flood of perfect piety"). Where Calvin would speak of "faith and piety," Luther speaks simply of "faith." In this he remains faithful to the vocabulary of the Latin Bible which, with the exception of Ecclesiastes and the letters of Timothy, only rarely used the word "piety." It does not seem that Calvin borrowed it from the *devotio moderna.* In the *Imitation of Christ,* the fundamental virtue of the Christian is called "devotion," not "piety." In the rare cases where "piety" is used, it does not refer to a human virtue, but the "honor of piety" (IV.3.18 and IV.1.12) or the grace (IV.12.8) which God shows to man. I believe that Calvin's use of the word comes from Erasmus or Lefèvre. In Erasmus' *Enchiridion militis christiani* (1518), Er Op 5, "piety" and its cognates occur frequently, most often meaning a heart-felt knowledge of God, a "desire for God" (28 A), which leads man from the visible to the invisible (27 D), to "come to Christ" (25 E, 26 F) and to imitate him as the "unique model" (39 B–40 C). Erasmus says that piety is fed by knowledge of the Scriptures, but he does not link piety to faith. However, he does note that faith is nurtured by knowledge (25 F) or other "aids of piety" (32 E). Lefèvre d'Etaples gives the following definition: "Piety is the motion of a mind converted to God. . . . A pious and religious mind is an eye that is always directed to the sun, taking in by means of that light everything that it has made, and bringing everything into that light" (*Comm. in I Tim.* 2, fol. 199v). He also says that "devotion to God," or a filial fear of God, is bound to a "sincere worship of God" (ibid., fol. 196r). In sum, Calvin seems to have taken an entirely scriptural idea from Luther and used a word that originated with the humanists to express and develop it.

53. OS 1, 41; cf. 96: "But this is a secret and hidden philosophy which cannot be drawn from syllogisms; but surely they whose eyes God has opened learn it by heart, that in his light they may see light." The faithful are thus "learned in faith."

54. OS 1, 76.

55. OS 1, 59–60.

56. Ibid.

57. OS 1, 66: "He wishes to be worshiped with gratitude, and to be loved in gratitude; thus, I say, he approves him who, when all hope of receiving a reward has been cut off, nonetheless does not stop worshiping him."

58. OS 1, 62: "prompted by the Spirit and eager to obey God." Cf. 225: "[If]

... they hear God call them in fatherly gentleness, filled with joy, they will respond with great eagerness to the one who calls and follow him who leads. In sum, they who are bound by the yoke of the law are like slaves."

59. OS 1, 67.

60. OS 1, 52; cf. 232: "Let us consider that there is a twofold government in man: one is spiritual, by which conscience is instructed in piety and worship of God; the other is political."

61. OS 1, 221.

62. OS 1, 106.

63. OS 1, 52.

64. OS 1, 247 and 252. Cf. Erasmus, *Morias encomium,* Er Op 4, 485 E: "Princes ... abandon ... the desire for piety."

65. OS 1, 224; cf. 274: "that we live a peaceful and quiet life, in all piety and honesty."

66. OS 1, 108.

67. OS 1, 222.

68. OS 1, 146.

69. OS 1, 210. All of this is very Lutheran. Cf. *Babylonian Captivity,* WA 6, 513: "impious doctrines"; 520: "impious teachers." On the Mass: 513: "monstrosities of impiety"; 520: "impious temerity . . . good work" (cf. WA 2, 295: "impiety of masses"); 532: "impious and unfaithful . . . contradictions . . . against faith"; 529: "impiety of faithlessness." Impiety for Luther, as for Calvin, is fundamentally a sin against the faith.

70. OS 1, 20 and 241. Cf. WA 6, 539: "impious men by their own inventions"; 558: "impious . . . traditions of men."

71. OS 1, 250. Cf. WA 6, 544 and 547: "impious tyranny."

72. OS 1, 231.

73. OS 1, 168. Cf. WA 6, 520: "impious teachers."

74. OS 1, 190.

75. OS 1, 258; cf. 240.

76. OS 1, 31: "We worship and adore the one God and Christ the Lord in one accord with all faithful people, just as he has always been adored by all the pious."

77. Ibid.: "If the pious then demanded some visible form before their eyes, would they not immediately have become downcast in their hearts?"

78. OS 1, 67.

79. OS 1, 242.

80. OS 1, 265.

81. OS 1, 272.

82. OS 1, 22.

83. OS 1, 168: "I truly call all the pious to testify whether those idlers are coming together that they might defile the purity of the sacrament with their leaven."

84. OS 1, 22.

85. OS 1, 64.

86. OS 1, 250.

87. See esp. OS 1, 290, 295, 299, 327.

88. OS 1, 233: "I pass over the degree of impiety with which they observe their laws, while they teach us to seek from that observance the remission of sins and righteousness, and then they establish the whole sum of religion and piety upon that

observance." 262: "Those unmoved by the numerous testimonies of Scripture dare to reproach this sacred ministry, as though it were something abhorrent to religion and Christian piety—what else do they do but affront God himself?"

89. OS 1, 232: "Let us take notice that there is a twofold government in man: one is spiritual, by which his conscience is educated in piety and the worship of God; the other is political."

90. OS 1, 256: "Nevertheless, it must always be carefully stipulated concerning those observations, that they not be believed necessary for salvation and consequently bind consciences by religion, nor are they to be made part of the worship of God so that piety is placed in them."

91. See pp. 197–199 of our study.

92. IRC (1559) I.12.1, OS 3, 105. A translation of 1560, OC 3, 141: "As far as the word 'religion' is concerned, no matter how much Cicero tries to derive it from the word *relire,* his reasoning seems forced. . . . I, on the other hand, believe that this word is the opposite of the license and excess in which the majority of the people indulge. . . . Religion thus connotes restraint as well as responsible and well-founded discretion. For true piety to be steadfast and unwavering it must remain within its limits. It seems to me that superstition has been so named because it did not content itself with what was ordained of God, but has created a superfluous mass of vanity."

93. Cicero, *De natura deorum* II.28.78. The same as Zwingli in his *Commentary,* CR 90, 639.

94. Augustine, *The City of God* 10.3. Cf. F. Koenig, *Religionswissenschaftliches Wörterbuch* (Freiburg im Breisgau, 1956), cols. 703–704; *LThK,* vol. 8, col. 1164.

95. OS 1, 226.

96. OS 1, 161.

97. OS 1, 256.

98. CR 90, 639: "We distinguish religion from superstition by the addition of the words 'true' and 'false.'" Here Zwingli follows Erasmus, who also opposes the virtue of religion to the superstitious deviations of worship (Er Op 5, 31 D, E; 32 F; etc.). For Luther, "true religion" consists completely in believing that God freely forgives sins (WA 25, 287). But he does not analyze the concept.

99. OS 1, 24: "true religion, which is handed down in the Scriptures"; 43: "true religion was overwhelmed and overthrown"; 134: "We ought to be baptized into true religion." 166: "The true form of religion should be sought from the Scriptures"; 260: "Let not the true religion . . . be violated with sacrilegious impunity."

100. OS 1, 24. Cf. Er Op 5, 35 E: "Apostle: Are we seeking a better teacher of religion, especially since all of divine Scripture agrees with this one?"

101. OS 1, 240.

102. OS 1, 166.

103. OS 1, 152.

104. OS 1, 241.

105. OS 1, 43–44.

106. OS 1, 102. This theme was dear to Christian humanists. Er Op 5, 37 C: "Visible works are not damned, but spiritual ones are preferred. Outward worship is not damned, but God is not appeased except by unseen piety. God is spirit and is moved by spiritual sacrifices. Let it be a disgrace for Christians to be ignorant of what was known by a pagan poet, who teaches about piety: If God, he says, is soul, as the songs tell us, you must especially worship him with a pure mind."

107. OS 1, 253. This passage continues: "Many marvel why the Lord threatens so fiercely that he is going to astonish the people who worshiped him by commandments and teachings of men, and announces that he is worshiped in vain by the precepts of men."

108. OS 1, 226.

109. OS 1, 234. Cf. *Babylonian Captivity,* WA 6, 525: "And let him think on this, that the Gospel is to be preferred to all canons and collects composed by men." 526: "The sacrament [i.e., baptism] . . . is not tainted by human constitutions."

110. OS 1, 248: "that consciences not be burdened with new observances or the worship of God be tainted by our own inventions."

111. OS 1, 257.

112. OS 1, 158.

113. Ibid. Note that Luther also calls the celebration of the Eucharist a "sacrifice of praise" (WA 8, 483).

114. OS 1, 103. Such a sincere affirmation of the profound meaning of worship! In comparison, the ordinances of the provincial synod of Sens appeared quite superficial. They condemn several attitudes and abuses ("let them cease . . . foul and profane conversations, . . . lewd and wanton music," "lest actors and mimes enter the church," etc.), but they do not touch upon the root of these evils (Mansi 32, 1190).

115. OS 1, 114.

116. OS 1, 160.

117. OS 1, 161.

118. Cf. OS 1, 232, 233, 241, 253, 256, 262.

Chapter 21. Critique and Ideal of Doctrine

1. See pp. 173 and 176–177 of our study.

2. OS 1, 22; cf. 25.

3. It is the scholastic method which is targeted. No doubt Calvin knew the sarcasm which Erasmus had aimed against scholasticism in his *Praise of Folly* (Er Op 4, 406 C, 461 C, 463 BC, 464 C, 465 E, 469–471) or in the *Enchiridion* (Er Op 5, 30 Bff.) to stigmatize theologians as sophists—overly subtle, quarrelsome, partisan, and intolerant. He could borrow the formulas of Erasmus, but for his basic criticisms he is certainly indebted to Luther. Luther had already affirmed that scholastic theologians pretend to "measure" the infinite grandeur of God; see his *Randbemerkungen zu Petrus Lombardus* (1510), WA 9, 47: "They measure the infinite breadth of deity by the pinpoint of their nothingness." Luther had long ago made clear how scholasticism abuses reason in matters of faith, in his *Disputatio contra scholasticam theologiam* (1517), WA 1, 226ff.; that it is not comparable to biblical theology, in his *De Captivitate* (1520), WA 6, 511: "The Holy Spirit is greater than Aristotle. . . . Whatever philosophy does not grasp, faith does. And the authority of the Word of God is greater than the capacity of our mind." See also *Rationis Latomianae pro incendiariis Lovaniensis scholae sophistis redditae, Lutherana confutatio* (1521), WA 8, 44: "by the tyranny of sophistry"; 54: "The assembly of sophists is the synagogue of Satan" (cf. 5, 300); 69: "They hasten to destroy this worship of God and knowledge of the truth."

4. OS 1, 139.

5. OS 1, 143.

6. OS 1, 144.

7. OS 1, 187.

8. OS 1, 151; cf. *Rationis Latomianae,* WA 8, 69: "These consequentialists and circumstantialists [are] sophists who boast that they alone are the interpreters of Scripture, when they do nothing but tear it into so many tatters and render these ambiguous and obscure."

9. OS 1, 29. There was a similar tendency toward subtlety among the most cultivated preachers. One Olivier Maillard, for example, had the habit of beginning his sermons with "a striking theological question." The provincial synod of Sens (1518) also inveighed against this deviation, Mansi 32, 1199: "In those sacred gatherings let them stop . . . the empty proposals of questions that are subtle and for the most part futile."

10. OS 1, 173: "The things which the scholastic sophists have handed down about penance"; 144: "They seem to accomplish this beautifully in their syllogisms, but if it happens that their consciences be exercised by a more serious attitude, they would be easily dashed along with their own syllogisms." Cf. OS 3, 248, IRC (1559) II.2.6.

11. OS 1, 96. Cf. Er Op 5, 141 E: "Christian philosophy. . . . This type of philosophy is more truly seated in the affections than in syllogisms; it is life more than disputation, inspiration more than erudition, transformation more than reason." 6, 254 (on the subject of "Blessed are the poor in spirit"): "Here that heavenly Teacher opens his hidden philosophy; to convey this to his own followers he descended from heaven to earth. . . . These are certainly the truths that make Christians, not the cleverness of the sophists." Cf. 5, 139 E and 1183.

12. OS 1, 160; cf. 256: "They measure the worship of God with human inventions . . . when traditions are thought to be necessary for salvation."

13. OS 1, 169.

14. Ibid.

15. OS 1, 250: "the insolence with which they sow new doctrines, by which they turn the wretched fold utterly away from the genuine and simple purity of the Word of God."

16. OS 1, 162.

17. OS 1, 161–162.

18. For Luther on "traditions" and "human inventions," see *Babylonian Captivity,* WA 6, 522, 525, 527, 530, 544–545, 557–558, and esp. 553: "One must especially distinguish between those things which have been handed down by divine agency in the sacred writings and those which have been invented by men in the church, no matter how much they excel others in sanctity and learning."

19. Cf. OS 1, 217: "Doubtless they attempt an ingenious thing, to contrive a single religion from Christianity, Judaism, and paganism, like little patches sewn together." This syncretism was attributed to the scholastic theologians.

20. Cf. OS 1, 250.

21. See p. 94 of our study. Cf. Er Op 5, 8 F: "Divine wisdom lisps at us and like a dutiful mother accommodates her speech to our infancy."

22. OS 1, 43–44.

23. Cf. R. Peter, "L'abécédaire genevois ou catéchisme élémentaire de Calvin," *RHPhR* 45 (1965), no. 1, pp. 11–45.

24. OS 1, 21.

25. OS 1, 29. Cf. PL 44, 186.

26. Cf. *Babylonian Captivity,* WA 6, 509: "My opinion is very reasonable, especially that . . . there should be no violence done to the divine words, neither by man nor angel; rather these words, insofar as possible, should be ordered in their simplest sense."

27. OS 1, 139.

28. OS 1, 170. Cf. WA 6, 510: "What shall we say here, when we make Aristotle and human doctrines the censors of sublime and divine matters? Why do we not discredit this curiosity and cling simply to the words of Christ, willing to be ignorant of what might come of it and content with the presence of the true body of Christ through the power of the words?"

29. OS 1, 73: "But what keeps us from explaining in simpler words those things in the Scriptures which perplex and obstruct our understanding? Nevertheless, let these words serve the truth of Scripture itself religiously and faithfully, and let them be used sparingly, modestly, and not inappropriately." Cf. 166: "The true form of religion should be sought out and taught from the Scriptures."

30. OS 1, 23–24.

31. Cf. WA 5, 35: "The best way of interpreting and understanding the Scriptures is to bring the texts together and keep an unbroken train of thought." See also WA 8, 237, 239; 7, 639; 14, 556.

32. OS 1, 75. Cf. WA 6, 511: "Does it not seem right for us to have wished to continue in simple faith? . . . Nevertheless I shall hold my understanding captive to obeying Christ, and, clinging simply to his words, I shall firmly believe."

33. OS 1, 166.

34. OS 1, 21.

35. OS 1, 23.

36. OS 1, 236.

Chapter 22. Critique and Ideal of the Ecclesiastical Structures

1. See pp. 159–162 of our study.

2. Compare OS 1, 150 with WA 6, 504; OS 1, 152 with WA 6, 561; OS 1, 157 with WA 6, 512; OS 1, 177 with WA 6, 546–547; OS 1, 206–207 with WA 6, 563–564 and with WA 7, 58; OS 1, 212 with WA 6, 564; OS 1, 250 with WA 6, 509.

3. Cf. Lortz, *RD,* vol. 1, pp. 14–18, 73–75, vol. 2, pp. 26–29; Imbart de la Tour, *L'Eglise catholique,* pp. 50–65, underlines in particular the role of papal theologians, those absolutist "legislators of the spiritual monarchy."

4. Sylvester Prierias (1456–1523), that "great abettor of pontifical absolutism" (Léonard, *La Réformation,* pp. 54–55), one of Luther's principal adversaries, did not hesitate to state in his *In praesumptuosas Martini Lutheri conclusiones de potestate papae dialogus* (1518): "The universal Church is virtually the Roman Church; the Roman Church is, in terms of representation, the college of cardinals, and therefore virtually the *pontifex maximus*" (cited in WA 1, 656, n. 1). In Luther's view, it was impossible to identify, even "virtually," the universal Church with the Roman Church; cf. WA 6, 561: "For only what is approved by the universal Church, not just the Roman Church, is approved in faith."

5. OS 1, 31.

6. OS 1, 32. Here Calvin joins with Luther in raising a problem with conciliarism: Which councils are the authentic representatives of the Church? Who are its members? Cf. H. Küng, *Strukturen der Kirche* (Freiburg im Breisgau, 1962), pp. 36–104.

7. OS 1, 134, 250.

8. OS 1, 152. Cf. WA 6, 493: "I am certain that the papal kingdom is Babylon"; 537: "They want to be seen as pastors, although they are Antichrists. . . . The papacy is in fact nothing but the kingdom of Babylon and the true Antichrist"; 555: "And the pope . . . is Antichrist." Cf. H. Preuss, *Die Vorstellungen vom Antichrist im späten Mittelalter, bei Luther und der konfessionellen Polemik* (thesis, Leipzig, 1906).

9. OS 1, 152.

10. OS 1, 250. Since the Carolingian era, several Roman canonists presented the Church as the new "Roman Empire." Cf. J. B. Sägmüller, "Die Kirche als imperium Romanum im kanonischen Recht," *ThQ* 80 (1898), pp. 50ff. The antipapists continuously rejected that dangerous notion. Following Gerson and Almain, Erasmus also criticized the popes' involvement with temporal power and their spirit of domination. Er Op 5, 49 B: "Apostle, pastor, bishop are terms of service, not domination. Pope and abbot indicate charity, not power." Luther's radical protests are well known. Cf. *Babylonian Captivity,* WA 6, 543: "[Christ] did not establish empires, powers, or dominions in his Church, but ministries." He states clearly why he considers the pope to be the Antichrist, 537: "For who is the man of sin and the son of perdition but the one who increases sin and perdition by his own doctrines and statutes in the Church, while seated in the Church as if he were God. And papal tyranny has abundantly accomplished all this for many centuries now; it has snuffed out faith, obscured the sacraments, and oppressed the Gospel, while it has passed and infinitely multiplied laws not only impious and sacrilegious but even barbarous and utterly benighted." On "papal tyranny," see also 504, 507–508, 535, 543, and 553.

11. OS 1, 32–33.

12. Calvin wrote at a time when the Council was a very live issue. Erasmus warmly endorses the event in his *De amabili ecclesiae concordia* (1533). By the end of 1534, the recently elected Paul III was in the process of convening a council. In 1535, Vergerio obtained an agreement on principles with numerous Lutherans, and in 1536, Contarini was put in charge of making preparations. Calvin's mistrust represents the tendency which was to lead in 1537 to the Schmalkaldic League's refusal to participate. Cf. Imbart de la Tour, *L'évangélisme,* pp. 579–591.

13. Cf. Luther's contradictory statements on the councils: WA 2, 404–405.

14. OS 1, 246–247.

15. Calvin himself was a layman and a lawyer, and here he shows how he participated in the emancipation of the laity, along with other jurists who were also advocates of Luther's ecclesiology. In his *Appeal to the Christian Nobility* (1520), WA 6, 404–469, and in his *Babylonian Captivity* (1520), Luther attempts to break down the wall between the clerical state and the lay state. For example, WA 6, 525: "In the reality of the Mass and the sacrament, we are all equals, priests and laity"; 566: "Concerning this sacrament of orders, [they are] in no way better than the laity"; 567: "In brief, I do not see any reason why a man once made a priest could not again become a layman, since a priest in no way differs from a layman except in ministry." Cf. W. Köhler, *Luthers Schrift an den christlichen Adel deutscher*

Nation im Spiegel der Kultur- und Zeitgeschichte; K. Tuchel, "Luthers Auffassung vom geistlichen Amt," in *Luther,* 1958, pp. 61–98.

16. OS 1, 206–207.

17. Cf. WA 6, 566: "By tonsure and vestments? A pitiful priest, who is known only by his tonsure and garb"!

18. OS 1, 207.

19. OS 1, 187; cf. Bucer, EN I, 148d–149a.

20. OS 1, 150. On the negative sense attributed to the term "layman" by Calvin, see OS 1, 189 and 208: "whom they call laity." Cf. the entire first part of *Babylonian Captivity,* WA 6, 502–507, and WA 2, 742, 17, 501.

21. OS 1, 156; cf. *De abroganda missa privata* (1521), WA 8, 398–476.

22. OS 1, 157; cf. the provincial synod of Sens, Mansi 32, 1189, recognized and combated the abusive and self-serving multiplication of Masses. This is also true for Luther, WA 6, 520: "the endless business of profit and gain"; 52: "For thus the venerable testament of God has been restricted to the servitude of the most wicked search for profit."

23. Cf. WA 6, 546: "Confession in secret . . . is acceptable; . . . the word we receive from the mouth of a brother has been offered by God. Receiving the word in faith, we rest in the mercy of God who speaks to us through the brother"; 574: "Whatever you have bound. . . . For this was spoken to each and every Christian. . . . Christ obviously gave the power to absolve to each one of his followers." On the keys: 541 and 544. For the similar position of Bucer, see EN I, 22b; for that of Zwingli: CR 90, 822.

24. OS 1, 177; cf. 175–176.

25. OS 1, 55. Cf. *De votis monasticis iudicium* (1521), WA 8, 573–669. Luther says, p. 583, that monks live "outside of ordinary life" and that their monasteries are "brothels of Satan."

26. OS 1, 213. On the "complete separation of title and function," see Imbart de la Tour, *L'Eglise catholique,* pp. 277–283. Cf. *Babylonian Captivity,* WA 6, 550: "What is a bishop who does not preach or care for souls, except an idol in the world which has the name and form of a bishop?"; 566: "The office of the priest is to preach, and if he does not, he is no more a priest than a portrait is a man."

27. Note, however, that Calvin himself was, from 1539 to 1546, a prebend of the cathedral of Strasbourg. He no doubt accepted this title with its modest income in the conviction that the income was a legitimate remuneration for his pastoral activity in this city, which had lasted three years. According to J. Rott, "Documents strasbourgeois concernant Calvin, II. Calvin prébendier de la Cathédrale de Strasbourg," *RHPhR* 44 (1964), no. 4, pp. 312–325.

28. Allusion to the mitre worn by bishops. Cf. OS 1, 213: "mitered pontiffs."

29. OS 1, 214.

30. This statement by Calvin is corroborated by what we read in the thoroughly documented work of Toussaert, *Le sentiment religieux en Flandre,* pp. 564–565, on the occupations that certain diocesan statutes authorized for the priest: "He could be a gardener, nurseryman, shepherd, herdsman [the "mule drivers" of Calvin!], farmer, painter, scribe, 'bookseller,' apothecary, preacher; in Tournai, they could still be barbers, a tailor." Note that according to Lefranc, *Histoire du Collège de France,* p. x, "connections between Tournai and Noyon, formerly part of the same diocese, were still very strong in the sixteenth century."

31. OS 1, 215. Cf. 56, 417: "illiterate preachers leading the uneducated people astray"; Lortz, *GK,* vol. 2, p. 31: "It could happen that a sacristan be ordained without further training and take the place of his former priest"; F. W. Oediger, *Über die Bildung der Geistlichen im späten Mittelalter.* According to Toussaert, *Le sentiment religieux en Flandre,* p. 564, in the diocese of Tournai, the statutes of 1366 demanded that the candidates for ordination know the following: the formula of absolution, the fourth book of the *Sentences,* and the chapter on clerics in the *Decretals.* Not a word about knowledge of Scripture, theology, or homiletics! The acts of the provincial synod of Sens (1528), Mansi 32, 1185ff., reveal a similar situation in France. Here is the most that was customarily expected of the candidates: "Let them promote no one to the priesthood unless he know (insofar as human weakness allows) those things contained in the canon *Quae ipsis,* dist. 38." (This refers to the *Decretals of Gratian,* Pars I, Dist. 38, c. 5: "Those things which are necessary for priests to learn, that is, the book of sacraments, the lectionary, the antiphonary, the rite of baptism, the *computus,* the rules of penance, the psalter, the homilies for Sundays throughout the year and for individual feast days" [ed. Leipzig, 1879], col. 141.) The synod also demanded that every parish priest should be able to preach on the Ten Commandments and the Credo, always with this reservation: "If any of them were elders not trained in doctrine . . . , let them read one chapter of John Gerson from his three-part work." Finally the synod speaks again of the practice of fraud and vagrancy among the clerics, of their venality, and of their wretchedness ("not a few priests who are naked and begging"!).

32. OS 1, 215: "Is this tolerable even to hear, that they are called pastors of the church who never see anyone from their congregation, who violently take possession of a church as if it were an enemy's estate, who win it in courtroom fracases, who purchase it for a price, who earn it by obsequious and base means, who as children scarcely able to babble grew up to receive this as a heritage from uncles and relatives?" Imbart de la Tour, *L'Eglise catholique,* pp. 219–224, gives several striking examples of the "elections" of bishops and abbots whose outcomes were determined by force; p. 281, the election of adolescents to episcopal seats through papal dispensation; p. 282, nepotism in the allocation, transfer, and accumulation of offices; pp. 273–274, the court prelates surrounding the king. Note that the provincial synod of Sens, Mansi 32, 1185, while forbidding the ordination of those too young, avoids speaking of adolescent or unconsecrated bishops.

33. OS 1, 233. Cf. WA 6, 536: "To be subjected to their statutes and tyrannical laws is to become truly slaves of men." In numerous other passages of *Babylonian Captivity* the German reformer castigates "human constitutions" that oppress souls.

34. OS 1, 237.
35. OS 1, 210.
36. Ibid.
37. OS 1, 211.
38. OS 1, 187.
39. OS 1, 33. Cf. Léonard, *La Réformation,* p. 63, notes that in the diocese of Liège, around 1516, the majority of monks could live with a concubine if they paid a modest tax. The synod of Sens, Mansi 32, 1194, took severe measures against "unchaste priests and clerics who had concubines."
40. OS 1, 251.

41. OS 1, 33: "You shall recognize quite clearly . . . that the very doctrine which they say makes them the Church is a fatal execution."

42. OS 1, 24.

43. See pp. 190–192 of our study.

44. See p. 192 of our study.

45. OS 1, 250; cf. 23.

46. OS 1, 206–207.

47. OS 1, 207. For the royal priesthood of believers in Luther, see WA 7, 628: "All Christians are Spirit-filled and are priests"; 8:247: "All Christians are priests"; 8, 486–489, 492–493; 12, 307; WA DB 6, 298 (all written between 1521 and 1523); H. Storck, "Das allgemeine Priestertum bei Luther," *ThEx* 37 (1953).

48. OS 1, 158–159.

49. OS 1, 187. Cf. *Babylonian Captivity,* WA 6, 541: "From whence does it have this authority? From the keys? But these belong to everyone and are powerful over mere sins."

50. OS 1, 187.

51. The same for Luther and for the Augsburg Confession, BSLK 120–133, art. 28: "On the Power of Bishops," or "On Ecclesiastical Power."

52. OS 1, 52. Cf. Er Op 4, 481 B, 482 B, 482 A: "They do not even remember their own obligations, nor the terms suggested by the word 'bishop'; I mean 'work,' 'care,' and 'concern.' " WA 6, 535, 550: "evangelizing," "caring for souls"; 10/III, 156: "Therefore, whoever would be a true bishop must direct all his efforts to the end that he make his heart expert in, desirous of, and devoted to [the Word of God], and bravely make a stand against the false babblers through specific teachings"; 12, 389–390: "And here he uses a Greek word: *episcopuntes.* That is, 'bishop,' and it comes from the word 'episcopal,' or in German, 'overseer' or 'watchman,' who keeps guard or lookout in order to observe what everyone needs." (All writings prior to 1523.)

53. OS 1, 212. Cf. WA 6, 440: "For a bishop and a pastor are one and the same according to Paul, as Jerome also affirmed"; 12, 390: "So take note that a bishop and an elder are the same. Therefore it is false when they say that the office of bishop alone is worthy."

54. OS 1, 237.

55. OS 1, 211; cf. 237: "Therefore this one thing is left for the apostles and remains even now for their successors, that they diligently keep this law [and] . . . go out and teach."

56. OS 1, 213.

57. OS 1, 31; cf. BL 1, 26, which has "it certainly has another mark" for "is found [*contineri*] in another mark." Cf. Augsburg Confession, art. 7, BSLK 61: "For the Church is a congregation of saints, in which the Gospel is purely taught and the sacraments properly administered."

Chapter 23. The Outline of Calvin's Plan for Reformation

1. OS 1, 31.

2. OS 1, 215–216.

3. OS 1, 192.

4. OS 1, 25–26: "I certainly do not at all doubt that it is new to them, for whom

Christ is also new and the Gospel is new. . . . For we are not forging some recent Gospel." Luther also rejects the accusation of being an innovator. WA 41, 458: "We teach nothing new, but sweep away the filth of the pope"; cf. 33, 462ff.; 36, 357: The reformation is like cleaning a mirror that has become opaque; 46, 62; 47, 218: The smoky lamp must be restored.

5. OS 1, 25–26; cf. 22: "the truth of Christ . . . buried." On the "form of the Church" and its variations, see L. Célier, "L'idée de réforme à la cour pontificale du Concile de Bâle au Concile de Constance, *RQH* 86 (1909/II), p. 419: "To reform in the Middle Ages is to form once again something already in existence but deformed. It is to bring an institution weakened by time, reduced and corrupted by abuse, back to its original form which was excellent and healthy." Cf. Y. M.-J. Congar, *Vraie et fausse réforme dans l'église,* pp. 356ff., where this text, among others, is quoted.

6. On the theme of "restoring the Gospel," see Lefèvre, *Comm. init. in quatuor evang.,* preface, fol. a 3r: "During the restoration of the light of the Gospel, which was moving into the world again during this time, many were illumined by the divine light. This was in contrast to many other times, beginning from the period of Constantine, when that primitive Church began to decline gradually and then collapsed, and the proclamation of Christ's name did not go . . . to any areas of the earth beyond those of its time." Luther regularly designated the period prior to the reform as "this time before the renewal of the Gospel" (WA 43, 452) and his reform activity as a new beginning of the Gospel; WA 3, 551 and 665: "the beginning of the Gospel"; 40/III, 248: "when I began the Gospel"; ibid., 628: "in the beginning of the Gospel," 620: "in the beginning of the evangelical cause."

7. OS 1, 134.

8. Cf. OS 1, 32–33 and 246–247, cited above. Here Calvin shows his general distrust of conciliarism. Some years later, in 1543, he will again state his pessimism in his *Supplex exhortatio* addressed to Charles V (OC 6, 525–529).

9. Cf. Lortz, *RD,* vol. 1, pp. 224ff., on the circumstances of Luther's *Appeal to the Christian Nobility* (1520), WA 6, 404–465.

10. Dankbaar, *Calvin, sein Weg und sein Werk,* p. 166: "Calvin was convinced that the principal duty to reform the Church lay upon the ruling authorities who had been called to their positions by God himself."

11. OS 1, 23. A little farther on, Calvin says that he submits the doctrine supported by the evangelicals to the King, adding: "By reading our confession, you yourself can judge according to your own prudence."

12. OS 1, 261–262. Theologians opposed to Pope Gregory already underlined the sacred character of royal dignity in the eleventh century; they were inspired by David's example and the analogy between the anointing of the Messiah and the sovereign. This idea is found again in Calvin, but with some significant modifications. Cf. J. Bohatec, *Calvins Lehre von Staat und Kirche* (Breslau, 1930); E. Chenevière, *La pensée politique de Calvin;* Niesel, *Die Theologie Calvins,* pp. 226–244.

13. OS 1, 263.

14. OS 1, 260.

15. Ibid.

16. Of the 47 biblical quotations or references in the Dedicatory Epistle, 7 are taken from the prophets and 24 allude either directly or indirectly to the prophetic

writings. In the chapter on "Christian Freedom," the proportion is as follows: of 211 quotes, 41 are from the prophets and 52 allude to prophetic concepts. The most typical pages in this regard are OS 1, 34–35, 234–235, 245–246, and 276.

17. E.g., OS 1, 234–236, where Isaiah 6; Jeremiah 1 and 23; Ezekiel 3; Deuteronomy 17; and Malachi 2 are quoted.

18. Cf. OS 1, 23.

19. Cf. OS 1, 44.

20. OS 1, 23.

21. OS 1, 32.

22. BL 1, 32.

23. OS 1, 34.

24. Ibid.

25. OS 1, 33. Cf. WA 33, 462ff.: Luther admits that the Reformation was followed by an increase in sects, but he attributed this to the clever work of the devil. WA 41, 135f.: Reformation leads to division, but it is not the cause of it.

26. OS 1, 34. For Luther, the Reformation brought a "blessed tumult"; WA 7, 281: "It is a blessed discord, uproar, and tumult which the Word of God awakens, for it gives rise to true faith and struggles against false beliefs which are opposed to the success and true knowledge of the Christian people."

27. OS 1, 34–35.

Chapter 24. Conclusion to Part Three

1. See pp. 53–57 of our study.

2. BL 1, XVI, Introduction of Pannier: "The success was so great that a year afterward a copy could no longer be found for sale in Basle, and hardly fifty at Frankfurt."

3. Huizinga, *Herbst des Mittelalters,* p. 149: "What is expressed here is basically a materialistic spirit, which cannot free itself from thinking in terms of the body." From this attitude comes the extraordinary veneration of the body of a deceased saint, of relics, and the elaborate cult which focused on the bodily assumption of the Virgin.

4. Ibid., p. 186: "An everyday, good-natured irreverence and an easy-going attitude alternated with the most ardent excitement of an enthusiastic piety, which again and again unexpectedly gripped the people."

5. Febvre, *Le problème de l'incroyance au XVIe siècle,* p. 256.

6. See pp. 175–177 of our study.

7. Mansi 32, 1161ff.

8. See, e.g., ch. 11, on the sacrificial character of the Mass (cols. 1172–1173); the primary problem of the relationship between the unique sacrifice of Calvary and the Mass is completely obscured here, and the proof of the argument is centered on this ambiguous expression: "He instructed [them] to repeat." And here are some typical arguments to sustain the celibacy of priests (cols. 1167–1168): "Obviously matrimony burdens the soul and casts it to the ground; love of children makes one anxious and distressed." (Such words would have brought Luther to his feet in protest!) Finally: he who thinks that priests should be married "are numbered among the heretics, with all excuses cast aside."

9. Léonard, *La Réformation,* p. 157, correctly remarks in reference to the Augs-

burg Confession: "We must not forget that since Catholic theology had not yet been fixed by the Council of Trent, he [Melanchthon] may have thought that he was still in line with the ancient Church in matters of faith."

10. French translation of approximately 1525, quoted by Moore, *La réforme allemande,* p. 272. Cf. the words attributed to Leo X: "Let us enjoy the papacy, since God has granted it to us," quoted by Lortz, *GK,* vol. 2, p. 48.

11. Lortz, *GK,* vol. 2, p. 48: "The Renaissance is . . . essentially a lay movement. Many clerics, monks, popes, and bishops contributed to it and were representatives of the first rank. However, the latent or apparent tendency is lay-secular, not clerical-ecclesiastical."

12. Ibid., p. 13: "A starting point for a comprehensive description of the Church's situation at the beginning of the modern age is the unfulfilled reform of its head and members."

13. In reading the *Livre des martyrs* of J. Crespin (1554), one is struck by the similarity between the beliefs confessed by the persecuted evangelicals and several essential themes of the first *Institutes:* "Christ alone," the rejection of "idolatry," of purgatory, and certain sacraments, as well as the proclamation of "pure doctrine," etc. Cf. Léonard, *La Réformation,* pp. 270ff.

Chapter 25. The Problem of the Conversion

1. Cf. Büsser, *Calvins Urteil über sich selbst,* pp. 13–16; R. Stauffer, *"Les discours à la première personne dans les sermons de Calvin,"* *RHPhR* 45 (1965), no. 1, pp. 46–78.

2. Doumergue, *La jeunesse de Calvin,* p. 337. For this reason, the author recommends that "we maintain a legitimate skepticism" in exploring various hypotheses. However, he does not attempt to remedy our ignorance and is content with saying: "We call 'converted' a Christian who maintains the ideas and feelings expressed in Cop's discourse" (p. 338). And a little earlier: "during the period in question, Calvin was already genuinely converted to evangelical protestantism" (p. 337).

3. Sprenger, *Das Rätsel,* pp. 46ff.; cf. the appendix, pp. 99–100.

4. The Jerusalem Bible translates it in the psalms most frequently by "to return." E.g., Ps. 6:5; 22:28; 71:13, 20, 21; 80:4, 8, 20; 85:5.

5. A classic example: Zech. 1:3: "Be converted to me, says the Lord of hosts, and I will be converted to you."

6. Cf. art. *"Bekehrung,"* in *RGG,* vol. 1, col. 979; R. Bultmann, *Theologie des Neuen Testaments,* 3d ed. (Tübingen, 1958) (E.T. *Theology of the New Testament;* 1951–1955), pp. 317, 428.

7. Luke 1:17: "bring back"; 17:4: "return"; Acts 9:40: "turning toward."

8. It is God who opens the eyes (Acts 26:18) or the heart (Acts 16:14).

9. *RGG,* vol. 1, col. 979: "Conversion does not consist primarily in turning away from the past, but in turning toward the future. . . . Paul did not turn away from Judaism in disgust (Gal. 1:14; Phil. 3:6) and come to Christ by seeking something better. Instead, Christ appeared to him, and thereby he recognized the emptiness of his early life (Phil. 3:7)."

10. Luke 1:16: the mission of John the Baptist; Acts 26:18: "I send you"; James 5:20: conversion of the sinner, thanks to a brother.

11. Cf. PL 10/1, 915–946, *De correptione et gratia,* bk. 1; Seeberg, art. *"Bekehrung"* in *RE,* vol. 2, col. 542.

12. Cf. Altensteig, *Vocabularius Theologiae,* fol. LV rb–va, refers to the word *conversio.* Of the authors quoted, only Gerson is sufficiently "theological" to affirm: "Only this calling [namely, of God] is enough in itself to convert a man."

13. Cf. H. Pinard de la Boullaye, art. "Conversion" in the *Dictionnaire de spiritualité* (Paris, 1953), vol. 2/2, cols. 2235 and 2238.

14. Erasmus does not comment on the word ἐπιστρέφειν either in the footnotes of his New Testament or in his "Paraphrases."

15. Er Op 6, 773 F (2 Corinthians 11); cf. 17 E and 18 B (Matt. 3:1): "Repent. Μετανοεῖτε . . . But our commoners think that doing penance means to atone by a prescribed punishment for [sins] committed; . . . a serious error in certain theologians who distort what Augustine wrote about penance, that is, public satisfaction for the anguish of the soul which they call contribution. . . . The Greek word . . . is derived not from 'punishment' . . . but from 'recovering one's senses,' which changes the meaning."

16. *Operationes in Psalmos* (1519–1521), WA 5, 319–320: "For no one is completely converted, until he has tasted of heaven and hell, that is, until he experiences how evil and wretched he himself is and how sweet and good the Lord is. This is experienced above all in the threat of death and the horror of the Last Judgment and is known in hope and trust in the mercy of God."

17. *The Bondage of the Will* (1525), WA 18, 68: "But it does not follow from these things that a man is converted by his own power . . . But the election of God is required no less than the conversion of ourselves and all our precepts, since the election of God is our true conversion. And yet no one has ever attacked the notion of free choice on the basis of that rule of election." 682: "The word 'converting' is treated in the Scriptures in two senses: its legal use and its Gospel use. In the legal use it is the word of the enforcer and the commander. . . . In its Gospel sense it is the word of consolation and divine promise, by which nothing is demanded of us, but is offered to us by the grace of God." Cf. WA 18, 683–684, and 13, 551.

18. *Praelectiones in proph. minor.* (1524ff.), WA 13, 551: "Here conversion is undoubtedly twofold. One conversion is ours toward God, the other is God's toward us. . . . But God demands conversion from us, not because we can fulfill it in our own strength, but so that in acknowledging our weakness we may implore the help of the Spirit, by whose agency we can be converted." Cf. WA 74, 31: "When one turns to God, the Holy Spirit appears with his gift, which he does not bestow because man wants it."

19. Cf. WA 41, 37: "What did he [i.e., Paul] merit that he came to this conversion?" WA 52, 611–612: "One should remember and preach in the Church the story of Paul's conversion as a special miracle of the grace of our dear Lord God."

20. *Enarr. in Psal.* (1532), WA 40/II, 438 (Psalm 51): "I know that my entire nature is corrupted by sin; I cast myself upon your mercy. . . . It is therefore necessary, if you wish to be converted, to experience terror or ruin. . . . Then you must accept consolation, not through any effort of your own but through that of God, who for that reason sent his son Jesus Christ into this world."

21. WA 18, 684: "Let him be converted, that is to say, with a conversion which saves him from the punishment of death, and let him live, that is, have a good life and rejoice in a conscience free of care."

22. *Hauspostillen* (1544), WA 52, 617: "To repent means that he turns away from evil and has remorse and sorrow. To turn to God means he lives in Christ, that he is our mediator, and that through him we are to have eternal life. To this, one thing more should be added, that one bear good fruit or do the work of repentance."

23. OC 5, 9: "the citizens' enthusiasm which had been turned to him"; 10: "having turned to his friends"; 49: "We turn to someone"; 55: "from that which had been turned"; 70: "turning . . . his weapons . . . against the commonwealth"; 149: "To this we are directed; to this we are turned."

24. OC 5, 200: "Let the conversation be turned to those"; 213: "he who speaks from the reverse"; 224: "Let the sinners be turned to hell" (Ps. 9: 18); 225: "Let us turn to the examples of other saints."

25. OS 1, 170: "Since they saw that this word was understood in various ways in the Scriptures, others have posited two forms of repentance which they distinguish from one another by calling one legal; in this the sinner is wounded by the sting of sin and worn down by his terror of the wrath of God. Crushed in this anxiety, he is perplexed and unable to extricate himself. The other is the Gospel form, in which the sinner is seriously afflicted within himself; however, he rises up higher and perceives Christ as the medicine for his wound, consolation for his terror, and a haven for his wretchedness." Cf. the corresponding texts of Luther, above in nn. 16–21. The editors of the OS refer to the Augsburg Confession, art. 12 (BSLK 66–67), but we do not believe that this text sheds any light on Calvin's theory of penance. We must go directly to Luther.

26. OS 1, 170: "Therefore their penance was nothing other than an entrance to hell." WA 5, 319–320: "For no one is completely converted until he has tasted of heaven and hell."

27. OS 1, 170–171. Calvin's *Catechism* (1538) contains a similar definition: OS 5, 336: "Penance means conversion, by which, when we have been enjoined to be strong amid the perversity of this world, we betake ourselves to the way of the Lord."

28. For example in OS 1, 92, 112, 129, and 179.

29. OS 1, 292 and 294: "confession of piety"; 301: "confession of our religion."

30. Cf. *Iacobi Sadoleti epistola ad Genevates,* OS 1, 442: "They are seeking new powers for themselves and new honors"; 543: "concerning their ambition, their avarice, and their zeal for glory among the people."

31. Cf. ibid., 452, where Sadolet makes the person representing the ministers of the Gospel say: "And when I looked back and saw that I myself, who had given so many years to the study of letters and theology, nevertheless did not have a place in the Church which my labors merited."

32. OS 1, 461.

33. Cf. *Trois traités,* ed. A.-M. Schmidt (Paris and Geneva, 1934), p. 33: "A French translation, whose author is difficult to determine, appeared in Geneva in 1540; it was approved by Calvin and reviewed by him, as all the results of internal criticism indicate."

34. Ibid., p. 43. Note that G. Gloede, *Musste Reformation sein? Calvins Antwort an Kardinal Sadolet,* p. 12, translates this phrase a bit too freely: "Do you believe that hunger has driven them to us? Is it for that reason that they strayed away from you, and did they quite despair of making *this change* in order to find their refuge

at new feast tables? [*sic* for *ad novas tabulas,* "to new account books"]." (Emphasis mine.)

35. OC 1, 362–363; cf. OC 28, 624.

36. OC 1, 339.

37. OC 1, 688; cf. 689: "When we proclaim the conversion of our lives to God, we seek a transformation . . . in our very souls."

38. *Comm. Is.,* 19: 22, OC 36, 347.

39. *Comm. Acts,* 28: 27, OC 48, 572; cf. 36, 347.

40. *Comm. Acts,* 9: 1ff., OC 48, 199.

41. Cf. ibid., 200: "We also know how surprising it is that the defiance of men increases with their progress; wherefore the conversion of Paul was the more difficult because he had become more obstinate by continuing in his madness."

42. Ibid., 199.

43. Ibid., 202; cf. OS 3, 80: "Paul . . . was converted into a new man by a sudden and unexpected change."

44. *Comm. Acts,* 9: 1ff., OC 48, 200.

45. Cf. ibid., 205: "There was need therefore of testimony to his calling."

46. Ibid., 202.

47. Ibid., 204: "Therefore, so that faith might be established by a miracle, Paul's comrades see a light like a flash of lightning." 205: "That he says he had not eaten nor drunk for three days must be regarded as something of a miracle."

48. Ibid., 201.

49. Ibid., 202.

50. Ibid., 203.

51. *Comm. Acts,* 22: 6ff., OC 48, 492: "In this . . . present passage . . . Paul reviews the circumstances by which he proves that he was divinely converted. . . . Therefore, in order that his conversion not be suspect to anyone, Paul teaches that the author of it was God by calling into evidence the many miracles that attended it."

52. Ibid., 493: "What am I to do, Lord? The voice is that of a man who has been tamed. And this is true conversion to the Lord, when we lay aside all ferocity, subject our neck willingly to the yoke laid upon it, and are prepared to undertake whatever he enjoins upon us to do. In addition, the beginning of acting aright is to seek the face of the Lord. For they act in vain who think of repentance apart from his Word."

53. *Sermon 170 on Deut.,* 30, OC 28, 569–570.

54. *Sermon 175 on Deut.,* 31, OC 28, 624.

55. OC 31, 200: "Conversion . . . is regarded as renewal; therefore I did not hesitate to turn. For there are those who argue too subtly on this point concerning penance." 239: The Vulgate "he converts my soul" becomes in Calvin "he restores my soul." The reason for it is indicated: "For the restoration of the soul . . . means the same as to remake it or to renew it"; 753, 755, 757: "God, convert us" (Vulgate) = "restore" (Calvin); cf. 786.

56. OC 31, 85–86.

57. For example, OC 31, 201, 552, 834 (to turn); 611, 736, 787 (to change); 86, 105, 187, 233, 520, 567, 571, 662 (to come back).

58. OC 31, 233–235.

59. OC 31, 520.

60. OS 3, 80: "Paul . . . was converted . . . from a professed enemy . . . into a new man by a sudden and unexpected change."

61. Cf. Sprenger, *Das Rätsel,* pp. 99–100: for a complete list of all the references to *conversio* and to *convertere* in the 1559 *Institutes.*

62. OC 8, 113.

63. OC 38, 673.

64. OC 38, 466; cf. 38, 671; 40, 456; 42, 316; 44, 497.

65. OC 38, 595.

66. OC 38, 671.

67. OS 1, 134.

68. Ibid.

69. Ibid.

70. *Epistola ad Genevates,* OS 1, 451: "Let us create these two men of both types, that is, from both walks of life, who are brought before that dread tribunal of the most high judge"; 452: "Let one of these be imagined."

71. Doumergue, *La jeunesse de Calvin,* p. 347: Henry, Staehelin, Kampschulte, L. Bonnet, Lefranc, etc.

72. Ibid., p. 350: "What a struggle and how dramatic was Calvin's conversion as he describes it! To think that such a description could be purely literary and only a typical, contrived conversion of an ordinary man!" Wendel, *Calvin, sources et évolution,* p. 21: "It seems to us impossible not to attribute to Calvin himself the well-known passage of the *Reply to Sadolet* in which he attributes to a partisan of reform an account of his conversion." L. Cristiani, *Calvin tel qu'il fut* (Paris, 1955), p. 43: "We certainly find here an unmistakable personal accent. He thus has his fictional character speak, that is to say, himself."

73. Lang, "Die Bekehrung Calvins," p. 36, writes that this testimony is to be used only as a secondary source. K. Müller, "Calvins Bekehrung," p. 243: "Certainly Calvin could have expressed there many things that he himself experienced; however, one cannot distinguish these from what he expresses as general and typical for all preachers and members of the congregation." Sprenger, *Das Rätsel,* p. 35: "That Calvin is basically speaking of his own conversion will never be proven with complete certainty." Cf. Büsser, *Calvins Urteil über sich selbst,* p. 30.

74. The French translation reads: "tempting someone."

75. *Reply to Sadolet,* OS 1, 480.

76. Ibid.

77. OS 1, 482: "Therefore, I wanted to impart faithfully to the Church that which I did not doubt I learned from you."

78. OS 1, 481: "Doctrines born in men's brains are forced upon the Church as if they were your word" (French: "sowed in the Church").

79. OS 1, 483: "The apostles proclaimed that there would be no enemies of your Church more pestilential [French: enemies in your Church]."

80. OS 1, 482: "It was not my aim to wander beyond those limits. . . . Moreover, concerning their repeated charges that I am leaving the Church, I have no guilty conscience. . . . I maintain such great desire for unity"; 483: "But I did not think that I was dissenting from the Church . . . that denunciations against me about

deserting the Church did not terrify me at all. . . . I was aflame with such great desire for unifying your Church."

81. OS 1, 480.

82. OS 1, 481.

83. OS 1, 480–481.

84. OS 1, 482.

85. Ibid.; cf. 483: "What of the opponents? Did they not furiously rush to flames, crosses, and swords?"

86. OS 1, 484.

87. Ibid.

88. Ibid.

89. OS 1, 485.

90. Ibid.

91. Ibid.

92. OS 1, 486.

93. Ibid.

94. See above, n. 42.

95. See above, n. 44.

96. OC 31, 27: "for five whole years"; 29: "this five-year-long consideration."

97. OC 31, 30.

98. OC 31, 29: "Because I assert that the world is governed by the secret providence of God, shameless men rise up and contend that in this way God becomes the author of sin. . . . Others strive to overturn the eternal predestination of God which separates the elect from the reprobate."

99. OC 31, 27: "I had scarcely one moment of quiet, free from both external and internal conflicts"; 33: "So far I speak of internal enemies of the Church."

100. Ibid.: "I was forced to break up this deadly conflict with my own body"; 29: "[They] did not cease to attack me and my ministry"; 31: "Some scattered frivolous rumors about my immense power, and others about my treasures."

101. Another typical example of Calvin's imprecise chronology is found in the *Supplementa Calviniana,* vol. 1, p. 122: "And I might say that twenty or thirty years ago I was in such distress that I wished to be half dead, to remove this anguish before my eyes. At least I had wished that my tongue were cut off for not having spoken the word [of profession which would have given persecutors an opportunity to arrest me]." This passage is taken from a sermon in 1562. It is often quoted as evidence of Calvin's situation after his conversion.

102. OC 31, 21 and 23.

103. Wernle I, pp. 90–95.

104. OC 21, 29–30.

105. Wernle I, pp. 85–86: "However, this is immediately clear: it is not a historical reference; he wants to give his reader his reflection based on faith."

106. Sprenger, *Das Rätsel,* pp. 4 and 12.

107. This language seems to be conventional for the period to describe the passage from "superstitious" piety to evangelical faith. Michel d'Arande writes to Farel after the death of Lefèvre d'Etaples, in 1536: "Support me with your prayers so that I may not fall into the bottomless pit in which I am plunged." According to Lovy, *Les origines,* p. 166, Mathurin Cordier, at the end of his life, characterized his youth in these terms: "As I began my work in Paris, I was not yet enlightened as to the

true light of the Gospel, but was plunged into the deep darkness of superstition." Quoted by Doumergue, *La jeunesse de Calvin,* p. 62.

108. OC 31, 21 and 22.

109. Sprenger, *Das Rätsel,* pp. 36–41.

110. OC 48, 199–202; cf. OC 31, 21.

111. The idea of subduing is still emphasized by the image of the preceding sentence. Just like a masterfully ridden horse, Calvin changes his direction with the pull of the bridle. "But God by the secret bridle of his providence finally turned my course in another direction." In the French text: "By his secret providence God nevertheless finally pulled the bridle to the other side."

112. Cf. Sprenger, *Das Rätsel,* pp. 40–41.

113. Cf. Doumergue, *La jeunesse de Calvin,* p. 345: "Calvin seems to have summed up what happened when he left France, and in this summary it is not always possible to know the exact moment of each event."

114. OC 31, 15.

115. OC 31, 17; cf. 19: "that I might adopt for my present use whatever doctrine could be gathered."

116. OC 31, 19.

117. OC 31, 33. We also read: "Readers will also acknowledge, if I am not mistaken, that when I explain the intimate feelings of David and others, I am certainly speaking of things I have personally experienced." Cf. 31: "But here I have every right to complain, along with David"; in the French text, 32: "In this regard I may well have the right to complain as David did."

118. OC 31, 23: "as if God from heaven had placed his mighty hand upon me"; in the French text, 26: "as if God had extended his hand upon me from on high in order to stop me."

119. OC 31, 25.

120. OC 31, 21: "But, as he [David] was taken from the sheepfold for the office of highest honor, so God deemed me, who was drawn from obscure and meager beginnings, worthy of this honorable office, that I might be a preacher and minister of the Gospel."

121. OC 31, 33: "But since this was the condition of David, that he was clearly worthy of his people and was nevertheless hated by many . . . , it was great solace for me when I received undeserved hatred from those whose duty was to uphold me."

122. Doumergue, *La jeunesse de Calvin,* p. 345: "If one takes all the more or less chronological indications of Calvin literally, one is confronted with insurmountable difficulties."

123. A literal interpretation of "sudden conversion" forces historians to put Calvin's conversion in 1528 and to explain how the young convert could hide new convictions for five to eight years without being a "Nicodemite." Cf. Sprenger, *Das Rätsel,* pp. 28ff.: *War Calvin "Nicodemit"?* Pannier, *Recherches,* p. 43, tries to avoid the literal interpretation: "There may have been an involuntary exaggeration. Besides, 'sudden' does not always mean 'at a single moment,' but also 'in rapid progression.' Finally, 'sudden conversion' may simply signify 'after having undergone conversion.' " In my opinion, Pannier's ideas are not properly understood unless they are integrated into the theological-prophetic perspective of which we have spoken.

124. K. Müller, "Calvins Bekehrung," p. 208: "This 'sudden conversion' is therefore something entirely different from the development that we so far have been able to trace. This is not presented as a break or a sudden turn in either its beginning or its continuation."

125. OC 48, 200.

126. Cf. Sprenger, *Das Rätsel,* p. 37.

127. OC 31, 21; cf. 22, the French text: "the beginnings of my vocation as much as the discourse and the continuation of my responsibility."

128. OC 31, 13: "If the reading of my commentaries offers as much benefit to the Church of God."

129. OC 31, 19, 27, 33, and passim.

130. Lecoultre, "La conversion de Calvin," p. 24.

131. Lang, "Die Bekehrung Calvins," p. 37: Calvin "had . . . suddenly broken with all his earlier efforts and ideals and turned to a new view and conception of life. Since he was plunged more deeply than others in the errors of the old Church, he received a single blow from the hand of the God of truth. He had to follow him promptly, with no time for contemplation."

132. K. Müller, "Calvins Bekehrung," pp. 213–214.

133. Pannier, *Recherches,* p. 43.

134. Wendel, *Calvin, sources et évolution,* pp. 23–25.

135. Sprenger, *Das Rätsel,* pp. 14, 28, 61.

136. Ibid., p. 87: "Break with his Mother Church." But, later on the same page, the author affirms: "However, there is no thought of two Churches, one of which must have been established first." Contrary to Lecoultre.

137. Cf. P. Althaus, "Die Bekehrung in reformatorischem und pietistischen Licht," in *Um die Wahrheit des Evangeliums,* pp. 224ff.; Léonard, *La Réformation,* pp. 259–260: "The term 'sudden conversion' which he will use one day has been interpreted either in the sense of the 'conversion which he experienced' (and here we are on the threshold of predestination) or in the sense of an 'unexpected conversion.' But this conversion was not like Wesley's, which virtually neglects and denies the road which preceded grace and focuses only on the precise day and hour of the voluntary decision. Luther also spoke of a sudden enlightenment. It had nonetheless been preceded by a long search for salvation. Calvin's case was similar." Luther's text of 1545, to which the author alludes, is found in WA 54, 186: "Immediately all of Scripture took on a different appearance for me."

Chapter 26. The Problem of Schism

1. *Resolutiones Lutheri de potestate papae,* WA 2, 190.

2. Ibid.

3. *Wider das Papsttum zu Rom, vom Teufel gestiftet* (1545), WA 54, 206: "For the Roman Church is and should be a part or member of the holy Christian Church, not the head which only applies to Christ, the cornerstone."

4. *Enarr. in I Mose* (1535ff.), WA 42, 79: "For it is constituted by the Word of God."

5. *Contra Henricum Angl.* (1522), WA 10/II, 220: "The papist Church finds its unity in the external unity of its image, the pope."

6. *Annotationes in aliquot cap. Matth.* (1538), WA 38, 615: "Therefore it should

be declared first, that the Roman pontiffs have nothing at all to do with Peter, nor Peter with them. For there is nothing 'Petrine' about them, nor is there anything 'papal' about Peter. Peter confessed and taught that Christ was the Son of the living God, but the pope demands obedience to his own Satanical and avaricious laws and customs. Peter proclaimed the life to come, but the pope proclaims his temporal tyranny." 616: "Second, it must be declared, that the Church and bishops who have faith in Christ and confess that he is the Son of the living God . . . are truly the Church and the successors of Peter." Cf. WA 47, 422–423.

7. *Enarr. in I Mose* (1535ff.), WA 42, 412–413: "For the false Church is always the persecutor of the true Church."

8. Ibid., 187: "And here [i.e., concerning the sacrifices of Cain and Abel] the Church begins to be divided: in the Church which is the Church in name only, there is nothing but a hypocritical and bloodthirsty Church and things opposed [to the truth]"; 232: "[Cain] built the first city . . . [and thereby] showed not only that he neglected the true Church but also that he wished to oppress it." Cf. 193.

9. Ibid., 413: "not only spiritually through false doctrine and impious worship but also physically through sword and tyranny."

10. Ibid., 187: "The true Church is hidden, excommunicated, held up as heretical, slain." 289: "Noah and his relatives were damned as seditious, heretical detractors of political and ecclesiastical majesty." Cf. *Enarr. in Ps. 90* (1534–1535), WA 40/III, 505: "The Church is hidden and dispersed." E. Kinder, "Die Verborgenheit der Kirche nach Luther," in *Festgabe J. Lortz,* vol. 1, pp. 173–192.

11. WA 51, 477.

12. *Predigt über Joh.,* 7, 41 (1531), WA 33, 456: "However, the pope says: 'The Church should be respected.' Now we also say this: there are many of you in the papacy who belong to the Christian Church, just as there are many among the Turks . . . who belong to the Christian Church. They are baptized, they uphold the Gospel, they use the sacraments properly and are true Christians."

13. Ibid. "We readily admit . . . that they are in the Christian Church; however, they are not truly members of the Church, [and] do not belong to her. . . . They are within the Church, but [they are] not genuine [members]."

14. Ibid., 457: "has only the appearance . . . is in and among the Christian churches, just as mouse droppings with pepper."

15. Ibid.: "[The false Church] has only the appearance [of the Church], even though it also has the Christian offices. For a scoundrel can properly baptize, read the Gospel . . . , but he remains an evil scoundrel and is called neither a Christian nor a member of the Christian Church."

16. *Wider Hans Worst* (1541), WA 51, 505: "For we not only recognize that you come out of the true Church with us. . . . But we say that you are also in the Church and remain there. Yes, you sit therein and rule, as Paul wisely says in 2 Thessalonians 2, that the cursed Antichrist will sit in the temple of God (not in a cow shed), etc. However, you are no longer of the Church or members of the Church."

17. *Comm. in XV Ps. graduum* (1532–1533), WA 40/III, 136: "For it would be an act of extreme ingratitude not to recognize this miracle, that the Church abides, that there are those who truly teach, confess, and believe in Christ, no matter how Satan rages, how the world and false brothers lie in wait, and finally no matter how our flesh, like an untamed beast, struggles against the Word and faith."

18. *Comm. in Gal.* (1531), WA 40/I, 68.

19. Cf. *Bedencken D. Martini Lutheri, Auff dem Reichstage zu Augspurgk* (1530), WA Br 5, 592: "It is true that Christendom is holy and cannot err (as the Creed says, "I believe in one holy, catholic Church"). However, that is true insofar as it concerns the Holy Spirit, for the Church is holy in Christ and not in itself. Insofar as the Church is in the flesh, she is sinful, she can err, and she can go astray."

20. WA 51, 476–477: ". . . why the papists through their lackeys reproach us as heretics. And this is the reason they give, that we have fallen away from the holy Church and have founded another, new Church." See W. Höhne, *Luthers Anschauungen über die Kontinuität der Kirche.*

21. WA 51, 477: "Therefore, they must recognize . . . that they are not the Church and that we do not wish to be heretics. We have left what is not the Church. Yes, because there is no middle ground, we must be the Church of Christ and they the Church of the devil—or vice versa."

22. Ibid., 478–479: "However, it is we—since I have shown that we remain in the true, ancient Church—yes, it is we who are the true, ancient Church. But you have separated from us, that is, from the ancient Church, and you have established a new church over against the ancient Church." Cf. WA 6, 505: "If some are to be named heretics and schismatics, let it not be the Bohemians or the Greeks (because they relied upon the Gospel), but you Romans are heretics, and impious schismatics, who prefer your own imagination against the evidence of God's Scriptures." WA 51, 485, 487, 515: "in the new church of the papists"; 501–502.

23. Ibid., 507–508: "The Church is a sublime, deeply hidden thing, for no one can see or recognize it; but one must only believe and hold to baptism, the sacrament, and the Word. Human teachings, ceremonies, tonsures, long robes, bishops' hats, and the entire papist pageantry only lead away [from the Church] and into hell, not to mention the fact that all of this should set forth the Church. For to the Church belong also simple, ordinary children, husbands, and wives, peasants and townsmen."

24. OC 5, 173–174.

25. OC 5, 175–176.

26. OC 5, 171–172.

27. OS 1, 23.

28. OS 1, 26.

29. OS 1, 31.

30. Ibid.

31. OS 1, 32.

32. OS 1, 33.

33. OS 1, 32.

34. OS 1, 33.

35. OS 1, 22; cf. pp. 204–205 of our study.

36. OS 1, 86: "This is the catholic, that is, the universal society, because one may not find therein two or three societies." "They have been gathered and joined together in one body, which is the catholic Church, the mystical body of Christ."

37. OS 1, 134, 241, 250, etc.

38. OS 1, 134.

39. OS 1, 152: "And do we still weave such abominable pretexts in the name of the Church and make our defense on the basis of those pretexts? just as if either of those Antichrists, who with such ease trample down, scatter about, and invalidate

the teaching and institutions of Christ, were the Church; or the apostolic Church were not the Church in which the entire power of religion flourishes?"

40. OS 1, 210; cf. 206: "But it was a sacrilege to usurp this title [i.e., the title of "clergy"] for themselves when it belongs to the entire Church."

41. OS 1, 289, 302, 306–307, 309–310, 313–314.

42. OS 1, 303: "And yet, if the Lord shall ever grant that the churches which that master of juggler's tricks [i.e., the pope] has ruined with his false claims be completely purged, there should be no better procedure than that the churches which emerged from his teachings be utterly uprooted and thereby be corrected by a complete and (as they say) single erasure."

43. OS 1, 289 and 314.

44. OS 1, 289, 297, 322.

45. OS 1, 302.

46. OS 1, 292.

47. OS 1, 301.

48. OS 1, 327; cf. 304: "not to make yourself different from them by religion."

49. OS 1, 318; cf. 319: "to listen to the Mass in order to placate the adversaries of the Gospel truth."

50. OS 1, 332: "In appraising the office of the bishop . . . one must listen to the judgment of the one God, by whose authority that office is constituted and by whose laws it is defined."

51. OS 1, 334: "And yet the Lord asks no small amount from the ministers of his Church." 335: "What of the fact that the Lord has placed so great a burden of cares upon the ministers of his Church?"

52. OS 1, 332: "You have been made a bishop. The apostle Paul straightway urges you with his exhortation that you fulfill that ministry which you have received in the Lord (Col. 4, 17)."

53. OS 1, 335: "advise in a few words how much of a burden you sustain for as long as you keep the name and appearance of a bishop—even if you claim some other duty from the pastor of the church." 337: "After you hold the name and position of bishop, . . . you have pledged your faithfulness to the Church; on what pretext, I ask, shall you reject the office itself?"

54. OS 1, 338: "But you do not therefore cease to be obligated, because you have made a promise in the sacrament with God and men as witnesses, or, more correctly, before both God and men; . . . because you profess [this] on your responsibility. Because you are surely guilty of sacrilege whenever that which is consecrated by the Word of the Lord for the holy use of the Church is so perversely and wrongfully profaned by you. . . . Now I appeal to and call upon you, the protector of religion, . . . the leader and moderator of the people, to witness how assiduously you watch over public matters under your care."

55. OS 1, 335: "So do not think that the bishop has properly performed his duties unless he has with eager and prudent care watched out for these three matters: that he nourish the Church with the food of the Word, that he guard against the incursions of Satan by the protection of the Word, and, finally, that he show the way by holy living."

56. OS 1, 331.

57. OS 1, 340: "such is the present state of your Church, or, more truly, the ruin."

58. Ibid.

59. OS 1, 360: "Either you must put before all other matters that which you hear is required of a bishop, or you must quit the office of bishop." 359: "You should rather lay down your assigned duty than . . . administer it . . . unworthily."

60. OS 1, 359.

61. OS 1, 331 and 356; cf. 353: "kingdom of the pope"; 356: "O Rome (to embrace with one word the *R*oot *O*f *M*any *E*vils), how many people not otherwise ill-born do you corrupt?"

62. OS 1, 336: "False prophets, who . . . obscure the true and pure religion with pernicious lies, contaminate it with depraved dogmas, and shatter it through the contentions of dissidents."

63. OS 1, 351–354.

64. OS 1, 340: "I say rather that formerly there were a great many and even today there are not a few who are bishops not just in name, but are most worthy of the praise and admiration of all."

65. OC 10/b, 148.

66. This is the sense in which we interpret the meaning of the passage: "Or it is necessary to allude to how you make your opinion agree with the words of our Lord: 'Whatever you bind . . . .' "

67. Ibid., 149.

68. Ibid.

69. Ibid. However, note that Calvin does not seem to wish to treat his friend as a schismatic. He wishes to keep in contact with him (149–150): "I support you in this infirmity and certainly do not reject you any more than if you were among us."

70. Ibid., 163–178.

71. Forty times. The note that the editors of the *Opera* put at the head of the letter does not exactly correspond to the content: "He insists on recognizing the Church which he has reentered as true" (163).

72. OC 10/b, 170: "When writing to Timothy, St. Paul called the Church the pillar of truth; he spoke . . . not of a particular Church but of the catholic Church. . . . In this [catholic Church] are comprised all the individual churches."

73. Ibid., 169: "It is certainly true that our Lord has given signs by which one can recognize those who are his own, when he said: My sheep hear my voice."

74. Ibid., 167: "Your judgment of these churches, that they are only relics of God's blessing, does not satisfy me"; 166: "I confess that I recognize as the Church of God that to which I have returned."

75. Ibid.: "Neither you nor I would have had an efficacious baptism in Jesus Christ, if we had not been baptized by the true ministry of God."

76. Ibid., 168.

77. Ibid., 168–169.

78. Ibid., 170.

79. Ibid., 172–173.

80. Ibid., 167.

81. For example, du Tillet expresses his agreement with the principle of "the just shall live by faith" (166), defends freedom of conscience (166, 173), seems to criticize corrupt churches according to Calvin's concept of "piety" and "religion" (171, 175), and speaks of the "Church of God" (the catholic Church) which he is cautious about identifying with Rome or the papacy. One might say that there are shades of Gallicanism here.

82. At the end of the manuscript we read this note: "The preceding epistle cannot be attributed to Espeville (Calvin), who the following year was chased out of the city where he was preaching" (OC 10/b, 163).

83. OC 10/b, 272.

84. Cf. OC 5, XLV, where the editors of the *Opera* write of Sadolet: "famous for his great eloquence and scholarship and praised no less for the *sanctity* of his character, he himself was also touched by some *desire to reform the Church*. . . . Beza passed too severe a judgment on the man . . . ; there is no reason for us to doubt his *sincerity* and his conviction that all things would proceed in the best way for the greater glory of Christ, provided the business of reform was granted to the college of bishops." (Emphasis mine.)

85. OS 1, 442.

86. OS 1, 443.

87. OS 1, 446.

88. OS 1, 447–448: "We are not so prideful as to condemn the decrees of the Church . . . , we enter in humility and obedience; and those things which were determined and handed on to us by the authority of our elders, most holy and wise men, we accept in all faith as though they were dictated [*sic*] and taught in fact by the Holy Spirit."

89. OS 1, 450: "For the catholic Church is, to define it briefly, that which always and everywhere, in all times past and present, in all places on earth, unified and harmonious in Christ, is directed in spirit by the one Christ; in it there can exist no division, for it is all interconnected and acting in unison."

90. Ibid.: "Because if any dissension or disruption should take place, the great body of the Church remains the same. But an abscess appears in which some of the corrupt flesh is cut off by the spirit which animates the entire body; and it belongs no more to the substance of the rest of the body of the Church."

91. OS 1, 453.

92. OS 1, 454: "because these have attempted to pluck apart the one bride of Christ? because they have dared not only to divide but to shred that robe of the Lord? . . . Can anyone who knows Christ . . . not understand that this sort of tearing and tattering of the holy Church is the proper work of Satan and not God?"

93. OS 1, 464: "You are either hallucinating in the name of the Church or you knowingly and willingly deceive. . . . First, in its definition you pass over the fact that [the Word of the Lord] had helped you greatly in understanding it rightly."

94. OS 1, 466.

95. OS 1, 464: "Where in this matter is the Word of the Lord, that most visible mark which the Lord himself commends so often to us in designating the Church?" 465: "Because he foresaw how dangerous it would be to boast of the Spirit without the Word, he maintained that the Church was governed by a Spirit which was indeed Holy, but that governance . . . he bound to the Word." 465–466: "But the Word is like a touchstone, by which it [i.e., the Church] examines all doctrines."

96. OS 1, 465: "They always assign the first place to the Word."

97. OS 1, 466: "to that form of the Church which the apostles founded, in which nevertheless we have the unique exemplar of the true Church."

98. OS 1, 462, 467, 471: mention of the "ancient Church"; 473: "We did not do that except by consent of the ancient Church which supports us," "by a decree of the ancient Church," "in that purer age"; 474: "We are armed with the support of

the holy Fathers," "you differ from that holy age of antiquity"; 475: "Through us the ancient Church stands firm"; 479: "But we did not in the least shrink from seeing that the doctrine sanctified by the old canons should have its place today."

99. OS 1, 464.

100. OS 1, 466.

101. OS 1, 474: "I shall not allow you, Sadolet, to bring infamy to the Church, contrary to all that is holy and just, by your inscribing the name of the Church on scandals of this sort; nor that you create envy against us among the ignorant, as if we had declared war against the Church."

102. OS, 1, 482–483.

103. OS 1, 465; 462: "You call [us] cunning men, enemies of Christian unity and peace, changers of the old and properly instituted things, seditious"; 465: "since the Spirit has been sent forth not to reveal new doctrine but to impress the truth of the Gospel upon souls." Cf. 475.

104. OS 1, 488: "Had not the purity of the Church been assailed by alien doctrines, even violated by your faction?"

105. OS 1, 465: "We are beset by two sects, which appear to be very different from each other—for how is the pope similar in appearance to the anabaptists? And yet, so that you see that Satan never so transforms himself by his tricks as not to reveal himself in some way, both sects have the same special weapon with which they harry us. For when they scornfully boast of the Spirit, they certainly do so for no other purpose than to oppress and bury the Word of God in order to make room for their own lies."

106. OS 1, 461.

107. OS 1, 466; cf. 457: "the yoke of the Roman pontiff"; 459: "Roman Curia."

108. OS 1, 474.

109. OS 1, 461, 486, 488.

110. OS 1, 460.

111. OS 1, 467: "In what way would you have us assess your Church in order best to spare its honor?" There follows the close examination of the state of doctrine, sacraments, and discipline under the papacy.

112. OS 1, 469: "Also the crass ignorance of [the glory of Christ] which still abides in all your churches."

113. OS 1, 476.

114. Ibid. "It [i.e., the complete ruin] would certainly have taken place had not the singular goodness of God prevented it. So it is in all places occupied by the tyranny of the Roman pontiff; there scarcely appear the scattered and torn remnants by which one can recognize that half-buried churches lie there." 466: "ruins which are all that are left of it among you."

115. OS 1, 134.

116. OS 1, 477: "Therefore we confess that we must heed the pastors of the Church no differently than Christ himself. But these pastors must carry out the duties enjoined upon them. . . . Let your pontiff now pride himself, as he would, on the succession of Peter; and even if he should prove that succession, still nothing more would come of it than obedience would be owed to him by the Christian people for as long as he himself upholds his fidelity to Christ and does not deviate from the purity of the Gospel."

117. OS 1, 478: "From this [i.e., the Word] is born also that which we attribute

to the Church and which we want to preserve undiminished, [namely,] the power to judge." 479: "But we do not in the least deny that the discipline which was sanctified by the old canons should have a place today."

118. OS 1, 476: "You hear from the mouth of Paul that the seat of the Antichrist would not be elsewhere than in the middle of the sanctuary of God (2 Thess. 2:4)."

119. OS 1, 485: "They [i.e., the evangelical ministers] indicated that there was a great difference between someone who withdraws from the Church and one who strives to correct the vices with which the Church itself has been contaminated." According to the French version: "For they indicated that there was a great difference between leaving and abandoning the Church and working to correct the vices with which the Church itself is soiled and contaminated." Gloede, *Musste Reformation sein?* p. 46, translated this phrase in an imprecise and "confessional" sense: "If someone were to take the step of leaving the Church [*sic*], it should be noted—so one teaches me here—whether he is concerned to correct the errors by which the Church itself is stained." Dankbaar, *Calvin, sein Weg und sein Werk,* p. 25, gives a translation much more faithful to the original. I take this occasion to give several examples of the freedom with which Gloede treats Calvin's text. He puts "new festival tables" for "new tablets" (p. 12) [which refers to "new account books," and therefore a "new start"], "universal Church" for "catholic Church" (p. 16), "Would you like to force upon me such a Church" for "Will you force upon me for a Church" (p. 20), "those so-called impostors" for "those so-called prelates" (p. 32), "on command of the Lord" for "as if from the mouth of the Lord" (p. 34), "the possibility of the free judgment" for "the faculty of judging" (p. 36), "sanctified" for "holy" (p. 37), "perspectives on the world" for "profane opinions" (p. 40), "harmony" for "unity" (p. 42). P. 19, we read: "so that I refer back to the form of the Church which the apostles established," although the original text also contains a very important subordinate clause: "so that I recall that form of the Church which the apostles instituted, in which we nevertheless have a unique example of the true Church." P. 33, we read: "Far be it from us, Sadolet, to take from the Church its own right which has been granted to it through the goodness of God, but that which through many strong restrictions was simply claimed by her." The original, on the contrary, says: "It is not our doing, Sadolet, to take from the Church its own right, which not only has been granted to it by the goodness of God but also has been upheld by many rigid restrictions."

120. O. Weber, "Die Einheit der Kirche bei Calvin," in *Calvin-Studien 1959,* p. 131: "On the one hand, the issue was whether, to what extent, and above all why the Roman Church is the false Church, and similarly whether, to what extent and why the Church of the Gospel is the true Church. How is it then that we do not have a split of the one Church rather than its restoration? On the other hand, the issue was especially how the unity of the true Church is possible without harming love or truth."

121. Ibid., p. 134: "Nevertheless—there is certainly the frightening reality of the false Church! Calvin, like the other reformers, could not abide such a thing. However, he experienced this false Church pronouncing a formal 'anathema' upon the true Church!" In what follows, the author frequently uses the phrase "the papist Church."

122. OC 22, 164.

123. OC 1, 553.

124. OS 5, 30; cf. OC 4, 598: "Comparison of the false Church with the true."

125. OS 5, 37: "But it shall even now appear more certain what place all churches occupied by the tyranny of that Roman idol have for us"; 40: "If they are churches, then the Church is not the pillar of truth. . . . For if they are churches, then the power of the keys belongs to them. . . . Then again, if they are churches, the promise of Christ is effective in them. . . . Therefore, either the promise of Christ has vanished or they are not churches, at least not in this view." 42: "Under his tyranny also they remain churches. . . . I say they are churches."

126. OS 5, 31: "They at least grandly commend *their* Church to us, . . . they make into schismatics all who . . . withdraw their obedience from his Church as they portray it." 37: "Let them go now; they even proclaim that we who have withdrawn from their Church are heretics." 39: "Now when they want to force us into the communion of their Church, . . . that whatever honor, power, and jurisdiction that Christ granted to his Church, we might transfer to their own Church."

127. OS 5, 35: "Therefore, whatever temple, priesthood, and leftover masks of this sort they maintain, this empty splendor which dazzles the eyes of the simple ought not move us in the least to accept as a church a place in which the Word of God does not appear."

128. OS 5, 41: "Therefore, while we are simply not willing to concede the title of Church to the papists, we do not thereby refuse to acknowledge that there are churches among them"; 42: "It is clear from this therefore that we do not in the least deny that under his tyranny churches continue to exist, . . . in which Christ lies half buried, the Gospel is overturned, piety is ruined, and the worship of God is almost abolished. . . . In sum, I say that they are churches insofar as God miraculously preserves . . . remnants of his people in them, insofar as some symbols of the Church remain. . . . But . . . I say that each congregation and the whole group lack the legitimate form of the Church."

129. OS 5, 36; cf. IC (1560), OC 605: "We call heretical and schismatic those who, in leaving the Church, destroy its unity."

130. Ibid.

131. OS 5, 37.

132. Ibid. The passage continues as follows: "Nevertheless this in itself absolves us more than adequately, unless they also want to condemn the apostles as schismatic, with whom we share a common cause. Christ, I say, predicted to his apostles that they would be cast out of the synagogues because of his name (John 16:2)."

133. Ibid.

134. On the diet, see R. Stupperich, *Der Humanismus und die Wiedervereinigung der Konfessionen;* H. Stöcker, "Luthers Stellung zum Regensburger Religionsgespräch im Jahre 1541," *Allgemeine evangelische Kirchenzeitung,* 1941, pp. 114ff., 126ff., 134ff.; the collection *Das Ringen um die Einheit der Kirche im Jahrhundert der Reformation* (Stuttgart, 1957); cf. the bibliographical notes in Léonard, *La Réformation,* p. 216.

135. Léonard, *La Réformation,* p. 217: "After the Lutherans at Ratisbon and Worms, a young French theologian with a sharp mind named John Calvin resisted the appeals of sentiment and politics. When he spoke, it seemed that Melanchthon became more rigid."

136. Weber, "Einheit der Kirche," p. 134: "He belonged to those who sought to the end an agreement. . . . Regensburg failed and the way led to Trent. But it

continues to be noteworthy that Calvin belonged to the party that sought to avoid the rupture."

137. OC 11, 215: "I know that you will be amazed that our adversaries have conceded so much. . . . I know that you will want a clearer account, and you have my assent in this matter. But if you consider what men we were dealing with, you will agree that much was accomplished."

138. Ibid.: "Then they came to the issue of the Church. Opinions concurred on its definition, but they began to disagree on power. . . . They proceeded to the issue of the Supper. At that point there was an insuperable stumbling block."

139. OC 5, 513/514.

140. OC 5, 653–654.

141. OC 5, 546: "For there is only one episcopate, in which each participant has his own place. The Church, which has expanded and increased in numbers because of its fertile growth, is one. There are several rays of sunshine, but there is only one light." Cf. OS 5, 36: "Also following Paul, Cyprian derived the source of harmony in the entire Church from the unique episcopate of Christ. Afterward he added that the Church which extends more widely in many ways by prolific growth is one, just as the rays of the sun are many, but the light is one."

142. OC 5, 528–529: "Christ gave very certain signs by which this great house which is the Church of God may be easily recognized, such as holy doctrine, the correct use of the sacrament, and the bonds of charity and peace. The first characteristics separate the Gentiles, pagans, and heretics from the Church. The third attribute separates the schismatics from those who are justly excommunicated." Cf. OS 5, 36: "Heretics and schismatics are those who create disagreement and destroy community in the Church. This is controlled by two bonds: agreement on sound doctrine and brotherly love. Therefore Augustine makes this distinction between heretics and schismatics: the former corrupt the soundness of faith with false dogmas, while the latter . . . break the bonds of community."

143. OC 5, 593. Luther expresses the same idea: WA 51, 477.

144. OS 5, 37.

145. OC 6, 225ff. Letter dedicated to Melanchthon: OC 6, 229/230–231/232.

146. OC 6, 241.

147. OC 6, 518ff.

148. OC 6, 522.

149. OC 6, 520: "This is most important of all, not to separate the Church from Christ its head. . . . Those who depart . . . from the Church . . . also fall short of Christ"; 522: "established the source of ecclesiastical concord in the sole episcopate of Christ."

150. OC 6, 520: "Therefore, in order for our adversaries to convince us that they are the true Church, they must show above all that they have the pure doctrine of God."

151. OC 6, 519: "But now let them make this brief response: that we are not in disagreement with the Church, nor are we outside its communion." 521: "Similarly we bear witness that the unity of the Church, as described by Paul, is sacrosanct to us, and we pronounce an anathema against all who have violated it in any way."

152. OC 6, 519: "You will recall that there was strife between the masked church of its era and the prophets and apostles, such as you see today between us and the Roman pontiff and his entire cohort. . . . If someone who is instructed in the sole

truth of God opposes himself to the Church's regular authority, he violates the unity of the Church. He will be a prophet of schism who is not weakened by threats that he not persist in constantly warring against priestly impiety."

153. OC 8, 79ff.

154. OC 11, 215.

155. Werdermann, "Calvins Lehre von der Kirche," pp. 269–270: "We must certainly affirm that Calvin succeeded in developing his standpoint over against the Catholic Church. . . . It has already been said above that Calvin's doctrine of the Church was developed essentially in opposition to the Catholic conception of the Church." Cf. Mülhaupt, "Luther und Calvin," p. 110: "Calvin is above all, in a special sense, the founder of the Church of the Reformation."

156. Werdermann, "Calvins Lehre von der Kirche," pp. 273–274: "In all of this [the requirements of unity, universality, and discipline], he retained all the basic forms of Catholic doctrine; however, as we have already seen, he changed the content of those concepts and thoughts. . . . Therefore the sentence 'The Reformation is essentially a break with the Catholic conception of the Church' (cf. W. Hoenig, cited below, p. 43) still is correct, even though it is formulated improperly." (Cf. W. Hoenig, *Der katholische und protestantische Kirchenbegriff in ihrer geschichtlichen Entwicklung* [Berlin, 1894].) The author's affirmation might be explained by his misinterpretation of Catholic ecclesiology prior to the reform. See the extremely sketchy and simplistic table which he gives on pp. 270–273.

157. J. Koopmans, *Das altkirchliche Dogma in der Reformation,* p. 35.

158. Dankbaar, *Calvin, sein Weg und sein Werk,* p. 27: "No one means that Calvin intentionally and gladly broke with the Roman Catholic Church." P. 28: "To the true Church of God he wished to belong afterward as well as before. . . . Calvin sought *to restore the Roman Church, not to break away from it.* The break was actually forced upon him." P. 209: "Moreover, he never wished to break with the Catholic Church; rather, he wished to save the Church from the decay into which he saw it had fallen and to restore the Church to its original purity and obedience to Christ." (Emphasis mine.)

159. Sprenger, *Das Rätsel,* p. 86: "Thus the notion that there are several Christian Churches, especially the Catholic and Evangelical, and that one can move from one Church to another, contains no great intellectual difficulty for us today. But that was certainly not the case for Luther and Calvin. For them there was simply the Church and outside this Church there are at best 'sects.' " P. 87: "However, the thought of two Churches, of which one must have been founded first, is not even considered."

Chapter 27. Calvin's Consciousness of a Divine Call

1. OS 1, 22: "common cause with all the pious and thus the very cause of Christ."

2. OS 1, 23–29.

3. OS 1, 24.

4. OS 1, 29.

5. OS 1, 32: "Aaron . . . and his sons, who had now been appointed priests, nevertheless erred when they built the calf." The example of Micaiah follows, then that of Jeremiah.

6. OS 1, 207: "as though they alone have been made a kingdom and priesthood

of God through Christ." 237: "but that power, if it is compared to that by which those spiritual tyrants pretending to be bishops and leaders of souls have sold themselves to the people of God."

7. OS 1, 215–216: "Those who can look dry-eyed upon the face of the Church as it appears today are without feeling and impious. Those who can heal and do not take the trouble to do so are exceedingly inhuman."

8. OS 1, 288: "I think I will be doing something worthwhile if with a few words here I appeal to upright men and implore them in that awesome name of God not to receive any of these exhortations from the Word of God as if they were listening to a recital by a poet . . . , [but] to remember that the truth and the doctrine of life is being handed on to them. This is rightly approved by them only when they obey and think of this very doctrine as the Word of God, which they cannot with impunity take lightly." There follows an allusion to "the terrible divine judgment," then the quotation from Ezekiel (Jerusalem Bible).

9. OS 1, 291 (30: 1ff.); 295 (2:3); 296 (45:23); 297 (52:11); 300 (52:11); 302 (8:13).

10. OS 1, 296 (3:16); 297 (6:11, and 14:1ff.).

11. OS 1, 291 (6:8); 295 (4:2); 305 (3:5).

12. OS 1, 320 (5:3).

13. OS 1, 295, 298 ("glory of Christ"), 302, 312 ("confession of glory to Christ"), 317, etc.

14. OS 1, 296, 298–299, 301–302, 307, 309, 312–316.

15. OS 1, 289, 297, 314, 322.

16. OS 1, 294: "Upon [the prophets] whom the Lord appoints to the ministry of his Word, he imposes a public role, so that their voice is raised in public and over the rooftops and sounds forth like the blast of a trumpet."

17. According to the Jerusalem Bible: "Shout for all you are worth, raise your voice like a trumpet."

18. OS 1, 329: "Among the voices of so much rejoicing, I alone in my peevishness will shout against you, so that I deplore in you that very thing on which all the others are so eagerly congratulating you."

19. OS 1, 293: "They are caught up in the same error, so that if by luck they come upon this letter (but I not only allow them to come easily across my letters but vehemently wish they would), they think that it was also written to them."

20. OS 1, 330: "Wherefore I intend this letter for you in such a way that all who are in the same boat with you (so to speak) understand that it was written to them."

21. OS 1, 333: Isa. 62:6 and Ezek. 3:17; 334: Ezek. 33:7; 336: Ezek. 3:17 and 33:7; 342: Ezek. 34:1ff.; 357: Isa. 58:7; 360: Zech. 11:17.

22. OS 1, 342: Ezek. 34:1–10 (Jerusalem Bible).

23. The theme of the prophet's criticism of the deficient priesthood appears again in pages 340 (Isaiah castigates and encourages the shepherds of Israel) and 360 (Zechariah admonishes a "worthless pastor").

24. OS 1, 336: "Nothing more serious could be brought forward than that simply hideous denunciation which ought to sound constantly in the bishops' ears. For that very thing which the Lord once denounced to his own prophet pertains no less to them than to the prophet to whom it was once spoken. I have placed you, he says (Ezek. 3:17 and 33:7), as a watchman for my people."

25. Cf. Ganoczy, *Calvin, théologien,* pp. 157ff.

26. OS 1, 331: "[God] prefers to correct rather than to break"; cf. 336–339, 354–358.

27. OS 1, 351–353. Calvin especially considered the "Roman" doctrine of the Mass to be a serious doctrinal deviation.

28. OS 1, 331.

29. OS 10/b, 221.

30. OS 10/b, 241: "I believe that on your part you have more to reconsider, since our Lord would not at all have turned you aside thereby to stop and think, if there were nothing reprehensible about your administration." 242: "an opportunity to examine yourselves."

31. OS 10/b, 241–242: "taking it even for the word and truth of God . . . in order to make examples which do not at all follow from it."

32. OS 10/b, 242: "I doubt whether you would have had the just vocation of God, having been called only by men whom God had dismissed of any responsibility and who initiated you in the same way that they had received you, namely, by their own authority."

33. Ibid.: "I am quite sure that you have gone too far in believing that those churches, in which you received the beginnings of your Christianity and the advancement that you have experienced within the space of more than fifteen years, are of God."

34. OS 10/b, 243.

35. OS 10/b, 244: "It would certainly distress us to have fallen into such an error and then not to have confessed it and straightened it out as necessary. I very much wished that it would have been possible for you to desist from such. . . . I pray and beg of you to desist for the moment while at Basle and to involve yourself no further."

36. See his letter to Farel, Sept. 1538: OC 10/b, 246–147.

37. OC 10/b, 251–255.

38. OC 10/b, 270.

39. OC 10/b, 272: "Here I call upon the opinion of all wise men who think that their simple words have sufficient weight to condemn us."

40. OC 10/b, 270–271.

41. OC 10/b, 271.

42. OC 10/b, 272.

43. OC 10/b, 290–302.

44. OS 1, 457–458: "But I confess, Sadolet, that I am one of those whom you so hatefully attack and wound. For even though religion was already established and the form of the Church corrected, I was called there, since I not only approved the achievements of Farel and Viret, I even sought to preserve and strengthen them as far as I was able. I cannot keep my own cause separate from theirs."

45. *Trois traités*, ed. A.-M. Schmidt (Paris and Geneva, 1934), pp. 37–38. Latin text: OS 1, 458.

46. OS 1, 340.

47. OS 1, 459: "which I know to be from Christ I must vindicate with my own blood, if need be."

48. OS 1, 469: "since I held the position of pastor among them."

49. OS 1, 475: "We took care to purge of these and similar plagues the churches the Lord commended to us."

50. *Trois traités,* p. 53. Latin text: OS 1, 466; cf. 462: "in the manner of the early Church."

51. OS 1, 466: "And now will you call an enemy of antiquity one who is not content with the prevailing general corruption, but with zeal for ancient piety and sanctity will struggle to correct and restore to their original splendor those things which are dissipated and depraved in the Church?" Cf. 485: "A much different form of doctrine has been stirred up, not one which will lead us away from the Christian profession but which will lead it back to its sources and return it to its purity as if cleansed from the dregs. . . . For they were reminding me that it is quite different to secede from the Church and to strive to correct the vices by which the Church itself is contaminated."

52. OS 1, 482: "unless perchance he is to be considered a deserter who, when he sees soldiers scattered and wandering far from their ranks, calls them back to their own stations by taking up the leader's banner."

53. OS 1, 489: "It is well known that we sustained this entire burden by ourselves while you were at ease and snoring." The French text: "Now it is certain that while you and the others were sleeping and at ease, we alone have sustained all this great burden [i.e., with a view to warding off the danger of sectarianism]."

54. OS 1, 483: "I had before my eyes the examples of your prophets, by which I saw how great the contentions were with the priests and prophets of their age."

55. OC 11, 95.

56. OC 11, 158.

57. OC 6, 477–478: "Both of which have been and still are being faithfully done by us to this point, namely, both our books and our public discourses offer a brilliant testimony."

58. OC 6, 478.

59. OC 6, 519. Jeremiah 18:18 is then quoted. Cf. 523: "false mask of the hierarchy."

60. *Responsio contra Pighium,* OC 6, 244: "But what, I implore, were they about to do if we remained silent? After being pushed so hard, they now show less care and interest than if they were touched by no concern for the Church at all. The whole world proclaims that the utter destruction of the Church is imminent, unless a remedy is applied immediately. . . . We strongly criticize, as is proper, their torpor, or rather their frightful cruelty, because they do not hasten to help the imperiled Church."

61. OC 6, 524. "The calumny of our adversaries should not be heard while they accuse us of impious indiscretion and almost unpardonable boldness, because we have tried to purge the Church of impure doctrine and ceremonies, when the assent of the Roman pontiff was no longer expected. But they denied that this was proper for private men."

62. OC 6, 532: "the restoration of the Church. . . . However meager hope may be, God commands that we be encouraged, so that casting aside all fear, we eagerly prepare ourselves for the task."

63. OC 6, 521.

64. OS 5, 22: "In this matter, Christ himself, the apostles, and almost all the prophets provide us with an example."

65. Ibid. All these passages were kept in the definitive edition of 1559.

66. OS 5, 45–46.

67. On Luther, see OS 5, 390: "that they stop harming the notable apostle of Christ [namely, Luther], through whose ministry during this time the light of the Gospel shone upon them." OC 6, 250: "We esteem him a notable apostle of Christ." Calvin concerning himself: OC 13, 17 (letter to Somerset in 1548): "And indeed, since God willed me to be one of those through whose labor and effort he today restores to the world the pure doctrine of the Gospel." Cf. OC 9, 469.

68. OS 5, 51–52: "But surely, since all things in the sacred assembly are to be done decently and in order, nothing in it is to be preserved more diligently than the establishment of governance."

69. OS 5, 52. Cf. Ganoczy, *Calvin, théologien,* pp. 304ff.

70. Sermon 51 on Deuteronomy, OC 26, 501. Cf. the remarkable article by Stauffer, "Les discours à la première personne dans les sermons de Calvin," pp. 46–78. We have taken these quotations from Stauffer.

71. Sermon 55 on Deuteronomy, OC 26, 554.

72. Sermon 14 on Titus, OC 54, 552.

73. During the most active years of his ministry, Calvin commented on the books of the Old Testament from the pulpit: Deuteronomy, Psalms, Ezekiel, and Daniel.

74. Sermon 3 on Jacob and Esau, OC 58, 54; Sermon 2 on Psalm 119, OC 32, 502: "Here I do not speak only to be heard. But I must also be a student of God so that the word which proceeds from my mouth benefits me, otherwise may I be damned."

75. Sermon 42 on Deuteronomy, OC 26, 394–395; cf. OC 34, 427.

76. Sermon 18 on 1 Timothy, OC 53, 219.

77. Sermon 5 on Ezekiel, quoted by C.-O. Viquet and D. Tissot, *Calvin d'après Calvin* (Geneva, 1864), p. 296; Sermon 21 on Daniel, OC 41, 540: "If anyone alleged that I am not the prophet Jeremiah, it is true; but I am as much a prophet in the sense that I hear the same word that he proclaimed."

78. For more detail, see Ganoczy, *Calvin, théologien,* pp. 224–243.

79. WA 5, 24: Luther spoke of himself as Jeremiah; 4, 597: "I am a prophet. I understand the spiritual deceptions of the devil"; 41, 706: "I am the prophet of Germany"; cf. 30/II, 587; 30/III, 290; 51, 589; etc. At times he alludes only to his prophetic mission: WA 30/III, 496: "I am one of the antipopes, called by divine revelation for this purpose, that I might overthrow, destroy, and plow under that kingdom of evil"; 31/II, 297: "I do not dare oppose myself to all the monasteries, etc.; but [God himself] says, 'I have made you a threshing sledge' (Isa. 41:15)." Elsewhere he refuses the title of prophet, for he does not claim to be able to predict the future: WA 2, 217; 7, 313; 51, 64; 30/II, 411; etc.

80. Since the French version is contemporaneous with the Latin text, and since it was definitely approved, if not written, by Calvin himself, we shall refer to the French text and compare it occasionally with the Latin. On the general nature of this document, see E. Mülhaupt, *Der Psalter auf der Kanzel Calvins,* pp. 8–9.

81. OC 31, 14.

82. OC 31, 36.

83. OC 31, 18.

84. Cf. *Harm. evang. Matth.* (1555), OC 45, 474: "All the faithful, . . . united by faith, together make one temple."

85. OC 31, 18.

86. OC 31, 20.

87. Cf. OC 31, 34.

88. Cf. OC 53, 338–339, where David is also called a prophet. Note that numerous religious writers of the Middle Ages identify David with the prophets.

89. OC 31, 22. A little above, we read: "If I have something in common with him, I am quite happy to consider it, and to compare the one with the other." Farther on, cols. 28, 30, 32, 34, Calvin still compares himself to David.

90. WA 42, 657; cf. 43, 510: "He often thought: 'I am so weak; why did God call me?' "

91. OC 31, 22.

92. OC 31, 22 and 24.

93. The Latin text contains a beautiful antithesis between the "shadow" in which Calvin searched and the "light" where the Lord placed him.

94. OC 31, 24.

95. OC 31, 24 and 26.

96. OC 48, 199: the conversion of Saul.

97. Cf. Isa. 5:25; 9:12, 17, 21; Jer. 15:6; Ps. 55:1; Ps. 138:7; etc.

98. OC 31, 26 and 28.

99. OC 31, 28, 30, 32. Note that Luther uses very similar expressions to show that his vocation has nothing to do with his free will. For example, WA 18, 641: "Who I am and by what spirit and plan I was forced into these matters, I entrust to him who knows that all things were accomplished by his free will, not mine." WA 1, 529: "I unwillingly come before the public"; 2, 183: "I was dragged by force into public matters"; 3, 564: "God led me unknowingly into the contest"; 4, 25: "God miraculously called me for this purpose through many unforeseen circumstances."

100. OC 31, 28: "For as this holy King knows . . . , I was assailed from all sides to such an extent that it was with great difficulty and only seldomly that I found rest and that I always had to undergo some struggles, either from those without or from those within." 32: "And in this sense I may certainly complain rightfully as did David." 34: "Of the domestic enemies of the Church . . . I am able to protest as did David. . . . In describing the inner feelings of David as well as others, I speak of them as things with which I am very familiar."

101. Cf. Sprenger, *Das Rätsel,* p. 37: "As a result of this intentional comparison, we are compelled to assume that Calvin himself, even though he does not say so explicitly, clearly found a great similarity between his own experience and that of Paul."

102. Cf. *Ioannis Calvini testamentum,* OC 21, 162: "First of all, I give thanks to God because, having compassion on me, . . . he not only raised me out of the deep darkness of idolatry in which I was immersed that he might lead me into the light of his Gospel . . . , but he also exercised such clemency and gentleness with me that he deigned to use my efforts in preaching and promulgating the truth of his Gospel."

Chapter 28. Summary and Conclusions

1. *Life of Calvin,* OC 21, 75; cf. 30: "as an excellent instrument of the Lord"; 43: "as the mouthpiece of the Lord."

2. Ibid., 45–46: "There was great mourning in the city. For his followers deeply missed the prophet of the Lord"; cf. 42: "He played the role of the true prophet and

servant of God by proclaiming his doctrine with sincerity, and by strengthening them for the approaching storms." 91: "He was truly a prophet."

3. For example, Dankbaar, *Calvin, sein Weg und sein Werk,* p. 47: "One does not become a prophet and reformer of the Church for one's own pleasure. That was the experience of Moses and Jeremiah, as well as Paul, Augustine, and Luther." Cf. *John Calvin, Contemporary Prophet,* ed. J. T. Hoogstra.

4. Bouyer, *Du protestantisme à l'église,* pp. 90 and 96.

5. Congar, *Vraie et fausse réforme dans l'église,* p. 218.

6. P. Tillich, "Die bleibende Bedeutung der katholischen Kirche für den Protestantismus," *ThLZ,* col. 643: "Protestantism is the prophetic protest against the sacramental interpretation of the Gospel."

7. Congar, *Vraie et fausse réforme dans l'église,* p. 218.

8. Cf. Denz, pp. 315–362.

9. OS 1, 455.

10. Cf. *Conc. Vatic. I, Constitutio dogmatica de fide cath.,* Denz 3013 (1794): "Because of its admirable growth, its exceptional sanctity, and its inexhaustible richness in all good things, and because of Catholic unity and unsurpassed stability, the Church in itself is a perpetual and strong proof of its credibility and is an enduring witness to its divine mission." 3014 (1794): "As a result, like a standard raised for the nations, [the Church] invites [them] unto itself." Cf. Denz 150 (86), 684 (347), 854 (464), 870 (468), 1868 (999), 2888 (1686): "The true Church of Jesus Christ, with its fourfold character . . . , is established and set apart . . . [so that it] shines forth."

11. Cf. A. Ganoczy, *Calvin und Vatikanum II, Das Problem der Kollegialität.*

12. Cf. Paul VI's discourse on the reform of the Curia, 21 September 1963; *Osservatore Romano* 22.9.1963: "that continuous reform, of which the Church itself has perpetual need since it is a human and earthly institution." See also the pope's discourse to the observers, *Oss. Rom.* 1.10.1964: "The Catholic Church . . . is prepared to investigate the ways in which . . . the genuine treasures of truth and spirituality which you possess . . . can be acknowledged." And the opening discourse of the Third Session, *Oss. Rom.* 14–15.9.1964: "Wherefore we shall take care that, with the greatest fidelity to the one Church of Christ, we might better recognize and approve all things which are true and ought to be approved in the various communities of Christians still separated from us." Finally, the *Decretum de oecumenismo* of the Council, chap. 1, no. 4: "On the other hand it is necessary that Catholics joyfully acknowledge and appreciate the truly Christian good that comes forth from the common inheritance. This is also found among the brothers who have been separated from us. . . . Nor should it be overlooked that graces of the Holy Spirit which are manifested among the separated brothers can redound to our edification, as well."

13. See, e.g.: L. Schummer, *Le ministère pastoral dans l'Institution Chrétienne de Calvin à la lumière du troisième sacrement.*

BIBLIOGRAPHY

Sources

Altensteig, J. *Vocabularius Theologiae.* Mainz, 1517.

Beatus Rhenanus. *Briefwechsel.* Edited by A. Horawitz and K. Hartfelder. Leipzig, 1886.

Bucer, M. *Enarrationes perpetuae in sacra quatuor evangelia, recognitae nuper et locis compluribus auctae.* Strasbourg, 1530.

Calvin, J. *Opera quae supersunt omnia.* Edited in CR by G. Baum, E. Cunitz, and E. Reuss. 55 vols. Braunschweig and Berlin, 1863–1890.

———. *Opera Selecta.* Edited by P. Barth, W. Niesel, and D. Scheuner. Vol. 1 (1926), vol. 2 (1952), vol. 3 (2d ed., 1957), vol. 4 (1959), vol. 5 (1962). Munich.

Concilium Senonense (Concile provincial de Sens, 1528), "Decreta," in Mansi 32, 1149–1202.

Denzinger, H., and A. Schönmetzer. *Enchiridion Symbolorum, Definitionum et declarationum de rebus fidei et morum.* 32 ed. Freiburg im Breisgau, 1963.

Emser, H. *Canonis missae contra Huldricum Zuinglium defensio.* In CCath 28, 38–93.

Erasmus, D. *Opera Omnia.* 10 vols. Leiden, 1705.

———. *Opus epistolarum.* Edited by P. S. Allen. Oxford, 1922ff.

Faber Stapulensis, J. *S. Pauli Epistolae XIV, Commentarius.* Paris, 1515.

———. *Commentarii initiatorii in quatuor evangelia.* Basle, 1523.

———. *Commentarii in epistolas catholicas.* Basle, 1527.

Gerson, J. *Opera.* vol. 1. Paris, 1606.

Gratianus. *Concordantia discordantium canonum* (= *Decretum Gratiani*). In PL 187.

Lombardus, P. *Sententiarum libri quatuor,* lib. 4. In PL 192, 839–962.

Luther, M. *Parvus catechismus.* In BSLK (2d ed.), pp. 507–527.

———. *Werke.* Weimar, 1883ff.

———. *Briefwechsel.* Weimar, 1930ff.

———. *Die deutsche Bibel.* Weimar, 1906ff.

Major, J. *Inclitarum artium ac sacrae paginae doctoris acutissimi magistri Iohannis maioris Scoti libri quos in artibus in collegio montis acuti Parisius regentando in lucem emisit.* Lyon, 1513.

———. *Quartus sententiarum Ioannis Maioris ab eodem recognitus denuoque impressus.* Paris, 1512.

———. *In Quartum Sententiarum quaestiones utilissimae.* Paris, 1521.

————. *Commentarius in Mattheum.* Paris, 1518.

Melanchthon, Ph. *Loci Communes.* Edited by D. Th. Kolde, according to G. L. Plitt's edition. Leipzig, 1900.

Zwingli, H. *De vera et falsa religione commentarius,* in CR 90, 628–911.

Works and Articles

Adam, J. *Evangelische Kirchengeschichte der Stadt Strassburg.* Strasbourg, 1922.

Althaus, P. "Die Bekehrung im reformatorischen und pietistischen Licht," in *Um die Wahrheit des Evangeliums.* Stuttgart, 1962.

Aubert, F. "Recherches sur l'organisation du Parlement de Paris au XVIe siècle (1515–1586)," *Nouvelle Revue de l'Histoire de Droit français et étranger.* Paris, 1912.

Barnaud, J. *Pierre Viret, sa vie et son oeuvre (1511–1571).* Saint-Amans, 1911.

————. *Jacques Lefèvre d'Etaples, son influence sur les origines de la Réformation française.* Cahors, 1900.

Battenhouse, R. W. "The Doctrine of Man in Calvin and in Renaissance Platonism," *Journal of the History of Ideas* 9 (1948), pp. 447–471.

Baumgartner, A. *Calvin hébraïsant et interprète de l'Ancien Testament.* Paris, 1889.

Bavaud, G. *La dispute de Lausanne (1536): Une étape dans l'évolution doctrinale des réformateurs romands.* Fribourg, 1956.

Becker, Ph. A. "Marguerite, duchesse d'Alençon et Guillaume Briçonnet, évêque de Meaux, d'après leur correspondance manuscrite, 1521–1524," *BHPF,* 1900.

————. "Les idées religieuses de Guillaume Briçonnet, évêque de Meaux," *RThQR,* 1900.

Beekenkamp, W. H. "Calvijn en Sadoleto," *Veritatem in Caritate* 4 (1959), pp. 21–27.

Benoit, J. D. *Institution de la Religion Chrétienne.* Vol. 1, Introduction. Paris, 1957.

Berger, S. *Le procès de Guillaume Briçonnet au Parlement de Paris en 1525.* Paris, 1895.

Berthault, E. A. *Mathurin Cordier et l'enseignement chez les premiers calvinistes.* Paris, 1875.

Beyerhaus, G. *Studien zur Staatsanschauung Calvins mit besonderer Berücksichtigung seines Souveränitätsbegriffes.* Berlin, 1910.

Blanke, F. "Calvins Urteile über Zwingli," *Zwingliana* 11 (1942), pp. 66–92.

Bloch, O., and W. v. Wartburg. *Dictionnaire étymologique de la langue française.* 4th ed. Paris, 1964.

Bohatec, J. *Budé und Calvin.* Graz, 1950.

Boisset, J. *Sagesse et sainteté dans la pensée de Calvin: Essai sur l'humanisme du réformateur français.* Paris, 1959.

Borgeaud, Ch. *L'adoption de la réforme par le peuple de Genève.* Geneva, 1923.

Bourrilly, V. L. (ed.). *Le journal d'un bourgeois de Paris sous le règne de François I.* Paris, 1910.

Bourrilly, V. L., and N. Weiss. "Jean du Bellay, les protestants et la Sorbonne," *BHPF* 53 (1903), pp. 193–231.

Bouvier, A. *Henri Bullinger, réformateur et conseiller oecuménique.* Paris, 1940.

Bouyer, L. *Autour d'Erasme.* Paris, 1955.

————. *Du protestantisme à l'église.* Paris, 1959.

Bower, H. M. *The Fourteen of Meaux.* London, 1894.

Breen, Q. *John Calvin: A Study in French Humanism.* Grand Rapids, 1931.

Broussard, J. "L'Université d'Orléans au XVIe siècle," in *Humanisme et Renaissance* 5 (1939), pp. 223ff.

Brunner, P. *Nikolaus von Amsdorf als Bischof von Naumburg. Eine Untersuchung zur Gestalt des evangelischen Bischofsamtes in der Reformationszeit,* SVRG 179 (1961).

Bulaeus, C. E. *Historia universitatis parisiensis.* Vol. 6. Paris, 1665.

Burckhardt, P. *Geschichte der Stadt Basel von der Zeit der Reformation bis zur Gegenwart.* 2d ed. Basle, 1957.

———. *Basel in den ersten Jahren nach der Reformation.* Basle, 1946.

Büsser, F. *Calvins Urteil über sich selbst.* Zurich, 1950.

Cadier, J. *Institution chrétienne.* Vol. 1, Introduction. Geneva, 1955.

———. "Luther et les débuts de la réforme française," *Positions luthériennes,* 1958.

von Campenhausen, H. "Die Bilderfrage in der Reformation," *ZKG,* 1957, pp. 96–128.

Carrière, V. "La Sorbonne et l'évangélisme au XVIe siècle," *Aspects de l'Université de Paris.* Pp. 159–186. Paris, 1949.

Célier, L. "L'idée de réforme a la cour pontificale du Concile de Bâle au Concile de Constance," *RQH* 86 (1909/II).

Chenevière, E. *La pensée politique de Calvin.* Paris, 1938.

Choisy, E. "Calvin und Basel," *Kirchenblatt für die reformierte Schweiz* 86 (1930), pp. 274–279.

Clark, F. *Eucharistic Sacrifice and the Reformation.* London, 1960.

Clouzot, H. "Les amitiés de Rabelais en Orléans," *Revue des Etudes rabelaisiennes* 3, pp. 174ff.

Congar, Y. M.-J. *Vraie et fausse réforme dans l'église.* Paris, 1950.

Coulton, G. G. *Art and the Reformation.* New York, 1953.

Courvoisier, J. "Bucer et l'oeuvre de Calvin," *RThPh* 21 (1936), pp. 66–77.

Cramer, J. A. *De heilige Schrift bij Calvijn.* Utrecht, 1926.

Crespin, J. *Histoire des martyrs persecutez et mis a mort pour la verité de l'évangile, depuis le temps des apostres jusques à présent* (1619). Edited by D. Benoit. 3 vols. Toulouse, 1885–1889.

Crottet, A. *Correspondance française de Calvin avec Louis du Tillet (1537–1538).* Geneva, 1850.

Dagens, J. *Humanisme et évangélisme chez Lefèvre d'Etaples.* Paris, 1959.

Dankbaar, W. F. *Calvijn, zijn Weg en Werk.* Nijkerk, 1958. German translation by H. Quistorp: *Calvin, sein Weg und sein Werk.* Neukirchen, 1959.

de Groot, E. J. "Melchior Wolmar, ses rapports avec les protestants français et suisses," *BHPF,* 1934.

Delarue, H. "La première offensive évangélique à Genève, 1532–1533," *Bulletin de la Société d'Histoire et d'Archéologie de Genève* 9 (1948), pp. 83–102.

Desmay, J. "Remarques sur la vie de Jean Calvin hérésiarque, tirées des registres de Noyon, Rouen, 1621 and 1657," *Archives curieuses de l'histoire de France.* Vol. 5, pp. 387–398. Paris, 1835.

Doinel, J. "Jean Calvin à Orléans," *BHPF* 26 (1877), pp. 174ff.

Dörries, H. "Calvin und Lefèvre," *ZKG* 44 (1925), pp. 544–581.

Doucet, R. *Etudes sur le gouvernement de François Ier dans ses rapports avec le Parlement de Paris, 1515–1525.* 1921.

Douglas, R. M. *Jacopo Sadoleto, Humanist and Reformer.* Cambridge, Mass., 1959.

Doumergue, E. *Jean Calvin, les hommes et les choses de son temps.* Vol. 1: *La jeunesse de Calvin* (Lausanne, 1899); vol. 2: *Les premiers essais* (Lausanne, 1902).

Dufour, Th. *Un opuscule inédit de Farel, Le résumé des actes de la dispute de Rive, 1535.* Geneva, 1885.

Eells, H. "Martin Bucer and the Conversion of John Calvin," in *Princeton Theological Review* 22 (July 1924), pp. 402–419.

Enders, L. *Luther und Emser,* nos. 8 and 9 of *Flugschriften aus der Reformationszeit.* Halle, 1890–1892.

Erichson, A. *L'église française de Strasbourg au seizième siècle d'après des documents inédits.* Paris, 1886.

————. *Die calvinische und die altstrassburgische Gottesdienstordnung.* Strasbourg, 1894.

Febvre, L. "L'origine des placards de 1534," *Bibliothèque d'Humanisme et de Renaissance,* 1945, pp. 62–75.

————. "Le cas Briçonnet," *AEPHE,* 5th sec., 1946.

————. *Le problème de l'incroyance au XVIe siècle, le siècle de Rabelais.* 2d ed. Paris, 1947.

————. *Au coeur religieux du XVIe siècle.* Paris, 1957.

————. "Les origines de la réforme française et le problème des causes générales de la réforme," *RH,* 1929.

Feret, P. *Histoire de la Faculté de Théologie de Paris et de ses docteurs les plus célèbres,* Epoque moderne, vols. 1, 2 (Paris, 1900–1901).

Forster, H. D. "Geneva Before Calvin, 1387–1536: The Antecedents of a Puritan State," *AHR* 8 (1903), pp. 217–240.

Franz, A. *Die Messe im deutschen Mittelalter.* Freiburg im Breisgau, 1902.

Ganoczy, A. *Calvin und Vatikanum II. Das Problem der Kollegialität.* Wiesbaden, 1965.

————. *Calvin, théologien de l'église et du ministère.* Paris, 1964.

Gloede, G. *Musste Reformation sein? Calvins Antwort an Kardinal Sadolet.* Göttingen, 1954.

Godet, M. "Le Collège de Montaigu," *Revue des Etudes rabelaisiennes* 7 (Paris, 1909). (Cited as Godet I.)

————. *La congregation de Montaigu (1490–1580).* Paris, 1912. (Cited as Godet II.)

Goumaz, L. *La doctrine du salut d'après les commentaires de Jean Calvin sur le Nouveau Testament.* Lausanne, 1917.

Graf, K. H. *Essai sur la vie et les écrits de Jacques Lefèvre d'Etaples.* Strasbourg, 1842.

————. "Faber Stapulensis," *ZHTh* 22 (1852), pp. 1–86 and 165–237.

Guilliard, Ch. *La conquête du pays de Vaud par les Bernois.* Lausanne, 1935.

Haag, E. and E. *La France protestante.* Paris, 1846–1859.

Hagenbach, K. R. *Oswald Myconius.* Elberfeld, 1859.

Hari, B. "Les placards de 1534," *Aspects de la propagande religieuse.* Geneva, 1957.

Hashagen, J. "Die Devotio moderna und ihre Einwirkung auf Humanismus, Reformation, Gegenreformation und spätere Richtungen," *ZKG* 55 (1936), pp. 523ff.

Herminjard, A. L. *Correspondance des réformateurs dans les pays de langue française.* 9 vol. Geneva, 1871–1897. (Cited as Herminjard.)

Herzog, J. J. *Das Leben Johannes Oecolampads und die Reformation der Kirche zu Basel.* Basle, 1843.

Heyer, F. *Der Kirchenbegriff der Schwärmer,* SVRG 56 (1939).

Heyer, H. *Guillaume Farel, Essai sur le développement de ses idées théologiques.* Geneva, 1872.

Höhne, H. *Luthers Anschauungen über die Kontinuität der Kirche.* Arbeiten zur Geschichte und Theologie des Luthertums, vol. 12 (Berlin, 1963).

Holl, K. *Luther und Calvin.* Berlin, 1919.

Hoogstra, J. T. (ed.). *John Calvin, Contemporary Prophet.* Grand Rapids, 1950.

Hugo, A. M. *Calvijn en Seneca, Een inleidende studie von Calvijns commentaar op Seneca "De Clementia," anno 1532.* Groningen, 1957.

Huizinga, J. *Herbst des Mittelalters.* Stuttgart, 1952.

Hyma, A. *The Brethren of the Common Life.* Grand Rapids, 1950.

———. *Renaissance to Reformation.* Grand Rapids, 1951.

———. *The Christian Renaissance: A History of the "Devotio Moderna."* New York, 1925.

Imbart de la Tour, P. *Les origines de la réforme.* Vol. 1 (2d ed., Melun, 1948): *La France moderne;* vol. 2 (2d ed., Melun, 1946): *L'Eglise catholique: La crise et la Renaissance;* vol. 3 (Paris, 1914): *L'évangélisme;* vol. IV (Paris, 1935): *Calvin et l'Institution Chrétienne.*

Iserloh, E. "Die Kirchenfrommigkeit in der 'Imitatio Christi.' " In *Sentire Ecclesiam,* edited by J. Daniélou and H. Vorgrimmler, pp. 251–267. Freiburg im Breisgau, 1961.

———. *Der Kampf um die Messe.* Münster in Westfalen, 1952.

———. "Der Wert der Messe in der Diskussion der Theologen vom Mittelalter bis zum 16. Jahrhundert," *ZKTh* 83 (1961), pp. 44–79.

Jacobs, P. *Prädestination und Verantwortlichkeit bei Calvin.* Neukirchen, 1937.

Jacquemot, H. *Viret, réformateur de Lausanne.* Strasbourg, 1836.

James, W. *The Varieties of Religious Experience.* London, 1903.

Jansen, J. F. *Calvin's Doctrine of the Work of Christ.* London, 1956.

Jourda, P. *Marguerite d'Angoulême, duchesse d'Alençon, reine de Navarre, 1492–1549.* Paris, 1930.

———. *Correspondance de Marguerite d'Angoulême, duchesse d'Alençon, reine de Navarre, 1492–1549.* Paris, 1930.

Junod, L. *Farel, réformateur de la Suisse romande et pasteur de l'église de Neuchâtel.* Neuchâtel-Paris, 1865.

Kalkoff, P. *Die Vermittlungspolitik des Erasmus.* Berlin, 1903.

Kampschulte, F. W. *Johannes Calvin, sein Kirche und sein Staat in Genf.* Vol. 1. Leipzig, 1869.

Kawerau, G. *Hieronymus Emser.* Halle, 1898.

Kern, F. *Die Nachfolge Christi.* Olten, 1947.

Kinder, E. "Die Verborgenheit der Kirche nach Luther." In *Festgabe J. Lortz.* Vol. 1, pp. 173–192. Baden-Baden, 1958.

Köhler, W. *"Das Täufertum in Calvins Institutio von 1536,"* Mennonitische Geschichtsblätter 2, pp. 1–4.

———. *Luthers Schrift an den christlichen Adel deutscher Nation im Spiegel der Kultur- und Zeitgeschichte.* Halle, 1895.

——— (ed.). *Erasmus von Rotterdam, Briefe.* Vol. 2. Wiesbaden, 1947.

Kolfhaus, W. "Der Verkehr Calvins mit Bullinger," *Calvinstudien,* pp. 27–125. Leipzig, 1909.

Koopmans, J. *Das altkirchliche Dogma in der Reformation.* Thesis, Utrecht, 1938. Translated by H. Quistorp, Munich, 1955.

Köstlin, J. "Calvins Institutio nach Form und Inhalt," *ThStK* 41 (1868).

Krusche, W. *Das Wirken des Heiligen Geistes nach Calvin.* Göttingen, 1957.

Küng, H. *Rechtfertigung. Die Lehre Karl Barths und eine katholische Besinnung.* 3d ed. Einsiedeln, 1961.

Lang, A. *Der Evangelienkommentar Martin Butzers und die Grundzüge seiner Theologie.* Leipzig, 1900.

———. *Reformation und Gegenwart.* Pp. 72–87: "Luther und Calvin"; pp. 88–135: "Melanchthon und Calvin." Detmold, 1918.

———. "Die Bekehrung Johannes Calvins," *StGThK,* 1897, vol. 2, fasc. 1, pp. 1–56.

———. "Die Quellen der Institutio von 1536," *EvTh* 3 (1936), pp. 100–112.

Law, T. G. "John Major, Scottish Scholastic," *Scottish Review,"* 1892, pp. 344–376.

Le Bras, G. *Introduction à l'histoire de la pratique religieuse en France.* Paris, 1942.

Leclercq-Vandenbroucke-Bouyer. *La spiritualité du Moyen Age.* Pp. 512ff. Paris, 1961.

Lecoultre, H. "La conversion de Calvin," *RThPh,* 1890, pp. 5–30.

———. "Calvin d'après son commentaire sur le 'De Clementia' de Sénèque," *RThPh,* 1891, pp. 51–77.

Le Coultre, J. "Maturin Cordier et les origines de la pédagogie protestante dans les pays de langue française," *Mémoires de l'Université de Neuchâtel,* vol. 5 (1926).

Lefranc, A. "Les idées religieuses de Marguerite de Navarre d'après son oeuvre poétique," *BHPF,* 1897.

———. *Histoire du Collège de France.* Paris, 1893.

———. *La jeunesse de Calvin.* Paris, 1888.

Léonard, E. G. *Histoire générale du protestantisme.* Vol. 1: *La Réformation;* vol. 2: *L'établissement.* Paris, 1961.

Lindeboom, J. *Oorsprong en geschiednis van den naam Protestant.* Amsterdam, 1940.

Liston, R. T. L. *John Calvin's Doctrine of the Sovereignty of God.* Thesis, Edinburgh, 1930.

Lortz, J. "Luthers Vorlesung über den Römerbrief," *TThZ* 71 (1962).

———. *Geschichte der Kirche, in ideengeschichtlicher Betrachtung.* 21st ed. Vol. 1 (1962); vol. 2 (1964). Münster im Westfalen. (Cited as *GK.*)

———. *Die Reformation in Deutschland.* 4th ed. Freiburg im Breisgau, 1962. (Cited as *RD.*)

———. "Die Leipziger Disputation 1519," *BZThS* 3 (1926), pp. 12–37.

———. *Wie kam es zur Reformation?* 2d ed. Einsiedeln, 1954.

Lovy, R.-J. *Les origines de la réforme française.* Paris, 1959.

Lücker, M. A. *Meister Eckhart und die Devotio Moderna.* Leiden, 1950.

Mackay, A. J. G. "A Biography of the Author." In *A History of Greater Britain,* by John Major, edited by A. Constable. Edinburgh, 1892.

Mann, M. *Erasme et les débuts de la réforme française.* Paris, 1934.

Maugis, E. *Histoire du Parlement de Paris.* Vol. 1. Paris, 1913.

Maurer, W. "Franz Lambert von Avignon und das Verfassungsideal der 'Reformatio Ecclesiarum Hassiae,' " *ZKG,* 1929, pp. 208–260.

Mesnard, P. "Mathurin Cordier (1479–1564)," *Foi et Education,* April–June 1959, pp. 76–94.

Meyer, A. *Etude critique sur les relations d'Erasme et de Luther.* Paris, 1909.

Meylan, H., and R. Deluz. *La dispute de Lausanne.* Lausanne, 1936.

Moore, W. G. *La réforme allemande et la littérature française: Recherches sur la notoriété de Luther en France.* Strasbourg, 1930.

Moser, A. "Franz Lamberts Reise durch die Schweiz im Jahre 1522," *Zwingliana,* 1957, pp. 467–471.

———. "Die Anfänge der Freundschaft zwischen Zwingli und Oekolampad," *Zwingliana,* 1958, pp. 614–620.

Mousseaux, M. *Briçonnet et le mouvement de Meaux.* Paris, 1923.

Mülhaupt, E. "Luther und Calvin," *Luther,* 1959, pp. 97–113.

———. *Die Predigt Calvins.* Berlin, 1931.

———. *Der Psalter auf der Kanzel Calvins.* Neukirchen, 1959.

Müller, G. *Franz Lambert von Avignon und die Reformation in Hessen.* Marburg, 1958.

Müller, K. "Calvin und die 'Libertiner,' " *ZKG* 40 (1922), pp. 83–122.

———. "Calvins Bekehrung," *NGG,* 1905, pp. 188–255.

Naef, H. *Les origines de la réforme à Genève.* Geneva, 1936.

Nauta, D. "Calvijn en Luther," *Free University Quarterly* 2, Amsterdam, 1952, pp. 1–17.

Niesel, W. "Verstand Calvin deutsch?" *ZKG* 49 (1930), pp. 343ff.

———. "Calvin und die Libertiner," *ZKG* 48 (1929), pp. 58–74.

———. *Die Theologie Calvins.* 2d ed. Munich, 1957.

Oediger, F. W. *Über die Bildung der Geistlichen im späten Mittelalter.* Leiden-Cologne, 1953.

Otten, H. *Calvins theologische Anschauung von der Prädestination.* Munich, 1938.

Otto, W. "Religio und superstitio," in *Archiv für Religionswissenschaft,* 1909.

Owen, J. *Commentaries on the Twelve Minor Prophets by John Calvin.* Vol. 1. 2d ed. Grand Rapids, 1950.

Pannier, J. "Calvin savait-il l'allemand?" *BHPF* 78 (1929), pp. 344, 476.

———. "Recherches sur l'évolution religieuse de Calvin jusqu'à sa conversion," *RHPhR,* no. 8 (1924).

———. "Calvin à Strasbourg," *RHPhR,* no. 12 (1935).

Pauck, W. "Calvin und Butzer," *JR* 9 (1929), pp. 237–256.

Paulus, N. *Geschichte des Ablasses im Mittelalter.* Vol. 2. Paderborn, 1922f.

Pellens, K. "Kirchendenken in der 'Imitatio Christi.' " In *Nachfolge Christi in Bibel, Liturgie und Spiritualität,* edited by Th. Bogler, pp. 41–67. Maria Laach, 1962.

Peter, R. "L'abécédaire genevois ou catéchisme élémentaire de Calvin," *RHPhR* 45 (1965), no. 1, pp. 11–45.

Piaget, A. (ed.). _Actes de la dispute de Lausanne 1536, publiés intégralement d'après le manuscrit de Berne,_ in _Mémoires de l'Université de Neuchâtel._ Vol. 6, 1928.

Pierson, A. _Studien over Johannes Kalvijn._ Amsterdam, 1881.

Pollet, J. V. _Martin Bucer, études sur la correspondance._ Vol. 2. Paris, 1962.

Polman, A. D. R. "Calvijn en Luther," in _Vier redevoeringen over Calvijn._ Kampen, 1959.

Prantl, K. _Geschichte der Logik im Abendlande._ Vol. 4, pp. 247–251. Leipzig, 1855–1867.

Preuss, H. _Die Vorstellungen vom Antichrist im späten Mittelalter, bei Luther und der konfessionellen Polemik._ Thesis, Leipzig, 1906.

de Raemond, Florimond. _Histoire de la naissance, progrès et décadence de l'hérésie de ce siècle._ Paris, 1605, and Rouen, 1623.

Renaudet, A. _Erasme, sa pensée religieuse et son action d'après sa correspondance (1518–1521)._ Paris, 1926.

———. "L'humanisme et l'enseignement de l'Université de Paris au temps de la Renaissance," _Aspects de l'Université de Paris,_ 1949, pp. 133–155.

———. _Préréforme et humanisme à Paris pendant les premières guerres d'Italie (1494–1517)._ 2d ed. Paris, 1953.

———. "Jean Standonck, un réformateur catholique avant la réforme," _BHPF,_ 1908, pp. 5–81.

———. _Etudes érasmiennes, 1521–1529._ Paris, 1939.

Reulos, M. "Le décret de Gratien chez les humanistes, les Gallicans et les réformés français au XVIe siècle," _StG,_ vol. 2, 1954.

———. "Les attaches de Calvin dans la région de Noyon," _BHPF,_ 1964, pp. 193–201.

Reuter, K. _Das Grundverständnis der Theologie Calvins. Unter Einbeziehung ihrer geschichtlichen Abhängigkeiten,_ pt. 1. Neukirchen, 1963.

Rilliet, A., and Th. Dufour. _Le Catéchisme français de Calvin publié en 1537._ Geneva, 1878.

Ritschl, O. _Dogmengeschichte des Protestantismus._ Vol. 3. Göttingen, 1926.

Rolland, R. "Le dernier procès de Louis de Berquin," _Mélanges de l'Ecole française de Rome,_ 1892.

Roth, P. _Durchbruch und Festsetzung der Reformation in Basel._ Basle, 1942.

Rott, H. G. _Forschungen und Arbeiten zur Geschichte des Protestantismus im Elsass,_ AElsKG (1941), pp. 331–349.

Rott, J. "Documents strasbourgeois concernant Calvin, I. Un manuscrit autographe: la harangue du recteur Nicolas Cop; II. Calvin prébendier de la Cathédrale de Strasbourg," _RHPhR_ 44 (1964), no. 4, pp. 290–325.

Sägmüller, J. B. "Die Kirche als imperium Romanum im kanonischen Recht," _ThQ_ 80 (1898), pp. 50ff.

Schmidt, Ch. _Gérard Roussel, prédicateur de la reine Marguerite de Navarre._ Strasbourg, 1845.

———. "Gérard Roussel, inculpé d'hérésie à Meaux, 1525," _BHPF,_ 1861.

———. _Etudes sur Guillaume Farel._ Strasbourg, 1834.

Schmidt, U. "Calvins Bezeugung der Ehre Gottes." In _Festgabe für A. Schlatter._ Berlin, 1927.

Schroten, H. *Christus, de Middelaar bij Calvijn.* Utrecht, 1948.

Schulze, M. *Calvins Jenseits-Christentum in seinem Verhältnisse zu den religiösen Schriften des Erasmus untersucht.* Görlitz, 1902.

Schummer, L. *Le ministère pastoral dans l'Institution Chrétienne de Calvin à la lumière du troisième sacrement.* Wiesbaden, 1965.

Seeberg, R. *Lehrbuch der Dogmengeschichte,* 4th ed. Vol. 4/2. Basle, 1954.

Smits, L. *Saint Augustin dans l'oeuvre de Jean Calvin.* Vol. 1. Assen, 1957.

Soos, B. "Zwingli und Calvin," *Zwingliana* 6 (1937), pp. 306–327.

Sperl, A. *Melanchthon zwischen Humanismus und Reformation.* Munich, 1958.

Sprenger, P. *Das Rätsel um die Bekehrung Calvins.* Neukirchen, 1960.

Staehelin, E. *Johannes Calvin, Leben und ausgewählte Schriften.* Elberfeld, 1863. Vol. 4 of the collection *Leben und ausgewählte Schriften der Väter und Begründer der reformirten Kirche.*

————. *Das theologische Lebenswerk Johannes Oekolampads.* Leipzig, 1939.

————. *Das Buch der Basler Reformation.* Basle, 1929.

————. *Briefe und Akten zum Leben Oekolampads.* Leipzig, 1927 and 1934.

Stauffer, R. "Les discours à la première personne dans les sermons de Calvin," *RHPhR* 45 (1965), no. 1, pp. 46–78.

Stöcker, H. "Luthers Stellung zum Regensburger Religionsgespräch im Jahre 1541," *Allgemeine evangelische Kirchenzeitung,* 1941, pp. 114ff., 126ff., 134ff.

Storck, H. "Das allgemeine Priestertum bei Luther," *ThEx* 37 (1953).

Stricker, E. *Johannes Calvin als erster Pfarrer der reformierten Gemeinde zu Strassburg.* Strasbourg, 1890.

Strohl, H. "Bucer et Calvin," *BHPF* 87 (1938), pp. 354ff.

————. *Le protestantisme en Alsace.* Strasbourg, 1950.

Stupperich, R. *Der Humanismus und die Wiedervereinigung der Konfessionen.* Leipzig, 1936.

Subilia, Ch. *La dispute de Lausanne.* Lausanne, 1885.

Taverney, P. *Doctrines réformatrices et influences luthériennes à Paris et à Meaux.* Lausanne, 1934.

Thiers, J. B. *Traité des superstitions qui regardent les sacremens.* Avignon, 1777.

Tillich, P. "Die bleibende Bedeutung der katholischen Kirche für den Protestantismus," *ThLZ* 9 (1962), cols. 643–644.

Toussaert, J. *Le sentiment religieux en Flandre à la fin du Moyen Age.* Paris, 1963.

Toussaint du Plessis, D. *Histoire de l'église de Meaux.* Paris, 1781.

Tuchel, K. "Luthers Auffassung vom geistlichen Amt," *Luther,* 1958, pp. 61–98.

van't Veer, M. B. *Catechese en catechetische stof bij Calvijn.* Kampen, 1941.

Veerman, A. *De stijl van Calvijn in de Institutio christianae religionis,* Utrecht, 1943.

Viard, P. E. *André Alciat, 1492–1550.* Paris, 1926.

Wackernagel, R. *Humanismus und Reformation in Basel.* Basle, 1924.

Walker, W. *Jean Calvin, l'homme et l'oeuvre.* Geneva, 1909. Translated by N. Weiss from *John Calvin: The Organiser of Reformed Protestantism 1509–1564.* New York, London, 1906 and 1910.

Wallace, R. S. *Calvin's Doctrine of the Word and Sacrament.* Edinburgh, 1953.

Weber, O. "Die Einheit der Kirche bei Calvin," *Calvin-Studien,* Neukirchen, 1960, pp. 130–143.

Weiss, N. "Martin Luther, Jean Eck et l'Université de Paris, d'après une lettre inédite, 11 septembre 1519," *BHPF,* 1917.

———. "Réforme et Préréforme, Lefèvre d'Etaples," *RMM,* 1918.

———. "Louis de Berquin, son premier procès et sa rétractation, d'après quelques documents inédits, 1523," *BHPF,* 1918.

Weiss, N., and V. L. Bourrilly. "L'affaire des placards," *BHPF,* vol. 53 (1904).

Wendel, F. *Calvin, sources et évolution de sa pensée religieuse.* Paris, 1950.

Wentzlaff-Eggebert, F. W. *Deutsche Mystik zwischen Mittelalter und Neuzeit.* Pp. 139ff. Tübingen, 1947.

Werdermann, Th. "Calvins Lehre von der Kirche in ihrer geschichtlichen Entwicklung," *Calvinstudien,* Leipzig, 1909, pp. 246–338.

Wernle, P. "Noch einmal die Bekehrung Calvins," *ZKG* 27 (1906), pp. 84–99. (Cited as Wernle I.)

———. "Zu Calvins Bekehrung," *ZKG* 31 (1910), pp. 556–583. (Cited as Wernle II.)

———. *Calvin und Basel bis zum Tode des Myconius, 1535–1552.* Tübingen, 1909.

———. *Der evangelische Glaube nach den Hauptschriften der Reformatoren,* vol. 3: *Calvin.* Tübingen, 1919.

Wiedeburg, A. "Die Freundschaft zwischen Butzer und Calvin nach ihren Briefen," *HJ* 83 (1964), pp. 69–83.

Zahn, A. "Calvins Urteile über Luther," *Biblische Zeugnisse,* 1928.

Zanta, L. *La renaissance du stoïcisme au XVIe siècle.* Paris, 1914.

Zeeden, E. W. "Das Bild Luthers in den Briefen Calvins," *ARG* 49 (1958), pp. 177–195.